MUTUAL ASSISTANCE IN CRIMINAL MATTERS

International Co-operation in the Investigation and Prosecution of Crime

AUSTRALIA
LBC Information Services–Sydney

CANADA and USA
Carswell–Toronto

NEW ZEALAND
Brooker's–Auckland

SINGAPORE and MALAYSIA
Sweet & Maxwell Asia
Singapore and Kuala Lumpur

MUTUAL ASSISTANCE IN CRIMINAL MATTERS

International Co-operation in the Investigation and Prosecution of Crime

By

Lorna Harris LL.B. (Edinburgh)
Solicitor

&

Christopher Murray LL.B. (London)
Solicitor, Recorder of the Crown Court

LONDON
SWEET & MAXWELL
2000

Published in 2000 by
Sweet & Maxwell Limited of
100 Avenue Road
Swiss Cottage
London NW3 3PF
http://www.smlawpub.co.uk

Typeset by York House Typographic Ltd
Printed and bound in Great Britain
by MPG Ltd, Bodmin, Cornwall

No natural forests were destroyed
to make this product, only farmed
timber was used and replanted

ISBN 0 421 610 204

A CIP catalogue record for this book
is available from the British Library

For   John   Gunilla

                  Natalie   Tom

                  Alasdair   Alice

Foreword by the Director of Public Prosecutions

I have thoroughly enjoyed reading this excellent and very useful book, aimed principally at the busy practitioner whether prosecutor or defender. The authors have struck the right balance between the education of prosecutors in the different ways in which mutual legal assistence can be pursued and the education of defenders both as to their ability to use mutual legal assistance provisions and to ensure that the rights of their clients are not unfairly overridden.

The practice of repeating the same information under a number of chapters will make life much easier for practitioners to "dip in" to topics of immediate concern to them.

Both authors have years of experience on both sides of the fence and their ability to draw together the bewildering and ever-changing strands of this topic in a single and intensely readable way is remarkable.

The Crown Prosecution Service is of course concerned with hundreds of requests for assistance every year. The numbers have grown from 508 in 1997 to 567 in 1998 (to 67 countries as well as Jersey, Guernsey and the Isle of Man) with a similar percentage increase projected for 1999. The figures involved in international money-laundering are staggering — the National Criminal Intellegence Squad estimating that approximately £22 billion of the proceeds of crime is "laundered" in Europe each year.

This book is an excellent handbook for those involved in such cases. I whole-heartedly commend it.

David Calvert-Smith Q.C.
Director of Public Prosecutions
October 1999

Foreword by the Director of the Serious Fraud Office

I am delighted that Chris Murray and Lorna Harris have published this book at this time. It is extremely useful for practitioners to have recourse to a single volume which contains comprehensive and up-to-date information on all the conventions, treaties, statutes and case law on the subject of international mutual legal assistance.

The Serious Fraud Office plays an important role in both seeking and assisting with requests for international legal assistance in investigating cases of serious and complex fraud.

The pitfalls are many and the case law in this area is developing very rapidly. The scale of the demand for assistance can be measured by the workload of the UKCA, the Home Office department which deals with both incoming and outgoing requests for assistance. Every year, the UKCA handles on average about 2,200 incoming requests and more than half as many again from the U.K. for assistance, altogether involving some 150 countries. The Serious Fraud Office receives requests for assistance from about 15 countries each year and has made requests for assistance in cases we are investigating to almost as many. Effective arrangements for good, rapid mutual legal assistance, where requests are made in conformity with the requirements of the receiving country, are a key factor in a successful investigation.

There are a bewildering number of agreements at international level which cover international mutual legal assistance and currently under negotiation is a further draft Convention on Mutual Legal Assistance in Criminal Matters between the Member States of the E.U. and a draft Second Additional Protocol to the 1959 Convention in the Council of Europe which will require changes to the U.K.'s legislation and working practices in due course. U.K. domestic law in this area, both in terms of statute and case law, is developing as rapidly.

The authors of this book have particular expertise and experience in this field and have done a thorough and workmanlike job in bringing together the authorities and setting out the practical procedures with such clarity.

Rosalind Wright
Serious Fraud Office
August 1999

Preface

It is perhaps an eloquent observation upon the increasing importance of international co-operation in criminal matters that a former prosecutor and a defence practitioner should feel able to join forces to write a book on the topic.

Whilst there are two outstanding academic volumes available on the subject by Professors Gilmore and McClean, there is nothing aimed primarily at the practitioner whom we see increasingly being consulted in this area of law and practice. We have therefore set out to provide a practical guide to assist those setting foot in virgin territory. That we have failed is evident in the number of omissions that have come to light since we delivered the manuscript and which must await a second edition or update!

It was only when we went back over our working papers to draft a preface that we were struck, not just by the hours of effort we had put in ourselves, but by the magnitude of the debt we owe to those of whom we have made demands of time and friendship. Our friends and colleagues have put up with us over the period of gestation of this book and we owe them all our gratitude.

We would also wish to record our indebtedness and grateful thanks to the following (in no particular order): His Honour Judge Richard May at whose prompting the book was conceived; Alastair Brown; David Calvert-Smith Q.C., Director of Public Prosecutions; Philip Barden; Alun Jones Q.C.; The U.K. Central Authority and in particular, Geoffrey Sonnenberg and Simon Watkin; Chris Gane and Mark Mackarel from the University of Dundee; our publishers, Sweet & Maxwell; John Clitheroe; Di Stafford at The Commonwealth Secretariat for allowing us to reproduce the Commonwealth Scheme; Michael Bromley-Martin; Bruce Swartz for his help in relation to the "American scene"; Anne Heimola; Hans Nilsson; Edmund Lawson Q.C. for his semantic wisdom; Linda Saunt for casting a cautious eye over parts of the proof; Annabelle Bolt; Andrew Barron; Professor John Spencer; Professor William Gilmore and Professor David McClean.

We must both express gratitude to our respective "employers". To those at the Serious Fraud Office, thanks are due, in particular to its former Director, George Staple, for permitting Lorna to co-write the book, its current Director, Rosalind Wright for her foreword, Robert Wardle and finally, Helen Garlick for proof reading it and making essential corrections and suggestions which we believe materially improved the text.

We are also indebted to the partners and Criminal Department of Kingsley Napley upon whom an enormous extra burden has fallen to make it possible for Christopher to write the book. Particular thanks must go to Stephen Gentle who was responsible for the chapter upon Restraint and Confiscation and without whose help our task would have been much heavier. Thanks also to Nicola Bustin for her wise advice and commercial know-how.

Lastly, Chrissie Goater, who typed every word of several drafts and still stayed cheerful and relatively sane through deadline after deadline, deserves more thanks than we can give.

Finally, it is to our families, John, Natalie and Alasdair and Gunilla. Tom and Alice that we are most beholden for their patience and forbearance and from whom we must beg forgiveness!

We are only too conscious that the assistance we have received from others has been one-way and not mutual. Despite the help we have received, we should make it plain that the views expressed reflect those of the authors and no other body or organisation.

CM & LH
London.
November 1999

Table of Contents

Table of Cases

Table of International Cases

Table of Statutes

Table of Statutory Instruments

Table of Bilateral and Multilateral Agreements and Conventions

CHAPTER 1

Introduction

1.00 The importance of international judicial assistance in criminal matters is a relatively recent phenomenon. As little as half a century ago, when a crime was committed, the resultant investigation was nearly always confined within the jurisdiction in which the crime had occurred. For the most part investigative trails, however complex, could be followed without having to look outside the country for evidence. This was as true for the defence lawyer as for the prosecutor or investigator.

Before, those who had committed offences did not leave the jurisdiction themselves, nor did they leave any evidential trail beyond the limits of their own country, and an international dimension for criminal investigations was in the main unnecessary. In many cases, to leave the immediate area of the commission of the offence would be as far as the potential defendant would have to go to ensure that detection would at the least be difficult.

1.01 International travel fifty years ago was relatively uncommon, and certainly harder than it is today. Journeys which were then almost unimaginable are accepted today as routine. Today, not only is international travel itself more easy but in addition, the formalities required to cross national boundaries are constantly being reduced. Border crossing points and visa controls were at one time able to provide, at least in part, a trail of movements, but these are now, in many countries, at a minimum. Within the area of the European Union (E.U.), Article 2(1) of the 1990 Convention implementing the Schengen Agreement of June 14, 1985 states:

"Internal borders may be crossed at any point without any checks on persons being carried out".[1]

For the 13 Member States to which it applies (that is, all Member States of the E.U. with the exception of the United Kingdom and Ireland) its effect is to create almost a frontierless zone.

1.02 If that is the case for the movement of people, the same can also be said about the movements of money and financial transactions. While international trade and commercial activity are long established, the means by which they now take place are much less laborious than before, and, as a result, much faster. The development of computerised transactions, and the electronic transfer of funds around the globe, have revolutionised the concept of international trade and finance. Transactions which formerly were accomplished in days, or even weeks, now take seconds, and funds move from country to country, and from continent to continent, at the press of a button. The development of the Internet as a global communication system has also had its effect, and increases in the rate of its use, and in the diversity of purposes for which it is used will similarly affect international commercial transactions.

Such developments already stretch concepts of national law: for example, the Theft Act 1997 was enacted speedily to deal with a problem in substantive law emerging as a result of the decision of the House of Lords in the case of *R. v. Preddy and Slade; R.*

---

1 Internal borders are defined as the common land borders of the Contracting Parties, their airports for internal flights and their sea ports for regular transhipment connections exclusively from or to other ports within the territories of the Contracting Parties and not calling at any ports outside those territories.

v. Dhillon.[2] The difficulty arose because of the problem of assimilating a modern technical transaction within the wording of legislation which was at least 20 years old, drafted before the complexities of modern technology existed.

1.03   The average citizen may be hardly aware of the effect these developments have had on his or her everyday life, but criminals have adapted techniques to take advantage of them. They know that a transaction which takes them seconds to perform, moving funds from one jurisdiction to another for example, will take investigators months, if not years, to unravel. A multinational conspiracy, with participants from several states, and as a consequence witnesses from at least as many states, will increase the complexity for the investigator. Thus modern technology has provided a new impetus to criminal activity as well as to legitimate commercial enterprise.

Informal police co-operation is almost as old as individual police forces but formal judicial co-operation, which will usually be necessary to obtain evidence in admissible form, is a relatively recent phenomenon, and is unable to move with the speed of the activities it seeks to investigate. For modern criminal investigations to be effective and speedy, it is essential that, so far as possible, international boundaries cause as few problems to the investigators as they do to criminals. National boundaries still create a natural limit to the territorial activities of national law enforcement forces although the provisions of the Schengen Implementing Convention enable police officers of the Member States to have a limited right of hot pursuit of criminal suspects across international borders.[3]

1.04   International co-operation in criminal investigations has become increasingly important for the practitioner – both the prosecutor and the defence lawyer; it is not just in complex cases that there is a need for effective co-operation. Even the apparently most simple case involving, for example, a minor road traffic accident, may involve witnesses or accused persons from a jurisdiction other than the one in which the accident has occurred. Witnesses from abroad may need to be summonsed to attend court, official papers may have to be served or the evidence of witnesses may have to be obtained. In more complex cases, where for example there is a need to unravel a complex trail of financial dealing across many countries and perhaps several continents, an effective system of mutual legal assistance is essential for the speedy and effective investigation and prosecution of cases. In all such cases, the defence too may wish to obtain evidence in another jurisdiction, in order to present its case properly.

1.05   If the system of international judicial co-operation either fails to operate effectively, or is perceived to operate ineffectively, then international criminal activity will not only continue unchecked, but the system of criminal justice in our country will be brought into disrepute. Already, organised international criminal activity operates on a scale which dwarfs the economic output of some countries. Governments must urgently take what steps they can to enable international co-operative efforts to be effective against this threat. The growth of international crime, and the recognition of the threat that this poses to civilised society, particularly in its organised form, is seen as one of the most important items on the current international political agenda. Estimates of the funds generated by organised crime are notoriously difficult to make, but there is no doubt that organised crime is hugely profitable. In 1999 the United Nations Office for Drug Control and Crime Prevention (UNDCP) estimated the value of the world trade in illicit drugs alone as at least $500

---

2 [1996] A.C. 815, HL.
3 Schengen Convention, Art. 41.

billion. Estimates of the profits from all forms of organised crime are obviously much higher still.

1.06 Recent expressions of political will in Europe and elsewhere emphasise the need to "enhance the ability of national legal systems to work closely together."[4] This emphasis is nowhere more clear, both in terms of political will and practical effort and achievement, than in the E.U.

Article 29 of the revised Treaty of European Union is as follows:

> the Union's objective shall be to provide a high level of safety within an area of freedom, security and justice, by developing common action among Member States in the fields of police and judicial co-operation in criminal matters and by preventing and combatting racism and xenophobia.

An exceptional Heads of State meeting of the E.U. will take place in October 1999 in Tampere, Finland, during the Finnish Presidency, devoted to Justice and Home Affairs issues. Initiatives to improve further international judicial co-operation will be discussed at that time.

1.07 Within Europe, where the first international instrument in this field was agreed in 1959 (but only incorporated into United Kingdom law in 1991), there is currently a new draft Convention on Mutual Legal Assistance in Criminal Matters, and a second Protocol to the 1959 Convention is also being prepared. Further detail on these documents is given in Chapter 2. Also within the E.U. there is the European Union's Action Plan to combat organised crime,[5] which contains a number of measures specifically designed to enhance the level of co-operation between Member States in this area.

1.08 Apart from international judicial co-operation through mutual legal assistance, support for the mutual recognition of criminal judgments across international borders is growing. This concept has been recognised within Europe, at least, for many years, and led to the European Convention on the International Validity of Criminal Judgements in 1970, (a Counsel of Europe initiative) and more recently, the 1991 Convention between the Member States of the European Communities on the Enforcement of Criminal Sentences. Disappointingly, however, few Member States have signed these Conventions, and fewer still have ratified them. The opportunity which such instruments provide for a speedier co-operation model should not be overlooked. The European Council meeting in Cardiff in June 1998, (referred to above) highlighted the need to identify the scope for greater mutual recognition of decisions of Member States' courts in criminal cases. The recent (1998) E.U. Convention on Driving Disqualifications will be implemented by way of direct recognition of disqualifications imposed by criminal courts in other jurisdictions, and this marks a significant step forward towards greater mutual recognition.

Further work to explore the extent to which other judicial decisions could be directly enforced in another jurisdiction is under way – examples of areas which might prove fruitful are the execution of witness summons, or cross border freezing orders. Safeguards to such procedures would of course be necessary, but in the long term, such mutual recognition could greatly facilitate international investigations. Discussions to explore the extent to which further mutual recognition might be possible are at an early stage in the context of the E.U.

1.09 However it is achieved, as the threat from organised crime has been better recognised internationally, the need for enhanced international co-operation has

---

4 See, for this extract, the conclusions of the Cardiff E.U. Council, June 1998.
5 Adopted by the Council on April 28, 1997 and published in [1997] O.J. C251/1

become an accepted political imperative, and therefore one which is likely to see further development and progress over the next few years.

Knowledge of the practical possibilities which currently exist for such co-operation to take place is vital for the practitioner in this field. This guide is designed primarily for the practitioner and is intended to assist anyone who is involved in international judicial co-operation both to understand the background to the subject, and effectively use the tools which are now available.

The 1959 Convention and The Development of Mutual Legal Assistance in the United Kingdom

2.00 Having examined the background within which today's international assistance exists, it is necessary to examine in more detail both what mutual legal assistance is, and how it operates in the United Kingdom today.

Mutual legal assistance exists to provide within jurisdiction A a service for jurisdiction B connected with the administration of justice in B. It does not necessarily relate to the investigation of serious international crime, or even to crime at all. At its most simple, it may consist only in the service of documents from a court in one jurisdiction, on an individual in another. On the other hand, it may also involve complex evidence gathering operations in a criminal matter, with a request from A (the requesting state) that evidence in B (the requested state) be seized, for subsequent use in a judicial process in A.

As far as proceedings in criminal matters are concerned, the rules governing the circumstances in which such assistance can be given have developed since the 1950s, and are now, for the most part, contained in the principal United Kingdom legislation on the point, the Criminal Justice (International Co-operation) Act 1990. Before looking at the specific legislation, however, it is important to set it in its context internationally, and to trace the history of the international instruments which gave rise to this legislation.

2.01 As early as 1856, the Foreign Tribunals Evidence Act provided for assistance to be given to foreign tribunals by the taking of evidence in England. In 1870, the Extradition Act made it clear that this provision applied not only to civil proceedings but also to criminal proceedings[1]. (It is interesting to note that even at this early stage there was a link between developments in the law on extradition and the law on international mutual legal assistance. Further examples of the connection will be seen later.) Those provisions remained in force until the Evidence (Proceedings in Other Jurisdictions) Act of 1975, section 5 of which in turn has been repealed by the 1990 Act.

Due to the strong feeling that criminal law was exclusively a domestic issue, and one which was not susceptible to co-operative effort, early attempts to co-operate internationally were principally related to civil law and did not include criminal law. States initially seemed unwilling to contemplate working together in the field of criminal law, although this was in all probability a consequence of the fact that, at least until comparatively recently, the effects of criminal activity were normally restricted to the territory where the criminal activity had occurred. It was only when criminal activity began to involve more than one jurisdiction, and its effects began to be felt internationally, that it became necessary to develop rules and procedures to deal with the problem.

---

1 The Extradition Act 1870, s. 24.

2.02   In 1953, the Committee of Ministers of the Council of Europe convened a committee of governmental experts to examine the possibility of a European Convention on Extradition. In its report to the draft Convention, the committee noted that it had discussed the question of mutual assistance in criminal proceedings, and continued:

"This question which is connected with the problem of extradition was referred to during the committee's discussions. The committee was generally in favour of concluding a special convention on mutual assistance in criminal proceedings. So far, no multilateral convention on this subject has been drawn up."[2] This view reflected again the close connection between developments in extradition and mutual legal assistance.

2.03   The experts thought that this was a matter of great practical importance, and that a multilateral Convention should be drawn up between the member countries of the Council of Europe. They considered further that such a Convention would in fact be acceptable to more of the Council's members than the Convention on Extradition. In due course, the terms of reference of the committee of experts were widened, to include the preparation of a convention of mutual assistance in criminal proceedings. The committee of experts drafted and agreed the Convention on Extradition in 1957, and then, following further work carried out in 1957 and 1958, prepared the European Convention on Mutual Assistance in Criminal Matters. This Convention was opened for signature by the Member States of the Council of Europe on April 20, 1959, and on that date, eight of the states who are now Member States of the E.U. signed the convention. The United Kingdom did not sign the Convention until June 21, 1991 and implemented it by the enactment of the Criminal Justice (International Co-operation Act) 1990, which came into force on November 27, 1991. This legislation contains the major provisions of the 1959 Convention.

It should be borne in mind that, since this was a Council of Europe instrument, and that, in 1999, there are 37 signatories, its principles will also guide the legislation in many of the countries in which international judicial assistance is likely to be sought. As the process of expansion of the E.U. proceeds, further signatories are likely, since the Convention is a major instrument of the *acquis communautaire* to which applicant states subscribe.

The dates of signature of all countries as at March 31, 1999 are detailed in the table below:—

Austria, Belgium, Denmark, Germany, Greece, Italy, Luxembourg and Sweden signed the Convention on April 20, 1959. The other signatories to the Convention signed it on the following dates:—

Albania	May 19, 1998
Bulgaria	Sep. 30, 1993
Cyprus	Mar. 27, 1996
Czech Republic	Mar. 27, 1996
Estonia	Nov. 4, 1993
Finland	Jan. 29, 1981
France	Apr. 28, 1961
Hungary	Nov. 19, 1991
Iceland	Sep. 27, 1982

2 Explanatory report on the European Convention on Mutual Assistance in Criminal Matters, Strasbourg 1969 App. D).

Ireland	Oct. 15, 1996
Latvia	Oct. 30, 1996
Liechtenstein	Oct. 28, 1969
Lithuania	Nov. 9, 1994
Malta	Sep. 6, 1993
Moldova	May 2, 1996
Netherlands	Jan. 21, 1965
Norway	Apr. 21, 1961
Poland	May 9, 1994
Portugal	May 10, 1979
Romania	June 30, 1995
Russia	Nov. 7, 1996
Slovakia	Feb. 13, 1992
Slovenia	Feb. 26, 1999
Spain	July 24, 1979
Switzerland	Nov. 29, 1965
Turkey	Oct. 23, 1959
Ukraine	May 29, 1997
United Kingdom	June 21, 1991
Israel[2a]	Sep. 27, 1967

2.04 A number of guiding principles were laid down by the experts while they considered the draft Convention. It was decided that mutual assistance in criminal matters should be independent of extradition, in that it should be granted in minor criminal cases, as well as in respect of the more serious cases, and that as a general rule, assistance should be available even if the offence under investigation was not an offence under the law of both countries. It was recognised, however, that in respect of requests for search and seizure, requirements of dual criminality could be made by signatories, if they felt it necessary. It was also considered advisable to exclude cases of a military nature from the Convention, and to make it optional in the investigation of offences of a fiscal or political nature.

The aims of the committee of experts were to produce a convention which was simple and flexible enough to be adopted throughout the Member States which agreed to ratify it, while laying down a general principle that mutual assistance should be provided where at all possible in criminal proceedings. The Convention has been the corner stone for all European co-operation since 1959, and has proved its worth in achieving its objectives.

2.05 As the principles of the 1959 European Convention underpin so much of the current legislation on mutual legal assistance, both in the United Kingdom and elsewhere, an understanding of its main provisions is necessary. Although within the United Kingdom the Criminal Justice (International Co-operation) Act 1990 (the 1990 Act)[3] is the main legislative provision, familiarity with the provisions of the Convention itself will enable a greater understanding of both the reason for the existence of these provisions, and for the legislative provisions which exist in other Member States.

2.06 Article 1 of the Convention[4] sets the tone for the whole document. Under the first Article, the countries signing undertake:

2a Israel is not a Member State of the Council of Europe.
3 For full text see App. A.
4 For full text see App. B.

"to afford each other . . . the widest measure of mutual assistance in proceedings
in respect of offences the punishment of which, at the time of the request for
assistance, fall within the jurisdiction of the judicial authorities of the requesting
Party."

The Convention thus applies to minor as well as to more serious offences and
assistance must be accorded where the offence comes under the jurisdiction of the
requested party. It is not normally subject to the rules governing extradition,
although in relation to Article 5 (below) there are some principles in common.

2.07   The Convention applies only to judicial proceedings, as opposed to administrative proceedings, but is drafted very broadly, as it is intended that it should cover
all types of assistance, and not just those specifically mentioned in the Convention.
Each Member State will have definitions which differ slightly as to the dividing line
between judicial proceedings and administrative proceedings. From the United
Kingdom's perspective, any proceedings which could result in a criminal conviction
being recorded against a person will be treated as judicial proceedings. In other
jurisdictions there are proceedings by administrative courts which can also result in
penalties (usually monetary) being imposed. Such proceedings would not be covered
by the Convention.

In the Explanatory Report on the Convention, examples of proceedings which
would attract assistance are given, and these demonstrate the breadth of the provision. For example, applications for pardon, or review of sentence, proceedings for
compensation of persons found innocent, and claims by an injured party for damages
in criminal proceedings would all be considered as proceedings appropriate for
mutual legal assistance.

2.08   Article 2 of the Convention is a general provision relating to the circumstances in which assistance may be refused. In general terms, it is provided that
assistance *may be* refused if the request relates to a political or fiscal offence, or if the
requested State considers that execution of the request is likely to prejudice the
sovereignty, security, *ordre public* or other essential interest of the country. It is
important to emphasise that refusal on any of these grounds is only optional, and it
does not necessarily follow that a state will refuse to assist if any of the criteria are
met. *Ordre public* and essential interest are not defined in the Convention. In some
states, this lack or definition has led to refusal of assistance in circumstances which
would not have led to the same result in the United Kingdom. "Political" and "fiscal"
are not defined in the Convention. The mere fact that an offence concerns a politician
would not mean that it became ineligible for assistance. The conviction of Jonathan
Aitken for perjury in 1999 followed a plea of guilty, but had the matter been
contested, the fact that the defendant had been a prominent politician would not have
affected the availability of mutual legal assistance. On the other hand, a prosecution
for election rigging might well fall within the definition of a political offence, but since
the ground for refusal is merely optional, might in any event attract mutual legal
assistance if necessary.

Similar considerations will apply to fiscal offences. The fact that an offence involves
evidence from tax authorities will not qualify it automatically as a fiscal offence. As
Professor McClean points out in his book on *International Judicial Assistance*, p.
132,

"Even the Swiss, with their reputation for protecting all information in matters
fiscal, have decided that the information provided by Swiss authorities may be
used by a foreign state in the investigation of political and associated offences

and tax offences unless a condition expressly prohibiting this has been made by the relevant Swiss authority".

What is important, however, is not the definition in the requesting State, but the interpretation of the facts and circumstances by the requested State, since it is the latter that will make any decision on refusal.

2.09   Articles 3 to 6 of the Convention deal with the details of the handling of letters of request, referred to in the Convention as "letters rogatory." These are defined, in the Explanatory Report to the Convention published in Strasbourg in 1969, as "a mandate given by a judicial authority of one country to a foreign judicial authority to perform in its place one or more specified actions."[5]
The general rule, provided for in Article 3(1) is that the requested party should execute letters rogatory in the manner provided for by its law. This is an important provision, since it sets out the general principle that requests should, in normal circumstances, be executed according to the law of the requested State. The practical result of this provision is that the requesting State may have difficulty in using the evidence provided under a letter of request, since the evidence requested may be produced in a format which does not satisfy the requesting State's evidential criteria. The provisions of the new draft E.U. Convention[6] and the draft Protocol to the Council of Europe Convention[7] reverse this fundamental rule, and establish the principle that requests should be executed according to the law of the requesting State, unless the procedures requested are at variance with fundamental principles of the law of the requested State.[8]

2.10   Article 3 additionally provides, however, that where the request is that witnesses or experts give evidence on oath, the requested state shall comply with the request if its law does not prohibit it. This will enable a requested State to hear evidence on oath, even if, as a general rule, there is no provision in its general procedure for an oath to be taken, provided that this is not contrary to its law. The oath would in such circumstances however, be administered in accordance with the law of the requested State.

2.11   Article 4 provides that, on the express request of the requesting State, the requested State shall inform the requesting State of the date and place of execution of the request, so as to enable "officials and interested persons" (from the requesting state) to be present at the execution of a request, subject to the consent of the requested State. It is understood in this connection, that such consent may of course only be given where it is not contrary to the law of the requested State. It should be noted that within the Member States of the E.U. there are a number of countries that do not permit the presence of foreign investigators during the execution of at least some parts of a letter rogatory. For example, certain procedures under some judicial systems have to take place in private, and it would not be possible for an investigator from another country to be present during such a procedure.

2.12   Article 5 of the Convention contains the provisions relating to search and seizure. It provides that any of the contracting parties to the Convention may by declaration

"reserve the right to make the execution of letters rogatory for search or seizure of property dependent on one or more of the following conditions:

---

5 Explanatory Report, Art. 3 (App. D).
6 App. F.
7 App. G.
8 See later para 2.25.

(a) that the offence motivating the letters rogatory is punishable under both the law of the requesting party and the law of the requested party.

(b) that the offence motivating the letters rogatory is an extraditable offence in the requested country.

(c) that execution of the letters rogatory is consistent with the law of the requested party"[8a].

In essence therefore, the Convention enables a State to refuse to execute requests where search or seizure are involved, on three possible grounds, and each State may form a view as to which conditions it wishes to apply. The first is dual criminality, that is that the circumstances giving rise to the criminal offence under investigation must be an offence in both the requested and the requesting States. It should be emphasised that what is important is the circumstances, and not the name of the offence. The fact that an offence is described as offence A in the requesting State, but would according to the facts given be described as offence B in the requested State, is enough to establish dual criminality. The second condition introduces the concept of equivalence with extradition, where a State may refuse to execute a request involving search or seizure in a case unless the offence is one where it would be prepared to grant a request for extradition. This condition, where invoked, will have the effect of excluding requests involving search or seizure if the alleged offences are relatively minor. The third condition makes it clear that requests for search or seizure should only be granted where the search or seizure is consistent with the law of the requested State.

The United Kingdom's reservations and declarations to the Convention[9] contain the following statement in relation to Article 5:

"the Government of the UK reserves the right to make the execution of letters rogatory for search and seizure of property dependent on the following conditions:

(a) that the offence motivating the letters rogatory is punishable under both the law of the requesting party and the law of the UK; and

(b) that execution of the letters rogatory is consistent with the law of the United Kingdom."

2.13 Article 6 relates to the transmission of material recovered as a result of the execution of a letter of request. In normal course, according to Article 3(3), certified copies are to be sent, but there is provision for the requested State to make every effort to transmit originals, if this is specifically requested.[10] Article 6 requires that the requesting party shall as soon as possible return any property which was handed over in execution of the letters rogatory, unless the requesting party waives its right to such return. Where the property obtained consists of the photocopies of business records, in most cases the requested State will not want to have the material returned, but it should be remembered that in all cases the requested State has the right to require its return.

2.14 The next series of provisions (Articles 7–12) relates to the service of writs and judgments, and the appearance of witnesses. In practice, the greatest number of requests for international legal assistance is in this area, where courts in one

---

8a Art. 5(1).
9 App. C.
10 Art. 3.3.

jurisdiction wish to have documents relating to a process there served on a person residing in another jurisdiction. Provisions relate to how that service can be achieved, and what formality can be requested, as well as what the requested State has to do to comply with the request. Provision is also made for various methods of service on the person concerned, according to whether the requesting party does or does not specify the form of service to be employed. There is also provision for expenses to be forwarded to witnesses to allow them to undertake travel to the requesting State.

The Convention makes it clear, however, that a witness in a foreign country cannot be compelled by the service of a summons from another country to attend court in that other country, even if the summons has been lawfully served on him or her in accordance with these provisions. It remains a matter for the person served to decide whether to comply with the witness order. Failure to comply will not result in any proceedings against that person, in either the requesting or the requested State.

2.15 Article 13 requires that a requested State shall communicate, on request, extracts from "judicial records" requested by a foreign judicial authority and needed in a criminal matter.

2.16 The next chapter of the Convention, from Article 14 to Article 20, deals with procedural aspects of letters rogatory, and details the necessary contents of such letters. Article 14 provides that a request should include:

(a) the authority making the request

(b) the object of, and reason for the request

(c) where possible, the identity and the nationality of the person concerned, and

(d) where necessary, the name and address of the person to be served.

Furthermore, where requests are made under Articles 3, 4 or 5 of the Convention, (that is, formal requests for evidence, rather than requests for the service of documents, etc.) they should also detail the offence and contain a summary of the offence alleged.

This part of the Convention also deals with the channels through which letters rogatory should be sent. It provides that they should be addressed by the Ministry of Justice of the requesting state to the Ministry of Justice of the requested state, although there is also a provision that urgent requests can be transmitted directly between the judicial authorities of the two countries concerned. A declaration to Article 15 made by the United Kingdom on signing the Convention defines the Home Office as the Ministry of Justice for the purposes of the Convention.

2.17 The next important procedural point, contained in Article 16, concerns translations of requests. The Convention states that translations shall not be required, unless the State makes a declaration on signing the Convention that requests and annexed documents shall be addressed to it accompanied by a translation into the language of the state, or into either of the official languages of the Council of Europe, or into one of those languages, as specified by it.

The United Kingdom has made such a declaration in relation to this Article, and has stipulated that requests and all annexed documents shall be addressed to it accompanied by translations into English.

2.18 Article 19 provides that reasons shall be given for any refusal of mutual assistance. Although refusal to grant assistance should not be confused with failure to grant assistance, it is important to remember this provision, since one of the more frequently voiced complaints about the operation of mutual legal assistance is that, on occasions, no reply is ever received from a requested state and there would thus appear to be refusal. There is a clear obligation on the requested State under this Article to give reasons in cases where it refuses to grant assistance. Giving of reasons is important, since it may enable the requesting State to remedy any defects in the request and re-submit it.

The final provisions of the Convention are of a more formal and procedural character, and shall be considered in detail where appropriate in the following text.

2.19 Despite the importance of this Convention, the United Kingdom did not ratify it until 1990, with the passing of the Criminal Justice (International Co-operation) Act. Before the Act was passed, the Minister of State at the Home Office, when introducing the Bill into Parliament acknowledged the comparatively poor record of the United Kingdom as a mutual assistance partner:

"Our inability to give assistance to other countries has ... meant that our prosecuting authorities have encountered serious difficulties in obtaining from overseas evidence which was crucial to cases which were being investigated in this country. Part 1 of the Bill will put this right. It fills the gaps which at present exist in our legislation and it will enable us to seek – and to provide – the full range of assistance which is often needed."[11-12]

The United Kingdom eventually implemented this legislation (and thus also ratified the Convention) when the Criminal Justice (International Co-operation) Act 1990 came into force on November 27, 1991. Until 1991, international assistance both to and from the United Kingdom was possible to a limited extent under the pre-existing legislation, which, although not as wide-ranging, allowed the United Kingdom to participate in international assistance. It is not proposed to deal further with the earlier legislation (latterly the Evidence (Proceedings in Other Jurisdictions) Act 1975).

2.20 The 1959 Convention was not the end of work in this area in Europe however, and as practical experience developed, it became apparent that improvements in the way that the Convention operated were both possible and desirable. A committee within Europe began examining the operation of the Convention, and as a result of its deliberations, an Additional Protocol to the 1959 Convention was signed in Strasbourg on March 17, 1978, and entered into force in 1982. The text can be found in full at Appendix E.

2.21 Chapter 1 (Articles 1 and 2) of the Protocol extends the 1959 Convention to fiscal matters, by removing (Article 1) the right under Article 2(a) of the Convention to refuse assistance solely on the ground that the request concerns an offence which is considered by the requested State to be a fiscal offence. Article 2 provides that where a State requires dual criminality for search or seizure, then this condition shall be fulfilled for fiscal offences, if the offence is punishable under the law of the requesting State, and corresponds to an offence of the same nature under the law of the requested State. Secondly, it provides that a request may not be refused on the ground that the law of the requested State does not impose the same kind of tax or duty as the law of the requesting State. For example, a request relating to an offence concerning a tax which uniquely existed in country A could not be refused by country B because it did not recognise the tax.

Chapter 2 (Article 3) applies the 1959 Convention to the service of documents concerning the enforcement of sentences, the recovery of fines, and the payments of

---

11-12 *Hansard*, 513, H.L. O.R. col 1216 (December 12, 1989).

costs of proceedings, and also to measures relating to the enforcement of sentences. These provisions extend the scope of the original Convention to the enforcement of penalties, which was not originally encompassed by the Convention.

Chapter 3 (Article 4) contains ancillary provisions relating to the exchange of information regarding convictions.

Chapter 4 (Articles 5–12) contains the remaining provisions, and relates to signature of the Protocol, and reservations and declarations.

This Protocol was also signed by the United Kingdom on June 21, 1991 and its provisions were brought into force by the Criminal Justice (International Co-operation) Act 1990.

However matters have moved on since 1978. In the same way that criminal ingenuity and activity have developed in the years since 1959, so has the need for ever greater international co-operation in the fight against it. For this reason, solutions and methods which were considered adequate then (and in 1978) have proved no longer to be so, and accordingly there is considerable current development in the field of international mutual legal assistance. Within Europe, there are currently two new initiatives in this field. In the first place, there is the draft E.U. Convention on Mutual Assistance on Criminal Matters,[13] currently under discussion within the E.U., and secondly there is a further Protocol to the 1959 Convention.[14] Neither document replaces the 1959 Convention, both rather amplify and enhance its provisions. The new draft Convention expresses that its purpose is to "supplement" the provisions and facilitate the application of, *inter alia*, the 1959 Convention, while the Council of Europe Protocol explains that it aims to "facilitate the application of the European Convention on Mutual Assistance in Criminal Matters", and also to supplement that Convention in certain aspects.

2.22   The new E.U. Convention will of course only be open to agreement between the Member States of the E.U., as opposed to the broader application of the Council of Europe instrument. The E.U. Convention seeks to tackle some of the more difficult issues in mutual legal assistance procedure which may have caused difficulties in operation over the years, and aims to simplify arrangements for co-operation between judicial and prosecuting authorities, and as a result to speed up procedures. It must be remembered that the text of both documents is only in draft, and negotiations continue. Discussions on the possibilities for the interception of tele-communications where more than one jurisdiction is involved are proving particularly difficult. The drafts show the areas where developments may be expected over the coming years, however. Article 1 of the draft Convention ensures that more favourable mutual assistance arrangements, under bilateral or multilateral arrange-ments, for example, will not be adversely affected. This provision reflects the provision in Article 26 of the 1959 Convention.

2.23   The first provisions also extend mutual legal assistance to administrative as well as criminal matters, and further provide a fundamental shift in balance. Under the 1959 Convention, as has been seen, assistance is to be offered generally in the manner provided for by the law of the requested State. The new Convention will provide that assistance shall be given in the manner indicated by the requesting State, unless that is contrary to the law of the requested State. This is an important provision, which will affect the way the requests of other countries are interpreted, as well as the way in which assistance may be given by other countries. It is perhaps more important for the United Kingdom, as one of the two common law countries in

---

13 App. F.
14 App. G.

the E.U. (along with Ireland), than for the other civil law jurisdictions, who are more accustomed to matters proceeding in a manner which is more familiar to them. The common law principle of orality is virtually unknown in civil law jurisdictions, for example, while the civil law *procès verbal* is unfamiliar to common law practitioners.

2.24   Article 2 of the draft Convention makes clear the procedures in connection with which assistance should be made available. These include proceedings brought by the administrative authorities in respect of offences which are punishable under the national law of the requesting or requested Member State, and also criminal or administrative proceedings for which a legal person may be liable in the requesting State. Another innovation in the draft Convention is that Article 3 will, as currently drafted, require Member States to execute requests as soon as possible, taking account of deadlines indicated by the requesting State. There are also established arrangements under which a requested State will be obliged to inform the requesting State if its request cannot be executed in accordance with either its requirements or its deadlines.

Another departure from 1959 procedures relates to the service of procedural documents, which under the new E.U. Convention may be served directly on a foreign resident by the authorities in another country, without the necessity of involving a central point.[15]

2.25   One of the more significant changes proposed by the draft E.U. Convention is that it envisages the direct transmission of requests for mutual legal assistance between judicial authorities, without the involvement of central authorities, although the involvement of central authorities will remain possible in particular circumstances. This provision is clearly designed to speed up the communication channels by omitting a number of links in the chain, although within the U.K. the Home Office will still be the appropriate authority for receipt and transmission of requests.

The new Convention will also provide a basis for co-operation in the use of modern methods of technology, for example, the hearing of evidence by live video link. This will extend to cases where the defendants do not have to be brought to court themselves but can follow the court proceedings from prison via a video link, should a country wish to take advantage of this. This provision was proposed by Italy, who face extreme difficulties in trials of Mafia suspects, where the number of defendants in any one trial may be considerable and the consequent security problems are unsurmountable if the defendants have to be brought to court for trial. Within its domestic law now, provision is made for defendants in such cases to remain in prison, and follow the proceedings in court via television link.

When this Convention is eventually agreed, it will need to be ratified and implemented by individual Member States. However, the political will for ensuring that effective levels of judicial co-operation are maintained, should result in a rapid timetable being adopted for the enactment of any necessary new legislation.

2.26   The second international development lies with the Council of Europe, which has a draft Second Additional Protocol to the 1959 Convention. This draft protocol also seeks to extend mutual legal assistance to administrative offences, and deals with a number of other ancillary matters to make the workings of the 1959 Convention smoother. In a number of instances, the matters covered by the new draft Protocol are either similar to, or indeed identical to the provisions of the new draft E.U. Convention. In particular, it deals with the direct transmission of requests between judicial authorities, service of procedural documents by post, and the

---

15 See generally Chap. 4.

hearing of witnesses by live television link. A text of the draft Protocol is included in Appendix G.

2.27   Both the E.U. Convention, and the Protocol to the 1959 Convention are currently being actively discussed within their respective fora. It is impossible to anticipate when agreement will be reached, but negotiations are currently taking place in respect of both texts. It should be remembered, however, that Member States of the E.U. and the Council of Europe will require to implement the new instruments once they have been agreed. In the United Kingdom, further primary legislation may be necessary, in respect of those provisions not currently encompassed by existing legislation.

Commonwealth scheme

2.28   Whilst considerable attention has been given to the European Convention and the Protocols, the United Kingdom is also party to the Commonwealth Scheme relating to mutual assistance in criminal matters within the Commonwealth. The Commonwealth is not like many other international organisations, not being created by treaty. Its members do not in the main deal with each other in the field of legal co-operation under treaties but rather on a "family" basis, which makes the Commonwealth unique, in the mutual recognition between members of each other's laws and practices, rather than their reliance upon treaties.

2.29   In 1983, at one of its regular meetings, the Commonwealth Law Ministers, in recognition of the need to develop co-operation in the prosecution and investigation of crime, authorised senior officials to draw up a mutual assistance scheme in relation to criminal matters. Those officials, having referred to the European Convention and other bilateral treaties, produced the Commonwealth Scheme on Mutual Assistance in Criminal Matters which, with Professor McClean's detailed commentary, appears at Appendix H. The Scheme, which reflects the desire on the part of the Commonwealth to keep pace with the developments within Europe, was made by law ministers in April 1990, having been conceived in Harare in August 1986. As Professor McClean has made clear elsewhere,[16] the scheme does not create binding international obligations, and is not registered under Article 102 of the UN Charter; it represents more an agreed set of recommendations for legislative implementation by each government relying on each country to enact domestic legislation enabling it to provide the assistance proposed in the scheme.[17]

2.30   Two aspects of the Scheme bear comment for their innovative effect:

    (a)   the extended grounds for refusal of requests, which are more extensive than those arising under the European Convention, under which refusals are restricted to essential state interests, fiscal and political offences which are detailed elsewhere. The Commonwealth Scheme also identifies the following grounds for refusing assistance:

        (i)   military offences
        (ii)   double jeopardy
        (iii)   discrimination – where compliance would, in the belief of the requesting State result in prosecution or prejudice on racial, national or political grounds.

---

16 "Mutual Assistance in Criminal Matters: The Commonwealth Initiative" (1988) 37 I.C.L.Q. 177 at p. 180.
17 See App. A for statutory provisions enacted by Commonwealth members.

(b) the inclusion of assistance in tracing, seizing and confiscating proceeds and instrumentalities of crime, which has since become a major weapon in the international war against transnational crime. These provisions were an effective forerunner of the Vienna Convention (the United Nations Convention against illicit traffic in Narcotic Drugs and Psychotropic Substances in 1988) to which the United Kingdom is a party, and which was itself a spur to the 1990 Strasbourg Convention, the Council of Europe Convention on Laundering, Search, Seizure and Confiscation of the Proceeds from Crime.

2.31   Finally, reference should be made to the work done by the Commercial Crime Unit of the Commonwealth Secretariat, Legal and Constitutional Affairs Division, which was set up at up at the request of the Commonwealth Law Ministers, in recognition of the vulnerability of the smaller Commonwealth countries, some of whom have experienced major economic damage at the hands of unscrupulous international criminals. These countries lack the financial and investigative "muscle" to combat the fraudsters who may be attracted to off-shore islands to launder their funds. From its original task of giving assistance in investigations and training in the identification of the different types of financial crime, it now helps in developing legislation to ensure its members are able to participate in international efforts to fight crime.

The Secretariat assists its members by supplying draft laws, guides on national practice and procedure in criminal mutual assistance, together with guidance upon confiscation of crime proceeds, and closer co-operation between regulators. The Secretariat can be contacted at Marlborough House, Pall Mall, London SW1Y 5HX: Tel: 0171-839 3411: Fax: 0171-930 0827.

General

2.32   The provision of mutual assistance in criminal matters is governed by the Criminal Justice (International Co-operation) Act 1990. It does not confine this assistance merely to those countries covered by the treaties to which the United Kingdom is a party. Similarly, the United Kingdom does not require the existence of bilateral treaties or agreements before assistance can be given and evidence provided.[18]

In cases where the laws of the requesting state require a treaty before that state can provide full reciprocal assistance to the United Kingdom, then the United Kingdom may consider it appropriate to enter into a bilateral agreement with the state in question. Otherwise, in the absence of treaties or other international agreements (the terms of which, including United Kingdom reservations and declarations, will apply to requests made under them) the provisions of the Act will apply to the supply of mutual assistance to countries not covered by the various Agreements. If there is any doubt about the scope of the 1990 Act, then the European Convention should be referred to to resolve such problems. In the case of *Atlan*,[19] it was stated that "any uncertainty can, indeed must, be resolved by resorting to the (European) Convention which it is the purpose of the Act to follow".

---

18 Save in relation to the confiscation of criminal assets, in which event the United Kingdom will normally require a multi or bilateral confiscation agreement prior to granting such assistance.
19 (Unreported) June 10, 1996, 91/4809/S1 & 92/6348/51

CHAPTER 3
Central Authorities

3.00   As international judicial co-operation arose out of the need for independent States to work together to fight cross border criminal activity, at its most simple, it consisted of a diplomatic request from one State to another for assistance. Gradually, the links formalised, but the diplomatic basis remained, and accounts for the formal language in which many requests are still framed. It also explains the development in many countries of a central point within a jurisdiction as the route for all incoming and outgoing requests. This central point is often situated within the Ministry of Justice of a country, although it may be situated either independently, or in another government department (for example, in the Ministry of Foreign Affairs). Requests for assistance are routed through this central point both on their outward and inward journey, although in many countries the point acts as little more than a post box, ensuring that requests are correctly addressed, etc., but otherwise adding little of value to the request.

3.01   There is a central point in the United Kingdom, located in the Home Office, and it is now known as the Mutual Legal Assistance Section in the Judicial Co-operation Unit (the MLA Section).[1] Although based in the Home Office, it is the MLA Section for requests to all parts of the United Kingdom including all three separate jurisdictions – Scotland, and Northern Ireland as well as England and Wales. Its functions are much more than that of a post box, however, and it is involved in respect of all incoming and outgoing requests. It is, for example, the MLA Section which determines, on receipt of an international letter of request, to which authority it shall be allocated for execution, and checks that all the documentation is in order before it sends it out for execution. It also receives all outgoing requests, and checks them for completeness before transmission. Although currently, under Article 15(2) of the 1959 Convention, requests may be transmitted directly between competent judicial authorities in the case of urgency, such cases will by definition be the exception rather than the rule.

3.02   Developments within Europe, however, make the examination of the role of a central authority important. Firstly, under the Schengen Implementation Convention, Article 53 provides that, "Requests for assistance may be made directly between judicial authorities and returned via the same channels." This means that for all Member States of the E.U. which have signed the Schengen Implementation Convention, (all Member States with the exception of the United Kingdom and Ireland), direct transmission of requests between competent authorities in all (including non-urgent) cases is possible. Even in those states which have signed the Schengen Implementation Convention, however, direct transmission is not used in all cases. Although the United Kingdom and Ireland have not signed the Schengen Implementation Convention, the provisions of a Protocol to the Treaty of Amsterdam of 1997 relate to the position of the United Kingdom, and make it clear that it can apply to opt in to particular provisions of the Convention when it chooses to do so. In May 1999,

---

1 MLA Section, The Home Office, Queen Anne's Gate, London, SW1H 9AT (Tel: 0171-273 2437; Fax: 0171-273 4400/4584).

the United Kingdom announced its intention of applying to opt in to those provisions of the Schengen Implementation Agreement which are contained in Title 3, and relate to police co-operation, (with the exception of one article on police co-operation which is outside the scope of this work), mutual assistance in criminal matters, the application of the *non bis in idem* principle, extradition, the transfer of the enforcement of criminal judgements, narcotic drugs, firearms and ammunition. The principal effect of this decision on the United Kingdom's position as a Mutual Legal Assistance partner is that Articles 48 to 53 (Chapter 2), relating to mutual assistance in criminal matters, will in due course be incorporated into United Kingdom law.

3.03   The main provisions of Chapter 2 of Title 3 of the Schengen Convention are:

(a)   Article 48 provides that the provisions of Chapter 2 are intended to supplement the 1959 Convention, but should not affect the broader provisions of any bilateral agreements between parties.

(b)   Article 49 extends the provision of mutual legal assistance to certain administrative offences.

(c)   Article 50 extends the provision of mutual legal assistance to certain customs, excise and value added tax offences.

(d)   Article 51 restricts the possible reservations to search and seizure provisions to cases where the offence under investigation is punishable under the laws of both states by a maximum sentence of imprisonment of at least six months.

(e)   Article 52 provides that procedural documents may be sent directly by post to persons who are in the territory of another signatory to the Convention.

(f)   Article 53 provides that requests for assistance may be made directly between judicial authorities and returned via the same channels.

The full text of these Articles is contained in Appendix J.

In relation to Article 48, separate agreements, for example between the Benelux countries (Belgium, the Netherlands and Luxembourg), and between the Nordic countries, already provide for an informal and direct approach to judicial co-operation, and it is the efficient model which these countries provide which demonstrate the future for European co-operation generally.

3.04   The second development is contained in the new (draft) EU Mutual Legal Assistance Convention.[2] In Article 5, it states, (as currently drafted): "Requests for mutual assistance ... shall be made directly between judicial authorities with territorial competence for their service and execution, and returned through the same channels ..." Once agreed, this would appear to envisage the direct transmission of all requests as in the Schengen Convention, but the precise effect of this provision on the United Kingdom, and the subsequent role of the MLA Section, is not clear. One possibility would be that the United Kingdom could expressly reserve its position, with a declaration to the effect that, because its judicial authorities do not in general have authority to execute requests received directly, as envisaged by the draft proposals, requests or information should therefore continue to be sent via the MLA Section. A second possibility would involve a much more direct approach, with those

---

2 App. F (and see general comments on draft Convention in chap. 2 above).

authorities which currently execute requests receiving them directly from their counterparts abroad. The matter remains under discussion, and since the Convention is still in draft, a final solution is not currently required.

3.05 With the application to opt in by the United Kingdom to those provisions of Schengen which refer to direct transmission of requests for judicial assistance, and the possibility also of agreement being reached with regard to an E.U. Mutual Legal Assistance Convention which contains provisions on direct transmission of requests, it is clear that the role of central authorities in connection with letters of request is bound to undergo change in the future. It is also clear that there is a considerable move to decentralise the operation of international judicial co-operation within Europe as a whole. Within the civil law jurisdictions, it can be expected that much greater use will be made of the direct transmission route, and practitioners in the United Kingdom should be aware of the new provisions, to understand the approach of their continental colleagues. Already, following the adoption by the Member States of the relevant Schengen provisions, this is happening. In some Member States, although statistics are difficult to come by, it is thought that at least as many requests now proceed by direct transmission as through a central authority.

3.06 The MLA Section is staffed by, and is currently situated within, the Home Office. The staff of the section are experienced administrators working exclusively on requests for legal assistance. The Section works closely, and on a daily basis with the International Division of the National Criminal Intelligence Office (NCIS) situated at Vauxhall, in London. Normally, all requests to the United Kingdom for judicial assistance in criminal matters are channelled through the Home Office, and further, all outgoing requests are transmitted through it. The only current exceptions would be requests which, for reasons of urgency, have been transmitted directly to the judicial authority involved (1959 Convention, Article 15(2)). However, it is unusual for incoming requests to be transmitted directly to the judicial authority in the United Kingdom, since it will be unlikely for the foreign authority to know which will be the appropriate authority to execute the request, and time could in fact be wasted by direct transmission. In the case of outgoing requests, judicial authorities in the United Kingdom may transmit these directly to the competent authority abroad in case of urgency (through the intermediary of Interpol), but in such cases, a copy may also be sent to the Home Office.

3.07 With incoming requests, the MLA Section liaises with law enforcement authorities or the NCIS about execution, since in nearly all cases, the involvement of some law enforcement authority will be necessary. Requests for police co-operation (for example, directly from an examining magistrate abroad), do not need to be sent to the Home Office, but if they are, the Home Office will pass them on to the appropriate police channels, through NCIS. The need for close co-operation between the MLA Section and the NCIS is therefore obvious. Currently, requests for the service of documents are also sent through the Home Office although this is likely to change if the provisions proposed in the new draft E.U. Convention are brought into force. These provisions provide for the direct service of procedural documents by post from one Member State to a person in a second Member State. It is thought that such direct service already occurs, although it is not possible to be certain about the extent of the practice.

3.08 In the case of outgoing requests, many authorities, in addition to sending the request through the Home Office send an additional copy through Interpol. The 1959 Convention provides that where direct transmission is permitted under the Convention, (*i.e.* as a result of urgency) it may take place through Interpol. This means that in the case of urgent requests which are to be directly transmitted under Article 15 of the 1959 Convention, the request may be sent through Interpol and there is no need for a further copy to be sent through any other channels. As a matter of practice, however, a further copy is usually sent to the Home Office for information only. This is not necessary.

3.09 The numbers of requests dealt with by the MLA Section have risen gradually over recent years. The figures reproduced in the table below relate to total incoming and outgoing requests between the dates specified.

	Number of incoming requests received	Number of outgoing requests processed
Apr. 1, 1994– Mar. 31, 1995	1,929	1,072
Apr. 1, 1995– Mar. 31, 1996	2,522	1,101
Apr. 1, 1996– Mar. 31, 1997	2,353	1,051
Apr. 1, 1997– Sep. 30, 1998	3,851 (2,610 received between Oct. 1, 1997 and Sep. 30, 1998)	2,000

It will be noted that the United Kingdom sends approximately half as many requests out as it receives. Regarding the total numbers of requests, by comparison, some European countries with much smaller populations deal with many times the number of requests as does the Home Office, in both directions.[3] There is no obvious reason for this, apart perhaps from a feeling in civil law countries that somehow assistance within a common law jurisdiction will be unduly difficult.

3.10 The figures for Scotland, although low, are showing considerable recent increases. For the year 1997/1998, there were 57 criminal letters of request, and for the year 1998/1999 there were 92. These figures include incoming and outgoing requests, but exclude all requests relating merely to the service of documents.

In terms of numbers, France makes by far the largest number of requests to the United Kingdom – accounting in some years for approximately half of the number of requests received – but many of these are fairly routine matters (such as traffic offences). A number of countries – among them the Netherlands, Spain, the USA, France – all receive frequent requests from the United Kingdom authorities, but there is not one country which predominates in respect of numbers of outgoing requests.

3.11 Many of the requests received relate to the service of documents. In the 12 months ending on September 30, 1998, of the 2,610 requests received by the MLA Section, 1,420, or more than half, were known to be for the service of documents. The total number of requests containing substantial matters requiring investigation in the United Kingdom is therefore at a level of about half the numbers shown in the above table. As far as outgoing requests are concerned, the United Kingdom's policy is to seek assistance only in respect of fairly substantial matters, and there is relatively little material sent from the United Kingdom relating to the service of documents. This factor contributes to the disparity in numbers between incoming and outgoing requests.

---

3 Note that figures for last period cover 18 months.

3.12 The MLA Section at the Home Office performs an important function in respect of both incoming and outgoing requests. In essence, in respect of incoming requests, it arranges for the execution of all requests, ensuring that priority is given to the most urgent cases. It will ensure that requests are sent to the appropriate authorities for execution, (police, courts, Customs and Excise, the Scottish authorities, Serious Fraud Office (SFO), *etc.*) and initially ensures that all documentation is complete. In the event that documents are incomplete, it will also take steps to remedy that situation. If, for example, a request relates to serious fraud, and it appears that a reference to the SFO will be appropriate, the Home Office will ensure the necessary undertakings are included in the documentation.[3a] It will also, in such cases, liaise with the SFO about whether or not the case is an appropriate one for the SFO to take on with a view to the execution of the requests. It will ensure that requests for assistance are in conformity with United Kingdom law and its international obligations, *e.g.* that the requests emanate from a competent authority and are for the proper purposes of criminal proceedings or investigations. Similarly it will ensure that public policy considerations are observed, *e.g.* double jeopardy, national security, etc.

The MLA Section will ensure that courts, police and other authorities are aware, if there is a need, for requested evidence to be obtained in the presence of foreign investigators and/or lawyers (both protection and defence). Whilst costs are normally met by the requested authority in accordance with established international practice, it will seek the agreement of requesting authorities to pay extraordinary costs of executing requests. The transmission of evidence to requesting authorities is also made by the MLA Section who will also check whether any part of the request remains outstanding.

3.13 The Home Office has produced and published guidelines, and while these are predominantly designed for those seeking assistance from the United Kingdom, much valuable information is contained within them about the functions of the MLA Section and the assistance it can provide. The Guide is available in French, German, Italian and Spanish, as well as English, and a new edition, published in 1999, is included in Annex K.

The Home Office has also drawn up a Code of Practice, which is included in the guidelines, and this document sets out the levels of service which can be expected from the MLA Section. The Code of Practice, which was drawn up following the Joint Action referred to in paragraph 3.15 below, relates both to incoming and outgoing requests, although the guidelines themselves are of principal use to those who wish to submit requests to the United Kingdom for assistance.

3.14 The Code of Practice is a direct result of the Joint Action adopted by the Council of the European Union on June 29, 1998, on good practice in mutual legal assistance in criminal matters.[4] This Joint Action provides for certain minimum standards to be adhered to by all Member States in the execution of requests. The United Kingdom was instrumental in promoting the agreement to this Joint Action during its Presidency of the E.U. in the first half of 1998, and under its terms, Member States are required to deposit with the General Secretariat of the Council of the European Union within twelve months of its adoption, statements of good practice. These statements should include practices in executing requests, including the transmission of results, from other Member States and sending requests to other Member States for legal assistance in criminal matters. The United Kingdom's statement,

---

3a See Chap. 12 below.
4 [1998] O.J. L191 (App. L).

submitted in June 1999, is included in the latest version of the guidelines referred to above.

3.15 The Joint Action requires that the statements of practice shall include undertakings by Member States to promote the following practices in accordance with their own national law and legal procedures:

(a) When requested to do so by the requesting Member States, to acknowledge all requests and written enquiries concerning the execution of requests unless a substantive reply is sent quickly; the requesting Member State may not require an acknowledgement unless the request is marked"urgent"by that Member State or in its view, an acknowledgement is necessary in the circumstances of the case.

(b) When acknowledging such requests and enquiries, to provide the requesting authority with the name and contact details, including telephone and fax numbers, of the authority, and if possible the person, responsible for executing the request.

(c) To give priority, so far as it is not contrary to the law of the requested Member State, to requests which have clearly been marked "urgent" by the requesting authority; and to treat requests, whether or not marked "urgent" no less favourably than comparable enquiries made in the requested Member State on behalf of the Member State's own authorities.

(d) Where the assistance requested cannot be executed in whole or in part, to give the requesting authorities a written or oral report explaining the difficulty and where possible offering to consider jointly with the requesting authority how the difficulty might be overcome.

(e) Where it is foreseeable that the assistance cannot, or cannot fully, be provided within any deadline set by the requesting Member State, and that this will impair proceedings in the requesting Member State, promptly to give its authority a written or oral report, and any further reports requested by that authority explaining when the assistance requested is likely to be provided.

(f) To submit requests for assistance as soon as the precise assistance needed is identified, and where a request is marked"urgent"or a deadline is indicated, to explain the reasons for the urgency or deadline; the Statement shall also include an undertaking not to mark as "urgent" requests which are of minor importance.

(g) To ensure that requests are submitted in compliance with the relevant treaty or other international arrangements.

(h) When submitting requests for assistance, to provide the requested authorities with the name and contact details, including telephone and fax numbers, of the authority, and if possible, the person responsible for issuing the request.

3.16 The Joint Action also contains provisions to ensure that within a Member State, the statement of good practice shall be brought to the attention of the judicial or competent authorities: "inviting them to promote measures within their competence as may be necessary with a view to its implementation." This should ensure that all concerned in the process of mutual legal assistance are aware of their international obligations, and the particular responsibilities which lie on them.

The Joint Action does not prescribe maximum time limits for the execution of letters of request, since this depends almost entirely on the type of assistance requested. However, the United Kingdom's Code of Practice goes further than is required in the Joint Action, and does lay down time scales within which various activities can be expected from it. For example, it provides that where the request is for the service of summonses or other procedural documents, then the request will be executed within X working days of its receipt in the Home Office. This initiative is a major step forward in the execution of international requests for assistance, since it is the first time that the execution of international requests has been the subject of agreement as to minimum performance levels.

3.17 Worries about the delays which appeared to be involved when international requests for judicial assistance were necessary were a major reason for another recent European initiative. This initiative is part of the European Union's Action Plan against organised crime,[5] and consists of the establishment of a mechanism to effect mutual evaluations of the application and implementation of international instruments in criminal matters. The first such mutual evaluation was started in 1998, (following the procedures laid down in Joint Action[6]) and is concerned with delays in international mutual legal assistance. Evaluation of all Member States will be carried out between 1998 and 2000, and recommendations will be made both to the individual country concerned and to the E.U. generally, with a view principally to reducing the delays in the execution of requests for mutual legal assistance. The preliminary conclusions of this process are beginning to appear and the Member States of the E.U. are concerned to ensure that the recommendations which emerge are implemented as soon as possible.

3.18 A further initiative within the E.U. which is of considerable importance in the field of international judicial co-operation is the European Judicial Network (the EJN). This was set up as a result of another Joint Action of June 29, 1998 (Appendix M), and adopted by the Council on the basis of Article K3 of the Treaty on European Union. Initial meetings of the EJN have taken place, and it is slowly developing into a useful aid to international assistance. As the title suggests, it consists of a network of contact points between the Member States. Each Member State has nominated a number of "contact points", bearing in mind internal rules and internal division of responsibilities, and taking care to ensure effective coverage of the whole of its territory and all forms of serious crime. Each Member State has also to ensure that its contact points have an adequate knowledge of a language of the European Union other than its own national language, bearing in mind the need to be able to communicate with the contact points in the other Member States.

The head of the MLA Section at the Home Office has taken on the role of one of the contact points for the European Judicial Network, and should be contacted in the first instance in respect of any queries in relation to international judicial assistance involving Member States of the E.U.

3.19 In terms of the Joint Action, the EJN will operate in particular in the following three ways:—

(a) it shall facilitate the establishment of appropriate contacts between the contact points in the various Member States in order to carry out the functions which the Joint Action lays down for them (see below);

(b) it shall organise periodic meetings of the Member States' representatives;

---

5 [1997] O.J. 251/1.
6 Joint Action of Dec. 5, 1997 [1997] O.J. L344/7.

(c)   it shall constantly provide a certain amount of up to date background information, notably by means of an appropriate telecommunications network.

3.20   The functions of the contact points are set out in the Joint Action. Their first function is to act as active intermediaries with the task of facilitating judicial co-operation between Member States, particularly in action to combat forms of serious crime. To this end, they should be available to enable local judicial authorities and other competent authorities in their own country, contact points in the other countries, and local judicial and other competent authorities in the other countries to establish the most appropriate direct contacts.

Secondly, they should be able to provide the legal and practical information necessary to the local judicial authorities in their own country, to the contact points in the other countries, and to the local judicial authorities in the other countries to enable them to prepare an effective request for judicial co-operation or to improve judicial co-operation in general.

Their third function is to improve co-ordination of judicial co-operation in cases where a series of requests from the local judicial authorities in a Member State necessitates co-ordinated action in another Member State.

3.21   The function of the contact points is therefore not necessarily to provide all the answers to queries themselves, but through their network of international contacts, to be able to find an answer. Within the United Kingdom, queries should be addressed to the United Kingdom's contact points, and not to the contact points in other countries. It will be the function of the United Kingdom contact point to make that further contact for any information required which he or she does not have. Within the United Kingdom, the nominated contact points are firstly, the head of the MLA Section at the Home Office, who will be the first contact for general queries. (The contact details are contained in Appendix K).

3.22   The development of a telecommunications network for the European Judicial Network is a logical next step, and discussions are actively taking place to promote such a system, subject to suitable safeguards relating to confidentiality of the material to be transmitted. CD Roms containing the texts of the relevant international instruments have been prepared and distributed. Further CD Roms will contain synopses of the relevant domestic legislation in individual Member States, to enable checks to be made about proposed requests. One tangible sign of the EJN's existence is its own website: its address is http://www.eu.ue.rje and this site contains the text of all the international Conventions and instruments on which international judicial co-operation is based. It is constantly updated. This initiative, and others referred to in this Chapter reflect the dynamic nature of the field of international mutual legal assistance and the evolving roles of the principal players in that field. The rate of change is dramatic. It is less than ten years since the United Kingdom signed the 1959 Convention and implemented it with the 1990 legislation. Already, much has changed, and within the next ten years much more change and development can be anticipated. Among these changes, those affecting the role of the MLA Section will be as fundamental as any other, and the shape of international judicial co-operation will alter considerably as a consequence.

CHAPTER 4

Service of Overseas Process in the United Kingdom, and Service of United Kingdom Process Overseas

4.00   Sections 1 and 2 of the Criminal Justice (International Co-operation) Act 1990 as amended, are the sections which generally cover the service of overseas process in the United Kingdom, and the service of United Kingdom process overseas.

Current European developments are likely to affect these provisions and are specifically dealt with at heading C: Recent developments, (paragraph 4.11 *et seq.* below).

A. The service of overseas process in the United Kingdom

Section 1 is as follows:—

"1.(1)   This section has effect where the Secretary of State receives from the government of, or other authority in, a country or territory outside the United Kingdom—

(a)   a summons or other process requiring a person to appear as defendant or attend as a witness in criminal proceedings in that country or territory; or

(b)   a document issued by a court exercising criminal jurisdiction in that country or territory and recording a decision of the court made in the exercise of that jurisdiction, together with a request for it to be served on a person in the United Kingdom.

(2)   The Secretary of State or, where the person to be served is in Scotland, the Lord Advocate may cause the process or document to be served by post or, if the request is for personal service, direct the chief officer of police for the area in which that person appears to be to cause it to be personally served on him.

(3)   Service by virtue of this section of any such process as is mentioned in subsection (1)(a) above shall not impose any obligation under the law of any part of the United Kingdom to comply with it.

(4)   Any such process served by virtue of this section shall be accompanied by a notice—

(a)   stating the effect of subsection (3) above;

(b)   indicating that the person on whom it is served may wish to seek advice as to the possible consequences of failing to comply with the process under the law of the country or territory where it was issued; and

    (c)   indicating that under that law he or she may not, as a witness, be accorded the same rights and privileges as would be accorded to him or her in criminal proceedings in the United Kingdom.

(5)   Where a chief officer of police is directed under this section to cause any process or document to be served he or she shall after it has been served forthwith inform the Secretary of State or, as the case may be, the Lord Advocate when and how it was served and (if possible) furnish him or her with a receipt signed by the person on whom it was served; and if the chief officer has been unable to cause the process or document to be served he or she shall forthwith inform the Secretary of State or, as the case may be, the Lord Advocate of that fact and of the reason.

(6)   In the application of this section to Northern Ireland for references to chief officer of police there shall be substituted references to the Chief Constable of the Royal Ulster Constabulary."

Summons/process to attend

4.01   This section will apply in respect of any documents or process from a foreign tribunal or court which it is desired to serve on a person in the United Kingdom. The wording of the section clearly indicates that the summons or other process should be judicial in its nature. Thus a letter from lawyers seeking the attendance of a witness for either prosecution or defence would not qualify. All such requests should be in writing and be sent to the Mutual Legal Assistance Section in the Judicial Co-operation Unit (the MLA Section) at the Home Office, which has been nominated by the Secretary of State as the appropriate authority to execute such requests. The Home Office has indicated it will not normally act on oral requests; as with all requests, advanced faxed copies will be acted upon if accompanied by an undertaking to forward the original request by airmail or courier within a reasonable period,[1] normally seven days. Where personal service is not necessary, then the MLA Section will serve by post on the addressee in the United Kingdom, using recorded delivery postal service. If, however, the foreign authority has requested that the process be served personally, then the MLA Section may, through Interpol, check the address of the person to be served before asking the local police force to serve personally on the addressee. In cases where the whereabouts in the United Kingdom of the addressee are clear and certain, the Home Office may send the documents direct to the local police force for service.

    4.02   The requirements of section 1(4) mean that a notice must be served with any procedural documents which explains that the service does not place the addressee under any obligation under United Kingdom law with regard to the documents served. The notice should also indicate that under the law of the foreign country a potential witness may not be accorded the same rights and privileges as would be accorded to him or her in criminal proceedings in the United Kingdom. For instance, the privilege against self-incrimination may not be available or in certain circumstances he or she may be compelled to give evidence. The Home Office has prepared such a document, which is included with all process to be served, whether postally, or personally. If the person is served personally, he or she is asked to sign a receipt, acknowledging that the document or process concerned has been received and this receipt is in due course returned to the Home Office. If the documents are served by the police, then, under section 1(5), the police inform the Secretary of State (the MLA

---

1 U.K. Guidelines, para. 14.

Section) of the details of service, and also obtain from the person served a receipt if possible. The evidence of service, including where appropriate the certificate of recorded delivery, or the notice from the chief officer of police as required in subsection (5), together with the receipt from the person served, will be transmitted by the MLA Section to the foreign authority as proof of service.

4.03   There is no requirement that the person to be served has to be a United Kingdom national. The only requirement is that the person should be in the United Kingdom at the time. Obviously, however, it is essential that there is a clear address provided, so that service can be effected. Although the MLA Section can ask local police to assist in locating individuals there must be some basic information provided before this can be possible and if no clear information is provided, then the Home Office will have no alternative but to return the papers to the requesting authority. There is also no requirement that the offence in respect of which any criminal proceedings are in course in the foreign country constitutes an offence under United Kingdom law.

4.04   Documents sent for service in the United Kingdom where the original material is not in English should be accompanied by a translation into English. The Home Office ask that requests for service of summonses, judgments and other procedural documents should include:

(a)   the original document(s) with a translation or, if the original documents cannot be provided, a translation certified as a true copy of the original.

(b)   the identity, date of birth and location of any person on whom a summons or judgment is to be served; details of that person's connection with the proceedings; and details of any particular way in which the summons or judgment should be served.

(c)   details of any allowances and expenses to which a person asked to appear in proceedings abroad is entitled; the address of the court where the proceedings are to take place; and the name and telephone number of an official of the court from whom the person asked to appear can seek further information if necessary.

Good practice however suggests that additionally the following should be included:

(a)   Details of the authority making the request

(b)   Details of the purposes and reason for the request

(c)   Description of the offences under investigation.

It is important to note that service of process in relation to the possible attendance of a witness in proceedings abroad will place the potential witness under no obligation to attend those proceedings. This is a reflection of Article 8 of the European Convention deriving from the international custom by which witnesses are completely free not to go to the requesting country. The notice accompanying the documents will also indicate that the person who is served may wish to seek legal advice as to the consequence of his or her non-compliance with the process under the law of the issuing state. If, however, the witness is willing to attend the proceedings, then the service of the document will have the desired effect. In many cases, however, the authorities abroad will have made preliminary informal enquiries to establish the willingness or otherwise of witnesses to attend foreign proceedings, and the service of the summons will be a formality. It is also possible that, in the case of a willing witness, there will be no formal process to serve at all – contact will be made informally and arrangements will be made directly between the witness and the judicial authority abroad. There is nothing to stop such informal contact being made.

4.05 There may be many reasons why a witness in one jurisdiction declines to attend in court in a foreign jurisdiction. The absence of a witness however, may be crucial to the success of either a prosecution or a defence case, and it is for that reason that developments are current in relation to the transmission of a witness's evidence from one jurisdiction to another by live television link. Particularly where a witness lives at a considerable distance from the court, it may be economically beneficial to arrange for this procedure to be put in place. Both the new (draft) E.U. Mutual Legal Assistance Convention, and the draft additional Protocol to the Council of Europe Convention make provision for such arrangements to be made.

B. The service of United Kingdom process overseas

4.06 Section 2 of the Criminal Justice (International Co-operation) Act 1990 as amended is as follows:—

"2.(1)   Process of the following descriptions, that is to say—

    (a)   a summons requiring a person charged with an offence to appear before a court in the United Kingdom; and

    (b)   a summons or order requiring a person to attend before a court in the United Kingdom for the purpose of giving evidence in criminal proceedings, may be issued or made notwithstanding that the person in question is outside the United Kingdom, and may be served outside the United Kingdom in accordance with arrangements made by the Secretary of State.

  (2)   In relation to Scotland subsection (1) applies to any document which may competently be served on any accused person or on any person who may give evidence in criminal proceedings.

  (3)   Service of any process outside the United Kingdom by virtue of this section shall not impose any obligation under the law of any part of the United Kingdom to comply with it, and accordingly failure to do so shall not constitute contempt of any court or be a ground for issuing a warrant to secure the attendance of the person in question or, in Scotland, for imposing any penalty.

  (4)   Subsection (3) above is without prejudice to the service of any process (with the usual consequences for non-compliance) on the person in question if subsequently effected in the United Kingdom."

These provisions broadly mirror those in section 1, and allow for the service abroad of documents relating to court proceedings in the United Kingdom. In the same way as for section 1, potential witnesses abroad cannot be forced to attend court in the United Kingdom, although subsection 3 makes it clear that if, subsequently, service on the person is effected in the United Kingdom, immunity from proceedings for non-compliance will not continue.

4.07 Article 12 of the 1959 European Convention provides that a witness or expert, whatever his or her nationality, responding to such process by attending before the judicial authorities of the requesting State, shall not be prosecuted or detained or subjected to any other restriction of his or her personal liberty in the territory of that State, in respect of acts or convictions anterior to his or her departure from the territory of the requested State. This is an immunity that ceases at the expiry of 15 days from the date when his or her presence is no longer required, if he or she has had the opportunity of leaving the jurisdiction, has remained or, having left, has voluntarily returned. A similar provision appears in the Commonwealth Scheme. This immunity is the subject of an express reservation by the United Kingdom government whereby the United Kingdom may claim the reciprocal benefit of Article 12 only in so far as it has been specifically requested by the person to whom the immunity would apply or by the appropriate authorities of the party from whom assistance is requested. Further, the reservation also provides that a request for immunity will not be granted where the judicial authorities of the United Kingdom consider that granting it would not be in the public interest. It is by no means certain that such protection would apply in the absence of the Convention, Treaty or other agreement and it would be advisable therefore for the witness or suspect or his or her advisers, to establish with the requesting state via the Home Office the extent, if any, to which a witness would have immunity and, if appropriate, request immunity.

Documents for service abroad should be sent through the Home Office in the normal way.

4.08 Pursuant to section 10 of the 1990 Act, Rules of Court have been made governing the procedure for Magistrates Courts and Crown Courts in relation to summons or orders issued under section 2. The Magistrates Courts (Criminal Justice (International Co-operation) Rules 1991[2] provide for the way in which a summons or order is issued. The Justices Clerk must send it to the Secretary of State with a view to its being served in accordance with arrangements made by the Secretary of State. Service of the summons or order may be proved in any legal proceedings by a certificate given by or on behalf of the Secretary of State. A statement in any such certificate that a summons has been served, the manner in which service was effected and the date of service is admissible as evidence of any facts stated as such. Similar provisions obtain in the Crown Court whereby the Crown Court Rules 1982 have been amended[3] to provide for the witness summons or order issued by the Crown Court in accordance with section 2(1) to be sent to the Secretary of State to be served in accordance with arrangements made by him or her.

4.09 Where a court in the United Kingdom requires to hear the evidence of a witness abroad, and the witness is unwilling or unable to travel to the United Kingdom to give that evidence, live television links may provide the answer. Under the Criminal Justice Act 1988, section 32, evidence can be given through a live television link, other than from the defendant, if the witness is outside the United Kingdom, and with the leave of the court, in a limited category of cases. These include the offences of murder, manslaughter, and proceedings being conducted by the Director of the Serious Fraud Office (SFO), as well as some offences of assault and some offences against children. In several cases already, notably those involving prosecutions brought by the SFO, the evidence of witnesses present in other jurisdictions has been transmitted live to courts in the United Kingdom. Once the evidence which the potential witness can give has been ascertained, whether itself by letter of request or otherwise, a separate letter of request will be necessary to the foreign

---

2 S.I. 1991 No. 1074 (App. N).
3 S.I. 1991 No. 1288 (App. O).

authorities, requesting that the witness be summoned to a court or other place in that jurisdiction. The requesting authority will make arrangements for a live television link to be set up between the foreign venue and the United Kingdom court, and will send to the foreign country representatives of the court, the prosecution and the defence, and the evidence will be taken in the usual way.[4]

The main difficulty surrounding such proceedings is in connection with the consequences of the witness giving perjured evidence. In such a case, where the witness gives evidence in France, for example which is transmitted to a court in the United Kingdom, it is necessary to consider what could be done, and under what jurisdiction, if that witness commits perjury in the proceedings.

4.10 The current draft E.U. Mutual Legal Assistance Convention contains a provision that each Member State shall take the necessary measures to ensure that its national law applies, where witnesses or experts are being heard within its territory in conformity with the provisions of the Convention, and refuse to testify when under an obligation to testify, or do not testify according to the truth, in the same way as if the hearing had taken place in a national procedure. According to this provision therefore, if a witness is being heard in proceedings in the United Kingdom, but is actually in France, French legislation will allow any perjury committed by the witness to be prosecuted in France according to French law, even though the perjured evidence was given in proceedings in the United Kingdom. With this type of safeguard the new provision will provide an additional practical facility to those involved in the prosecution and defence of offences with an international element.

C. Recent developments

4.11 Current developments will enable postal service of procedural documents directly by judicial authorities on an addressee in another country and the postal service of documents from foreign judicial authorities on persons resident in the United Kingdom.

Article 7 of the 1959 Convention requires a requested state to effect service of writs and records of judicial verdicts transmitted to it for that purpose by a requesting state. Arrangements are being made in Article 4 of the draft E.U. Convention and in Articles 9 and 9 *bis* of the draft Council of Europe Protocol which will permit summonses and other documents to be sent directly by a state to a person in another state by post. Article 52 of the Schengen Implementation Convention contains similar provisions. The role of the Central Authority in this process is therefore being gradually reduced.

4.12 Under Article 4 of the E.U. Convention as currently drafted, the general rule will be that, subject to certain exceptions set out in paragraph 2, "procedural documents" addressed to a person in the territory of other Member States will be sent by post. No definition of what constitutes a procedural document has been provided and the intention is that the term should be interpreted broadly. Article 9 of the Council of Europe Protocol as currently drafted enables summonses to be posted to a witness or expert in another state and Article 9 *bis* makes similar provision in respect of writs and judicial verdicts. For the purpose of summonses dealt with under the Council of Europe Protocol, a state will be entitled to make a declaration that it requires copies of summonses posted to persons on its territory to be copied to its Ministry of Justice or another authority.

4.13 In so far as languages are concerned, Article 4 of the draft E.U. Convention

---

4 Further consideration of cases where it was sought to introduce evidence by television link is made at paragraph 5.48 below.

requires that translations of at least the most important portions of the documents be provided in a language of the Member State where the addressee is, or some other language if the issuing Member State is aware that the addressee only understands that other language. Summonses served under Article 9 of the draft Council of Europe Protocol will have to be translated into the language of the state to which they are posted, unless the addressee is a national of the issuing State. The translation arrangements for writs and judicial verdicts, dealt with under Article 9 *bis* of the draft Protocol, are similar to those which apply under the draft E.U. Convention.

4.14 Paragraph 4 of the draft E.U. provision imposes an obligation on the issuing state to enclose a report, appropriately translated if necessary, indicating where the addressee may obtain information regarding his or her rights and obligations arising out of the relevant documents. A summons which has been sent by post under Article 9 of the draft Council of Europe Protocol must include a descriptive notice of its application.

4.15 The E.U. text currently specifically provides for the application of certain matters in respect of witnesses and others by virtue of Articles 8 (non-punishment for failure to obey a summons), 9 (expenses) and 12 (immunity from prosecution) of the 1959 Convention and also under the Benelux Treaty. Paragraph 3 of Article 9 of the Council of Europe Protocol states that Article 8 of the 1959 Convention will apply by analogy.

CHAPTER 5

Overseas Evidence for Use in the United Kingdom

5.00 Section 3 of the Criminal Justice (International Co-operation) Act 1990 as amended is the section which generally covers the application by authorities in the United Kingdom for evidence to be obtained from abroad.

Section 3 of the 1990 Act is as follows:

"**3.**(1) Where, on an application made in accordance with subsection (2) below, it appears to a justice of peace or a judge or, in Scotland, to a sheriff or a judge—

    (a) that an offence has been committed or that there are reasonable grounds for suspecting that an offence has been committed; and

    (b) that proceedings in respect of the offence have been instituted or that the offence is being investigated,

      he may issue a letter ("a letter of request") requesting assistance in obtaining outside the United Kingdom such evidence as is specified in the letter for use in the proceedings or investigation.

(2) An application under subsection (1) above may be made by a prosecuting authority or, if proceedings have been instituted, by the person charged in those proceedings.

(3) A prosecuting authority which is for the time being designated for the purposes of this section by an order made by the Secretary of State by statutory instrument may itself issue a letter of request if

    (a) it is satisfied as to the matters mentioned in subsection (1)(a) above; and

    (b) the offence in question is being investigated or the authority has instituted proceedings in respect of it.

(4) Subject to subsection (5) below, a letter of request shall be sent to the Secretary of State for transmission either—

    (a) to a court or tribunal specified in the letter and exercising jurisdiction in the place where the evidence is to be obtained; or

    (b) to any authority recognised by the government of the country or territory in question as the appropriate authority for receiving requests for assistance of the kind to which this section applies.

(5) In cases of urgency a letter of request may be sent direct to such a court or tribunal as is mentioned in subsection (4)(a) above.

(6) In this section "evidence" includes documents and other articles.

(7) Evidence obtained by virtue of a letter of request shall not without the consent of such authority as is mentioned in subsection (4)(b) above be used for any purpose other than that specified in the letter; and when any document or other article obtained pursuant to a letter of request is no longer required for that purpose (or for any other purpose for which such consent has been obtained), it shall be returned to such an authority unless that authority indicates that the document or article need not be returned.

(8) In exercising the discretion conferred by section 25 of the Criminal Justice Act 1988 (exclusion of evidence otherwise admissible) in relation to a statement contained in evidence taken pursuant to a letter of request the court shall have regard

    (a) to whether it was possible to challenge the statement by questioning the person who made it; and

    (b) if proceedings have been instituted, to whether the local law allowed the parties to the proceedings to be legally represented when the evidence was taken.

(9) In Scotland evidence obtained by virtue of a letter of request shall, without being sworn to by witnesses, be received in evidence in so far as that can be done without unfairness to either party.

(10) In the application of this section to Northern Ireland for the reference in subsection (1) to a justice of the peace there shall be substituted a reference to a resident magistrate, and for the reference in subsection (8) to section 25 of the Criminal Justice Act 1988 there shall be substituted a reference to Article 5 of the Criminal Justice (Evidence, etc.) (Northern Ireland) Order 1988."

5.01 The first three subsections make it clear that there are two categories of person entitled to issue a letter of request for evidence to be obtained from abroad. The first, under subsection (1) is a judge, (as defined in the section, according to the court and jurisdiction) who makes the request on application by either the prosecuting authority, or if proceedings have been instituted, the person charged in those proceedings. The second category (under subsection (3)) is that of "a prosecuting authority which is for the time being designated for the purposes of this sub-section" who is entitled to issue the letter of request itself.

5.02 A Designation Order[1] has been made in respect of:

(i) the Attorney General for England & Wales;

(ii) the Director of Public Prosecutions and any Crown Prosecutor;

(iii) The Director of the Serious Fraud Office and any person designated under section 1(7) of The Criminal Justice Act 1987;

(iv) the Secretary of State for Trade & Industry;

(v) the Commissioners of Customs & Excise;

---

1 The Criminal Justice (International Co-operation) Act 1990 (Designation of Prosecuting Authorities) Order 1991 (S.I. 1994 No. 1224) which effectively implements the Declaration of the U.K. Government in relation to Article 24 of the 1959 Convention.

   (vi) The Lord Advocate;

   (vii) any Procurator Fiscal;

   (viii) the Attorney General for Northern Ireland;

   (ix) the Director of Public Prosecutions for Northern Ireland.

All of these individuals or groups of individuals are therefore themselves entitled to make requests.

5.03   Requests by designated prosecuting authorities are by far the most common type of requests made. (Of the 2,000 outgoing requests processed through the Home Office from April 1, 1997 to September 30, 1998, the number of letters of requests issued by courts was in single figures only). It should be borne in mind when framing requests that some jurisdictions are reluctant to accept a letter of request if it has not been issued by a court, or by an authority which is recognised by them as equivalent to a court. For this reason, all letters of request should make explicit the authority under which they are issued, avoiding terms which might be ambiguous. For example, in Denmark, the Chief Constable is a judicial authority by virtue of the fact that he or she is also the chief prosecutor for the area, but a letter of request signed merely by the Chief Constable will be rejected in many jurisdictions. The Danish authorities include in any request the alternative designation of the Chief Constable as the Chief Prosecutor to satisfy other states.

Grounds for request

5.04   A justice of the peace or a judge, (or in Scotland, a sheriff or a judge) may issue a request under section 3(1) of the Act, following an application made under section 3(2) where it appears to him or her that:—

   (a)   an offence has been committed or there are reasonable grounds for suspecting that an offence has been committed (Section 3(1)(a)), and

   (b)   proceedings in respect of the offence have been instituted or the offence is being investigated (Section 3(1)(b)).

5.05   A Designated Prosecuting Authority may itself issue a letter of request, *i.e.* without the need for an application to a justice of the peace or a judge, if it is satisfied,

   (a)   as to the matters mentioned in section 3(1)(a) (*i.e.* that an offence has been committed or that there are reasonable grounds for suspecting that an offence has been committed (Section 3(3)(a)) and

   (b)   the offence in question is being investigated or the authority has instituted proceedings in respect of it (Section 3(3)(b)).

The request, in both cases, and however the application originates, is in the form of a letter requesting assistance in obtaining such evidence outside the United Kingdom as is specified in the letter for use in the proceedings or investigation.

Must the offence be committed and proceedings be instituted in the United Kingdom?

5.06   Whilst the purpose of the section is clearly to enable prosecutors, persons charged or investigators in the United Kingdom to obtain evidence from abroad to use in the proceedings or investigations in the United Kingdom, the section does not so limit itself in its wording.

This point was taken in *Cuoghi v. Governor of Brixton Prison*[2] which was an application for leave to appeal against an earlier order that a letter of request should not be issued to the proper and competent judicial authority in Geneva. "C" was the subject of extradition proceedings brought by the Swiss Government in the course of which he initiated an application for *habeas corpus*, alleging therein that the accusations against him were made in bad faith. He asked the court to request the Swiss authorities to investigate the matter, with a view to obtaining further evidence in Switzerland to assist him in his *habeas corpus* application. It was argued that the word "offence" in section 3 was not confined to an offence in the United Kingdom and should equally apply to an offence in Switzerland. Further, "proceedings in respect of the offence" could cover proceedings in the United Kingdom (not just Switzerland), including the extradition and *habeas corpus* proceedings relating to an offence committed in Switzerland. Such an interpretation would allow the court to issue a letter of request to the Swiss for use in the United Kingdom *habeas corpus* proceedings.

5.07 Whilst the court below indicated that this was a possible reading of the subsection, if the subsection stood alone, in the context of section 4 of the Act such a reading was unsustainable; this case did not fall within section 3.

Hirst L.J. in the Court of Appeal was strongly inclined to agree with the court below, however he stated "it seems to me that this point is just arguable and that it is in the public interest that so important a question should be authoritatively decided".

The court did not hold out strong prospects of success on the point. In fact it was never decided, for the appeal was dismissed on other grounds. It remains to be decided authoritatively, therefore, whether offences or proceedings in other countries will be covered by the words used in section 3.

Who can make the request to the Court for the issue of a request under section 3(1)?

Prosecuting authority

5.08 The section makes it plain that an application to the Court for a letter of request may be made by a "prosecuting authority" (section 3(2)). The powers conferred by section 3(3), however, are conferred on *designated* prosecuting authorities. Therefore, section 3(2) will include applications from *any* prosecuting authority, while the powers conferred by section 3(3) will be restricted to those prosecuting authorities designated for the time being by the Secretary of State. As the designated prosecuting authority does not need to make application to the Court to issue a letter of request, the power conferred on prosecuting authorities by section 3(2) will for the most part be exercised only by those prosecuting authorities which are not for the time being designated. This provision therefore will apply both to private prosecutors and those who conduct investigations and prosecutions but who are not Designated Prosecuting Authorities (for example, local authority prosecutions, or prosecutions by a government department not included in the list of designated prosecuting authorities). Of the total of outgoing requests annually, between 5 and 10 per cent are from non-designated prosecuting authorities whose requests therefore are routed through the courts under section 3(2).

---

2 *Cuoghi v. Governor of Brixton Prison* [1997] 1 W.L.R. 1346, CA.

In Scotland, although the right to private prosecution is preserved, in practice all prosecutions are carried out by the Procurator Fiscal. As he or she is a designated prosecuting authority, there is effectively no scope in Scotland for applications for letters of request made by non-designated prosecuting authorities.

The person charged

5.09 It is also clear that an application may be made by a person "charged in those proceedings" (section 3(2)). Thus, a defendant may make an application via the court, for a letter of request to be issued, but only after proceedings have been instituted against him or her.[3] He or she may make such an application at any stage of the proceedings after charge, and in particular, may make an application during the trial process itself. The procedure is, however, not available to a potential defendant, who may be seeking to dissuade a prosecuting authority from commencing proceedings. Further, it follows from the statutory provisions detailed above, that the defendant himself cannot issue a letter of request in the same way that the designated prosecuting authority is enabled to do.

5.10 Applications by or on behalf of the person charged are not frequently made, but it is an important facility which the defence has, and should not be overlooked. If, following an application made on behalf of the person charged, to a justice of the peace or judge, the justice of the peace or judge refuses to issue a letter of request, then the defence may appeal this decision. There is no statutory provision for such procedure, but the matter would, it is submitted, be subject to appeal in the same way as any other ruling. If the case is at pre-trial stage, then the appropriate mechanism would be by judicial review. However, if the case is actually at trial stage, then a refusal by the judge to issue a letter of request could only form part of the ground of appeal if the matter resulted in conviction, as it would appear that such a decision is "a matter relating to trial on indictment" within the wording of section 29(3) Supreme Court Act 1981 and thus excluded from judicial review (see *Re Smalley*).[4] Refusal by a judge at preparatory hearing stage in a trial (for example in an SFO case) would raise the possibility of an interlocutory appeal under section 9(11) of the Criminal Justice Act 1987. Since appeals under this section are restricted to the matters raised under sections 9(3)(b) or 9(3)(c), (that is (b) any question as to the admissibility of evidence, and (c) any other question of law relating to the case) the appellant would have to satisfy the court that his or her appeal fell within these subsections.

5.11 In the case of Forsyth[5] there was an application under section 3(2) of the 1990 Act made on behalf of the defendant, during the course of the trial, to the judge in the case. (The case was appealed on other grounds, and the judgment in the Court of Appeal is not on this point). The application was to the effect that the trial judge should issue a letter of request (in this case, the hearing of witnesses by television link) requesting assistance from the authorities in the Turkish Republic of northern Cyprus. The judge summarised the matter thus:

> "Since 1983 the so-called Turkish Republic of northern Cyprus has not been recognised by the United Kingdom, nor by any other country except for Turkey itself. Thus it is impossible to obtain extradition of any fugitive from justice from northern Cyprus. The fact of non-recognition seems to me to present an insuperable obstacle to the issue of a letter of request since by section 3(4) such

---

3 However, see below under s. 1782 of the United States Code.
4 [1985] A.C. 622 and see also *ex parte Rees, The Times*, May 7, 1986.
5 *R. v. Forsyth* [1997] 2 Cr. App. R. 299

a letter has to be sent to the Secretary of State for the Home Department of Her Majesty's Government for transmission to the court of northern Cyprus. The Secretary of State would be unable and unwilling to comply with that requirement since to do so would necessarily imply recognition of the so-called Turkish Republic of northern Cyprus. Mr Robertson (on behalf of the defendant) has submitted that there are a number of respects in which the authorities of the United Kingdom and of northern Cyprus co-operate with each other not least in certain investigations made by the Serious Fraud Office in this or in an associated case. He urges me to take the view that it would not amount to recognition for me to write to a judge in northern Cyprus but in my opinion this Act does not envisage the writing of letters on that basis, and does not empower me to do so. In my view the provisions of the Criminal Justice (International Co-operation) Act 1990 do not extend to the requesting of assistance in obtaining evidence from states which are not recognised by the United Kingdom. Accordingly I have no jurisdiction to grant the application and I therefore refuse it."

5.12 The decision to refuse the application on behalf of the defence was thus made on the somewhat unusual ground that the foreign country where the evidence was sought was not recognised by Her Majesty's Government. The merits or otherwise of the application were not considered. In most cases, it is thought that courts will try to accede to defence applications to obtain evidence from abroad, wherever this is possible in accordance with the statutory provisions.

Indeed, the Court of Appeal, in Forsyth (at page 311) stated that:

"In general, once it is shown that there is difficulty in obtaining the attendance of witnesses abroad whose evidence is relevant to the defence, we consider the court should lean in favour of permitting evidence to be given in this way, though in particular cases, there may be reasons to refuse it".

United States code, section 1782

5.13 Although applications can only be made by or on behalf of the defendant under the 1990 Act when he or she is charged, the situation may be different, if the evidence which an actual or potential defendant seeks is in the U.S. In those circumstances, he or she may be able to use the provisions of section 1782 of the US Code, and seek to obtain the evidence at an earlier stage.

This section, which was revised by Congress in 1964 to liberalise United States "procedures for assisting foreign ... tribunals and litigants in obtaining oral and documentary evidence in the United States"[6] states:

"1782 Assistance to foreign and international tribunals and to litigants before such tribunals

(a) The district court of the district in which a person resides or is found may order him to give his testimony or statement or to produce a document or other thing for use in a proceeding in a foreign or international tribunal. The order may be made pursuant to a letter rogatory issued, or request made, by a foreign or international tribunal or upon the application of any interested person and may direct that the testimony or statement be given or the document or other thing be produced, before a person appointed by the court. By virtue of his appointment, the person appointed has power to

---

6 1964 Senate Report at 3788.

administer any necessary oath and take the testimony or statement. The order may prescribe the practice and procedure, which may be in whole or part practice or procedure of the foreign country or the international tribunal, for taking the testimony or statement or producing the document or other thing. To the extent that the order does not prescribe otherwise, the testimony or statement shall be taken, and the document or other thing produced, in accordance with the Federal Rules of Civil Procedure.

A person may not be compelled to give his testimony or statement or to produce a document or other thing in violation of any legally applicable privilege.

(b)   This chapter does not preclude a person within the United States from voluntarily giving his testimony or statement, or producing a document or other thing, for use in a proceeding in a foreign or international tribunal before any person and in any manner acceptable to him."

5.14   In effect then, section 1782 permits a United States federal court to order United States style discovery for use in foreign proceedings. Whilst this section is the normal vehicle by which corporations or individuals involved, or about to become involved, in non-United States arbitration or litigation, request through the United States courts that a potential witness in the United States provide statements or produce documents for use in those proceedings, it has also been used in criminal proceedings and in some cases in criminal investigation. Letters rogatory in aid of foreign criminal proceedings are authorised. The Crown Prosecution Service of the United Kingdom is "an interested person" within the meaning of the federal statute governing foreign applications for judicial assistance.[7]

5.15   It is not necessary for proceedings to have been commenced before an application under section 1782 may be granted. However, the various circuits have applied different tests, both to "discoverability" (see below) and also to imminence of proceedings. For instance in *Re International Judicial Assistance (Letter Rogatory) for the Federative Republic of Brazil*[8] it was held that the district court may order production of evidence pursuant to a foreign government's letter rogatory in the absence of pending adjudicative proceedings but only if such proceedings are imminent, that is, very likely to occur within a brief interval from the request; it is not sufficient that adjudicative proceedings are merely "probable".

In *Re Letter of Request from Crown Prosecution Service of United Kingdom*[9] it was held that United Kingdom criminal proceedings were not required to be pending in order for the Crown Prosecution Service to be entitled to request assistance in a criminal investigation, but rather it was sufficient that judicial proceedings be within reasonable contemplation. In the same case it was held the lack of pending judicial proceedings did not prohibit the District Court under section 1782 from ordering a United States citizen to give deposition testimony and to provide documents to assist the United Kingdom authorities during a criminal perversion of justice investigation upon application via a letter rogatory.

It was held in the application of *Asta Medica SA*,[9a] that in determining whether an interested person has established that the information sought would be discoverable in the foreign jurisdiction, the district court need not explore whether the information

7 *Re Letter of Request from Crown Prosecution Service of U.K.* 1989, 870 F.2d686, 276 U.S. pp. D.C. 272.
8 C.A.2 N.Y. 1991, 936 F.2D 702.
9 *ibid.*
9a CA1 (Me.) 1992, 981 F2D 1.

being sought by the applicant would be admissible in the foreign jurisdiction, or indeed any other issue of foreign law. Further, the courts have held that witnesses cannot object to a district court's action in issuing *subpoena*s in response to letters rogatory from a foreign court on the grounds that the testimony to be taken might not be admissible in the trial in the foreign country.[10]

5.16   The procedure by which an "interested person" initiates a request under section 1982 will depend upon the circuit in which the request is sought. Depending upon that circuit and its local rules a request generally comprises a brief *ex parte* application, which is accompanied by a copy of the proposed order and the memorandum of the appropriate law. The United States court will issue the *subpoena* or other order, which may be challenged, according to the United States Federal Rules of Procedure.

A witness in the United States who is *subpoena*ed in relation to an investigation being conducted in the United States cannot rely upon any statute provided that a person before a foreign or international tribunal cannot be compelled to give testimony or to produce documents in violation of any legally applicable privilege.[11]

Clearly the prospects of success of any such application will depend not only upon the circuit in which the proposed witness resides but upon technical questions of United States law and procedure and obviously therefore any applicant should seek advice from specialist American counsel. As the section is available as an alternative to the letters rogatory route, it has clear advantages of speed and wider applicability for actual and potential defendants. This procedure is equally available to a prosecutor or investigator as "interested persons", but because a designated prosecutor can issue a letter of request at any stage of the investigation it is unlikely to offer advantages over the United Kingdom statutory route, unless of course severe delay is anticipated.

Confidentiality of requests

5.17   To allay fears about the confidentiality of requests, the Home Office seeks to ensure that defence requests will remain confidential. It should be remembered, however, that such safeguards may not exist once the request has been received by the requested state.

In this regard, defence requests are no more vulnerable than prosecution requests, as in some jurisdictions the substance of a letter of request is disclosed as a matter of routine to the subject of the letter. Considerations of the desirability of this may affect the timing of letters of request to foreign authorities. For example, if a request relates to the obtaining of details of a bank account in a foreign country, in some jurisdictions the letter of request may itself be served on the account holder, who may be a suspect. The grounds for suspicion, and the course of the investigation to date (as outlined in the letter of request) may well not be known to the suspect, and the premature disclosure could have adverse consequences on the investigation. Although disclosure of the content of the letter by the prosecution to the defence may take place at a later stage in line with the provisions of the Criminal Procedure and Investigation Act 1996,[12] care should be taken to avoid the possibility of disclosure at an inappropriate time.

---

10 *Re Letter Rogatory from Tokyo District*, Japan C.A.9(Cal) 539F2D 1216 (1976).
11 *Re Doe* C.A.2(N.Y.) 860 F2D 40 (1988).
12 See para. 5.34 *et seq.*

5.18 For further information as to the likely disclosure of a particular letter of request within a foreign jurisdiction, it is recommended that contact is made with the MLA Section at the Home Office. Within Europe, the European Judicial Network may be able to provide an answer, and further afield, the staff in the Home Office may have experience which will assist in relation to a particular country.

United Kingdom Court Procedure

5.19 Section 10 of the Act provides for rules of court to be made for any purpose for which it appears to the authority having power to make the rules, that it is necessary or expedient to do so in connection with any of the provisions of the Act.

Accordingly, rules have been made under section 3 of the Act in relation to applications for letters of request.

England and Wales

Magistrates' Courts

Under the Magistrates' Court (Criminal Justice (International Co-operation)) Rules 1991[12a] it is provided that notice of an application should be given to the clerk of the court and shall

- (a) be in writing, except that the court may in exceptional circumstances dispense with the need for notice

- (b) state the particulars of the offence which it is alleged has been committed, or the grounds for suspecting that an offence has been committed

- (c) state whether proceedings in respect of the offence have been instituted or the offence is being investigated, and

- (d) include particulars of the assistance requested in the form of a draft letter of request.

5.20 An application under section 3(1) shall be heard in a petty sessional court house, and may be heard *ex parte*. When hearing an application under section 3(1) of the Act, the court may, if it thinks necessary in the interests of justice, direct that the public be excluded from the court. Where the matter is urgent, the provisions of section 3(5) apply, and the letter of request may be sent direct to the court or tribunal specified in the letter of request. In such circumstances, however, the Magistrates Courts Rules provide that a copy of the letter shall also be sent to the Secretary of State.

Crown Court

5.21 The Crown Court Amendment Rules 1991[13] added a new Rule to the 1982 Crown Court Rules. This Rule (Rule 31) makes similar provision to the rules for the magistrates' courts. Notice of an application under section 3(1) of the Act should be given to the appropriate officer of the Crown Court and shall:

- (a) be in writing, except that the court may in exceptional circumstances dispense with the need for notice;

12a S.I. 1991 No. 1047.
13 S.I. 1991 No. 1228.

(b) state the particulars of the offence which it is alleged has been committed or the grounds upon which it is suspected that an offence has been committed;

(c) state whether proceedings in respect of the offence have been instituted or the offence is being investigated;

(d) include particulars of the assistance required in the form of a draft letter of request.

5.22 As in the magistrates' court, the application may be heard *ex parte*, and the court may, if it thinks necessary in the interests of justice, direct that the public be excluded from the court. Similar provisions to the magistrates' court also apply where, in a case of urgency, the Crown Court sends a letter of request direct to the foreign tribunal. In this case also, a copy of the letter of request should also be sent to the Secretary of State.

Scotland

5.23 In Scotland the relevant provisions of section 3 of the 1990 Act are supplemented by section 272(1)(a) of the Criminal Procedure (Scotland) Act (which consolidated earlier similar provisions contained in section 32 of the Criminal Justice (Scotland) Act 1980), and by the Act of Adjournal (Criminal Procedure Rules) 1996.[14] Chapter 23 of the Act of Adjournal, Rules 23.1–23.6 deals with the procedures to be followed in making applications to both the High Court and the Sheriff Court.

Because, as has been said, all prosecutions in Scotland are conducted by the Procurator Fiscal, and he or she is a designated prosecuting authority, the only application likely to be made to the court in connection with evidence to be obtained from abroad are applications on behalf of the defence. These rules have therefore had limited use. In addition, a restrictive interpretation on the use of the section has been given by the courts, following the decision in *Muirhead*[14a], and this has further restricted their application.

5.24 There are no guidelines as to which will be the appropriate United Kingdom court for an application for a letter of request in any given case; it is assumed that the court from whom the letter of request is sought will be the court having conduct of the matter at the time of the request, *i.e.* if the offence is summary, or the matter is prior to transfer/committal then the Magistrates' Court will be the appropriate court. If the case has been transferred/committed or is already before the Crown Court then the request will be made to the Crown Court.

REQUESTS FROM DESIGNATED PROSECUTING AUTHORITIES

5.25 The more common method for requests to be made is by designated prosecuting authorities themselves. Where a designated prosecuting authority is either investigating an offence, or has instituted proceedings in respect of the offence, and it becomes apparent that evidence is required from a foreign jurisdiction, he or she may prepare a letter of request to the foreign authority, asking for assistance in respect of particular matters. He or she may issue the letter of request either before or after proceedings have been instituted.

---

14 S.I. 1996 No. 513.
14a 1983 S.C.C.R. 133.

Transmission of requests

5.26   Under section 3(4) of the Act, all letters of request, whether issued by the Court on application, or by a designated prosecuting authority are passed to the Home Office for the Secretary of State to transmit them, either to the court specified in the letter and exercising jurisdiction in the place where the evidence is to be obtained or to any authority recognised by the overseas government as the appropriate authority for receiving requests for assistance in the provision of evidence.

The exception to this rule (provided for in section 3(5)) is that in cases of urgency, letters of request may be sent directly to the court or tribunal to whom the letter is addressed, which exercises jurisdiction in the place where the evidence is to be obtained. This provision derives from Article 15(2) of the 1959 Convention, which provides for direct contact in cases of urgency. However, the Convention also provides that in such cases, the evidence obtained shall be returned through the channels of the Ministry of Justice of the respective countries.

5.27   Both the Schengen Convention, to whose provisions on this topic the United Kingdom has applied to opt in and the (new) (draft) Mutual Legal Assistance Convention within the E.U. provide for direct transmission of requests for assistance in all cases, and not only those requiring urgent action. The position of the United Kingdom, with regard to opting in to the Schengen provisions regarding Mutual Legal Assistance, has already been considered. Since foreign authorities are, by and large, unfamiliar with United Kingdom procedures, the immediate result of the move towards greater use of direct transmission will inevitably be a number of requests to the United Kingdom being received by an inappropriate authority with consequent delays. For example, a foreign authority may send a request in a fraud case for execution to the SFO, when the case does not meet SFO criteria. In such an eventuality, the SFO would itself have to transmit the case to the authority best placed to deal with the request. The United Kingdom could, by declaration, reserve its position *vis à vis* its MLA Section. Such a move might be appropriate where, as in the case of the United Kingdom, a country's judicial authorities cannot in general execute requests from abroad, although it would be inconsistent with the principle of direct transmission contained in Article 15(2) of the 1959 Convention and to which the United Kingdom already subscribes. The final position of the United Kingdom in this matter remains to be decided.

5.28   At the same time as the request is sent through official channels – in normal circumstances, through the Home Office, but possibly directly to the foreign judicial authority – some requests are also sent to Interpol. The result of this is that the police authorities in the requested state will be aware of the request (and may have made some preliminary informal enquiries) before the "official" copy of the request is received through official channels. This may speed up the ultimate execution of the request. If the request asks for members of the investigation team to travel to the requested State, then the request should always be copied to Interpol, so that the necessary administrative arrangements can be made. Where urgent requests are transmitted direct to the foreign authority for execution, they may be copied to the Home Office for information, but there is no requirement for this to happen.

General information about requests

5.29   It is impossible to be prescriptive about the precise contents of a letter of request, since each request will depend on the circumstances of the case. Section 3 does not give any guidance as to what must be contained in a letter of request, but the

1959 Convention does lay down certain minimum requirements. These are contained in Article 14, which states that as a minimum the request should contain details of:

(a) the authority making the request

(b) the object of and the reason for the request

(c) where possible, the identity and the nationality of the person concerned

(d) where necessary, the name and address of the person to be served

(e) the offence involved and a summary of the facts.

From the outset, it is important to remember that it is essential to be specific about the assistance required. The foreign authority will know nothing about the case, and will need detailed information to enable it to make the necessary enquiries requested. Additional information may also have to be provided in order to comply with a requested state's legislation, or to make a request more comprehensible. The Home Office Guidelines (prepared, it should be remembered, primarily to facilitate incoming requests) contain a useful checklist of information which should be included if at all possible.

5.30 The Home Office guidelines suggest that, in forming requests, the following instructions should be observed. For the complete text of the guidelines, see Appendix K:

"All relevant information must be included. This will vary according to the nature of the assistance required. Omission of any relevant information may delay execution of the request. Wherever possible all requests should include:

(a) Any information which is likely to help the Home Office arrange for execution of the request in accordance with the requirements of the requesting authority.

Letters of request must include the following details:

(a) Details and the address of the judicial or prosecuting authority conducting the investigation or proceedings to which the request relates, and the name, telephone and fax details of the responsible official(s) there.

(b) Full name(s) of the subject(s) of the investigation or proceedings.

(c) A summary of the facts of the offence(s) and details of the offence(s)[15] committed or alleged. Where evidence is required, the request should make clear that there are reasonable grounds for suspecting that the offence has been committed and that proceedings have been instituted in relation to the offence or, if proceedings have not been instituted, that the offence is being investigated.

(d) A description of the evidence or material or other assistance required, clearly stating whether original evidence or certified copies are required.

(e) The purpose for which the evidence or material or other assistance is required and the relevance of the assistance to the investigation or proceedings.

---

15 This is important in case dual criminality is involved, since it is this description of the alleged offences which will enable the foreign authority to see if the behaviour described would also constitute an offence under its law.

Requests should also state, to the extent necessary and possible:

(a)   The date of the trial or hearing and any other dates relevant for the purposes of executing the request; and any reasons why the request is urgent, for example because the accused person or suspect is in detention.

(b)   The full name, date of birth and location of any person from whom evidence is required making clear whether they are a witness or an actual or potential accused.

(c)   Available information on the identity and whereabouts of any person to be located.

(d)   Details, including the telephone number, of any British law enforcement officer who is familiar with the investigation.

(e)   The request should also say whether *and why* the presence of officers or officials of the requesting authorities is required during the execution of the request. The names of such persons should be provided (in general, such officers or officials may observe, but may not participate in, the execution of requests).

If the request is for the evidence of a witness, it should include the following items additionally:

(a)   Where evidence is required to be taken *on oath* before a court this should be expressly stated in the request. Expressions such as *"to hear"* or *"to examine"* witnesses or suspects should be avoided as they may have an ambiguous meaning. For the avoidance of doubt the requesting authority should set out as clearly as possible the conditions under which any interview or examination should be conducted.

(b)   A list of questions to be asked.

(c)   Details of the procedure to be followed in taking the evidence, including any rules on privilege which a person or suspect may be entitled to claim.

(d)   Any caution or formal notification of rights which should be given to the witness or suspect according to United Kingdom law.

(e)   If banking evidence is required, the request must provide the name or number of the account and the address or number of the branch of the bank where the account is held.

(f)   It should be remembered that in some countries, *e.g.* France, centralised bank account records are held from all banking institutions – this will facilitate the location of a particular account, but does not replace the need for specific details to be provided, nor justify "fishing expeditions".

Requests for search and seizure of evidence should include:

(a)   The full address or a precise description of any place to be searched; full details of the specific material or type of material to be seized and a full description of the criminal conduct concerned. In most countries, there is a requirement of dual criminality for search and seizure provisions to be applied. A description of the offence will be essential if this is to be satisfied. (For further details on search and seizure, see Chapters 8–10 below).

(b) An explanation why the material requested is considered both relevant and important evidence to the investigation or proceedings; why the evidence is thought to be on the particular premises or in the possession of the particular person concerned and why the material would not be produced voluntarily.

(c) Appropriate undertakings for the safekeeping and return of any seized evidence. (These are technically unnecessary in the case of requests between signatories to the 1959 Council of Europe Convention, since Article 6(2) provides that property (including documents and original records) shall be returned by the requesting state to the requested state as soon as possible unless the requested state waives the return of them. Some countries, *e.g.* Ireland, however, insist on them).

Requests for the restraint (freezing) of property should include:

(a) The name, address, nationality, date and place of birth and present location of the defendant(s) or person(s) whose criminal conduct has given rise to civil confiscation proceedings.

(b) Details of the offence with which the defendant has been, or is about to be, charged (or the civil action brought or about to be brought).

(c) Details of the law applicable to the charges and the evidence against the defendant.

(d) Particulars of the property which it is intended to restrain, the persons holding it and details of the link between the defendant and the property (this is important if the property to be restrained is held in the name of a third party such as a company or another person).

(e) State clearly whether prior assistance in the case (including asset tracing assistance) has been provided by the requested State and, if so, give particulars of the enforcement or other authority involved and details of the assistance already received.

(f) Where applicable, details of any court orders already made in the United Kingdom against the defendant in respect of his or her property. If any court order has been made a duly authenticated copy should he included with the request – that is a true copy of that order certified by a person in his or her capacity as a United Kingdom judge, magistrate or officer of the relevant court or by an official of the MLA section in the Home Office.

When assistance should be sought

5.31 While the request for assistance should be as focused as possible, there is always a dilemma for the investigator, as to whether he or she should issue a letter of request as soon as the need for it is apparent, when information may be limited, or whether it would be better to wait until he has more information, at which stage the request may be urgent, and place the foreign authority under pressure of time. There is no easy solution to this problem, but broadly, a request should be issued as soon as the information is available which makes a request both necessary and possible. Supplementary requests are always possible, as the investigation progresses and indeed are very common in complex investigations. It is possible to request material which it is not anticipated will be used at the trial, that is, material which may lead to the discovery of evidence. "Fishing expeditions" will not be permitted, however, and letters of request should be focussed enough to avoid such criticism. This matter was raised in the *Finninvest* case.[16]

Translations

5.32   Translation of requests into the language of the requested State may also be necessary. Article 16(1) of the 1959 Convention states that subject to paragraph 2 of the Article translations of requests and annexed documents shall not be required. However, paragraph 2 provides that on signing the Convention, or on depositing the instrument of ratification, states may reserve the right by declaration to stipulate that requests and annexed documents shall be accompanied by a translation into:

(a)   its own language, or

(b)   either of the official languages of the Council of Europe, (French or English) or

(c)   one of the latter languages,

as specified by it.

5.33   The United Kingdom, in its reservations and declarations handed over at the time of the deposit of the instrument of ratification on August 29, 1991, has reserved the right to stipulate that requests and annexed documents shall be addressed to it accompanied by translations into English. Many other signatories to the 1959 Convention have made reservations in this connection too. In some cases, states have made it possible to accept letters of request in one of a number of languages. For practical purposes, however, it is normally advisable to make a translation of an outgoing request into the language of the requested state, since failure to do so could result in a delay in the foreign state while they seek a translation. It also ensures that translations are made to the standard required by the requesting state, and avoids the possibility that a translation made locally in a requested state does not fully or accurately reflect the requesting authority's intentions. The Home Office will be able to advise on the correct language for translations for an individual letter of request. It should also be remembered that in some countries there are two or more official languages. Care should be taken that the correct language is selected. For example, with requests to Switzerland, it would be unacceptable to send a request translated into German to Geneva or a request translated into French to Zurich. Mistakes of this type will cause delays in the execution of requests.

Since a letter of request is addressed directly to a foreign authority, the request should be restricted to matters which lie within the jurisdiction of that authority. Although a letter of request may (and often does) contain multiple requests to the one authority, requests relating to other authorities should not be included. A separate request will be necessary for each separate foreign authority. In this connection it is important to remember that within one country there may be more than one jurisdiction, and therefore with countries such as Switzerland and Germany separate requests (translated perhaps into different languages as appropriate) will be required for evidence from separate cantons or *lander*. If there is any doubt about the matter, then the Home Office will advise as to the correct procedure.

---

16 R. v. *Secretary of State for the Home Department ex parte Finninvest SpA* [1997] 1 All E.R. 942 (for further details of the issues raised in this case, see para. 6.04 *et seq.*)

Disclosure of request

5.34   Mention has already been made of the need for care in the preparation of letters of request, since they may obtain a wider circulation in the requested state than the author envisaged. This is as much true for letters prepared by the prosecution as for letters prepared by the defence. However, the question of disclosure of letters of request within England and Wales must also be considered, in terms of the Criminal Procedure and Investigation Act 1996 (CPIA). It should be remembered that the provisions of this Act do not apply to summary only cases, but it is thought likely that the number of such cases in which there are letters of request is small.

Under the Act, all material "relevant to the investigation" must be retained. Under the Code of Practice issued under the CPIA, material will be relevant to an investigation if it appears to any member of the case team that it has some bearing on any offence under investigation, or any person being investigated, or on the surrounding circumstances of the case, unless it is incapable of having any impact on the case. Thus a letter of request falls to be considered as material relevant to the investigation. That docs not mean, however, that it will necessarily ultimately be disclosed to the defence. It does mean, however, that the disclosure officer has a responsibility to examine all retained material, with a view to determining whether there is a duty to disclose it.

5.35   The Criminal Procedure and Investigations Act lays down the regime for the disclosure of what was previously called the "unused material" in a case. The first task of the prosecution will be to review the unused material in its hands, and decide if any of it falls to be considered as sensitive. It is possible, although unlikely, that a letter of request would fall into this category.

The main disclosure obligation on the prosecution is to disclose to the defence any prosecution material which has not previously been disclosed and which in the opinion of the prosecutor might undermine the case for the prosecution against the accused. (Primary disclosure; section 3(1) of the CPIA). He must also give a schedule of the unused non-sensitive material to the defence. Assuming that the letter of request is not sensitive, it will normally form part of that schedule of material. Once the defence has obtained the schedule of unused non-sensitive material, it will be possible for the defence to seek to see specific items from the schedule. Where the prosecution has issued a letter of request in a case, however, and the letter has been executed by a foreign state, then the evidence produced as a result of the letter of request will normally form part of the prosecution case at committal or transfer.

5.36   There is no corresponding obligation on the defence to disclose any letters of request which have been issued as a result of its application to the Court. Since these may have been made *ex parte*, the prosecution may well have no knowledge of them, although if the evidence obtained as a result of them forms a material plank of the defence case, it will have been disclosed in the defence's statement, which is the statutory obligation conferred by CPIA on the defence.

Refusal of assistance

5.37   Under Article 2 of the 1959 Convention, states are entitled to refuse assistance:

(a)   if the request concerns an offence which the requested party considers a political offence, an offence connected with a political offence, or a fiscal offence

(b)   if the requested Party considers that execution of the request is likely to prejudice the sovereignty, security, *ordre public* or other essential interests of its country.

Having Article 2(a) particularly in mind it is important that a requesting authority makes clear the use to which the evidence, if obtained, will be put, since the requested state could refuse assistance if the conditions in the Article are met. The grounds for refusal under Article 2 are however, discretionary, and each application will be considered on its merit.

Use limitation

5.38   Section 3(7) provides that evidence obtained shall not, without the consent of the authority recognised by the overseas country as the appropriate authority for receiving requests for assistance, be used for any purpose other than that specified in the letter of request.[17]

The case of *R. v. Gooch*[18] demonstrates the restrictive application of this provision. In the Court of Appeal, G was appealing *inter alia* against the trial judge's findings as to the benefit which he had received from drug trafficking. G had been convicted of offences in relation to the importation of cannabis and sentenced to eleven years' imprisonment. In addition, having been found to have benefitted from drug trafficking in the sum of £4,728,208.90, his realisable assets were assessed at £650,000 and a confiscation order was made against him in that sum.

In the Appeal Court, it was argued that certain foreign evidence had been used to prove the proceeds figure of £4,728,208.90, and that without that foreign evidence, the benefits figure would have been £1.2 million less. Mantell L.J. said, in giving the judgment of the Court,

> "The admissibility of the foreign evidence is challenged on the ground that the letters of request did not state that the evidence sought was to be used in a confiscation enquiry under the Drug Trafficking Offences Act 1986, and that evidence obtained by this procedure can be used only for the purposes identified in the letter.
>
> There are three letters of request ... Each letter refers to a prosecution which has been instigated against (G and others) on a charge that they were knowingly concerned in the smuggling into the United Kingdom of 550 kilogrammes of herbal cannabis ... Each letter is expressed in terms which can only be regarded as a request for assistance in obtaining evidence *for use in the trial* of the appellant and others upon the charge identified in the letter. Although the allegation ... was a live allegation (at that time) ... the appellant was not convicted of the offence identified in the letters. That offence was not even the subject of the trial proceedings ... when the appellant was convicted ...
>
> Each of the letters expressed the request contained therein as being pursuant to the Single Convention on Narcotic Drugs 1961 ... In our judgment the Single Convention of 1961 has now to be read within the context of more recent legislation, namely the Criminal Justice (International Co-operation) Act ... The Act came into force on June 10, 1991. It was thus in force when each of the three letters of request was written. (He then detailed the provisions of section 3(7)). On behalf of the defendant it is submitted that section 3(7) debarred the

---

17 Compare the position on incoming requests below.
18 *The Times*, July 15, 1998.

admission of the foreign evidence in the confiscation proceedings. The respondent has argued that section 3(7) does not preclude use of the foreign evidence for the purpose of questioning a defendant. If, during questioning, so runs the argument, the defendant accepted the primary facts disclosed by the evidence and thereafter in the proceedings did not challenge the evidence, once it had been admitted, he cannot complain. That is precisely what happened here.

In our judgment the language of section 3(7) is clear. The stated purpose in the letters was equally clear ... If the prosecution had wished to use this evidential material in the confiscation proceedings, the consent of the appropriate authority in Switzerland and in Liechtenstein should first have been obtained. Such consent was not even sought. The evidence was nonetheless used in the proceedings. In our judgment, as the evidence was used for a purpose "other than specified in the (letters)" the use contravened section 3(7). This material should not have been before the court in the confiscation proceedings. In our judgment the fact that the appellant had not challenged the evidence itself (he had challenged its admissibility) and that, once admitted, he had sought to rely upon it as a vehicle for argument cannot render admissible that which the 1990 Act provides should not have been used.

...(CA)We have come to the clear conclusion that the material obtained as a result of the letters of request should not have been used in the confiscation proceedings nor should it have been used for the purpose of interviewing the appellant if (as it was) the sole purpose of the interview was the preparation of a section 3 statement."

5.39 Thus, evidence obtained in accordance with section 3 may not be used, for example, in civil proceedings for asset recovery arising out of the same subject matter as the criminal proceedings, unless the appropriate consent has been obtained from the foreign authority.

It does not appear that there is power in the court to allow the use of the evidence in other proceedings.[19] Wherever asset recovery is a possibility, specific permission should be sought in advance.

Execution of letters of request

5.40 In straightforward cases, once a letter of request is dispatched to the Home Office for transmission to the requested state, nothing more is heard until the requested evidence is received via the same channels. Even if the letter of request is sent directly to the foreign authority, the evidence, as has been seen, will be transmitted back formally through the Home Office. However, in many cases there is considerable contact between the requesting authority and the requested authority as regards the details of the execution of the request, especially if the request is complex, or involves a number of different aspects. Direct contact is encouraged at least at the European level, where normally, language is not an insuperable barrier. Further, it is one of the specific reasons for the formation of the European Judicial Network, whose functioning is described more fully at Chapter 3. The United Kingdom's principal "contact point" within the Network is the Head of the Mutual Legal Assistance Section at the Home Office. For further information about contacting foreign authorities direct, contact in the first instance should be made with that contact point.

---

19 Compare with the position of documents obtained in criminal proceedings in United Kingdom *Marcel v. Metropolitan Police Commissioner* [1992] Ch.225.

Travel to the requested State by United Kingdom investigators and representatives of the person charged

5.41 It often assists a foreign authority in the execution of a request if a member of the United Kingdom investigating authority is prepared to travel to the foreign country to assist in the execution of the letter of request. If that is desired, then a request to this end must be included in the original letter of request. It is possible, however, that such a stipulation could delay the execution of the request, since separate authorisation may have to be given by the foreign authorities, and travel arrangements will have to be made. In some circumstances, too, foreign authorities, may be unable to agree to the presence of a member of a foreign investigating authority as a result of their internal legislation. For example, there are some aspects of the preliminary procedure in Belgium and France which have to be conducted in private, and it would be impossible to obtain agreement to the presence of any third party including United Kingdom investigators, at such proceedings. Even in such circumstances, however, it should be possible for the United Kingdom investigators to assist their foreign counterparts, particularly where the case is complicated, by preparing lists of questions which should be asked of particular witnesses, or areas which should be covered in questioning.

In some cases, too, the prosecution may be requested by the defence to allow representatives of the defence to be present when a witness is examined abroad. Although this will ultimately be a matter for the court in the foreign jurisdiction, consideration of section 3(8) of the 1990 Act suggests that the presence of such representatives will increase the likelihood of the statement of the witness being admitted in United Kingdom court proceedings in due course.

The type of evidence requested

5.42 A letter of request can seek to obtain any evidence which it is believed is in a foreign country. This can consist of documentary records, (whether contained in bank records or elsewhere), statements of witnesses, searches of property, official records, or, in terms of section 3(1) "such evidence as is specified in the letter for use in the proceedings or investigation." For some types of request, the requested state may impose a dual criminality requirement (most usually those involving search and seizure). For this reason, it is essential that the elements giving rise to the allegation of criminality are clearly stated, to enable the requested state to satisfy itself that the acts alleged would constitute a crime within its own jurisdiction. This does not mean that the foreign State would have to be satisfied that it would have jurisdiction in identical circumstances. However, it must be able to be satisfied that the conduct alleged and described in the request would constitute an offence (however described) within its jurisdiction.

5.43 Under the 1959 Convention (Article 3) the requested State is obliged to execute any letter of request "in the manner provided for by its law" This can lead, on occasions, to evidence being returned to the requesting State in a form which is difficult to assimilate in the requesting State's procedures. At worst, it may even not be in a form in which it can be used at all in the courts of the requesting State. The emphasis has moved since 1959, however, and current practice normally involves a requested State making efforts to ensure that what it produces is a product which will be of use to the requesting authority. This development will be recognised in the (new) draft Mutual Legal Assistance Convention (as far as contact between E.U. Member States is concerned). This provides that letters of request should be executed in the manner requested by the requesting State, so far as it is not inconsistent with the requested State's laws and practices. Negotiations as to what may or may not be acceptable are an important part of the liaising function which is so necessary in dealing with foreign requests. It is another potentially invaluable aspect of the European Judicial Network.

The development towards the execution of requests in the manner requested by the requesting State is particularly important for requests between civil and common law countries. The common law principal of orality, where all evidence should be heard orally in court, is largely unknown on the continent, and often, civil law authorities are unable to understand the United Kingdom insistence on the attendance of witnesses at trial, when a signed statement has already been obtained.

Return of evidence to the United Kingdom

5.44 In normal cases, evidence obtained as a result of a letter of request is returned through official channels from the foreign Ministry of Justice to the Home Office and from there to the requesting authority. One of the most frequently voiced criticisms of the system of foreign letters of request is that they take too long to execute, and it is in fact the case that there can be a considerable lapse of time between the issue of a letter and the receipt of evidence in response to that letter. Indeed, in a disappointing number of cases, there are still instances where no reply is ever received, either favourable or unfavourable to the original letter of request, despite the best endeavours of the Home Office to speed things up. At least within Europe, this is relatively uncommon now, although further afield there may still be problems.

Continuity in respect of documentary evidence is an area where great care must be taken, to avoid attack at proceedings in United Kingdom courts. The importance of precision and detail in the letter of request in this regard cannot be over emphasised.

Duration of letter of request – the effect of delay

5.45 In *R. v. Central Criminal Court ex parte Hunt*[20] a letter of request was issued to Switzerland, pursuant to section 3(l) of the Act, on March 10, 1992, at an early stage of the United Kingdom proceedings against four defendants. In due course, two defendants left the jurisdiction for countries from which they could not be extradited and the criminal proceedings against the two remaining defendants came to a conclusion. In 1995, an application was made by Hunt (one of those who had fled the jurisdiction) for a ruling that the letter of request was no longer valid.

> "The point which is now being considered is what remaining force there is in the letter of request of March 10, 1992. The investigating authorities in the United Kingdom wish to pursue their investigation by obtaining further assistance from the Swiss authorities. The Swiss authorities are concerned to know what the attitude of this Court (and indeed of the English law) is to the letter (of request)."

The court held that as the letter was one of request to the Swiss authorities, it must be a decision for them whether in 1995 they were prepared to offer further assistance to a letter three years old. In reaching such a conclusion, the Swiss authorities would be entitled to have information as to what had happened in the United Kingdom over that period.

---

20 *The Times*, February 21, 1995.

The Divisional Court could not see how it could properly be its function to express a view as to how the Swiss authorities should respond in 1995 to a request that had been made three years before. If they decided that in the circumstances they could offer no further assistance, then it was open to the United Kingdom authorities to make a fresh request under section 3 of the Act.

In the light of these comments, if significant delay has ensued in the proceedings in the requesting state since the issue of the letter of request, the designated prosecuting authority (or the party applying for the letter of request) should keep the foreign authorities informed of developments.

When evidence obtained is finished with

5.46   Under section 3(7) it is provided that where any document or article obtained pursuant to a letter of request is no longer required for that purpose or any other purpose for which consent has been obtained, it shall be returned, unless the authority indicates that it need not be returned. In the case of documentary exhibits, if certified copies have been obtained, and also in the case of statements of witnesses, it is sensible to arrange with the foreign authority that these should not be returned. Original documents, however, should be returned at the end of the proceedings for which they were obtained.

Return of material after execution

5.47   Article 6(2) of the 1959 Convention provides that "any property, as well as original records or documents, handed over in execution of letters rogatory shall be returned by the requesting party to the requested party as soon as possible, unless the latter party waives the return thereof".

Since, under Article 3 of the 1959 Convention, the requested party is entitled to transmit certified copies or certified photostat copies of records or documents requested, unless the requesting party expressly requests the transmission of originals, in most cases, the requested party will not seek the return of such copies. However, the right of the requested party to have material returned as soon as the need for it is finished, should not be overlooked.

The use of the evidence in proceedings in the United Kingdom

By oral evidence

5.48   There will obviously be occasions where the party adducing the evidence will wish to have the maker of the statement present in court to give oral evidence. In normal circumstances, the evidence of the witness living abroad will have been served on the other party, and an indication received as to whether the witness is required personally to attend court to give evidence. If the witness is required, then a witness order could be obtained, but since that would have no force in the foreign country, it is usually more effective for the party which wishes to call the witness to make contact directly with the witness and arrange for his attendance in court. He or she cannot be forced to attend court in the United Kingdom.

In the case that the witness is willing to give evidence, but is unwilling or unable to travel to the United Kingdom to give that evidence, the possibility of the witness giving evidence by remote television link should be explored. At present, the use of this is limited to the offences listed in section 32 of the Criminal Justice Act 1988. If that solution is likely to be viable, then a supplementary letter of request to the foreign authorities will be necessary, requesting that the witness be summoned to an agreed venue in the foreign country where television recording/transmission facilities have been arranged. The witness can then be questioned and the answers transmitted live to the court in the United Kingdom. Practically, although there are no set rules for this procedure, it will be normal for representatives of three parties to travel to the foreign country to be present while the examination of the witness is taking place – the prosecution, the defence and the court itself. Although the questions will be put to the witness by Counsel in the case in the United Kingdom (and not by Counsel present in the foreign country), the presence of these representatives will ensure that there can be no allegations that the witness was improperly influenced in giving evidence.

The United Kingdom has used this procedure on several occasions, notably in Serious Fraud Office trials, and it has proved successful. The reasons for the witness's unwillingness to travel to the United Kingdom should be fully explored, however. If the witness has genuine personal or professional reasons which preclude travel, then the solution will be appropriate. If, however, the witness wishes to avoid travel to the United Kingdom because of fear of prosecution, for example, then it will be less likely that this procedure will be appropriate.

In the case of *Forsyth*, application was made to the trial judge to issue a letter of request to the authorities in northern Cyprus, to allow a number of witnesses to give evidence by live television link. Application was made not only for the issue of a letter of request under section 3(2) of the 1990 Act, but also under section 32 of the Criminal Justice Act 1988 for evidence to be taken in this way. The trial judge refused both applications, and in respect of the application under section 32, on the ground that he had no jursidiction to permit the link, because the witness could not be extradited from northern Cyprus to stand trial for perjury. The Court of Appeal allowed the appeal on other grounds, so did not decide whether on a review of all the relevant circumstances it would have held that the judge should have permitted evidence to be given by video link. The court emphasised however, the importance of leaning in favour of permitting defence evidence to be given in this way, where such evidence has been shown to be relevant to the defence.

The use of live television recording of the evidence of witnesses is a major provision of the new draft E.U. Mutual Legal Assistance Convention, since, although the United Kingdom is currently able to make use of the facility in specific cases, in many other European countries, it is not possible to reciprocate. The Convention, and the implementing legislation in other countries should change that situation.

Written evidence

Section 23 and 24 Criminal Justice Act 1988

5.49   These provisions contain important exceptions to the hearsay rules as far as statements in documents are concerned, allowing the reception of hearsay evidence in certain circumstances in the absence of the maker of the statement. To come within these exceptions it will, however, still be necessary for the party seeking to adduce overseas evidence under section 23 of the 1998 Act to establish that the maker of the statement is outside the United Kingdom and that it is not reasonably practicable to secure his or her attendance (section 23(2)(b)).

They must also satisfy the court, on the balance of probabilities that a statement not prepared in accordance with section 3 of the 1990 Act was in fact made by its purported maker[21] and that it was a statement the accuracy of which the maker had in some way acknowledged.

---

21 *R. v. McGillivray* [1993] 97 Cr. App. R. 232.

5.50   In *Director of Prosecutions v. Boo*[22] the defendant was accused of being in charge of a car with an excess of alcohol in his breath/blood or urine. He denied being the driver and claimed that the real driver had returned to Columbia.

The defendant produced a fax from the "real" driver addressed to the Magistrates but sent to the defence solicitors. Despite CPS objections to its admissibility, the Justices admitted it under section 23 and section 26 of the 1988 Act. The Crown appealed, by case stated, the Justices' decision to acquit. Whilst the fax purported to come from Columbia, it came from no identifiable address, and it was not produced with any evidence as to its source. It was not even evident from the fax stamp that it came from outside the United Kingdom (let alone Columbia), or indeed from its purported maker as it was not even signed. The appeal court held that the fax should not have been admitted, and allowed the appeal.

5.51   The amended wording of section 24(4) of the Criminal Justice Act 1988 introduced by Schedule 4 of the Criminal Justice (International Co-operation) Act 1990, *i.e.* "A statement prepared in accordance with section 3 of the Criminal Justice (International Co-operation) Act 1990"suggests that section 3 of this Act in fact prescribes a form for such statements, which it does not. It is submitted that the amendment refers to the procedure under which evidence is obtained from abroad rather than the form (simpliciter) in which it is produced, *i.e.* an unsolicited fax sent direct to the defence solicitors from a potential witness abroad does not comply with the requirements of section 3 of the 1990 Act.

5.52   The case of *Foxley*[23] is relevant to the admissibility of business records produced consequent to a letter of request. In *Foxley*, the appellant was employed by the Ministry of Defence and had direct influence over the placement of all substantial ammunition contracts. He was charged with having corruptly placed contracts with three foreign manufacturing companies. The prosecution produced evidence obtained consequent to letters of request, such as credit notes, invoices and credit invoices recovered from these companies. These documents were introduced under sections 24 and 25 of the Criminal Justice Act 1988. It was contended on appeal *inter alia*, that under these sections, it must be separately proved that the document was created in the course of a trade or business; that the information contained in it was supplied by a person with personal knowledge of its contents, and that the document was authentic. It was held, dismissing the appeal, that the purpose of sections 24 and 25 was to enable a document to speak for itself, and Parliament's intention would be defeated if in every case the creator or keeper of the document or the supplier of the information had to be called. Parliament's intention had clearly been that the courts could draw such inferences as they thought proper from the documents themselves and from the method or route by which they had been produced before the court.

> "Is direct oral evidence required either from the officer of the appropriate authority in the foreign country that he has seized the documents in accordance with the laws of his country or from an officer of the company that these were indeed documents from his company created in the course of business containing information supplied by a person who had or may reasonably be supposed to have had personal knowledge of the matters dealt with? In our judgement such direct evidence is not essential, although it will often be desirable to have such evidence." [*per* Roch L.J. at p. 538].

5.53   Discretion to exclude admissible evidence

22 (Unreported) (CO/2538/97, January 29, 1998).
23 [1995] 2 Cr. App. R. 523.

Under section 25 of the Criminal Justice Act 1988, if the court is of the opinion that, in the interests of justice, a statement which is admissible by virtue of section 23 or section 24 of the Act nevertheless ought not to be admitted, it may so direct.

In exercising its discretion to exclude admissible evidence, section 3(8) of the 1990 Act provides that in relation to a statement contained in evidence taken pursuant to a letter of request, the court shall have regard:—

(a) to whether it was possible to challenge the statement by questioning the person who made it, and

(b) if proceedings have been instituted, whether the local court allowed the parties to the proceedings to be legally represented when the evidence was being taken.[24]

5.54   In *R. v. Virani* (1994) the trial judge, Hutchinson J., heard expert evidence upon the procedure adopted in Leichtenstein at Commission Rogatoire proceedings. This involved all questions being put by a judge which could have included defence questions had they been notified of the hearing. This failure on the part of the SFO to notify the defence was, he found, compensated by the defence's ability under section 3 of the 1990 Act to make its own request.

However, in a far reaching decision in relation to the use of "foreign" evidence, the Court of Appeal in *R. v. Radak*[25] considered whether, as a matter of discretion under section 26 of the Criminal Justice Act 1988, it was in the interests of justice to grant leave to admit the written statement of S, a prosecution witness living in the United States who refused to attend court to give evidence (allegedly through fear). The defendant's right to equality of arms with the prosecution, as to the summoning and examining of witnesses, had to be safeguarded, to comply with Article 6(3)(d) of the European Convention for the Protection of Human Rights and Fundamental Freedom 1950. S's evidence was essential to the prosecution case. The prosecution had known from the outset that S might not attend voluntarily, yet had done nothing. The defendant's rights under the Convention would have been safeguarded if they had been able to cross examine S. That could have been achieved had his evidence been taken pursuant to section 3 of the 1990 Act. The prosecution should have anticipated the problem regarding S's attendance in sufficient time to enable his evidence to be obtained on commission. That they did not do so was a relevant consideration under section 26 of the Criminal Justice Act 1988. In the circumstances, the court considered on balance that S's statement ought not to have been admitted in the interests of justice. The appeal was allowed.

5.55   It is interesting to note that this case was decided in 1998, under the provisions of the Criminal Justice Act 1998. Arguments involving the Human Rights Convention were deployed, although the legislation in the United Kingdom was neither passed nor implemented. It is anticipated that increasingly, human rights arguments will be made, when judges are asked to exercise their discretion in one way or another.

Statement prepared in accordance with section 3 of the 1990 Act for the purpose of:

(a) pending or contemplated criminal proceedings, or

(b) a criminal investigation

---

24 These factors are additional to those required to be considered under s. 25(2).
25 *The Times*, October 7, 1998.

do not have to fulfill the conditions of admissibility of business documents under section 24(1). This means that, even though the attendance of the maker of the statement in the business document could be secured, the document can, nonetheless, be admissible in the maker's absence (section 24(4), Criminal Justice Act 1988).

CHAPTER 6

Obtaining Evidence in the United Kingdom for Use Overseas

6.00 Section 4 of the Criminal Justice (International Co-operation) Act 1990 as amended is the section which covers the application by authorities abroad for evidence to be obtained in the United Kingdom.[1]

Section 4 of the Act is as follows:—

"(1) This section has effect where the Secretary of State receives—

    (a) from a court or tribunal exercising criminal jurisdiction in a country or territory outside the United Kingdom or a prosecuting authority in such a country or territory; or

    (b) from any other authority in such a country or territory which appears to him to have the function of making requests of the kind to which this section applies,

a request for assistance in obtaining evidence in the United Kingdom in connection with criminal proceedings that have been instituted, or a criminal investigation that is being carried on, in that country or territory.

(2) If the Secretary of State or, if the evidence is to be obtained in Scotland, the Lord Advocate is satisfied—

    (a) that an offence under the law of the country or territory in question has been committed or that there are reasonable grounds for suspecting that such an offence has been committed; and

    (b) that proceedings in respect of that offence have been instituted in that country or territory or that an investigation into that offence is being carried on there,

he may, if he thinks fit, by notice in writing nominate a court in England, Wales or Northern Ireland or, as the case may be, Scotland to receive such of the evidence to which the request relates as may appear to the court to be appropriate for the purpose of giving effect to the request.

(2A) Except where the evidence is to be obtained as is mentioned in subsection (2B) below, if the Secretary of State is satisfied—

    (a) that an offence under the law of the country or territory in question has been committed or that there are reasonable grounds for suspecting that such an offence has been committed, and

    (b) that proceedings in respect of that offence have been instituted in that country or territory or that an investigation into that offence is being carried on there,

---

1 See Chap. 13 for the procedure adopted where a request is referred to the SFO.

and it appears to him that the request relates to an offence involving serious or complex fraud, he may, if he thinks fit, refer the request or any part of the request to the Director of the Serious Fraud Office for him to obtain such of the evidence to which the request or part referred relates as may appear to the Director to be appropriate for giving effect to the request or part referred.[2]

(2B) Where the evidence is to be obtained in Scotland, if the Lord Advocate is satisfied as to the matters mentioned in paragraphs (a) and (b) of subsection (2A) above and it appears to him that the request relates to an offence involving serious or complex fraud, he may, if he thinks fit, give a direction under section 51 of the Criminal Justice (Scotland) Act 1987.[3]

(3) Where it appears to the Secretary of State or, as the case may be, the Lord Advocate that the request relates to a fiscal offence in respect of which proceedings have not yet been instituted he shall not exercise his powers under subsection (2) [(2A) or (2B)] above unless—

(a) the request is from a country or territory which is a member of the Commonwealth or is made pursuant to a treaty to which the United Kingdom is a party; or

(b) he is satisfied that the conduct constituting the offence would constitute an offence of the same or a similar nature if it had occurred in the United Kingdom.

(4) For the purpose of satisfying himself as to the matters mentioned in subsection (2)(a) and (b) [or (2A)(a) and (b)] above the Secretary of State or, as the case may be, the Lord Advocate shall regard as conclusive a certificate issued by such authority in the country or territory in question as appears to him to be appropriate.

(5) In this section "evidence" includes documents and other articles.

(6) Schedule 1 to this Act shall have effect with respect to the proceedings before a nominated court in pursuance of a notice under subsection (2) above."[4]

6.01   It will be appreciated immediately that the provisions under this section apply only to evidence being received by a nominated court. If the request can be complied with without the formality of court nomination (which of course requires willing co-operation) then the Secretary of State will not be required to make a nomination under Section 4, but the Mutual Legal Assistance Section (MLA Section) at the Home Office will liaise directly with the appropriate law enforcement authority (normally a police force) which will itself arrange for the provision of the evidence requested. This will normally take place by way of interviewing the requested person, taking a statement from him, and transmitting this to the Home Office for further transmission to the requesting state. It should be appreciated that in many civil law jurisdictions, the concept of sworn statements is unknown, and that therefore this less formal procedure will often suffice. In some cases, however, it may be necessary, depending on the requirements of the requesting state, for the statement to be sworn

---

2 See Chap. 13.
3 Subss. (2A), (2B) and the words in square brackets in subss. (3), (4) were inserted by the Criminal Justice and Public Order Act 1994, s. 164(1).
4 See App. A for the entire statute.

before a court, in which case the Secretary of State may make a nomination under section 4(2) of the 1990 Act. If the witness is unwilling, a nomination will always be necessary to obtain the testimony of the witness by the use of a witness summons.

Preconditions

6.02   For a request to be executed under this section, it must be received by the Secretary of State from a *court or tribunal exercising criminal jurisdiction in the requesting state, a prosecuting authority in that state or from any other authority in that state which appears to the Secretary of State to have the function of making requests* of the kind to which section 4 applies. It is the responsibility of the M.L.A. Section in the Home Office to ensure that this precondition is fulfilled.

The Secretary of State must also be satisfied:—

(i)   that an offence under the law of the requesting state has been committed or that there are reasonable grounds for suspecting that such an offence has been committed; and

(ii)   that proceedings in respect of that offence have been instituted in the requesting state or that an investigation into that offence is being carried on there.

Certificate

6.03   For the purpose of satisfying himself that an offence under the law of the requesting state has been committed or that there are reasonable grounds for suspecting that such an offence has been committed *and* that proceedings have been instituted or an investigation is being carried on, the Secretary of State shall regard as conclusive any certificate issued by the requesting State. (Section 4(4)).

In the absence of a Certificate, however, the Secretary of State has to satisfy himself on the information contained in the letter of request itself that the conditions specified in section 4(2)(a) and 4(2)(b) or, in cases to be referred to the SFO, section 4(2A)(a) and 4(2A)(b) are satisfied.

Ministerial discretion

6.04   Having satisfied himself of the matters contained in section 4(2) the Secretary of State thereafter has a discretion. If he thinks fit, he may by notice in writing nominate a court to receive such of the evidence to which the request relates as may appear to the court to be appropriate for the purpose of giving effect to the request.[5]

The question of ministerial discretion was considered in the *Finninvest* case.[6] The applicants in the case were Finninvest itself, which was a large Italian corporation with advertising, publishing and broadcasting interests, its President, and its previous President Silvio Berlusconi, principal shareholder, leader of the Forza Italia political party and a former Prime Minister of Italy.

6.05   It was alleged by the Italian prosecuting authorities that the applicants were involved in a large fraud whereby in excess of £50 million was secretly removed from the company and used for criminal purposes. Mr Berlusconi was the subject of criminal proceedings, for allegedly bribing Revenue officials and making illegal donations to another former Prime Minister, Mr Craxi. Their illegality arose from the

5 Subject to the provisions of s. 4(3) relating to fiscal offences
6 R. v. *Secretary of State for the Home Department ex parte Finninvest SpA* [1997] 1 All E.R. 942.

fact that they were made without the authority of the Finninvest board and without proper records. Further investigations were being made into allegations of false accounting within the Finninvest group carried out in order to conceal the true source of the large sums concerned. In connection with that investigation, the Secretary of State for the Home Department had received from the Italian authorities a letter of request, sent under the provisions of the 1959 European Convention on Mutual Assistance, which had been implemented by the 1990 Act.

6.06   The letter of request sought assistance in obtaining documents relevant to the allegations of false accounting and in particular, documents held by CMM Corporate Services Ltd (CMM) at an address in Regent Street; CMM had been founded by a solicitor. The Home Secretary referred the request to the Director of the SFO under section 4(2A) of the 1990 Act (as amended by the Criminal Justice and Public Order Act 1994). The request was implemented by the SFO, using its powers under the Criminal Justice Act 1987, which were similarly amended in 1994 to provide for a reference by the Home Secretary under section 4(2A) and they sought and obtained a search warrant, authorising entry to CMM's premises to search there for specified documents. They further implemented the request by serving upon the solicitor a notice under section 2(3) of the Criminal Justice Act 1987 requiring him to produce specified documents.[7]

That search warrant was issued by Bow Street Magistrates' Court and executed the same day upon CMM. The documents that were removed were examined by representatives of the Italian authorities to ascertain which were relevant[8] and which were required for transmission to Italy. There were various challenges in relation to different aspects of the matter, many of which are dealt with elsewhere. The question for examination in this chapter was the extent to which the Home Secretary was bound to consider whether or not the request concerned "a political offence (or) an offence connected with a political offence" (within the meaning of Article 2(a) of the 1959 European Convention).

Article 2 provides, "Assistance may be refused:

> (a)   if the request concerns an offence which the requested Party considers a political offence, an offence connected with a political offence, or a fiscal offence;(CA)..."

6.07   It was argued by Counsel for the Secretary of State that the Home Secretary was not bound to consider Article 2(a) at all,[9] for there was no requirement in the 1990 Act that he should do so, in contrast to the express provision in section 4(3) relating to fiscal offences.

Simon Brown L.J. found such an argument unsound. He ruled that Section 4(3) deals merely with some, but by no means all fiscal offence requests in effect by removing the discretion which would otherwise exist in regard to them.

> "This leaves other fiscal offence requests to be considered, just like any political offence requests under the remaining provisions of Section 4, which expressly confer upon the Home Secretary a general discretion in the matter. It seems to me quite impossible to contend that in exercising this general discretionary power the Home Secretary is entitled to ignore the express discretion arising under Article 2. The Secretary of State would, in my judgement, plainly be overlooking

---

7 For the powers of the Director of the SFO, see Chap. 13 below
8 As to relevance see Chap. 11, para. 11.29 *et seq.*
9 In fact he had paid regard to it.

a material consideration if, for example, he simply forgot the existence of Article 2(a)."

6.08   It is clear therefore that by use of the words *"he may, if he thinks fit* by a notice in writing nominate a court . . ."* in section 4(2) of the 1990 Act, the Statute invests the Home Secretary with a general discretion which must be exercised prior to nominating a court. As to the considerations that must be taken into account when exercising this general discretion assistance is provided by reference to the relevant Conventions and in particular the European Convention of 1959 and the United Kingdom reservations thereto and the Commonwealth Scheme[10] and the grounds for refusal of assistance. These are dealt with below under the heading "Refusal of Assistance".

6.09   The manner in which the Secretary of State exercised his general discretion was further alluded to in *Finninvest*. The court, having confirmed that Section 4 of the 1990 Act expressly conferred general discretion upon the Home Secretary, ruled that in exercising that general discretion he is not entitled to ignore the express discretion which arises under Article 2 of the 1959 Convention, for to do so would be to overlook a material consideration.

Simon Brown, L.J. continued:

> "That is not to say, however, that the Secretary of State was bound to reach a decision as to whether or not these offences were themselves, or were connected with, political offences. He could instead, had he wished, have decided that whether or not they were – whether or not in other words a discretion arose under Article 2(a) – he would not in any event exercise it to refuse co-operation with the Italian authorities in the particular circumstances of this case. Had he followed that course – or, indeed had he deposed in the present proceedings that, even had he reached a contrary view on the political offence question, he would still have decided to comply with the request – his decision would in my judgment be proof against this particular ground of challenge, irrespective of whether or not he directed himself correctly on the substantive issue".

6.10   Unfortunately, the Secretary of State had approached the issue in a different manner. As the letter of request had referred to "illicit payments to politicians" he had considered that the payments in question were offences of bribery and corruption and had not considered the offences described in the request to be political offences. Thus, although he stated he had had Article 2(a) in mind, he had taken the view that he did not need to consider possible refusal of assistance under the Article. The court therefore did not know what decision he would have taken had he thought the offences were political, in which event it was necessary for the court to address the question of whether or not the offences were political.

The nature of the minister's discretion was further examined by Latham J. in *R. v. Bow Street Magistrates' Court ex parte Zardari*.[11]

6.11   The applicant, the husband of Miss Benazir Bhutto, the former Prime Minister of Pakistan, was arrested and taken into custody following his wife's removal from office by the President of Pakistan. A letter of request was sent to the United Kingdom by the Pakistani authorities to obtain of evidence under Section 4 of the Criminal Justice (International Cooperation) Act 1990. The applicant sought judicial review of two separate decisions:

---

10 Scheme Relating to Mutual Assistance in Criminal Matters within the Commonwealth (App. H).
11 (Unreported) CO/1593/98, April 29, 1998, QBD.

(a) The decision of the stipendiary magistrate at Bow Street who had been nominated under section 4 to collect evidence and who had declined to consider any argument to the effect that the proceedings before him constituted an abuse of process of the court; and

(b) The decision of the Secretary of State to decline to consider a similar submission.

It was contended that the assertions made by the Government of Pakistan when it sought mutual assistance from the United Kingdom Government were fraudulent. As the learned judge put it:

"In other words, the information upon which it persuaded the United Kingdom Government to act was untrue ... The fraud which is alleged to have been perpetrated by the Pakistani Government, relates to whether or not there have indeed been any proceedings instituted in respect of the relevant offence."

6.12   Having considered the wording of section 4(2), the learned judge indicated that there were clearly two discretions within the sub-section; that of the Secretary of State as expressed in the phrase "if he thinks fit" and that of the magistrates' court once nominated to receive such of the evidence to which the request relates "as may appear to it to be appropriate". He rejected the argument that the magistrates' court had any other discretion. It did not have a discretion, once nominated to decline to carry out what on its face was its statutory obligation, to receive such of the evidence to which the request relates "as may appear to the court to be appropriate". Rather, he continued, this was the

"sort of issue which could properly be the sort of material which the Secretary of State is entitled to consider in the exercise of his discretion as to whether to nominate a court under Section 4(2). It is also, it seems to me, arguable that the Secretary of State's discretion is one which he is entitled to exercise, not merely by way of nomination, but also by way of retraction of that nomination, if material comes to his attention which would suggest that the conditions, which he considered were present so as to justify his nomination in the first instance, no longer exist."[12]

Latham J., having concluded that there was no arguable case that the stipendiary magistrate was wrong in law in declining to hear the argument which was sought to be put before him, did however indicate that it was an argument "which arguably the Secretary of State could and should have considered".

Refusal of assistance[13]

General considerations

6.13   In its 1991 guidelines upon international mutual legal assistance[14] the MLA Section, indicated that the United Kingdom will render the maximum possible

---

12 The report of the case does not make it clear whether the minister had before him a Certificate under s. 4(4) of the Act.
13 "For good measure Art. 19 (European Convention) provides that "reasons should be given for any refusal of mutual assistance" *per* Simon Brown L.J. in *R. v. Secretary of State for the Home Dep. ex parte Finninvest SpA* [1997] 1 All E.R. 942.
14 U.K. Guidelines on International Mutual Assistance in Criminal Matters, August 1991, para. 40, however see Chap. 4.

assistance and anticipates that cases of refusal will be rare. It indicates that the normal practice, with the exception of clear-cut cases, will be for it to consult with the requesting state before finally concluding that a request could not be executed (either wholly or in part) and to discuss with the requesting state any possibilities for overcoming such difficulties. Article 19 of the 1959 Convention provides that reasons shall be given for any refusal of mutual legal assistance. In addition, the Joint Action of June 29, 1998 (Appendix L) on good practice in mutual legal assistance in criminal matters (Article 3(d)) makes clear the obligation on states to give to requesting authorities a written or oral report explaining any difficulty where a request cannot be executed in whole or in part and where possible, offer to consider jointly how the difficulties might be overcome. This principle is reflected in the statement of good practice contained in the Home Office Guidelines (see Appendix K).

It has been seen that the Secretary of State retains, in all cases, an overriding discretion whether or not to comply with the request. Earl Ferrers, at the second reading of the Bill,[15] made it clear that, in relation to requests from Convention states (member of the Council of Europe) it would be assumed that the Secretary of State would comply. Requests, of course, will also be received from non-Convention states and even from states with which the United Kingdom has no agreement at all. In addressing the circumstances where requests may be refused, one should have regard to the various Conventions and also to the legislation.

A. European Convention on Mutual Assistance in Criminal Matters 1959 article 2

"Assistance may be refused:—

(a) If the request concerns an offence which the requested Party considers a *political offence*, an *offence connected with a political offence*, or a *fiscal offence*;

(b) If the requested Party considers that execution of the request is *likely to prejudice the sovereignty, security, ordre public or other essential interests of its country*."

B. United Kingdom Reservations to the European Convention on Mutual Assistance Criminal Matters 1959[16]

The Government of the United Kingdom of Great Britain and Northern Ireland reserved the right to refuse assistance in respect of Article 2, if the person who is the subject of a request for assistance has been convicted or acquitted in the United Kingdom or in the third state of an offence which arises from the same conduct as that giving rise to proceedings in the requesting State in respect of that person. (This principle is known as *ne bis in idem*).

C. The Commonwealth Scheme[17]

Under the Commonwealth Scheme, refusal of assistance is dealt with under paragraph 7.

---

15 (1989) 513 H.L.R. 1232.
16 The subject of reservations to the Convention by the U.K. is currently under review as far as relations with other Member States of the E.U. are concerned.
17 Scheme Relating to Mutual Assistance in Criminal Matters within the Commonwealth. See App. H.

7(1) The requested country may refuse to comply in whole or in part with a request for assistance under this Scheme if the criminal matter appears to the MLA Section of that country to concern:—

    (a)   conduct which would not constitute an offence under the law of that country.

         Although double criminality, which is what this subparagraph refers to, is a standard precondition in extradition treaties, it is not a standard feature of mutual legal assistance agreements, other than where search and seizure (and to a limited extent, fiscal offences) are involved. In this context, however, its presence is explained in the commentary to the scheme[18] as a consequence of criminal law reform, in certain parts of the world, which has been influenced by particular regions or ideological considerations, and which defines offences as punishable with heavy penalties which are accepted or much more lightly punished, in other countries. It was implicit in the discussions giving rise to this text however, that the use of this discretionary power would be regarded as exceptional and in no way automatic.

    (b)   an offence or proceedings of a *political character*.

         This is also an optional ground for refusal under the 1959 Convention, Article 2(a); or

    (c)   conduct which in the requesting country is an offence only under *military law* or a law relating to *military obligations*[19]; or

    (d)   conduct in relation to which the person accused or suspected of having committed an offence has been acquitted or convicted by a court in the requested country.

         This ground is covered also in the United Kingdom's reservation to Article 2 of the 1959 Convention.

(2) The requested country may refuse to comply in whole or in part with a request for assistance under this Scheme:—

    (a)   to the extent that it appears to the MLA Section of that country that compliance *would be contrary to the Constitution of* that country, or *would prejudice the security, international relations or other essential public interests of that country*; or

    (b)   where there are substantial grounds leading the MLA Section of that country to believe that compliance would facilitate the prosecution or punishment of any person on account of his or her *race, religion, nationality or political opinions* or would cause prejudice for any of these reasons to any person affected by the request.

Paragraph 7(2)(d) contains provisions similar to those in Article 2 of the 1959 Convention. Paragraph 7(2)(b) is not replicated in the 1959 Convention.

(3) The requested country may refuse to comply in whole or in part with a request for assistance to the extent that the *steps required to be taken in*

---

18 App. H.
19 Art. 1(2) of the 1959 Convention expressly excludes offences contrary to military law.

order to comply with the request cannot under the law of that country be taken in respect of criminal matters arising in that country.

(4)   An offence shall not be an offence of a political character for the purpose of this paragraph if it is an offence within the scope of any international convention to which both the requesting and requested countries are parties and which imposes on the parties thereto an obligation either to extradite or prosecute a person accused of the commission of the offence.

D. United Nations Model Treaty on Mutual Assistance in Criminal Matters 1990

Reference should also be made to the United Nations Model Treaty on Mutual Assistance in Criminal Matters 1990.

The treaty includes the following suggested grounds for refusal of assistance.

Article 4(1)

Assistance may be refused if:

(a)   the requested state is of the opinion that the request, if granted, would prejudice its *sovereignty, security, public order* or other essential public interest;

(b)   the offence is regarded by the requested state as being of a *political nature*;

(c)   there are substantial grounds for believing that the request for assistance has been made for the purpose of prosecuting a person account of that person's *race, sex, religion, nationality, ethnic origin* or *political opinions* or that the person's position may be prejudiced for any of those reasons;

(d)   the request relates to an offence that is subject to investigation or prosecution in the requested state where the prosecution of which in the requesting state would be *incompatible with the requested state's law on double jeopardy (ne bis in idem)*;

(e)   the assistance requested required the requested state to carry out compulsory measures that are inconsistent with its law and practice had the offence been the subject of investigation or prosecution under its own jurisdiction;

(f)   the act is an offence under *military law*, which is not also an offence under ordinary criminal law.

The relevance of the model treaty relates to requests from jurisdictions where mutual assistance treaties have accepted this model.

Article 19(1)

No person shall be compelled in response to a request under this scheme to give any evidence in the requested country which he could not be compelled to give:

(a)   in criminal proceedings in that country; or

(b)   in criminal proceedings in the requesting country.

Article (19)2

For this purposes of this paragraph, any reference to giving evidence includes references to answering any question and to producing any document."

Refusal of assistance in relation to political offences

6.14   The question of whether the Home Secretary should have refused a request for mutual assistance in respect of a political offence or an offence connected with a political offence was considered by the Divisional Court in *R. v. Secretary of State for the Home Dept ex parte Finninvest SpA*, the facts of which are set out above.[20]

In that case, whilst the offences under investigation were "illicit payments to politicians", the Secretary of State considered that these were ordinary offences of bribery and corruption and therefore did not consider that the offences described in the mutual assistance request, namely false accounting and illicit payments to politicians were political offences, or offences connected with political offences. In those circumstances the Secretary of State, although he had Article 2(a) of the 1959 European Convention in mind, felt no need to consider possible refusal of assistance under Article 2(a).

The court went on to consider the substantive question, not knowing what decision the Home Secretary would have taken, had he concluded that the allegations were or were connected with political offences.

6.15   As a preliminary issue, the court had to decide according to whose law is the question of whether or not an offence is political to be determined, that of the requesting or the requested state. The court referred to the express words of Article 2(a), "An offence which the requested Party considers a political offence". This distinguished it from the position normally arising under international Conventions where the courts seek to maintain consistency between the decisions of different jurisdictions. In the Divisional Court's judgement, the issue falls to be determined according to English law.

6.16   Reference has been made above to the Home Secretary's conclusion that the illicit payments to politicians involved offences of bribery and corruption. In fact this turned out to be mistaken, as the illegality of certain of the payments derived from the fact that they were made without the requisite transparency and authority. The court stressed therefore that a requesting state should in future give sufficient detail of the facts to the Secretary of State, in order that he can exercise his discretion under Article 2(a) with a proper understanding of those facts.

The court then proceeded to consider what it described as "the appropriate question":—

> "Whether, had the true facts been known to him, the Home Secretary would, or even could, have regarded these offences as political." (at p. 958)

It was necessary for the applicants to establish that the making of illicit political donations is a political offence.

> "The whole concept of political crime is well recognised to be one of consider-able difficulty." (at p. 959)

Recognising the numerous reported cases on the topic and the large number of judicial utterances upon various aspects of the problem, the court concentrated upon

---

20 See p. 59; [1997] 1 All E.R. 942.

three key passages. Whilst the court was ready to assume that there are certain offences of an intrinsically political character, it found it impossible to regard the present offence as political *per se*, *i.e.* political irrespective of motive or circumstance.

As Simon Brown L.J. expressed it:—

"The applicants argue that it is so simply because it relates to the funding of the political process. I disagree. Rather, it seems to me merely an offence against the ordinary law enacted for the proper ordering of the democratic process in Italy – no different from, say, voting twice at an election. It is, of course, an offence committed in a political context. In my judgement, however, that does not make it a political offence." (at p. 959)

6.17 The applicants relied upon the dictum of Lord Lloyd in *T. v. Home Secretary, House of Lords*.[21]

"A crime is a political crime for the purposes of Article 1(F)(b) of the Geneva Convention (a provision excluding the protection of asylum for those guilty of "serious non-political crimes") if, and only if:

(1) it is committed for a political purpose, that is to say, with the object of overthrowing or subverting or changing the Government of a state or *inducing it to change its policy*; and
(2) there is a sufficiently close and direct link between the crime and the alleged political purpose.

In determining whether such a link exists, the court will bear in mind the means used to achieve the political end, and will have particular regard to whether the crime was aimed at a military or governmental target, on the one hand, or a civilian target on the other, and in either event whether it was likely to involve the indiscriminate killing or injuring of members of the public."

6.18 The applicants drew particular attention to Lord Lloyd's use of the words, "inducing (the Government) to change its policy". They submitted that it was an obvious inference that the present offence was indeed committed to influence Government policy in some way, as one did not secretly pay large amounts of money to a political party unless one had such a purpose. The court was disposed to accept such a submission and to draw the suggested inference but what it could not accept was "that any offence committed with a view to inducing a change in Government policy is *ipso facto* to be regarded as a political offence. The difficulty comes in defining just when it will be and when it will not" (at p. 960).

In seeking to decide when such an offence properly can be characterised as political by virtue of the offender's purpose or motivation, the court found considerable help in a passage from Lord Radcliffe's speech in *Strachs v. Government of Israel*[22]:

"In my opinion the idea that lies behind the phrase "offence of a political character" is that the fugitive is at odds with the state that applies for his extradition on some issue connected with the political control or Government of the country. The analogy of "political" in this context is with "political" in such phrases as "political refugee", "political asylum" or "political prisoner". It does

21 [1996] 2 All E.R. 865 at 800.
22 [1964] A.C. 556 at 591.

indicate, I think, that the requesting state is after him for reasons other than the enforcement of the criminal law in its ordinary, what I may call its common or international, aspect. It is this idea that the judges were seeking to express in the two early cases of *Re Castioni* and *Re Meunier* when they connected the political offence with an uprising, a disturbance, an insurrection, a civil war or struggle for power: and in my opinion it is still necessary to maintain the idea of that connection. It is not departed from by taking a liberal view as to what is meant by disturbance or these other words, provided that the idea of political opposition as between fugitive and requesting state is not lost sight of: but it would be lost sight of, I think, if one were to say that all offences were political offences, so long as they could be shown to have been committed for a political object or with a political motive or for the furtherance of some political cause or campaign. There may, for instance, be all sorts of contending political organisations or forces in a country and members of them may commit all sorts of infractions of the criminal law in the belief that by so doing they will further their political ends: but if the central Government stands apart and is concerned only to enforce the criminal law that has been violated by these contestants, I see no reason why fugitives should be protected by this country from its jurisdiction on the ground that they are political offenders."

6.19   Finally, the court referred itself to Lord Diplock's speech in *R. v. Governor of Pentonville Prison ex parte Cheng*[23]:

"The purpose of the restriction (again Section 3(1) of the Extradition Act 1870), as it seems to me, was twofold. First, to avoid involving the United Kingdom in the internal political conflicts of foreign states. Today's Garibaldi may well form tomorrow's Government and, secondly, the humanitarian purpose of preventing the offender being surrendered to a jurisdiction in which there was a risk that his trial or punishment might be unfairly influenced by political considerations. As indicated by the inclusion of the second part of the restriction (barring extradition where it is sought "with a view to trial punishing for an offence of a political character") it was suspicion of the motives of requestioning states in seeking the surrender of fugitive criminals who were political opponents of the Governments of those states which underlie both requirements of Section 3(1) of the Act."

6.20   Drawing these strands together, Simon Brown L.J. stated the court's conclusions on the political issue as follows:

"I do not accept for one moment that the Italian magistracy's desire to expose and punish corruption in public and political life, and the conflict that that has created between the judges and the politicians there, operates to transform the present offences into political ones. It is a misuse of language to describe the magistrate's campaign as being "for political ends" or their approach to Mr Berlusconi as one of political persecution. On the contrary, all that I have read in this case suggests rather that the magistracy are demonstrating both their proper independence from the executive and an even handedness in dealing equally with the politicians of all political parties. If one applies Lord Radcliffe's dictum that there should be no protection for offenders "if the central Government stands apart and is concerned only to enforce the criminal law", one finds in the present context the magistracy standing apart as the relevant arm of central Government

---

23 [1973] A.C. 931.

and the politicians (or some of them) as the offenders against whom "the criminal law in its ordinary . . . aspect" is being enforced. More fundamentally, however, I reject the applicant's basic proposition that making payments to politicians or political parties – whether by way of bribes or illicit donations to my mind matters not – constitutes political offending in any relevant sense. It is not intrinsically political, nor is it made so because the offender hopes to change policy by buying political influence, nor because the judiciary by prosecuting hope to clean up politics. In short, none of the applicant's arguments, whether taken individually or cumulatively, begin to persuade me that the present offences are political. I just cannot see corrupt political contributors as "today's Garibaldis" (*per* Lord Diplock) or "seekers for freedom" (*per* Lord Reed), or "political prisoners" (*per* Lord Radcliffe).

Refusal of assistance in relation to fiscal offences

6.21 The United Kingdom Parliament was concerned, when the legislation was under consideration, at the potential use of the provisions by overseas authorities in proceedings for fiscal offences and the consequent threat to confidentiality under United Kingdom banking law.

Under the Act, where it appears to the Secretary of State that the request relates to a fiscal offence in respect of which proceedings have not yet been instituted he shall not exercise his powers under section 4(2) unless:

(i)   the requesting state is a member of the Commonwealth, or

(ii)   the request is made pursuant to a treaty to which the United Kingdom is a party,[24] or

(iii) the Secretary of State is satisfied that the conduct constituting the offence would constitute an offence of the same or a similar nature if it occurred in the United Kingdom. (*i.e.* dual criminality).

It is anticipated, therefore, that the issue of dual criminality in relation to fiscal offences will arise rarely and only in those cases where a request is received from a non-treaty partner. In all cases, however, the Secretary of State retains a discretion as to whether to meet a request and issues such as threats to confidentiality under domestic banking laws will be taken into account when exercising that discretion.

Granting of assistance under section 4

6.22 The assistance which can be granted under this section is the nomination by the Secretary of State of a court to receive such of the evidence to which the request relates as may appear to the court to be appropriate, for the purpose of giving effect to the request. In most cases, the court to be nominated will be the magistrates court nearest to the witness whose evidence is sought. Where there are a number of witnesses in different locations, the Secretary of State will in normal circumstances choose a court conveniently situated for the majority of those witnesses and will ask that court to liaise with them about the taking of the evidence requested.

If the evidence is particularly complex, or appears to involve complex questions of law, then it is open to the Secretary of State to nominate a Crown Court or the High Court to hear the evidence requested.

When a court has been nominated by the Secretary of State as above, it will be the responsibility of that court to execute the request. This will usually involve co-

---

24 *e.g.* European Convention 1959.

operation with the court police liaison officer, who will make enquiries as to the whereabouts of the witness, and arrange for his or her appearance in court. If the witness is willing, a witness summons will not be necessary, but if the witness is unwilling, or if he or she requires a court order, for example to produce business records or other confidential material, then a witness summons may be issued by the court under paragraph 1 of Schedule 1 of the 1990 Act to secure his or her attendance at Court.

Where the witness is willing and co-operative, the police may be able to agree with the witness, before the court hearing, to take a statement setting out the main matters to be dealt with in his or her statement and the court hearing may involve no more than a formal adoption in court under oath of the police statement. Provision is made under paragraph 2 of schedule 1 of the 1990 Act for the proceedings in the court to be under oath.

Proceedings before the nominated court

6.23   In *R. v. Secretary of State for the Home Department ex parte Zardari.*[25] Lord Bingham C.J. described the court procedure under section 4 as follows:

> "It is, however, quite plain that the process envisaged by Section 4 is not a trial; it is a process of gathering evidence. The use to be made of the evidence so gathered is a matter for the requesting state. If the evidence taken in an English court is to be used as primary evidence in the requesting state, then one would ordinarily expect, if the requesting state's legal system is at all analogous to our own, that the requesting state would recognise the need for the suspect to have a full and fair opportunity to contest the evidence either here or in its own court. If the evidence taken in England were not to be used as evidence in the requesting state then the need for a full and fair opportunity to contest that evidence in this country would be much less and might not exist at all."

6.24   Proceedings before the nominated court are regulated by the Magistrates Courts (Criminal Justice (International Co-operation)) Rules 1991[26] and also by the corresponding Crown Court Rules.[27] These Rules provide that the Court may, if it thinks necessary in the interests of justice, direct that the public be excluded from the court. It is also provided that the power to exclude the public is in addition and without prejudice to any other powers of the court to hear proceedings in camera.

If the letter of request has included a request that representatives of the requesting authority, or representatives of the defence from the requesting state be present during the taking of the witness's evidence, then this request will be acceded to, so far as possible, in the execution of the request. However, if it is impossible, for example for practical reasons, to arrange a court hearing for the witness at a time that suits the foreign representatives, then the hearing may have to go ahead in the absence of those representatives. It would be made clear to the requesting authorities in such circumstances that their request could not be executed in full, *e.g.* in the presence of the representatives of the defence, because of the urgency attached to the request. Whether in some circumstances this could be interpreted as a refusal to allow defence participation and thereby give rise either to an application for judicial review in this country or to the appropriate application in the requesting country remains to be tested.

---

25 CO/0345/98, March 11, 1998, QBD.
26 See App. N.
27 See App. O.

6.25   The Court Rules under the 1990 Act impose a duty on the clerk of the court (whether in the magistrates court or the Crown Court) to make a note of the proceedings, and in particular, to record

(a)   which persons with an interest in the proceedings were present

(b)   which of the said persons were represented and by whom

(c)   whether any of the said persons were denied the opportunity of cross examining a witness as to any part of his testimony.

The Secretary of State is entitled to request a copy of this record of proceedings.

6.26   In *R. v. Bow Street Magistrates' Court, ex parte Zardari*[27a] Mr Justice Latham indicated that the court's discretion is, as set out in Section 4(2)(b), to receive such of the evidence to which the request relates, "as may appear to the court to be appropriate".

"In those circumstances, it seems to me that the statute does not envisage the court having any other discretion than that identified in the sub-section".

Thus the question of whether the assertions made by the requesting state were fraudulent was not a matter for the discretion of the nominated court, but rather for the Secretary of State. The court thereby rejected a claim that the proceedings had been brought as an abuse.

As is mentioned above, paragraph 1 of Schedule 1 empowers the court to compel witnesses to attend court, or to produce documents, in the same way as for other proceedings before the court. Further, under paragraph 2, the court may in the proceedings take evidence on oath. For a detailed consideration of the procedural provisions governing the issue of witness summonses see p. 78.

6.27   In relation to Article 3 of the 1959 Convention, referring to the taking of evidence generally, the United Kingdom reserved the right not to take the evidence of witnesses, or require the production of records, or other documents, where its law recognised in relation thereto privilege, non-compellability or other exemption from giving evidence.[28]

The non-compellability of witnesses in respect of evidence which they may be called on to give before nominated courts is covered by paragraph 4 of Schedule 1 to the 1990 Act. Under this paragraph, it is provided that:

4(1) A person shall not be compelled to give in the proceedings any evidence which he could not be compelled to give—

(a)   in criminal proceedings in the part of the United Kingdom in which the nominated court exercises jurisdiction; or

(b)   subject to subparagraph (2) below, in criminal proceedings in the country or territory from which the request for the evidence has come.

In relation to possible claims for non-compellability under paragraph 4(1) above, three topics fall to be considered:—

a)   Privilege against self-incrimination

b)   Compellability of witnesses

27a (Unreported) CO/1593/98, April 29, 1998, QBD.
28 See App. C.

c)   Legal Professional privilege

Privilege against self incrimination

In United Kingdom proceedings

6.28   The classic formula is set out in *Blunt v. Park Lane Hotel*,[29] by Goddard L.J.,

> "The rule is that no-one is bound to answer any question if the answer thereto would, in the opinion of the judge, have a tendency to expose (that person) to any criminal charge, penalty or forfeiture which the judge regards as reasonably likely to be preferred or sued for."

Under the rule a witness is entitled to refuse to answer questions in court. The privilege extends also to the production of records and other documents (similarly recognised in the United Kingdom reservation to Article 3 of the European Convention) and enables a *subpoena*ed witness appearing before the nominated court under section 4 of the 1990 Act to refuse to produce documents, should they have a tendency to incriminate him or her.

This protection is confirmed by paragraph 4(6) of Schedule 1 to the 1990 Act: "In this paragraph references to giving evidence include references to answering any question and to producing any document or other article . . ."

6.29   There must be "a tendency to expose" and clearly this is a matter upon which the court must judge. In order for the witness to be entitled to remain silent

> "the court must see from the circumstances of the case and the nature of the evidence which the witness is called to give, that there is reasonable ground to apprehend danger to the witness from being called to answer. The danger . . . must be real and appreciable with reference to the ordinary operation of law in the ordinary course of things; not a danger of an imaginary and insubstantial character."[30]

It may be necessary for the judge to hear the witness in camera and for him or her to give evidence as to his or her fear of prosecution. Relevant considerations that a court must take into account are whether the line of questioning might form a significant link in the chain of evidence required for a prosecution.[31] Similarly harmless questions may in combination with other material lead to damaging inferences being drawn.[32] If, however, the evidence against the witness is already sufficiently strong that proceedings are likely to be taken whether or not the witness refused to answer, then it is unlikely that a claim for privilege will succeed. The judge must look at all the circumstances and determine whether the additional evidence, if given, might increase the risk of proceedings being taken.[33]

6.30   The privilege is against self-incrimination and is personal to the witness claiming it; it must arise from a fear of being prosecuted following the disclosure of facts or documents; it cannot be claimed by someone on his or her behalf. Thus, it

---

29 [1942] 2 K.B. 253 at 257. In relation to witnesses in civil proceedings see s. 14 Civil Evidence Act 1968.
30 *R. v. Boyes* [1861] 1 B&S 3.11 *per* Cockburn C.J.
31 *Beldam L.J. in Sociedade Nacional de Combustiveis de Angola U.E.E. v. Lundquvist* [1990] 3 All E.R. 283.
32 See Coburn C.J. in *R. v. Boyes*.
33 *Rio Tinto Zinc Corporation v. Westinghouse Electric Corporation* [1978] A.C.E. 547.

follows that a witness cannot claim the privilege if his or her answers are likely to incriminate others whether they be strangers or his or her spouse.[34]

However, in some foreign jurisdictions a person cannot be compelled to answer questions that might tend to incriminate his or her spouse or immediate family in which event the protection is extended to preclude compulsion.

6.31 Due to its personal nature, that is, self incrimination, an employee whilst able to claim the privilege on his or her own behalf, cannot do so if the answers given in evidence would tend to incriminate the company which employs him or her. This may have specific relevance to the growing liability of corporations to penalties under EEC regulations. In *Sociedade Nacional de Combustiveis de Angola U.E.E. v. Lundqvist*[35] Beldam L.J. ruled that a company cannot refuse to answer questions which would tend to incriminate its office holders.

Incrimination in foreign proceedings

6.32 In United Kingdom trial proceedings, the fact that an answer or the production of a document might tend to expose the witness to proceedings in another country does not provide the privilege against self-incrimination to the witness.

In relation to mutual assistance proceedings before a nominated court, however,

"The court has to consider when faced with an application involving the production of documents, any claim made by a person not to have to produce the documents as if the proceedings were domestic English proceedings. Thus English law and English considerations must apply"

per Collins J. in *R. v. Bow Street Magistrates' Court ex parte King.*[36] Thus it is submitted that the sole test is – if the proceedings in the requesting state were proceedings in an English court would the production of documents/evidence tend to incriminate the witness? In answering such a question, it is submitted that the facts should also be hypothetically imported to the English jurisdiction.

e.g. Y is charged with making a corrupt payment to D (an Italian civil servant) in England. D is *subpoena*ed as a witness by Y. D can refuse to answer any question that Y seeks to put that might expose him to prosecution in the United Kingdom. If there is no risk of United Kingdom proceedings against him or her, the danger of prosecution against him in Italy will not be privileged.

If, however, criminal proceedings are under way in Italy against Y and a letter of request is sent to the United Kingdom for evidence to be taken from D who is resident in the United Kingdom then D, if *subpoena*ed to a British court to give such evidence or produce documents, could claim the privilege against self-incrimination in relation to the Italian proceedings.

There appears to be no absolute privilege against self-incrimination under foreign law but it was held in *Arab Monetary Fund v. Hashim*[37] that the possibility of self-incrimination or indeed the incrimination of others under foreign law is a factor which can be taken into account under in deciding whether, and on what terms, a

---

34 See Lord Diplock in *Rio Tinto Zinc Corporation v. Westinghouse Electric Corporation ibid* but see below as to the effect of Sched. 1 4(1)(b).
35 [1990] 3 All E.R. 283.
36 (Unreported) CO/3489/97, October 8, 1997, QBD.
37 [1989] 3 All E.R. 466

disclosure order should be made. It was indicated that non-disclosure should normally be limited to cases where disclosure might have serious consequences for persons still resident in the requesting state.[38]

Claim against compulsion

6.33 In addition to the terms of paragraph 4(i) of Schedule 1 of the 1990 Act, reproduced at p. 71 above, which restrict the circumstances in which a witness may be compelled to give evidence before a nominated court in the United Kingdom, there must also be considered the terms of paragraphs 4(2) – (5) of the same schedule which are:—

> (2) Sub-paragraph (1)(b) above shall not apply unless the claim of the person questioned to be exempt from giving the evidence is conceded by the court, tribunal or authority which made the request.

> (3) Where such a claim made by any person is not conceded as aforesaid he may (subject to the other provisions of this paragraph) be required to give the evidence to which the claim relates but the evidence shall not be transmitted to the court, tribunal or authority which requested it if a court in the country or territory in question, on the matter being referred to it, upholds the claim.

> (4) Without prejudice to sub-paragraph (1) above a person shall not be compelled under this Schedule to give any evidence if his doing so would be prejudicial to the security of the United Kingdom; and a certificate signed by or on behalf of the Secretary of State or, where the court is in Scotland, by or on behalf of the Lord Advocate to the effect that it would be so prejudicial for that person to do so shall be conclusive evidence of that fact.

> (5) Without prejudice to sub-paragraph (1) above a person shall not be compelled under this Schedule to give any evidence in his capacity as an officer or servant of the Crown.

The effect of these paragraphs is that:

> (i) A person shall not be compelled to answer questions or produce any document or article which he could not be compelled to give:
>
> > (i) in criminal proceedings in the part of the United Kingdom in which the nominated court exercises jurisdiction (paragraph 4(1)(a)); or
> > (ii) in criminal proceedings in the requesting state, provided that the claim to be exempt is conceded by the requesting state or Authority (paragraphs 4(1)(b) and 4(2))

6.34 Where the claim to be exempt is not conceded, the witness may be required to give evidence but it will not be transmitted to the requesting court or authority if a court in the requesting state upholds the claim. The evidence is liable not to be transmitted until the claim of privilege has been determined by the foreign state (paragraph 4(3)).

In addition, a witness may not be required to give evidence if by so doing it would

---

38 *Arab Monetary Fund v. Hashim (No. 2)* [1990] 1 All E.R. 673.

be prejudicial to the security of the United Kingdom, or in his capacity as an officer of the Crown (Schedule 1, paragraph 4(4) & (5)).

It will therefore be seen that the protection is effectively dual. If the witness could be compelled, under the test in United Kingdom criminal proceedings, he or she will be compellable before the nominated court. If, however, he or she could be compelled in British criminal proceedings, he or she may still be protected, if it becomes apparent from the letter of request, that exemption applies in the requesting state. An interesting example of this relates to German letters of request, where the rule against self-incrimination applies not only to the witness, but also to the spouse of the witness and to immediate family members. Thus the witness could claim in the proceedings in a nominated court the privilege against self-incrimination if by answering the questions or producing the documents sought, his or her answers would tend to incriminate his or her spouse – a protection not available in criminal proceedings in the United Kingdom.

6.35   It will further be seen, that if the witness's claim to be exempt under the law of the requesting state is not conceded, he or she may be required to give evidence but that evidence will be withheld pending his or her claim being upheld in the requesting state. In practice, witnesses wishing to make such a claim should make representations to the Mutual Legal Assistance Section in the Home Office in advance or to the court, which will in all likelihood request clarification from the Ministry of Justice of the requesting state. In effect therefore, it is unlikely that the disputed evidence would be taken prior to clarification. In the absence of such clarification there are powers to exclude persons from the court[39] while the evidence is being taken and representations should be made to the court to exclude any representatives from the requesting state in order to secure the protection.

Encroachments on the privilege

6.36   It has become more common over recent years for statutes to compel witnesses in certain circumstances to answer questions, despite the fact that the answers might incriminate them. Some, though by no means all, of such statutory provisions allow use to be made of such answers, for the purpose for which the questioning was authorised.

By far the most common instance of this is under section 2 of the Criminal Justice Act 1987 (see Chapter 13) under which the Director of the SFO may require a person under investigation for a suspected offence involving serious or complex fraud (or any other person) to answer questions, furnish information and produce documents. However, under section 2(8) a statement in response to such a requirement may only be used in evidence against the maker (a) for an offence of knowingly or recklessly making a false or misleading statement, or (b) in a prosecution for some other offence where in giving evidence the witness makes a statement inconsistent with it. Of similar importance is the provision under section 434 of the Companies Act 1985 under which officers and agents of a company and others possessing relevant information are obliged to answer questions put by Board of Trade Inspectors appointed to investigate suspected fraud in the conduct or management of the company.[40] Recognising the risk implicit in such powers, particularly if the self-incriminatory answers were transmitted to a foreign jurisdiction, similar restrictions

---

39 The Magistrates' Courts (Criminal Justice (International Co-operation) Rules 1991 and the Crown Court Amendment Rules 1991.
40 See also s. 42 Banking Act 1987; s. 77 Criminal Justice Act 1986; ss133, 236, 290 Insolvency Act 1986.

to those contained in section 2(8) of the Criminal Justice Act 1987 are imposed on information obtained on behalf of a foreign authority. Those foreign authorities are required to sign an undertaking that no such statement made by any person to the SFO in the exercise of its coercive powers will be used against that person in a prosecution without the prior consent of the Secretary of State for the Home Department (see below Chapter 13, p. 170).

In cases where statute has removed the privilege, the judge still has discretion under sections 76 and 78 PACE 1984 to exclude the material – see *R. v. Saunders*; *R. v. Parnes*; *R. v. Ronson*; *R. v. Lyons*[41] below.

Self incrimination and the European Convention on Human Rights

6.37   In *Funke v. France*[42] the European Court of Human Rights held that a conviction under the French Customs Code for refusal to supply documents relating to alleged customs offences breached the right to fair trial under Article 6 of the Convention. The court indicated that it was implicit in the Article that an accused should not be required to provide evidence for the case against him.

Similarly, in *Saunders v. United Kingdom*,[43] the Court of Appeal's decision in *R. v. Saunders* (see above) was reviewed. The trial judge had allowed the prosecution to produce as evidence, transcripts of the accused's compulsory interviews by inspectors under section 434(5) Companies Act 1985; the Court of Appeal upheld the trial judge.

The European Court of Human Rights found the use of the transcripts in such a fashion in breach of Article 6, distinguishing the requirement upon a person to produce relevant evidence, (*e.g.* documents/blood/urine samples) against himself, which was compatible with the Convention, and the infringement of the right to remain silent in breach of Article 6, as had occurred in the trial.

6.38   Clearly this ruling will be highly relevant to the court's exercise of its discretion; the full effect of the decision is set out in the judgment of Judge Walsh:—

> "In my opinion the privilege against self-incrimination extends further than answers which themselves will support a conviction. It is sufficient to sustain the privilege where it is evident from the implications of the questions and the setting in which they are asked that a responsive answer to the question or an explanation as to why it cannot be answered could also be dangerous because injurious disclosure could result."

Compellability of witnesses

A defendant

6.39   The Criminal Evidence Act 1898 made the accused a competent but not a compellable witness for the defence in all criminal proceedings. Thus an accused in foreign proceedings cannot be compelled to give evidence before a nominated court in the United Kingdom.

In a recent mutual assistance request in which the Central Criminal Court was nominated[44] D, a Jersey resident, had pleaded guilty in Jersey to various offences some years previously, including one of forgery. In the course of his police interview by

---

41 (1996) 1 Cr. App. Rep. 463.
42 Case 82/1991/334/407, Series A, Vol 256 – A.
43 (1997) 23 E.H.R.R. 313.
44 *Application under the Criminal Justice (International Co-operation) Act 1990 re Christopher Delaney*, CCC (Unreported) October 1, 1996.

Jersey Fraud Squad, he implicated P, a Swiss citizen in that offence of forgery. The allegedly forged documents, which were produced by D in Jersey, had been presented before an Italian court, as part of the defence of a the defendant in one of the Banco Ambrosiano trials. An Italian examining magistrate brought proceedings in Italy against D and P and others responsible for introducing the allegedly forged documents into the earlier proceedings. D was in fact serving a sentence of imprisonment for the Jersey offences (including that of forgery) in England. The Italian magistrate sought to have D provide evidence to the Central Criminal Court for use against P in the Italian proceedings to which D was also a party. D was allowed by the Central Criminal Court to refuse to give such evidence, on the grounds of autrefois convict, that answers given by him might tend to incriminate him and finally, that as a co-accused he was thereby non-compellable.

Autrefois acquit/convict – double jeopardy

6.40 In the context of *autrefois acquit* (and *autrefois convict*) (*res judicata* in Scotland) the Reservation to Article 2 of the 1959 Convention should be borne in mind.[45] The United Kingdom reserves the right to refuse assistance if the person who is the subject of the request for assistance has been convicted or acquitted of an offence in the United Kingdom or in a third state of an offence which arises from the same conduct as that giving rise to proceedings in the requesting state in respect of that person.

Section 80(3) of the Police & Criminal Evidence Act 1984

6.41 This section provides that:

> In any proceedings the wife or husband of the accused shall, subject to sub-section (4) below, be compellable to give evidence for the prosecution ... if and only if—

> (a) the offence charged involves an assault on, or injury or a threat of injury, to the wife or husband of the accused or a person who was at the material time under the age of 16; or

> (b) the offence charged is a sexual offence alleged to have been committed in respect of a person who was at the material time under that age, or

> (c) the offence charged consists of attempting or conspiring to commit, or of aiding, abetting, counselling, procuring or inciting the commission of, an offence falling within paragraph (a) or (b) above.

6.42 The phrase "in any proceedings" would appear to cover the situation whereby a requesting state seeks to compel the spouse of the accused who is resident within the requested state to provide evidence against his or her spouse. The non-compellability of the spouse ceases when the parties are no longer married.

> "In any proceedings, a person who has been but is no longer married to the accused shall be competent and compellable to give evidence as if that person and the accused had never been married."[46]

---

45 App. B.
46 s. 80(5) Police and Criminal Evidence Act 1984.

Sovereign and diplomatic immunity

6.43   The heads of other Sovereign states are not compelled to give evidence. Reference should be made to the Diplomatic Privileges Act 1964, Consular Relations Act 1968, International Organisations Act 1968, Diplomatic and Other Privileges Act 1971 and State Immunity Act 1978 in order to examine the different degrees of immunity from compellability in the case of diplomats, consular officials and officers of prescribed international organisations.

Legal professional privilege (LPP)

6.44   For a detailed consideration of LPP, reference should be made to Chap. 10.
   Alongside the question of compellability is the sometimes overlapping question of *admissibility*.

Admissibility

Witness summons

6.45   The standard procedure whereby nominated courts obtain the evidence sought under section 4 of the 1990 Act is (in the absence of voluntary testimony) to issue a witness summons directed to the third party.
   In the Crown Court, the power to do so is contained in the Criminal Procedure (Attendance of Witnesses) Act 1965 (the 1965 Act).
   The arrangements for issuing witnesses summonses to attend the Crown court under sections 2 and 2A-E of the 1965 Act have been modified by section 66 of the Criminal Procedure and Investigations Act 1996 (CPIA). These new procedures were implemented on April 1, 1999 applying to any proceedings for the purpose of which no witness summons has been issued under section 2 of the 1965 Act prior to that date.

   (a)   The applicant for a potential summons must satisfy the court that the witness is able to give material evidence or produce any document or thing which is likely to be material evidence;

   (b)   The application must also satisfy the court that the potential witness will not give, or provide documentary evidence voluntarily;

   (c)   An application for the production of documentary evidence must be supported by an affidavit which includes information which will enable the potential witness to identify the evidence and the grounds for believing that the witness will be able to provide material evidence.

   This effectively requires the applicant to have approached the potential witness to discover whether they do in fact possess material evidence or to seek voluntarily disclosure before making any applications for a witness summons;

   (d)   In the case of applications for the production of a document or thing the potential witness has the opportunity to oppose the application for a witness summons and to attend the hearing before it is issued.

   (e)   If a witness summons is issued, a potential witness may apply to the Crown Court to make it ineffective, if he/she satisfies the court that they:

   (i)   have not received notice of the application to issue the summons; and

    (ii)   have not been present or represented at any hearing on the issue of the summons; and

    (iii) would not be able to give any material evidence, produce any document or thing likely to be material evidence.

In the magistrates' court the equivalent power is contained in section 97 of the Magistrates' Courts Act 1980:

"(1) Where a Justice of the Peace ... is satisfied that any person in England or Wales is likely to be able to give material evidence, or produce any document or thing likely to be material evidence ... and that that person will not voluntarily attend as a witness or will not voluntarily produce the document or thing, the Justice shall issue a summons directed to the person requiring him to attend before the court at the time and place appointed in the summons to give evidence or to produce the document or thing".

The meaning of "evidence"

6.46   The proper approach to be followed, when considering an application for the production of documents from a third party to criminal proceedings, is most conveniently set out in the judgment of Simon Brown, L.J. (as approved subsequently by the House of Lords) in *R. v. Reading Justices ex parte Berkshire County Council.*[47] After reviewing the authorities, he said:

"The central principles to be derived from those authorities are as follows:—

(i)   To be material evidence, documents must be not only relevant to the issue arising in the criminal proceedings, but also documents admissible as such in evidence;

(ii)   Documents which are desired merely for the purpose of possible cross examination are not admissible in evidence and thus are not material for the purposes of section 97;

(iii)   Whoever seeks production of documents must satisfy the Justices, with some material, that the documents are "likely to be material" in the sense indicated, the likelihood for this purpose involving a real possibility, although not necessarily a probability.

(iv)   It is not sufficient that the applicant merely wants to find out whether or not the third party has such material documents. This procedure must not be used as a disguised attempt to obtain discovery."[48]

    Whilst these principles apply to documentary evidence, the relevant sections in the legislation refer to "giving material evidence" or producing documents "likely to be

---

47 [1996] 1 Cr.App.R. 239 at p.247.

48 In *R. v. Milner* (Unreported) July 5, 1993, CCC. His Honour Judge Laughland, Q.C. held that a summons must specify, with a reasonable particularity, the document, or item, required to be produced. Identification can either be by reference to a class of documents or things, such that the object of the witness summons can recognise the obligation placed on him by the court, or by individual identification of the document itself. If the recipient is required to exercise his judgment as to relevance, then the summons is neither proper nor effective. He found the summonses in question, "in very broad terms, designed to trawl through the files of social work department and other agencies, such as the NSPCC, to produce not merely the produce of such searches to the court, but to seek to force their production for prior inspection by parties to the litigation", constituted an abuse of the process of the court.

    In *R. v. H.(L.)* [1997] 1 Cr.App. R. 176, Sedley J. indicated that the issue of a largely speculative summons may well amount to an "unproper, unreasonable or negligent act" capable of attracting a wasted costs order.

material evidence". "Materiality" is clearly common to both, and thus oral evidence must be subject to the same principles.

6.47   The principles of the *Reading Justices* case in relation to a mutual assistance request were tested in the case of *R. v. Bow Street Magistrates' Court, ex parte King and Anor*[49]. The case concerned the boxing promoter Don King, who was charged before a United States court with wire fraud. On a re-trial, and on a defence request, the trial judge made a request for documents, comprising contingency and/or non-appearance policies, issued by a Lloyds syndicate between January 1, 1985 and the date of the Divisional Court hearing. The relevance of these policies was directed towards an allegation that Don King had fraudulently made claims under insurance policies, when a participant in a boxing match, promoted by him, had sustained injury in the course of training and had thus been unable to appear at the scheduled fight. The American prosecutor had produced evidence as to the interpretation of a specific term within the policy and Don King's lawyers were concerned to try to obtain evidence to contradict such assertions. Accordingly, they wished to look at all previous policies brokered by the same broker, in order to discover whether, in previous policies, different definitions had been adopted and in relation to claims under policies, the appropriate term had been interpreted contrary to the assertions of the prosecution witnesses. The defence request, as made by the American judge, was exceedingly wide but having been made, it was transmitted to the United Kingdom under section 4 of the 1990 Act. In due course, the Secretary of State nominated Bow Street Magistrates' Court as the relevant court. The magistrate declined to give effect to the letter of request, a decision challenged by the applicants by way of judicial review.

6.48   Having considered the facts and also recited the relevant provisions of Schedule 1 of the 1990 Act, Collins J. stated:

> "It is clear from those provisions that the English court (the Stipendiary Magistrate in this case) has to consider, when faced with an application which involves the production of documents, any claim made by a person that he does not have to produce the documents as if the proceedings were domestic English criminal proceedings. Thus, English law and English considerations must apply.
>   . . . it seems to me quite unarguable that even in paragraph 4(1)(a) proceedings, the court has to consider the admissibility or the compellability, to put it in its precise terms, of the material in the foreign proceedings".
> "The Stipendiary Magistrate was, in my judgment, clearly correct to approach this matter on the basis of what English law would have allowed. That means, as was the case here, that in certain circumstances a request made by a foreign court may not be met, but that stems from the form in which this particular legislation is enacted. The English court can only, of course, apply the law as laid down by Parliament in this particular Act."

6.49   The judge then drew attention to the principles as set out by Simon Brown, L.J. in *R. v. Reading Justices, ex parte Berkshire County Council*[50] and proceeded to apply those rules of admissibility to the request:

> "I am wholly satisfied that if this were English law, those documents could not be admissible for the purpose of construing the contract or for the purpose of discovering what the relevant words meant.

49 (Unreported) CO/3489/97, October 8, 1997, QBD.
50 [1996] 1 Cr.App. R. 239 at 247.

I appreciate that the law in the United States appears to be different. It may be, although objections of course have been made ... and I assume for the moment that that evidence will be admitted before the jury for the purpose of establishing what the prosecution say is the true meaning of (the) expression. One can well understand the applicants' concern that this is potentially unfair because they are not able to get their hands, they say, on material which would show that what the witnesses said is not right. That is a matter, I am afraid, which I cannot take into account in deciding upon admissibility and, more importantly, it is a matter which the magistrate could not take into account."

6.50 Whilst the judge ruled that it was not a matter he had to decide in terms, he indicated that, were he sitting at first instance, on the material before him, he would have found it difficult, *prima facie*, to be persuaded that the exercise was, in reality, more than disguised discovery. Accordingly, leave to move for judicial review was refused.

Judicial inspection

6.51 If the materiality of the matter sought under the summons is questioned, although the judge may accept such an assertion, he has a discretion to examine the material himself[51].

In the event that the recipient of a witness summons objects to production of the material sought, on the grounds that public interest immunity attaches to it, it is the duty of a judge to inspect the material.[52]

Relevance

6.52 By introducing the concept of relevance, the courts have imposed duties upon those collecting evidence, whether under section 4 of the Act, or under section 7, to assess the relevance of the material to the request. To date, no authority exists for the principles to be applied by the nominated court in this connection but assistance can be obtained, by referring to the views expressed by the civil courts in relation to civil letters of request.

As recently as 1998, in *First American v. Sheikh Al-Nahyan*[53] Sir Richard Scott V.-C. stated:

"The question as to what evidence would, and what evidence would not, be relevant to an issue in the foreign action is primarily a matter for the foreign court. The House of Lords held in *re Asbestos Insurance Coverage Cases* [1985] 1 All E.R. 716 at 722/723 *per* Lord Fraser:

'It would be quite inappropriate, even if it were possible, for this House or any English court to determine in advance the matters relevant to the issues before the Californian courts on which each of these witnesses is in a position to give evidence.'

In my opinion, therefore, an English court must look at the issue of the relevance of the requested testimony, if it is raised, in broad terms, leaving to the foreign court, in all but the clearest cases, the decision as to whether particular answers, or answers on particular topics, would constitute relevant admissible evidence."

---

51 *R. v. W(G) & W(E)* [1997] 1 Cr.App. R. 166.
52 *R. v. Kay (Trevor Douglas)* [1997] Cr.App. R. 342.
53 [1998] 4 All E.R.

6.53 These two dicta must be compared with the dictum of Collins J. in *R. v. Bow Street Magistrates' ex parte King*,[54] where clear weight was placed on what English law and English considerations would dictate in the proceedings.

In the absence of authority in relation to proceedings before a nominated court in a criminal matter, bearing in mind the provisions of paragraph 4(1) of Schedule 1 of the 1990 Act, it is submitted that the approach of Collins J. is more likely to be followed.

Having said that, however, as will become apparent below, the courts often find themselves reviewing the issues and the relevance of the proposed evidence in assessing their materiality, in the light of the principles as set out in Reading Justices.

6.54 In *First American Corporation v. Sheikh Zayed Al-Nahyan*,[55] the Vice-Chancellor did make the point that it is not always possible to draw a sharp distinction between the different types of questioning. No objection could be made to a request on the basis that it was "a fishing exercise", if there was sufficient ground for believing that the intended witness might have relevant evidence to give, on topics relevant to the issues in the action.

> "Moreover, it is not always possible to draw a sharp distinction between, on the one hand, questions 'designed to establish allegations of fact' and, on the other hand, questions designed to extract 'information which may lead to obtaining evidence in support of a party's case'[56] There may be some questions which are obviously one, or obviously the other. But a number of questions may, potentially, lead either to an answer which is probative of an allegation of fact or to an answer which prompts a further line of enquiry without being probative, or to both. In framing questions to ask a witness from whom no proof has been taken, the questioner can be expected to ask a number of preliminary questions in order to feel his way in. This is not fishing. It is a normal technique of examination. A topic for legitimate questioning may have merely background significance."

Oppression

6.55 It is interesting to observe that the judge in *R. v. Bow Street Magistrates Court, ex parte King*[57] expressly although obiter, raised the issue of "oppression", a concept considered by the civil courts on numerous occasions, in relation to letters rogatory, under the Evidence (Proceedings in Other Jurisdictions) Act 1975 and Order 80 of the Rules of the Supreme Court.

One can detect, in certain of the recent authorities, a willingness on the part of the courts to refer to and apply to criminal mutual assistance requests certain of the criteria adopted by the civil courts. Within the civil jurisdiction, the United Kingdom courts have narrowed proposed questioning, when matters for examination are uncertain, vague or otherwise unfair and thereby oppressive.

In *First American v. Sheikh Al-Nahyan*[58] Sir Richard Scott V.-C. drew the court's attention to the dissenting judgment of Ralph Gibson, L.J. in *Re State of Norway's application*[59]. He indicated that Ralph Gibson, L.J. had agreed that a witness ought not to be required to comply with a letter of request, if it appeared to the court – "that

---

54 (Unreported) October 8, 1997 CO/3489/97.
55 [1998] 4 All E.R. 439.
56 See per Kerr L.J. in Re. Norway's (State) Application (No. 1) [1989] 1 All E.R. 661 at p. 684.
57 October 8, 1997, CO/3489/97.
58 [1998] 4 All E.R. 439.
59 (No. 1) [1989] 1 All E.R. 661 at 695.

the request is 'irrelevant, or fishing, or speculative or oppressive'. See *Senior v. Holdsworth*[60] *per* Lord Denning, M.R.

> "... that is the test which the court will apply in deciding to set aside a *subpoena* so as to excuse a witness from being required to give evidence at all. It has been held that the fact that the witness is clearly able to give relevant evidence and that nothing more is sought from him is not decisive: the *subpoena* may be set aside if, on balancing the value of the evidence to the applicant against the burden upon the witness, and the degree of intrusiveness of the proposed questioning and all other circumstances, it seems to the court that the request is oppressive."

6.56 Sir Richard referred in his judgment to *State of Minnesota v. Phillip Morris Inc*[61] in which the Court of Appeal gave judgment on July 30, 1997, Lord Woolf M.R. holding,

> "Because of the need to hold the balance between the requesting court and the witnesses who are to be examined, if the request is given effect, the court will not allow uncertain, vague or other objectionable requests to be implemented. A witness is entitled to know within reasonable limits the matters about which he or she is to be examined."

6.57 In the First American[62] case itself, the Court of Appeal was unwilling to uphold letters of request for the testimony of Price Waterhouse witnesses who, it was alleged by the plaintiffs, had been knowingly involved in a fraud. The court took the view that it was oppressive to hold as a sword of Damocles above the head of witnesses the possibility of their being joined as defendants in a civil action and thereby being the target of allegations of fraud but contemporaneously asking for the opportunity of cross examining two of the witnesses, on matters which would form the basis of a future civil action. The Court of Appeal effectively said that the plaintiffs should "put up or shut up" and decide whether they wish to join Price Waterhouse as defendants or give undertakings that they would not bring proceedings. The requests were held as oppressive.

It is submitted that, in criminal mutual assistance, the requesting State should be compelled to confirm the status of the proposed witness, whether he or she is viewed as a witness, or as a potential accused and that any attempt to avoid doing so may be challengeable on the grounds of oppression.[63]

6.58 In *England v. Purves*[54] before Mr Justice Evans-Lombe, JNTF and F, both in liquidation in and Australia, brought proceedings against HSBC and HKBA alleging, *inter alia*, that they had knowingly assisted F's directors in a dishonest breach of trust, in respect of an indemnity agreement and ship mortgage entered into by F and that they were therefore liable as constructive trustees. In the course of the proceedings, JNTF and F's liquidator, E, obtained orders from the Australian court for oral examination of P, S and M, senior officers of HSBC, said to be closely concerned in the relevant transactions. Pursuant to those orders, the Australian court submitted letters of request to the English court under the Insolvency Act 1986 section 426 and applied to the English court for examination of P, S and M, who were resident in

---

60 [1975] 2 All E.R. 1009 at 1016.
61 (1997) CA transcript 1741.
62 [1998] 4 All E.R. 439.
63 See also *England v. Purves* below.
64 *The Times*, January 29, 1998.

England. Refusing the applications, the court held that it would comply with a letter of request issued pursuant to section 426, provided there were no compelling reasons to do otherwise. Public policy was not the only reason why assistance might not be offered and the court had a discretion as to what form the assistance might take. An order for examination of a witness could be made either under the 1986 Act, section 236, or under the Australian Corporation's Law section 596 B and, while the powers conferred on the court under each statute appeared to be similar, there was a substantial difference in the way those powers were exercised by the English and Australian courts respectively. While the English courts would generally refuse to order an examination in respect of a witness against whom the liquidator had commenced proceedings, that was not considered a ground for refusing an examination in Australia. In the circumstances, given that an application under section 236 would almost certainly have been refused as oppressive in the light of the allegations made against P, S and M, the applications and request for assistance were refused.

The effect of proceedings under section 4 upon the PACE safeguards

6.59 "... the process envisaged by section 4 is not a trial; it is a process of gathering evidence." (*per* Lord Bingham C.J. in *R. v. Secretary of State for the Home Department ex parte Zardari*[64a].) Section 4 introduces for the first time into the English criminal process the concept of a United Kingdom court undertaking an investigatory function. The court is being used to collect evidence, a concept more familiar to civil than common law jurisdictions. This anomaly provides foreign investigators requesting evidence from the United Kingdom with powers which, in some circumstances, exceed those available to British officers in domestic investigations. A practical example will serve to illustrate.

If a foreign investigation agency (for example, the FBI in the United States) is investigating allegations of dishonesty by its citizens, and has information that funds have been transferred by a suspect to an account held by a third party in the United Kingdom, it will seek to trace the funds. The third party, however, may have passed all the papers relating to the transaction to his or her accountant, to sort out his or her tax position. The FBI will initially seek informal access to the accountant's records, but this may be denied. In those circumstances, a formal letter of request will be issued by the U.S. authorities. In due course, a court will be nominated under section 4 of the 1990 Act, (most usually a magistrates court) and the accountant will be summoned to the court to produce his or her files and give evidence in relation thereto.

If however, the investigation had been entirely domestic, the situation would have been different, and obtaining the evidence of the accountant would have been more complicated.

6.60 At the *investigation* stage, no United Kingdom court has locus to compel a person to give evidence or to produce evidence (other than by such coercive measures as search warrants, in which event safeguards exist). There are, after all, no proceedings. The investigators must therefore rely upon their search and seizure powers.

The accountant's papers are "special procedure material"[65] and in normal circumstances only a Crown court judge (not a magistrate as in the example given above) can order production of the papers but only:

    (a)   after an *inter partes* hearing (unless it is suggested that the accountant may seek to destroy the file); and

---

64a (Unreported) CO/6345/98, March 11, 1998, QBD.
65 See below s. 14 PACE 1984 and Chap. 10.

(b)   upon being satisfied that the material is likely to be

   (i)   of substantial value (whether by itself or together with other material) to the investigation; and
   (ii)   relevant; and
   (iii) in the public interest having regard to the benefit likely to accrue to the investigation and to the circumstances under which the person in possession of the material holds it, and

(c)   if one or other of the access conditions has been satisfied.[66]

6.61   In effect, the confidentiality safeguards enshrined in the Police and Criminal Evidence Act 1984 (PACE) and protected by the courts are circumvented (see in particular *R. v. Maidstone Crown Court ex parte Waitt*[67] and *R. v. Southampton Crown Court ex parte J and P*[68]) in which the courts emphasise that circuit judges (Crown Court judges) are to take the utmost care in deciding whether to grant applications for access to special procedure material and to be scrupulous in ensuring that all the requirements are satisfied, before performing the balancing process necessary in determining these applications. The special procedure provisions are a serious in-road into the liberty of the subject, the more so when an application is ex-parte. No case perhaps illustrates this more forcibly than *R. v. Crown Court at Lewes ex parte Hill*[59] concerning an application for access to material held by various banks. Bingham, L.J. (as he then was) stated:

"The Police and Criminal Evidence Act governs a field in which there are two very obvious public interests. There is, first of all, a public interest in the effective investigation and prosecution of crime. Secondly, there is a public interest in protecting the personal property rights of citizens against infringements and invasion. There is an obvious tension between these two public interests . . ."

6.62   There is a heavy burden placed upon the police to submit to the Crown Court judge detailed information, which should be as precise and complete as possible, in order to enable him to perform the balancing process properly.
   As if to underline the importance of these personal property rights being protected by the Crown Court and the balancing exercise carried out by its judges he continued:

"The judge should be shown such material as is necessary to enable him to be satisfied of the matters of which he is required to be satisfied before making the order, and the judge should be told of anything to the knowledge of the party applying which might weigh against making an order."

As will be seen from the authorities of *Gross v. The Crown Court at Southwark, The Secretary of State for the Home Department and The Commissioner of Police for the Metropolis*[70] and *R. v. Maidstone Crown Court, ex parte Waitt*,[71] if a circuit judge makes an order, it is essential he set out clearly his reasons for making it, particularly

---

66 PACE Sched. 1.
67 [1988] Crim. L.R. 384.
68 [1993] Crim. L.R. 962.
69 [1991] 93 Cr. App. R. 60.
70 (Unreported) CO/1759/98, July 24, 1998, QBD.
71 [1988] Crim. L.R. 384.

where the order is made on an *ex parte* application. It will of course be appreciated that the vast majority of summonses issued by magistrates' courts are *ex parte*.

All of these detailed safeguards built up by the courts over the years are effectively wholly bypassed by the practice of nominated courts issuing witness summonses to those holding special procedure material.

6.63   United Kingdom police officers, when serving witness summonses, on occasions explain to the recipient that the summons serves as a safeguard against the recipient breaching the confidentiality owed to the person on whose behalf he or she holds the papers. Whilst this may be the practical effect, Parliament clearly did not intend to bypass the safeguards contained in PACE, in so far as they protect confidentiality, and in so doing to give to foreign investigators greater powers in the United Kingdom than are given to British investigators within their own country.

Earl Ferrers stated to the House of Lords, at the Bill stage of the 1990 Act, that however much the Government wished to assist other countries, it could not allow Parliament to make greater powers available on behalf of overseas authorities, than are available to United Kingdom police or prosecuting authorities in domestic cases.[72]

6.64   In the quotation from *ex parte Hill*,[73] cited above, Bingham L.J. drew attention to the careful balance provided by PACE between the sometimes competing public interests of investigation and prosecution of crime on the one hand, and the protection of personal and property rights of individuals against infringement and invasion on the other.

> "The 1984 Act seeks to effect a carefully judged balance between these interests and that is why it is a detailed and complex Act. If the scheme intended by Parliament is to be implemented, it is important that the provisions laid down in the Act should be fully and fairly enforced(CA)...
>
> It is in my judgment clear that the courts must try to avoid any interpretation which would distort the parliamentary scheme and so upset the intended balance."

There seems to have arisen a similar imbalance to that rectified by the House of Lords in *R. v. Southwark Crown Court ex parte Bowles*.[74] In that instance the safeguards provided by PACE in relation to the issue of production orders by circuit judges authorising the search for seizure of confidentially held material, (see below under Chapter 10) were being by-passed by investigators proceeding under the apparently conflicting (and more draconian) provisions of section 93H of the Criminal Justice Act 1988 (as amended) (CJA 1988). (See p. 137.)

6.65   Lord Hutton in his speech, in rejecting this practice, stated: "In my opinion it was not the intention of Parliament in enacting section 93H (of the CJA 1988) to take away in respect of the investigation of criminal offences involving the obtaining of money or other property, the safeguards to the citizen given in the detailed provisions of Schedule 1 to PACE." Sentiments, it is submitted, that could equally apply in relation to section 4 of the Criminal Justice (International Co-operation) Act 1990.

Whilst this apparent conflict awaits judicial resolution, foreign investigators will continue to have greater compulsive powers of investigation in the United Kingdom than their British counterparts.

---

72 513 H.L. Official Report Col. 1217 December 12, 1989.
73 *R. v. Crown Court at Lewes ex parte Hill* 1991 93 Crim. App. R. 60.
74 [1998] 2 All E.R. 193.

6.66 The practical effects of this anachronism will clearly be of concern to the defence practitioner, for the domestic investigator acts as the agent of the foreign investigator and as such, will have access to information and evidence to which he or she is not entitled under his domestic powers. It is facile to believe that use is not made of such material in a domestic context, indeed the recent authority of *R. v. Bow Street Magistrates & Another, ex parte M.*[75] makes it clear that the English investigator has a positive duty to inspect the material and to assess its relevance before passing it to the requesting State (see pp. 153, 157). In most cases, there will of course be no British interest, the duty of inspection being a separate issue, to ensure that the terms of the warrant are complied with.

Disclosure of letter of request

6.67 Consideration has already been given to the eventual disclosure of outgoing letters of request under the CPIA[76] in United Kingdom proceedings.

The Home Office, observing established international practice, discloses neither the existence, nor the contents of a letter of request, other than to Government departments, agencies, the courts or United Kingdom enforcement agencies. Whilst this policy is subject to modification, if appropriate, when evidence is being obtained in proceedings in the United Kingdom, disclosure is limited to what is absolutely necessary to obtain the witness' co-operation. In general, letters of request will neither be shown, nor copied, to the witness, nor will the witness be told the identity of other witnesses.

Is a witness who is required to give evidence or produce documents to a nominated court pursuant to a foreign letter of request entitled to have sight of that letter?

Whilst the Act is silent on this point, it is difficult to envisage how a witness can raise issues of legal privilege, self incrimination or admissibility of evidence in ignorance of the contents of the letter of request.

6.68 It is therefore suggested that it is good practice for the legal representatives of those acting for prospective witnesses to seek from the nominated court a copy of the incoming request (and any accompanying documents) to which the witness is to be referred, and in the event that disclosure is refused, consider the possibility of judicially reviewing such a refusal.

Those advising prospective witnesses must take care in scrutinising the request, not only to consider questions of compellability and any objections that may arise, but also its scope. Whilst the content of the request might be wide (see *Finninvest*), the class of material sought must be clearly identified. Similarly, if documents are sought, the letter should describe their nature, the dates within which they are sought and the names of those from whom they are sought.

Transmission of evidence[77]

6.69 Once the evidence has been obtained by the court, it must be furnished to the Secretary of State, for transmission to the court, tribunal or authority that made the request, together with any certificate, affidavit or verifying document required by the requesting state or authority. There is no provision in the Act for it to be provided to the overseas authorities direct,[78] or to visiting officers or officials from the overseas

---

75 CO/4287/97 & CO/3263/97, 7 April, 1998, QBD.
76 See p. 47.
77 See more generally Chapter 11.
78 See the position regarding search and seizure material *per* Laws J. in *ex parte Propend Finance Property Limited* (1996) Cr. App. R. 26.

country, or via diplomatic missions in the United Kingdom. This is the case even where officers from the requesting state have been present in court when the evidence was obtained.

However, officers of the requesting state who are present will of course be able to act on any evidence which they have heard or seen prior to its transmission, and it would be unrealistic to exclude this possibility.[79]

Costs

6.70   There is no provision in the 1959 Convention in relation to the costs of executing requests, which normally fall to the requested state. Any costs of obtaining evidence must normally be met by the nominated court, or by the police, in accordance with arrangements made with them by the court. In the event that the court, after consultation with the police, is of the opinion that the costs would be extraordinary, the court should inform the MLA Section, before obtaining the evidence and the overseas authority might then be asked to meet the cost in whole, or in part. If agreement cannot be reached with the overseas authorities, then the request may be refused on such grounds.

---

79 See R. v. Secretary of State for the Home Department ex parte Finninvest SpA [1997] 1 All E.R. 942.

Transfer of Prisoners for the Purpose of Giving Evidence or Assisting Investigations

7.00 Under Article 11 of the European Convention, signatories are required to make provision allowing for prisoners to be transferred to requesting states, to give evidence, or to assist investigations.

Sections 5 and 6 of the 1990 Act contain the relevant provisions.

These provisions are little used. There are only a few such applications in each direction every year. The cost of escorting a prisoner from and to the departure and arrival points in the United Kingdom and the costs of holding the prisoner in the requesting country are borne by the requesting authorities.

Transfer of United Kingdom prisoners

7.01 Section 5 of the Criminal Justice (International Co-Operation) Act 1990, as amended contains the relevant provisions as follows:

5. Transfer of United Kingdom prisoner to give evidence or assist investigation overseas

(1) The Secretary of State may, if he thinks fit, issue a warrant providing for any person ("a prisoner") serving a sentence in a prison or other institution to which the Prison Act 1952 or the Prisons (Scotland) Act 1989 applies to be transferred to a country or territory outside the United Kingdom for the purpose—

  (a) of giving evidence in criminal proceedings there; or
  (b) of being identified in, or otherwise by his presence assisting, such proceedings or the investigation of an offence.

(2) No warrant shall be issued under this section in respect of any prisoner unless he has consented to being transferred as mentioned in subsection (1) above and that consent may be given either—

  (a) by the prisoner himself; or
  (b) in circumstances in which it appears to the Secretary of State inappropriate, by reason of the prisoner's physical or mental condition or his youth, for him to act for himself, by a person appearing to the Secretary of State to be an appropriate person to act on his behalf;

but a consent once given shall not be capable of being withdrawn after the use of the warrant.

(3) The effect of a warrant under this section shall be to authorise—

(a) the taking of the prisoner to a place in the United Kingdom and his delivery at a place of departure from the United Kingdom into the custody of a person representing the appropriate authority of the country or territory to which the prisoner is to be transferred; and

(b) the bringing of the prisoner back to the United Kingdom and his transfer in custody to the place where he is liable to be detained under the sentence to which he is subject.

(4) Where a warrant has been issued in respect of a prisoner under this section he shall be deemed to be in legal custody at any time when, being in the United Kingdom or on board a British ship, British aircraft or British hovercraft, he is being taken under the warrant to or from any place or being kept in custody under the warrant.

(5) A person authorised by or for the purposes of the warrant to take the prisoner to or from any place or to keep him in custody shall have all the powers, authority, protection and privileges—

(a) of a constable in the part of the United Kingdom in which that person is for the time being; or

(b) if he is outside the United Kingdom, of a constable in the part of the United Kingdom to or from which the prisoner is to be taken under the warrant.

(6) If the prisoner escapes or is unlawfully at large, he may be arrested without warrant by a constable and taken to any place to which he may be taken under the warrant issued under this section.

(7) In subsection (4) above—

"British aircraft" means a British-controlled aircraft within the meaning of section 92 of the Civil Aviation Act 1982 (application of criminal law to aircraft) or one of Her Majesty's aircraft;

"British hovercraft" means a British-controlled hovercraft within the meaning of that section as applied in relation to hovercraft by virtue of provisions made under the Hovercraft Act 1968 or one of Her Majesty's hovercraft;

"British ship" means a British ship for the purposes of the Merchant Shipping Acts 1894 to 1988 or one of Her Majesty's ships;

and in this subsection references to Her Majesty's aircraft, hovercraft or ships are references to aircraft, hovercraft or, as the case may be, ships belonging to or exclusively employed in the service of Her Majesty in right of the Government of the United Kingdom.

(8) In subsection (6) above "constable", in relation to any part of the United Kingdom, means any person who is a constable in that or any other part of the United Kingdom or any person who, at the place in question has, under any enactment including subsection (5) above, the powers of a constable in that or any other part of the United Kingdom.

(9) This section applies to a person in custody awaiting trial or sentence and a person committed to prison for default in paying a fine as it applies to a

prisoner and the reference in subsection (3)(b) above to a sentence shall be construed accordingly.

(10) In the application of this section to Northern Ireland for the reference in subsection (1) to the Prison Act 1952 there shall be substituted a reference to the Prison Act (Northern Ireland) 1953.

Request

7.02 The Home Office recommends that the letter of request should contain the following specific information.

(a) Dates on which the presence abroad of the prisoner is required, including the dates on which the court or other proceedings for which the prisoner is required will commence and are likely to be concluded;

(b) Information for the purpose of obtaining the prisoner's consent to the transfer and satisfying the UK authorities that arrangements will be made to keep the prisoner in secure custody such as:

(i) whether the prisoner will have immunity from prosecution for previous offences;

(ii) details of proposed arrangements for collecting the prisoner from and returning the prisoner to the United Kingdom;

(iii) details of the type of secure accommodation in which the prisoner will be held in the requesting State;

(iv) details of the type of escort available abroad to and from the secure accommodation.

7.03 If the prisoner is to give evidence, the request must detail any rules on privileges which the prisoner may be entitled to claim, together with any caution which, if possible, should be given under the law of the requesting state. Where evidence is to be taken, details should be provided of whether the evidence is to be taken before a court, and whether it is to be given on oath or affirmation; if a less formal (*e.g.* police) interview, is to take place, neither on oath nor on affirmation, this should be confirmed.

A description should also be given of the evidence sought and a list of any particular questions to be asked. Sufficient information must be provided to ensure that the prisoner's consent is given on an informed basis, and to satisfy the United Kingdom prison authorities that suitable arrangements will be made to secure the prisoner's custody. They should also include details of any prisoners' privileges, such as visits and letters, to which the prisoner will be entitled whilst abroad.

Consent

7.04 No transfer can take place unless the prisoner gives his or her consent; no compulsion can be applied and if it appears to the Secretary of State that it would be inappropriate for the prisoner to act for himself or herself, by reason of his or her physical or mental condition, or his or her youth, an appropriate person should act on his or her behalf and will be required to give consent for him or for her. Once given, after issue of the warrant, consent cannot be withdrawn.

Refusal

7.05 If the Secretary of State receives a request to which the prisoner consents (either directly himself or, if applicable, through "an appropriate person") he has a discretion, "if he thinks fit", to issue a warrant. Refusal may be on political, security or national interests grounds;

The minister is likely to refuse a request, or at least to delay the transfer, if the prisoner is nearing date of release in the United Kingdom, or is required for proceedings before a court in the United Kingdom; to establish whether or not a prisoner is required for such purposes in the United Kingdom, the Home Office will contact all relevant departments.

If granting the request would contravene U.K. law or established practice, it will be refused.

Whilst one would not expect the prisoner to consent, if to do so might result in double jeopardy, (for instance, retrial for the offence for which he or she is serving his or her sentence in the United Kingdom) in theory it would appear that the Secretary of State retains a discretion in such circumstances, to refuse transfer, despite the prisoners' consent.

Unfortunately, the availability of free legal advice to a prisoner is limited, despite its need, in relation to questions of legal privilege, self-incrimination and issues of admissibility, central to reaching the "informed consent" required.

Warrant and transfer

7.06 Having received a request with which he is prepared to comply, the Secretary of State will issue a warrant, which will authorise the prisoner's transfer to a place of departure in the United Kingdom.

The prisoner will be handed over to the custody of a person representing the appropriate authority, in the requesting state to which he or she is to be transferred to give evidence, or to assist in an investigation, and the warrant will also authorise his or her return to the United Kingdom and his or her transfer back into custody to complete his sentence.

At any time when the prisoner is in the United Kingdom, on board a British ship, aircraft or hovercraft, the prisoner is deemed under the warrant to be in legal custody. Whilst the Act does not specifically provide, the prisoner is presumably in legal custody whilst held abroad; it would also appear that, for the purposes of calculating the time spent in custody, the prisoner will be deemed to be serving his or her sentence whilst abroad, on transfer.

Transfer of overseas prisoners

7.07 Section 6 of the 1990 Act contains the relevant provisions which are as follows:—

> **6. Transfer of overseas prisoner to give evidence or assist investigation in the United Kingdom**
>
> (1) This section has effect where—
>
> > (a) a witness order has been made or a witness summons or citation issued in criminal proceedings in the United Kingdom in respect of a person ("a prisoner") who is detained in custody in a country or territory outside the United Kingdom by virtue of a sentence or order of a court or tribunal exercising criminal jurisdiction in that country or territory; or
> >
> > (b) it appears to the Secretary of State that it is desirable for a prisoner to be identified in, or otherwise by his presence to assist, such proceedings or the investigation in the United Kingdom of an offence.

(2) If the Secretary of State is satisfied that the appropriate authority in the country or territory where the prisoner is detained will make arrangements for him to come to the United Kingdom to give evidence pursuant to the witness order, witness summons or citation or, as the case may be, for the purpose mentioned in subsection (1)(b) above, he may issue a warrant under this section.

(3) No warrant shall be issued under this section in respect of any prisoner unless he has consented to being brought to the United Kingdom to give evidence as aforesaid or, as the case may be, for the purpose mentioned in subsection (1)(b) above but a consent once given shall not be capable of being withdrawn after the issue of the warrant.

(4) The effect of the warrant shall be to authorise—

    (a) the bringing of the prisoner to the United Kingdom;

    (b) the taking of the prisoner to, and his detention in custody at, such place or places in the United Kingdom as are specified in the warrant; and

    (c) the returning of the prisoner to the country or territory from which he has come.

(5) Subsections (4) to (8) of section 5 above shall have effect in relation to a warrant issued under this section as they have effect in relation to a warrant issued under that section.

(6) A person shall not be subject to the Immigration Act 1971 in respect of his entry into or presence in the United Kingdom in pursuance of a warrant under this section but if the warrant ceases to have effect while he is still in the United Kingdom—

    (a) he shall be treated for the purposes of that Act as if he has then illegally entered the United Kingdom; and

    (b) the provisions of Schedule 2 to that Act shall have effect accordingly except that paragraph 20(1) (liability of carrier for expenses of custody etc of illegal entrant) shall not have effect in relation to directions for his removal given by virtue of this subsection.

(7) This section applies to a person detained in custody in a country or territory outside the United Kingdom in consequence of having been transferred there—

    (a) from the United Kingdom under the Repatriation of Prisoners Act 1984; or

    (b) under any similar provision or arrangement from any other country or territory,

    as it applies to a person detained as mentioned in subsection (1) above.

7.08 The reciprocal provisions of section 6 essentially mirror those of section 5. However the following additional matters should be borne in mind:—

Section 6(1)(a) refers to the issue of a witness summons in United Kingdom criminal proceedings in respect of the overseas prisoner. The admissibility requirements set out in *R. v. Reading Justices ex parte Berkshire County Council*[1] and the

---

1 [1996] Cr. App. R. 239.

provisions of section 2 Criminal Procedure (Attendance of Witnesses) Act 1965 (as amended) are clearly relevant and reference should be made to Chapter 6.

7.09 By virtue of its reservation to Article 12 of the European Convention, the United Kingdom will only consider granting immunity under Article 12 when this is specifically requested by the person to whom it would apply or by the appropriate authorities of the country from whom assistance is requested. Thus, where the United Kingdom has requested the appearance of an overseas prisoner to assist in proceedings in the United Kingdom, immunity from prosecution cannot be automatically conferred[2]; such immunity requests will be carefully considered, but the United Kingdom authorities will not grant immunity where this would be contrary to public interest.

The Secretary of State has to issue a warrant for a fixed period of detention in the U.K. which in some instances, due to prolonged proceedings, may require extension.

Requesting authorities should therefore exercise care in requesting a period of transfer, since extension may be administratively complex to arrange.

---

2 A similar exception or adaptation is made to para. 25 of the Commonwealth Scheme.

Search and Seizure in the United Kingdom for the Purpose of Investigations and Proceedings Abroad-General Principles

Section 7 of the 1990 Act and its effect

8.00   Search and seizure has always been a fertile area for the courts and the effect of the provisions of section 7 of the Act will in all likelihood be subjected to closer scrutiny and greater judicial intervention than any other section. Whilst the Act has yet to reach its tenth birthday, a significant number of cases has been decided upon the proper interpretation of section 7.

One must therefore examine not only the provisions of the section but also the general law relating to search and seizure and in particular the relevant parts of the Police and Criminal Evidence Act 1984 (PACE).

8.01   Section 7 of the Act provides for the use in the United Kingdom of search and seizure powers for the purpose of foreign proceedings and the relevant provisions are as follows;

7. Search, etc. for material relevant to overseas investigation

(1)   Part II of the Police and Criminal Evidence Act 1984 (powers of entry, search and seizure) shall have effect as if references to serious arrestable offences in section 8 of and Schedule 1 to that Act included any conduct which is an offence under the law of a country or territory outside the United Kingdom and would constitute a serious arrestable offence if it had occurred in any part of the United Kingdom.

(2)   If, on an application made by a constable, a justice of the peace is satisfied—

(a)   that criminal proceedings have been instituted against a person in a country or territory outside the United Kingdom or that a person has been arrested in the course of a criminal investigation carried on there;

(b)   that the conduct constituting the offence which is the subject of the proceedings or investigation would constitute an arrestable offence within the meaning of the said Act of 1984 if it had occurred in any part of the United Kingdom; and

(c)   that there are reasonable grounds for suspecting that there is on premises in the United Kingdom occupied or controlled by that person evidence relating to the offence other than items subject to legal privilege within the meaning of that Act,

he may issue a warrant authorising a constable to enter and search those premises and to seize any such evidence found there.

(3)   The power to search conferred by subsection (2) above is only a power to search to the extent that is reasonably required for the purpose of discovering such evidence as is there mentioned.

(4)   No application for a warrant or order shall be made by virtue of subsection (1) or (2) above except in pursuance of a direction given by the Secretary of State in response to a request received—

(a)   from a court or tribunal exercising criminal jurisdiction in the overseas country or territory in question or a prosecuting authority in that country or territory; or

(b)   from any other authority in that country or territory which appears to him to have the function of making requests for the purposes of this section;

and any evidence seized by a constable by virtue of this section shall be furnished by him to the Secretary of State for transmission to that court, tribunal or authority.

(5)   If in order to comply with the request it is necessary for any such evidence to be accompanied by any certificate, affidavit or other verifying document the constable shall also furnish for transmission such document of that nature as may be specified in the direction given by the Secretary of State.

(6)   Where the evidence consists of a document the original or a copy shall be transmitted, and where it consists of any other article the article itself or a description, photograph or other representation of it shall be transmitted, as may be necessary in order to comply with the request.

(7)   The Treasury may by order direct that any powers which by virtue of this section are exercisable by a constable shall also be exercisable by, or by any person acting under the direction of, an officer commissioned by the Commissioners of Customs and Excise under section 6(3) of the Customs and Excise Management Act 1979[1]; and the Secretary of State may by order direct that any of those powers shall also be exercisable by a person of any other description specified in the order.

8.02   The effect of section 7(1) of the 1990 Act is to extend the scope of section 8 and Schedule 1 of the Police and Criminal Evidence Act 1984 (PACE) to cover offences committed abroad provided they would constitute a *serious arrestable offence* had they occurred in the United Kingdom.

The limited effect of section 7(2) is to provide for the issue of a search warrant to search premises in the United Kingdom occupied or controlled by a person who is being proceeded against abroad, or who has been arrested for an offence in that country, which would have been an *arrestable offence* within the meaning of section 24 PACE.[2]

---

1 The Criminal Justice (International Co-operation) Act 1990 (Exercise of Powers) Order 1991 (S.I. 1991 No. 1297), made pursuant to s. 7(7) of the 1990 Act, empowers an officer of Customs & Excise or any person acting under the direction of such an officer, to apply for a warrant to search premises and seize evidence.

2 It would seem that the arrest need not be within the requesting State, in which event such a procedure could be used in extradition proceedings being brought in the United Kingdom by another country to obtain evidence in those proceedings, if the subject of those proceedings has been arrested (in the United Kingdom).

"Serious arrestable offences"

8.02 The term *"serious arrestable offence"* is defined by section 116 of PACE and Schedule 5 to the Act. Certain arrestable offences count as "serious" in all circumstances. These are:—

> Treason; murder; manslaughter; rape; kidnapping; incest or intercourse with a girl under thirteen; buggery with a boy under sixteen or someone who has not consented; indecent assaults which amount to gross indecency; possession of firearms with intent to injure; carrying firearms with criminal intent; use of firearms or imitation firearms to resist arrest; causing explosions likely to endanger life or property; hostage taking; hijacking and certain offences under sections 1, 9 and 10 of the Prevention of Terrorism (Temporary Provisions) Act 1984; hijacking channel tunnel trains or seizing/exercising control of the tunnel system; indecent photographs of children; publication of obscene matter; various offences under section 1 of the Drugs Trafficking Act 1994.

Additionally, any other arrestable offence may be treated as "serious" for the purpose of exercising the relevant powers, if it has or is likely to lead to:—

> serious harm to the security of the State or public order; serious interference with the administration of justice or with the investigation of offences; the death of anyone; serious injury to anyone; substantial financial gain to any person, or serious financial loss to any person.

"Arrestable offences"

8.03 An *arrestable offence* is defined in section 24 of PACE as an offence for which the penalty is fixed by law; offences carrying a penalty of five or more years' imprisonment; various statutory offences, including offences of indecent assault on a woman; causing prostitution of women; procuring a girl under twenty-one; taking a motor vehicle or other conveyance without authority; going equipped for stealing and certain offences for which a person may be arrested under Customs and Excise Acts.

Dual criminality

8.04 The requirement of dual criminality appears only twice in the 1990 Act, that in relation to the search and seizure provisions of section 7 of the Act (which are the subject of the following chapter), and in relation to fiscal offences under section 4(3) (see p. 69).

Under Article 5 of the 1959 Convention, a State may, by declaration, reserve the right to make the execution of letters rogatory for search or seizure of property dependent, *inter alia*, on a condition of dual criminality. It has been noted that the United Kingdom made a reservation to Article 5, to the effect that letters rogatory for search and seizure should be dependent on dual criminality. This reservation is reflected in section 7, which requires that the conduct concerned should be both an offence in the requesting state and a "serious arrestable offence" in the United Kingdom.

Dual criminality fell for consideration in *Finninvest*.[3] In this case, more fully discussed at page 59 the Home Secretary referred the Italian authorities' letter of

---

3 *R. v. Secretary of State for the Home Department, ex parte Finninvest SpA.* [1997] 1 All E.R. 942.

request to the Serious Fraud Office (SFO); his decision to do so was challenged, on the basis that, before making such a referral, he was required, but failed, to consider whether there was dual criminality. The challenge relied on the wording of section 4(2A) of the 1990 Act, whereby it was a precondition to a referral that, "it appears to (the Home Secretary) that the request relates to an offence involving serious or complex fraud".

8.05   Under section 1(3) of the Criminal Justice Act 1987, the SFO's powers only arise in cases involving "serious or complex fraud". It was submitted by the applicants that the offence in question must necessarily always constitute such an offence, prosecutable under English law.

This was described by the judge as "a hopeless argument". The Criminal Justice (International Co-operation) Act 1990 indicates clearly when dual criminality is required and when it is not.

In so far as search and seizure was concerned, the court drew attention to the provisions of Article 5 of the European Convention on Mutual Assistance 1959 which allows any contracting party

> "to reserve the right to make the execution of letters rogatory for search or seizure of property dependent upon one or more of the following conditions:
>
> (a)   that the offence motivating the letters rogatory is punishable under both the law of the requesting Party and the law of the requested Party".

The court drew attention to the United Kingdom's reservation of that right, so that when, in due course, Parliament came to deal with search or seizure, in section 7 of the Criminal Justice (International Co-operation) Act 1990, it provided, in terms, that the offence in question "must constitute a serious arrestable offence if it had occurred in any part of the United Kingdom".

8.06   The court stressed that the only other requirement of dual criminality to be found in the 1990 Act was in relation to fiscal offences, under section 4(3), which, it stated, was permissible not because of Article 5 of the 1959 Convention, but rather because of Article 2(a), which permits assistance to be refused not only if the request concerns a political offence, but also if it concerns a fiscal offence, and which therefore allowed conditions to be imposed, as in the subject case, in section 4(3)(b).

The court indicated the striking contrast between these instances and the language of section 4(2)(A)(a) which required only that the offence should be one "under the law of the country or territory in question".

The SFO had deposed in its information that "the facts set out in the request would, if they had taken place in England, constitute offences of, inter alia, conspiracy to defraud and false accounting." The court felt that it was impossible to suppose that the Home Secretary himself, had he addressed the point, could have concluded otherwise.

Principles governing grant of assistance

8.07   The powers of search and seizure may only be exercised:—

(a)   *in performance of a direction given* by the Secretary of State in response to a request received from:

(b)   *a court or tribunal exercising criminal jurisdiction* in the overseas country or territory or *a prosecuting authority* in that country or territory; or

(c) *any other authority* in that country or territory *which appears to him to have the function of making* requests for the purposes of the section, and

(d) **with the authority of a court.**

With the authority of a court

8.08   Under the Police and Criminal Evidence Act 1984 search and seizure may follow upon the exercise of the following police powers:—

(a) those to stop and search an individual or his or her vehicle; or

(b) those permitting entry, search and seizure in relation to persons suspected of or arrested for crime, or

(c) those exercisable by virtue of court order.

(a) and (b) are concerned with police powers exercisable in relation to persons either suspected of, or under arrest for, a criminal offence, or property controlled by such persons and are of little relevance to international requests. It is in relation to those falling under (c) that section 7 of the 1990 Act is concerned.

CHAPTER 9

Search and Seizure in the United Kingdom for the Purpose of Investigations and Proceedings Abroad-Applications to the Courts for Authority to Search and Seize

9.00　The basic provisions granting police the power to search and seize are those contained in sections 8 and 9 and Schedule 1 of PACE. It is important that they are fully understood so that the operation of section 7 of the 1990 Act can be seen against the backdrop of the domestic legislation.

The nature of the material sought effectively dictates the appropriate court to which the application should be made.

Non-confidential material

9.01　Section 8 of PACE gives a magistrate the power to issue a warrant to search for and seize evidence of relevance to "a serious arrestable offence".

> "There is no mystery about the word "warrant"; it simply means a document issued by a person in authority under power conferred in that behalf authorising the doing of an act which would otherwise be illegal"[1]

Confidential material

9.02　A Circuit Judge has power under section 9 and Schedule 1 of PACE to order the production of confidential material or to issue a warrant to search for and seize such material in relation to a "serious arrestable offence" or if the confidential material could have been the subject of a magistrate's warrant before PACE, the offence need not be a serious arrestable offence.

Material to which legal professional privilege attaches can never be seized.

Section 8 PACE – Power of justice of the peace to authorise entry and search of premises[2]

(1)　If on an application made by a constable a justice of the peace is satisfied that there are reasonable grounds for believing—

    (a)　that a serious arrestable offence has been committed; and

    (b)　that there is material on premises specified in the application which is

---

1 *I.R.C. v. Rossminster Ltd* [1980] A.C. 952 *per* Lord Wilberforce.
2 As modified by s. 7(1) Criminal Justice (International Co-operation) Act 1990.

likely to be of substantial value (whether by itself or together with other material) to the investigation of the offence; and

(c)   that the material is likely to be relevant evidence; and

(d)   that it does not consist of or include items subject to legal privilege, excluded material or special procedure material; and

(e)   that any of the conditions specified in subsection (3) below applied,

he may issue a warrant authorising a constable to enter and search the premises.

(2)   A constable may seize and retain anything for which a search has been authorised under subsection (1) above.

(3)   The conditions mentioned in subsection (1)(e) above are -

(a)   that it is not practical to communicate with any person entitled to grant entry to the premises;

(b)   that it is practicable to communicate with a person entitled to grant entry to the premises but it is not practicable to communicate with any person entitled to grant access to the evidence;

(c)   that entry to the premises will not be granted unless a warrant is produced;

(d)   that the purpose of a search may be frustrated or seriously prejudiced unless a constable arriving at the premises can secure immediate entry to them.

(4)   In this Act "relevant evidence", in relation to an offence, means anything that would be admissible in evidence at a trial for the offence.

(5)   The power to issue a warrant conferred by this section is in addition to any such power otherwise conferred.

Application for a warrant in the magistrates' court

9.03   The provisions relating to applications for and the contents of, a search warrant are set out in section 15 of PACE.

15 Search warrants – safeguards

(1)   This section and section 16 below have effect in relation to the issue to constables under any enactment, including an enactment contained in an Act passed after this Act, of warrants to enter and search premises; and an entry on or search of premises under a warrant is unlawful unless it complies with this section and section 16 below.

(2)   Where a constable applies for any such warrant, it shall be his or her duty—

(a)   to state—

(i)   the ground on which he or she makes the application; and

(ii)   the enactment under which the warrant would be issued;

(b)   to specify the premises which it is desired to enter and search; and

(c)   to identify, so far as is practicable, the articles or persons to be sought.

(3)   An application for such a warrant shall be made *ex parte* and supported by an information in writing.

(4)   The constable shall answer on oath any question that the justice of the peace or judge hearing the applications asks him or her.

(5)   A warrant shall authorise an entry on one occasion only.

(6)   A warrant—

(a)   shall specify—

(ii)   the name of the person who applies for it;
(ii)   the date on which it is issued;
(iii)   the enactment under which it is issued; and
(iv)   the premises to be searched; and

(b)   shall identify, so far as is practicable, the articles or persons to be sought.[3]

(7)   Two copies shall be made of a warrant.

(8)   The copies shall be clearly certified as copies.

The duty of the court

"[Section 8 of the Act . . .] confers a draconian power and it is of vital importance that it should be clearly understood by all concerned that it is for the justice to satisfy himself that there are reasonable grounds for believing the various matters set out. The fact that a police officer, who has been investigating the matter, states in the information that he considers there are reasonable grounds is not enough."[4]

9.04   Circuit Judges and magistrates hearing applications for warrants under section 8 or Schedule. 1 PACE may ask questions. The officer shall answer on oath any questions put to him by the court hearing the application.

In deciding whether or not to grant an application for a search warrant, the court must balance the public interest in ensuring that police investigations are not hampered by their inability to gather evidence in relation to serious arrestable offences against the public interest of the citizen in protecting his or her rights of security of property. The court must satisfy itself that the grounds for issuing the warrant are indeed established.

Similar considerations apply to the issuing of search warrants under statutory provisions other than PACE, for example, Criminal Justice Act 1987, section 2 (SFO powers) and Theft Act 1968.

Duty of the police/applicant

9.05   An application for a search warrant can be made by any police officer but Code B 2.4[5] requires each application to be approved by at least an inspector or, in relation to confidential information, a superintendent.[6]

The application is heard *ex parte*. It must be supported by an information in

---

3 In *R. v. C.C.C. ex parte AJD Holdings* [1992] C.L.R. 669, the warrant was held to be invalid as it failed to identify the subject matter as being records of financial business details of the company which was not the subject of the search.
4 *Per* Parker L.J. in *R. v. Guildhall Magistrates' Court, ex parte Primlaks Holding Co. (Panama) Inc.* [1990] 1 Q.B. 261 at p. 272.
5 PACE Code of Practice.
6 See *Gross v. The Crown Court at Southwark* (Unreported) CO/1759/98, July 24, 1998, QBD.

writing.[7] The officer is under a duty to state the grounds of the search, the statute under which the search is required, the premises to be entered and searched and, so far as practicable, the articles or persons sought.

Code B of PACE at 2.1 and 2.3 requires the police to check that the information received is accurate, recent and supplied in good faith, not provided maliciously and, if based on an anonymous source, that corroboration has been sought; and to make reasonable enquiries to establish what, if anything is known about the likely occupier, the nature of the premises and whether they have been previously searched.

These general provisions apply equally to applications for search and seizure following foreign letters of request as to similar applications in purely domestic cases.

9.06 The importance of full disclosure and precision, in relation to mutual assistance warrant applications, has recently been underlined in *R. v. Bow Street Magistrates' Court ex parte M.*[8] Two letters of request were received from the United States in July and August 1998, seeking assistance to obtain evidence, for the purposes of a criminal investigation in relation to Mrs M. Requests were made for the seizure of evidence held by her and her former husband, and by her solicitors, both at his office and at his home, together with the contents of a safety deposit box at Selfridges. Assistance was also sought to freeze her assets and those of others.

In exercise of his powers under section 4(2A) of the 1990 Act, the Home Secretary requested the Director of the SFO to use her powers under section 2(1A)(b) of the Criminal Justice Act 1987 as amended.

9.07 Section 2(4) of the 1987 Act provides:—

> Where, on information on oath laid by a member of the SFO, a justice of the peace is satisfied, in relation to any documents, that there are reasonable grounds for believing—
>
> (a) that:
>   (i)   a person has failed to comply with an obligation under this section to produce them;
>   (ii) it is not practicable to serve a notice under sub-section (3) above in relation to them; or
>   (iii) the service of such a notice in relation to them might seriously prejudice the investigation; and
>
> (b) that they are on premises specified in the information, he or she may issue such a warrant as is mentioned in sub-section (5) below.
>
> The warrant referred to above is a warrant authorising any constable:—
>
> (a) to enter (using such force as is reasonably necessary for the purpose) and search the premises, and
> (b) to take possession of any documents appearing to be documents of the description specified in the information or to take in relation to any documents so appearing any other steps which may appear to be necessary for preserving them and preventing interference with them.

---

7 The occupier, whilst entitled to a copy of the warrant, is not entitled to see the sworn information upon which the warrant was issued (*R. v. Aylesbury Justices, ex parte Wisbey* [1965] 1 All E.R. 602).
8 *R. v. Bow Street Magistrates' Court & Anor ex parte M.*; *R. v. SFO ex parte SFO* (Unreported) April 7, 1998.

9.08 The information, together with copies of the letters of request, were left overnight with the Stipendiary Magistrate by the SFO representative, before application was made on September 5, 1997, the following day, for the warrants, which were issued.[9]

The information failed to disclose to the magistrate that the safety deposit box had been opened by the Metropolitan police nine months before, under the order of a Circuit Judge and discovered to contain "over $2m pounds in certificate of deposit"(*sic*). The deponent accepted in his later affidavit to the Divisional Court, when the warrants were challenged, that he had read of this in a draft affidavit, two days before his application for the warrants.

The court stated:

> "In his second affidavit Mr D (the deponent) persists in his statement that a warrant was required to obtain access to the safety deposit box at Selfridges. Plainly it was not required because he knew, or ought to have known, that entry to the box had been obtained without a warrant and its contents were already known to the police. The more general point is in relation to the submission of Mr Alun Jones, Q.C., for the first, second and third applicants, that an important aspect of the September 1997 operation was a debt collection exercise. The warrant has enabled assets, the bearer bonds, to be collected. I do not need to hold, and do not hold, that Mr D was aware of what was in the deposit box at Selfridges and deliberately withheld that information from the Stipendiary Magistrate. I do, however, hold that he should have known what was in it and the information should have been disclosed to the magistrate. In the event, the value of the search warrant was in obtaining possession of an asset of the third applicant, valuable bearer bonds. Had the magistrate been aware of that, he would have appreciated that there was at least a debt collecting element in the application and assessed it accordingly.
>
> When the validity of search warrants is considered, each case will depend upon its own facts. Judicial statements in the context of one case may have little value in the context of another. I propose to cite only a few statements of principle from earlier cases before considering the facts of the present case."

In *Williams v. Somerfield* [1972] 2 Q.B 512, 518 Lord Widgery C.J. stated:

> "Generations of justices have, or I would hope have, been brought up to recognise that the issue of a search warrant is a very serious interference with the liberty of the subject and a step which would only be taken after the most mature careful consideration of all the facts of the case".

In *R. v. Kensington Income Tax Commissioners ex parte Princess Edmond De Polignac* [1917] 1 Q.B. 486, 509 Warrington L.J. stated:

> "It is perfectly well settled that a person who makes an *ex parte* application to the court – that is to say in the absence of the person who will be affected by that which the court is asked to do – is under an obligation to the court to make the fullest possible disclosure of all material facts within his knowledge, and if he does not make that fullest possible disclosure, then he cannot obtain any advantage from the proceedings, and he will be deprived

---

9 The court commented upon this practice: "The delivery of pages to the magistrate on the day before the hearing rather than at the hearing is not in itself a reason for a less thorough presentation of the application to the magistrate. The failure by those applying for the warrant to keep a note of the proceedings before the magistrate was most unfortunate". Pill L.J.

of any advantage he may have already obtained by means of the order which has thus wrongly been obtained by him. That is perfectly plain and requires no authority to justify it".

That passage was cited with approval by Donaldson J. in *Bank Mellat v. Nikpour* [1985] F.S.R. 87 when considering an *ex parte* application for a freezing order (Mareva injunction). Donaldson J. added: "The rule requiring full disclosure seems to me to be one of the most fundamental importance". In my judgment, it is at least as important when application is made for search warrants.

In *R. v. Crown Court at Lewes, ex parte Hill* [1991] 93 Cr. App. R. 60, 69 Bingham L.J. stated

> "the judge should be shown such material as is necessary to enable him to be satisfied of the matters of which he is required to be satisfied before making order, and the judge should be told anything to the knowledge of the party applying which might weigh against making an order."

In *R. v. Leeds Crown Court ex parte Switalski* [1991] C.L.R. 359 Neill L.J. stressed the importance of attention being given to legal privilege when search warrants were sought in respect of a solicitor's practice files and documents. Neill L.J. considered the difficulty of deciding in advance what items might be covered by legal privilege and what might not be excluded from protection under the criminal exception (see p. 111).

> "Two conflicting public interests had to be weighed – investigating crime and the maintenance of confidentiality of communications between clients and their legal advisers. Maintaining confidentiality was of the greatest importance as vital for confidence in the legal system".

Nine search warrants were obtained and four of them are challenged upon this application. The operation was aimed at the first applicant by means of warrants covering the home of the first applicant and her husband, the premises of her solicitors and premises where she or her husband were believed to have safe deposit boxes. It is in my view appropriate to consider the operation as a whole in assessing the validity of the warrants.

In my judgment, the operation was seriously flawed and each of the warrants must be quashed. I propose to refer to the main features which in the circumstances I consider unsatisfactory.

The purpose of the operation was in my judgment insufficiently thought out and insufficiently brought to the attention of the magistrate. The application for search warrants was linked with an application for a restraint order. The letters of request were essentially requests to obtain documents, though in the supplementary request the expression "as well as for the purpose of the freeze application" also appears. In his information, Mr D follows the same line. It is documents which are sought. However, in his affidavit sworn for the purposes of this hearing, Mr D referred, in the passages already mentioned, to finding and recovering assets. If this was a purpose of the warrants, it should have been made clear to the magistrate. The Selfridges warrant can only have been justified on that ground, the contents of the safe deposit box already being known to the Serious Fraud Office. The magistrate should have had the opportunity to consider the true purpose or purposes of the operation. The restraint aspect is not considered in the information laid before the magistrate even though at the briefings on 8 September, described by police officers in their affidavits, restraint was very much in mind."

9.09   Having dealt with the issue of non-disclosure the court turned its attention to the extent of the warrant which the applicants claimed authorised seizure of material in terms which were excessively wide and uncertain.

"The Berkeley Street (the solicitors' offices) warrant I regard as excessively wide. In *R. v. C.C.C. ex parte AJD Holdings* [1992] C.L.R. 669, Nolan L.J. quashed a warrant which purported to give the warrant holder "a free hand to seek and seize all documents of the kind described irrespective of whether or not they fell within the scope of the investigation to which the information relates". While the information does describe the investigation into the first applicant's conduct and refers to "documents relevant to the investigation", there is no such limitation in the warrant. The only limitation in the warrant is in relation to V where a connection "with the matter" is mentioned. The "matter" is undefined. Moreover, once it is recognised that there is a "matter" by which the relevance of that material can be assessed, there is no reason why the limitation should not apply to all material. I also regard the warrant as insufficiently clear in its terms. The words "beneficially or otherwise" are unclear in themselves and it is not clear to what they relate. The words "financial affairs" which appear in the M (Mrs M's home) warrant do not appear."

CHAPTER 10

Protecting Confidentiality under the Criminal Justice (International Co-operation) Act 1990

10.00   The role of the United Kingdom court is pivotal in the provision of evidence to foreign jurisdictions for, whether it is acting as a nominated court under section 4 of the 1990 Act (see Chapter 6), or is authorising search and seizure under section 7 of the Act (see Chapter 11), it has the power to compel the production of evidence, oral or otherwise.

These powers are however subject to various safeguards[1], certain of which seek to protect the citizen's right to confidentiality.

For example, in Chapter 6, it has been noted that paragraph 4 of Schedule 1 to the 1990 Act provides, *inter alia*, that a witness shall not be compelled to give evidence before a nominated court which he or she could not be compelled to give in criminal proceedings in the part of the United Kingdom in which the nominated court exercises jurisdiction. Thus a witness could not be forced to disclose in evidence communications with his lawyer.

10.01   Similarly, the general power given to police under section 19 of PACE to seize material is qualified by subsection (6) which provides—

> "No power of seizure conferred on a constable under any enactment [including an enactment contained in an Act passed after this Act] is to be taken to authorise the seizure of an item which the constable exercising the power has reasonable grounds for believing to be subject to legal privilege."

In the context of examining the exercise of the court's powers under sections 4 and 7 of the 1990 Act, it is convenient to adopt the "headings" of confidentiality defined in PACE, namely:—

1.   Legal privilege.

2.   Excluded material.

3.   Special procedure material.

LEGAL PRIVILEGE

Confidentiality

10.02   It is an implied term of every contract between the lawyer and his/her client that any information passing between the two of them will not be divulged to an outside party without the consent of a client.

---

1 *e.g.* the material sought must be relevant (s.8 & Sched. 1 PACE); the privilege against self incrimination.

The Law Society of England & Wales in its Guide to the Professional Conduct of Solicitors states that:—

> A solicitor is under a duty to keep confidential to his or her firm the affairs of clients and to ensure that the staff do the same.

However, as was recently emphasised by Toulson J. in *General Mediterranean Holdings S.A. v. Patel*[2]:

> "Not every communication between lawyer and client will give rise to a duty of confidentiality. In *R. v. Cox and Railton*,[3] Stephen J. stated that a communication in furtherance of a criminal purpose does not "come into the ordinary scope of professional employment" and therefore could not give rise to a duty of confidence. And as Diplock L.J. observed in *Parry-Jones v. Law Society* [1969] 1 Chap. 1, at p. 9, a duty of confidence is subject to, and overridden by, the duty of any party to comply with the law of the land. A few statutes have overridden legal confidentiality (for example, sections 93A and 93B of Criminal Justice Act 1988 and sections 50 to 52 of the Drug Trafficking Act 1994 in relation to the suspected laundering of the proceeds of criminal conduct) . . ."

Many confidential matters will also be the subject of privilege.

Legal Professional Privilege (LPP)

10.03   LPP is the protection afforded to certain communications between lawyer[4] and client and "has no life outside litigation".[5]

In *Parry-Jones v. The Law Society*[6] Diplock L.J. said:

> "Privilege, of course, is irrelevant when one is not concerned with judicial or quasi-judicial proceedings because, strictly speaking, privilege refers to a right to withhold from a court, or a tribunal exercising judicial functions, material which would otherwise be admissible in evidence."

Such "judicial or quasi-judicial proceedings" will clearly cover proceedings in the Crown and magistrates' courts.

The rule

(a)   A client need not in civil or criminal proceedings give in evidence communications between him/her and his/her lawyers.

(b)   A lawyer *cannot* give in evidence in such proceedings, such communications without the client's consent.

10.4   The justification for such a rule was recently reiterated by the House of Lords in the landmark case of *R. v. Derby Magistrates' Court ex parte B.*[7]

---

2 (Unreported) July 19, 1999, QB (Commercial) 1995 No. 111.
3 [1884] 14 Q.B.D. 153.
4 Which includes solicitors, counsel, "in-house" counsel (*Alfred Crompton Amusement Machines Ltd v. Customs & Excise Commissioners (No. 2)* [1974] A.C. 405) and overseas lawyers (*Re Duncan* [1968] p.306).
5 Foster, Wynn and Ainley *Disclosure and confidentiality: A Practitioner's Guide* (1st ed. 1996).
6 [1969] 1 Ch. 1.
7 [1995] All E.R. 526.

"The principle which runs through all the(se) cases . . . is that a man must be able to consult his lawyer in confidence, since otherwise he might hold back half the truth. The client must be sure that what he tells his lawyer in confidence will never be revealed without his consent. LPP is thus much more than an ordinary rule of evidence, limited in its application to the facts of a particular case. *It is a fundamental condition on which the administration of justice as a whole rests.*" [authors' emphasis][8]

Which communications are privileged?

(a) Those made between a lawyer and his or her client for the purposes of seeking or giving legal advice – "advice privilege".

(b) Those made between a lawyer and his or her client, or the lawyer or the client and a third party, which come into existence for the dominant purpose of use in connection with actual or pending litigation – "litigation privilege".

LPP outside judicial proceedings

10.05 The Parry-Jones case confirms the limits of privilege to disclosure in judicial or quasi-judicial proceedings.

However, numerous statutory provisions[9] have extended the protection of material otherwise qualifying for LPP in judicial proceedings, to circumstances where no court proceedings are in existence. This ensures that "LPP communications" are protected from disclosure to investigating agencies and others with statutory rights to compel the production of evidence in the discharge of their functions.

Items subject to legal privilege

10.06 For the purpose of this work, the most obvious, and pertinent, examples are the provisions in PACE 1984.

The police are not permitted to obtain access to items which are the subject of legal professional privilege (LPP), either under a warrant or under any powers of seizure under section 18 and 19 of PACE.

Police and Criminal Evidence Act 1984 section 10 (PACE)

10.07 This Act governs the powers of police and most investigating authorities. Under its search and seizure provisions[10], the Act defines those items that are capable of seizure, or those to which conditions are imposed on seizure. As to LPP items, whilst section 10 restates the common law[11], it is worthwhile to set out the provisions here:

---

8 (*Per* Lord Taylor, *C.J. in R. v. Derby Magistrates' Court ex parte B*). B was charged in 1978 with murder having admitted to police that he had strangled a girl. He changed his story before trial, alleging S had killed her. He was acquitted. S in 1991 was charged with the murder and B gave evidence at the committal proceedings against him. In cross examination, B refused to answer questions about his original instructions to his solicitors, before he changed his story. The defence obtained a witness summons under s.97 of the Magistrates' Courts Act 1980, addressed to B's former solicitors, seeking production of the privileged documentation relating to B's original instructions.
9 See in particular PACE 1984 (ss.8, 9, 10, 19(6)); The Criminal Justice Act 1987 (s.2); The Criminal Justice (International Co-operation) Act 1990.
10 See below.
11 *Francis & Francis (a firm) v. Central Criminal Court* [1988] 3 All E.R. 775.

10 Meaning of "items subject to legal privilege"

(1) Subject to subsection (2) below, in this Act "items subject to legal privilege" means—

    (a) communications between a professional legal adviser and his client or any person representing his client made in connection with the giving of legal advice to the client;

    (b) communications between a professional legal adviser and his client or any person representing his client or between such an adviser or his client or any such representative and any other person made in connection with or in contemplation of legal proceedings and for the purposes of such proceedings; and

    (c) items enclosed with or referred to in such communications and made—

        (i)   in connection with the giving of legal advice; or

        (ii) in connection with or in contemplation of legal proceedings and for the purposes of such proceedings,

    when they are in the possession of a person who is entitled to possession of them.

(2) Items held with the intention of furthering a criminal purpose are not items subject to legal privilege.

10.08 LPP therefore attaches to three categories of material when in the possession of a person who is entitled to possession of it:

(i) Communications between a professional legal adviser and his or her client, or any person representing his or her client, made in connection with the giving of legal advice to the client.
It therefore follows that material arising within a solicitor/client relationship but not concerned with the giving of legal advice is not privileged. In *R. v. Crown Court at Inner London Sessions ex parte Baines & Baines*[12] it was held that material which comprised merely documents relating to the financing and purchasing of a house were not legally privileged.[13]

(ii) Communications between a professional legal adviser and his or her client or any person representing his or her client or between any of these people and a third person, made in connection with or in contemplation of and for the purpose of legal proceedings.
This, of course, will also cover communications with potential expert witnesses, as happened in the case of *R. v. R.*,[14] where a blood sample was provided by the defendant to his lawyer, for provision to defence experts, for a DNA test to be carried out. This was held to be the subject of legal professional privilege and the prosecution were not permitted to call the expert, to give evidence of his analysis of the specimen of the blood.

(iii) Items enclosed with or referred to in such communications and made in connection with the giving of legal advice or in connection with or in contemplation of and for the purpose of legal proceedings.

---

12 [1988] 1Q.B. 579.
13 It will however be special procedure material. See below, p. 124.
14 *The Times*, February 2, 1994.

Pre-existing material

10.09   Material which has been sent to a solicitor, together with correspondence, for the purpose of obtaining legal advice, is not covered by LPP, if it was pre-existing material and was not made in connection with the giving of legal advice, or in connection with, or in contemplation of legal proceedings and for the purpose of such proceedings.[15]

10.10   Forged material requires special consideration. A forged receipt passed to a solicitor is not subject to LPP; not because of the effect of section 10(2), but because it pre-exists the seeking of legal advice.[16] If passed to an expert, no LPP is thereby acquired, however his report falls within section 10(1)(c) and is protected by LPP.[17] Such forged documents cannot be received in confidence, there being "no confidence in iniquity",[18] neither can they be special procedure material in the solicitor's hands.[19] Thus, they can be the subject of a Magistrates' Court warrant, either under section 8 PACE or under section 7 Forgery and Counterfeiting Act 1981.

Privilege only attaches to documents *prepared* for the purpose of obtaining legal advice. Thus, pre-existing documents cannot be protected, merely by passing them to a solicitor in order to obtain advice upon them, or for that matter, lodging them with the solicitor for safekeeping. They acquire no greater protection in the hands of the solicitor than they had in the hands of the client. In *R. v. Justice of the Peace for Peterborough, ex parte Hicks*[20] a client sent a forged document to his solicitor, in order to obtain legal advice and a warrant was issued to search the solicitor's office, in order to seize the document. The document would have been open to seizure by warrant from the client and therefore it was not privileged in the hands of the solicitor.

10.11   In *Crown Prosecution Service on behalf of DPP for Australia v. Holman Fenwick & Willan* (a firm)[21], an appeal by way of case stated, the Divisional Court considered the question of whether LPP attached to an agreement and declaration of trust, a licence letter and a letter of valuation, annexed to an affidavit in a chancery action. These documents were sought by the DPP for Australia under section 4 of the Criminal Justice (International Cooperation) Act 1990; before the magistrate the respondent claimed they were confidential and covered by LPP, a view with which the magistrate agreed. Applying the test set out in *R. v. Inner London Crown Court ex parte Baines & Baines* (a firm of solicitors)[22], the Divisional Court held that none of the documents sought came into existence for the dominant purpose of giving legal advice. The first three documents were the fruits of legal advice; the fourth, the valuation letter, was not sought for legal purposes at all and in the event, none of the documents were covered by LPP.

Communications in furtherance of an unlawful course of conduct – section 10(2) PACE

10.12   If a client consults his lawyer in order to further a criminal purpose there is no relationship of confidence and hence nothing to be protected.

---

15 *R. v. Guildhall Magistrates' Court ex parte Primlaks Holdings Co. (Panama) Inc.* [1988] 89 Cr. App. R. 215.
16 *R. v. Crown Court at Northampton ex parte DPP* [1991] 93 Cr. App. R. 376.
17 *R. v. King* [1983] 1 All E.R. 929.
18 *Gartside v. Outram* (1856) 26 L.J. Ch. 113 at 114.
19 *R. v. Leeds Magistrates' Court ex parte Dumbleton* [1993], Crim. L.R. 866.
20 [1977] 1 W.L.R. 1371.
21 (Unreported) December 13, 1993.
22 [1988] 1 Q.B. 579.

(a) Section 10(2) PACE (above) does not alter the common law – "furthering a criminal purpose" means the same as "fraud" under the common law.

(b) If the legal adviser *does not know* that the client's purpose in seeking the advice is to facilitate a crime or a fraud, the communications are, on the grounds of public policy, deemed not privileged[23].

(c) If the legal adviser *does know* of the dishonest purpose, and gives advice nevertheless, he or she does not act as a lawyer and therefore communications between him/her and his/her client are not legally privileged.

Items held with the intention of furthering a criminal purpose

10.13   In *Francis & Francis (a firm) v. C.C.C.*[24] the House of Lords ruled that the intention referred to does not need to be that of the person holding the document; it can be the intention of any other person. In that case, conveyancing documents which were innocently held by solicitors, with regard to the purchase of a property by an innocent client but intended to be used by a third party, who was related to the client, for the criminal purpose of laundering the proceeds of drugs trafficking, were not items subject to legal privilege.

Death of the client

10.14   LPP survives the death of the client and vests in his/her personal representatives or the person entitled to his/her estate. Those persons are also entitled to waive the privilege.[25]

Bagging-up

10.15   In order to protect the sanctity of LPP material, a practice has grown up, by agreement between the police and lawyers present at a search, to isolate material which might attract a claim of privilege. Any material, or items to which privilege might attach, are separated, uninspected by police, and placed in sealed bags. These bags are then removed and kept in secure conditions, opened only in the presence of the lawyer acting for the client whose privilege is claimed, to enable him to inspect the documents and, where appropriate, claim privilege. Such a practice was used extensively in the Maxwell case.

10.16   Judicial doubt has recently been expressed upon the legality of such a practice. In *Gross v. The Crown Court at Southwark*[26] the officer informed the Circuit Judge, who heard the *ex parte* application for a warrant under Schedule 1, that he proposed, at the search of Mr and Mrs Gross' home, to remove the material and sift it later, to see what was privileged and what was not. The Divisional Court held that the combined effect of sections 9 and 14, together with Schedule 1 of PACE, made it clear that removal of legally privileged material from the premises which are the subject of the warrant is not permitted. It was incumbent upon a Circuit Judge on an application for a production warrant to indicate that such material should not be taken at all.

This poses considerable practical problems for the investigator and for the defence lawyer. Effectively, officers executing search warrants will have to remain on the premises and examine all material that they propose to seize, firstly to exclude LPP

---

23 *R. v. Cox & Railton* [1884] 14 Q.B.D. 153.
24 [1988] 3 All E.R. 775.
25 *R. v. Patrick Molloy* [1997] 2 Cr.App.283.
26 (Unreported) CO/1759/98, July 24, 1998, QBD.

material and thereafter to identify such material authorised under the warrant. This will be a particularly time consuming exercise, the more so in relation to material held on computer disks.

Searching solicitors' offices

10.17   Searches of solicitors' offices present additional practical problems, as warrants under section 8 cannot authorise the search for and seizure of LPP material, or excluded, or special procedure material. Magistrates' clerks, in exercising their advisory function, should examine applications, to ensure that warrants are not inadvertently issued to search for such material. In the *Primlaks*[27] case two search warrants were issued by the magistrates, authorising the search of two firms of solicitors for correspondence, which included items subject to LPP and special procedure material. The Divisional Court held that there was no material on which the justices could have held that there were reasonable grounds for believing that the correspondence did not include an item within the definition of section 10(1) PACE, or that if it did, it was not privileged by virtue of section 10(2) or any item which was not special procedure material as defined by section 14 PACE. Nor could the justices have been satisfied that any of the grounds specified in section 8(3) PACE applied, namely, that it was not practicable to communicate with the person entitled to grant access to the premises and/or the evidence. Mention is made elsewhere of the draconian nature of these powers and the need for judicial care. Where the police are aware that the items sought may include items subject to LPP, the correct procedure is to make an application under section 9(2) and Schedule 1 PACE.

10.18   In *R. v. Crown Court at Leeds, ex parte Switalski*,[28] on a judicial review application of a decision where search warrants under section 9 and Schedule 1 had been granted in respect of a solicitor's office, it was pointed out by Leonard J. that the Circuit Judge has to balance two conflicting public interests – the interest in the prevention of crime and the interest in maintaining the confidentiality of communications between clients and their legal advisers. He said:

> "I regard this second interest ... as of the greatest importance and indeed vital for the maintenance of confidence in the legal system. Therefore, the police who have obtained warrants, such as the present, have a very special responsibility to ensure that any information obtained, however inadvertently, is not misused. I would anticipate that in some cases it may well be thought right that the police will be required to give an express undertaking as to the way in which the information will be used so as to emphasise the gravity of the matter."

10.19   In *Propend*,[29] an *ex parte* application was made at the Central Criminal Court by the Metropolitan Police for warrants to search for and seize documents at the premises of solicitors and accountants, pursuant to a direction of the Secretary of State, under section 7 of the Criminal Justice (International Co-operatoin) Act 1990. No earlier approach had been made to either firm. One of the officers seeking the warrants was asked by the Circuit Judge whether other efforts had been made to obtain the material sought. He was informed that they had not, because "we knew we were bound to fail". The officer stated his firm belief that, if approached, they would claim privilege and not hand the documents over. The other (Australian) officer,

27 *R. v. Guildhall Magistrates' Court, ex parte Primlaks Holdings Co. (Panama) Inc.* [1988] 89 Cr. App. R. 215.
28 [1991] Crim. L.R. 559.
29 *R. v. C.C.C. ex parte Propend Finance Property Limited* (1996) Cr. App. R. 26.

attending on behalf of the requesting state, asserted that the (highly reputable) legal and accountancy firms, if put on notice, might take steps to remove, or destroy, evidence which might otherwise be available. Having been assured that no material subject to legal privilege was present, the judge ordered the warrant. Laws J. ruled that this was an inappropriate case for an *ex parte* application and order. No material was placed before the judge which was capable of demonstrating any risk that either set of professionals would destroy the documents, had an *inter partes* notice been served upon them.

> "In effect (the judge) had nothing but the assertion of a long standing association between the clients and the firms as a basis upon which to issue an ex parte order. This was manifestly not enough [*per* Laws J]."

10.20   In *R. v. Crown Court at Southampton, ex parte J & P*[30] the Solicitors Complaints Bureau were, together with the police, investigating a firm of solicitors, regarding allegations of theft from an elderly client. The police sought access to the firm's accounting records and client files, by obtaining warrants under section 9 and Schedule 1 of PACE. The application was made *ex parte*, on the grounds that notice of the application might seriously prejudice the investigation.[31]

The warrants were challenged on three grounds:

(a)   That they were too widely drawn and extended to material not the proper subject of an investigation. Because the police believed that other suspected unspecified offences had been committed, access was extended to all the firms' accounts;

(b)   That the warrants included material subject to LPP; and

(c)   That the application should have been *inter partes*.

10.21   The Divisional Court allowed the application and the warrant was quashed on all three grounds. On the question of LPP, whilst it was agreed that the accounting records were unlikely to contain LPP material, the clients' files of course would. The Divisional Court gave guidance on the factors to take into account in balancing the competing interests of a criminal investigation against the confidentiality of communications between solicitor and client.

The police are under an obligation to draw to the attention of the judge the material which is arguably the subject of LPP and to provide sufficient information to enable the judge to reach a decision, as to whether or not it is privileged. In cases of doubt, legal advice may be necessary to assist the judge. Whilst it may not be possible to satisfy the judge that every document in a file, or every file in a specific category, was not the subject of LPP, if the investigation was narrow, it should be possible to exclude privileged material with precision.

10.22   It was agreed by the court that an *inter partes* hearing would have been more appropriate as:

(a)   the Law Society had already seen the accounts;

(b)   the police already had some of the ledger sheets;

(c)   an *inter partes* order would, in any event, have frozen the material in the possession of the firm;

---

30 December 21, 1992.
31 See below under access conditions, pp. 125–6.

(d)   the firm had been aware of the investigations for some nine months, and finally

(e)   the solicitors were, in any event, under a duty to account to their clients which provided an alternative source of investigation.

10.23   A further practical problem is how the privileged material is to be identified. If officers are not allowed to search for and seize material subject to LPP, who decides whether the material is privileged or not? If it is to be the lawyer acting on behalf of his or her client who claims the privilege, how can the police know that they can trust him/her? Alternatively, if it is to be the officer, once he/she inspects the material, there is a risk that the confidentiality that the privilege seeks to protect will be lost.

10.24   Whether the police actually are permitted to sift through all the material to exercise their powers is uncertain. In *Frank Truman Export Ltd v. Metropolitan Police Commissioner*,[32] decided before PACE, Swanwick J. said:

"The question seems to me to be one of balance of public policy and the discretion in the exercise of an equitable remedy on the facts and in the circumstances of the particular case. On the one hand, there was here a warrant authorising entry and search for forgery. The search must involve sorting. The method of sorting was consented to and the documents handed over for that purpose".

"Some sorting there must be in order to execute the warrant, but in conducting a search in the offices of a solicitor who is not suspected of complicity in any criminal activity, that sorting should, in my view, as far as possible, take place in the solicitor's office and be so conducted that documents which are clearly both privileged and inadmissible . . . can be eliminated at once and without perusal of their text".

10.25   There are obvious dangers in such a sifting exercise, that the absolute nature of LPP, as emphasised by the House of Lords in *Derby Magistrates Court ex parte B*, will be threatened.

The difficulties of searching solicitors' premises in the context of mutual assistance was considered in *R. v. Bow Street Magistrates' Court ex parte M*.[33] Warrants had been issued in relation to the solicitor's business and home addresses. However, as the court stated:—

"Notwithstanding the contents of the briefings and the presence of legally qualified persons at the search, the issue of legal privilege was dealt with in an unsatisfactory manner, especially when the search was directed to the premises of solicitors. I cannot accept Mr Radcliffe's submission that, against the background of events in this case, all documents relevant to the criminal investigation and to the recovery of assets were covered by the criminal exception.

The first applicant (Mrs M) could legitimately obtain advice as to the legality and effect of court orders in the United Kingdom and, with the help of such advice, has successfully challenged the English restraint order. The line between what is legitimate advice to a client in dealing with assets and what is subject to the criminal exception is a difficult one to draw. It was not given sufficient consideration. The second respondent (SFO) was, for example, in possession of a detailed letter of 11 August 1993 from the fourth applicant (S, the solicitor) to a Swiss bank in which he analyses and comments on the position and conduct of the first applicant (Mrs M) in the context of her wish to transfer funds. This was not brought to the attention of the magistrate and apparently not considered relevant. The magistrate was also not told that of the financial claims, only the claim for interest was outstanding, something which might well have influenced his view of the conduct over the years of each of the applicants.

The lack of consideration of legal privilege was notable at (S's home address). A computer and eight floppy disks were taken. A vast amount of information was recorded on the disks. It included information subject to legal professional privilege and information relating to family trusts and other clients of the fourth applicant (S himself) unrelated to the United States investigation. It included obviously irrelevant material such as games and computer software. General consideration of the circumstances in which disks containing a vast amount of information can be seized and the procedure to be followed if they are seized may fall for consideration in another case".

10.26   As chance would have it, in another case within three months, a differently constituted Divisional Court, (Brooke L.J. and Rougier J.)[34] in a judgment on another issue, disagreed with the court in *ex parte M.* and made it plain that removal of legally privileged material from the premises which are the subject of the warrant, is not permitted. The practice of "bagging up" which had been adopted in *ex parte M.*, was ruled unlawful.

In *ex parte M.*, Counsel for the SFO had sought to argue that the effect of the wording of section 2(5)(b) of the Criminal Justice Act 1987[35] demonstrated the breadth of the Director's powers and enabled her "to take any other steps which may be necessary" making it possible to hold and detain documents until any issues of legal professional privilege which may arise could be resolved. As described by Counsel "it provides a breathing space". Clearly, the court in Gross rejected this interpretation.

10.27   The court in *ex parte M.* continued its criticism of the manner in which the LPP material had been seized, by imposing upon those who had seized the material, a duty of assessing its relevance, to which further reference will be made below.[36]

"In this case those who seized the disks made no attempt to sort the information and retain only what was relevant[37] and they do not appear to have appreciated the problems involved. Moreover, among the documents seized at (the home address of S) was exhibit 40, which the SFO recorded as 'legal opinion documents' and exhibit 22 "envelope containing papers marked lawsuit against us".

Challenging orders granting access to LPP material

10.28   If an order has been made by a Circuit Judge, seeking access to material which is subject to LPP, then unless the client agrees to waive the privilege, applica-

---

34 *Gross v. The Crown Court at Southwark*, CO/1759/98, unreported, July 24, 1998.
35 (5) The warrant referred to above is a warrant authorising any constable—
   (b) to take possession of any documents appearing to be documents of the description specified in the information or to take in relation to any documents so appearing any other steps which may appear to be necessary for preserving them and preventing interference with them.
36 See p. 153 *et seq.*
37 *i.e.* before transmitting it to the USA.

tion should be made on notice to the Circuit Judge issuing the original order, to seek its variation, or discharge, in accordance with Rule 25(B) of the Crown Court (Amendment) Rules 1986. Should this fail, application should be to the Divisional Court for *certiorari*. The privilege, of course, belongs to the client and not to the legal adviser and thus the lawyer is under a duty to assert the privilege, unless the client agrees to waive it.

"Tipping off"

10.29 Certain orders to produce documents or material contain a provision making it a criminal offence to "tip off", that is, to make any disclosure which is likely to prejudice an investigation.

For example, section 58 of the Drug Trafficking Act 1994 provides that where, under section 55 of the Act, an order has been made, or applied for and not refused, or where under section 56, a warrant issued, it is an offence for any person, knowing or suspecting that the investigation is taking place, to make any disclosure which is likely to prejudice the investigation. It is a defence for a person charged with such an offence to prove, on the balance of probabilities, that he or she did not know, or suspect, that disclosure was likely to prejudice the investigation, or that he or she had lawful authority, or reasonable excuse, for making the disclosure.

The difficulties that such provisions will cause legal advisers is recognised by section 58(3), which provides that it is not an offence for a professional legal adviser to disclose any information, or other matter:—

(a) To, or to a representative of, a client of his/her in connection with the giving by the adviser of legal advice to the client; or

(b) To any person—

(i) in contemplation of, or in connection with, legal proceedings; and

(ii) for the purpose of those proceedings.

10.30 The sub-section provides a similar exclusion to that appearing in section 10(2) of PACE, in that section 58(3) does not apply in relation to any information or other matter which is disclosed with a view to furthering a criminal purpose.

Similar provisions apply under the Proceeds of Crime Act 1995.

Bearing in mind that the privilege belongs to the client and not to the lawyer, it may be lawful for a lawyer, when these provisions apply, to seek his or her client's instructions in relation to the order. The statutory exclusion could be said to give a degree of protection; Lord Griffiths in *ex parte Francis & Francis*[38] which was decided prior to the legislation under consideration, stated obiter that he had no doubt that the solicitor/client relationship provides a reasonable excuse for taking a client's instructions.

10.31 Similar considerations obtain where those holding special procedure material (see below under Schedule 1 PACE) are served with a notice of an application for a production order. By definition, that person holds the material subject to an undertaking of confidentiality to his or her client, or in the case of a bank, to the customer who will be the subject of the police investigation. If the special procedure material that is sought is held by a lawyer,[39] then it would seem that no offence would be committed by that lawyer, in disclosing the service of a notice of application, if that

---

38 *Francis & Francis v.C.C.C.* [1988] 3 All E.R. 775.
39 See below under "status of lawyers' files", p. 124.

is done in connection with the giving by the adviser of legal advice to the client, or in contemplation of, or in connection with legal proceedings and for the purpose of those proceedings as contemplated above.

This does not mean that a lawyer must always inform the client of such an application for it will be appreciated that it is the lawyer's purpose in informing the client that will determine whether a tipping-off offence is committed: if the purpose is that described in the section there is no offence: if it is not, there may be.

10.32   Others holding special procedure material but who are not legal advisers do not have the same protection under the tipping-off provisions, and should be careful not to make any disclosure which is likely to prejudice the investigation, if it is an investigation subject to those provisions.

10.33   In relation to investigations not the subject of tipping-off provisions, the Court of Appeal in *Barclays Bank plc v. Taylor*[40] held that, whilst banks are under no duty to inform a customer, it is by no means clear that they are under a legal duty *not* to inform the customer. Whilst Lord Donaldson, the Master of the Rolls, expressed his surprise and disappointment at the prospect of banks informing customers, when requested by the police not to, he accepted that they appeared to be free to ignore such a request.

LPP and the European Convention on Human Rights

10.34   Article 6 provides:

"Right to a fair trial.

1.   In the determination of his civil rights and obligations or of any criminal charge against him, everyone is entitled to a fair and public hearing within a reasonable time by an independent and impartial tribunal established by law ..."

Article 8 provides:

"Right to respect for private and family life.

1.   Everyone has the right to respect for his private and family life, his home and his correspondence.
2.   There should be no interference by a public authority with the exercise of this right except such as is in accordance with the law and is necessary in a democratic society in the interests of national security, public safety or the economic well-being of the country, for the prevention of disorder or crime, for the protection of health or morals, or for the protection of the rights and freedoms of others."

10.35   It is arguable that the right to a fair trial under Article 6 includes the right of a person to consult a lawyer confident that what he/she says will not be revealed without his or her consent, unless there is reasonable cause to believe that the communication was made with the intention of furthering a criminal act. In relation to Article 8, the right to respect for a person's private and family life, home and correspondence, would appear to include the right to respect for communications between himself/herself and his/her lawyer, this being important for the furtherance

---

40 [1989] 3 All E.R. 563.

of a person's rights under Article 6; and that no interference should be permitted under Article 8(2) unless again there is reasonable cause to believe that the purpose for which the right exists is being abused.[41]

Silver and *Campbell* related to privacy of prisoners' correspondence. In *Campbell* the court said at pages 160–161:

> "46. It is clearly in the general interest that any person who wishes to consult a lawyer should be free to do so under conditions which favour full and uninhibited discussion. It is for this reason that the lawyer – client relationship is, in principle, privileged.
>
> 48. . . . the court sees no reason to distinguish between the different categories of correspondence which, whatever their purpose, concern matters of a private and confidential character. In principle, such letters are privileged under Article 8. This means that the prison authorities may open a letter from a lawyer to a prisoner when they have reasonable cause to believe that it contains an illicit enclosure which the normal means of detection have failed to disclose. The letter should, however, only be opened and should not be read. Suitable guarantees preventing the reading of the letter should be provided, *e.g.* opening the letter in the presence of the prisoner. The reading of a prisoner's mail to and from a lawyer, on the other hand, should only be permitted in exceptional circumstances when the authorities have reasonable cause to believe that the privilege is being abused in that the contents of the letter endanger prison security or the safety of others or are otherwise of a criminal nature."

10.36 In *Niemietz*, which concerned a search of a lawyer's offices by police looking for information revealing the identity and whereabouts of a person who was the subject of a criminal investigation, the court held that the search violated Article 8, recognising that activities of a professional character could fall within the notions of private life and correspondence. It also recognised that, where a lawyer was involved, an encroachment on professional secrecy might have repercussions on the proper administration of justice and hence on the rights guaranteed by Article 6.

EXCLUDED MATERIAL

10.37 Section 8(1)(d) of PACE also exempts from search and seizure under that section "Excluded Material".

Meaning of "excluded material"

10.38 Section 11 of PACE defines excluded material.

(1) Subject to the following provisions of this section, in this Act "excluded material" means—

    (a) personal records which a person has acquired or created in the course of any trade, business, profession or other occupation or for the purposes of any paid or unpaid office and which he holds in confidence;

---

41 See *Silver v. U.K.* (1983) 5 E.H.R.R. 347, *Campbell v. U.K.* (1992) 15 E.H.R.R. 137 and *Niemietz v. Germany* (1992) 16 E.H.R.R. 97.

(b) human tissue or tissue fluid which has been taken for the purposes of diagnosis or medical treatment and which a person holds in confidence;

(c) journalistic material which a person holds in confidence and which consists—

(i)   of documents; or
(ii) of records other than documents

(2) A person holds material other than journalistic material in confidence for the purposes of this section if he holds it subject—

(a) to an express or implied undertaking to hold it in confidence; or

(b) to a restriction on disclosure or an obligation of secrecy contained in any enactment, including an enactment contained in an Act passed after this Act.

(3) A person holds journalistic material in confidence for the purposes of this section if—

(a) he holds it subject to such an undertaking, restriction or obligation; and

(b) it has been continuously held (by one or more persons) subject to such an undertaking, restriction or obligation since it was first acquired or created for the purposes of journalism.

Meaning of "personal records"

10.39 "Personal records" are defined by section 12 of PACE as follows:

In this Part of this Act "personal records" means documentary and other records concerning an individual (whether living or dead) who can be identified from them and relating—

(a) to his physical or mental health;
(b) to spiritual counselling or assistance given or to be given to him; or
(c) to counselling or assistance given or to be given to him, for the purposes of his personal welfare, by any voluntary organisation or by any individual who—

(i)   by reason of his office or occupation has responsibilities for his personal welfare; or

(ii) by reason of an order of a court has responsibilities for his supervision.

Meaning of "journalistic material"

10.40 "Journalistic material" is defined by section 13 of PACE as follows:

(1) Subject to subsection (2) below, in this Act "journalistic material" means material acquired or created for the purposes of journalism.

(2) Material is only journalistic material for the purposes of this Act if it is in the possession of a person who acquired or created it for the purposes of journalism.

(3) A person who receives material from someone who intends that the

recipient shall use it for the purposes of journalism is to be taken to have acquired it for those purposes.

Effect of legislation

10.41 Essentially, with the exception of journalistic material, excluded material can best be described as personal confidential material. In balancing the public interest in the detection of crime, against the privacy of the individual, Parliament decided that it should exclude access to such material, save in the following two cases:

(1) where a warrant could previously have been issued, authorising the search for and seizure of such material,[42] and

(2) search and seizure by H.M. Customs & Excise.

This exception arises under regulation 6 of PACE (Application to Customs & Excise) Order (Section I. 1987/439)) which effectively removes the protection of Schedule 1 from "material in the possession of persons who acquired or created it in the course of any trade, business, profession, or other occupation or for the purpose of any paid or unpaid office and which relates to an unassigned matter".

Effectively, warrants obtained by Customs Officers under Customs legislation, to search for and seize business records, proceed in the normal way, without reference to Schedule 1 of PACE.

Excluded material falls under three headings:

(1) personal records;

(2) human tissue or tissue fluid taken for the purposes of diagnosis or medical treatment and/or

(3) journalistic material.

Personal records

10.42 This will cover personal records which a person has acquired or created in the course of any trade, business, profession or other occupation or for the purpose of any paid or unpaid office and which he or she holds in confidence. Under section 12 of PACE "personal records" are defined as documentary or other records (which will include computerised records) concerning an individual (whether living or dead) who can be identified from them and relating:

(a) to his or her physical or mental health – this will obviously cover records kept by hospitals, medical practitioners and those concerned with the physical and mental health of individuals, including midwives, health visitors, etc. There is no requirement for professional qualifications and thus it will also cover osteopaths, hypnotists, chiropractors, etc.;

(b) spiritual counselling or assistance given or to be given to him/her – whilst clearly this will cover the accepted spiritual advisers, *e.g.* priests, rabbis, *etc.* the use of the word "spiritual" would appear to include those who belong to religious sects and give religious advice; or

(c) to the counselling or assistance given, or to be given to him/her, for the purposes of his/her personal welfare, by any voluntary organisation or by any individual who—

---

42 See the second set of access conditions under Sched. 1 below, p. 126.

(i)   by reason of his or her office or occupation has responsibility for his or her personal welfare, or

(ii) by reason of an order of the court has responsibilities for his supervision.

This will include records maintained by social workers, Relate, those in charge of refuges, Citizens Advice Bureaux, etc.

Human tissue or tissue fluid

10.43   This covers such items removed from an individual and held in confidence by someone connected with a hospital, clinic or laboratory. It is limited to human tissue or tissue fluid. It will not therefore cover items removed from a body. These items must have been "taken for the purposes of diagnosis or medical treatment". It seems unlikely that this would cover samples taken from the victim of crime for forensic comparison.

Journalistic material

10.44   The requirement is that the material be "acquired or created" by a person for the purposes of journalism "which is not confined merely to newspapers or professional journalists". It will cover, therefore, the journalist's research papers and unsolicited material if the supplier intended it should be used for the purposes of journalism, in which event its recipient is to be taken as having received it for such a purpose.

The material must not only be held in confidence but it should be held continuously subject to such an undertaking, restriction or obligation from its first acquisition or creation for the purposes of journalism.

This is of importance in relation to leaked documents which are passed to a journalist who then passes them through his or her internal chain of command and up to his/her editor. So long as each one in the chain receives it for the purposes of journalism it remains excluded material. If, however, the document is passed to a non-journalist for whatever reason, *e.g.* authentication, whilst the confidentiality requirement obtains throughout, a link in the continuity of purpose is missing, for the person asked to evaluate the document does not acquire it for the purpose of journalism. Thus, documents passed to and held by the newspaper's lawyers seem to lose their excluded material protection and as they have not been prepared for the purpose of receiving legal advice, they do not have the protection of legal professional privilege. They would seem, however, to have become special procedure material (see below, p. 123).

SPECIAL PROCEDURE MATERIAL

Meaning of "special procedure material"

10.45   Special procedure material is the third category of material excluded by section 8(1)(d) PACE and is defined in section 14 of PACE as:

(1)   In this Act "special procedure material" means—

(a)   material to which subsection (2) below applies; and

(b)   journalistic material, other than excluded material.

(2)   Subject to the following provisions of this section, this subsection applies to

material, other than items subject to legal privilege and excluded material, in the possession of a person who—

(a) acquired or created it in the course of any trade, business, profession or other occupation or for the purpose of any paid or unpaid office; and

(b) holds it subject—
   (i) to an express or implied undertaking to hold it in confidence; or
   (ii) to a restriction or obligation such as is mentioned in section 11(2)(b) above.

Nature of special procedure material

10.46 As its name implies, special procedure material is available to police, provided an application is made in accordance with the special procedure set out under Schedule 1 of PACE. It falls into two categories:

(1) journalistic material which is not excluded material, and

(2) material to which section 14(2) PACE applies.

Journalistic material other than excluded material

10.47 Only if journalistic material consists of:—

(1) documents or

(2) records other than documents; and

(3) is continuously held in confidence

is it excluded material.

Thus, unless all of these requirements are met, the material held will not be excluded material but will be special procedure material. For example, as referred to above, journalistic material which is passed to the journalist's legal advisers loses its "continuous holding" and becomes special procedure material.

The section was considered in *R. v. Crown Court at Bristol, ex parte Bristol Press & Picture Agency Ltd.*[43] During the St Paul's riots in Bristol, photographs were taken by the press, which were sought by the police. It was claimed that they were excluded material. The court held that, whilst they were "documents or records other than documents", they were not held in confidence (whether continuously or not), clearly having been "created for the purposes of journalism"; they were thus not excluded material but were special procedure material.

Special procedure to which section 14(2) applies

10.48 Material is special procedure material if it:

(i) is not legally privileged or excluded material;

(ii) it is in the possession of a person who acquired or created it in the course of any trade, business, profession or other occupation or for the purposes of any paid or unpaid office; and

---

43 1986 85 Cr. App. R. 190.

(iii) it is held in confidence or subject to a restriction on disclosure or an obligation of secrecy contained in any enactment.

The most common holders of such special procedure material are banks, building societies, accountants, brokers and lawyers.

Status of lawyers' files

(a) All documents and other records in the possession of a solicitor in relation to the affairs of his clients are special procedure material unless they are subject to legal privilege.[44]

(b) Items which under section 10(2) PACE have been held with the intention of furthering a criminal purpose and which have thereby lost their legal privilege status, become special procedure material.[45]

10.49   In *R. v. Leeds Magistrates' Court, ex parte Dumbleton*[46] the Divisional Court held that where a forged document is handed to a solicitor by a fraudulent client, it is not special procedure material, because its nature is such that it could not have been acquired, made or created in the course of the profession of a lawyer.

Interestingly, in *R. v. Singleton*,[47] which concerned dental records (excluded material) the Court of Appeal held that the object of the PACE provisions regarding excluded and special procedure material was to safeguard the maker or holder of such material and not the suspect; in which event, the holder of the records could disclose the material voluntarily – if he or she chose not to, then the Schedule 1 procedure must be followed.

10.50   Before voluntarily disclosing special procedure material held by them, care should be exercised by lawyers who seek to rely upon the authority of Singleton. The items they hold as special procedure material will be of two types:—

(1) those which are held in confidence but are not subject to LPP, because they do not fall under the definition of section 10(1) PACE. They are still held in confidence and the lawyer will be subject to his/her normal duty of confidentiality to his/her client;

(2) those which have lost their privileged status under the criminal purpose exception of section 10(2) PACE. Strong *prima facie* evidence is required before the lawyer can consider himself released from LPP.[48] In such a case, his/her role is not that of lawyer, and no confidentiality attaches to the relationship. In these circumstances, the documents or communications would not have been received in confidence, there being no confidence in iniquity (*Gartside v. Outram*[49]). In *Finers v. Miro*[50] the court indicated that it has jurisdiction to give a solicitor directions as to how he or she should deal with funds held or controlled on behalf of a client, against whom there was *prima facie* evidence that he/she had obtained such funds or assets fraudulently. Notwithstanding the solicitor's professional duty of con-

---

44 Per Lord Bridge in *R. v. C.C.C., ex parte Francis & Francis* [1989] A.C. 347 at 370.
45 *R. v. Guildhall Magistrates' Court, ex parte Primlaks Holding Co. (Panama) Inc.* [1990] 1Q.B. 261.
46 [1993] Crim. L.R. 866.
47 [1995] 1 Cr. App. R. 431.
48 *Derby & Co. Ltd. v. Weldon (No.7)* [1990] 1 W.L.R. 1156.
49 [1856] 26 L.J. Ch.113 at p. 114, cited with approval in *R. v. Leeds Magistrates' Court, ex parte Dumbleton* [1993].
50 [1991] 1 All E.R. 182.

fidentiality towards his/her client, such directions could include notification being given to third parties, who might have a claim against the client or his/her assets, or possibly even to police investigating the fraud. A solicitor holding assets in such a situation might consider himself in potential breach of the provisions of the money laundering legislation, in which event a report to police would not in fact amount to a breach of confidentiality.[51]

ORDERS FOR OBTAINING ACCESS TO EXCLUDED OR SPECIAL PROCEDURE MATERIAL

Special provisions as to access

10.51 Section 9 of PACE provides:

(1) A constable may obtain access to excluded material or special procedure material for the purposes of a criminal investigation by making an application under Schedule 1 below and in accordance with that Schedule.

(2) Any Act (including a local Act) passed before this Act under which a search of premises for the purposes of a criminal investigation could be authorised by the issue of a warrant to a constable shall cease to have effect so far as it relates to the authorisation of searches—

(a) for items subject to legal privilege; or
(b) for excluded material; or
(c) for special procedure material consisting of documents or records other than documents.

Whilst the effect of section 9(1) is straightforward, that of section 9(2) is less so. Under the sub-section any statutory provisions existing before PACE, which authorised the issue of a search warrant to a constable, cease to have effect, so far as they relate to the authorisation of searches for items subject to LPP, excluded material, or special procedure material consisting of documents or records other than documents. Therefore magistrates are prevented from issuing a warrant under an Act pre-dating PACE, where the material sought falls into one of those categories.[52]

PACE Schedule 1 – the statutory provisions

10.52 LPP material can never be obtained but in relation to excluded material, or special procedure material in documentary form, an application must be made to a Circuit Judge under Schedule 1, either for an order requiring the person in possession of the material to produce it to the police, or for a warrant authorising a constable to enter and search premises for the material.

Schedule 1: Special Procedure – Section 9[53]

Making of orders by Circuit Judge
1. If on an application made by a constable a Circuit Judge is satisfied that one or other of the sets of access conditions is fulfilled, he/she may make an order under paragraph 4 below.

---

51 See, *e.g.* s.93 Criminal Justice Act 1988; ss.50 & 51 Drug Trafficking Act 1994, p. 117 above.
52 See the second set of access conditions, p. 126 below.
53 As amended by Criminal Justice (International Cooperation) Act 1990.

2. The first set of access conditions is fulfilled if—

    (a) there are reasonable grounds for believing—

        (i)   that a serious arrestable offence has been committed;
        (ii) that there is material which consists of special procedure material or also includes special procedure material and does not also include excluded material on premises specified in the application;
        (iii) that the material is likely to be of substantial value (whether by itself or together with other material) to the investigation in connection with which the application is made; and
        (iv) that the material is likely to be relevant evidence;

    (b) other methods of obtaining the material—

        (i)   have been tried without success; or
        (ii) have not been tried because it appeared that they were bound to fail; and

    (c) it is in the public interest, having regard—

        (i)   to the benefit likely to accrue to the investigation if the material is obtained; and
        (ii) to the circumstances under which the person in possession of the material holds it,

    That the material should be produced or that access to it should be given.

3. The second set of access conditions is fulfilled if—

    (a) there are reasonable grounds for believing that there is material which consists of or include excluded material or special procedure material on premises specified in the application;
    (b) but for section 9(2) above a search of the premises for that material could have been authorised by the issue of a warrant to a constable under an enactment other than this Schedule; and
    (c) the issue of such a warrant would have been appropriate.

4. An order under this paragraph is an order that the person who appears to the Circuit Judge to be in possession of the material to which the application relates shall—

    (a) produce it to a constable for him/her to take away; or
    (b) give a constable access to it,

    not later than the end of the period of seven days from the date of the order or the end of such longer period as the order may specify.

5. Where the material consists of information contained in a computer—

    (a) an order under paragraph 4(a) above shall have effect as an order to produce the material in a form in which it can be taken away and in which it is visible and legible; and
    (b) an order under paragraph 4(b) above shall have effect as an order to give a constable access to the material in a form in which it is visible and legible.

6. For the purposes of sections 21 and 22 above material produced in pursuance of an order under paragraph 4(a) above shall be treated as if it were material seized by a constable.

Notices of applications for orders

7. An application for an order under paragraph 4 above shall be made *inter partes*.[54]

11. Where notice of an application for an order under paragraph 4 above has been served on a person, he shall not conceal, destroy, alter or dispose of the material to which the application relates except—

   (a) with the leave of a judge; or
   (b) with the written permission of a constable, until—

      (i) the application is dismissed or abandoned; or
      (ii) he has complied with an order under paragraph 4 above made on the application.

Issue of warrants by circuit judge

12. If on an application made by a constable a Circuit Judge—

   (a) is satisfied—

      (i) that either set of access conditions is fulfilled; and
      (ii) that any of the further conditions set out in paragraph 14 below is also fulfilled; or

   (b) is satisfied—

      (i) that the second set of access conditions is fulfilled; and

   (c) that an order under paragraph 4 above relating to the material has not been complied with, he may issue a warrant authorising a constable to enter and search the premises.

13. A constable may seize and retain anything for which a search has been authorised under paragraph 12 above.

14. The further conditions mentioned in paragraph 12(a)(ii) above are—

   (a) that it is not practicable to communicate with any person entitled to grant entry to the premises to which the application relates;
   (b) that it is practicable to communicate with a person entitled to grant entry to the premises but it is not practicable to communicate with any person entitled to grant access to the material;
   (c) that the material contains information which—

      (i) is subject to a restriction or obligation such as is mentioned in section 11(2)(b) above; and
      (ii) is likely to be disclosed in breach of it if a warrant is not issued;

---

[54] The parties are the police and the person in possession of the material, not the owner of the material who may be the subject of the investigation. See *R. v. Crown Court at Leicester, ex parte Director of Public Prosecutions* [1978] 3 All E.R. 654.

(d)   that service of notice of an application for an order under paragraph 4 above may seriously prejudice the investigation.

15. (1)   If a person fails to comply with an order under paragraph 4 above, a Circuit Judge may deal with him/her as if he/she had committed a contempt of the Crown Court.

(2)   Any enactment relating to contempt of the Crown Court shall have effect in relation to such a failure as if it were such a contempt.

The balancing process

10.53–10.59   "The special procedure under section 9 and Schedule 1 is a serious in-road upon the liberty of the subject. The responsibility for ensuring that the procedure is not abused lies with Circuit Judges.[55] It is of cardinal importance that Circuit Judges should be scrupulous in discharging that responsibility.[56]"

"Generations of justices have, or I would hope have, been brought up to recognise that the issue of a search warrant is a very serious interference with the liberty of the subject, and a step which would only be taken after the most mature, careful consideration of all the facts in the case.[57]"

10.60   These are but two of the numerous passages in the authorities underlining the enormous care to be taken by Circuit Judges in deciding whether to grant applications under Schedule 1 of PACE. Similar care is to be exercised by judges when considering applications under section 7 of the 1990 Act.

". . . it is noteworthy that if premises in England and Wales are to be searched for special procedure material or excluded material at the request of an overseas country, all the protections afforded by PACE will be available before a judge will issue a warrant for such a search."[58]

10.61   In *R. v. Southwark Crown Court & Anor, ex parte Sorsky Defries*,[59] following a request from the United States authorities, the Secretary of State for the Home Department directed Customs and Excise to apply for a search warrant under section 9 and Schedule 1 of PACE, pursuant to his powers under section (4) of the Criminal Justice (International Cooperation) Act 1990. On that same day, Customs and Excise applied *ex parte* to Southwark Crown Court for a search warrant and the application was granted. It was executed four days later at the applicant's premises, who were a firm of accountants. It was common ground that the judge had never seen an application like this before. The entire proceedings took a couple of minutes before the judge; he was referred to virtually nothing and approached the application on the basis that he could rely upon what was contained in the affidavit of the Customs officer, without applying his own mind to being satisfied as to the various matters upon which it was necessary for him to be satisfied.

"What is plain is that such an intrusion into the liberty of the subject cannot be

---

55 A recorder has no jurisdiction to order production. *R. v. C.C.C. ex.parte Francis & Francis* [1989] A.C. 347.
56 *R. v. Maidstone Crown Court ex parte Waitt* [1988] Crim. L.R. 384 *per* Lloyd L.J.
57 *Per* Lord Widgery C.J. in *Williams v. Summerfield* [1971] 2Q.B. 512.
58 *Per* Brooke L.J. in *R. v. Manchester Stipendiary Magistrates' Court, ex parte Granada Television Limited*, [1999] C.L.R. 162.
59 [1966] Crim. L.R. 195.

allowed to go through on the nod . . . as to whether, however, he could have been satisfied that the material was likely to be of substantial value and material evidence is a matter upon which I would require further argument. Certain I am, however, that the judge could not possibly have been so satisfied in the time available. Simply to read the information in fifteen minutes would be good going, but to have analysed it and sorted out what evidence related to which company and individual in that time is beyond belief." [*per* McCowan L.J.]

10.62 In *R. v. Crown Court at Lewes, ex parte Hill*,[60] which concerned an order in relation to material held by several banks, Bingham LJ stated:

"The Police & Criminal Evidence Act governs a field in which there are two very obvious public interests. There is, first of all, a public interest in the effective investigation and prosecution of crime. Secondly, there is a public interest in protecting the personal property rights of citizens against infringements and invasions. There is an obvious tension between these two public interests . . .

The 1984 Act seeks to effect a carefully judged balance between these interests and that is why it is a detailed and complex Act. If the scheme intended by Parliament is to be implemented, it is important that the provisions laid down in the Act should be fairly and fully enforced. It would be quite wrong to approach the Act with any preconception as to how these provisions should be operated, save insofar as such preconception is derived from the legislation itself."

Information to be submitted in support of an application

10.63 Paragraph 8 of Schedule 1 provides that a notice of application for a production order is to be served upon the person believed to be in possession of the information or material that is sought.

In *R. v. C.C.C., ex parte Adegbesan*[61] Watkins L.J. stated that the duty of the police "is to set out in the Notice which goes to a person whose assistance is required, a description of all that is sought to be produced or to be discovered, notwithstanding the risk that such evidence might be destroyed". The failure, in that case, of the Notices to specify the material, went to the very root of the procedure properly to be applied under Schedule 1.

In *R. v. C.C. at Inner London Sessions, ex parte Baines & Baines*[62] the court held that although the police were not obliged to provide an "information" setting out the evidence in support of an application, if they did so, it was to be served on all parties and not just the court and where no advance information was given, an adjournment could be sought.

10.64 In order to satisfy the judge that the material is "likely to be of substantial value (whether by itself or together with other material) to the investigation" it is clearly necessary for the police to describe the offence under investigation, what other evidence there is and how the material sought relates to the investigation. "Relevant evidence" in relation to an offence means anything that would be admissible in evidence at a trial for the offence (section 8(4) PACE) and thus, in order that the judge can properly perform the balancing exercise, it is vital that the police information is as precise as possible.

In *R. v. C.C. at Lewes, ex parte Hill*[63] Bingham L.J. stated that:

---

60 [1991] 93 Cr. App. R. 60.
61 [1987] 84 Cr. App. R. 219.
62 [1987] 77 Cr. App. R. 111.
63 [1991] 93 Cr. App. R. 60.

"The judge should be shown such material as is necessary to enable him to be satisfied of the matters of which he is required to be satisfied before making the order, and the judge should be told of anything to the knowledge of the party applying which might weigh against making an order".

In *Gross* (which concerned a mutual assistance request)[64] Rougier J. stated:

"The procedure under Part II of PACE has been correctly likened to the Anton Pillar orders in the civil jurisdiction, and there is abundant authority that it is the duty of the applying party to make the fullest disclosure of all facts which may be relevant, whether those facts are favourable to him or adverse."

10.65   In *Gross*, the United States authorities sent a letter of request to the Secretary of State who, in accordance with his powers under section 7 of the 1990 Act, made a direction to the Metropolitan Police Fraud Department, "that an application be made for a warrant under paragraph 12(a) of Schedule 1 to the Police and Criminal Evidence Act 1984". The material sought, which was excluded material, was held by Professor & Mrs Gross, having been sent to them from the United States by their son, the subject of deception and false accounting charges in the United States. These charges alleged that he had submitted claims to various medical insurers for treatment of patients, when in fact no such treatment had been given.

It was submitted that there was a failure to make reasonable, or indeed any enquiry, as to the sort of person Professor Gross was, still less to inform the judge of the various matters concerning his life and personality.

"In point of fact, the Professor at the time was 73 years old, a recently retired professor of business studies with a distinguished record of service in the United States Air Force during World War II and in criminal law terms, of good character."

10.66   This tended to suggest that, even though he was the father of the accused, he would be highly unlikely to assist in the criminal offence of attempting to pervert the course of justice, by putting the material out of reach. It was never suggested by anyone that there was a possibility of Mrs Gross acting in such a fashion.

It was held that "no less than ten mistakes of varying degrees of seriousness were made in connection with what was, after all, an invasion of Professor Gross' home under the authority of the State. An American living in Upminster is just as much entitled as his English neighbours to regard his home as his castle". Amongst the relevant mistakes catalogued by the court were:

1. The enquiries to establish what, if anything, was known about Professor Gross fell short of what was reasonable.

2. No authority was obtained from a police officer, of at least the rank of Inspector, before the application for a warrant was made.

3. Inadequate disclosure was made to the court about Professor Gross, and the judge asked no questions to satisfy himself that the requirements of paragraph 14(d) of Schedule 1 were satisfied.

4. The judge was given information which was, perhaps accidentally, untrue

---

64 *Gross v. The Crown Court at Southwark, (Unreported) CO/1759/98, July 29, 1998.*

about the total amounts contained in the actual charges against Professor Gross.

5.   The judge gave no reasons for his decision to grant a warrant, despite a number of injunctions in decisions of the Divisional Court that he should do so.

The application hearing

(a) Application for a production order

10.67   The hearing of the application should be *inter partes*.[65]

The onus is upon the police to satisfy the judge, on the balance of probabilities,[66] that the access conditions contained in Schedule 1 paragraph 2 or 3 above are fulfilled.

Normally, the officer in the case will set out in an information sufficient details of the offence that is being investigated and the grounds upon which he/she believes the access conditions are fulfilled. The similarity of the conditions set out in the first set of access conditions to those governing the issue of a warrant by magistrates under section 8 PACE, requires similar considerations to be taken into account by the court.

It is not enough for the officer "blandly to assert that these conditions were met", because the schedule imposed a duty on the judge to be satisfied and the judge had, using Lloyd L.J.'s words in *ex parte Waitt*, "to be scrupulous in discharging that responsibility if the interests of the absent defendant were to be adequately protected."[67] In *ex parte Hill*[67a], an order was first obtained under the Bankers' Books Evidence Act 1879 to inspect bank records relating to Mr Hill and an order was then sought and obtained under section 9 and Schedule 1 of PACE, giving access to the same bank records. However, the officer failed to disclose to the judge that the Bankers' Books Evidence Act application had not been fully utilised.

10.68   The Divisional Court emphasised that the practical effect of recipients such as banks allowing such applications to go by default, was to convert an *inter partes* hearing into an *ex parte* one. Since the customer in such circumstances would be unaware of the application and it was his interests which were most closely affected by it, there was a strict duty on the party applying, to make full disclosure of all matters which might affect the court's decision to make or refuse the order and in particular, to make disclosure of all matters known to the party applying, which might militate against the making of an order,

(a)   if the judge before whom the application is made is to be satisfied of the specific matters listed in paragraph 2 before making an order, he/she must be given sufficient material to form a reliable judgment;

(b)   if he/she has no details of the charges against the defendant, he/she cannot be satisfied that there are reasonable grounds for believing the material is likely to be of substantial value;

(c)   if he/she is not told of the dates covered by the charges, he/she cannot be satisfied there are reasonable grounds for believing the material is likely to be relevant;

---

65 There is no duty on a bank to inform its customer of an application made under PACE nor are they under a duty to contest the application – *Barclays Bank plc v. Taylor* [1989] 3 All E.R. 563.
66 *R. v. Norwich Crown Court ex parte Chethams* [1991] C.O.D. 271.
67 *R. v. Maidstone Crown Court, ex parte Waitt* [1988] Crim. L.R. 384, DC.
67a *R. v. Crown Court at Lewes ex parte Hill* (1991) 93 Cr. App.R. 60.

(d)   unless he/she is told what other efforts have been tried and their outcome, he/she cannot be satisfied that other methods of obtaining the material have been tried without success;

(e)   similarly, he/she cannot be satisfied that a production order would be in the public interest,[68] having regard to the benefit likely to accrue to the investigation, if the material is obtained without any idea of what material already existed.[69]

10.69   Clearly, the officer must describe the offence which is the subject of the investigation in sufficient detail to satisfy the judge that the material sought is "likely to be of substantial value" and that it is likely to be "relevant evidence" – that is, admissible in evidence at a trial for the offence.[70]

10.70   In *R. v. Lewes Crown Court & Chief Constable of Sussex ex parte Weller & Co*[71] a Circuit Judge issued a warrant to enter and search the offices of a firm of solicitors after an *ex parte* application. Unfortunately the judge gave no reasons for his decision. It was contended by the applicant, in relation to the first set of access conditions, that they did not apply when excluded materials are involved. In the circumstances of the case it was submitted that, had the judge addressed his mind to whether the warrant might be directed towards, *inter alia*, excluded material, he must have concluded that excluded material was indeed involved, because the files sought would contain medical records, psychiatric records and social enquiry reports. The court noted, "The reality is that on the information before him the judge could not be satisfied that the first set of access conditions was fulfilled because excluded material was involved".

10.71   Of particular relevance to mutual assistance is the correlation between evidence sought under section 4 of the Criminal Justice (International Co-operation) Act 1990 and that to be obtained under section 7 of the Act.

It is clear from the authorities, and in particular *R. v. Crown Court at Lewes, ex parte Hill*[72] in which Bingham L.J. ruled that,

"the plain intention of the Schedule [1 of PACE] is that the judge should not make an order under the schedule unless he is satisfied that the application is substantially the last resort . . . I do not say that the application can be impugned because it is possible to find some very minor and partial remote step which could have been, and has not been taken, but I do think that the Act requires the judge to be satisfied that other practical methods of obtaining disclosure have been substantially exhausted without success".

Thus, if a request is made and a court nominated under section 4 of the Act, it is

---

68 The public interest requirement in Sched. 2, para. 2(c)(ii) doubtless refers to the duty of confidence owed by the holder of the material to the third party and the release from that duty pursuant to a judicial order.
69 In *R. v. Lewes Crown Court & Chief Constable of Sussex ex parte Nigel Weller & Co.* May 12, 1999 CO/2890/98 the Divisional Court noted that when issuing a warrant to search a solicitor's office "public interest" is not simply a reference to legal privilege because there would be no order for disclosure for material which enjoys such privilege (see s.19(6)) except where the material is held with the intention of furthering a criminal purpose (see s.10(2) PACE) and the value and importance of legal privilege, and the importance of not restricting its scope, was stressed recently by the House of Lords in *R. v. Derby Magistrates' Court ex parte "B"* [1966] 1 A.C. 487. The form of the warrant in the case suggested that no attention had been paid to the problems to which legal privilege would inevitably give rise.
70 s.8(4) PACE.
71 (Unreported) CO/2890/98, May 12, 1999.
72 [1991] 93 Cr. App. R. 60.

submitted that it would be inappropriate to seek a production order under section 7, until all steps have been taken to obtain evidence from the relevant witness under section 4.

This would suggest that if the requesting state fails to obtain the requested evidence through the procedures available under section 4, after service of a witness summons by the nominated court, this can be rectified, subject to the question of oppression (see Chapter 6) by an application under section 7. For instance, if a witness refuses to produce documents, on the grounds that to do so might tend to incriminate him/her but the officer is able to satisfy the other access conditions, namely that the documents sought are both relevant, *i.e.* admissible, and of substantial value to the investigation, they might be obtainable by a later section 7 application under section 9 and Schedule 1 PACE for a production order or if the material sought is non confidential, a search warrant under section 8 PACE. The officer must however first exhaust the section 4 option.

10.72 What does "relevant" mean in these circumstances? In the *Reading Justices*[73] case Simon Brown L.J. ruled that a witness summons could not be used to obtain documents merely required for the possibility of cross examination of a witness for they were not admissible in evidence.

This would suggest that if the purpose of a production order or search warrant is merely to obtain documents required for the possibility of cross examination, these would not be admissible, and if not admissible they could not be "relevant evidence" (as defined in PACE), in which event a judge or magistrate should refuse an application for a production order or search warrant. Some doubt is cast upon such a proposition by remarks made also by Simon Brown L.J. in the *Finninvest*[74] case where it was argued by the applicants that the search warrant and section 2(3) notice, as well as the letter of request, were too wide.

10.73 They argued that the word "evidence" in sections 4(1)(b) and 4(2A) of the Criminal Justice (International Co-operation) Act 1990 had a special meaning in relation to mutual assistance. Reliance was placed by the applicants on Viscount Dilhorne's speech in *Rio Tinto Zinc Corporation v. Westinghouse Electric Corporation*[75] in which he defined the evidence required as "... direct evidence for use at a trial as contrasted with information which may lead to the discovery of evidence ..." and upon Kerr L.J.'s definition of "fishing" in *Re* State of Norway's application.[76]

> "[Fishing] arises in cases where what is sought is not evidence as such, but information which may lead to a line of enquiry which would disclose evidence. It is the search for material in the hope of being able to raise allegations of fact, as opposed to the elicitation of evidence to support allegations of fact, which have been raised bona fide with adequate particularisation".

10.74 Simon Brown L.J. stated that the meaning of "evidence" in the context of an application under the 1990 Act was not identical to that made under the legislation applicable to the authorities quoted immediately above, the Evidence (Proceedings in Other Jurisdictions) Act 1975.

That Act was limited to evidence required for civil proceedings whether instituted or contemplated, and criminal proceedings once instituted. The 1990 Act, however, provided for the obtaining of evidence in connection with a criminal investigation.

---

73 R. v. Reading Justices ex parte Berkshire County Council [1996] 1 Cr. App. R. 239.
74 R. v. The Secretary of State for the Home Department ex parte Finninvest SpA [1997] 1 All E.R. 942.
75 [1978] A.C. 547 at 619.
76 [1987] 1Q.B. 433 at 482.

"Inevitably there is some flexibility in the whole concept of evidence – not even the applicants submit, for example, that what may be sought under the 1990 Act must be "likely to be material evidence" within the meaning of section 97(1) of the Magistrates' Courts Act 1980 as explained in *R. v. Reading Justices ex parte Berkshire County Council*.[77] When, therefore, one is speaking of "evidence" in the context of a criminal investigation, the permissible area of search must inevitably be wider than once that investigation is complete and the prosecution's concern is rather to prove an already investigated and "instituted" case.

The 1990 Act in short created a wholly new scheme for mutual assistance with regard to criminal investigations. A scheme under which it would plainly be necessary to examine altogether more material than would ultimately constitute evidence at any trial."

10.75   He could not accept that by the use of the word "evidence" Parliament could have intended to confine assistance within the narrow parameters of *Westinghouse* and *Re Norway*.

In applying these remarks to the warrant itself which arose at the investigative stage of an enquiry into a wide-ranging, multi-faceted international fraud, he ruled that there could not be greater particularisation of the offences than that given in the letter of request which was as precise and focussed as such a request could be in the circumstances.

10.76   It is unfortunate that in the context of the case itself, no argument appears to have been directed at the test of relevance that the magistrate was required to undertake prior to the issue of the search warrant, other than in the context of the argument that the search warrant authorised a fishing expedition.

Rather, the court imposed a duty upon those assisting the requesting state in the search, in this instance, the SFO, to assess the relevance of the material once it had been seized.

"It is impossible to know just what documents are both in London and relevant. To discover that, it is necessary to find, examine and appraise them . . . Insofar as any of the documents seized prove not to be, they will not be transmitted . . ."

Unfortunately he did not define "relevance" in such a context although it would seem sensible to assume that it meant either relevant to an issue arising in the criminal proceedings or "admissible in evidence at a trial for the offence" (PACE).

It is clear that he anticipated in his remarks that material could lawfully be seized that was not relevant hence the need for the post search examination and elimination.

There appears to be a contradiction in the interpretation of relevance which can perhaps only be reconciled in Simon Brown L.J.'s explanation that if the evidence is sought at the investigative stage, the test of relevance is much wider than that once proceedings have commenced.

10.77   The second set of access conditions arise from the effect of section 9(2) PACE which prevents a magistrate from issuing a warrant under a pre-existing statute if the material sought is legally privileged, excluded or special procedure material in documentary form. Whilst the former can never be obtained, the latter two categories can be obtained, after application to a Circuit Judge under Schedule 1 paragraph 3. Such material would, were it not for section 9(2) PACE, have been obtainable under

---

a warrant issued by a magistrates' court. It should be noted that the offence in question need not be a serious arrestable offence.

(b) Application for a warrant to search for excluded and special procedure material

10.78   It is hardly surprising that the only effective difference between the provisions of Schedule 1 paragraphs 12 to 14, which apply to an application for a warrant under Schedule 1 of PACE, and the provisions of section 8 PACE (see page 95 above) is that contained in paragraph 14(c), that the material sought is subject to a restriction, or obligation of confidentiality, which disclosure of the material sought will breach, unless a warrant is issued.

Thus the considerations obtaining to applications for warrants are of similar applicability to those in relation to applications for warrants under Schedule 1.

Whilst in normal circumstances the application will be made *ex parte*, there may be circumstances, particularly in relation to a warrant issued when the first set of access conditions are satisfied, when the application can be made inter partes.[78]

10.79   Code B at 2.4 provides that no application for a production order may be made without the authority of an officer of at least the rank of superintendent; Code B 2.7 provides that an application for a search warrant under paragraph 12(a) of Schedule 1 to PACE shall, where appropriate, indicate why it is believed that service of notice of an application for a production order may seriously prejudice the investigation.

Specific reference was made by the court in *Gross*[79] to the authority of *R. v. Southampton Crown Court, ex parte J & P.*[80] Lord Justice Brooke stated that it would, in his judgment, be desirable if the following passage of the former Deputy Chief Justice was drawn to the attention of every Circuit Judge who is likely to be concerned with applications to grant search warrants under Schedule 1 of PACE:

"The Act does not require a Circuit Judge to give reasons when making an order inter partes or issuing a warrant *ex parte* for access to special procedure material. However, challenges to decisions of Circuit Judges which have come before this court demonstrate, in my opinion, especially as to ex parte applications, the need for this to be done. Reasons need not be elaborate, but they should be recorded and be sufficient to identify the substance of any relevant information or representation put before the judge in addition to the written information. They should set out what inferences he has drawn from the material relevant to the statutory conditions governing the content and form of the order or warrant sought. Where he has considered the question of legal privilege he should explain why, if he does, he has included in the order or warrant material which is prima facie privileged, or why he has excluded material as subject to privilege. In the latter case, where the excluded material consists of particular documents or categories of documents which might otherwise be included in the material to which access is given, he should carefully describe and identify them in the order or warrant.

These requirements may seem onerous for the exercise of a power to which the police often seek recourse as a matter of urgency but a Circuit Judge has responsibility not only to assist the effective investigation of crime, but also to

---

78 See *R. v. Crown Court at Southampton, ex parte J & P* [1993] Crim. L.R. 962 and below.
79 [1998] C.O.D. 445, QBD.
80 [1993] Crim. L.R. 962.

protect as needs be the holder of and person in respect of whom he holds material in confidence from unjustified intrusion into their private affairs."

10.80 In *R. v. Lewes Crown Court & Chief Constable of Sussex ex parte Nigel Weller & Co*[81] an application was made to a Circuit Judge *ex parte* under section 9 of PACE and a warrant issued to enter and search the offices of a firm of solicitors. The judge gave no reasons.

Kennedy L.J. noted:—

"A regrettable feature is that yet again a Circuit Judge exercising the necessary but draconian power granted to him by the 1984 Act has failed to give reasons for his decision."

10.81 Having referred to Watkins L.J.'s dicta in the *Southampton Crown Court* case he continued by accepting that if, despite the lack of reasons, the court was able to discern adequate reasons for the judge's decision, an appeal may fail. "Hard pressed Circuit Judges" may not always find it easy to remember to give reasons when they have no more assistance than that provided by a police officer on his own making what doubtless the officer regards as a formal ex parte application.[82]

However, as the court stated:—

"The reality is that—

(1)   the person or persons against whom an order has been made are entitled to know why it is made;
(2)   the requirement to give reasons should help to ensure that a judge does, as he must, address each of the statutory requirements before making the order; and
(3)   if it is necessary to review an order in this court, reasons will be of great assistance. We will know why the judge decided as he did".

Lord Justice Brooke continued in *Gross*:

"The courts will, of course, not place any obstacles in the way of those who act within the powers given to them by Parliament to investigate and prosecute serious crime. This case, however, has revealed a degree of sloppiness by those concerned with the seeking, granting and execution of warrants which is not acceptable, particularly as some of the submissions we receive from the respondents might be interpreted as evincing an attitude that adherence to the detailed rules set out by Parliament and in the Code of Police Practice does not really matter. It does."

10.82 As was highlighted in *Gross v. Crown Court at Southwark*,[83] Code B 5.13 stipulates that an officer of the rank of inspector or above should take charge of and be present at a search made under a warrant issued under Schedule 1, to ensure that the search is carried out with discretion and as little disruption as possible to business or other activities carried out on the premises. The court also emphasised that an amendment to the final draft of Code B (B.2.4) required the authority of an officer of

---

81 CO/2890/98, May 12, 1999.
82 Some Circuit Judges have indicated that such applications should preferably be made by Counsel.
83 *Gross v. The Crown Court at Southwark* [1998] C.O.D. 445, QBD.

at least the rank of superintendent for an application for a production order or a warrant under Schedule 1 of PACE, although this requirement was omitted, apparently by inadvertence, from the first three impressions of the Code published by HMSO.

Passing reference should also be made to other statutory provisions allowing access to the courts for search and seizure orders.

The Drug Trafficking Act 1994

10.83 This Act, which incorporates certain provisions of the Criminal Justice (International Co-operation) Act 1990 is aimed at empowering the United Kingdom courts to recover the proceeds of drug trafficking; its effectiveness will be discussed below in Chapter 12 in relation to forfeiture and confiscation.

Drug trafficking is almost by definition, international, and thus the relevant provisions of PACE are inadequate, as they are confined to serious arrestable offences within the jurisdiction. "Drug trafficking offences" to which this Act applies relates to acts and offences committed outside the jurisdiction of the United Kingdom. The major provisions are:

10.84 Section 55 This empowers the court to make an order for the purposes of an investigation into drug trafficking. Drug Trafficking is widely defined to include doing, or being concerned in the production, supply, transportation, importation or exportation of controlled drugs, manufacture or supply of scheduled substances, use of any ship for illicit traffic of controlled drugs, concealment or transfer, acquisition, possession or use or handling of the proceeds of drug trafficking.

The application is made *ex parte* to a Judge in Chambers, who need only be satisfied, on reasonable grounds for *suspicion*, that the person specified in the application has carried on, or has benefitted from drugs trafficking, or that the material to which the application relates is likely to be of substantial value to the investigation and does not consist of or include items subject to legal professional or excluded material. The requirement of reasonable grounds for belief in the public interest, similar to that under PACE Schedule 1 paragraph 2(c), is also necessary. It will be noted that only LPP and excluded material are accepted, as there is no reference to special procedure material. Due to the exceptionally draconian and *ex parte* nature of these powers, then clearly the courts will require particularity and full disclosure from the police.

Section 56 This section authorises the issue of a search warrant by a Circuit Judge in relation to drug trafficking offences which by the definition of the offence do not require to have been committed within the jurisdiction.

Tipping-off Particular care should be taken to ensure that, where an order under section 55 has been made, or a warrant issued under section 56, any person knowing or suspecting that an investigation is taking place makes no disclosure which is likely to prejudice the investigation. The exception in relation to legal advice has already been remarked upon above.[84]

Proceeds of Crime Act 1995

10.85 This Act amends Part VI of the Criminal Justice Act 1988 and empowers the court to confiscate the proceeds of certain offences both indictable and summary.

---

84 p. 117.

The most specific provisions are those contained in sections 93H to 93J of the Criminal Justice Act 1988 as amended by the Proceeds of Crime Act 1995. Under section 93H a constable may apply to a Circuit Judge for an order, similar to that under section 55 of the Drug Trafficking Act 1994, for the purpose of an investigation into whether a person has benefitted from any criminal conduct, or into the extent or the whereabouts of the proceeds of any criminal conduct, in relation to particular material, or material of a particular description. Legally privileged and excluded material are excepted from the scope of the order.

Under section 93J, a constable may apply to a Circuit Judge for a warrant authorising entry, search for and seizure of other than legally privileged or excluded material, which is likely to be of substantial value to an investigation, for which purpose the warrant was issued. This follows the form of the section 56 Drug Trafficking Act 1994 warrant provisions. The tipping-off provisions apply.

Criminal Justice Act 1987

10.86   Section 2 of the Act provides to the Serious Fraud Office investigative powers covered elsewhere at Chapter 13.

The Bankers' Books Evidence Act 1879

10.87   Schedule 1 paragraph 6 of the Criminal Justice (International Co-operation) Act 1990 states in relation to proceedings before a nominated court that: "For the avoidance of doubt it is hereby declared that the BBEA applies to the proceedings as it applies to other proceedings before the court".

Thus, proceedings before a nominated court under section 4 of the 1990 Act are to be proceedings to which the provisions of the Bankers' Books Evidence Act applies.

Prior to the passing of the Police and Criminal Evidence Act 1984 and the procedures provided by section 9(2) and Schedule 1 of the Act, reliance was often placed by the investigating authorities upon the provisions of section 7 of the Bankers' Books Evidence Act 1879. The section provides:

> 7 On the application of any party to a legal proceeding, a court or judge may order that such party be at liberty to inspect and take copies of any entries in a banker's book for any of the purposes of such proceedings. An order under this section may be made either with or without summoning the bank or any other party, and shall be served on the bank three clear days before the same is to be obeyed, unless the court or judge otherwise directs.

This provision, used now to a much lesser extent, is subject to the following qualifications:—

(a)   It is not confined to serious arrestable offences.

(b)   It is, however, confined to banks and bankers' books (which will not include other records such as notes, diaries etc).

(c)   Proceedings, whether civil or criminal, must have been instituted.

(d)   It does not require dual criminality unlike other provisions referred to above.

The early cases upon the proper interpretation of this section laid the grounds for the courts' unwillingness to countenance oppression under PACE: thus, fishing expeditions are excluded; the order must be limited, as to the period of disclosure of the bank account, to a period strictly relevant to the charge before the court.[85] Whilst the section expressly permits ex parte applications "there is much to be said for notice being given. There is much to be said for a frank attitude in all criminal proceedings."[86]

---

85 *Williams v. Summerfield* [1972] 2 Q.B. 513.
86 *R. v. Marlborough Street Magistrates' Court Metropolitan Stipendiary Magistrate, ex parte Simpson,* 70 Cr. App. R. 291.

Chapter 11

Search and Seizure in the United Kingdom for the Purpose of Investigations and Proceedings Abroad – Seizure and After

Execution of warrant and conduct of searches

11.00   The procedure for the execution of warrants is set out in section 16 of PACE and is supplemented by the Code of Practice.

The relevant provisions apply equally to warrants obtained as a result of an international letter of request and to warrants obtained under other legislations.

16 Execution of warrants

   (1)   A warrant to enter and search premises may be executed by any constable.

   (2)   Such a warrant may authorise persons to accompany any constable who is executing it.

   (3)   Entry and search under a warrant must be within one month from the date of its issue.

   (8)   A search under a warrant may only be a search to the extent required for the purpose for which the warrant was issued.

Who is authorised to enter and search?

Execution by a constable

11.01   A warrant may be executed "by any constable" – not a reference to rank but rather to office. The Home Office Consolidated Circulars (1977) suggest that wherever possible an officer of the rank of inspector of above should be in charge of executing a warrant. In relation to warrants issued under Schedule 1 of PACE, Code of Practice B 5.13 directs that "An officer of the rank of inspector or above shall take charge of and be present at any search".

Authority for other persons to be present

11.02   Under section 16(2) other persons may be authorised to accompany the constable who is executing the warrant.

In *R. v. Reading Justices, ex parte South West Meat Ltd*,[1] the police obtained a warrant on behalf of the Meat Intervention Board, a Government department with no powers to enter and search premises. The warrant failed to include officers of the Board and it was held they had no right to enter the premises.

---

1 [1992] C.L.R. 672.

This requirement is of considerable relevance to mutual assistance. Home Office Circular No. 16 of 1997 at paragraph 65 permits an overseas officer to observe only the application for the warrant and its execution and nothing else.

Where a request from a foreign country includes a request for its officers to attend at the execution of a search, the information will expressly narrate this and the warrant will include details of the names of the officers authorised to be present. They are of course not permitted themselves to search or to question the occupants. Their presence is solely to assist the United Kingdom searching officers in identifying "relevant material" (see below, p. 153).

11.03   In *Gross v. Southwark Crown Court & Ors*[2] the United States authorities sent a letter of request to the Secretary of State requesting seizure of certain documents. The Secretary of State made a direction to the Metropolitan Police Fraud Department that an application be made for a warrant under paragraph 12(a) of Schedule 1 of PACE.[3] Two Metropolitan Police officers executed the warrant, taking with them a Mr Moore, an official of the United States investigating agency that had been dealing with the matter since its inception but who was not named in the warrant. What happened at the premises was set out in the affidavit of one of the English officers:-

> "10. DC Richards, Mr Moore and I arrived at the address to be searched at about 8 am. The door was answered by Mr Jack Gross who was wearing a dressing gown. I introduced myself, DC Richards and Mr Fred Moore to Mr Gross and showed him my warrant card. I informed him that I had a search warrant authorising a search of the address. Mr Gross immediately invited us into the house and led us into the front room where we sat down. I then showed the original search warrant to Mr Gross. I explained that the American author-ities had sought the assistance of the Home Office in their investigation of his son and that a search warrant had been granted to search for and seize documents in relation to that case. Mr Moore showed his badge to Mr Gross ... There was then a brief conversation between Mr Moore and Mr Gross regarding an offer of immunity from prosecution to Mr Gross in return for assisting the DCIS and giving evidence against his son (the subject of the criminal proceedings in the United States in which the request for assistance had been made). Mr Gross dismissed this ... It was explained to Mr Gross that we had a warrant to search the premises and that we were looking for documents that his son had shipped over to this address. I informed Mr Gross that we would like Mr Moore to be present whilst we searched to identify any documents suitable for the investiga-tion. I reassured Mr Gross that Mr Moore would have no authority to be involved in the search. Mr Gross said that he was concerned about documents which were subject to legal privilege and concerned in the defence of his son's case and he did not wish Mr Moore to have sight of these documents, partic-ularly sworn affidavits. I reassured him again of the reason for Mr Moore's presence, which was to facilitate the search by identifying documents shown to him, but that he would not participate in the search itself. Mr Gross made no objection to this ... It must be borne in mind that we were expecting to have to search a vast number of documents. Mr Moore's presence in the house made the search much shorter than it would otherwise have been. I wish to stress that Mr Gross made no objection to Mr Moore's presence or to us assisting him in the way proposed."

---

2 [1998] C.O.D. 445, QB.
3 The manner in which that application was made falls for consideration below.

The officer described how they went to the garage where the documents were stored in cartons.

> "13. I left the room together with Mr Gross and Mr Moore whilst DC Richards finished writing down the questions and answers. Mrs Gross remained in the room for a few moments, but then followed us en route to the garage. DC Richards drew to my attention that there were legal documents in the garage relating to the defence of (her son) Robert Gross which they were particularly concerned Fred Moore would get sight of. I again informed Mr & Mrs Gross that we would still like Mr Moore to be present, but assured them that he would not be involved in a search nor have sight of these documents. I must emphasise again that there was no objection by Mr or Mrs Gross and had they objected at any time, I would have had no hesitation in telling Mr Moore to leave the premises and wait until the search was completed."

11.04   There was a factual dispute between the officer and Mr and Mrs Gross as to whether Mr Moore had started looking at the contents of the cartons whilst the two officers were absent.

There was considerable criticism over the role played by Mr Moore.

Brooke L.J. described the American criminal investigator's actions as those of someone "not named on the warrant, entering Mr Gross' house unlawfully as a trespasser when the warrant was executed and behaving inappropriately once he had entered it by seeking to bargain with him over immunity from prosecution".

11.05   In his judgment, Rougier J. stated,

> "Far more serious, however, to my mind, is the criticism concerning the presence and activities of Mr Moore. Mr Moore was not named on the warrant as being authorised to accompany the Detective Constables; according to the affidavit of Detective Constable Kingsford, when the door was opened by (Mr Gross) in his dressing gown, the three persons were introduced by no more than names, and it was not until he was inside the living room, admittedly by invitation, that any attempt was made to indicate who Mr Moore was or why he was there".

Having referred to the contents of Home Office Circular No. 16 of 1997, he continued,

> "In my judgment, if such a person is to be authorised to enter the premises he must be named on the warrant and if he is not, then any entry by him before his status and identity has been revealed to the occupier, and the latter's permission has been given, is unlawful and, in my judgment, that unlawfulness taints the entire proceedings of entry. It is also considerably aggravated by the fact that, almost at once, Mr Moore started offering Mr Gross some form of immunity from prosecution, an offer which contains a distinctly minatory corollary."

11.06   Counsel for the police sought to argue that, although Mr Moore was a trespasser in the circumstances in which he entered the Gross' house, there was no breach of section 16(2) of PACE. The court rejected this argument. Section 16(1) PACE provides that

> "a warrant to enter and search the premises may be executed by any constable, which has the inevitable inference that nobody else is permitted to do so and, in my view, the same reasoning applies to sub-section (2)".

In colourful language, the court continued,

> "If DC Kingsford had taken with him five burly members of what is colloquially referred to as "the Heavy Mob", with all their threatening implications, this would undoubtedly have constituted an unlawful entry; in my judgment, the unauthorised entry of Mr Moore, coupled with his officer, falls into the same category, although of a lesser degree."

Duration of validity of a warrant

A warrant must be executed within one month from the date of its issue. There are normally no problems in this connection.

The extent of the warrant and the procedure on search

11.07 The specific provisions of section 7(3) of the Criminal Justice (International Co-operation) Act 1990 apply to searches made pursuant to section 7(2) of the Act.

Thus if a warrant is issued to search premises in the United Kingdom, occupied or controlled by a person who has been proceeded against outside the United Kingdom, or who has been arrested in the course of an investigation in that country for an offence which would have been an arrestable offence within the meaning of section 24 PACE, the power to search those premises is limited to the extent that is reasonably required for the purposes of discovering such evidence as is mentioned in the warrant.

In general, the search may only extend to the purpose for which the warrant was issued (section 16(8) PACE).

11.08 The provisions of section 19 of PACE enable a constable, who is lawfully on any premises (which includes his/her presence in executing a search warrant) to seize anything which is on the premises if he/she has reasonable grounds for believing—

(a) that it is evidence in relation to an offence which he is investigating or *any other offence*; and

(b) that it is necessary to seize it in order to prevent the evidence being concealed, lost, altered or destroyed.

It is arguable that once an officer starts to search beyond the scope of the warrant he/she may no longer be acting lawfully and thereby the provisions of Section 19 would not apply.

The question arises as to whether this provision entitles the officer to seize evidence of any other offence in the Requesting State?

11.09 In *R. v. Southwark Crown Court & Anor ex parte Sorsky Defries*[4] the United States authorities sent a letter of request to the Secretary of State who, pursuant to section 7(4) of the 1990 Act, directed Customs and Excise to apply for a search warrant under section 9 and Schedule 1 of PACE. Customs and Excise applied (ex parte) to Southwark Crown Court for a search warrant to search the premises of the applicants who were a firm of accountants. The warrant was issued and executed. The applicants later successfully challenged the issue of the warrant on the grounds that the judge failed to act with the care and caution required in dealing with PACE

---

4 [1996] Crim. L.R. 195.

Schedule 1 applications for special procedure material.[5] Furthermore, the applicants challenged the seizure under the warrant of documents which they argued fell outside its scope. It was contended that those executing the warrant seized not only documents which were covered by it, but also some which were outside it. The respondents did not dispute this but contended that the documents falling without the warrant which were taken away were not searched for but "were stumbled upon in the course of the lawful search" and were seized because those conducting the search had reasonable grounds for believing that they were evidence "in relation to . . . any other offence" with in section 19(3) of PACE.

The court was in no doubt that "any other offence" in section 19 of the 1994 Act refers to *domestic* offences only.

> "On the passing of the Criminal Justice (International Cooperation) Act 1990 it was necessary to incorporate Section 7(1) to provide that Part II of the 1984 Act (PACE) was to have effect as if references to serious arrestable offences in Section 8 and Schedule 1 of that Act included any conduct which is an offence under the law of a country or territory outside the United Kingdom and would constitute a serious arrestable offence if it had occurred in any part of the United Kingdom. That section . . . confirms the view that without that amendment those offences would not have covered offences outside the United Kingdom. That very provision militates against a construction that allows "offence" elsewhere in Part II of the 1984 Act to include a foreign offence."

11.10 The court held that on that basis, even had the warrant been lawfully issued, the seizure of the documents without the warrant was unlawful. The search therefore went outside the purpose of the warrant, thereby rendering it unlawful. Furthermore, the seizure of documents actually covered by the warrant was unlawful as well.

Therefore, in executing a search warrant under section 7 an officer is not entitled to seize evidence of any other offence in the requesting state. If however, he/she sees evidence of offences not covered in the warrant, but appearing to be offences under English law, it is submitted that we would be entitled to seize this under section 19.

Execution of warrants between England and Wales and Scotland

11.11 Whilst the provisions described above permit the use of the provisions of Schedule 1 PACE to execute search warrants for excluded/special procedure material following upon a request from a foreign state, curiously such assistance is not available in relation to requests from within the United Kingdom.

If a police force in England and Wales wishes to obtain a warrant to search for excluded/special procedure material in Scotland, or the Scottish police require a similar warrant to search premises in England or Wales, there is no power for the warrant to be executed (*R. v. Manchester Stipendiary Magistrate, ex parte Granada Television Ltd* [1999] C.L.R. 162).[6]

Ministerial duty

11.12 Section 7 (4) of the 1990 Act provides that:

> "(4) No application for a warrant or order should be made by virtue of sub-

---

5 See pp. 128–9 below.
6 For a helpful analysis of the reasons, reference should be made to Elizabeth Franey "An anomalous state of affairs", *New Law Journal*, June 4, 1999.

section (1) or (2) above except in pursuance of a direction given by the Secretary of State in response to a request received—

(a) from a court or tribunal exercising criminal jurisdiction in the overseas country or territory in question or a prosecuting authority in that country or territory; or

(b) from any other authority in that country or territory which appears to him to have the function of making a request for the purposes of this section;

and any evidence seized by a constable by virtue of this section shall be furnished by him to the Secretary of State for transmission to that court, tribunal or authority."

11.13 If, in order to comply with the request, it is necessary for any such evidence to be accompanied by any certificate, affidavit or other verifying document, then the constable shall also furnish for transmission such document of that nature as may be specified in the direction by the Secretary of State.[7]

Where the evidence consists of a document, the original or a copy shall be transmitted, and where it consists of any other article, the article itself, or a description, photograph or other representation of it shall be transmitted, as may be necessary, in order to comply with the request.[8]

It seems clear from the judgment of Simon Brown L.J. in *Finninvest*[9] that provided only and always that the request is essentially one for evidence, the possibility that it extends too far is not something that need concern the Secretary of State; rather it is a matter for consideration by those applying for the warrant or order. Similarly, it would be a matter for the court in those cases where the Secretary of State nominates a court under section 4 (2) of the 1990 Act.

Aspects of the extent and nature of the Minister's duty have been considered by three separate Divisional Courts.

Propend[10]

Nature of Secretary of State's responsibilities

11.14 The nature of the Secretary of State's responsibilities under section 7 (4) of the 1990 Act was first considered by the Divisional Court by Laws J. in *R. v. C.C.C. ex parte Propend Finance Property Limited*.

In *Propend* the form of the direction made by the Secretary of State gave the Metropolitan Police a choice as to the nature of application they should make for search and seizure. Under the direction it was left to the police to decide whether they should make:—

(a) an application for a warrant under section 7 (2) of the 1990 Act; or

(b) an application for a warrant under section 8 of PACE; or

(c) an application for a production order under paragraph 4 of Schedule I of PACE; or

---

7 The Criminal Justice (International Co-operation) Act 1990, s. 7(5).
8 The Criminal Justice (International Co-operation) Act 1990, s. 7(6).
9 *R. v. Secretary of State for the Home Department ex parte Finnivest SpA* [1997] 1 All E.R. 942.
10 [1996] Cr. App. R. 26.

(d) an application for a search warrant under paragraph 12 of Schedule I of PACE.

11.15   This effectively left to the police the decision whether the documents that were sought included excluded material or special procedure material, and if they did, to decide which of the Schedule I remedies available from a Circuit Judge should be sought.

Laws J. accepted the submission that the Secretary of State was not entitled to confer a discretion on the police as to the route they were to follow. He must decide what type of application was appropriate and direct the police accordingly.

"The question is whether the statute can be construed so as to allow the Secretary of State to choose whether to give little, much, or no discretion to the police as to how the direction is to be fulfilled. How is he to arrive at such a choice? If he decides upon a unitary direction, that must be because he has concluded that no form of application save that which he has directed is appropriate; in that case he will himself have made a judgement that only the application which he has specified ought to be made. If he gives a multiple direction of the kind in question here, that could hardly be on the basis that any of the forms of application specified by him is appropriate – since, for example, any particular case cannot be fit both for an *ex parte* application for a warrant and an inter partes application for a production order, nor can any individual case be fit for both a section 8 application (which would not cover special procedure material) and a Schedule I application (which would).

In short, the different forms of application are in large measure mutually consistent. So the premise of a multi-direction must be that (1) the Secretary of State has made no judgment as to the aptness of any particular application and (2) one or more of the forms of application covered by the direction is actually inappropriate, since they cannot all be appropriate. Mr Richards' (Counsel for the Minister) submission thus involves the proposition that a direction may lawfully authorise forms of application at least one of which ought not to be made at all. It would be very surprising if that were right.

In the present case, the Secretary of State acknowledges that no application under section 7 (2) could be made (because no-one had been charged or arrested), even though such an application is covered by his direction. A multi-direction could only be lawful if, on it's true construction, the statute contemplated that the police should have the duty to decide, if the Secretary of State chose to confer such a duty, whether any particular form of application should be made at all. We do no believe that the Act can be read as distributing such contingent and differential functions between the Secretary of State and the police force.

In our judgment, the Secretary of State has not only the responsibility of deciding whether assistance should be given to the requesting state; in our view he must also decide what assistance should so be given. *Section 7 (4) authorises only a unitary direction, specifying a particular form of application.* (author's emphasis). We reach this conclusion without assistance from Mr Jones' (Counsel for the applicant) submission that the construction of section 7 (4) is coloured by section 4, which in our view deals with an entirely different state of affairs from that contemplated by section 7.

It was submitted to us by Mr Richards that the police possess an experience and expertise in the administration of the PACE procedures which the Secretary of State does not share. But he has specific responsibilities under the Act of 1984 to oversee certain processes by the police: see section 66. So that submission does not, in our judgment, assist the Secretary of State. Accordingly we would conclude this point against the Secretary of State".

R. v. Bow Street Magistrates Court ex parte M; R. v. Serious Fraud Office ex parte S[11]

Transmission of evidence by the Secretary of State

11.16 On the question of transmission of the evidence obtained under the warrants, which were subsequently quashed, Pill L.J. considered as "a very unsatisfactory" feature of the operation, the fact that

> "the disks and documents taken from (the solicitors home address) were transmitted unsorted to the United States. No copies were taken. In the absence of an application for interim relief, it is submitted (the SFO) was entitled to forward and (the Home Secretary) to send the documents out of the jurisdiction. I reject that submission. Inaction by those subject to the search did not relieve (the SFO's) staff of the duty to retain only what they were entitled to retain and the duty to assess the relevance of what was seized and whether it is covered by legal privilege. To send the material out of the jurisdiction was to compound the error".

11.17 Having quashed the warrants, the court then turned to the Secretary of State's responsibility. It was submitted that he should not have transmitted to the United States documents forwarded to him by the SFO. The SFO argued that, while the Secretary of State has a discretion not to transmit the documents, he is not under a duty to review the evidence and form his own judgment on issues of relevance and legal privilege. As the warrants had been quashed for the reasons set out elsewhere, it was not necessary for the court to consider the extent of the Secretary of State's duty in these regards. However, the court indicated that "the statute does not empower the Secretary of State to send out of the jurisdiction documents unlawfully obtained. While the default may be that of the SFO the documents have been transmitted unlawfully".

Gross v. Crown Court at Southwark[12]

Transmission of evidence by Secretary of State

11.18 Having quashed the warrants, the Divisional Court considered the position of the Secretary of State. The only decision by the Secretary of State which was attacked was that to transmit to the United States the documents that had been seized in the execution of the warrant. The applicants sought, *inter alia*, a declaration that the Secretary of State acted irrationally, in allowing what turned out to have been only seven days to elapse, after the seizure, before transmitting the documents abroad, and a declaration that the Secretary of State acted unlawfully, in transmitting abroad legally privileged material, which was seized when the warrant was executed. In so doing they sought to rely upon the judgement of the Divisional Court in *ex parte* Montgomery.

11.19 However, with regret, the Divisional Court found itself unable to grant the relief sought.

---

11 (Unreported) April 7, 1998 DC. See pp. 103–106.
12 (Unreported) CO/1759/98, July 24, 1998.

"On the evidence before us the Secretary of State in good faith transmitted documents to the United States which had been seized by the police in execution of a warrant granted by a circuit judge. In my judgement there can be no question of his acting unlawfully, even if the warrant is subsequently set aside. The granting of the warrant by a judge made lawful what would otherwise have been unlawful, and the Secretary of State was bound to forward the purposes of Parliament in Section 7(4) of the Criminal Justice (International Cooperation) Act 1990 ("the 1990 Act"), once the evidence seized by the police by virtue of the direction he had given them was furnished by them to him for transmission abroad. The fact that we are today quashing the warrant does not make unlawful what was previously lawful – and, indeed, constituted the Secretary of State's duty – any more than the setting aside of a prison sentence by an appellate court renders the jailers liable for unlawfully detaining the prisoner in reliance on the order of the sentencing court until such time as the sentence was set aside."

Secretary of State's direction

11.20   Having disagreed with its brethren in *ex parte M*, the Court then turned to the judgment of Laws J. in *Propend*.

It was the Court's view that a direction in the unitary form recommended in *Propend*

"puts the police in a straight jacket if, after making the enquiries they are bound to make, they are not satisfied that the Schedule I criteria for applying *ex parte* for a search warrant, as opposed to applying inter partes for an order to produce documents, are fulfilled. Section 7(1) of the 1990 Act applies Part II of PACE for cases of this type, and in order to apply for a search warrant the circuit judge has to be satisfied that the service of the notice of an application for an order may seriously prejudice the investigation.

Code B2 of PACE places the responsibility to make appropriate enquiries fairly and squarely on the shoulders of the police who are considering whether to apply for a search warrant. Relevant paragraphs read:

> B2.3 The officer shall ... make reasonable enquiries to establish what, if anything, is known about the likely occupier of the premises ...
> B2.4 No application for a search warrant may be made without the authority of an officer of at least the rank of inspector ...

Indeed, it appeared from Archbold (1998 ed., p. 1247) that an amendment to the final draft of Code B required the authority of an officer, of at least the rank of superintendent, for an application for a production order or a warrant under Schedule I of PACE, although this requirement was omitted, apparently by inadvertence, from the first three impressions of the Code published by HMSO.

Paragraphs B2.6 and B2.7 provide that an application for a search warrant must be supported by an information in writing specifying *inter alia*, the grounds on which the application is made and if, as here, a search warrant under paragraph 12 (a) of Schedule I to PACE is sought, the application shall also indicate why it is believed that the service of notice of an application for a production order may seriously prejudice the investigation."

Having criticised the lack of enquiry made by the police into Professor Gross and his wife (see above, page 130) the court continued:

"It may be that if the police had made enquiries about Professor Gross of their United States counterparts they might have drawn a blank. It may be that if they had told the judge something about Professor Gross' history they might still have persuaded him to issue a search warrant, because the prohibition on disposing of the material, which is contained in paragraph 11 of Schedule I, appears, on the face of it, to lack teeth, although we did not hear argument on this point. But the fact that Code B places the onus on the police to make reasonable enquiries to establish what if anything is known about the likely occupier of the premises, made me doubtful about the correctness of Laws J.s conclusion that the Act cannot be read as distributing what he called contingent and differential functions between the Secretary of State and the police.

Unless the language of the statute forbids it, it appears to me to be desirable in a case of this kind that the Secretary of State, having considered the nature of the documents being requested and concluded that they consist of special procedure material, or include such material and do not include excluded material, should be able, if the request he has received permits it, to direct the police to apply for whichever of a production order or search warrant under Schedule I of PACE appears to them to be appropriate once they have completed the enquiries required by their Code of Practice.

When I turn back to section 7 of the 1990 Act, it appears to me that the Secretary of State is entitled to give such a direction. Once the police had completed their enquiries and have satisfied themselves as to the appropriateness of the remedy they were seeking, they would be making their application in pursuance of the direction of the Secretary of State and the requirements of Section 7 (4) of the Act would be satisfied.

It follows that I consider that Laws J. was wrong to construe section 7 quite so restrictively. I should add that I do not consider the fact that section 66 of PACE gives the Secretary of State a duty to issue Codes of Practice takes the argument any further. If anything turned on the point, therefore, I would not have been willing to follow Laws J. in that part of his judgment. It might be, however, that if the terms of the Letter of Request had been more widely framed, and the Secretary of State had not felt banned by the decision in *Propend* to make what Laws J. calls a "unitary direction", the police might have been more conscious of the responsibility which the Code of Practice lays on them to satisfy themselves, through an officer of the appropriate senior rank, that an application for a search warrant, as opposed to a production order, was justified."

Pre-transmission Disclosure

11.21 Evidence seized pursuant to a warrant or order under section 7 (1) or a warrant under section 7 (2) must be furnished by the police or customs officer to the Secretary of State for transmission to the requesting court, tribunal or authority, together with any certificate, affidavit or other verifying document specified in the Secretary of State's direction and required in order to comply with the request.

It is, of course, commonplace for officers from the requesting state to be present at the execution of a search warrant. In such circumstances they may become privy to the contents of the material seized and the question arises as to the extent to which those contents or the documents themselves can be passed on to the requesting state, in advance of formal transmission by the Secretary of State.

Pre-1990 Act

11.22   Prior to the passing of the Criminal Justice (International Co-operation) Act 1990 the position was covered by *R. v. Southwark Crown Court ex parte Customs and Excise Commissioners.*[13] Customs officers were investigating the involvement of General Noriega, the *de facto* Head of Panama, in the laundering of the proceeds of drug trafficking through banks and other financial institutions in the United Kingdom. As a result of a separate investigation into drug trafficking offences conducted by the United States, French and British Customs Officers, a number of people, including professional staff of BCCI were arrested in the United States and the United Kingdom. Customs and Excise authorities applied for orders pursuant to Section 27 of the Drug Trafficking Offences Act 1986[14] seeking production of the accounts of those managers held by the London branch of BCCI and orders were granted by circuit judges.

11.23   Whilst customs officers were searching the offices of one of those managers, they discovered files relating to the accounts held by Noriega and various members of his family. The files were not covered by the search warrant and Customs and Excise authorities applied to the circuit judge at Southwark Crown Court for an order seeking production of the files. The judge granted the order. The bank applied for an order to vary or discharge the original order. The judge varied the order relating to Noriega, to the extent that she imposed conditions that Customs and Excise authorities could not remove, or cause, or permit the removal of any of the documents from the jurisdiction, or show, or send copies to any foreign law enforcement agency. However she refused to impose any conditions of the orders made in respect of the two managers.

11.24   On applications for judicial review by Customs and Excise authorities, to quash the order imposing conditions on the order relating to General Noriega, and by the bank in respect of the refusal to impose conditions on the orders relating to the two managers, the Divisional Court held that the power to make an order under section 27 (1) of the Drug Trafficking Offences Act 1986 was not limited to an investigation conducted by customs officers in the United Kingdom. On the true construction of Section 22 of the PACE,[15] a customs officer was entitled to retain material as against it's owner or possessor, for as long as the Act of 1986 permitted, and he was entitled to make the information contained in the material available, provided that he did not, without further order, part with the material itself, to the foreign agency for whose investigation the material had been produced.

The court was at pains to emphasise the importance of international cooperation.

> "Such a construction of the legislation would serve suitably the ordinary obligations of our law enforcement agencies to cooperate with their foreign colleagues in achieving their common aims. International cooperation in the discovery of crime and the apprehension of criminals is a well established fact and constantly in use. We think, for example, in this regard of Interpol."[16]

---

13 *R. v. Southwark Crown Court ex parte Customs and Excise Commissioners; R. v. Southwark Crown Court ex parte Bank of Credit and Commerce International SA* (1990)1Q.B. 650.
14 Since replaced by the Drug Trafficking Act 1994.
15 "(1) ... anything which has been [produced in pursuance of an Order under s. 27 (2) to a customs officer] ... may be retained so long as is necessary in all the circumstances. (2) without prejudice to the generality of sub-section (1) above – (a) anything (so produced) may be retained ... (i) for use as evidence at a trial for an offence; or (ii) for forensic examination or for investigation (into drug trafficking); ..."
16 *Per* Watkins L.J. 662.

Post 1990

11.25 *Sorsky Defries* The position changed however with the passing of the 1990 Act and the matter first came before the courts for guidance in *R. v. Southwark Crown Court ex parte Sorsky Defries.*[17] Pursuant to a mutual assistance request from the authorities in the United States, the Secretary of State for the Home Department, in accordance with section 7 (4) of the Criminal Justice (International Co-operation) Act 1990, directed Customs and Excise to apply for a search warrant under section 9 and Schedule I of PACE. Customs and Excise applied *ex parte* to Southwark Crown Court for a search warrant which was granted. For the reasons given above the warrants were quashed.(See pages 143–4.)

Prior to furnishing the evidence seized under the warrants to the Secretary of State for onward transmission, the applicants had learned that access to the seized documents had been given to an employee of the United States Customs Service, who was an assistant attaché based at the American Embassy in London. The court was informed that the documents had been shown to her to obtain confirmation that the documents taken without the warrant (the basis on which the warrant was in due course quashed) were indeed evidence in relation to other offences. She had been allowed to make notes on them but not to take photocopies.

It was submitted by the applicant that this amounted to a breach of section 7(4), since it was outside the requirement on the police, to furnish the evidence to the Secretary of State for onward transmission. It was argued that, as a matter of law, Customs and Excise had no power to do anything to seized material, other than to furnish it to the Secretary of State. This argument was rejected by the court.

> "The section does not say that the constable is not permitted to do anything with the evidence except furnish it to the Secretary of State. All that it is saying is that the constable must furnish it to the Secretary of State so that he can in turn transmit it to the Authority that made the request to him".

Propend In *R. v. C.C.C. ex parte Propend Finance Property Limited and another,*[18] the Secretary of State, by letter, authorised submission of the evidence seized under a warrant direct to the requesting state rather than via the Home Office, in accordance with section 7 (4) of the 1990. Whilst the court emphasised that it expressed no final conclusion on this point, it did incline to the view that the Secretary of State lacked the authority to require transmission of seized documents direct to a requesting state, as it is at least doubtful whether such action constitutes a mode of furnishing the material to the Secretary of State, within the closing words of section 7(4).

Finninvest[19] The search warrant in question had been issued by the Bow St Metropolitan Stipendiary Magistrate on the April 15, 1996 and executed on the same day. The documents removed were, with the consent of the applicant's former solicitors, examined by the representatives of the Italian authorities (the requesting state), to ascertain which were relevant and which were required for transmission to Italy. Some of the documents seized were returned and the rest were furnished by the SFO to the Secretary of State. None has actually transmitted to the requesting state, although its representatives communicated certain information, as to the contents of

---

17 [1996] Crim. L.R. 195.
18 [1996] 2 Cr. App. R. 26.
19 *R. v. the Secretary of State for the Home Department ex parte Finninvest SPA* (1997) 1 All E.R. 942 – see above under Chap. 6 (p. 59) for a detailed consideration of the facts.

the documents seized, to the Italian prosecuting authorities. As a result of this, further arrests were made. The transmission of this information by the Italian representatives to their prosecuting authority was challenged, as breaching the requirement in section 2 (8A) of the Criminal Justice Act 1987, that any evidence obtained by the SFO should be furnished to the Secretary of State, for transmission abroad. This challenge was rejected by the court. Agreement had been reached with the applicant's former solicitors, that the Italian representatives would continue to examine the documents, as they had during the search itself, so as to limit what was to be sent to the Home Office to the documents, or copies, needed for the investigation.

> "The Italian representatives made no notes of the documents, a fact confirmed by the terms of a report which they wrote on return to Italy on April 19:
>   "... the information given in this report could contain some inaccuracies as it is simply the fruits of an effort to memorise the information made by the writer."
>   In those circumstances I accept the respondent's submission that it cannot be said that there has yet been any transmission to Italy of "evidence" – defined by section 4 (5) of the 1990 Act to include documents – contrary to section 2 (8A), or of the documents contrary to the assurance. Nor do I think it right to criticise the Italian representatives for reporting back to their superiors in Italy to the best of their ability, or the SFO for not seeking assurances from the Italians that they would not do so. This frankly seems to me to have been neither realistic or necessary. This challenge too, therefore, I would reject." [*per* Simon Brown L.J.]

11.26   *R. v. Southwark Crown Court* ex parte *Bowles*[20]   Attention has already been drawn above (page 137) to the different forms of production orders and warrants available under section 9(2) and Schedule I of PACE, the Drug Trafficking Act 1994 and the Proceeds of Crime Act 1995 as incorporated into the Criminal Justice Act 1988.

In *Bowles*, the House of Lords considered the relationship between section 93(H) of the Criminal Justice Act 1988 and section 9 of and Schedule I to the PACE and the purpose for which the police may obtain an order under the former section. The House ruled that section 93(H) is concerned with an investigation into the proceeds of crime to assist the authorities to obtain information which may enable an application to be brought for a restraint order or a confiscation order. This was in contra distinction to the purpose of section 9 of, and Schedule I to, PACE which related to the investigation of a crime for the purpose of obtaining evidence to prosecute an offender.

Safeguards

11.27   There have been many judicial pronouncement on the safeguards contained within PACE and the burden upon circuit judges when considering production order applications to be scrupulous in discharging their responsibility.

The safeguards protecting the rights of citizens under section 93(H) are however less stringent than in PACE. These were listed by the House of Lords in *Bowles* as follows:—

(i)   Applications under section 93(H) can be made ex parte; paragraph 7 of

---

20 [1998] 2 All E.R. 193.

Schedule I requires that applications under section 9 must be made inter partes;

(ii) Section 9 applications must relate to a "serious arrestable offence"; no such requirement arises under section 93(H);

(iii) A section 9 order can only be made where there are "reasonable grounds for believing" (paragraph 2 (a) (i) of Schedule I) that an offence has been committed; section 93(H) involves a lower threshold test, which is that there are "reasonable grounds for suspecting" that a person has benefited from criminal conduct;

(iv) Applications under section 9 are limited by the requirement in para 2(b) of Schedule I that other methods of obtaining the material have failed or have not been tried because they were bound to fail, but such a restriction does not apply to section 93(H).

In their Lordships' opinion it was not the intention of Parliament in enacting section 93(H) to take away, in respect of the investigation of criminal offences involving the obtaining of money or other property, the safeguards for the citizen given in the detailed provisions of Schedule I to PACE.

The House then went on to consider the answer to the question posed by Simon Brown L.J. in his judgment in the Divisional Court "What then is the touchstone by which to decide whether a section 93(H) application should be made by the prosecuting authority and, other conditions being satisfied, granted by the Court?"

Lord Hutton in his speech answered the question thus:—

"I consider that if the true and dominant purpose of an application under section 93(H) is to enable an investigation to be made into the proceeds of criminal conduct, the application should be granted even if an incidental consequence may be that the police will obtain evidence relating to the commission of an offence. But if the true and dominant purpose of the application is to carry out an investigation whether a criminal offence has been committed and to obtain evidence to bring a prosecution, the application should be refused."

11.28 The effect of this decision appears to impose an additional duty upon the Secretary of State, when giving a direction under section 7 of the 1990 Act. Whether the "unitary test" of *Propend* is adopted, or the wider test propounded in *Gross*, it seems that the Secretary of State should, prior to making a direction, determine the dominant purpose of the request for assistance. This imposes upon the requesting state the obligation of giving sufficient details to enable the Secretary of State to determine the dominant purpose for which the material is sought. Without such information, it is difficult to see how the Minister is able to decide what assistance should be given and thereby to direct the police properly.

Assessment of relevance of material sought

11.29 The provisions under section 7 of the Act are coercive by their nature. The courts have consistently underlined the necessity for safeguards to ensure that the appropriate balance is retained, between the need to investigate crime and the requirement to protect the citizen's rights of security of property.

Section 4 of the 1990 Act makes available coercive measures, to compel a witness, by virtue of a witness summons, to provide evidence to a nominated court. The courts have set themselves against "fishing expeditions" and ensured that tests of relevance and admissibility are observed and satisfied.[21]

Safeguards also exist in relation to applications under section 7. It is instructive to examine the various steps in the process, for checks are built in at each stage:—

(a) Upon receipt of the request the Secretary of State must give a direction whether assistance should be given to the requesting state and if so, what assistance should so be given.

(b) Section 4(2A) of the 1990 Act (as amended) provides that if the Secretary of State is satisfied—

"(i) that an offence under the law of the country or territory in question has been committed or that there are reasonable grounds for suspecting that such offence has been committed; and

(ii) that proceedings in respect of that offence have been instituted in that country or territory or that an investigation into that offence has been carried on there,

and it appears to him that the request relates to an offence involving serious or complex fraud, he may, if he thinks fit, refer the request or any part of the request to the Director of the SFO, for her to obtain such of the evidence to which the request or part referred relates, as may appear to the Director to be appropriate, for giving effect to the request or part referred"

Clearly therefore, in such instances, the Secretary of State's obligations require him solely to consider whether the request relates to an offence involving serious or complex fraud and gives him a discretion, if he thinks fit, to refer such a request, or any part of it, to the Director of the SFO. By so doing, he abrogates any responsibility for giving a direction to apply for a warrant and to particularise the appropriate form of search and seizure.

By virtue of section 2 of the Criminal Justice Act 1987 (as amended) the Director is given power by notice in writing to require a person to produce any specified documents which *appear to the Director to relate to any matter relevant to the investigation or any documents of a specified description which appear to her so to relate*; thus the Director clearly has an obligation to consider issues of relevance.

(c) (i) Under *Propend*[22] there should be a unitary direction specifying the particular form of application.

(ii) Under *Gross*[23] (the Secretary of State should consider the nature of the documents being requested and if he concludes that they consist of special procedure material or include such material and do not include the excluded material, he should direct the police to apply for whichever of a production order or search warrant under Schedule I of PACE appears to the police to be appropriate once they have completed enquiries they are required to make under the Code of Practice of PACE.

(d) (i) Code B2.3 requires an officer to make reasonable enquiries to establish what, if anything, is known about the likely occupier of premises;

---

21 See *R. v. Reading Justices ex parte Berkshire County Council* (1996) 1 Cr.App.R. 239.
22 [1996] 2 Cr. App. R. 26.
23 (Unreported) July 24, 1998.

(ii) B2.4 provides that no application for a search warrant may be made without the authority of an officer of at least the rank of Inspector;

(iii) B2.4 requires the authority of an officer of at least the rank of superintendent for an application for a production order or warrant under Schedule I of PACE;

(iv) B2.6 and B2.7 provide that an application for a search must be supported by information in writing specifying the grounds on which the application is made and if a search warrant under paragraph 12 (a) of Schedule I to PACE is sought why it is believed that service of notice of an application for production order may seriously prejudice the investigation.

(e) Bowles[24] requires prior consideration of the true and dominant purpose of an application for an order for the production of material under section 93(H) or Schedule 1 of PACE.

(f) Provided the request is essentially one for evidence, the Secretary of State need not concern himself with the width of the request for that is a matter for the party applying for the warrant.[25]

(g) Whether under section 8, Schedule I of PACE, section 2 of the Criminal Justice Act 1987 (as amended) or other provision, the powers of search for and seizure of material in the United Kingdom for purpose of investigations and proceedings abroad can only be exercised with the authority of a court.

● Both under section 8 and Schedule I paragraph 2 (a) (iv) of PACE, the court must be satisfied that there are reasonable grounds for believing that the material sought is likely to be relevant evidence. "Relevant evidence" in relation to an offence means anything that would be "admissible in evidence at a trial for the offence".

● Does this mean admissible at a trial in the United Kingdom or in the requesting state?

● In considering the question of relevance of evidence sought by a mutual assistance request under Section 4 of the 1980 Act, the issue of admissibility was considered in *R. v. Bow Street Magistrates Court ex parte King*.[26] It was held that when the Court is faced with an application involving the production of documents following the issue of a witness summons, any claim made by a person that he did not have to produce the documents had to be considered as if the proceedings were domestic English proceedings.

● A section 4 application is however subject to the provisions of Schedule I of the 1990 Act, which under the heading "Privilege of Witnesses", provides that a person cannot be compelled to give in proceedings any evidence which he could not be compelled to give in criminal proceedings in the United Kingdom. No such qualification arises in relation to section 7 applications.

● When applications are made under Section 7 for the issue of a warrant, unless the Courts are prepared to receive evidence as to admissibility of

---

24 [1998] 2 All E.R. 193.
25 *R. v. Secretary of State for the Home Department ex parte Finninvest* [1997] 1 All E.R. 942.
26 (Unreported) October 8, 1997, QBD. CO/3489/97, see pp. 79–80.

evidence in foreign proceedings, it is submitted that admissibility must be interpreted according to United Kingdom rather than foreign rules. The alternative interpretation would require the magistrate to have before him a certificate from the requesting state, to the effect that the evidence sought would be admissible within the foreign jurisdiction, for without such certificate, the magistrate would not be in a position to rule upon admissibility.

- Over and above these considerations as to admissibility is the court's overall duty to satisfy itself that there are reasonable grounds for believing the various matters set out in the application.

(h) Once material has been seized, pursuant either to an order or a warrant, the courts have indicated a further duty to assess relevance.

- In *Finninvest*[27] the court rejected the assertion that the request was vague and speculative, describing it as being as precise and focused as such a request could sensibly be in the circumstances. "It is impossible to know just what documents are both in London and relevant. To discover that, it is necessary to find, examine and appraise them. Given, however, that these are the type of documents invariably germane to any major company fraud investigation, and that these overseas companies are now administered by CMM, it is highly likely that that many will be relevant. And in so far as any of the documents seized prove not to be, they will not be transmitted to Italy. It is perhaps helpful in this regard to note also this passage from the judgment of the Swiss Federal Court dealing with the applicant's challenge to the Commission Rogatoire there:

  > "The question of knowing whether the information requested in the context of an application for assistance is necessary or of use in the proceedings underway in the applicant state, in general, it must be left up to the assessment of the latter's authorities. The state applied to does not, in fact, have the means to be able to pronounce on the advisability of adopting certain evidence and cannot, therefore, put it's own power of assessment in place of that of the foreign authority carrying out the enquiries."

- This test appears to suggest that the assessment of relevance should be undertaken by officers from the requesting state, as indeed happened in Finninvest. However, in *ex parte M*,[28] the Court found it necessary to criticise those seizing the documents for a failure to take any copies of the documents that were transmitted, unsorted, to the United States – the requesting state. "Inaction by those subject to the search did not relieve the (SFO's) staff of the duty to retain only what they were entitled to retain and the duty to assess the relevance of what was seized and whether it is covered by legal privilege. To send the material out of the jurisdiction was to compound the error." [*per* Pill L.J.]

- Thus a further duty to assess relevance would appear to fall upon representatives of the requested state.

  (i) As to whether the Secretary of State, prior to transmitting the docu-

---

27 [1997] 1 All E.R. 942.
28 (Unreported) April 7, 1998.

ments seized, is under a duty to review the evidence and form his own judgement on the issues of relevance and legal privilege, the Court in *ex parte M* declined to consider the question, ruling only that the Act did not empower the Minister to send out of the jurisdiction documents unlawfully obtained. Whilst the Court in *Gross* departed from this latter view it was prepared to rule that "the idea that the Secretary of State is under a duty to sift through materials seized himself, is not, in my judgement, properly tenable." His role was in the statutory scheme was described as "that of a conduit pipe". His only duty arose, if he was put on notice of any material irregularity whilst the documents were in his possession not to transmit them abroad before that question has been resolved.

CHAPTER 12

Mutual Assistance and Restraint and Confiscation Orders

The Legislative Framework

12.00 A detailed examination of the legislation governing restraint and confiscation orders is outside the scope of this work. However, it is important to be aware of the provisions as they relate to international co-operation in this area of practice. The relevant statutes are:—

(a) The Drug Trafficking Act 1994, section 39, and

(b) Part VI of the Criminal Justice Act 1988 as amended by the Criminal Justice Act 1993 and the Proceeds of Crime Act 1995 (section 96 of the 1988 Act).

Although the above statutes provide the primary legislation, it is two Orders in Council which provide the actual law, in relation to reciprocal enforcement of overseas restraint and confiscation orders. The relevant orders are:—

(a) The Drug Trafficking Act 1994 (Designated Countries & Territories) Order 1996 (S.I. 1996 No. 2880), and

(b) The Criminal Justice Act 1988 (Designated Countries & Territories) Order 1991 (S.I. 1991 No. 2873) and subsequent amendment orders.

For all practical purposes, it is the Orders in Council to which a practitioner should turn, in seeking guidance in relation to practice and procedure in this area.

The International Dimension

12.01 The law relating to this area in the United Kingdom operates within a network of international conventions, memoranda of understanding and bilateral agreements. Chief amongst the conventions are:

(a) The 1988 UN Convention Against Illicit Traffic in Narcotic Drugs & Psychotropic Substances ("The Vienna Convention"), and

(b) The Council of Europe Convention on Laundering, Search, Seizure & Confiscation.

As well as formal binding bilateral confiscation treaties, which are registerable at the United Nations, there are also informal arrangements between parties and semi-formal agreements, (such as the memorandum of understanding with Colombia, in relation to the proceeds of drug trafficking).

In general terms, the agreements set out the practice and procedure in relation to the relevant orders, including details of who may make the requests, through which official channels requests may be made, the contents of requests and the costs of proceedings.

Designation

12.02   The United Kingdom can only offer assistance in freezing assets and confiscating the proceeds of crime, be it drugs related, or other serious offences, if the country in question is designated under an Order in Council. The primary legislation provides for this designation and the Orders in Council list those countries originally designated. Subsequent Amending Orders add further countries.

A country may be designated either as a result of signing a Convention, or of a bilateral agreement. Once a country is designated, it may issue and enforce proceedings in the High Court. Designation does not in itself mean that the United Kingdom may automatically receive co-operation from the jurisdiction of the designated country. However, according to the Home Office Guide for Enforcement Authorities, "in relation to confiscation and money laundering practice, countries are designated where the United Kingdom has an expectation of reciprocal confiscation assistance". Whether the United Kingdom could enforce restraint or confiscation proceedings overseas in a non-designated country would depend on the local law.

12.03   In general terms, there are more designated countries in relation to drugs trafficking offences than "all crimes" offences, although the number of countries implementing domestic legislation in relation to restraining or confiscating the proceeds of all crime is increasing. One can expect a corresponding increase in mutual assistance in the future.

There may be more than one arrangement in place in relation to one country, *e.g.* Italy is designated in relation to drug trafficking matters by two multilateral Conventions and also a bi-lateral agreement.

It would be misleading to provide a list of countries which have been designated. Practitioners are advised to contact the Confiscation Section of the MLA Section of the Home Office (Telephone: 0171-273 3801 Fax: 0171-273 4422) for information on a case by case basis.

United Kingdom Requests for Assistance

12.04   United Kingdom requests for assistance may take place at two distinct stages. These are:—

(a)   the investigation stage (including once proceedings have commenced), and

(b)   the post conviction stage.

The investigation stage

12.05   Once an investigation has commenced in the United Kingdom, the authorities may require assistance from overseas in:—

(i)   Obtaining information in connection with the defendant's assets.

Information in relation to a defendant's assets may be obtained using the machinery of general mutual legal assistance.

(ii)   Restraining or freezing assets, to prevent their dissipation in the course of the proceedings.

> The investigator must first establish whether the country to which the request is sent is designated. Although requests may be made to non-designated countries, they may well be refused. Any request to a non-designated country should be referred to the confiscation section of the Home Office.

The investigator must then establish which is the relevant convention or treaty, as this will set out the formalities of the request.

In order to obtain information about a defendant's assets overseas, a request may be made through the MLA Section, under the provisions of a bi-lateral agreement or a relevant Convention.

12.06 As regards requests in relation to drug trafficking, an investigator must decide whether to frame the request in compliance with the provisions of the 1988 Vienna Convention, or the Council of Europe Convention. The Home Office recommends that, generally, the latter should provide the most appropriate framework, as it is a specialist convention. If there is a bilateral treaty in force, then it is the terms of that treaty which should be complied with.

The MLA Section should be aware of the requirements of the designated country and a request should therefore be framed accordingly. In general it will need to comply, at the very least, with the terms of section 3 of the Criminal Justice (International Co-operation) Act.

Assuming that there is reasonable cause to believe that the defendant may be or has been convicted of an offence from which he/she has benefitted, an investigating body may seek to restrain a defendant from dealing in assets in which he/she has an interest, in order to prevent their dissipation before the conclusion of any trial.

12.07 Sections 62(2) of the Drug Trafficking Act and section 102(3) of the Criminal Justice Act defines realisable property as being property "wherever situated". In theory at least, the defendant's property worldwide may therefore be available to an investigator, for the purposes of restraint and eventual confiscation. The purpose of the order is to ensure sufficient assets will be available to allow the English court to make an appropriate confiscation order, if a conviction is obtained in England or Wales against the defendant in question. The order may be served on a defendant in the jurisdiction of the High Court, or under Rule 11 of the Rules of the Supreme Court, the High Court may, on an application from the prosecutor, give leave for the service of the Notice of Motion out of the jurisdiction. Breach of the order would render the person or third party on whom the order had been served liable to proceedings for contempt.

Clearly, the practical effect of serving an order on a defendant, or a third party, who is out of the jurisdiction, in relation to property which is also out of the jurisdiction, is extremely slight.

As regards third parties who have a presence in this country **and** in the overseas jurisdiction in question, case law in this country suggests that they must comply with the terms of an order served here, giving effect to it in their overseas incarnation. However, in most cases, the party served will only comply with the terms of the English order to the extent that it does not conflict with local law.

Ancillary to a restraint order, a repatriation order may be made, requiring the defendant to return identified property from overseas to the jurisdiction of the High Court, where the restraint order would then bite.

The High Court also has power to make disclosure orders against both defendants and third parties.

It is important to note that a restraint order operates *in personam* not *in rem*.

The post conviction stage

12.08 Once a confiscation order has been made in this country, it may be enforced in the jurisdiction where the asset is situated, as long as that particular jurisdiction is a signatory to a bilateral agreement or a Convention. The practical operation of this enforcement will be a matter for local law and costs will be also be borne by the requested jurisdiction. Sums realised will accrue to the enforcing jurisdiction, although there are asset sharing arrangements between countries. As regards drugs trafficking there is a Seized Assets Fund in the United Kingdom, which recycles funds seized from convicted drugs offenders into anti-drugs programmes.

Requests for assistance from overseas authorities

12.09 Overseas authorities may request assistance in the United Kingdom in relation to the same categories as above, *i.e.* at the investigation stage or subsequently at the post conviction stage.

The investigation stage

12.10 Requests for assistance in relation to an investigation into property in England and Wales may be made under bilateral agreement or under a relevant Convention. The investigation will then be carried out in the United Kingdom, as though it were a domestic investigation. All domestic powers are available to the investigator, including PACE warrants, warrants under section 93H of the Criminal Justice Act, or warrants under section 55 of the Drug Trafficking Act. Powers under section 7 of the Criminal Justice (International Co-operation) Act 1990 are also available. This latter section allows the onward transmission of evidence seized to the requesting jurisdiction.

A letter of request is the means by which a designated country may ask the United Kingdom authorities to assist in an investigation into property in England and Wales (under the general mutual legal assistance arrangements) or in obtaining a restraint order. The letter of request for the restrained property should contain the following information:—

(a) Personal details of the defendant.

(b) Details of the offence with which the defendant has been, or is about to be charged and/or details of the civil action against the defendant.

(c) Details of the law applicable to the charges and evidence against the defendant.

(d) Particulars of the property which it is intended to restrain in the United Kingdom generally and England and Wales in particular, as well as details of the persons holding this property.

(e) Particulars of the link between the defendant and the property.

(f) Details of any court orders made in the designated country against the defendant in respect of the property and brief general details of all property held by the defendant outside the United Kingdom. This may, for practical purposes, be limited to property in the designated country.

12.11 A request for restraint should be accompanied by:—

(a) A certificate issued by or on behalf of the MLA Section of the designated country stating:

(i)   that proceedings have been instituted in the designated country and have not been concluded, or that proceedings are to be instituted in the designated country and, if so, when; and

(ii)   where no confiscation order has yet been made, that the confiscation order, which it is expected the court in the designated country will make, has the purpose of recovering property, or the value of property received, in connection with drug trafficking, or other serious crime; and

(iii) A duly authenticated copy of any court order made in the designated country against a defendant in respect of property. This may not be available but should be supplied if an order has been made.

12.12   Having received the request, the MLA Section will pass the matter on to the appropriate prosecuting authority in this country. Under section 39 of the Drug Trafficking Act 1994, or section 96 of the Criminal Justice Act 1988 (or rather the relevant Orders in Council – see above), the High Court has the power to make a restraint or charging order against realisable assets in this jurisdiction in response to a request from overseas, similar to that in domestic proceedings. An order may be made providing:—

(i)   proceedings have been instituted in the designated country; and

(ii)   proceedings have not been concluded; and

(iii) an external confiscation order has been made or it appears to the High Court that an order may be made.

The "institution of proceedings" is defined (for each country) in the Appendices to the Orders in Council. The order may be made against any person having an interest in the property.

12.13   As has been said above, it is outside the scope of this chapter to deal with the procedure for obtaining a restraint or charging order in the High Court but in effect, an application is made by the designated prosecutor in the United Kingdom, acting on behalf of the overseas authority, by notice of motion, supported by an affidavit complying with the terms of section 79A of the Criminal Justice Act or section 10 of the Drug Trafficking Act. The affidavit should state the nature of the property to be restrained in as much detail as possible, as well as full details of its location. A draft restraint order is normally prepared and when the order is made, there should be specific provision made for service on the defendant and any other person outside the jurisdiction who is touched by the proceedings.

The procedure for enforcement of overseas restraint orders, charging orders, garnishee orders, and confiscation orders is set out in Order 115 of the Rules of the Supreme Court.

The post conviction stage

12.14   As with restraint and charging orders, the procedure for enforcing an external confiscation order of a designated country is commenced by the MLA Section receiving a letter of request containing the following information:—

1.   The name (including any aliases), address, date and place of birth of the defendant;

2.   A summary of the relevant law in the designated country, the facts of the

case and any other matters which give rise to a belief that an external confiscation order may be made against the defendant;

3. Full particulars of the realisable property in respect of which the order is sought, including as much information as possible as to the nature, location and extent of the defendant's known assets; and

4. If a restraint order has been granted in the designated country, it is helpful to append a copy to the letter of request. This is not, however, obligatory, nor is it an essential prerequisite to the obtaining of an order, that a similar order is in force in a designated country.

5. Details of any other parties' interest.

12.15 Once the MLA Section receives the request, it is forwarded on to the relevant designated prosecutor.

The enforcement of an overseas confiscation order takes place in two stages. First, the order must be registered under Section 40 of the Drug Trafficking Act or Section 97 of the Criminal Justice Act and secondly the order must be enforced.

(a) Registration

The High Court may register an external confiscation order as long as:—

(i) It is satisfied that at the time of registration the order is in force and not subject to appeal;

(ii) It is satisfied, where the person against whom the order is made did not appear in the proceedings, that he/she received notice of the proceedings in sufficient time to enable him/her to organise a defence; and

(iii) It is of the opinion that enforcing the order in England and Wales would not be contrary to the interests of justice.

12.16 The person against whom the order is to be registered, as well as a copy of the external confiscation order, should accompany the application for registration. The document must also be properly authenticated, by an appropriate authority or person of the designated country.

The designated country's appropriate authority should issue a certificate stating that:—

(i) proceedings have been instituted and have not been concluded or that proceedings are to be instituted there;

"proceedings" and "the Appropriate Authority" are defined in the Order in Council. (This provision is relevant in relation to requests for restraint orders).

(ii) that an external confiscation order is in force and is not subject to appeal;

(iii) that all, or a certain amount, of the sum payable under an external confiscation order remains unpaid in the designated country, or that other property recoverable under an external confiscation order remains unrecovered there;

(iv) that any person has been notified of any proceedings, in accordance with the law of the designated country; or

(v) that the order has the purpose of recovering payment, or other rewards received, in connection with drug trafficking or other serious crime, or their value.

12.17   The summary of the facts should also be supplied to the court.

An officer of the United Kingdom competent authority should swear an affidavit in support of the registration of the external confiscation order, which deals with the above.

Once registered, the person against whom the external confiscation order has been made must be served.

(b) Enforcement

12.18   Enforcement is through the High Court and can occur through voluntary settlement, garnishee proceedings or the appointment of a receiver in respect of realisable property within the jurisdiction of the High Court.

Voluntary settlement may occur, by the defendant paying voluntarily to the designated jurisdiction, or paying through the repatriation of restrained funds to the requesting country.

The appointment of a receiver is carried out in the same way as in domestic proceedings, with slight variations. Practitioners should refer to the relevant order (Order 115) for the full detail.

As regards garnishee orders, the applicant is the Crown Prosecution Service, or H.M. Customs and Excise and it is the High Court who is the actual garnishor. This procedure is used where the asset in question is *a debt owed to the defendant*. Practitioners should refer to Order 49, which governs this procedure. Essentially, the application is made without notice to a judge, supported by an affidavit. The order nisi must be served on the garnishee 15 days before the hearing for the absolute order and then on the judgment debtor at least seven days after and seven days in advance of the hearing. It may then be made absolute.

CHAPTER 13
Serious Fraud

Criminal Justice Act 1987

13.00   The investigation and prosecution of serious and complex fraud cases in the United Kingdom underwent revision in 1987, with the Criminal Justice Act 1987 and the Criminal Justice (Scotland) Act 1987. In Scotland, the legislation was somewhat more restricted, concentrating principally on the introduction of special powers of questioning in serious fraud cases, but for the rest of the United Kingdom, the changes were more radical. Although similar special powers of questioning were introduced both north and south of the border, the Criminal Justice Act was more wide ranging in its effect on the investigation and prosecution of serious fraud, and among other innovations, set up the Serious Fraud Office (SFO).

The Criminal Justice Act gave to the SFO extensive powers of investigation, mainly through the use of the compulsory powers contained in section 2 of the Act. (In Scotland similar powers are granted by section 51 of the Criminal Justice (Scotland) Act 1987 to the person nominated by the Lord Advocate.) From the outset these powers have been used widely and effectively in the investigation of cases of serious or complex fraud.

13.01   The powers contained in section 2 of the Criminal Justice Act 1987 are restricted as to their use to "the purposes of an investigation under section 1" (section 2(1)). This is, under section 1(3), an investigation into "any suspected offence which appears to the Director on reasonable grounds to involve serious or complex fraud."

Since section 17(1) restricts the extent of the Act to England and Wales, (and in the case of section 2, to Northern Ireland and Scotland also), the powers contained in section 2 were not available to the SFO, if the investigation related to a suspected offence of serious or complex fraud, which had occurred other than in the United Kingdom of Great Britain and Northern Ireland.

The effectiveness of the use of the compulsory powers in the investigation of cases of serious or complex fraud in the United Kingdom was such that it was quickly apparent that they could, to advantage, be extended into investigations in similar cases for the assistance of foreign authorities.

Modern technology has had an enormous impact on financial dealings and commercial transactions now take place electronically in seconds: money moves across international boundaries as quickly as it moves within one jurisdiction. Fraudsters are aware of the benefits which distance can bring to an evidential trail and use this to their advantage. Transactions which move through six foreign jurisdictions in as many minutes will take at least six letters of request (and often many more) and many months of difficult investigation to unravel. In addition, the institutions from which evidence is sought guard jealously the secrets of their clients and evidence gathering in such cases is fraught with difficulty. The investigative powers of the SFO were introduced in an attempt to facilitate investigation in such cases. Their success prompted the desire to extend the powers for the benefit of foreign investigations in similar cases.

Extension of SFO powers

13.02   In 1995, by virtue of section 164 of the Criminal Justice and Public Order Act 1994, the Criminal Justice (International Co-operation) Act 1990 was amended, to empower the SFO to assist foreign authorities in their own criminal investigations into serious or complex fraud, by adding to their armoury the SFO's coercive powers to compel disclosure of material and information.

The effect of the 1994 amendment was to amend section 4 of the 1990 Act, in respect of requests from foreign authorities to the United Kingdom. The section now provides (section 4(2A), inserted by section 164 of the 1994 Act) that, if the Secretary of State is satisfied:

(a)   that an offence under the law of the country or territory in question has been committed or that there are reasonable grounds for suspecting that such an offence has been committed, and

(b)   that proceedings in respect of that offence have been instituted in that country or territory or that an investigation into that offence is being carried on there, and

it appears to him that the request relates to an offence involving serious or complex fraud, then he may if he thinks fit, refer the request to the Director of the SFO, for him to obtain such of the evidence to which the request, or part referred, relates, as may appear to the Director to be appropriate, for giving effect to the request or part referred. (section 4(2A)). The section also allows the Secretary of State to refer appropriate cases to the Lord Advocate, where the request relates to assistance which may be provided in Scotland.

13.03   Section 164(2) of the 1994 Act made a consequential amendment to section 2 of the Criminal Justice Act 1987, to enable the powers of the SFO to be exercised in respect of cases referred by the Secretary of State under this provision. Section 164(3) of the 1994 Act makes similar amendments to the Criminal Justice (Scotland) Act.

Statutory provisions

13.04   The relevant part of the text of the Criminal Justice Act 1987 (with 1994 amendments in italics) follows:

"2(1) The powers of the Director under this section shall be exercisable, but only for the purposes of an investigation under section 1 above, or on a request made by an authority entitled to make such a request, in any case in which it appears to him that there is a good reason to do so for the purpose of investigating the affairs, or any aspect of the affairs, of any person.
(1A) The authorities entitled to request the Director to exercise his powers under this section are:

(a)   *the Attorney General of the Isle of Man, Jersey or Guernsey, acting under legislation corresponding to section 1 of this Act and having effect in the Island whose Attorney General makes the request: and*
(b)   *the Secretary of State acting under section 4(2A) of the Criminal Justice (International Co-operation) Act 1990, in response to a request received by him from an overseas court (an "overseas authority").*

(1B) The Director shall not exercise his powers on a request from the Secretary of State acting in response to a request received from an overseas authority within subsection (1A) (b) above unless it appears to the Director on reasonable grounds that the offence in respect of which he has been requested to obtain evidence involves serious or complex fraud:"

13.05 Similarly, where the evidence is to be obtained in Scotland, the Lord Advocate may, if the request appears to him to involve serious or complex fraud, give a direction under section 51 of the Criminal Justice (Scotland) Act 1987. The investigation in the United Kingdom of international serious or complex fraud therefore now has the benefit of the use of the compulsory powers contained in section 2 of the Criminal Justice Act.

The use of extended powers

13.06 The effect of these provisions is that the Director of the SFO (and in Scotland, members of the Procurator Fiscal Service following a direction by the Lord Advocate) may in cases to which this section applies, use the compulsory powers which statute has given him to collect evidence.

The SFO has been using these powers since February 1995. In the first full year for which figures are available (April 1995 to March 1996) the SFO received 35 requests from the Secretary of State (the Home Office), for it to use its powers on behalf of a foreign state. Of these 28 were accepted.[1] In the next year (to March 1997), these figures had increased to 57 and 54 respectively, and for the Year to April 1998, the figures were 23 and 19 respectively. In the most recent year for which figures are available (to March 1999) there were 22 requests referred, of which 10 were accepted.

Although the figures in the last two years have dropped, in fact the level of work being undertaken on behalf of other jurisdictions has remained fairly constant, since the complexity of requests themselves is increasing, and most cases involve at least one, and often many, supplementary requests. In the year ending March 1999, for example, in addition to the 10 requests which were accepted, the SFO received 25 supplementary requests, relating both to that year's cases and also to cases from earlier years. In fact, a feature of the SFO's involvement in these cases is the extent of some of the investigations required. An indication of this aspect can be seen from the fact that although only 10 new cases were accepted in 1998–99, in the same period 124 notices under section 2 of the Criminal Justice Act 1987 were executed.

In total, over the time that the SFO has been involved in work of this nature, it has been able to assist numerous separate jurisdictions in the investigation of cases of serious or complex fraud, and many of the cases with which it has been involved have been of considerable international importance.

SFO case selection criteria

13.07 There is no definition of "serious" or "complex"in any of the legislation. Seriousness and complexity are understood in their ordinary meanings. For domestic cases, the SFO uses (1999) as one of its selection criteria a threshold of value of one million pounds, and the same limits are applied to international cases. That does not mean that cases of less than £1 million will be turned away, since the value of the case is only one of the factors used in its assessment, but it is a guide. For international cases, it means that the case in its country of origin should be the same type of case

---

1 See SFO Annual Reports, HMSO.

which the SFO would be likely to accept if it had been a domestic case. Note that a case, for acceptance by the SFO does not have to be serious *and* complex, but serious *or* complex.

The SFO would not accept a case for investigation on behalf of a foreign authority, however, unless there was some advantage to be gained from using its compulsory powers. If the evidence sought was of such a nature that it could be obtained by the police acting on their own, or by the nomination of a court to receive the evidence of a witness, albeit that the case involved serious or complex fraud, there would be no point in the referral. Therefore, normally the cases which are referred (and which are most likely to be accepted) are those where some special feature of the SFO's investigative skills will be relevant or necessary to the investigation requested, *e.g.* that accountancy skills are required, or that the use of compulsory powers under section 2 will be necessary to obtain the evidence requested.

13.08 Under the current legislation, therefore, when a request is received by the Secretary of State from a foreign authority, if he is satisfied that

1. an offence under the law of the requesting state has been committed or there are reasonable grounds for suspecting that such an offence has been committed, and

2. either proceedings in respect of that offence or an investigation into that offence are under way in the requesting state; and

3. the request relates to an offence involving serious or complex fraud

then he may refer the request, or any part of it to the Director of the SFO for execution of the whole or part of the request.

13.09 The Director of the SFO, on receipt of a request from the Secretary of State, then goes through a "vetting" procedure similar to that embarked on for purely domestic cases, to decide whether the case is appropriate for acceptance. It will have been observed from the figures quoted above, that not all cases submitted by the Secretary of State are accepted, but if the Director decides that it is an appropriate case to accept, then the Secretary of State is informed accordingly, and the investigative powers available to members of the office, when investigating domestic cases under the Criminal Justice Act 1987, become available to those executing the request.

Requests for execution by the SFO are the same as other requests, in that they will be made by the competent foreign authority, either when an offence has been committed in the foreign country, or when it is suspected that an offence has been committed. It is not necessary that there should be a person either arrested or charged, nor need formal proceedings have been commenced.

SFO section 2 powers

13.10 Section 2 of the Criminal Justice Act 1987 confers on the Director of the SFO wide powers of compulsion in relation to the investigation of serious or complex fraud. The provisions of section 2 which are relevant here (and these are unamended by the 1994 legislation) are:

2(2) The Director may by notice in writing require the person whose affairs are to be investigated ("the person under investigation") or any other person whom he has reason to believe has relevant information to answer questions or otherwise furnish information with respect to any matter relevant to the investigation at a specified place and either at a specified time or forthwith.

(3) The Director may by notice in writing require the person whose affairs are to be Investigated (the person under investigation") or any other person to produce at such place as may be specified in the notice and either forthwith or at such time as may be so specified any specified documents which appear to the Director to relate to any matter relevant to the investigation or any documents of a specified description which appear to him so to relate;

(4) Where on information on oath laid by a member of the SFO a justice of the peace is satisfied, in relation to any documents, that there are reasonable grounds for believing—

   (a)   that—

      (a)   a person has failed to comply with an obligation under this section to produce them;

      (b)   it is not practicable to serve a notice under subsection (3) above in relation to them;

      or

      (c)   the service of such a notice in relation to them might seriously prejudice the investigation; and

      (d)   that they are on the premises specified in the information,

      he may issue such a warrant as is specified in subsection (5) below.

(5) The warrant referred to above is a warrant authorising any constable:

   (a)   to enter (using such force as is reasonably necessary for the purpose) and search the premises and

   (b)   to take possession of any documents appearing to be documents of the description specified in the information or to take in relation to any documents so appearing any other steps which may appear to be necessary for preserving them and preventing interference with them.

((6)–(7) not reproduced here)

(8) A statement by a person in response to a requirement imposed by virtue of this section may only be used in evidence against him

   (a)   on a prosecution for an offence under subsection (14) below; or

   (b)   on a prosecution for some other offence where in giving evidence he makes a statement inconsistent with it.

13.11   The full text of the Criminal Justice Act as amended is contained in the Appendix. Using the compulsory powers under section 2 of the 1987 Act, extended to these cases by the 1994 Act, members of the SFO can investigate cases referred from foreign authorities, by requiring answers to questions, or the production of documents and explanations to those documents, or in the last resort, can apply to the court for a warrant, in respect of specified documents.

SFO mutual assistance investigations

13.12   The Investigations carried out by the SFO are carried out by members of the SFO, including lawyers, accountants and financial investigators, assisted where appropriate by members of the Metropolitan Police Fraud Squad International Co-operation Section. Very often, these investigations are greatly facilitated if a member of the investigation team from the foreign country attends at the SFO.

Bearing in mind that these cases are by their nature serious or complex, an officer from the "home"team can make the conduct of the enquiries much easier. Such a foreign official can have a variety of backgrounds – he/she could be a lawyer, an accountant or a police officer. If the assistance requested is to interview witnesses, then the foreign official can actually take part in the interviews, and for this purposes can be authorised by the Director of the SFO to use the powers conferred by section 2 of the 1987 Act. This power is contained in section 2(11) of the 1987 Act. This can be very useful for the SFO investigators. It should be remembered, however, that because section 2 powers are not available to police officers, the Director will not make them available to foreign police officers, but only to those who would be entitled to use them, if they were members of the SFO.

Limitation on use

13.13 There may be an additional requirement made, when a case is referred to the SFO, which is not present in other cases. Because there are restrictions on the use to which statements so obtained can be put, in respect of domestic cases, (section 2(8)) the same restrictions are imposed on statements obtained on behalf of a foreign authority. Therefore, if the case is one which is to be referred by the Secretary of State to the SFO, and is one where it is likely that the powers under section 2 will be used to obtain statements from prospective witnesses, it will be necessary to obtain an undertaking from the foreign authority, to the effect that no statement made by any person to the SFO, as a result of their coercive powers, will be used against that person in a prosecution, without the prior consent of the Secretary of State for the Home Department. If a letter of request does not contain that undertaking, and the Secretary of State is considering a referral to the SFO, then the request will be returned to the requesting state for the undertaking to be completed. The SFO will not accept a case where statements are to be obtained using the powers contained under section 2, without the undertaking. It should be remembered however, that since the restriction on the use of evidence under section 2(8) only refers to "a statement", then if the information sought by the letter of request is of a formal nature, for example documentary material from a bank, then such an undertaking will not be necessary. It may of course be difficult at an early stage to be certain as to the nature of evidence which will emerge during the course of a letter of request, and in those circumstances, it would always be safer, if the requesting authorities included the appropriate undertaking at an early stage.

13.14 Where search warrants are to be applied for under the Criminal Justice Act 1987 in respect of a foreign authority, then the same principles will apply as apply for search warrants generally. Chapters 8 to 11 should be referred to for details of the procedures which will be applied, even although the application to the magistrates' court will be under section 2 of the 1987 Act.

Many of the recent challenges to the operation of the 1990 Act have in fact been made in relation to investigations on behalf of foreign authorities carried out by the SFO (for example *Finninvest and R. v. Bow Street Magistrates Court ex parte Montgomery*) and these are extensively covered elsewhere at the appropriate part of this book.

The SFO has prepared a guide to Obtaining Evidence in the United Kingdom in respect of cases of serious or complex fraud. This can be obtained from the SFO, and is available in translation to other European languages also.

CHAPTER 14
Mutual Assistance Apart From the 1990 Act

14.00 Whilst the aim of this book is to examine the machinery of mutual assistance in criminal matters and thus the provisions of the 1990 Act and their practical effect, it would present a partial picture, if other forms of international co-operation were completely ignored.

Nothing in the Act in any way alters the well-established and vital channels of communication and evidence gathering that have grown up internationally, on a formal and informal basis, between police, customs, the DTI and tax authorities, under various bilateral arrangements and memoranda of understanding.

The explanatory report on the European Convention on Mutual Assistance in Criminal Matters (Council of Europe, Strasbourg 1969),[1] whose object is to facilitate understanding of the Convention, rather than to provide an authoritative guide on its interpretation, makes it plain that the clear intention of the framers of the Convention (as was that of the United Kingdom Parliament) was to complement, not derogate from, these arrangements.

It is outside the scope of this book to attempt an exhaustive review of these arrangements or their provisions; one must necessarily be selective and highlight only those areas which are most likely to impact upon the practitioner.

Memoranda of Understanding (MOU)

14.01 Rather than enter into formal treaties, regulators and government departments have favoured the use of the informal MOU, which is much simpler, faster, more flexible and, above all, confidential. There is no requirement for them to be registered with any organisation nor need they be published. They do however provide an agreed framework between the parties, for assisting each other in the collection and transfer of information and are an invaluable means both of ensuring close appreciation of respective regulatory systems and of enhancing closer international co-operation.

> "The request by the relevant foreign agency would not, and would not be intended to, give rise to a binding legal obligation to provide the assistance requested; it would provide a facility to the domestic agency to provide the assistance requested in appropriate cases".[2]

MOUs will tend to be used in circumstances where formal letters of request are not necessary. They will facilitate informal contacts and exchanges of information.

---

1 App. D.
2 *Mutual Assistance between Business Regulatory Agencies: A paper by the Australian Attorney-General's Department in Commonwealth Secretariat*, 1990 Meeting of Commonwealth Law Ministers: Memoranda Part 1 (1991) p. 250.

An MOU will set out the procedure which is to be followed when making a request for information, with definitions of the relevant legal rules and requirements, together with the grounds upon which assistance will be refused.[3]

Police to police/customs to customs

14.02 There has been considerable development over recent years in relation to specialist law enforcement agencies, in particular with regard to the police, the work of Interpol and the creation of Europol.[4]

In the field of customs co-operation, the Customs Co-operation Council, with its headquarters in Brussels, through its Enforcement Committee, is responsible for the international organisation of co-operation between various customs bodies. Of particular relevance in this area are the Naples and Nairobi Customs Co-Operation Arrangements.[5] These Conventions deal with various aspects of international customs work, including assistance on requests in relation to surveillance operations, the appearance of customs officials before foreign courts and co-ordinated enforcement and intelligence operations, with regard to drugs.

Requests which can be dealt with directly by police or customs, are sent through Interpol or customs channels[6] and not through the Home Office unless this is demanded by the requesting judicial authority. Not only requests from foreign police forces fall into this category. The requirement is rather that the police (or customs) can execute the request, without the need to comply with any of the provisions of the 1990 Act. Such requests may come not only from foreign police forces (hence "police to police" enquiries) but often from foreign magistrates. They do not require the formality of a letter of request.

14.03 The areas in which such informal arrangements are most commonly utilised are:—

(a) the interviewing of witnesses and suspects in criminal investigations, who are willing to co-operate without appearing before a nominated court in the United Kingdom and whose evidence can be provided unsworn;

(b) sharing information with another state, regarding investigations into United Kingdom offences;

(c) the provision of details relating to medical or dental records, where the patient has consented in writing to disclosure[7];

(d) the provision of details of keepers of United Kingdom registered motor vehicles and of United Kingdom issued driving licences;

(e) providing details of previous convictions; if these are required purely for intelligence purposes, then no fingerprints need be provided; if however the details are required for the purposes of a police investigation, a certified copy of the person's previous convictions will be provided, on receipt of a copy of the person's fingerprints;

(f) providing telephone subscriber details;

---

3 By way of example in the field of criminal law see the MOU between the U.K. and the Russian Federation, App. W.
4 Council Act of July 26, 1995 drawing up the Convention on the Establishment of a European Police Office (Europol Convention).
5 See App. R.
6 The U.K. National Central Bureau of Interpol, part of NCIS (National Criminal Intelligence Service) London.
7 See Chap. 10 for the procedure where consent is withheld – "excluded material", page 125 *et seq.*

(g) providing passport details held by the United Kingdom Passport Agency (including photographs);

(h) providing medical samples, obtained with the consent of the person from whom they were obtained;

(i) if a person in the United Kingdom is in possession of property stolen abroad and is suspected of knowing that the property is stolen, the United Kingdom police can seize and secure that property;

14.04 These enquiries will either be handled by customs or by NCIS, or routed to a local police force. NCIS co-ordinates international enquiries, and, within the NCIS office is the United Kingdom National Central Bureau of Interpol.[8]

In its evidence to the House of Lords Select Committee, Customs and Excise stated:

"Customs & Excise authorities, as well as using the formal channels of assistance available under the legislation, also use a procedure known as Mutual Administrative Assistance (MAA). MAA involves the provision of information between agencies in different countries, but all information is given on a voluntary basis and can only be sent to the requesting agency if the person from whom the information is obtained consents. If subsequently it becomes necessary to formulate that information as evidence, in the strict definition of the term, then the formal channels of mutual legal assistance must be gone through as in normal cases."[9]

Dissemination of intelligence material outside the United Kingdom

14.05 The draft European Convention on Mutual Assistance in Criminal Matters contains provisions in relation to agreements between Member States as to covert investigations into crime.

Dissemination of intelligence material outside the European Economic Area (EEA)[10] is carried out in order to prevent or detect international crime and terrorism.[11]

Dissemination of intelligence material to foreign law enforcement agencies will be conducted where it is deemed a necessary means to achieve the desired result and it does not concern "confidential material"[12] unless due account has been taken of any restrictions on its use or requirement for special handling imposed by the officer who authorised its collection. If the material is to be passed to a country outside the EEA

---

8 The role of Interpol should be clearly distinguished from that of Europol. Europol, established by Convention in 1995 was set up to provide strategic overviews and analyses to assist Member States in the investigation of the mandated crime areas. These include terrorism, unlawful drug trafficking and other serious forms of international crime, where there are factual indications that an organised criminal structure is involved, and two or more Member States are affected. Europol is not an operational police force.

9 *Prosecuting Fraud on the Communities' Finances – the Corpus Juris*, European Communities Committee 9th Report 1998–99 H.L. Paper 62 (HMSO, London; ISBN 0 10 406299 1); see pp. 183–4.

10 The EEA comprises all Member States of the E.U. together with Iceland, Liechtenstein and Norway.

11 The Data Protection Act 1998 prohibits the transfer of personal data to countries outside the EEA unless that country ensures an adequate level of protection for the rights and freedoms of data subjects in relation to the processing of personal data, or a substantial public interest would be served by such dissemination. In such cases NCIS, Customs and Excise and the Metropolitan Police maintain secure liaison arrangements to ensure that such dissemination outside the EEA is only conducted after an assessment of the risk to the data subject and within the liaison arrangement.

12 Effectively material subject to legal professional privilege, excluded and journalistic material as defined in the Police Act 1997, ss. 98, 99 and 100.

which is judged not to possess an adequate level of protection, it is necessary first to assess the risks to the subject arising from the transfer of the intelligence material.

14.06 Dissemination is subject to authorisation depending upon its destination:—

(a) to foreign law enforcement agencies within the EEA it may be given:

(i) in the case of police, the National Crime Squad and the Scottish Crime Squad, by an officer subject to the supervision of an inspector; outside the EEA, authorisation must be given by an officer subject to the supervision of a superintendent;

(ii) in the case of NCIS and Customs and Excise, by an officer subject to the supervision of an officer of equivalent rank; outside the EEA, authorisation must be given by an officer subject to the supervision of an officer of equivalent rank.

Records must be maintained of the material disseminated together with any restrictions on its use or further dissemination, the addressee of the material and the objective of the dissemination. If the material is "confidential" a record must be kept of any restrictions on use or further dissemination and any requirements for special handling imposed by the officer who authorised its collection. In relation to countries outside the EEA where a risk assessment has been made due to the prior judgement that it did not possess adequate levels of protection, the risk assessment to the data subject concerned must be recorded.

Mutual assistance between regulators

14.07 The rapid growth in criminal mutual assistance merely mirrors the internationalisation of serious crime. In like fashion, the global securities and futures markets have flourished, driven by the massive advances in computers and communications, which have, in turn, bred interdependence between the world's major trading partners. Investments are now diversified globally, with increasing use of foreign debt and equity markets to raise finance.

Scavenging in the wake of this explosion is the transnational criminal. Mutual assistance in criminal matters is insufficient on its own to combat such a threat, for it can be cumbersome and slow.

This has been recognised by the steady growth in the sharing of information between regulatory bodies and the use of their sanctions to complement, where necessary, the criminal process.

14.08 Of particular importance in the international regulatory field is the MOU entered into between the United States Security & Exchange and Commodities Futures Trading Commission on the one hand and the United Kingdom DTI and SIB on the other, on September 25, 1991, which followed the changes made by the 1990 Act and which is reproduced at Appendix T.[13]

It would be wrong however to assume that such co-operation is limited to MOU's; there are many other bilateral and multilateral treaties, of which one of the most significant is the 1989 Council of Europe Convention on Insider Trading and its Protocol.

H.M. Treasury's consultation document upon the Financial Services and Markets Bill sets out how the Bill will ensure that, when the FSA becomes aware of problems or potential problems with a regulated firm, it will be able to act immediately, to

---

13 See App. T.

protect the interests of consumers and to ensure that steps are taken by the firm to remedy the situation. It will have the power to impose sanctions, in order to deter and punish unacceptable behaviour and the Bill gives the FSA a range of effective powers, to intervene in a regulated firm's business and to discipline wrong doers.

14.09   The FSA will have statutory intervention and disciplinary powers and a wide discretion to take the action it thinks appropriate. This may, in serious cases, involve the revocation of authorisation or, in less serious cases, restricting the firm's business activities, or imposing controls on how it handles its assets.

It will also be able to apply for orders to freeze assets. These powers will be exercised internationally,

> "The Financial Services industry operates across national boundaries. A number of recent events, such as the collapse of Barings, have underlined the need for extensive co-operation with regulatory bodies and other countries. The Bill enables the FSA to use its intervention powers at the request of, or to assist, an overseas regulator. It is intended that the Bill, as introduced, will also give the FSA new powers to conduct investigations on their behalf".[14]

Companies Act 1989

14.10   In September 1991 the International Organisation of Securities Commissions (IOSCO) held its sixteenth conference. It issued a set of principles for MOU's[15], as a "conspectus" for use by securities and futures regulatory authorities in developing MOU's with their foreign counterparts, in order to develop effective tools for fighting fraud and other abuses in the securities and futures markets. Principle 7 is particularly relevant:—

> "MOU should provide that the authorities will take all reasonable steps to ensure that they can utilise their full domestic powers to execute requests for assistance. The available assistance should include, whether the requested authority has such powers, obtaining documents and the statements or testi-mony of witnesses, granting access to the requested authorities non-public files, and conducting inspections of regulated entities."

In line with this principle are sections 82 to 91 of the Companies Act 1989.

Scope of requests

14.11   Provisions exist under the 1989 Companies Act, for requests for information or evidence to be made to the United Kingdom by an authority which has specialist regulatory functions, similar to those undertaken by the United Kingdom authorities, in respect of a company's financial services (including insider dealing, insurance or banking). The Secretary of State for Trade and Industry has powers under the Act, which he may exercise, in order to assist the requesting authority.

Scope of powers

14.12   The Secretary of State, or his authorised investigators, has power to compel persons to answer questions put to them and can examine those persons on oath and require production of any documents specified by the investigators. Investigators can

---

14 H.M. Treasury Financial Services & Markets Bill, a Consultation Document, Part I, Overview of Financial & Regulatory Forum.
15 App. S.

also require production of documents or information from banks, in certain circumstances. They do not, however, have power to exercise search warrants.

Reciprocity

14.13 This is not a pre-condition. In deciding whether to exercise the powers, the Secretary of State may take into account in particular:

(a) Whether corresponding assistance would be given in that country or territory to an authority exercising regulatory functions in the United Kingdom.

(b) Whether the enquiries relate to the possible breach of a law or other requirement which has no close parallel in the United Kingdom or involves the assertion of a jurisdiction not recognised by the United Kingdom.

(c) The seriousness of the matter to which the enquiries relate, the importance to the enquiry of the information sought in the United Kingdom and whether the assistance could be obtained by other means; whether it is otherwise appropriate in the public interest to give the assistance sought.

Principles governing grant of assistance

14.14 During the passage of the Bill through Parliament, the then Secretary of State for Trade & Industry indicated the considerations he would take into account when exercising his powers:—

(a) There must be a belief on his part that the request was made in good faith.

(b) Confidentiality must be protected and therefore it would only be released:—

    (i) under arrangements, (e.g. bilateral MOU's) covering the exchange of regulatory information and containing provisions limiting use and disclosure by the representing authority; and

    (ii) in the absence of such arrangements, subject to the imposition of broadly similar conditions imposed on an ad hoc basis.

The Secretary of State would have a discretion, if there was reason to suspect non-observation of these conditions, not to set up an investigation, or not to provide some, or all of the information collected during an investigation.[16]

Cost

14.15 Finally, the Secretary of State may decline to exercise his powers unless the overseas regulatory authority undertakes to make such contribution towards the cost of their exercise as the Secretary of State considers appropriate.

Effectively the 1989 Act provides two forms of assistance:—

(a) that of allowing disclosure to overseas regulatory authorities of information obtained under existing investigative powers, or contained in other legislation, which was amended accordingly:—

---

16 *Hansard* H.C. Parl. Deb., Vol. 504 col. 107.

(i) Banking Act 1987 section 84(1) amended by Companies Act 1989 section 81(2).

(ii) Building Societies Act 1986 section 53(7)(6)(iii) inserted by Companies Act 1989 section 80.

(iii) Financial Services Act 1986 section 180(1)(99) added by Companies Act 1989 section 76(3)(f).

(iv) Companies Act 1985 section 449(1)(m) as substituted by Companies Act 1989 section 65(2)(i) which provides that information or documents produced under section 447 of the 1985 Act can be disclosed for the purposes of enabling or assisting an overseas regulatory authority to exercise its regulatory functions.[17]

(b) that of providing powers to assist "overseas regulatory authorities" (section 82–91 of the Act).

The inter-reaction between regulatory and criminal assistance

14.16 Whilst MOU's rarely stand alone and will normally supplement those co-operation systems, both formal and informal, already in place, difficulties may arise when the actions under scrutiny are criminal in their nature, and thus vulnerable to the machinery of formal criminal mutual assistance provisions existing between the parties.

Whilst safeguards exist under the criminal mutual assistance structure to protect the rights of criminal suspects, these are often absent from the provisions of MOU's. Indeed their confidentiality may, by definition, preclude them.

The 1993 Commonwealth statement declared that the availability of assistance by other means and especially through existing routes governing the provisions of mutual assistance in criminal matters, was of relevance in exercising discretion as to whether or not assistance should be granted.[18]

The Companies Act 1989 poses an additional problem, in that it provides an alternative statutory route to the foreign investigator, who may feel spoilt for choice. In a sense, the decision may, in part, be made for him by the Home Office, for if, upon receipt of a request under the 1990 Act, the MLA Section concludes that the 1989 Companies Act powers are more appropriate, it will pass the request to the DTI.

14.17 In a paper delivered to the 1992 Oxford Conference on International and White Collar Crime,[19] Bridget Chase offered the following guidance to her foreign counterparts:—

(a) Are the investigations/proceedings civil or administrative rather than penal in nature?

If they are, then it is unlikely that the 1990 Act procedure will be appropriate.

(b) Is the information required as evidence in criminal proceedings?[20]

If criminal evidence is required, it may be that the Companies Act, with its limitations as to the method and form in which the information can be

---

17 Companies Act 1985, s. 449(1)(c) as substituted by Companies Act 1989, s. 65(2)(d) authorises disclosure for the purposes of assisting the Secretary of State to discharge his functions under Part III of the 1989 Act, which includes responding to assistance from overseas regulatory authorities.
18 See also Companies Act 1989, s. 82(4)(c).
19 B. Chase "*Mutual Assistance to Overseas Business Regulatory Bodies – Action Against Trans-national Criminality*".
20 But see the Proceeds of Crime Act 1996.

obtained, is simply not appropriate. The 1990 Act will permit evidence to be taken in a form which is more likely to be admitted in the criminal proceedings which follow.

(c)   Is there a clear idea of which witnesses are required to be summoned in court and a clear list of questions to be put to them?

Magistrates will require detailed background and questions, such as it is only possible to prepare when all the facts are known.

(d)   Is the request really to discover what has been happening?

If enquiries are at an early stage and the real need is to know the story, it may be better to address a request to the DTI/Treasury, since the 1989 Act powers and indeed the DTI personnel, used as they are to fact-finding enquiries, may be most appropriate.

(e)   Is confidential information needed from banks?

The 1989 Act is tailor-made for the obtaining of this sort of evidence and its restricted disclosure provisions could give comfort to those from whom the information is sought.[21]

(f)   Are foreign investigators to be involved directly with the United Kingdom investigations requested or can they support these investigations indirectly?

If it is possible for overseas investigators to be authorised, without causing conflict of interest problems, it may assist the fact finding investigations to have them directly involved, particularly where they may have background knowledge of a case.

(g)   Are witnesses to be questioned in private rather than in open court?

The 1989 Act provides for a confidential investigation using inquisitorial methods. The 1990 Act uses open court, with its accusatorial procedure, giving an opportunity for Counsel to put questions to a witness.

14.18   In conclusion, whichever method is employed to deal with requests, it is clear that means now exist in the United Kingdom which provide not only for fact finding investigations but also the provision of evidence which is admissible in overseas proceedings. It is clear that the United Kingdom cannot be considered a haven for those involved in white collar crime committed overseas. All those who are involved in the enforcement process are anxious to see that the new powers are used to the full in the fight against such crime and are always glad to assist overseas authorities in determining the choice of route and the contents of their request.

Mutual assistance between foreign revenue departments

14.19   Exchange of information with foreign Revenue departments would arise under the provisions of relevant Double Taxation agreements and in particular the EEC Mutual Assistance Directive.[22]

This Directive, No. 77/799/EEC, was issued on December 19, 1977 by the Council of the European Communities and required Member States' Revenue authorities to

---

21 See App. V.
22 Extended to VAT by Directive 79/1070.

provide each other, on request, with information regarding income and gains by tax payers in the relevant Member State. This Directive was initially implemented by section 77 of the Finance Act 1978, which removed the obligation of secrecy from United Kingdom Revenue officials, in relation to authorities of other Member States. This, however, provided only partial co-operation, for whilst the Revenue was authorised to pass on information obtained for its own purposes, it had no authority to make a special reciprocal request for information required for the purposes of tax liability in another Member State. Full compliance with the Directive was achieved by section 125 of the Finance Act 1990 which extended the powers in the Taxes Management Act 1970 (TMA) section 20 to permit the issue of a notice to require production of documents and information necessary to determine liability to tax on income or capital in a Member State other than the United Kingdom. Prior thereto the power under section 20 TMA was confined to material considered necessary to determine liability only to United Kingdom income, corporation and capital gains taxes.

It should be noted, however, that these wider powers are subject to the same conditions and restrictions as are applicable to the production of documents for United Kingdom purposes. Thus

(a) The Board may only issue a section 20(2) TMA notice without the consent of a General or Special Commissioner for information required or sought by a Member State where there has been serious non-compliance with the tax laws of that State (Finance Act 1990 section 125(2)(a)).

(b) If there is an appeal, review or similar proceedings in the Member State in relation to the tax in question, documents or information may not be required (Finance Act 1990 section 125(2)(b)).

(c) Where a document originating six years prior to the issue of the notice is required, a General or Special Commissioner must be satisfied that tax has been or may be lost to the Member State as a result of the tax payer's fraud (TMA 1970 section 20B(6) and Finance Act 1990 section 125(2)(c)).

Under the Directive, the following points should be noted:—

(a) Article 2 enables a request for information to be made between two Member States, however the competent authority of the requested state has a discretion whether or not to comply if it appears that its opposite number in the requesting state has not exhausted its own usual information which it could have used in the circumstances of the case to obtain the information sought without jeopardising its objective;

(b) Enquiries are made by the competent authority of the request state (Article 2(2));

(c) Whilst in normal circumstances requests will only be made in the course of an investigation in the requesting state, under Article 4, provision is made for the "spontaneous exchange" of information by the competent authority of a Member State *without prior request*. It may forward information of which it has knowledge to its opposite number in a fellow Member State:— if the competent authority of the one Member State has grounds for supposing there may be a loss of tax in the other Member State;

(d) A person liable to tax obtains a reduction in or exemption from tax in the one Member State which would give rise in an increase to tax or to liability to tax in the other Member States;

(e) Business dealings between a person liable to tax in a Member State and a person liable to tax in another Member State are conducted through one or more countries in such a way that a saving in tax may result in one or the other Member State or in both;

(f) The competent authority of a Member State has grounds for supposing that a saving of tax may result from artificial transfers of profits within groups of enterprises;

(g) Information forwarded to the one Member State by the competent authority of the other Member State has enabled information to be obtained which may be relevant in assessing to tax in the latter Member State.

14.20 There are secrecy provisions relating to the information supplied under Article 7(1) to the effect that information made known to a fellow Member State should be subject to the same secrecy provisions as under its domestic legislation.

Article 8 provides limits to the exchange of information in that no obligation is imposed by the Directive either to carry out enquiries or to provide information if the requested state is prevented by its laws or administrative practices from carrying out the enquiries or from collecting or using the information for its own purposes.

Similarly, information will be refused if it would lead to the disclosure of a commercial, industrial or professional secret or of a commercial process or of information whose disclosure would be contrary to public policy.

Thus, foreign tax authorities will be limited to obtaining only that which could be obtained by Customs & Excise or the Inland Revenue; similarly if United Kingdom tax investigators seek information from other E.U. Member States they will be limited to information which is obtainable by the tax authority in the requested state.

14.21 The SCO London Liaison Unit, (Angel Court, 199 Borough High Street, London, SE1 1HZ) assumes a role similar to the MLA in relation to the majority of exchanges of information with foreign Revenue departments. It will provide advice to United Kingdom Revenue officials on whether it is appropriate to request information from overseas and it will also send information spontaneously to foreign Revenues.

International Co-operation under section 426 Insolvency Act 1986

14.22 Mention should be made of the provisions of section 426(4) of this Act which provides for co-operation between United Kingdom courts and those in other jurisdictions[23] exercising jurisdiction in relation to insolvency. The relevant sub-sections read:—

426(4)–

"The courts having jurisdiction in relation to insolvency law in any part of the United Kingdom shall assist the courts having the corresponding jurisdiction in any other part of the United Kingdom or any relevant country or territory."

426(5)–

"For the purposes of sub-section (4) a request made to a court in any part of the

---

23 A country or territory must be designated by the Secretary of State before its courts may make a request for assistance.

United Kingdom by a court in any other part of the United Kingdom or in a relevant country or territory is authority for the court to which the request is made to apply, in relation to any matters specified in the request, the insolvency law which is applicable by either court in relation to comparable matters falling within its jurisdiction.

In exercising its discretion under this sub-section, a court shall have regard in particular to the rules of private international law."

14.23 Whilst 426(4) provides that the United Kingdom "shall" give assistance, implying a mandatory obligation, the courts have been unwilling to abandon their discretion.

Reference should be made to *Re. BCCI (No. 9)* [1993] B.C.C. 787; *Re Focus Insurance* [1996] B.C.C. 659 and in particular *Hughes v. Hannover* [1997] 1 B.C.L.C. 497 in which the Court of Appeal [Morritt L.J.] stated that there was nothing in the wording of the section which limited the jurisdiction or powers of the court, the section indicating which courts had an obligation to assist a requesting court. On receipt of a request the court could use its general jurisdiction, the Insolvency Act 1986, and any specified sections of the Company Directors' Disqualification Act 1986, and finally, the law of the requesting country if this did not conflict with the United Kingdom law under section 426(5). The court's duty was to decide whether assistance could properly be given in accordance with these three sources.

CHAPTER 15

The Future Role of Mutual Legal Assistance

"First, having recognised the inadequacies of our existing legislation, we have been determined to secure arrangements which will place us in the first rank internationally in our ability to co-operate with other countries in this most important of areas.

Secondly, we have sought to ensure that once the measures which are proposed in the Bill are enacted, we will be able to seek assistance from other countries to just the same extent, and in the same ways, as we are able to offer help to them.

Thirdly, we have been conscious that however much we may wish to assist other countries, we cannot allow Parliament to make greater powers available on behalf of overseas authorities than are available to our own police or prosecuting authorities in domestic cases."

15.00   So were the principles of the forthcoming Criminal Justice (International Co-operation) Act 1990 described by Earl Ferrers, the Minister of State in December 1989.[1]

There can be no doubt that in the ten years that have passed since the Minister's statement, the United Kingdom has advanced significantly and is now, as Earl Ferrers had hoped, in the first rank internationally in its ability to co-operate with other countries, in what is increasingly recognised as a crucial weapon in the fight against international and organised crime.

There are alternative approaches to the problem of the increased need for international co-operation, and these are being canvassed in a number of international fora, and being supported with varying levels of enthusiasm by international practitioners.

Corpus Juris

15.01   A more novel approach to the question of international criminal activity, and appropriate investigation and prosecution, and one which could render traditional measures of mutual legal assistance to an extent obsolete has been offered in the form of the so called "Corpus Juris", a study financed by the European Commission and involving eight European Professors. The background to this study is concern about fraud and corruption that directly or indirectly affects the E.U. budget. Frustrated by, among others, the failure of European Member States to ratify or implement those instruments which existed to help protect them against serious criminality, the European Commission sought an alternative approach.

"We propose a radically new response to the absurdity, widely condemned but still tolerated, which consists in opening up borders to criminals whilst closing

---

1 513 H.L. Off. Rep. col. 1217, December 12, 1989.

them to law enforcement agencies, at the risk of transforming our countries into havens for crime"[2]

15.02 The Corpus Juris envisages, for cases of crimes against the financial interests of the European Union, a standard set of offences and prosecution procedures. This would result in prosecution for any of the specified and defined offences being possible in any of the Member States notwithstanding where the offence was actually committed. (The creation of a so called "European Judicial space"). The Corpus Juris also envisages a European Director of Public Prosecutions for such offences with local deputies, and it follows that investigations would be possible within the area of all Member States without the formality of seeking international judicial co-operation by traditional methods, or even extradition. Although the proposal as it stands is strictly limited to financial crimes affecting the E.U. budget, it goes without saying that the solutions it proposes could also be applied to other forms of transnational crime. This proposal is still being developed under the aegis of the European Commission, and it remains to be seen how much support it obtains. At this stage, however, it has received a mixed reception in Member States of the E.U. Some States are clearly more enthusiastic than others, and in the United Kingdom, there has been, broadly, a degree of interest, but additionally, a degree of scepticism as to how such radical proposals could work in practice. Some lurid headlines, (*e.g.* "Freedom's flame flickers" (*The Times*, March 23, 1999)) have exaggerated the effect of the proposals, and have generated an unmerited atmosphere of hostility to a genuine attempt to deal with the problems of pan-European criminal activity.

The U.K. Government's position on Corpus Juris was set out on April 28, 1999 by Lord Williams of Mostyn in a written answer:

> "The Government notes that, although the European Parliament welcomes Corpus Juris as a possible example for future developments, it said that it was not seeking the creation of a European Penal Code. The Government fully shares the objective of fighting fraud against the Community budget, but disagrees with many of the recommendations of the "Corpus Juris" study, including the proposal to establish a European public prosecutor. The Government also rejects the idea that the European public prosecutor should be given control over Europol. "Corpus Juris" has not been submitted to the Council of Ministers, but if this were to happen, unanimous agreement would be needed for its proposals to be adopted and come into effect."

15.03 The House of Lords in its report on the E.U. Corpus Juris raised serious objection on a number of grounds:—

(a) The need for major changes in United Kingdom criminal law and procedure.

(b) Its questionable feasibility.

(c) The European Director of Public Prosecutions' democratic unaccountability.

(d) The threat to defendants' human rights, demonstrated most vividly by the proposal that suspects be remanded in custody for several months prior to charge.

---

2 Corpus Juris, 1997, p.40.

15.04   Lord Hope of Craighead noted:

"In our view, however, this scheme does not offer an acceptable way forward. There are too many conflicts with our system of criminal justice, and the concept of a single legal area cannot be justified in the present climate of public opinion. We think that energy and resources would be better directed towards improvements in mutual legal assistance and better practical co-operation in criminal matters between E.U. Member States."[3]

Another approach which has recently been ventilated at a European level is the so called "EuroJust". EuroJust can perhaps be described as a European clearing house. It would be a structure containing a number of lawyers from Member States, who would be contacted when it appeared that a case involved serious international crime. If the case were accepted by EuroJust, then the lawyers would be able to call on their colleagues within EuroJust to facilitate and expedite investigations in the countries concerned. This could enable a speedier completion of investigation, and a full discussion of the appropriate venue for any trial in the case, bearing in mind the knowledge of all the various circumstances involved. The idea of EuroJust has only recently been mooted, and much further discussion on the subject is likely over coming months.

Criminal Justice Act 1993 – Part I

15.05   Other developments have emphasised the increasing reliance that will be placed upon mutual legal assistance in the future.

On June 1, 1999 Part I of the Criminal Justice Act 1993 was finally implemented. This contains important provisions on extra territorial jurisdiction which will require intense international co-operation in their implementation.

The provisions contained in Part I of the Act in sections 1–6 extend the jurisdiction of the United Kingdom courts in respect of a number of offences in specific ways.

Two groups of offences are defined:

Group A

Theft
Obtaining Property by Deception
Obtaining a pecuniary advantage by deception
False accounting
False statements by Company Directors
Procuring the execution of a valuable security by deception
Blackmail
Handling stolen goods
Obtaining services by deception
Avoiding liability by deception
Forgery
Copying a false statement
Using a copy of a false statement
Offences under section 5 of the Forgery & Counterfeiting Act 1971 relating to money orders, share certificates, passports, etc.
Cheating the public revenue

---

3 *Prosecuting Fraud on the Communities' Finances – the Corpus Juris*, European Communities Committee, 9th Report 1998–99 H.L. Paper 62 (HMSO, London; ISBN 0 10 406299 1).

Group B

Conspiracy to commit a Group A offence
Conspiracy to defraud
Attempting to commit a Group A offence
Incitement to commit a Group A offence

15.06   Section 2(3) provides that a person may be guilty of a Group A offence, "if any of the offences which are relevant events in relation to the offence occurred in England or Wales". A "relevant event" is defined under section 2(1) as "any omission or other event, proof of which is required for conviction of the offence".

Thus, from the implementation of the section, there will be offences which will for the first time be subject to the jurisdiction of the English courts. This is relevant to considerations of mutual legal assistance, since the cases which fall to be prosecuted under this section may be cases which, before the implementation of the legislation, would have been prosecuted elsewhere (if they were prosecuted at all) and might have been the subject of letters of request from foreign authorities for evidence. This legislation will extend the capacity of the English courts to try cases, where the criminality extends across several jurisdictions, and will enable the English authorities themselves to take action.

15.07   The provision in section 71 of the Act however, has been in effect for some time already. This section was enacted in direct response to the Keith Report on the Enforcement Powers of the Revenue Departments, which recommended the enactment of a provision to deal with multi-territory frauds in the European community. Under section 71, a person is guilty of a serious offence in the United Kingdom if, in the United Kingdom, he "assists in or induces any conduct outside the United Kingdom which involves the commission of a serious offence against the law of another Member State". The section defines the serious offences to which the section refers and these include a number of matters relating to community duties and taxes, provided that the maximum term of imprisonment for the offence is at least twelve months.

The need for caution

15.08   Increased reliance upon mutual legal assistance will, however, require constant monitoring to ensure that United Kingdom domestic law is observed and that the rights of United Kingdom citizens are protected.

In his statement to the House of Lords,[4] Earl Ferrers identified the danger of making available to foreign authorities greater powers than are available to our own police or prosecuting authorities in domestic cases.

This has, to a limited extent, already occurred – see Chapter 6 (page 84). Under section 4 of the 1990 Act, witnesses holding special procedure material may be required, upon service of a witness summons issued by a magistrates' court, to produce that material to the court and thence for transmission to the foreign investigator. A British investigator would be required not only to apply to a circuit judge in the Crown Court for access to such material, but also to satisfy the stringent safeguards of PACE.

Other areas will doubtless call for intervention from the courts, particularly in the provision of evidence and the search for and seizure of materials, where the needs of prosecutors and investigators are often in conflict with the rights of the citizen. Whilst

---

4 513 H.L. Off. Rep. col. 1217, December 12, 1989.

safeguards are built into the various mutual assistance instruments, statutory or otherwise, their effectiveness is limited.

What safeguards currently exist?

15.09   There are numerous exclusions and reservations, aimed primarily at the grounds upon which mutual legal assistance will be refused. The major multilateral agreements[5] identify the standard safeguards.

In general, assistance may be refused by the requested State:—

(a)   If the offence is regarded as being of a **political nature**;

(b)   If the request is made for the purpose of prosecuting a person on account of that person's **race, sex, religion, nationality, ethnic origins or political opinions**;

(c)   If prosecution for the offence in the requesting state would be incompatible with the requested state's laws on **double jeopardy**;

(d)   If the request requires evidence from witnesses or production of material in circumstances which are **protected by privilege or non-compellability** in the requested state[6].

(e)   Unless the request for **search and seizure** and delivery of materials to the requesting state are consistent with the law and practice of the requested state.

15.10   There is some concern that these safeguards are insufficient to protect the fundamental rights of those the subject of requests, or affected by them as, on occasion, treaties are ignored and on other occasions, adherence to the treaty leads to rights abuse.[7]

Bypassing the Treaty

Unilateral extra territorial jurisdiction

15.11   The analysis above indicates the requirement that evidence sought, whether in proceedings or by means of search and seizure, must be obtainable under the laws of the requested State. Thus, if Country A requires the production of evidence from Country B, if under the law of Country B it is forbidden to provide that evidence or material, Country A will be unable under the treaty to obtain it. The existence of such a prohibition recognises a right of non-disclosure or non-production, on the part of the holder of the material.

---

5 The European Convention on Mutual Assistance in Criminal Matters, 1959; The Scheme Relating to Mutual Assistance in Criminal Matters within the Commonwealth; The United Nations Model Treaty on Mutual Assistance in Criminal Matters, 1990.

6 The Commonwealth Scheme specifically widens this condition to include non-compulsion in criminal proceedings in the requesting State; the United Kingdom has qualified its position in the latter regard in circumstances where the requesting State concedes exemption, failing which the evidence will be taken but not transmitted pending determination of the claim by the requesting state. It is of interest that the United States. Supreme Court has recently ruled that the 5th Amendment does not protect a witness from giving evidence in United States proceedings that might incriminate that witness in foreign proceedings. See *United States v. Aloyzas Balsys*, June 25, 1998.

7 We are greatly indebted to G. Gane and M. Mackarel for their excellent paper "The Admissibility of Evidence Obtained from Abroad into Criminal Proceedings the Interpretation of Mutual Legal Assistance Treaties and Use of Evidence Irregularly Obtained" *European Journal of Crime, Criminal Law & Justice* 1996–2, which has been an invaluable source of a number of foreign authorities referred to herein.

15.12 In-roads into the protection of such rights (and their recognition in the relevant treaties to which the countries themselves are party) have been made by the unilateral approach of the courts in certain jurisdictions (the United States in particular). The existence of a treaty has been ignored and alternative methods sought to obtain evidence which would not be forthcoming under it.

In *Re Sealed Case*[8] which arose out of the Arms to Iran investigation, the appellant was *subpoena*ed by a United States grand jury to produce financial documentation which belonged to companies in Switzerland. He refused to comply with the sub-poena on the grounds that the documents themselves were protected by Swiss secrecy laws, that the *subpoena* could not override those laws and that under Swiss law, compliance with the *subpoena* was forbidden. Had the appellant complied, he would have risked prosecution in Switzerland, a point confirmed by the Swiss Government which appeared as amicus. It was argued that the United States/Switzerland MLAT treaty was the proper means of obtaining the material, which had the United States authorities relied upon it, would have precluded production of the documentation.

The District of Columbia Court of Appeal held that mere signature of the treaty did not limit the United States Government's powers to obtain evidence to those contained under the MLAT. The court held that despite the fact that the evidence could not be obtained lawfully under the treaty, and despite the fact that to provide it would have rendered the object of the *subpoena* in breach of Swiss law, the appellant had no option but to comply with the *subpoena*.

15.13 A similar decision was made in *Marsoner v. United States*,[9] where the appellant was ordered to authorise disclosure of Austrian bank accounts. He refused so to do and was not only fined but also imprisoned for civil contempt of court, this despite the fact that compulsion to sign such a disclosure violated Austrian law and Articles 3, 6 and 8 of the European Convention of Human Rights, which are incorporated into it.

It would appear that, only if there is in place a specific exclusion within the treaty that such compulsory measures are in breach of the spirit of the MLAT, will such unilateral action be avoided[10].

Relying upon illegally obtained evidence

15.14 The existence of informal evidence gathering techniques between investigating agencies of different countries may lend itself to abuse by those agencies either in their own, or more likely, in foreign states[11].

One or two examples may suffice:—

(a) In *United States v. Verdugo-Urquidez*[12] after the United States Government had obtained an arrest warrant based upon a complaint charging an alien who was a citizen and resident of Mexico with various narcotics related offences, Mexican police officers apprehended the alien and transported him to a border patrol station, where United States Marshalls arrested him. United States DEA agents, working in concert with Mexican police officers

---

8 *Re Sealed Case* (1987), 832 F.2d 1268 United States Ct of Appeals for Dist. of Columbia.
9 *Marsoner v. United States re Grand Jury proceedings*; *Marsoner v. United States* (1994), 40F.3d.959, United States Court of Appeal 9th Circuit.
10 Under Art. 17 of the United Kingdom-United States Treaty concerning the Cayman Islands and Mutual Legal Assistance in Criminal Matters 1987, parties are specifically precluded from enforcing any compulsory measures (including a grand jury *subpoena*) for the production of documents located in the territory of the other party with respect to any criminal offence within the scope of the Treaty.
11 See also below under "Informal Intelligence".
12 *United States v. Verdugo-Urquidez* (1990) 110 S.Ct.1056.

then searched the alien's residences in Mexico seizing certain documents; these searches were illegal as no warrant was obtained. When the prosecution sought to produce the evidence, the defendant challenged its admission alleging that the searches were in violation of the 4th Amendment to the United States Constitution which protects the citizen against unreasonable searches and seizures.

A majority of the Supreme Court refused to reject the evidence, holding that the protection of the 4th Amendment was only available to United States nationals or "those with sufficient connection to the country" and the defendant having been returned under arrest to the United States appeared to have no voluntary connection with the United States such as might afford him that protection. It did not apply to the search and seizure by United States agents of property that was owned by a non-resident alien and located in a foreign country where at the time of the search, the alien, who had been lawfully but involuntarily present in the United States for only a matter of a few days prior to the search, was a citizen and resident of Mexico with no voluntary attachment to the United States and the place searched was in Mexico.[13]

(b) The United States courts only appear willing to reject such illegally obtained evidence if to admit it would "shock the conscience" of the court – a test laid down in *United States v. Marzano*,[14] in which case the defendant had absconded to the Cayman Islands from the United States where he was suspected of being involved in a bank theft. He was arrested in Cayman, by a local police officer, together with two FBI agents. His possessions were seized and handed over to the FBI agents and he was put on a plane to Miami without being informed that he could travel to any other destination. He was arrested in the United States, tried and convicted. The court was able to conclude that the FBI agents had played no part in any of the events taking place in the Cayman Islands and accordingly admitted the evidence in the proceedings.

Similarly the English courts refuse to exclude relevant admissible evidence solely on the ground that it was obtained by improper or unfair means.[15] The court is not concerned with how the evidence was obtained, the only fetters upon such malpractice being the court's discretion under Section 78 of the Police and Criminal Evidence Act 1984 (PACE) or its own inherent jurisdiction to prevent abuse of its process. It follows that the obtaining of illegal evidence will not necessarily preclude its admissibility despite the safeguards embodied in the mutual assistance treaties or legislation.

(c) In an English case, *R. v. Governor of Pentonville Prison ex parte Chinoy*,[16] the defendant was wanted by the United States for money laundering offences, having previously been a manager at the BCCI Bank in Paris. Contrary to French law, United States agents had unlawfully intercepted his telephone in France. Knowing that such information would be excluded in

---

13 This was despite the fact that the relevant MLAT between the United States and Mexico, concluded after Verdugo-Urquidez's arrest but before the Supreme Court hearing, expressly forbids one party "to undertake in the territorial jurisdiction of the other, the exercise and performance of the functions or authority exclusively entrusted to the authorities of that other party by its national laws or regulations".
14 *United States v. Marzano* (1976) 537 F.2d.257.
15 *R. v. Sang* [1979] 2 All E.R. 1222.
16 *R. v. Governor of Pentonville Prison ex parte Chinoy* [1992] 1 All E.R. 317.

extradition proceedings in France, as it contravened both French law and the European Convention on Human Rights, it was arranged by the United States that Chinoy should be arrested by the English police, when he visited the United Kingdom. It was anticipated (as it happened, correctly) that in all likelihood he would be extradited from the United Kingdom, as no breach of English law had taken place, only French law. On seeking to overturn his committal for extradition, Chinoy asserted that the American action in arranging for him to be arrested in the United Kingdom was an abuse of process of the United Kingdom court and, additionally, the court should have excluded much of the prosecution evidence, using its Section 78 PACE[17] discretion.

The court took a robust view, applying the test of *Sang*[18] and expressing its lack of concern with how the evidence was obtained. The events complained of took place prior to the jurisdiction of the English courts and therefore could not be held to be an abuse of their process; the only test to apply was whether the prejudicial effect of the evidence outweighed its probative value.

(d)   Somewhat similar considerations came before the House of Lords two years later in *Bennett*[19] where the Court, by a majority, recognised the extent of the power of at least the High Court, to intervene where there has been some gross unfairness preceding the criminal proceedings. In *Bennett* the ruling was made on the premise that he had been unlawfully brought to the United Kingdom for his trial. Lord Griffiths stated at p 64.

> "In the present case there is no suggestion that the appellant cannot have a fair trial, nor could it be suggested that it would have been unfair to try him if he had been returned to this country through extradition procedures. If the court is to have power to interfere with the prosecution in the present circumstances, it must be because the judiciary accepts a responsibility for the maintenance of the rule of law that embraces a willingness to oversee executive action and to refuse to countenance behaviour which threatens either basic human rights or the rule of law ... I have no doubt that the judiciary should accept this responsibility ... if it comes to the attention of the court that there has been a serious abuse of power, it should, in my view, express its disapproval by refusing to act upon it".

Lord Lowry at p.74 spoke of the power to stay proceedings being exercisable "because it offends the court's sense of justice and propriety to be asked to try the accused in the circumstances of a particular case."

The seeking of evidence by means not available under one's own jurisdiction.

15.15   Assuming that the request is made formally and both states proceed in accordance with their respective treaty obligations, in spite of the standard safeguards, rights of citizens in both the requesting and requested states may be threatened. Whilst the following examples are by no means exhaustive, they are emerging as potential areas for challenge.

---

17 Police and Criminal Evidence Act 1984.
18 [1979] All E.R. 1222.
19 *R. v. Horseferry Magistrates Court ex parte Bennett* [1994] 1 A.C. 42.

Whilst the United Kingdom courts have yet to rule upon the propriety of obtaining evidence from a foreign jurisdiction by means that would not be available in the United Kingdom, other jurisdictions have done so. The classic example is the recent Canadian decision of *Schreiber*.[20] The respondent, Schreiber, a Canadian citizen residing both in Canada and in Europe, had an interest in bank accounts in Switzerland. The Federal Department of Justice sent a letter of request to the Swiss authorities seeking their assistance with respect to a criminal investigation in Canada. The Swiss Government accepted the request and issued an order for the seizure of documents and records relating to S's accounts. Prior to delivery of the letter of request, no search warrant or other judicial authorisation had been obtained in Canada. The issue before the Supreme Court was whether the Canadian standard for the issuance of search warrants was required to be satisfied, before the Minister of Justice submitted the letter of request to the Swiss Authorities.

Section 8 of the Canadian Charter of Rights and Freedoms protects the individual from intrusions upon his privacy by the Government of Canada through unreasonable use of the power of search and seizure.

15.16 The majority of the court held that, by itself, the sending of a letter of request did not engage section 8 of the Charter. All of the actions that relied upon State compulsion, in order to interfere with the appellant's privacy interest, were undertaken in Switzerland, by Swiss authorities and were not subject to Charter scrutiny. Drawing a line between the Canadian actions, which did not implicate the Charter and the actions by the Swiss authorities, that would have so implicated the Charter, had they been undertaken by the Canadian authorities, was consistent with the Supreme Court's jurisprudence on matters involving Canada's international co-operation in criminal investigations and prosecutions. The safeguard was the court's power to exclude evidence obtained abroad, through foreign officials, where it is necessary to preserve the fairness of the trial.

15.17 The Chief Justice, however, reasoned thus: the Charter generally applies to the letter of request, as it is prepared by Canadian officials within Canada. However, the reasonableness of the search or seizure is measured by balancing the State's interest in law enforcement against the individual's interest in privacy. Accordingly, section 8 is only triggered if the individual can show that he or she had a reasonable expectation of privacy, in the place searched, or the material seized. The information was clearly the sort of information which the individual could expect to remain confidential, but the records were located in Switzerland and furthermore were obtained in a manner consistent with Swiss law. A Canadian residing in a foreign country should expect his or her privacy to be governed by the laws of that country. A search carried out by foreign authorities in a foreign country in accordance with foreign law does not infringe a person's reasonable expectation of privacy as he or she cannot reasonably expect more privacy than he or she is entitled to under that foreign law. "In this case there is no evidence that the appellant's records were seized illegally in Switzerland, and it therefore cannot be said that his reasonable expectation of privacy was violated." This is an interesting comment, for it implies that, had the records been seized illegally in Switzerland, then that expectation of privacy would have been violated and the Canadian court would have found an infringement of section 8 of the Charter, thereby running contrary to the United Kingdom and United States authorities cited above.[21]

---

20 *Schreiber v. Canada (Attorney General)* [1998] 5 B.H.R.C. 145.
21 *Verdugo-Urquidez, Marzano* and *Chinoy*, above.

15.18   The court considered the earlier Canadian authorities of *R. v. Plant*[22] and *R. v. Terry*.[23] Terry concerned the conduct of American authorities acting in the United States, who took statements from suspects in a manner that, although consistent with the American Bill of Rights, was inconsistent with the Charter. The court had held that the Charter could not govern the actions of foreign authorities acting in a foreign country.

Similar difficulties have arisen in the Belgian and English courts, and it is interesting to note the manner in which they have approached the problem.

Both Belgian cases involved the obtaining of evidence by the use of telephone taps applied outside Belgium. This was a method of investigation which was contrary to Belgian law, which provided that evidence upon which a criminal prosecution is to be founded must have been lawfully obtained and that no conviction could be founded upon evidence unlawfully obtained.

15.19   In the first case[24] the Netherlands police had intercepted telephone calls from the suspect (who was being investigated in Belgium) and a Dutch drugs trafficker in Holland. This intercept had been carried out at the request of the Belgian authorities. The intercepts were relied upon to convict the suspect in Belgian court proceedings. The conviction was upheld; provided the evidence had been obtained in conformity with the laws of the Netherlands and in circumstances compatible with the requirements of Article 8 of the European Convention on Human Rights, its use in Belgium did not violate the protection afforded by the Constitution to correspondence, nor the legislation prohibiting telephone intercepts.

In the second case[25] the intercept was carried out in France, as part of a French investigation, wholly independent from the Belgian authorities, or their investigation. The evidence was again permitted. As a criminal prosecution and conviction could only be based upon evidence that had been lawfully obtained, the Belgian courts had to ensure such evidence was lawfully obtained, whether that evidence was obtained abroad or not. It was not enough that the evidence had been obtained in conformity with the requirements of the foreign law. That French law had also been held by the European Court of Human Rights to comply with the requirements of the European Convention on Human Rights. The court suggested that whilst it was not for the Belgian court to determine the legality of procedures adopted in foreign states, the Belgian courts were entitled to refuse to rely upon evidence obtained by procedures which were incompatible with the European Convention on Human Rights.

15.20   The English courts have adopted a broadly similar approach. In *R. v. Governor of Belmarsh Prison ex parte Martin*,[26] the court sanctioned the admission in extradition proceedings of evidence of telephone conversations obtained by interception abroad.

Also in *R. v. Aujla (Ajit Singh)*[27] the trial judge ruled as admissible evidence of a telephone conversation between the accused in the United Kingdom and someone in the Netherlands, which had been lawfully intercepted by the Netherlands authorities. The Court of Appeal held that the 1985 Interception of Communications Act did not prohibit the use in United Kingdom proceedings of material gained through the

---

22 [1993] 3 S.C.R. 281.
23 [1996] 2 S.C.R. 207.
24 Cour de Cassation (2ième ch., sect.néerl) January 26, 1993 (en cause de Co.D). Revue de droit pénal, 1993, p. 768.
25 Cour de Cassation (2ième ch., sect.néerl) October 12, 1993 (en cause de Co.D). Revue de droit pénal, 1993, p. 792.
26 [1995] 2 All E.R. 548.
27 [1998] 2 Cr. App.R. 16.

tapping of telephone communications abroad and the circumstances did not constitute a breach of Article 8 of the 1950 Convention. The trial judge acted within his discretion, when deciding not to exclude the evidence under section 78 PACE and there was no abuse of process.

Interception of communications

15.21 At present the United Kingdom does not comply with requests to intercept communications with subjects on United Kingdom territory. There are in place mutual legal assistance arrangements between most Member States which are used by them for the purpose of intercepting communications of persons on the territory of other Member States.

Advances in telecommunications have made it increasingly difficult for law enforcement agencies in the E.U. (and elsewhere) to maintain these existing interception capabilities.

In order to address this problem provisions in the draft Convention on Mutual Legal Assistance are aimed at providing the appropriate framework specifically for intercepts. The draft Convention will, if it is to be ratified, require changes to current United Kingdom legislation.

15.22 Two major legal bases will be provided for:—

a)   Seeking technical assistance to implement an interception warrant against a person on the territory of the intercepting Member State.

The draft Convention places the requested Member State under an obligation to provide assistance where it is satisfied that a valid interception warrant has been issued by the requesting Member State.

b)   Seeking the co-operation of another Member State to intercept a person on its territory.

Under the draft Convention the requirements of national law will apply to both requesting and requested Member States, providing thereby double protection. In other words, unless the Secretary of State would be able to issue a warrant in accordance with the provisions of United Kingdom law, he will not agree to a request from another Member State to intercept a target on United Kingdom territory. He will also be able to impose the same conditions upon the use of intercept material by Member States that he would be able to impose under domestic United Kingdom law.

Limitation on use

15.23 The UN Model Treaty (Article 8) imposes a limitation upon the use of information or evidence provided by a requested state. Unless the requested state consents, such material is only to be used in the investigation or proceedings stated in the request.

No such limitation is to be found in the European Convention or under the Commonwealth Scheme. The 1990 Act (section 3(7)) provides that in relation to outgoing requests, evidence received shall not be used for any purpose other than that specified in the letter of request (without the consent of the relevant authority).

15.24 Under the United Kingdom legislation, when a request is received for *evidence*, the Secretary of State need only be satisfied that an offence has been committed in the requesting state, or that there are reasonable grounds for suspecting that it has; that proceedings have been instituted, or an investigation is being carried on, in respect of that offence; and that the evidence sought is relevant to the investigation or proceedings.[28]

With regard to *search and seizure* requests, there is no power in the court to limit the use to which material properly seized under a warrant can be put. The English courts have demonstrated a distaste for excessively wide search warrants, thereby introducing a fetter of relevance; *i.e.* that the material seized should be relevant to the matter the subject of the request, an exercise that is to be undertaken by those in the requested state who are drafting the warrant and executing the request.[29]

It is to be hoped that such judicial strictures will encourage greater particularity in letters of request thereby introducing an element of use limitation. Two United States authorities serve as warnings.

In *United States v. Sturman*[30] the United States requested and received banking records and information from the Swiss authorities, in relation to an investigation into an organised crime. The United States/Switzerland Treaty specifically excludes assistance in connection with tax offences. The defendant was tried for, and convicted of, tax offences, the evidence provided by the Swiss in accordance with the request being used against the defendant at his trial. On appeal, the court held that the request contained "no serious misrepresentations" – the only circumstances in which it envisaged overturning the conviction being "serious governmental misconduct", which one can assume would be an analogous to an abuse of process under English law. Just how serious the misconduct must be, is difficult to gauge; clearly governmental misrepresentation is insufficient.

In an earlier United States decision, *United States v. Johnpoll*,[31] the United States received evidence pursuant to a request relating to allegations of a conspiracy involving stolen securities. Whilst the evidence received was used at the defendant's trial for the conspiracy, it was also used to support customs offences, which were expressly excluded from the treaty. The appeal court had no difficulty in accepting such a practice, holding that as long as the material was used in relation to offences covered by the treaty, this did not prevent its use in relation to other offences.

Whilst many treaties do contain specific use limitation provisions, the United States cases reveal that the protection provided may be illusory.

Informal intelligence

15.26 In 1987 a British army officer named Simon Hayward was arrested in Sweden driving a Jaguar motor car, which was found to contain a large consignment of cannabis. This car, which belonged to his brother, had been driven by him from Ibiza. The case attracted enormous interest in both the British and Swedish press, due in the main to the regiment to which he belonged, the Household Cavalry, and his last tour of duty, undercover work in Northern Ireland. Simon Hayward denied from the outset any knowledge of the drugs, insisting that he was merely delivering the car to an associate of his brother.

As a consequence, the Swedish judicial system was put under the spotlight. At one stage of the investigation Swedish police were in contact with two officers from the United Kingdom National Drugs Intelligence Unit, (NDIU) and were provided with intelligence suggesting that an unnamed informant had information to the effect that

---

28 Criminal Justice (International Co-operation) Act 1990, s. 4(2).
29 See in particular *R. v. Bow Street Magistrates Court & Anr ex parte Montgomery and Others*; *R. v. SFO ex parte S* (Unreported) April 7, 1998; see pp. 103–106.
30 *United States v. D Sturman, R Levine, R Sturman, M Kaminsky* (1991), 951 f.2d. 1466 US Ct of App. 6th Cir.
31 198 *United States v. Johnpoll* (4), 739 F.2d.702.

Simon Hayward was aware of the drugs. This intelligence was introduced in the Swedish trial as evidence, despite the protestations of the NDIU. Under common law jurisdictions the concept of third-hand hearsay is anathema.

Such an incident dramatically highlights the dangers that will increasingly arise under informal investigator-to-investigator mutual assistance arrangements where the participants come from differing legal systems. The danger can only grow with the increasing reliance upon international databases bypassing any formal information exchange machinery. See however the safeguards set out at pages 173–4 above.

Obstacles to judicial co-operation and progress

15.27   In October 1998, at a conference in Avignon on Judicial Co-operation, the Home Secretary recognised four main obstacles to progress in this area.

"1.   The use by law enforcement agencies of 19th Century mechanisms to fight 21st Century crime.

Modern technology, information and financial networks and greater free-dom of movement of goods and people, especially within the E.U., mean that opportunities for criminals are expanding. All the developments which facilitate the conduct of business across the E.U. also facilitate the business of crime. In the meantime, however, investigators, magistrates and prose-cutors have to operate within the constraints of national jurisdictions.

2.   The administrative burden of making these mechanisms work.

The current arrangements for mutual legal assistance in particular are not easy to operate efficiently, and it is well known that prosecutors often encounter delays. There is a continuing need to heighten the awareness of local practitioners and to overcome the natural tendency of some of them to give priority to domestic cases over requests from other countries. Some countries like the United Kingdom channel incoming requests through an MLA Section, which can oversee performance and co-ordinate cases requir-ing a response from more than one agency. The more decentralised approach used under the Schengen system allows an examining magistrate to send his request for legal assistance direct to a magistrate in another Member State. This has its advantages, but may mean less central oversight of national performance and less capacity for co-ordination in complex cases. Whichever approach is used, the arrangements for mutual legal assistance require regular attention by Governments to keep them working efficiently.

3.   The disparity in criminal law

The third obstacle is the disparity in criminal law. For example, differences in the criteria for search and seizure, or for the use of other coercive powers, mean that a prosecutor in one Member State may be prevented from obtaining evidence such as bank records to which his own courts would have granted him access. The rules for exercising coercive powers tend to be politically sensitive and are therefore especially difficult for Member States to bring into alignment.

4.   Jurisdiction

The difficulty arises in finding a jurisdiction in which to mount a prosecution. "Conduct which is an offence in one State may not be illegal in another, or may be regarded less seriously. Gaps can arise if there is a poor fit between the criminal jurisdiction of one State and another, with the result that a criminal who participates in a fraud or conspiracy in several Member States may be beyond the reach of the law. The E.U. has begun to address this problem, for example through the Fraud Convention and the proposed Joint Action on Participation in a Criminal Organisation. But further alignment of criminal laws is likely to be needed."

15.28   The Home Secretary suggested various possible solutions to these problems, in particular the European Judicial Network, the Joint Action on Good Practice in Mutual Legal Assistance adopted by the Council in June 1998 and mutual evaluation of each Member State's mutual assistance system by a team of experts drawn from other Member States.

Finally, he noted the E.U. Action Plan which is set for completion by the end of 1999, the proposed simplification within the E.U. of the Council of Europe Conventions on Extradition and Mutual Assistance and plans for strengthening further the arrangements for tracing and seizing criminal assets.

15.29   An alternative approach would be that of increased recognition of the judgments of the courts of other countries. This topic was also mentioned in the Home Secretary's Avignon speech referred to above, and is an approach which has considerable merit, although there are many practical and ideological difficulties inherent.

This idea of mutual recognition outlined by Straw was not new at least in relation to questions arising post conviction. He cited how the 1990 Council of Europe Convention on Money Laundering and Asset Confiscation provided for the mutual enforcement of confiscation orders. The Convention on the Transfer of Sentenced Prisoners and the Driving Disqualification Convention were further examples.

"What we now need to consider, I suggest, is the possibility of applying this same principle of mutual recognition to the earlier stages in criminal procedure ... mutual recognition of all court decisions is unlikely to be achievable straight away, but we should aim to develop a new work programme heading in that direction."

One example of mutual recognition that he proposed was the possible agreement between Member States to limit or abolish dual criminality restrictions on extradition and mutual legal assistance.

"There will certainly be difficulties along the way. Issues of sovereignty and constitutional principles, reflecting long traditions in each of our countries, are at stake and I suspect that, in each of our countries, the public may not yet be ready to accept the direct application of decisions by courts in other Member States, particularly where the decision affects our own nationals. There is undoubtedly a need for much greater public understanding than exists at present of the judicial procedures in other E.U. countries. There would need to be confidence about such matters as how police treat suspects, different sentencing patterns and adequate standards of interpretation for foreign defendants.

There is also the fact that controls and criteria for the exercise of coercive powers differ. Some approximation of minimum standards may be needed before we could seek public acceptance of the direct enforcement of such powers.

In short, mutual recognition is by no means an easy option; but it is one which I believe deserves very serious consideration as being a method of proceeding incrementally rather than trying to force major changes in all our countries at one time. I would see this being taken forward under a long term coherent programme which would be designed to achieve full mutual recognition for judicial co-operation over a period of years – and I will not attempt at this stage to specify how many. I would hope, however, that agreement might be reached soon on a timetable and priorities."

15.30   Most recently, in October 1999, at a special meeting of the European Council in Tampere, Finland, on the creation of an area of freedom, security and justice, the commitment of the European Council to reinforce the fight against serious organised and transnational crime was emphasised. It was agreed that a balanced development of Union-wide measures against crime should be achieved while protecting the freedom and legal rights of individuals and economic operators.

15.31   One of the conclusions of the Tampere Council took a stage further the idea of Eurojust which has been referred to above (page 184). The text of the conclusion is as follows (conclusion No. 46)

"To reinforce the fight against serious organised crime, the European Council has agreed that a unit (EUROJUST) should be set up composed of national prosecutors, magistrates or police officers of equivalent competence, detached from each Member State according to its legal system. EUROJUST should have the task of facilitating the proper co-ordination of national prosecuting authorities and of supporting criminal investigations in organised crime cases, notably based on Europol's analysis, as well as of co-operating closely with the European Judicial Network, in particular in order to simplify the execution of letters rogatory. The European Council requests the Council to adopt the necessary legal instrument by the end of 2001".

15.32   Mutual recognition (discussed at paragraph 15.29 above) also featured in the Tampere conclusions (conclusion No. 35) as follows

"Enhanced mutual recognition of judicial decisions and judgements and the necessary approximation of legislation would facilitate co-operation between authorities and the judicial protection of individual rights. The European Council therefore endorses the principle of mutual recognition which, in its view, should become the cornerstone of judicial co-operation in both civil and criminal matters within the Union. The principle should apply both to judgements and to other decisions of judicial authorities".

15.33   It is inevitable therefore with the political impetus of Tampere, and continuing developments in practice that considerable change will continue to take place in the field of international mutual legal assistance in the coming months and years.

Appendix A

CRIMINAL JUSTICE (INTERNATIONAL CO-OPERATION) ACT 1990

(1990, c. 5)

Arrangement of Sections

Part I
Criminal Proceedings and Investigations

Mutual service of process

Part II
The Vienna Convention

Offences at sea

Supplementary

PART IV

GENERAL

SCHEDULES

An Act to enable the United Kingdom to co-operate with other countries in criminal proceedings and investigations; to enable the United Kingdom to join with other countries in implementing the Vienna Convention against Illicit Traffic in Narcotic Drugs and Psychotropic Substances; and to provide for the seizure, detention and forfeiture of drug trafficking money imported or exported in cash [5 April 1990]

PART I

CRIMINAL PROCEEDINGS AND INVESTIGATIONS

Mutual service of process

Service of overseas process in United Kingdom

1.—(1) This section has effect where the Secretary of State receives from the government of, or other authority in, a country or territory outside the United Kingdom—

(a)   a summons or other process requiring a person to appear as defendant or attend as a witness in criminal proceedings in that country or territory; or

(b)   a document issued by a court exercising criminal jurisdiction in that country or territory and recording a decision of the court made in the exercise of that jurisdiction,

together with a request for it to be served on a person in the United Kingdom.

(2) The Secretary of State or, where the person to be served is in Scotland, the Lord Advocate may cause the process or document to be served by post or, if the request is for personal service, direct the chief officer of police for the area in which that person appears to be to cause it to be personally served on him.

(3) Service by virtue of this section of any such process as is mentioned in subsection (1)(a) above shall not impose any obligation under the law of any part of the United Kingdom to comply with it.

(4) Any such process served by virtue of this section shall be accompanied by a notice—

(a)   Stating the effect of subsection (3) above;

(b)   indicating that the person on whom it is served may wish to seek advice as to the possible consequences of his failing to comply with the process under the law of the country or territory where it was issued; and

(c)   indicating that under that law he may not, as a witness, be accorded the same rights and privileges as would be accorded to him in criminal proceedings in the United Kingdom.

(5) Where a chief officer of police is directed under this section to cause any process or document to be served he shall after it has been served forthwith inform the Secretary of State or, as the case may be, the Lord Advocate when and how it was served and (if possible) furnish him with a receipt signed by the person on whom it was served; and if the chief officer has been unable to cause the process or document to be served he shall forthwith inform the Secretary of State or, as the case may be, the Lord Advocate of that fact and of the reason.

(6) In the application of this section to Northern Ireland for references to a chief officer of police there shall be substituted references to the Chief Constable of the Royal Ulster Constabulary.

Service of United Kingdom process overseas

2.—(1) Process of the following descriptions, that is to say—

(a)   a summons requiring a person charged with an offence to appear before a court in the United Kingdom; and

(b)   a summons or order requiring a person to attend before a court in the United Kingdom for the purpose of giving evidence in criminal proceedings.

may be issued or made notwithstanding that the person in question is outside the United Kingdom and may be served outside the United Kingdom in accordance with arrangements made by the Secretary of State.

(2) In relation to Scotland subsection (1) above applies to any document which may competently be served on any accused person or on any person who may give evidence in criminal proceedings.

(3) Service of any process outside the United Kingdom by virtue of this section shall not impose any obligation under the law of any part of the United Kingdom to comply with it and accordingly failure to do so shall not constitute contempt of any court or be a ground for issuing a warrant to secure the attendance of the person in question or, in Scotland, for imposing any penalty.

(4) Subsection (3) above is without prejudice to the service of any process (with the usual consequences for non-compliance) on the person in question if subsequently effected in the United Kingdom.

Mutual provision of evidence

Overseas evidence for use in United Kingdom

3.—(1) Where on an application made in accordance with subsection (2) below it appears to a justice of the peace or a judge or, in Scotland, to a sheriff or a judge—

(a)   that an offence has been committed or that there are reasonable grounds for suspecting that an offence has been committed; and

(b)   that proceedings in respect of the offence have been instituted or that the offence is being investigated,

he may issue a letter ("a letter of request") requesting assistance in obtaining outside the United Kingdom such evidence as is specified in the letter for use in the proceedings or investigation.

(2) An application under subsection (1) above may be made by a prosecuting authority or, if proceedings have been instituted, by the person charged in those proceedings.

(3) A prosecuting authority which is for the time being designated for the purposes of this section by an order made by the Secretary of State by statutory instrument may itself issue a letter of request if—

(a)   it is satisfied as to the matters mentioned in subsection (1)(a) above; and

(b)   the offence in question is being investigated or the authority has instituted proceedings in respect of it.

(4) Subject to subsection (5) below, a letter of request shall be sent to the Secretary of State for transmission either—

(a)   to a court or tribunal specified in the letter and exercising jurisdiction in the place
      where the evidence is to be obtained; or
(b)   to any authority recognised by the government of the country or territory in
      question as the appropriate authority for receiving requests for assistance of the
      kind to which this section applies.

(5) In cases of urgency a letter of request may be sent direct to such a court or tribunal as is
mentioned in subsection (4)(a) above.

(6) In this section "evidence" includes documents and other articles.

(7) Evidence obtained by virtue of a letter of request shall not without the consent of such an
authority as is mentioned in subsection (4)(b) above be used for any purpose other than that
specified in the letter: and when any document or other article obtained pursuant to a letter of
request is no longer required for that purpose (or for any other purpose for which such consent
has been obtained), it shall be returned to such an authority unless that authority indicates that
the document or article need not be returned.

(8) In exercising the discretion conferred by section 25 of the Criminal Justice Act 1988
(exclusion of evidence otherwise admissible) in relation to a statement contained in evidence
taken pursuant to a letter of request the court shall have regard—

(a)   to whether it was possible to challenge the statement by questioning the person who
      made it; and
(b)   if proceedings have been instituted, to whether the local law allowed the parties to
      the proceedings to be legally represented when the evidence was being taken.

(9) In Scotland evidence obtained by virtue of a letter of request shall, without being sworn
to by witnesses, be received in evidence in so far as that can be done without unfairness to either
party.

(10) In the application of this section to Northern Ireland for the reference in subsection (1)
to a justice of the peace there shall be substituted a reference to a resident magistrate and for the
reference in subsection (8) to section 25 of the Criminal Justice Act 1988 there shall be
substituted a reference to Article 5 of the Criminal Justice (Evidence, Etc) (Northern Ireland)
Order 1988.

United Kingdom evidence for use overseas

4.—(1) This section has effect where the Secretary of State receives—

(a)   from a court or tribunal exercising criminal jurisdiction in a country or territory
      outside the United Kingdom or a prosecuting authority in such a country or
      territory; or
(b)   from any other authority in such a country or territory which appears to him to have
      the function of making requests of the kind to which this section applies.

a request for assistance in obtaining evidence in the United Kingdom in connection with
criminal proceedings that have been instituted, or a criminal investigation that is being carried
on, in that country or territory.

(2) If the Secretary of State or, if the evidence is to be obtained in Scotland, the Lord Advocate
is satisfied—

(a)   that an offence under the law of the country or territory in question has been
      committed or that there are reasonable grounds for suspecting that such an offence
      has been committed; and
(b)   that proceedings in respect of that offence have been instituted in that country or
      territory or that an investigation into that offence is being carried on there.

he may, if he thinks fit, by a notice in writing nominate a court in England. Wales or Northern
Ireland or, as the case may be, Scotland to receive such of the evidence to which the request
relates as may appear to the court to be appropriate for the purpose of giving effect to the
request.

[(2A) Except where the evidence is to be obtained as is mentioned in subsection (2B) below,
if the Secretary of State is satisfied—

(a)   that an offence under the law of the country or territory in question has been
      committed or that there are reasonable grounds for suspecting that such an offence
      has been committed: and
(b)   that proceedings in respect of that offence have been instituted in that country or
      territory or that an investigation into that offence is being carried on there.

and it appears to him that the request relates to an offence involving serious or complex fraud, he may, if he thinks fit, refer the request or any part of the request to the Director of the Serious Fraud Office for him to obtain such of the evidence to which the request or part referred relates as may appear to the Director to be appropriate 'for giving effect to the request or part referred.

(2B) Where the evidence is to be obtained in Scotland, if the Lord Advocate is satisfied as to the matters mentioned in paragraphs (a) and (b) of subsection (2A) above and it appears to him that the request relates to an offence involving serious or complex fraud, he may, if he thinks fit, give a direction under section 51 of the Criminal Justice (Scotland) Act 1987.]

(3) Where it appears to the Secretary of State or, as the case may be, the Lord Advocate that the request relates to a fiscal offence in respect of which proceedings have not yet been instituted he shall not exercise his powers under subsection (2) [(2A) or (2B)] above unless—

(a)   the request is from a country or territory which is a member of the Commonwealth or is made pursuant to a treaty to which the United Kingdom is a party: or
(b)   he is satisfied that the conduct constituting the offence would constitute an offence of the same or a similar nature if it had occurred in the United Kingdom.

(4) For the purpose of satisfying himself as to the matters mentioned in subsection (2)(a) and (b) [or (2A)(a) and (b)] above the Secretary of State or, as the case may be, the Lord Advocate shall regard as conclusive a certificate issued by such authority in the country or territory in question as appears to him to be appropriate.

(5) In this section "evidence" includes documents and other articles.

(6) Schedule 1 to this Act shall have effect with respect to the proceedings before a nominated court in pursuance of a notice under subsection (2) above.

Note
Sub-ss. (2A), (2B) and the words in square brackets in sub-ss. (3), (4) were inserted by the Criminal Justice and Public Order Act 1994, s. 164(1).

Transfer of United Kingdom prisoner to give evidence or assist investigation overseas

5.—(1) The Secretary of State may, if he thinks fit, issue a warrant providing for any person ("a prisoner") Serving a sentence in a prison or other institution to which the Prison Act 1952 or the Prisons (Scotland) Act 1989 applies to be transferred to a country or territory outside the United Kingdom for the purpose—

(a)   of giving evidence in criminal proceedings there; or
(b)   of being identified in, or otherwise by his presence assisting, such proceedings or the investigation of an offence.

(2) No warrant shall be issued under this section in respect of any prisoner unless he has consented to being transferred as mentioned in subsection (1) above and that consent may be given either—

(a)   by the prisoner himself; or
(b)   in circumstances in which it appears to the Secretary of State inappropriate, by reason of the prisoner's physical or mental condition or his youth, for him to act for himself, by a person appearing to the Secretary of State to be an appropriate person to act on his behalf;

but a consent once given shall not be capable of being withdrawn after the issue of the warrant.

(3) The effect of a warrant under this section shall be to authorise—

(a)   the taking of the prisoner to a place in the United Kingdom [??] his delivery at a place of departure from the United Kingdom into the custody of a person representing the appropriate authority of the country or territory to which the prisoner is to be transferred; and
(b)   the bringing of the prisoner back to the United Kingdom and his transfer in custody to the place where he is liable to be detained under the sentence to which he is subject.

(4) Where a warrant has been issued in respect of a prisoner under this section he shall be deemed to be in legal custody at any time when, being in the United Kingdom or on board a British ship, British aircraft or British hovercraft, he is being taken under the warrant to or from any place or being kept in custody under the warrant.

(5) A person authorised by or for the purposes of the warrant to take the prisoner to or from any place or to keep him in custody shall have all the powers, authority, protection and privileges—

(a)   of a constable in the part of the United Kingdom in which that person is for the time being; or

(b)   if he is outside the United Kingdom, of a constable in the part of the United Kingdom to or from which the prisoner is to be taken under the warrant.

(6) If the prisoner escapes or is unlawfully at large, he may be arrested without warrant by a constable and taken to any place to which he may be taken under the warrant issued under this section.

(7) In subsection (4) above—

"British aircraft" means a British-controlled aircraft within the meaning of section 92 of the Civil Aviation Act 1982 (application of criminal law to aircraft) or one of Her Majesty's aircraft;

"British hovercraft" means a British-controlled hovercraft within the meaning of that section as applied in relation to hovercraft by virtue of provisions made under the Hovercraft Act 1968 or one of Her Majesty's hovercraft;

"British ship" means a British ship for the purposes of the [Merchant Shipping Act 1995] or one of Her Majesty's ships;

and in this subsection references to Her Majesty's aircraft, hovercraft or ships are references to aircraft, hovercraft or, as the case may be, ships belonging to or exclusively employed in the service of Her Majesty in right of the Government of the United Kingdom.

(8) In subsection (6) above "constable", in relation to any part of the United Kingdom, means any person who is a constable in that or any other part of the United Kingdom or any person who, at the place in question has, under any enactment including subsection (5) above, the powers of a constable in that or any other part of the United Kingdom.

(9) This section applies to a person in custody awaiting trial or sentence and a person committed to prison for default in paying a fine as it applies to a prisoner and the reference in subsection (3)(b) above to a sentence shall be construed accordingly.

(10) In the application of this section to Northern Ireland for the reference in subsection (1) to the Prison Act 1952 there shall be substituted a reference to the Prison Act (Northern Ireland) 1953.

Note
The words in square brackets in sub-s (7) were substituted by the Merchant Shipping Act 1995, s. 314(2), Sched. 13, para. 87.

Transfer of overseas prisoner to give evidence or assist investigation in the United Kingdom

6.—(1) This section has effect where—

(a)   a witness order has been made or a witness summons or citation issued in criminal proceedings in the United Kingdom in respect of a person ("a prisoner") who is detained in custody in a country or territory outside the United Kingdom by virtue of a sentence or order of a court or tribunal exercising criminal jurisdiction in that country or territory; or

(b)   it appears to the Secretary of State that it is desirable for a prisoner to be identified in, or otherwise by his presence to assist, such proceedings or the investigation in the United Kingdom of an offence.

(2) If the Secretary of State is satisfied that the appropriate authority in the country or territory where the prisoner is detained will make arrangements for him to come to the United Kingdom to give evidence pursuant to the witness order. Witness summons or citation or, as the case may be, for the purpose mentioned in subsection (1)(b) above, he may issue a warrant under this section.

(3) No warrant shall be issued under this section in respect of any prisoner unless he has consented to being brought to the United Kingdom to give evidence as aforesaid or, as the case may be, for the purpose mentioned in subsection (1)(b) above but a consent once given shall not be capable of being withdrawn after the issue of the warrant.

(4) The effect of the warrant shall be to authorise—

(a)   the bringing of the prisoner to the United Kingdom;

(b)   the taking of the prisoner to, and his detention in custody at, such place or places in the United Kingdom as are specified in the warrant; and

(c)   the returning of the prisoner to the country or territory from which he has come.

(5) Subsections (4) to (8) of section 5 above shall have effect in relation to a warrant issued under this section as they have effect in relation to a warrant issued under that section.

(6) A person shall not be subject to the Immigration Act 1971 in respect of his entry into or presence in the United Kingdom in pursuance of a warrant under this section but if the warrant ceases to have effect while he is still in the United Kingdom—

(a)   he shall be treated for the purposes of that Act as if he has then illegally entered the United Kingdom; and

(b)   the provisions of Schedule 2 to that Act shall have effect accordingly except that paragraph 20(1) (liability of carrier for expenses of custody etc of illegal entrant) shall not have effect in relation to directions for his removal given by virtue of this subsection.

(7) This section applies to a person detained in custody in a country or territory outside the United Kingdom in consequence of having been transferred there—

(a)   from the United Kingdom under the Repatriation of Prisoners Act 1984; or

(b)   under any similar provision or arrangement from any other country or territory.

as it applies to a person detained as mentioned in subsection (1) above.

Additional co-operation powers

Search etc for material relevant to overseas investigation

7.—(1) Part II of the Police and Criminal Evidence Act 1984 (powers of entry, search and seizure) shall have effect as if references to serious arrestable offences in section 8 of and Schedule 1 to that Act included any conduct which is an offence under the law of a country or territory outside the United Kingdom and would constitute a serious arrestable offence if it had occurred in any part of the United Kingdom.

(2) If, on an application made by a constable, a justice of the peace is satisfied—

(a)   that criminal proceedings have been instituted against a person in a country or territory outside the United Kingdom or that a person has been arrested in the course of a criminal investigation carried on there;

(b)   that the conduct constituting the offence which is the subject of the proceedings or investigation would constitute an arrestable offence within the meaning of the said Act of 1984 if it had occurred in any part of the United Kingdom; and

(c)   that there are reasonable grounds for suspecting that there is on premises in the United Kingdom occupied or controlled by that person evidence relating to the offence other than items subject to legal privilege within the meaning of that Act,

he may issue a warrant authorising a constable to enter and search those premises and to seize any such evidence found there.

(3) The power to search conferred by subsection (2) above is only a power to search to the extent that is reasonably required for the purpose of discovering such evidence as is there mentioned.

(4) No application for a warrant or order shall be made by virtue of subsection (1) or (2) above except in pursuance of a direction given by the Secretary of State in response to a request received—

(a)   from a court or tribunal exercising criminal jurisdiction in the overseas country or territory in question or a prosecuting authority in that country or territory; or

(b)   from any other authority in that country or territory which appears to him to have the function of making requests for the purposes of this section:

and any evidence seized by a constable by virtue of this section shall be furnished by him to the Secretary of State for transmission to that court, tribunal or authority.

(5) If in order to comply with the request it is necessary for any such evidence to be accompanied by any certificate, affidavit or other verifying document the constable shall also furnish for transmission such document of that nature as may be specified in the direction given by the Secretary of State.

(6) Where the evidence consists of a document the original or a copy shall be transmitted, and where it consists of any other article the article itself or a description, photograph or other representation of it shall be transmitted, as may be necessary in order to comply with the request.

(7) The Treasury may by order direct that any powers which by virtue of this section are exercisable by a constable shall also be exercisable by, or by any person acting under the direction of an officer commissioned by the Commissioners of Customs and Excise under section 6(3) of the Customs and Excise Management Act 1979; and the Secretary of State may by order direct that any of those powers shall also be exercisable by a person of any other description specified in the order.

(8) An order under subsection (7) above shall be made by statutory instrument subject to annulment in pursuance of a resolution of either House of Parliament.

(9) In the application of this section to Northern Ireland for references to the Police and Criminal Evidence Act 1984, to Part II and section 8 of and to Schedule 1 to that Act there shall be substituted references to the Police and Criminal Evidence (Northern Ireland) Order 1989, to Part III and Article 10 of and to Schedule 1 to that Order.

Search etc for material relevant to overseas investigation: Scotland

8.—(1) If, on an application made by the procurator fiscal, it appears to the sheriff—

(a)   that there are reasonable grounds for believing that an offence under the law of a country or territory outside the United Kingdom has been committed; and

(b)   that the conduct constituting that offence would constitute an offence punishable by imprisonment if it had occurred in Scotland,

the sheriff shall have the like power to grant warrant authorising entry, search and seizure by any constable as he would have at common law in respect of any offence punishable at common law in Scotland.

(2) No application for a warrant shall be made by virtue of subsection (1) above except in pursuance of a direction given by the Lord Advocate in response to a request received by the Secretary of State—

(a)   from a court or tribunal exercising criminal jurisdiction in the overseas country or territory in question or a prosecuting authority in that country or territory; or

(b)   from any other authority in that country or territory which appears to him to have the function of making requests for the purpose of this section,

and any evidence seized by the constable by virtue of this section shall be furnished by him to the Lord Advocate for transmission to that court, tribunal or authority

(3) If in order to comply with the request it is necessary for any such evidence to be accompanied by any certificate, affidavit or other verifying document the constable shall also furnish for transmission such document of that nature as may be specified in the direction given by the Lord Advocate.

(4) Where the evidence consists of a document the original or a copy shall be transmitted, and where it consists of any other article the article itself or a description, photograph or other representation of it shall be transmitted, as may be necessary in order to comply with the request.

(5) The Treasury may by order direct that any powers to enter, search or seizure granted by virtue of subsection (1) above which may be exercised by a constant constable shall also be exercisable by, or by any person acting under the direction of, an officer commissioned by the Commissioners of Customs and Excise under section 6(3) of the Customs and Excise Management Act 1979; and the Secretary of State may by order direct that any of those powers shall also be exercisable by a person of any other description specified in the order.

(6) An order under subsection (5) above shall be made by statutory instruments subject to annulment in pursuance of a resolution of either House of Parliament.

Enforcement of overseas forfeiture orders

9.—(1) Her Majesty may by Order in Council provide for the enforcement in United Kingdom of any order which—

(a)   is made by a court in a country or territory outside the United Kingdom designated for the purposes of this section by the Order in Council:

(b)   is for the forfeiture and destruction, or the forfeiture and other disposal, of anything in respect of which an offence to which this section applies has been committed or which was used [or intended for use] in connection with the commission of such an offence.

[(1A) Without prejudice to the generality of subsection (1) above the provision that may be made by virtue of that subsection includes provision which, for the purpose of facilitating the enforcement of any order that may be made, has effect at times before there is an order to be enforced.]

(2) Without prejudice to the generality of subsection (1) above an Order in Council under this section may provide for the registration by a court in the United Kingdom of any order as a condition of its enforcement and prescribe requirements to be satisfied before an order can be registered.

(3) An Order in Council under this section may include such supplementary and incidental provisions as appear to Her Majesty to be necessary or expedient and may apply for the purposes of the Order (with such modifications as appear to Her Majesty to be appropriate) any provisions relating to confiscation or forfeiture orders under any other enactment.

(4) An Order in Council under this section may make different provision for different cases.

[(5) An Order in Council under this section shall be subject to annulment in pursuance of a resolution of either House of Parliament.]

(6) This section applies to any offence which corresponds to or is similar to an offence under the Misuse of Drugs Act 1971, a drug trafficking offence as defined in [section 1(3) of the Drug Trafficking Act 1994], an offence to which section 1 of the Criminal Justice (Scotland) Act 1987 relates or [an offence to which Part VI of the Criminal Justice Act 1988 applies or an offence to which Part I of the Proceeds of Crime (Scotland) Act 1995 applies or an offence in respect of which a suspended forfeiture order may be made under section 18 of the said Act of 1995].

Note

The words in square brackets in sub-s. (1) were inserted by the Criminal Justice Act 1993, s. 21(1). Sub-s. (1A) was inserted by the Proceeds of Crime Act 1995, s. 14(3) with retrospective effect. Sub-s. (5) was substituted by the Criminal Justice Act 1993, s. 21(2), (3). In sub-s (6), the words in the first set of square brackets were substituted by the Drug Trafficking Act 1994, s. 65(1), Sched. 1, para. 25 and the words in the second set were substituted by the Criminal Procedure (Consequential Provisions) (Scotland) Act 1995, s. 5, Sched. 4, para. 76.

Supplementary

Rules of court

10.—(1) Provision may be made by rules of court for any purpose for which it appears to the authority having power to make the rules that it is necessary or expedient that provision should be made in connection with any of the provisions of this Part of this Act.

(2) Rules made for the purposes of Schedule 1 to this Act may, in particular, make provision with respect to the persons entitled to appear or cake part in the proceedings to which that Schedule applies and for excluding the public from any such proceedings.

(3) An Order in Council under section 9 above may authorise the making of rules of court for any purpose specified in the Order.

(4) Rules of court made under this section by the High Court in Scotland shall be made by Act of Adjournal.

(5) This section is without prejudice to the generality of any existing power to make rules.

Application to courts-martial etc

11.—(1) Section 2 above applies also to a summons requiring a person charged with a civil offence to appear before a service court (whether or not in the United Kingdom) or to attend before such a court for the purpose of giving evidence in proceedings for such an offence; and a warrant may be issued under section 6 above where—

    (a)   such a summons has been issued in respect of a prisoner within the meaning of that section: or

(b) it appears to the Secretary of State that it is desirable for such a prisoner to be identified in, or otherwise by his presence to assist, such proceedings or the investigation or such an offence.

(2) Section 5 above applies also to a person serving a sentence of detention imposed by a service court or detained in custody awaiting trial by such a court.

(3) In this section "a civil offence" has the same meaning as in the Army Act 1955, the Air Force Act 1955 and the Naval Discipline Act 1957 and "service court" means a court-martial constituted under any of those Acts or a Standing Civilian Court.

PART II

THE VIENNA CONVENTION

Substances useful for manufacture of controlled drugs

12.—(1) It is an offence for a person—

(a) to manufacture a scheduled substance; or
(b) to supply such a substance to another person,

knowing or suspecting that the substance is to be used in or for the unlawful production of a controlled drug.

[(1A) A person does not commit an offence under subsection (1) above if he manufactures or, as the case may be, supplies the scheduled substance with the express consent of a constable.]

(2) A person guilty of an offence under subsection (1) above is liable—

(a) on summary conviction, to imprisonment for a term not exceeding six months or a fine not exceeding the statutory maximum or both;
(b) on conviction on indictment, to imprisonment for a term not exceeding fourteen years or a fine or both.

(3) In this section "a controlled drug" has the same meaning as in the Misuse of Drugs Act 1971 and "unlawful production of a controlled drug" means the production of such a drug which is unlawful by virtue of section 4(1)(a) of that Act.

(4) In this section and elsewhere in this Part of this Act "a scheduled substance" means a substance for the time being specified in Schedule 2 to this Act.

(5) Her Majesty may by Order in Council amend that Schedule (whether by addition, deletion or transfer from one Table to the other) but—

(a) no such Order shall add any substance to the Schedule unless—

(i) it appears to Her Majesty to be frequently used in or for the unlawful production of a controlled drug; or
(ii) it has been added to the Annex to the Vienna Convention under Article 12 of that Convention; and

(b) no such Order shall be made unless a draft of it has been laid before and approved by a resolution of each House of Parliament.

Note
Sub-s. (1A) was inserted by the Criminal Justice (International Co-operation) (Amendment) Act 1999, s.1.

13.—(1) The Secretary of State may by regulations make provision—

(a) imposing requirements as to the documentation of transactions involving scheduled substances;
(b) requiring the keeping of records and the furnishing of information with respect to such substances;
(c) for the inspection of records kept pursuant to the regulations;
(d) for the labelling of consignments of scheduled substances.

(2) Regulations made by virtue of subsection (1)(b) may, in particular, require—

(a)   the notification of the proposed exportation of substances specified in Table I in Schedule 2 to this Act to such countries as may be specified in the regulations; and

(b)   the production, in such circumstances as may be so specified, of evidence that the required notification has been given;

and for the purposes of section 68 of the Customs and Excise Management Act 1979 (offences relating to exportation of prohibited or restricted goods) any such substance shall be deemed to be exported contrary to a restriction for the time being in force with respect to it under this Act if it is exported without the requisite notification having been given.

(3) Regulations under this section may make different provision in relation to the substances specified in Table I and Table II in Schedule 2 to this Act respectively and in relation to different cases or circumstances.

(4) The power to make regulations under this section shall be exercisable by statutory instrument subject to annulment in pursuance of a resolution of either House of Parliament.

(5) Any person who fails to comply with any requirement imposed by the regulations or, in purported compliance with any such requirement, furnishes information which he knows to be false in a material particular or recklessly furnishes information which is false in a material particular is guilty of an offence and liable—

(a)   on summary conviction, to imprisonment for a term not exceeding six months or a fine not exceeding the statutory maximum or both;

(b)   on conviction on indictment, to imprisonment for a term not exceeding two years or a fine or both.

(6) No information obtained pursuant to the regulations shall be disclosed except for the purposes of criminal proceedings or of proceedings under the provisions of the [Drug Trafficking Act 1994] or the Criminal Justice (Scotland) Act 1987 relating to the confiscation of the proceeds of drug trafficking or corresponding provisions in force in Northern Ireland.

Note

In sub-s. (6) the words in square brackets were substituted by the Drug Trafficking Act 1994, s.65, Sched.1, para.26.

14.–17. (Ss 14, 16 were repealed (s.14 as to England and Wales only) by the Drug Trafficking Act 1994, ss67, 68, Sched.3; s.14 was repealed as to Northern Ireland by S.I. 1996 No. 1299 (N.1.9.); s.15 was repealed by the Criminal Procedure (Consequential Provisions) (Scotland) Act 1995, s.6, Sched.5; s.17 was repealed by the Criminal Justice (Scotland) Act 1995, s.117, Sched.6, Pt II, Sched.7, Pt II.)

Offences at sea

Offences on British Ships

18.—Anything which would constitute a drug trafficking offence if done on land in any part of the United Kingdom shall constitute that offence if done on a British ship.

Ships used for illicit traffic

19.—(1) This section applies to a British ship, a ship registered in a state other than the United Kingdom which is a party to the Vienna Convention (a "Convention state") and a ship not registered in any country or territory.

(2) A person is guilty of an offence if on a ship to which this section applies, wherever it may be, he—

(a)   has a controlled drug in his possession; or

(b)   is in any way knowingly concerned in the carrying or concealing of a controlled drug on the ship,

knowing or having reasonable grounds to suspect that the drug is intended to be imported or has been exported contrary to section 3(1) of the Misuse of Drugs Act 1971 or the law of any state other than the United Kingdom.

(3) A certificate purporting to be issued by or on behalf of the government of any state to the effect that the importation or export of a controlled drug is prohibited by the law of that state shall be evidence, and in Scotland sufficient evidence, of the matters stated.

(4) A person guilty of an offence under this section is liable–

(a) in a case where the controlled drug is a Class A drug–

(i) on summary conviction, to imprisonment for a term not exceeding six months or a fine not exceeding the statutory maximum or both;

(ii) on conviction on indictment, to imprisonment for life or a fine or both;

(b) in a case where the controlled drug is a Class B drug–

(i) on summary conviction, to imprisonment for a term not exceeding six months or a fine not exceeding the statutory maximum or both;

(ii) on conviction on indictment, to imprisonment for a term not exceeding fourteen years or a fine or both;

(c) in a case where the controlled drug is a Class C drug–

(i) on summary conviction, to imprisonment for a term not exceeding three months or a fine not exceeding the statutory maximum or both;

(ii) on conviction on indictment, to imprisonment for a term not exceeding five years or a fine or both.

(5) In this section "a controlled drug" and the references to controlled drugs of a specified Class have the same meaning as in the said Act of 1971; and an offence under this section shall be included in the offences to which section 28 of that Act (defences) applies.

Enforcement powers

20.—(1) The powers conferred on an enforcement officer by Schedule 3 to this Act shall be exercisable in relation to any ship to which section 18 or 19 above applies for the purpose of detecting and the taking of appropriate action in respect of the offences mentioned in those sections.

(2) Those powers shall not be exercised outside the landward limits of the territorial sea of the United Kingdom in relation to a ship registered in a Convention state except with the authority of the [Commissioners of Customs and Excise]; and [they] shall not give [their] authority unless that state has in relation to that ship—

(a) requested the assistance of the United Kingdom for the purpose mentioned in subsection (1) above; or

(b) authorised the United Kingdom to act for that purpose.

Note

The words in square brackets in sub-ss. (2)–(4), (6) were substituted by the Criminal Justice Act 1993, s.23(2).

Jurisdiction and prosecutions

21.—(1) Proceedings under this Part of this Act or Schedule 3 in respect of an offence on a ship may be taken, and the offence may for all incidental purposes be treated as having been committed, in any place in the United Kingdom.

(2) No such proceedings shall be instituted—

(a) in England or Wales except by or with the consent of the Director of Public Prosecutions or the Commissioners of Customs and Excise;

(b) in Northern Ireland except by or with the consent of the Director of Public Prosecutions for Northern Ireland or those Commissioners.

(3) Without prejudice to subsection (2) above no proceedings for an offence under section 19 above alleged to have been committed outside the landward limits of the territorial sea of the United Kingdom on a ship registered in a Convention state shall be instituted except in pursuance of the exercise with the authority of the Commissioners of Customs and Excise of the powers conferred by Schedule 3 to this Act; and section 3 of the Territorial Waters Jurisdiction Act 1878 (consent of Secretary of State for certain prosecutions) shall not apply to those proceedings.

Note

The words in square brackets in sub-s.(3) were substituted by the Criminal Justice Act 1993, s.23(2)(b).

Supplementary

Extradition

22.—(1) The offences to which an Order in Council under section 2 of the Extradition Act 1870 can apply shall include drug trafficking offences.

(2) In paragraph 15 of Schedule 1 to the Extradition Act 1989 extradition offences treated as with jurisdiction of foreign states) after paragraph (i) there shall be inserted—

"(j)   a drug trafficking offence within the meaning of the Drug Trafficking Offences Act 1986; or

(k)   an offence to which section 1 of the Criminal Justice (Scotland) Act 1987 relates;".

(3) At the end of subsection (2) of section 22 of the said Act of 1989 (extradition offences under Conventions) there shall be inserted–

"(h)   the United Nations Convention against Illicit Traffic in Narcotic Drugs and Psychotropic Substances which was signed in Vienna on 20th December 1988 ("the Vienna Convention")."

and at the end of subsection (4) of that section there shall be inserted "and

(h)   in relation to the Vienna Convention–

(i)   any drug trafficking offence within the meaning of the Drug Trafficking Offences Act 1986; and

(ii)   an offence to which section 1 of the Criminal Justice (Scotland) Act 1987 relates;".

Application of ancillary provisions of Misuse of Drugs Act 1971

23.—(1) The Misuse of Drugs Act 1971 shall be amended as follows.

(2) In section 12(1) (prohibition direction on practitioner etc. in consequence of conviction) after paragraph (b) there shall be inserted—

"(c)   of an offence under section 12 or 13 of the Criminal Justice (International Co-operation) Act 1990;".

(3) In section 21 (offences by bodies corporate) after the words "an offence under this Act" there shall be inserted the words "or Part II of the Criminal Justice (International Co-operation) Act 1990".

(4) In section 23 (power to search and obtain evidence) after subsection (3) there shall be inserted—

"(3A) The powers conferred by subsection (1) above shall be exercisable also for the purposes of the execution of Part II of the Criminal Justice (International Co-operation) Act 1990 and subsection (3) above (excluding paragraph (a)) shall apply also to offences under section 12 or 13 of that Act, taking references in those provisions to controlled drugs as references to scheduled substances within the meaning of that Part."

23A. (This section, which was inserted by the Criminal Justice Act 1993, s.77, Sched.4, was repealed as to England and Wales by the Drug Trafficking Act 1994, ss 67, 68, Sched.3 and as to Northern Ireland by S.I. 1996 No. 1299 (N.1.9).)

Interpretation of Part II

24.—(1) In this Part of this Act—

"British ship" means a ship registered in the United Kingdom or a colony;

"Convention state" has the meaning given in section 19(1) above;

"scheduled substance" has the meaning given in section 12(4) above;

"ship" includes any vessel used in navigation;

"the territorial sea of the United Kingdom" includes the territorial sea adjacent to any of the Channel Islands, the Isle of Man or any colony;

"the Vienna Convention" means the United Nations Convention against Illicit Traffic in Narcotic Drugs and Psychotropic Substances which was signed in Vienna on 20th December 1988.

(2) Any expression used in this Part of this Act which is also used in the [Drug Trafficking Act 1994] has the same meaning as in that Act [and, in section 22(1), "drug trafficking offences" includes drug trafficking offences within the meaning of the Criminal Justice (Confiscation) (Northern Ireland) Order 1990].

(3) In relation to Scotland, any expression used in this Part of this Act which is also used in the Criminal Justice (Scotland) Act 1987 has the same meaning as in that Act and "drug trafficking offence" means an offence to which section of that Act relates.

(4) If in any proceedings under this Part of this Act any question arises whether any country or territory is a state or is a party to the Vienna Convention, a certificate issued by or under the authority of the Secretary of State shall be conclusive evidence on that question.

Notes
In sub-s(2), the words in the first set of square brackets were substituted by the Drug Trafficking Act 1994, s.65, Sched.1, para. 28 and the words in the second set were added by the Criminal Justice (Confiscation) (Northern Ireland) Order 1990, S.I. 1990 No. 2588, art. 38, Sched. 2.

25.–29. (*Repealed by the Drug Trafficking Act 1994, s. 67, Sched. 3.*)

PART IV
GENERAL

Expenses and receipts

30.—(1) Any expenses incurred by the Secretary of State under this Act shall be defrayed out of money provided by Parliament.

(2), [(3)] . . .

Notes
Sub-s.(3), which was added by the Criminal Justice Act 1993, s.25 was repealed, together with sub-s.(2), by the Drug Trafficking Act 1994, s.67, Sched.3.

Consequential and other amendments, repeals and revocation

31.—(1) The enactments and instruments mentioned in Schedule 4 to this Act shall have effect with the amendments there specified, being amendments consequential on or otherwise relating to the provisions of this Act.

(2) . . .

(3) The enactments mentioned in Schedule 5 to this Act are hereby repealed to the extent specified in the third column of that Schedule.

(4) Article 9 of the Criminal Justice (Evidence, Etc) (Northern Ireland) Order 1988 is hereby revoked.

Note
Sub-s.(2) was repealed by the Drug Trafficking Act 1994, s.67, Sched. 3.

Short title, commencement and extent

32.—(1) This Act may be cited as the Criminal Justice (International Co-operation) Act 1990.

(2) This Act shall come into force on such day as may be appointed by the Secretary of State by an order made by statutory instrument and different days may be appointed for different provisions and different purposes and for different parts of the United Kingdom.

(3) This Act extends to Northern Ireland.

(4) Her Majesty may by Order in Council direct that the provisions of this Act [and those provisions of the Drug Trafficking Act 1994 which re-enact provisions of this Act] shall extend, with such exceptions and modifications as appear to Her Majesty to be appropriate, to any of the Channel Islands, the Isle of Man or any colony.

Note
The words in square brackets in sub-s.(4) were inserted by the Drug Trafficking Act 1994, s.65, Sched.1, para. 29.

SCHEDULES

SCHEDULE 1

Section 4(6)

UNITED KINGDOM EVIDENCE FOR USE OVERSEAS: PROCEEDINGS OF NOMINATED COURT

Securing attendance of witnesses

1. The court shall have the like powers for securing the attendance of a witness for the purpose of the proceedings as it has for the purpose of other proceedings before the court.
   2. In Scotland the court shall have power to issue a warrant to officers of law to cite witnesses for the purpose of the proceedings and [section 156 of the Criminal Procedure (Scotland) Act 1995] shall apply in relation to such a witness.

Power to administer oaths

3. The court may in the proceedings take evidence on oath.

Privilege of witnesses

4.—(1) A person shall not be compelled to give in the proceedings any evidence which he could not be compelled to give—

  (a)   in criminal proceedings in the part of the United Kingdom in which the nominated court exercises jurisdiction; or
  (b)   subject to sub-paragraph (2) below, in criminal proceedings in the country or territory from which the request for the evidence has come.

(2) Sub-paragraph (1)(b) above shall not apply unless the claim of the person questioned to be exempt from giving the evidence is conceded by the court, tribunal or authority which made the request.

(3) Where such a claim made by any person is not conceded as aforesaid he may (subject to the other provisions of this paragraph) be required to give the evidence to which the claim relates but the evidence shall not be transmitted to the court, tribunal or authority which requested it if a court in the country or territory in question, on the matter being referred to it, upholds the claim.

(4) Without prejudice to sub-paragraph (1) above a person shall not be compelled under this Schedule to give any evidence if his doing so would be prejudicial to the security of the United Kingdom; and a certificate signed by or on behalf of the Secretary of State or, where the court is in Scotland, by or on behalf of the Lord Advocate to the effect that it would be so prejudicial for that person to do so shall be conclusive evidence of that fact.

(5) Without prejudice to sub-paragraph (1) above a person shall not be compelled under this Schedule to give any evidence in his capacity as an officer or servant of the Crown.

(6) In this paragraph references to giving evidence include references to answering any question and to producing any document or other article and the reference in sub-paragraph (3) above to the transmission of evidence given by a person shall be construed accordingly.

Transmission of evidence

5.—(1) The evidence received by the court shall be furnished to the Secretary of State or, in Scotland, the Lord Advocate for transmission to the court, tribunal or authority that made the request.

(2) If in order to comply with the request it is necessary for the evidence to be accompanied by any certificate, affidavit or other verifying document, the court shall also furnish for transmission such document of that nature as may be specified in the notice nominating the court.

(3) Where the evidence consists of a document the original or a copy shall be transmitted, and where it consists of any other article the article itself or a description, photograph or other representation of it shall be transmitted, as may be necessary in order to comply with the request.

Supplementary

6. For the avoidance of doubt it is hereby declared that the Bankers Books' Evidence Act 1879 applies to the proceedings as it applies to other proceedings before the court.
7. No order for costs shall be made in the proceedings.

Note
In para.2, the words in square brackets were substituted by the Criminal Procedure (Consequential Provisions) (Scotland) Act 1995, s.5, Sched.4, para. 76.

Sections 12 and 13   SCHEDULE 2

Substances Useful for Manufacturing Controlled Drugs

TABLE I

Ephedrine
Ergometrine
Ergotamine
Lysergic acid
1-Phenyl-2-propanone
Pseudoephedrine
The salts of the substances listed in this Table whenever the existence of such salts is possible.

TABLE II

Acetic anhydride
Acetone
Anthranilic acid
Ethyl ether
Phenylacetic acid
Piperidine
The salts of the substances listed in this Table whenever the existence of such salts is possible.

SCHEDULE 3

Section 20

Enforcement Powers in Respect of Ships

Preliminary

1.—(1) In this Schedule "an enforcement officer" means—

    (a)   a constable;

(b) an officer commissioned by the Commissioners of Customs and Excise under section 6(3) of the Customs and Excise Management Act 1979; and

(c) any other person of a description specified in an order made for the purposes of this Schedule by the Secretary of State.

(2) The power to make an order under sub-paragraph (1)(c) above shall be exercisable by statutory instrument subject to annulment in pursuance of a resolution of either House of Parliament.

(3) In this Schedule "the ship" means the ship in relation to which the powers conferred by this Schedule are exercised.

Power to stop, board, divert and detain

2.—(1) An enforcement officer may stop the ship, board it and, if he thinks it necessary for the exercise of his functions, require it to be taken to a port in the United Kingdom and detain it there.

(2) Where an enforcement officer is exercising his powers with the authority of the [Commissioners of Customs and Excise] given under section 20(2) of this Act the officer may require the ship to be taken to a port in the Convention state in question or, if that state has so requested, in any other country or territory.

Powers in respect of suspected offence

4. If an enforcement officer has reasonable grounds to suspect that an offence mentioned in section 18 or 19 of this Act has willing to receive it.

(3) For any of those purposes he may require the master or any member of the crew to take such action as may be necessary.

(4) If an enforcement officer detains a vessel he shall serve on the master a notice in writing stating that it is to be detained until the notice is withdrawn by the service on him of a further notice in writing signed by an enforcement officer.

Power to search and obtain information

3.—(1) An enforcement officer may search the ship, anyone on it and anything on it including its cargo.

(2) An enforcement officer may require any person on the ship to give information concerning himself or anything on the ship.

(3) Without prejudice to the generality of those powers an enforcement officer may—

(a) open any containers;

(b) make tests and take samples of anything on the ship;

(c) require the production of documents, books or records relating to the ship or anything on it;

(d) make photographs or copies of anything whose production he has power to require.

Powers in respect of suspected offence

4. If an enforcement officer has reasonable grounds to suspect that an offence mentioned in section 18 or 19 of this Act has been committed on a ship to which that section applies he may—

(a) arrest without warrant anyone whom he has reasonable grounds for suspecting to be guilty of the offence; and

(b) seize and detain anything found on the ship which appears to him to be evidence of the offence.

Assistants

5.—(1) An enforcement officer may take with him, to assist him in exercising his powers—

  (a)   any other persons; and
  (b)   any equipment or materials.

  (2) A person whom an enforcement officer takes with him to assist him may perform any of the officer's functions but only under the officer's supervision.

Use of reasonable force

6. An enforcement officer may use reasonable force, if necessary, in the performance of his functions.

Evidence of authority

7. An enforcement officer shall, if required, produce evidence of his authority.

Protection of officers

8. An enforcement officer shall not be liable in any civil or criminal proceedings for anything done in the purported performance of his functions under this Schedule if the court is satisfied that the act was done in good faith and that there were reasonable grounds for doing it.

Offences

9.—(1) A person is guilty of an offence if he—

  (a)   intentionally obstructs an enforcement officer in the performance of any of his functions under this Schedule;
  (b)   fails without reasonable excuse to comply with a requirement made by an enforcement officer in the performance of those functions; or
  (c)   in purporting to give information required by an officer for the performance of those functions—

       (i)   makes a statement which he knows to be false in a material particular or recklessly makes a statement which is false in a material particular; or
       (ii) intentionally fails to disclose any material particular.

  (2) A person guilty of an offence under this paragraph is liable on summary conviction to a fine not exceeding level 5 on the standard scale.

Note
In para 2(2) the words in square brackets were substituted by the Criminal Justice Act 1993, s. 23(2).

SCHEDULE 4

Section 31(1)

CONSEQUENTIAL AND OTHER AMENDMENTS

The Misuse of Drugs Act 1971

1. In section 27(1) of the Misuse of Drugs Act 1971 after "1986" there shall be inserted the words "or an offence to which section 1 of the Criminal Justice (Scotland) Act 1987 relates".

The Magistrates' Courts Act 1980

2. After section 97(2) of the Magistrates' Courts Act 1980 there shall be inserted—

"(2A) A summons may also be issued under subsection (1) above if the justice is satisfied that the person in question is outside the British Islands but no warrant shall be issued under subsection (2) above unless the justice is satisfied by evidence on oath that the person in question is in England or Wales.".

The Criminal Justice Act 1982

3. At the end of Part II of Schedule 1 to the Criminal Justice Act 1982 there shall be inserted–

"Criminal Justice (International Co-operation) Act 1990 (c. 5) Section 14 (concealing or transferring proceeds of drug trafficking)."

4., 5. . . .

The Criminal Justice Act 1988

6.—(1) The Criminal Justice Act 1988 shall be amended as follows.
(2) In sections 24(4) and 26 for the words "section 29 below" there shall be substituted the words "section 3 of the Criminal Justice (International Co-operation) Act 1990".
(3) In paragraph 6(1) of Schedule 13 for the words "In section 29 above 'criminal proceedings' does not include proceedings before a Service court" there shall be substituted the words "No application shall be made under section 3 of the Criminal Justice (International Co-operation) Act 1990 in relation to any offence which is or is to be the subject of proceedings before a Service court".

The Magistrates' Courts (Northern Ireland) Order 1981

7. In Article 118(2) of the Magistrates' Courts (Northern Ireland) Order 1981 after the words "a person" there shall be inserted the words "in Northern Ireland".

The Criminal Justice (Evidence, Etc.) Northern Ireland) Order 1988

8. In Articles 4(4) and 6 of the Criminal Justice (Evidence, Etc.) (Northern Ireland) Order 1988 for the words "Article 9" there shall be substituted the words "section 3 of the Criminal Justice (International Co-operation) Act 1990".

Notes
Para. 4 was repealed by the Drug Trafficking Act 1994, s.67(1), Sched.3. Para.5 was repealed by the Criminal Procedure (Consequential Provisions) (Scotland) Act 1995, s.6(1), Sched.5.

Section 31(3)   SCHEDULE 5

REPEALS

Chapter	Short title	Extent of repeal
36 & 37 Vict. c. 60	The Extradition Act 1873	Section 5.
1975 c. 34	The Evidence (Proceedings in Other Jurisdictions) Act 1975	Section 5
1978 c. 26	The Suppression of Terrorism Act 1978	In section 1, subsection (3)(d) together with the word "and" immediately preceding it, in subsection (4) the words from "and that subsection (3) (d)(ii)" onwards and subsection (5)(b) together with the word "and" immediately preceding it.

Chapter	Short title	Extent of repeal
1987 c. 43	The Criminal Justice (Scotland) Act 1987	In section 5(2) the words from "at the date" to the "first occurs)", the words "on that date" and the words "as at that date".
1988 c. 33	The Criminal Justice Act 1988	Section 29.
1989 c. 33	The Extradition Act 1989	In section 22(4)(f)(ii) the word "and". In Schedule 1, in paragraph 15(h) the word "or" where it last occurs.

EUROPEAN CONVENTION ON MUTUAL ASSISTANCE IN CRIMINAL MATTERS, 1959

Source: Council of Europe, Strasbourg

PREAMBLE

The Governments signatory hereto, being Members of the Council of Europe,

Considering that the aim of the Council of Europe is to achieve greater unity among its Members;

Believing that the adoption of common rules in the field of mutual assistance in criminal matters will contribute to the attainment of this aim;

Considering that such mutual assistance is related to the question of extradition, which has already formed the subject of a Convention signed on 13th December 1957,

Have agreed as follows:

CHAPTER I
GENERAL PROVISIONS

Article 1

1. The Contracting Parties undertake to afford each other, in accordance with the provisions of this Convention, the widest measure of mutual assistance in proceedings in respect of offences the punishment of which, at the time of the request for assistance, falls within the jurisdiction of the judicial authorities of the requesting Party.

2. This Convention does not apply to arrests, the enforcement of verdicts or offences under military law which are not offences under ordinary criminal law.

Article 2

Assistance may be refused:

    (*a*)   if the request concerns an offence which the requested Party considers a political offence, an offence connected with a political offence, or a fiscal offence;

    (*b*)   if the requested Party considers that execution of the request is likely to prejudice the sovereignty, security, *ordre public* or other essential interests of its country.

CHAPTER II
LETTERS ROGATORY

Article 3

1. The requested Party shall execute in the manner provided for by its law any letters rogatory relating to a criminal matter and addressed to it by the judicial authorities of the requesting

Party for the purpose of procuring evidence or transmitting articles to be produced in evidence, records or documents.

2. If the requesting Party desires witnesses or experts to give evidence on oath, it shall expressly so request, and the requested Party shall comply with the request if the law of its country does not prohibit it.

3. The requested Party may transmit certified copies or certified photostat copies of records or documents requested, unless the requesting Party expressly requests the transmission of originals, in which case the requested Party shall make every effort to comply with the request.

Article 4

On the express request of the requesting Party the requested Party shall state the date and place of execution of the letters rogatory. Officials and interested persons may be present if the requested Party consents.

Article 5

1. Any Contracting Party may, by a declaration addressed to the Secretary General of the Council of Europe, when signing this Convention or depositing its instrument of ratification or accession, reserve the right to make the execution of letters rogatory for search or seizure of property dependent on one or more of the following conditions:

(a)   that the offence motivating the letters rogatory is punishable under both the law of the requesting Party and the law of the requested Party;
(b)   that the offence motivating the letters rogatory is an extraditable offence in the requested country;
(c)   that execution of the letters rogatory is consistent with the law of the requested Party.

2. Where a Contracting Party makes a declaration in accordance with paragraph 1 of this Article, any other Party may apply reciprocity.

Article 6

1. The requested Party may delay the handing over of any property, records or documents requested, if it requires the said property, records or documents in connection with pending criminal proceedings.

2. Any property, as well as original records or documents, handed over in execution of letters rogatory shall be returned by the requesting Party to the requested Party as soon as possible unless the latter Party waives the return thereof.

CHAPTER III
SERVICE OF WRITS AND RECORDS OF JUDICIAL VERDICTS – APPEARANCE OF WITNESSES,
EXPERTS AND PROSECUTED PERSONS

Article 7

1. The requested Party shall effect service of writs and records of judicial verdicts which are transmitted to it for this purpose by the requesting Party.

Service may be effected by simple transmission of the writ or record to the person to be served. If the requesting Party expressly so requests, service shall be effected by the requested Party in the manner provided for the service of analogous documents under its own law or in a special manner consistent with such law.

2. Proof of service shall be given by means of a receipt dated and signed by the person served or by means of a declaration made by the requested Party that service has been effected and stating the form and date of such service. One or other of these documents shall be sent immediately to the requesting Party. The requested Party shall, if the requesting Party so requests, state whether service has been effected in accordance with the law of the requested Party. If service cannot be effected, the reasons shall be communicated immediately by the requested Party to the requesting Party.

3. Any Contracting Party may, by a declaration addressed to the Secretary General of the Council of Europe, when signing this Convention or depositing its instrument of ratification or accession, request that service of a summons on an accused person who is in its territory be transmitted to its authorities by a certain time before the date set for appearance. This time shall be specified in the aforesaid declaration and shall not exceed 50 days.

This time shall be taken into account when the date of appearance is being fixed and when the summons is being transmitted.

Article 8

A witness or expert who has failed to answer a summons to appear, service of which has been requested, shall not, even if the summons contains a notice of penalty, be subjected to any punishment or measure of restraint, unless subsequently he voluntarily enters the territory of the requesting Party and is there again duly summoned.

Article 9

The allowances, including subsistence, to be paid and the travelling expenses to be refunded to a witness or expert by the requesting Party shall be calculated as from his place of residence and shall be at rates at least equal to those provided for in the scales and rules in force in the country where the hearing is intended to take place.

Article 10

1. If the requesting Party considers the personal appearance of a witness or expert before its judicial authorities especially necessary, it shall so mention in its request for service of the summons and the requested Party shall invite the witness or expert to appear.

The requested Party shall inform the requesting Party of the reply of the witness or expert.

2. In the case provided for under paragraph 1 of this Article the request or the summons shall indicate the approximate allowances payable and the travelling and subsistence expenses refundable.

3. If a specific request is made, the requested Party may grant the witness or expert an advance. The amount of the advance shall be endorsed on the summons and shall be refunded by the requesting Party.

Article 11

1. A person in custody whose personal appearance as a witness or for purposes of confrontation is applied for by the requesting Party, shall be temporarily transferred to the territory where the hearing is intended to take place, provided that he shall be sent back within the period stipulated by the requested Party and subject to the provisions of Article 12 in so far as these are applicable.

(a) if the person in custody does not consent,

(b) if his presence is necessary at criminal proceedings pending in the territory of the requested Party.

(c) if transfer is liable to prolong his detention, or

(*d*)   if there are other overriding grounds for not transferring him to the territory of the requesting Party.

2. Subject to the provisions of Article 2, in a case coming within the immediately preceding paragraph, transit of the person in custody through the territory of a third State, Party to this Convention, shall be granted on application, accompanied by all necessary documents, addressed by the Ministry of Justice of the requesting Party to the Ministry of Justice of the Party through whose territory transit is requested.

A Contracting Party may refuse to grant transit to its own nationals.

3. The transferred person shall remain in custody in the territory of the requesting Party and, where applicable, in the territory of the Party through which transit is requested, unless the Party from whom transfer is requested applies for his release.

Article 12

1. A witness or expert, whatever his nationality, appearing on a summons before the judicial authorities of the requesting Party shall not be prosecuted or detained or subjected to any other restriction of his personal liberty in the territory of that Party in respect of acts or convictions anterior to his departure from the territory of the requested Party.

2. A person, whatever his nationality, summoned before the judicial authorities of the requesting Party to answer for acts forming the subject of proceedings against him, shall not be prosecuted or detained or subjected to any other restriction of his personal liberty for acts or convictions anterior to his departure from the territory of the requested Party and not specified in the summons.

3. The immunity provided for in this Article shall cease when the witness or expert or prosecuted person, having had for a period of fifteen consecutive days from the date when his presence is no longer required by the judicial authorities an opportunity of leaving, has nevertheless remained in the territory, or having left it, has returned.

CHAPTER IV
JUDICIAL RECORDS

Article 13

1. A requested Party shall communicate extracts from and information relating to judicial records, requested from it by the judicial authorities of a Contracting Party and needed in a criminal matter, to the same extent that these may be made available to its own judicial authorities in like case.

2. In any case other than that provided for in paragraph 1 of this Article the request shall be complied with in accordance with the conditions provided for by the law, regulations or practice of the requested Party.

CHAPTER V
PROCEDURE

Article 14

1. Requests for mutual assistance shall indicate as follows:

(*a*)   the authority making the request,
(*b*)   the object of and the reason for the request,
(*c*)   where possible, the identity and the nationality of the person concerned, and
(*d*)   where necessary, the name and address of the person to be served.

2. Letters rogatory referred to in Articles 3, 4 and 5 shall, in addition, state the offence and contain a summary of the facts.

Article 15

1. Letters rogatory referred to in Article 3, 4 and 5 as well as the applications referred to in Article 11 shall be addressed by the Ministry of Justice of the requesting Party to the Ministry of Justice of the requested Party and shall be returned through the same channels.
2. In case of urgency, letters rogatory may be addressed directly by the judicial authorities of the requesting Party to the judicial authorities of the requested Party. They shall be returned together with the relevant documents through the channels stipulated in paragraph 1 of this Article.
3. Requests provided for in paragraph 1 of Article 13 may be addressed directly by the judicial authorities concerned to the appropriate authorities of the requested Party, and the replies may be returned directly by those authorities. Requests provided for in paragraph 2 of Article 13 shall be addressed by the Ministry of Justice of the requesting Party to the Ministry of Justice of the requested Party.
4. Requests for mutual assistance, other than those provided for in paragraphs 1 and 3 of this Article and, in particular, requests for investigation preliminary to prosecution, may be communicated directly between the judicial authorities.
5. In cases where direct transmission is permitted under this Convention, it may take place through the International Criminal Police Organisation (Interpol).
6. A Contracting Party may, when signing this Convention or depositing its instrument of ratification or accession, by a declaration addressed to the Secretary General of the Council of Europe, give notice that some or all requests for assistance shall be sent to it through channels other than those provided for in this Article, or require that, in a case provided for in paragraph 2 of this Article, a copy of the letters rogatory shall be transmitted at the same time to its Ministry of Justice.
7. The provisions of this Article are without prejudice to those of bilateral agreements or arrangements in force between Contracting Parties which provide for the direct transmission of requests for assistance between their respective authorities.

Article 16

1. Subject to paragraph 2 of this Article, translations of requests and annexed documents shall not be required.
2. Each Contracting Party may, when signing or depositing its instrument of ratification or accession, by means of a declaration addressed to the Secretary General of the Council of Europe, reserve the right to stipulate that requests and annexed documents shall be addressed to it accompanied by a translation into its own language or into either of the official languages of the Council of Europe or into one of the latter languages, specified by it. The other Contracting Parties may apply reciprocity.
3. This Article is without prejudice to the provisions concerning the translation of requests or annexed documents contained in the agreements or arrangements in force or to be made between two or more Contracting Parties.

Article 17

Evidence or documents transmitted pursuant to this Convention shall not require any form of authentication.

Article 18

Where the authority which receives a request for mutual assistance has no jurisdiction to comply therewith, it shall, *ex officio*, transmit the request to the competent authority of its country and shall so inform the requesting Party through the direct channels, if the request has been addressed through such channels.

Article 19

Reasons shall be given for any refusal of mutual assistance.

Article 20

Subject to the provisions of Article 10, paragraph 3, execution of requests for mutual assistance shall not entail refunding of expenses except those incurred by the attendance of experts in the territory of the requested Party or the transfer of a person in custody carried out under Article 11.

CHAPTER VI

LAYING OF INFORMATION IN CONNECTION WITH PROCEEDINGS

Article 21

1. Information laid by one Contracting Party with a view to proceedings in the courts of another Party shall be transmitted between the Ministers of Justice concerned unless a Contracting Party avails itself of the option provided for in paragraph 6 of Article 15.
2. The requested Party shall notify the requesting Party of any action taken on such information and shall forward a copy of the record of any verdict pronounced.
3. The provisions of Article 16 shall apply to information laid under paragraph 1 of this Article.

CHAPTER VII

EXCHANGE OF INFORMATION FROM JUDICIAL RECORDS

Article 22

Each Contracting Party shall inform any other Party of all criminal convictions and subsequent measures in respect of nationals of the latter Party, entered in the judicial records. Ministries of Justice shall communicate such information to one another at least once a year. Where the person concerned is considered a national of two or more other Contracting Parties, the information shall be given to each of these Parties, unless the person is a national of the Party in the territory of which he was convicted.

CHAPTER VIII

FINAL PROVISIONS

Article 23

1. Any Contracting Party may, when signing this Convention or when depositing its instrument of ratification or accession, make a reservation in respect of any provision or provisions of the Convention.
2. Any Contracting Party which has made a reservation shall withdraw it as soon as circumstances permit. Such withdrawal shall be made by notification to the Secretary General of the Council of Europe.
3. A Contracting Party which has made a reservation in respect of a provision of the Convention may not claim application of the said provision by another Party save in so far as it has itself accepted the provision.

Article 24

A Contracting Party may, when signing the Convention or depositing its instrument of ratification or accession, by a declaration addressed to the Secretary General of the Council of Europe, define what authorities it will, for the purposes of the Convention, deem judicial authorities.

Article 25

1. This Convention shall apply to the metropolitan territories of the Contracting Parties.
2. In respect of France, it shall also apply to Algeria and to the overseas Departments, and, in respect of Italy, it shall also apply to the territory of Somaliland under Italian administration.
3. The Federal Republic of Germany may extend the application of this Convention to the *Land* of Berlin by notice addressed to the Secretary General of the Council of Europe.
4. In respect of the Kingdom of the Netherlands, the Convention shall apply to its European territory. The Netherlands may extend the application of this Convention to the Netherlands Antilles, Surinam and Netherlands New Guinea by notice addressed to the Secretary General of the Council of Europe.
5. By direct arrangement between two or more Contracting Parties and subject to the conditions laid down in the arrangement, the application of this Convention may be extended to any territory, other than the territories mentioned in paragraphs 1, 2, 3 and 4 of this Article, of one of these Parties, for the international relations of which any such Party is responsible.

Article 26

1. Subject to the provisions of Article 15, paragraph 7, and Article 16, paragraph 3, this Convention shall, in respect of those countries to which it applies, supersede the provisions of any treaties, conventions or bilateral agreements governing mutual assistance in criminal matters between any two Contracting Parties.
2. This Convention shall not affect obligations incurred under the terms of any other bilateral or multilateral international convention which contains or may contain clauses governing specific aspects of mutual assistance in a given field.
3. The Contracting Parties may conclude between themselves bilateral or multilateral agreements on mutual assistance in criminal matters only in order to supplement the provisions of this Convention or to facilitate the application of the principles contained therein.
4. Where, as between two or more Contracting Parties, mutual assistance in criminal matters is practised on the basis of uniform legislation or of a special system providing for the reciprocal application in their respective territories of measures of mutual assistance, these Parties shall, notwithstanding the provisions of this Convention, be free to regulate their mutual relations in this field exclusively in accordance with such legislation or system. Contracting Parties which, in accordance with this paragraph, exclude as between themselves the application of this Convention shall notify the Secretary General of the Council of Europe accordingly.

Article 27

1. This Convention shall be open to signature by the Members of the Council of Europe. It shall be ratified. The instruments of ratification shall be deposited with the Secretary General of the Council.
2. The Convention shall come into force 90 days after the date of deposit of the third instrument of ratification.
3. As regards any signatory ratifying subsequently the Convention shall come into force 90 days after the date of the deposit of its instrument of ratification.

Article 28

1. The Committee of Ministers of the Council of Europe may invite any State not a Member of the Council to accede to this Convention, provided that the resolution containing such invitation obtains the unanimous agreement of the Members of the Council who have ratified the Convention.
2. Accession shall be by deposit with the Secretary General of the Council of an instrument of accession which shall take effect 90 days after the date of its deposit.

Article 29

Any Contracting Party may denounce this Convention in so far as it is concerned by giving notice to the Secretary General of the Council of Europe. Denunciation shall take effect six months after the date when the Secretary General of the Council received such notification.

Article 30

The Secretary General of the Council of Europe shall notify the Members of the Council and the Government of any State which has acceded to this Convention of:

(a) the names of the Signatories and the deposit of any instrument of ratification or accession;
(b) the date of entry into force of this Convention;
(c) any notification received in accordance with the provisions of Article 5 – paragraph 1, Article 7 – paragraph 3, Article 15 – paragraph 6, Article 16 – paragraph 2, Article 24, Article 25 – paragraphs 3 and 4, or Article 26 – paragraph 4;
(d) any reservation made in accordance with Article 23, paragraph 1;
(e) the withdrawal of any reservation in accordance with Article 23, paragraph 2;
(f) any notification of denunciation received in accordance with the provisions of Article 29 and the date on which such denunciation will take effect.

In witness whereof the undersigned, being duly authorised thereto, have signed this Convention.

DONE at Strasbourg,

this 20th day of April 1959, in English and French, both texts being equally authoritative, in a single copy which shall remain deposited in the archives of the Council of Europe. The Secretary General of the Council of Europe shall transmit certified copies to the signatory and acceding Governments.

Appendix C

UNITED KINGDOM

Reservations and Declarations handed over at the time of the deposit of the instrument of ratification on 29 August 1991 – Or. Engl.

RESERVATIONS

Article 2

In respect of Article 2, the Government of the United Kingdom of Great Britain and Northern Ireland reserves the right to refuse assistance if the person who is the subject of a request for assistance has been convicted or acquitted in the United Kingdom or in the third State of an offence which arises from the same conduct as that giving rise to proceedings in the requesting State in respect of that Person.

Article 3

In respect of Article 3, the Government of the United Kingdom of Great Britain and Northern Ireland reserves the right not to take the evidence of witnesses or require the production of records or other documents where its law recognises in relation thereto privilege, non-compellability or other exemption from giving evidence.

Article 5 paragraph 1

In accordance with Article 5, paragraph 1, the Government of the United Kingdom of Great Britain and Northern Ireland reserves the right to make the execution of letters rogatory for search and seizure of property dependent on the following conditions:

    a.   that the offence motivating the letters rogatory is punishable under both the law of the requesting Party and the law of the United Kingdom; and

    b.   that execution of the letters rogatory is consistent with the law of the United Kingdom.

Article 11 paragraph 2

The Government of the United Kingdom of Great Britain and Northern Ireland is unable to grant requests made under Article 11, paragraph 2 for a person in custody to transit through its territory.

Article 12

The Government of the United Kingdom of Great Britain and Northern Ireland will only consider the granting of immunity under Article 12 where this is specifically requested by the person to whom the immunity would apply or by the appropriate authorities of the party from whom assistance is requested. A request for immunity will not be granted where the judicial authorities of the United Kingdom consider that granting it would not be in the public interest.

Article 21

The Government of the United Kingdom reserves the right not to apply Article 21.

DECLARATIONS

Declaration 1

Article 15 paragraph 1

In respect of the Government of the United Kingdom of Great Britain and Northern Ireland, references to the "Ministry of Justice" for the purposes of Article 11, paragraph 2, Article 15, paragraphs 1, 3 and 6 and Article 21, paragraph 1 and Article 22 are to the Home Office.

Declaration 2

Article 16 paragraph 2

In accordance with Article 16, paragraph 2, the Government of the United Kingdom reserves the right to stipulate that requests and annexed documents shall be addressed to it accompanied by translations into English.

Declaration 3

Article 24

In accordance with Article 24 for the purposes of the Convention, the Government of the United Kingdom deems the following to be judicial authorities:

— Magistrates' courts, the Crown Court and the High Court;
— the Attorney General for England and Wales;
— the Director of Public Prosecutions and any Crown Prosecutor;
— the Director and any designated member of the Serious Fraud Office;
— the Secretary of State for Trade and Industry in respect of his function of investigating and prosecuting offences;
— any Assistant Secretary (Legal) in charge of Prosecution Division of HM Customs and Excise;
— District Courts and Sheriff Courts and the High Court of Justiciary;
— the Lord Advocate;
— any Procurator Fiscal;
— the Attorney General for Northern Ireland;
— the Director of Public Prosecutions in Northern Ireland.

Appendix D

1969 EXPLANATORY REPORT ON THE EUROPEAN CONVENTION ON MUTUAL ASSISTANCE IN CRIMINAL MATTERS, 1959

Source: Council of Europe, Strasbourg

General Considerations

The work of the Council of Europe on mutual assistance in criminal matters follows on that relating to the preparation of the European Convention on Extradition signed in Paris on 13 December 1957.

The Convention drafted by the experts deal with such matters as letter rogatory for the examination of witnesses or experts, service of official documents and judicial verdicts, summoning of witnesses, experts, or persons in custody and transmission of information from judicial records.

A number of guiding principles were laid down for mutual assistance in criminal matters. It was decided that such assistance should be independent of extradition in that it should be granted even in cases where extradition was refused. For example, it was agreed that assistance should be granted in the case of minor offences and that as a general rule the offence need not be an offence under the law of both countries. In the case of letters rogatory for search and seizure, however, the Contracting Parties could derogate from these rules under Article 5 of the Convention.

It was considered advisable to exclude mutual assistance in cases of a military nature from the application of the Convention and to make it optional to refuse assistance in cases of a political or fiscal nature.

Mutual assistance in the prosecution of nationals of the requested country was not excluded. A clause was inserted, however, in order to protect their interest (see commentary on Article 7, paragraph 3). An expert considered that, in this respect, aliens or stateless persons domiciled in the requested country should receive the same treatment as nationals.

Assistance must be given even if the offence is one which may be prosecuted by the authorities of *both* the requesting and the requested Parties.

It should be pointed out that some States, including Austria, the Federal Republic of Germany and Norway, make no distinction between "letters rogatory" and "other requests for mutual assistance" such as the "service of writs" or "communication of information from judicial records." For those States, all these forms come under the single concept of "mutual assistance" and should be dealt with as a whole. The special situation of those countries was accordingly taken into account, particularly in designing the arrangements of the Convention. Thus, for example, the experts were led to group the provisions concerning "channels" for the transmission of requests for mutual assistance in a single Article.

The experts examined certain other points which were not regulated in the draft Convention.

In the first place, the committee debated whether a provision should be drawn up to enable single items of information concerning a criminal matter to be exchanged directly between *"police authorities acting in an auxiliary capacity to the judicial authorities."* The majority of the experts were in favour of making no such provision. They thought it best not to force the existing practice of the police into a rigid mould, besides which, the Statute of the International Criminal Police Organisation (Interpol) already regulated mutual assistance between police authorities. However, it was stipulated in paragraph 5 of Article 15 relating to channels of communication that, in all cases where direct transmission is permitted, it may take place through Interpol.

Second: the question was raised whether provision should be made for an *"arbitral body"* to settle any disputes over the interpretation or application of the Convention.

The committee thought that arbitration would be out of place, as Article 2 enabled Contracting Parties to refuse assistance on the grounds specified therein, which are to be assessed according to the practice of the requested country.

Some experts then asked whether it would not be advisable to consider setting up a "Committee" which would be responsible for establishing a "common interpretation" of the provisions of the Convention. The experts were unable to come to an agreement on this question.

Third: The question was brought up whether *officials and magistrates* of one Party should not be authorised to engage in *certain activities in the territory of another* Party with a view to the continued pursuit and arrest of a fugitive offender. It was explained that such activities would be subject to the condition that the offender, after arrest, should be immediately handed over to the local authorities.

The experts thought that this matter should be the subject of bilateral arrangements, as it affected only countries with a common frontier.

The European Convention on Mutual Assistance was, by a decision taken by the Committee of Ministers sitting at Deputy level, at its 71st meeting (April 1959), opened for signature by the Member States of the Council of Europe on 20 April 1959.

COMMENTARIES ON THE ARTICLE OF THE CONVENTION

Article 1

Paragraph 1 applies to the whole Convention, the Contracting Parties giving an undertaking in principle to afford each other the widest measure of mutual assistance in proceedings in respect of offences the punishment of which falls within the competence of the judicial authorities of the requesting Party. Provision is thus made for minor offences as well as for other, serious, offences; furthermore, mutual assistance is not subject to the rules governing extradition (but see commentary on Article 5). Mutual assistance must also be accorded in cases where the offence comes under the jurisdiction of the requested Party.

The Convention applies only to judicial proceedings as opposed to administrative proceedings. As regards the concept of "judicial authorities" mentioned in that paragraph, some experts pointed out that in their countries "public prosecutors" were regarded as administrative authorities, whereas in certain others they were judicial authorities. A provision (Article 24) was accordingly adopted in order to enable the Parties to state which authorities they consider as judicial authorities within the meaning of this Convention (see commentary on Article 24).

This paragraph, which is of a general character, is to be interpreted in a broad sense. It covers not only those forms of mutual assistance specifically mentioned in the Convention, but also every other kind of mutual legal assistance, including requests for assistance made in connection with:

(i) proceedings in respect of an *Ordnungswidrigkeit* under German law; an *Ordnungswidrigkeit* is an offence which, while not classified as a criminal offence, is punishable by a fine imposed by an administrative authority; the accused person has, however, a right of appeal to the ordinary courts. To make it quite clear that mutual assistance can only be invoked in the judicial stage of such proceedings, the Committee of Experts inserted the phrase "at the time of the request for assistance" in this paragraph;

(ii) injured party claims for damages in criminal proceedings;

(iii) application for pardon or review of sentence;

(iv) proceedings for the compensation of persons found innocent.

In Austria the amount of compensation payable to persons found innocent was a matter not for criminal jurisdiction but for the civil courts. Under Turkish legislation compensation could be obtained only by application to the administrative authorities.

It was specified in *paragraph* 2 that this Convention does not apply to "arrests and the enforcement of verdict". These words were substituted for the words "enforcement of judgments" employed in the preceding text of the experts since this expression was not sufficiently precise; for instance, it did not cover arrest warrants and imprisonment for debt which are generally to be excluded from the application of mutual assistance. Furthermore, this paragraph excluded military offences which are not offences under ordinary law from the field of application of the Convention. Other treaties or agreements may provide for assistance in cases of military offences. A similar clause appears in Article 4 of the European Convention on Extradition.

Article 2

This Article sets forth a number of exceptions.

Sub-paragraph (a) concerns political and fiscal offences. Assistance will not, however, always be refused in these cases since the text of this Article leaves the matter to the discretion of the requested State.

Several experts pointed out that in such cases it might still be in the interest of an accused person that assistance should be granted since he would then be informed of the charge and could prepare his defence. Hearing witnesses might also operate in favour of the accused.

With regard to fiscal offences, it was agreed that the requested Party might in certain circumstances consider it desirable to grant assistance even if such a course was unfavourable to the accused.

Sub-paragraph (b) mentions other cases in which the requested State may refuse assistance.

The phrase "essential interests" refers to the interests of the State, not of individuals. Economic interests may, however, be covered by this concept.

During the drafting it was suggested to add to Article 2 a clause worded as follows:

"The execution of letters rogatory may be refused if such execution does not lie within the competence of the judicial authorities of the requested State."

This proposal was taken from Article 11 (3) of the Convention on Civil Procedure signed at The Hague on 11 March 1954. It was not adopted by the experts, however, on account of its restrictive character.

Another proposal would have resulted in a provision being inserted to the effect that assistance may be refused if the requested Party has substantial grounds for believing that the proceedings against the person concerned have been instituted for the purpose of prosecuting or punishing him on account of his race, religion, nationality or political opinions. A similar provision appears in Article 3 (2) of the European Convention on Extradition.

This suggestion was not accepted by the committee, which considered such a clause unnecessary in the case of mutual assistance under Council of Europe arrangements.

With reference to Article 8 and 9 of the European Convention on Extradition, it was proposed to provide an optional clause whereby the requested Party would retain the right to refuse assistance:

(a) if the person charged is being proceeded against by the authorities of the requested Party or by the judicial authorities of a third State for the offence or offences which have given rise to the proceedings in the requesting country, or

(b) if the person charged has been finally convicted or acquitted by the judicial authorities of the requested Party or those of a third State in respect of the offence or offences which have given rise to the proceedings in the requesting country or if the aforesaid authorities have decided either not to institute or to terminate proceedings in respect of the same offence or offences.

This proposal was not adopted. It was considered that the insertion of this clause would have reduced the scope of the Convention. Moreover, in certain cases, such a clause might harm not only the interests of the requesting Party — which would still have to take a decision in the criminal matter in question even though it has not received the assistance requested, but also the interests of the requested Party which might require certain information concerning the accused person from the requesting Party, which Party would then apply to it reciprocity. Hence this proposal was not adopted; however, it was accepted that governments may enter a reservation to that effect.

Article 3

This Article concerns the execution of letters rogatory.

Paragraph 1 sets forth the purposes for which letters rogatory may be sent. By "letter rogatory", in this Article, is meant a mandate given by a judicial authority of one country to a foreign judicial authority to perform in its place one or more specified actions.

The expression "procuring evidence" refers, inter alia, to the hearing of witnesses, experts or accused persons, the transport involved as well as search and seizure. The words "criminal matter" mean any proceedings within the meaning of Article 1 (1).

It follows from this text that letters rogatory must be executed in the manner provided for by the laws of the requested Party. No condition of substance is stipulated and the rule of culpability in both countries, which is one of the guiding principles of the European Convention on Extradition, has not been retained in the present Convention, because mutual assistance does not have exactly the same effects as extradition. Nevertheless, provision is made in Article 5 (1) for an exception in the case of search and seizure.

In respect of the Federal Republic of Germany, the term "judicial authorities of the requesting Party" denoted also the judicial authorities of the *Länder*.

According to *paragraph 2*, experts and witnesses may give evidence on oath only if the law of the requested Party does not prohibit it. Under this provision, the requested Party may hear evidence given on oath even if, as a general rule, there is no provision in its judicial practice for the taking of an oath, provided that this is not contrary to its law. It was also agreed that the oath would be administered in accordance with the rules of the requested Party.

Paragraph 3 does not call for special comment.

Article 4

This concerns notice of execution of letters rogatory.

The object of this clause is to enable the authorities of the requesting Party or the interested persons, if they expressly so request, to be present at the execution of letters rogatory if the requested Party agrees to this course. It is understood that consent may be given only if the law of the requested party does not prohibit it.

It was also agreed that where this "express request" is not contained in the letters rogatory it should be transmitted by the channels laid down for such letters.

The Italian expert said during the elaboration of the Convention that under Italian law the interested persons could not be present at the execution of letters rogatory because judicial enquiries were secret. Only the foreign authorities could be allowed to attend.

Article 5

This Article lays down the conditions governing execution of letters rogatory for search or seizure.

Under Article 1 and 3, mutual assistance is not subject to the rules of extradition or to those of culpability in both countries; but *paragraph 1* of Article 5 enables the Parties concerned to require the application of one or both of those rules to cases of search or seizure. According to sub-paragraph (*c*), moreover, a Party may declare that it will only authorise the execution of a letter rogatory for search or seizure if such execution is consistent with its law.

Paragraph 2 makes it possible for reciprocity to be invoked in regard to any Party which has made use of the optional provisions of the preceding paragraph.

Article 6

This concerns the handing over of property to the requesting Party in execution of letter rogatory.

Paragraph 1 is based on paragraph 3 of Article 20 of the European Convention on Extradition.

The property referred to in *paragraph 2* means (*a*) property seized in pursuance of letter rogatory, (*b*) property seized on a previous occasion in connection with other proceedings and handed over to the requesting Party, (*c*) property handed over without previous seizure. The word "property" refers to the "evidence" mentioned in Article 3, paragraph 1.

It was agreed that in accordance with this text the requesting Party may not dispose of such property even in a case where under its own legislation it is obliged to decide the question of its ownership.

Article 7

This refers to service of writs and records of judicial verdicts. The word "service" is to be understood in a broad sense as referring to both simple transmission and official notification. It is not, however, necessary that the document in question be handed personally to the person to be served unless this is stipulated in the law of the requested Party or is consistent with this law and desired by the requesting Party.

According to *paragraph 1*, the requested Party is obliged to serve writs and records of judicial verdicts sent to it by the requesting Party on the persons concerned. This text refers in particular to the summoning of accused persons, witnesses and experts to hearings in the requesting country. Provision is made for various methods of service on the persons concerned according as to whether the requesting Party does or does not specify the form of service to be employed.

(*a*)   If the requesting Party does not specify the method of service, "service may be effected by simple transmission". This clause was given an optional form in order to enable the requested Party either to transmit the papers to the person to be served without further formality or to serve them in a manner provided for under domestic law. The requested Party can thus choose the method of service to be employed.

(*b*)   If the requesting Party expressly so requires, the requested Party must serve the documents in a manner provided for under its law or in a special manner compatible with such law.

With regard to *paragraph 2*, it was explained that receipts could be made out in any form desired. The requested Party was not therefore bound to use whatever form was attached to the documents to be served.

Paragraph 3: Before commenting on this text, it should be recalled that the criminal courts of the Scandinavian countries proceed on the basic principle that no accused person may be convicted without having been informed in good time of the charge preferred against him. Moreover, under the legislation of the Scandinavian countries, judgment by default is allowed only in exceptional cases.

It follows that in criminal cases, judgment by default, which is the practice of many Council of Europe States, is unknown to the Scandinavian courts. This divergency between the Scandinavian system and that of these other countries arises not only from a difference in the conduct of criminal proceedings but also from a difference of tradition in the administration of justice. With regard to procedure, for example, it is to be noted that Scandinavian courts may, at their discretion – and here they probably have much wider powers than those of the courts in other countries – compel the accused to appear in court in person.

The final text of paragraph 3 is the result of a compromise between the various legal systems.

According to the *first sentence of this paragraph*, Contracting Parties having exercised the right provided therein might request that the writ should reach them a given time before the date set for appearance. This time, which must not exceed 50 days, is to be specified by the Parties themselves in their "declaration". Its purpose is to enable the requested Party to transmit the writ in good time to the accused so that he may prepare his defence and travel to the place where he is due to appear.

According to the second *sub-paragraph of this paragraph*, this time-limit "shall be taken into account". Under this provision the requesting Party is obliged to fix the date of the appearance of the accused and to serve the writ in time to allow the accused to observe this date. This clause does not make it compulsory for the law to provide that the courts of the requesting Party may not give a judgment by default if, due to special circumstances, the writ could not be transmitted to the requested Party within the stipulated time-limit.

Article 8

This Article refers to all witnesses and experts, whether their personal appearance (see Article 10) has or has not been expressly requested.

The rule laid down is derived from an international custom by which witnesses and experts are completely free not to go to the requesting country.

The word "penalty" refers to all forms of restraint, including fines.

Article 9

This Article refers to all witnesses or experts whether their personal appearance has or has not been expressly requested (See Article 10).

The phrase "rates at least equal" implies that experts and witnesses will always receive at the very least the amount payable under the scales and rules in force in the requesting country. Thus the requesting Party, which is alone empowered to decide in the matter, may grant them a larger sum.

Article 10

Implicit provision is made in Article 7 (1) for the summoning of witnesses or experts for the purpose of giving evidence.

Paragraph 1 of Article 10 supplements paragraph 1 of Article 7 in that it obliges a requesting Party which attaches particular importance to the personal appearance of a witness or expert to say so in its request for service. In this case, the obligation of the requested Party will be to "invite" the witness or expert to comply with the summons. It was agreed that such invitation would be merely a "recommendation". It follows, quite apart from the provisions of Article 8, that witnesses or experts cannot be compelled by force or otherwise to appear before a court in the requesting country.

Paragraphs 2 and 3 apply only in the case provided for in the preceding paragraph, i.e. when the requesting Party has mentioned in its request that it considers the personal appearance of a witness or expert to be especially necessary.

Article 11

This Article is concerned with the transfer of persons in custody.

According to *paragraph 1*, persons in custody whose personal appearance is requested must in principle be transferred. Such transfer may be refused only in the cases provided for in the second sub-paragraph of paragraph 1 which contains four derogations. Of these the fourth is to be regarded as a general clause.

Paragraphs 2 and 3 call for no special comment.

Article 12

This Article concerns immunity.

Paragraph 1 applies to both witnesses and experts summoned to appear in the territory of the requesting Party.

Paragraph 2 is in essence identical with paragraph 1 and applies to a person summoned on a charge. This person may not be prosecuted or detained in respect of an offence or a former conviction not mentioned in the summons.

Persons summoned as witnesses, experts, or accused enjoy immunity only in respect of offences or convictions preceding their departure and may be prosecuted for offences committed subsequently.

Paragraph 3 is similar to paragraph 1 (*b*) of Article 14 of the European Convention on Extradition.

Article 13

This Article refers to information in judicial records. It should not be confused with "exchange of information from judicial records" referred to in Article 22.

Paragraph 1 applies to requests from a judicial authority in connection with a "criminal matter".

Paragraph 2 deals with cases where the requests are made by judicial authorities without jurisdiction in criminal matters, for example civil courts, or by administrative authorities. The word "practice" has been inserted in view of the fact that in some countries such matters are not governed by law or regulation.

Article 14

Paragraph 1 specifies what must be contained in requests for assistance.

Paragraph 2 deals with the content of letters rogatory. It was emphasised that it would be useful to add to such letters a list of questions that might be put to the witnesses or experts. This list would be indicative and not restrictive.

Article 15

This Article specifies the channels of transmission to be used in mutual assistance. However, it was recognised that whatever the channel adopted, the requesting Party could always use the diplomatic channel if it deemed this to be necessary for special reasons.

Paragraph 1 specifies the channels of transmission for letters rogatory and applications for the personal appearance of a person in custody; these must, in principle, pass through the Ministries of Justice of the two Parties, but there is provision for some exceptions with regard to letters rogatory (see paragraphs 2 and 6 below).

The Irish and Swedish experts said that in their countries the Foreign Ministry took the place of the Ministry of Justice for the transmission of letters rogatory. The Ministry of Justice of the requesting Party should therefore apply to the Department of External Affairs in Ireland or the Foreign Ministry in Sweden.

Paragraph 2 makes an exception in respect of the letters rogatory referred to in Articles 3, 4 and 5 by introducing the rule of direct communication in urgent cases; its application, however, is optional. Nevertheless, after the execution of letters rogatory, documents must be returned by the Ministry of Justice of the requested Party to the Ministry of Justice of the requesting Party.

The Irish expert stated that communications could not be made directly between judicial authorities abroad and judicial authorities in Ireland, even in urgent cases.

Paragraph 3 specifies the channels for the transmission of requests for information, including extracts, from the judicial records. Two channels are laid down according to whether the request is made in pursuance of paragraph 1 or paragraph 2 of Article 13.

If the request is made in accordance with paragraph 1 of Article 13, it "may be addressed directly" to the appropriate department of the requested Party, that is the competent local authority. This channel is thus not obligatory, and the requesting Party is therefore also free to apply to the Ministry of Justice (for example, if it does not know the competent local authority).

On the other hand, if the request is made in accordance with paragraph 2 of Article 13, it must needs be transmitted through the Ministries of Justice.

Paragraph 4 specifies the channels for the transmission of requests for assistance other than those mentioned in paragraphs 1 and 3 discussed above. These include requests for service of writs and records of judicial verdicts as well as requests for investigation preliminary to prosecution made by the Public Prosecutor. Direct channels are provided for, but their use is optional.

It was specified that the word "proceedings" under German law referred to *die gerichtliche Strafverfolgung*.

Paragraph 5 allows direct transmission to take place through the International Criminal Police Organisation (Interpol). A similar provision appears in Article 16 of the European Convention on Extradition.

Paragraph 6 was drawn up because some delegations could not accept all the channels provided for in the preceding paragraphs, in particular direct transmission. This provision will allow the Parties concerned freely to choose in all cases the channel of transmission they consider the most appropriate.

According to *paragraph 7*, this Article is without prejudice to the provisions of bilateral agreements or arrangements which provide for the direct transmission of requests for assistance. This clause had to be inserted because, under Article 26 (1), such agreements will be superseded upon the entry into force of this Convention. Without this paragraph, the countries concerned would have to draw up new agreements on this particular point.

Article 16

This Article concerns the translation of requests for mutual assistance and annexed documents.

Paragraph 1 lays down the principle that translations shall not be required and, at least for some countries, confirms existing practice.

Paragraph 2 gives Parties the right to derogate from the principle laid down in the preceding paragraph by enabling them to request a translation either into their own language or into either of the official languages of the Council, namely French or English, or into one of the latter languages specified by it. It was thought advisable to allow such derogation, since it is the local authorities (and not, as in extradition matters, the central authorities) who are required to act on requests for assistance and they are, as a rule, familiar only with their own tongue; but reciprocity may be applied. It was agreed that the "declaration" provided for in this paragraph could name countries from which translations would be required.

In the event of the requesting Party having difficulty in securing a translation of the documents to be transmitted into the language of the requested Party, it could always ask the latter to arrange for such translation but would undertake to bear the cost thereof itself. The requested Party shall comply with this request in so far as it is able.

Paragraph 3 is essentially the same as paragraph 7 of Article 15. It stipulates that its provisions shall be without prejudice to those of agreements or arrangements in force or to be made in the matter of the translation of requests or annexed documents. It follows from this text that, where such agreements already exist, a Contracting Party may not exercise the right set forth in paragraph 2 with regard to a Party to the said agreement or arrangement.

Article 16 will not apply to the exchange of information from judicial records referred to in Article 22.

Article 17

It was agreed that the phrase "any form of authentication" also covers every additional formality such as "certification of competence" in German law.

Article 18

Only those local authorities that have received a request for assistance through direct channels are required to inform the requesting authority that the request has been transmitted to the competent local authority.

This is not, however, the case where transmission has taken place through the Ministries of Justice, since in the latter event the requesting Party is not directly interested in knowing which local authority in the requested country is competent.

Article 19

The expression "any refusal" includes refusal in part.

Article 20

This Article calls for no special comment.

Article 21

This provision enables any Contracting Party to request another Party to institute proceedings against an individual. It refers in particular to cases where a person, having committed an offence in the requesting country, takes refuge in the territory of the requested country and cannot be extradited.

In this situation it is clear that the requesting Party shall itself afford the widest measure of mutual assistance which could be requested of it by the requested Party in such a case.

The Irish expert explained that in his country, except in a limited number of cases, a person could not be charged with or punished for an offence committed abroad.

Article 22

This Article, which is not to be confused with Article 13, introduces the rule of automatic communication of information from judicial records and relates to nationals of other Contracting Parties. According to this text, "criminal convictions" and "subsequent measures" need only be notified if they are entered in the judicial records of the country where sentence was passed.

The words "criminal convictions" must be construed in a broad sense. The "subsequent measures" refer, more particularly, to rehabilitation.

Information – such as is available – must be communicated once a year: it is not necessary for it to be communicated within a year of being entered.

Article 23

This Article which concerns reservations is identical with Article 26 of the European Convention on Extradition.

Article 24

As mentioned in the commentary on Article 1, paragraph 1, the term "judicial authorities" has a different connotation in different countries. In some countries "Public Prosecutors" come within the term, whereas in others they do not. Accordingly, it was agreed that any country could at the time of signature or of deposit of its instruments of ratification define how it would construe "judicial authorities" for the purposes of the Convention, so as to allow, if considered desirable, for the inclusion of "Public Prosecutors".

Article 25

This Article which concerns the territorial application of the Convention follows the text of Article 27 of the European Convention on Extradition, except for the second sentence of paragraph 2 and paragraph 4.

It should be noted that when depositing its instruments of ratification, the French Government made a declaration excluding from the field of application of the Convention Algeria which has become independent.

Article 26

This Article concerns the relationship between this Convention and existing or future bilateral and multilateral agreements.

Paragraph 1 is based on paragraph 1 of Article 28 of the European Convention on Extradition. Under Article 15 (7) and Article 16 (3), the provisions of former treaties relating to the direct transmission of requests for assistance and the translation of requests and annexed documents will remain in force.

Paragraph 2 lays down that clauses relating to specific aspects of mutual assistance in bilateral or multilateral conventions shall not be affected by the present Convention. The Contracting Parties will therefore be bound to respect these clauses. However, if these international conventions are incomplete in this respect, the corresponding provisions of this Convention will have to be applied accordingly. As a general rule, however, the provisions of these conventions shall to the extent they deal with particular aspects of mutual assistance always take precedence with regard to these particular aspects over those of the Council of Europe.

Paragraph 3 is based on paragraph 2 of Article 28 of the European Convention on Extradition. It was accepted that the "agreements" referred to in this paragraph could provide for keeping in force certain provisions of international instruments superseded by virtue of paragraph 1.

Paragraph 4 is based, mutatis mutandis, on paragraph 3 of Article 28 of the European Convention on Extradition. Thus Parties having a system of mutual assistance "on the basis of uniform legislation" (Scandinavian countries) may regulate their mutual relations exclusively in accordance with that system. The reference to a "special system providing for the reciprocal application in their respective territories of measures of mutual assistance" was inserted in order to protect any reciprocal arrangements that might exist between Ireland and the United Kingdom.

Article 27

This Article which concerns the signature, ratification and entry into force of the Convention, reproduces the text of Article 29 of the European Convention on Extradition.

Article 28

This Article which concerns accession reproduces the text of Article 30 of the European Convention on Extradition.

Article 29

This Article which concerns denunciation of the Convention reproduces the text of Article 31 of the European Convention on Extradition.

Article 30

This Article which concerns notifications corresponds to Article 32 of the European Convention on Extradition.

Appendix E

ADDITIONAL PROTOCOL OF 1978 TO THE EUROPEAN CONVENTION ON MUTUAL ASSISTANCE IN CRIMINAL MATTERS, 1959

Source: Council of Europe, Strasbourg

The member States of the Council of Europe, signatory to this Protocol,
  Desirous of facilitating the application of the European Convention on Mutual Assistance in Criminal Matters opened for signature in Strasbourg on 20 April 1959 (hereinafter referred to as "the Convention") in the field of fiscal offences;
  Considering it also desirable to supplement the Convention in certain other respects,
  Have agreed as follows:

Chapter I

Article 1

The Contracting Parties shall not exercise the right provided for in Article 2.a of the Convention to refuse assistance solely on the ground that the request concerns an offence which the requested Party considers a fiscal offence.

Article 2

1. In the case where a Contracting Party has made the execution of letters rogatory for search or seizure of property dependent on the condition that the offence motivating the letters rogatory is punishable under both the law of the requesting Party and the law of the requested Party, this condition shall be fulfilled, as regards fiscal offences, if the offence is punishable under the law of the requesting Party and corresponds to an offence of the same nature under the law of the requested Party.
  2. The request may not be refused on the ground that the law of the requested Party does not impose the same kind of tax or duty or does not contain a tax, duty, customs and exchange regulation of the same kind as the law of the requesting Party.

Chapter II

Article 3

The Convention shall also apply to:

  a.   the service of documents concerning the enforcement of a sentence, the recovery of a fine or the payment of costs of proceedings;

b.   measures relating to the suspension of pronouncement of a sentence or of its enforcement, to conditional release, to deferment of the commencement of the enforcement of a sentence or to the interruption of such enforcement.

CHAPTER III

Article 4

Article 22 of the Convention shall be supplemented by the following text, the original Article 22 of the Convention becoming paragraph 1 and the below-mentioned provisions becoming paragraph 2:

"2. Furthermore, any Contracting Party which has supplied the above-mentioned information shall communicate to the Party concerned, on the latter's request in individual cases, a copy of the convictions and measures in question as well as any other information relevant there to in order to enable it to consider whether they necessitate any measures at national level. This communication shall take place between the Ministries of Justice concerned."

CHAPTER IV

Article 5

1. This Protocol shall be open to signature by the member States of the Council of Europe which have signed the Convention. It shall be subject to ratification, acceptance or approval. Instruments of ratification, acceptance or approval shall be deposited with the Secretary General of the Council of Europe.

2. The Protocol shall enter into force 90 days after the date of the deposit of the third instrument of ratification, acceptance or approval.

3. In respect of a signatory State ratifying, accepting or approving subsequently, the Protocol shall enter into force 90 days after the date of the deposit of its instrument of ratification, acceptance or approval.

4. A member State of the Council of Europe may not ratify, accept or approve this Protocol without having, simultaneously or previously, ratified the Convention

Article 6

1. Any State which has acceded to the Convention may accede to this Protocol after the Protocol has entered into force.

2. Such accession shall be effected by depositing with the Secretary General of the Council of Europe an instrument of accession which shall take effect 90 days after the date of its deposit.

Article 7

1. Any State may, at the time of signature or when depositing its instrument of ratification, acceptance, approval or accession, specify the territory or territories to which this Protocol shall apply.

2. Any State may, when depositing its instrument of ratification, acceptance, approval or accession or at any later date, by declaration addressed to the Secretary General of the Council of Europe, extend this Protocol to any other territory or territories specified in the declaration and for whose international relations it is responsible or on whose behalf it is authorised to give undertakings.

3. Any declaration made in pursuance of the preceding paragraph may, in respect of any territory mentioned in such declaration, be withdrawn by means of a notification addressed to the Secretary General of the Council of Europe. Such withdrawal shall take effect six months after the date of receipt by the Secretary General of the Council of Europe of the notification.

Article 8

1. Reservations made by a Contracting Party to a provision of the Convention shall be applicable also to this Protocol, unless that Party otherwise declares at the time of signature or when depositing its instrument of ratification, acceptance, approval or accession. The same shall apply to the declarations made by virtue of Article 24 of the Convention.

2. Any State may, at the time of signature or when depositing its instrument of ratification, acceptance, approval or accession, declare that it reserves the right:

    a.   not to accept Chapter I, or to accept it only in respect of certain offences or certain categories of the offences referred to in Article 1, or not to comply with letters rogatory for search or seizure of property in respect of fiscal offences;

    b.   not to accept Chapter II;

    c.   not to accept Chapter III.

3. Any Contracting Party may withdraw a declaration it has made in accordance with the foregoing paragraph by means of a declaration addressed to the Secretary General of the Council of Europe which shall become effective as from the date of its receipt.

4. A Contracting Party which has applied to this Protocol a reservation made in respect of a provision of the Convention or which has made a reservation in respect of a provision of this Protocol may not claim the application of that provision by another Contracting Party; it may, however, if its reservation is partial or conditional claim the application of that provision in so far as it has itself accepted it.

5. No other reservation may be made to the provisions of this Protocol.

Article 9

The provisions of this Protocol are without prejudice to more extensive regulations in bilateral or multilateral agreements concluded between Contracting Parties in application of Article 26, paragraph 3, of the Convention.

Article 10

The European Committee on Crime Problems of the Council of Europe shall be kept informed regarding the application of this Protocol and shall do whatever is needful to facilitate a friendly settlement of any difficulty which may arise out of its execution.

Article 11

1. Any Contracting Party may, in so far as it is concerned, denounce this Protocol by means of a notification addressed to the Secretary General of the Council of Europe.

2. Such denunciation shall take effect six months after the date of receipt by the Secretary General of such notification.

3. Denunciation of the Convention entails automatically denunciation of this Protocol.

Article 12

The Secretary General of the Council of Europe shall notify the member States of the Council and any State which has acceded to the Convention of:

a. any signature of this Protocol;

b. any deposit of an instrument of ratification, acceptance, approval or accession;

c. any date of entry into force of this Protocol in accordance with Articles 5 and 6;

d. any declaration received in pursuance of the provisions of paragraphs 2 and 3 of Article 7;

e. any declaration received in pursuance of the provisions of paragraph 1 of Article 8;

f. any reservation made in pursuance of the provisions of paragraph 2 of Article 8;

g. the withdrawal of any reservation carried out in pursuance of the provisions of paragraph 3 of Article 8;

h. any notification received in pursuance of the provisions of Article 11 and the date on which denunciation takes effect.

In witness whereof the undersigned, being duly authorised thereto, have signed this Protocol.

Done at Strasbourg, this 17th day of March 1978, in English and in French, both texts being equally authoritative, in a single copy which shall remain deposited in the archives of the Council of Europe. The Secretary General of the Council of Europe shall transmit certified copies to each of the signatory and acceding States.

APPENDIX F

(Preparatory Acts pursuant to Title VI of the Treaty on European Union)

DRAFT COUNCIL ACT
Establishing the Convention on Mutual Assistance in Criminal Matters between the Member States of the European Union

(1999/C 251/01)
(Text submitted to Coreper on 14 July, 1999)

THE COUNCIL OF THE EUROPEAN UNION,

Having regard to the Treaty on European Union, and in particular Article 34(2)(d) thereof.

Whereas, for the purposes of achieving the objectives of the Union, the Member States regard the rules governing mutual assistance in criminal matters between the Member States of the European Union as a matter of common interest coming under the cooperation provided for in Title VI of the Treaty.

HAVING DECIDED that the Convention signed today by the representatives of the Governments of the Member States of the European Union, the text of which is reproduced in the Annex, is hereby established.

RECOMMENDS that it be adopted by the Member States in accordance with their respective constitutional requirements.

Done at ...

For the Council
The President

Draft Convention

ESTABLISHED BY THE COUNCIL IN ACCORDANCE WITH ARTICLE 34 OF THE TREATY ON EUROPEAN UNION, ON MUTUAL ASSISTANCE IN CRIMINAL MATTERS BETWEEN THE MEMBER STATES OF THE EUROPEAN UNION

THE HIGH CONTRACTING PARTIES to this Convention, Member States of the European Union,

REFERRING to the Council Act establishing the draft Convention on Mutual Assistance in Criminal Matters between the Member States of the European Union.

DESIRING to improve judicial cooperation in criminal matters between the Member States of the Union.

POINTING OUT that the Member States have a common interest in ensuring that mutual assistance between the Member States is provided in a fast and efficient manner compatible with the basic principles of their national law, including the principles of the European Convention for the Protection of Human Rights and Fundamental Freedoms, signed in Rome on 4 November 1950.

EXPRESSING their confidence in the structure and functioning of their legal systems and in the ability of all Member States to guarantee a fair trial.

TAKING INTO ACCOUNT the importance of concluding a Convention between the Member States of the European Union to supplement the European Convention on Mutual Assistance in Criminal Matters of 20 April 1959 and other Conventions in force in this area.

CONSIDERING that the provisions of those Conventions remain applicable for all matters not covered by this Convention,

CONSIDERING that the Member States attach importance to strengthening judicial co-operation, while continuing to apply the principle of proportionality.

RECOGNISING that this Convention does not affect the exercise of the responsibilities incumbent on Member States with regard to the maintenance of law and order and the safeguarding of internal security, and that it is a matter for each Member State to determine, in accordance with Article 33 of the Treaty on European Union, under which conditions it will maintain law and order and safeguard internal security.
HAVE AGREED ON THE FOLLOWING PROVISIONS:

TITLE I

REQUESTS FOR MUTUAL ASSISTANCE

Article 1

General provisions

1. The purpose of this Convention is to supplement the provisions and facilitate the application between the Member States of the European Union, of:

— the European Convention on Mutual Assistance in Criminal Matters of 20 April 1959, hereinafter referred to as the "European Mutual Assistance Convention",
— the Additional Protocol of 17 March 1978 to the European Mutual Assistance Convention.
— the Convention of 19 June 1990 applying the Schengen Agreement of 14 June 1985 on the Gradual Abolition of Checks at their Common Borders, in the context of relations between the Member States party to that Convention, and
— Chapter 2 of the Treaty on Extradition and Mutual Assistance in Criminal Matters between the Kingdom of Belgium, the Grand Duchy of Luxembourg and the Kingdom of the Netherlands of 27 June 1962, as amended by the Protocol of 11 May 1974, hereinafter referred to as the "Benelux Treaty", in the context of relations between the Member States of the Benelux Economic Union.

2. Paragraph 1 shall not affect the application of more favourable provisions in bilateral or multilateral agreements between Member States or, as provided for in Article 26(4) of the European Mutual Assistance Convention, arrangements in the field of mutual assistance in criminal matters agreed on the basis of uniform legislation or of a special system providing for the reciprocal application of measures of mutual assistance in their respective territories.

Article 2

Procedures in connection with which assistance is to be afforded

1. Mutual assistance shall also be afforded in proceedings brought by the administrative authorities in respect of offences which are punishable under the national law of the requesting or the requested Member State, or both, by virtue of being infringements of the rules of law, where the decision may give rise to proceedings before a court having jurisdiction in particular in criminal matters.

2. Mutual assistance shall also be afforded in connection with criminal proceedings and procedures as referred to in paragraph 1 which relate to offences or infringements for which a legal person may be held liable in the requesting Member State.

Article 3

Criminal investigation

For the purposes of Title III of this Convention, a "criminal investigation" is an investigation following the commission of a specific criminal offence in order to identify and arrest, charge, prosecute or deliver judgment on those persons responsible.

Article 4

Compliance with the formalities and procedures indicated by the requesting Member States

1. Where mutual assistance is afforded and provided that such formalities and procedures are not contrary to the fundamental principles of law in the requested Member State, the Member States shall undertake to comply, unless otherwise provided in this Convention, for the purposes of executing letters rogatory, with formalities and procedures expressly indicated by the requesting Member State. The requested Member State shall execute the request for assistance as soon as possible and shall take as full account as possible of any deadlines set by the requesting Member State. The requesting Member State shall explain the reasons for the deadline.
2. Where the request cannot, or cannot fully, be executed in accordance with the requirements set by the requesting Member State, the authorities of the requested Member State shall promptly inform the authorities of the requesting Member State and indicate the conditions under which it might be possible to execute the request. The authorities of the requesting and the requested Member State may subsequently agree on further action to be taken concerning the request, where necessary making such action subject to the fulfillment of those conditions.
3. If it is foreseeable that the deadline set for execution of the request cannot be complied with, and if the reasons referred to in paragraph 1, third sentence, indicate in a concrete way that this will lead to substantial impairment of the proceedings being conducted in the requesting Member State, the authorities of the requested Member State shall promptly indicate the estimated time needed for execution of the request. The authorities of the requesting Member State shall promptly indicate whether the request is to be upheld none the less. The authorities of the requesting and requested Member States may subsequently agree on further action to be taken concerning the request.

Article 5

Sending and service of procedural documents

1. Each Member State shall send procedural documents intended for persons who are in the territory of another Member State to them directly by post.
2. Procedural documents may be sent via the competent authorities of the requested Member State only:

— if the address of the person for whom the document is intended is unknown or uncertain, or
— if the relevant procedural law of the requesting Member State requires proof other than proof that can be obtained by post of the service of the document on the addressee, or
— if it has not been possible to serve the document by post or
— if the requesting Member State has justified reasons for considering that dispatch by post will be ineffective or is inappropriate.

3. Where there is reason to believe that the addressee does not understand the language in which the document is drafted, the document, or at least the important passages thereof, must be translated into (one of) the language(s) of the Member State in the territory in which the

addressee is staying. If the authority by which the procedural document was issued knows that the addressee understands only some other language, the document, or at least the important passages thereof, must be translated into that other language.

4. All procedural documents shall be accompanied by a report stating that the addressee may obtain information from the authority by which the document was issued or from other authorities in that Member State regarding his or her rights and obligations concerning the document. Paragraph 3 shall also apply to that report.

5. Articles 8, 9 and 12 of the European Mutual Assistance Convention and Articles 32, 34 and 35 of the Benelux Treaty shall apply.

Article 6

Transmission of requests for mutual assistance

1. Requests for mutual assistance and the communications referred to in Article 7 shall be made directly between judicial authorities with territorial competence for their service and execution, and returned through the same channels unless otherwise specified in this Article.

Any charge brought by a Member State for proceedings before the courts of another Member State within the meaning of Article 21 of the European Mutual Assistance Convention and Article 42 of the Benelux Treaty may be the subject of direct communications between the competent judicial authorities.

2. Paragraph I shall not prejudice the possibility of requests being sent or returned in specific cases:

  (a) between a central authority of a Member State and a central authority of another Member State, or

  (b) between a judicial authority of one Member State and a central authority of another Member State.

3. A Member State may declare, in a statement to be sent to the depositary of this Convention, that its judicial authorities do not, or do not in general, have authority to execute requests received directly as envisaged in paragraph 1, or requests received from a central authority as envisaged in paragraph 2(b), and that requests and information must therefore be sent via the central authority or authorities of the Member State to the extent indicated in the statement. The Member State may at any time amend its statement by means of a communication to be made to the depositary and any such amendment shall be for the purpose of giving greater effect to paragraph 1.

4. Any request as referred to in paragraph 1 may, for the sake of speed, be made via the International Criminal Police Organisation (Interpol) or any body competent under provisions introduced pursuant to the Treaty on European Union.

5. Where, in respect of requests pursuant to Articles 12 or 14, the competent authority is a judicial authority or a central authority in one Member State and a police or customs authority in the other Member State, requests may be made and answered directly between these authorities. Paragraph 4 shall apply to these contacts.

6. Where, in respect of requests for assistance in relation to proceedings as envisaged in Article 2(1) the competent authority is a judicial authority or a central authority in one Member State and an administrative authority in the other Member State, requests may be made and answered directly between these authorities.

7. Any Member State may declare, when giving the notification provided for in Article 23(2), that it is not bound by the first sentence of paragraph 5 and/or by paragraph 6 or that it will only apply those paragraphs under certain conditions which it shall specify. Such a declaration may be withdrawn or amended at any time.

8. The following requests or communications shall be made through the central authorities of the Member States:

  (a) requests for temporary transfer or transit of persons held in custody as referred to in Article 9 of this Convention, in Article 11 of the European Mutual Assistance Convention and in Article 33 of the Benelux Treaty.

  (b) notices of judgments as referred to in Article 22 of the European Mutual Assistance Convention and Article 43 of the Benelux Treaty. However, requests for copies of convictions and measures as referred to in Article 4 of the Additional Protocol to the

European Mutual Assistance Convention may be made directly to the competent authorities.

Article 7

Spontaneous exchange of information

1. The competent authorities of the Member States may, within the limits of their national law and without a request to that effect, exchange information relating to criminal offences as well as the infringements of the rules of law referred to in Article 2(I), the punishment or handling of which falls within the competence of the receiving authority at the time the information is provided.
2. The providing authority may, pursuant to its national law, impose conditions on the use of such information by the receiving authority.
3. The receiving authority shall be bound by those conditions.

TITLE II
REQUESTS FOR CERTAIN SPECIFIC FORMS OF MUTUAL ASSISTANCE

Article 8

Restitution

1. At the request of the requesting Member State and without prejudice to the rights of bona fide third parties, the requested Member State may place articles obtained by criminal means at the disposal of the requesting State with a view to their return to their rightful owners.
2. In applying Article 3 and 6 of the European Mutual Assistance Convention and Article 24(2) and 29 of the Benelux Treaty, the requested Member State may waive the return of articles supplied to the requesting Member State if the restitution of such articles to the rightful owner may be facilitated thereby. The rights of bona fide third parties shall not be affected.
3. In the event of any such waiver as referred to in paragraph 2, the requested Member State shall exercise no security right or other right of recourse under tax or customs legislation in respect of surrendered articles, other than those owned by the rightful owner.

Article 9

Temporary transfer of persons held in custody for purposes of investigation

1. Where there is agreement between the competent authorities of the Member States concerned, a Member State which has requested an investigation for which the presence of a person held in custody on its own territory is required may temporarily transfer that person to the territory of the Member State in which the investigation is to take place.
2. The agreement shall cover the arrangements for the temporary transfer of the person and the date by which he must be returned to the territory of the requesting Member State.
3. Where consent to the transfer is required from the person concerned, a statement of consent or a copy thereof shall be provided promptly to the requested Member State.
4. The period of custody in the territory of the requested Member State shall be deducted from the period of detention which the person concerned is or will be obliged to undergo in the territory of the requesting Member State.
5. Articles 11(2) and (3), 12 and 20 of the European Mutual Assistance Convention and Articles 33, 35 and 46 of the Benelux Treaty shall apply.
6. Each Member State may declare when giving the notification provided for in Article 23(2) that, before reaching an agreement under paragraph 1 of this Article, the consent referred to in paragraph 3 of this Article will be required or will be required under certain conditions indicated in the declaration.

Article 10

Hearing by video conference

1. If a person is in one Member State's territory and has to be heard as a witness or expert by the judicial authorities of another Member State, the latter may, where it is not desirable or possible for the person to be heard to appear in its territory in person, request that the hearing take place by video conference, as provided for in paragraphs 2 to 8.

2. The requested Member State shall agree to the hearing by video conference provided that the use of the video conference is not contrary to its fundamental principles of law and on condition that it has the technical means to permit the hearing. If the requested Member State has no access to the technical means for video conferencing, such means may be made available to it by the requesting Member State by agreement between them.

3. Applications for a hearing by video conference shall contain, in addition to the data referred to in Article 14 of the European Mutual Assistance Convention and Article 37 of the Benelux Treaty, the reason why it is not desirable or possible for the witness or expert to attend, the name of the judicial authority and of the persons who will be conducting the hearing.

4. The judicial authority of the requested Member State shall summon the person concerned to appear in accordance with the forms laid down by its legislation.

5. With reference to hearing by video conference, the following rules shall apply:

(a)   a judicial authority of the requested Member State shall be present during the hearing, where necessary assisted by an interpreter, and shall also be responsible for ensuring both identification of the person to be heard and respect for the fundamental principles of the law of the requested Member State. If the judicial authority of the requested Member State judges that during the hearing the fundamental principles of the law of the requested Member State are infringed, it shall immediately take the necessary measures for the continuation of the hearing in accordance with the said principles;

(b)   measures extending to the protection of the person to be heard may be agreed between the competent authorities of the requesting and the requested Member States;

(c)   the hearing shall be conducted directly by, or under the direction of, the judicial authority of the requesting Member State in accordance with its own laws:

(d)   at the request of the requesting Member State the requested Member State shall ensure that the person to be heard is assisted by an interpreter, if necessary:

(e)   the person to be heard may claim the right not to testify which would accrue to him or her under the law of either the requested or the requesting Member State:

6. Without prejudice to any measures agreed for the protection of persons, the judicial authority of the requested Member State shall on the conclusion of the hearing draw up minutes indicating the date and place of the hearing, the identity of the person heard, the identities and functions of all other persons participating in the hearing, any oaths taken and the technical conditions under which the hearing took place. The document shall be forwarded by the competent authority of the requested Member State to the competent authority of the requesting Member State.

7. The cost of establishing the video link, costs related to the servicing of the video link in the requested Member State, the remuneration of interpreters provided by it and allowances to witnesses and experts and their travelling expenses in the requested Member State shall be refunded by the requesting Member State to the requested Member State, unless the latter waives the refunding of all or some of these expenses.

8. Each Member State shall take the necessary measures to ensure that its national law applies where witnesses or experts are being heard within its territory in accordance with this Article and refuse to testify when under an obligation to testify or do not testify according to the truth, in the same way as if the hearing took place in a national procedure.

9. Member States may at their discretion also apply the provisions of this Article, where appropriate and with the agreement of their competent judicial authorities, to hearings by video conference involving an accused person. In this case, the decision to hold the video conference, and the manner in which the video conference shall be carried out, shall be subject to agreement between the Member States concerned, in accordance with their national law and relevant international instruments, including the 1950 European Convention on Human Rights.

Any Member State may, when giving its notification pursuant to Article 23(2), declare that it will not apply the first subparagraph. Such a declaration may be withdrawn at any time.

Hearings shall only be carried out with the consent of the accused person. Such rules as may prove to be necessary, with a view to the protection of the rights of accused persons, shall be adopted by the Council in a legally binding instrument.

Article 11

Hearing of witnesses and experts by telephone conference

1. If a person is in one Member State's territory and has to be heard as a witness or expert by a judicial authority of another Member State the latter may, where its national law so provides, request assistance of the former Member State to enable the hearing to take place by telephone conference, as provided for in paragraphs 2 to 5.
2. A hearing may be conducted by telephone conference only if the witness or expert agrees that the hearing take place by that method.
3. The requested Member State shall agree to the hearing by telephone conference where this is not contrary to its fundamental principles of law.
4. An application for a hearing by telephone conference shall contain, in addition to the data referred to in Article 14 of the European Convention on Mutual Assistance and Article 37 of the Benelux Treaty, the name of the judicial authority and of the persons who will be conducting the hearing and an indication that the witness or expert is willing to take part in a hearing by telephone conference.
5. The practical arrangements regarding the hearing shall be agreed between the Member States concerned. When agreeing such arrangements, the requested Member State shall undertake:

— to notify the witness or expert concerned of the time and the venue of the hearing.
— to ensure the identification of the witness or expert,
— to verify that the witness or expert agrees to the hearing by telephone conference.

The requested Member State may make its arrangement subject, fully or in part, to the relevant provisions of Article 10(5) and (8). Unless otherwise agreed, the provisions of Article 10(7) shall apply *mutatis mutandis*.

Article 12

Controlled deliveries

1. Each Member State shall undertake to ensure that, at the request of another Member State, controlled deliveries may be permitted on its territory in the framework of criminal investigations into extraditable offences.
2. The decision to carry out controlled deliveries shall be taken in each individual case by the competent authorities of the requested Member State, with due regard for the national law of that State.
3. Controlled deliveries shall take place in accordance with the procedures of the requested Member State. Competence to act and to direct operations shall lie with the competent authorities of that Member State.

Article 13

Joint investigation teams

1. By mutual agreement, the competent authorities of two or more Member States may set up a joint investigation team to carry out criminal investigations in one or more of the Member States setting up the team. A joint investigation team for the purposes of this Article shall be composed of members of the authorities of the Member States concerned responsible for or participating in criminal investigations and may, in particular, include judicial, police and customs officers. Where necessary, officials of international organisations or bodies may be part of the team.

A joint investigation team may in particular be set up where:

- – a Member State's inquiries into serious criminal offences require difficult and demanding investigations having links with other Member States,
- – a number of Member States are conducting investigations in which the circumstances of the case necessitate coordinated, concerted action in the Member States involved.

A request for the setting up of a joint investigation team may be made by any of the Member States concerned. The investigation team shall be set up in one of the Member States in which the investigations are expected to be carried out.

2. In addition to the information referred to in Article 14 of the European Convention on Mutual Assistance in Criminal Matters and Article 37 of the relevant Benelux Treaty, requests for the setting up of a joint investigation team shall include proposals for the composition of the team.

3. A joint investigation team shall operate in the territory of the Member States setting up the team under the following general conditions:

- (a) it shall be set up only for a specific purpose and for a limited period:
- (b) the team shall be headed by an official from the Member State in which the team is operating. This official shall coordinate and lead the activities of the team in the territory of that Member State;
- (c) the Member State in which the team operates shall make the necessary organisational arrangements for it to do so.

4. The officials seconded to a joint investigation team by a Member State shall be bound by the law of the Member State in which the team operates. They shall come under the leadership of the team's head appointed in accordance with paragraph 3(b) and be required to follow his instructions.

5. The seconded officials shall have the following rights within the territory of the State of operation;

- (a) they shall be entitled to be present in the State of operation in the course of the investigation team's investigations;
- (b) by agreement between the Member States concerned, and in accordance with the law of the State of operation, they may in individual cases be entrusted with the task of taking criminal procedural steps. The State of operation may lay down conditions regarding the procedural steps to be taken, including for example that a member of that State's law enforcement authorities is present when the steps are taken in order to ensure compliance with its law.

6. When a joint investigation team is set up, the Member States involved may agree on further arrangements for its operation. They may in particular agree that requests for mutual assistance relating to the team's investigations, by way of derogation from Article 6 of the Convention, can be submitted by officials seconded to the team directly to the competent authorities in the State of operation.

7. A seconded official may for the purpose of a criminal investigation supply information lawfully available to him to the joint investigation team in accordance with Article 7(1) and (2). The use of such information in the State of operation shall be governed by Article 7(3).

8. Information lawfully obtained by an official while forming part of a joint investigation team based in another Member State may be used for the purposes of criminal investigations in the seconding Member State under the same conditions as if the information had been obtained by way of mutual assistance.

9. This Article shall be without prejudice to any other provisions or arrangements on the setting up or operation of joint investigation teams.

Article 14

Covert investigations

1. The requesting and the requested Member State may agree to assist one another for the operation of investigations into crime by officers acting under covert or false identity (covert investigations).

2. The decision on the request is taken in each individual case by the competent authorities of the requested Member State with due regard to its national law and procedures. The duration of the covert investigation, the detailed conditions, the legal status of the officers concerned and liability for any offence committed or damage caused during covert investigations shall be agreed between the Member States with due regard to their national law and procedures.

3. Covert investigations shall take place in accordance with the national law and procedures of the Member State on the territory of which the covert investigation takes place. The Member States involved shall cooperate on the preparation and supervision of the covert investigation, including arrangements for the security of the officers acting under covert or false identity.

4. Any Member State may when giving the notification provided for in Article 23(2) declare that it is not bound by this Article. Such a declaration may be withdrawn at any time.

TITLE III

INTERCEPTION OF TELECOMMUNICATIONS

Article 15

Authorities competent to order interception of telecommunications

For the purpose of the application of the provisions of Articles 16, 17 and 18, "competent authority" shall mean a judicial authority, or, where judicial authorities have no competence in this area, an equivalent competent authority, specified pursuant to Article 21(1)(e) and acting in the framework of a criminal investigation.

Article 16

Requests for interception of telecommunications

1. For the purpose of a criminal investigation, a competent authority in any Member State (the requesting Member State) may, in accordance with the requirements of its domestic law, make a request to a competent authority in another Member State (the requested Member State) for:

   (a)   the interception and immediate transmission to the requesting Member State of telecommunications; or

   (b)   the interception, recording and subsequent transmission to the requesting Member State of the recording of telecommunications.

2. Requests under paragraph 1 may be made in relation to the use of means of telecommunications by the subject of the interception, if this subject is present:

   (a)   in the requesting Member State, and where the requesting Member State needs the technical assistance of the requested Member State to intercept his communications;

   (b)   in the requested Member State, and where his communications can be intercepted in that Member State;

   (c)   in a third Member State, which has been informed pursuant to Article 18(1)(a), and where the requesting Member State needs the technical assistance of the requested Member State to intercept his communications.

3. By way of derogation from Article 14 of the European Mutual Assistance Convention and Article 37 of the Benelux Treaty, requests under this Article shall include the following:

   (a)   an indication of the authority making the request;

   (b)   confirmation that a lawful interception order or warrant has been issued in connection with a criminal investigation;

   (c)   information for the purpose of identifying the subject of the interception:

   (d)   an indication of the criminal conduct under investigation;

   (e)   the desired duration of the interception;

   (f)   if possible, the provision of sufficient technical data to ensure that the request can be met (in particular the relevant network connection number).

4. In the case of a request pursuant to paragraph 2(b), a request shall also include a summary of the facts. The requested Member State may require any further information necessary to enable the requested Member State to decide whether the request would be granted if it had been made by a national authority of that Member State.

5. The requested Member state undertakes to comply with requests under paragraph 1(a):

(a)   in the case of a request pursuant to paragraph 2(a) and 2(c), on being provided with the information in paragraph 3. The requested Member State may allow the interception to proceed without further formality;

(b)   in the case of a request pursuant to paragraph 2(b), on being provided with the information in paragraphs 3 and 4 and where the request would be granted if it had been made by a national authority of that Member State. The requested Member State may make its consent subject to any conditions which it would impose had the request been made by one of its own national authorities.

6. Where immediate transmission is not possible, the requested Member State undertakes to comply with requests under paragraph 1(b) on being provided with the information in paragraphs 3 and 4 and where the request would be granted if it had been made by a national authority of that Member State. The requested Member State may make its consent subject to any condition which it would impose had the request been made by one of its own national authorities.

7. Any Member State may declare when giving the notification provided for in Article 23(2) that it is bound by paragraph 6 only when it is unable to provide immediate transmission. In this case the other Member States may apply the principles of reciprocity.

8. When making a request under paragraph 1(b), the requesting Member State may, where it has a particular reason to do so, also request a transcription of the recording. The requested Member State shall consider such requests in accordance with its national law and procedures.

9. The Member State receiving the information provided under paragraphs 3 and 4 shall keep that information confidential in accordance with its national law.

Article 17

Interceptions of subjects on national territory by the use of service providers

1. For the purposes of lawful interceptions of telecommunications, Member States shall permit the international telecommunication systems operating on their territory and providing telecommunications services in more than one Member State to be directly accessible, by the use of the service providers present on their territory, to the other Member States.

2. In the case provided for in paragraph 1, the competent authorities of a Member State, for the purposes of a criminal investigation and in accordance with the applicable national law, shall carry out the interception on the condition that the subject of the interception is present in that Member State.

3. Paragraph 2 shall also apply where the competent authority of a Member State makes a request to another Member State, pursuant to Article 16(2)(b), for the interception of a person present on the territory of that other State.

4. Where direct access is not used, the Member State hosting the international telecommunications systems provided for in paragraph 1 shall reply to the request for assistance using the ordinary forms. In that case, the reasons for refusal provided for in Article 2 of the European Mutual Assistance Convention shall be indicated.

Article 18

Interception of subjects on the territory of another Member State without technical assistance of this Member State

1. Where for the purpose of a criminal investigation, the interception of telecommunications is authorised by the competent authority of one Member State, and the telecommunication address of the subject specified in the interception order is being used on the territory of another

Member State from which no technical assistance is needed to carry out the interception, the first mentioned Member State shall inform the other Member State on the interception:

(a) prior to the interception in cases where it knows when ordering the interception that the subject is on the territory of that Member State;

(b) immediately after it knows that the subject of the interception is on the territory of that Member State in other cases.

2. The information to be provided by the intercepting Member State includes;

(a) an indication of the authority ordering the interception;

(b) confirmation that a lawful interception order or warrant has been issued in connection with a criminal investigation;

(c) information for the purpose of identifying the subject of the interception;

(d) an indication of the criminal conduct under investigation;

(e) the expected duration of the interception.

3. On receipt of the information listed in paragraph 2, the competent authority of the Member State concerned:

(a) may contact the competent authority in the intercepting Member State in order to coordinate any criminal investigations already conducted by it relating to the subject of the interception with the investigation conducted by the intercepting Member State;

(b) shall have 96 hours in which to agree to the interception from the time at which it was informed by the intercepting Member State. If no reply is received within that period, the intercepting State must immediately suspend the interception, and may not use the material collected as evidence in criminal proceedings from the time at which it became aware that the subject was on the territory of the State visited. The absence of a reply from the State visited shall be considered to constitute a refusal and must subsequently give rise to a written statement of reasons, based on one of the reasons mentioned in subparagraph (d);

(c) may request from the competent authority in the intercepting Member State a summary of the facts of the case and any further information. In that event a further period of 96 hours shall commence from the time when that request is made by the State visited and the provisions of subparagraph (b) shall apply *mutatis mutandis*;

(d) may require the interception not to be carried out or to be interrupted where the interception would not be permissible pursuant to its national law or for the reasons specified in Article 2 of the European Mutual Assistance Convention. Where a Member State imposes such a requirement it must give reasons for its decision, in writing; it may also require the intercepting Member State not to use the intercepted material from the time at which it is established that the subject was on its territory.

Member States shall take the measures necessary to ensure that a reply can be given within the 96-hour period.

4. The Member State receiving the information provided under paragraph 2 shall keep that information confidential in accordance with its national law.

5. Where the intercepting Member State is of the opinion that the information disclosed by paragraph 2 is of a particularly sensitive nature, it may be transmitted to the competent authority through a specific authority where that has been agreed on a bilateral basis between the Member States concerned.

6. Any Member State may declare, when giving its notification under Article 23(2), or at any time thereafter, that it will not be necessary to provide it with the information on interceptions as envisaged in this Article.

Article 19

Responsibility for charges made by telecommunications operators

Costs which are incurred by telecommunications operators or service providers in executing requests pursuant to Article 16 shall be borne by the requesting Member State.

Article 20

Bilateral arrangements

Nothing in this Title shall preclude any bilateral or multilateral arrangements between Member States for the purpose of facilitating the exploitation of present and future technical possibilities regarding interception of telecommunications.

TITLE IV

FINAL PROVISIONS

Article 21

Statements

1. When giving the notification referred to in Article 23(2), each Member State shall make a statement naming the authorities which, in addition to those already indicated in the European Mutual Assistance Convention and the Benelux Treaty, are competent for the application of this Convention and the application between the Member States of the provisions on mutual assistance in criminal matters of the instruments referred to in Article 1(1), including in particular:

(a) the competent administrative authorities or services within the meaning of Article 2(1), if any,

(b) one or more central authorities for the purposes of applying Article 6 as well as the authorities competent to deal with the requests referred to in Article 6(8)(b).

(c) the police or customs authorities competent for the purposes of Article 6(5), if any.

(d) the administrative authorities competent for the purposes of Article 6(6), if any, and

(e) the authority or authorities competent for the purposes of the application of Articles 16 and 17 and Article 18(1) to (4).

2. Statements made in accordance with paragraph 1 may be amended in whole or in part at any time by the same procedure.

Article 22

Reservations

No reservations may be entered in respect of this Convention, other than those for which it makes express provision.

Article 23

Entry into force

1. This Convention shall be subject to adoption by the Member States in accordance with their respective constitutional requirements.

2. Member States shall notify the Secretary-General of the Council of the European Union of the completion of the constitutional procedures for the adoption of this Convention.

3. This Convention shall enter into force 90 days after the notification referred to in paragraph 2 by the State, member of the European Union at the time of adoption by the Council of the Act establishing this Convention, which is last to complete that formality.

4. Until this Convention enters into force, any Member State may, when giving the notification referred to in paragraph 2 or at any other time, declare that as far as it is concerned this

Convention shall apply to its relations with Member States which have made the same declaration. Such declarations shall take effect 90 days after the date of deposit thereof.
5. This Convention shall apply only to requests for mutual assistance submitted after the date on which it enters into force or is applied as between the requested Member State and the requesting Member State.

Article 24

Accession of new Member States

1. This Convention shall be open to accession by any State which becomes a member of the European Union.
2. The text of this Convention in the language of the acceding State, drawn up by the Council of the European Union, shall be authentic.
3. The instruments of accession shall be deposited with the depositary.
4. This Convention shall enter into force with respect to any State which accedes to it 90 days after the deposit of its instrument of accession or on the date of entry into force of this Convention if it has not already entered into force at the time of expiry of the said period of 90 days.
5. Where this Convention is not yet in force at the time of the deposit of their instrument of accession, Article 23(4) shall apply to acceding Member States.

Article 25

Depositary

1. The Secretary-General of the Council of the European Union shall act as depositary of this Convention.
2. The depositary shall publish in the *Official Journal of the European Communities* information on the progress of adoptions and accessions, statements and reservations and also any other notification concerning this Convention.

    Done at ... on ... in a single original in the Danish, Dutch, English, Finnish, French, German, Greek, Irish, Italian, Portuguese, Spanish and Swedish languages, all texts being equally authentic, such original being deposited in the archives of the General Secretariat of the Council of the European Union.

Appendix G

European Committee on Crime Problems (CDPC)

Committee of Experts on the Operation of European Conventions in the Penal Field (PC-OC)
PRELIMINARY DRAFT SECOND ADDITIONAL PROTOCOL TO THE EUROPEAN CONVENTION ON MUTUAL ASSISTANCE IN CRIMINAL MATTERS

Strasbourg, 26 March 1999

Secretariat Memorandum prepared by the Directorate of Legal Affairs

NB: *This paper is based on the draft reproduced in doc. PC-OC (98) 11. It is intended to reflect the discussions at the 38th meeting of the Committee (22–25 February 1999).*

The member States of the Council of Europe, signatory to this Protocol,

Desirous of facilitating the application of the European Convention on Mutual Assistance in Criminal Matters opened for signature at Strasbourg on 20 April 1959 (hereinafter referred to as "the Convention");

Considering it also desirable to supplement the Convention in certain aspects,

Have agreed as follows:

Article 0
Scope

Article 1 of the Convention shall be replaced by the following provisions:

"1. The Parties undertake promptly to afford each other, in accordance with the provisions of this Convention, the widest measure of mutual assistance in proceedings in respect of offences the punishment of which, at the time of the request for assistance, falls within the jurisdiction of the judicial authorities of the requesting Party.

"2. This Convention does not apply to arrests, the enforcement of verdicts or offences under military law which are not offences under ordinary criminal law.

"3. Mutual assistance may also be afforded in proceedings brought by the administrative authorities in respect of offences which are punishable under the national law of the requesting or the requested State by virtue of being infringements of the rules of law, where the decision may give rise to proceedings before a court having jurisdiction in particular in criminal matters.

"4. Mutual assistance shall not be refused solely on the grounds that it relates to facts for which a legal person may be held liable in the requesting State."

Article 1
Procedure

Notwithstanding the provisions of Article 3 of the Convention, where requests specify formalities or procedures which are necessary under the law of the requesting State, even if unfamiliar to the requested State, the latter shall comply with such requests to the extent that the action sought is not contrary to fundamental principles of its law.

Article 4
Hearing by video conference

1. If a person is in one Party's territory and has to be heard as a witness or expert by the judicial authorities of another Party, the latter may, where it is not desirable or possible for the person to be heard to appear in its territory in person, request that the hearing take place by video conference, as provided for in paragraphs 2 to 9.
2. The requested Party shall agree to the hearing by video conference provided that the use of the video conference is not contrary to its fundamental principles of law and on condition that it has the technical means to permit the hearing. If the requested Party has no access to the technical means for video conferencing, such means may be made available to it by the requesting Party by agreement between them.
3. Applications for a hearing by video conference shall contain, in addition to the data referred to in Article 14 of the Convention, the reason why it is not desirable or possible for the witness or expert to attend, the name of the judicial authority and of the persons who will be conducting the hearing.
4. The judicial authority of the requested Party shall summon the person concerned to appear in accordance with the forms prescribed by its legislation.
5. With reference to hearing by video conference, the following rules shall apply:

    (a)   a judicial authority of the requested Party shall be present during the hearing, where necessary assisted by an interpreter, and shall also be responsible for ensuring both identification of the person to be heard and respect for the fundamental principles of the law of the requested Party. If the judicial authority of the requested Party judges that during the hearing the fundamental principles of the law of the requested Party are infringed, it shall immediately take the necessary measures for the continuation of the hearing according to the above-mentioned principles;

    (b)   measures extending to the protection of the person to be heard may be agreed between the competent authorities of the requesting and the requested Parties;

    (c)   the hearing shall be conducted directly by, or under the direction of, the judicial authority of the requesting Party in accordance with its own laws;

    (d)   at the request of the requesting Party the requested Party shall ensure that the person to be heard is assisted by an interpreter, if necessary;

    (e)   the person to be heard may claim the right not to testify according to the law of either the requested or the requesting Party;

6. Without prejudice to any measures agreed for the protection of persons, the judicial authority of the requested Party shall on conclusion of the hearing draw up minutes indicating the date and place of the hearing, the identity of the person heard, the identities and functions of all other persons participating in the hearing, any oaths taken and the technical conditions under which the hearing took place. The document shall be forwarded by the competent authority of the requested Party to the competent authority of the requesting Party.
7. [see Article 12.4]
8. Each Party shall take the necessary measures to ensure that its national law applies where witnesses or experts are being heard within its territory in conformity with this Article and refuse to testify when under an obligation to testify or do not testify according to the truth, in the same way as if the hearing took place in a national procedure.
9. Parties may at their discretion also apply the provisions of this Article, where appropriate and with the agreement of their competent judicial authorities, to hearings by video conference involving an accused person or suspect. In this case, the decision to hold the video conference, and the manner in which the video conference shall be carried out, shall be subject to agreement between the Parties concerned, in conformity with their national law and relevant international instruments, including the European Convention on Human Rights. Hearings of accused persons or suspects shall only be carried out with their consent.

Article 4 bis
Hearing by telephone conference

1. If a person is in one Party's territory and has to be heard as a witness or expert by a judicial authority of another Party the latter may, where its national law so provides, request assistance

of the former Party to enable the hearing to take place by telephone conference, as provided for in paragraphs 2 to 5.

2. A hearing may be conducted by telephone conference only if the witness or expert agrees that the hearing take place by that method.

3. The requested Party shall agree to the hearing by telephone conference where this is not contrary to its fundamental principles of law.

4. An application for a hearing by telephone conference shall contain, in addition to the data referred to in article 14 of the Convention, the name of the judicial authority and of the persons who will be conducting the hearing and an indication that the witness or expert is willing to take part in a hearing by telephone conference.

5. The practical arrangements regarding the hearing shall be agreed between the Parties concerned. When agreeing such arrangements, the requested Party shall undertake to:

–   notify the witness or expert concerned of the time and the venue of the hearing;
–   **ensure the identification of the witness or expert;**
–   verify that the witness or expert agrees to the hearing by telephone conference.

The requested Party may make its agreement subject, fully or in part, to the provisions of Article 4(5) and 4(8). Unless otherwise agreed, the provisions of Article 4(7) shall apply mutatis mutandis.

Article X
Statements of voluntary witnesses

1. Police or other officials of one State may take voluntary statements from a witness who consents to do so, and who is present in the territory of a second State, provided that notice is given to the second State of the intention to take such a statement and that State has given its permission for such a procedure.

2. The notice to the second State of the intention to take a statement from a voluntary witness shall include the name and address of the witness, the fact that the witness consents to give such a statement, a short summary of the facts of the case and of the criminal offences involved, and the names and capacities of the officials who propose to travel to the second State to take the statement.

3. The notice to the second State, its consent to the procedure and other communications on the matter shall be through the Interpol channels or directly between the officials involved.

4. If the second State so requires, an official of that State may be present while such statement is taken.

5. The taking of the statement may take place at a consulate of the first State or at a location agreeable to the witness and to the second State.

Article X bis
Presence of officials of the requesting Party

Article 4 of the Convention shall be supplemented by the following text, the original Article 4 of the Convention becoming paragraph 1 and the under-mentioned provisions becoming paragraph 2:

"2. Requests for the presence of such officials or interested persons should not be refused when that presence is likely to assist in being more responsive to the needs of the requesting Party and therefore being likely to prevent supplementary requests for assistance."

Article 6
Spontaneous information

1. Without prejudice to its own investigations or proceedings, a Party may without prior request, forward to another Party information obtained within the framework of its own

investigations, when it considers that the disclosure of such information might assist the receiving Party in initiating or carrying out investigations or proceedings, or might lead to a request by that Party under the Convention or its Protocols.

2. The providing Party may, pursuant to its national law, impose conditions on the use of such information by the receiving Party.

3. The receiving Party shall be bound by those conditions.

Article 7
Restitution of tangible and intangible property

1. Property and money obtained through an offence and seized by the requested Party may be returned to the requesting Party for the purpose of its restitution, having due regard to any claim concerning rights of property raised by a third person.

2. In applying Articles 3 and 6 of the Convention, the requested Party may decide to waive the return of any property or money, provided for in paragraph 2 of Article 6 of the Convention, in particular if this is likely to facilitate rapid restitution of the property.

Article 8
Temporary transfer to the requested Party of persons held in custody

1. Where there is agreement between the competent authorities of the Parties concerned, a Party which has requested an investigation for which the presence of a person held in custody on its own territory is required, may temporarily transfer that person to the territory of the Party in which the investigation is to take place.

2. The agreement shall cover the arrangements for the temporary transfer of the person and the date by which the person must be returned to the territory of the requesting Party.

3. Where the person concerned's consent to being transferred is required, a statement of consent or a copy thereof shall be provided promptly to the requested Party.

4. The period of custody in the territory of the requested Party shall be deducted from the period of detention which the person concerned is or will be obliged to undergo in the territory of the requesting Party.

5. The provisions of Articles 11, paragraphs 2 and 3, and 12 of the Convention shall apply.

Article 9
Summons by post and service by post

1. The competent judicial authorities of the requesting Party may directly address, by post, summons to appear in its territory, as well as writs and records of judicial verdicts, to persons who are in the territory of the requested Party.

2. Summons and procedural documents shall be written in the language of the requesting Party. If there are reasons to believe that the recipient does not understand the language in which the summons or the documents are drafted, the summons and the documents, or at least the most important passages of the documents, shall be translated into the – or one of the – language(s) of the Party in whose territory the recipient is. If the authority that issued the summons or the document knows that the addressee understands only some other language, the summons and the documents, or at least the most important passages of the documents, shall be translated into that other language.

3. The provisions of Articles 8, 9 and 12 of the Convention shall apply. The summons must include a descriptive notice of its application.

4. Any Contracting State may at any time, by means of a declaration addressed to the Secretary General of the Council of Europe, declare that it requires that a copy of the summons be forwarded to its Ministry of Justice or to any other authority designated for that purpose.

5. All documents shall be accompanied by a report stating that the addressee may obtain information from the authority that issued the document or from other authorities in that Party regarding his or her rights and obligations concerning the document. Paragraph 2 above shall apply to that report.

OBS re para 3: . . ."shall apply" to the extent that they are applicable . . .
Decision: This Article was agreed upon.

Article 10
Right to decline evidence

1. A person, whatever his nationality, appearing on a summons before the judicial authorities of the requesting Party, may claim a right to decline evidence on the basis of:

   a.   any provision of the law of the requesting Party which has application to his evidence, or
   b.   any provision of the law of the requested Party which has application to his evidence and which would apply were the witness giving evidence in the territory of the requested Party.

2. Where a person claims a right to decline evidence under the law of the requested Party and there is doubt about the existence of such a right, the requesting Party may ask the requested Party for a declaration. The requested Party shall promptly provide the requested declaration. If the requested Party declares that its law does not confer such right, the judicial authority of the requesting Party is no longer bound to take the claimed right into consideration.

3. The provisions of paragraphs 1 and 2 of this Article shall apply:

   (a) where a person, whatever his nationality, appears on a summons before the judicial authorities of the requested Party;
   (b) where a person, whatever his nationality, whilst being present on the territory of the requested Party, is heard, either directly or through audio or video means, by the judicial authorities of the requesting Party.

Article 11
Personal appearance of transferred sentenced persons

The provisions of Articles 11 and 12 of the Convention shall apply to persons who are in custody in the requested Party pursuant to having been transferred in order to serve a sentence passed in the requesting Party, where their personal appearance for purposes of review of the judgment is applied for by the requesting Party.

Article 12
Costs

Article 20 of the Convention shall be replaced by the following provisions:
   "1. Parties shall not claim from each other the refund of any costs resulting from the application of this Convention, except:

   (a) costs incurred by the attendance of experts in the territory of the requested Party;
   (b) costs incurred by the transfer of a person in custody carried out under Articles 8 or 11 of this Protocol, or Article 11 of the Convention;
   (c) costs that result from the requested Party's complying with requests that specify any given procedure or any procedural requirement;
   (d) reasonable expenses associated with storing, keeping, protecting and transporting property under seizure;
   (e) costs of a substantial or extraordinary nature.

2. If it appears that compliance with a request for assistance will entail costs of a substantial or extraordinary nature, the Parties shall consult with each other, with a view to determining the conditions under which the request may be executed as well as making arrangements for the payment of the costs.

3. Parties shall consult with each other with a view to making arrangements for the payment of claimable costs as listed above.

4. The cost of establishing a video link, costs related to the servicing of a video link in the requested Party, the remuneration of interpreters provided by it and allowances to witnesses

and experts and their travelling expenses in the requested Party shall be refunded by the requesting Party to the requested Party, unless the Parties agree otherwise."

Article 14
Cross-border observations

1. Police officers of one of the Parties who, within the framework of a criminal investigation, are keeping under observation in their country, a person who is presumed to have taken part in a criminal offence to which extradition may apply, shall be authorised to continue their observation in the territory of another Party where the latter has authorised cross-border observation in response to a request for assistance which has previously been submitted. Conditions may be attached to the authorisation.

On request, the observation will be entrusted to officers of the Party in whose territory it is carried out.

The request for assistance referred to in the first subparagraph must be sent to an authority designated by each of the Parties and having jurisdiction to grant or to forward the requested authorisation.

2. Where, for particularly urgent reasons, prior authorisation of the other Party cannot be requested, the officers conducting the observation shall be authorised to continue beyond the border the observation of a person presumed to have committed offences listed in paragraph 7, provided that the following conditions are met:

(a)   The authorities of the Party designated under paragraph 5, in whose territory the observation is to be continued, must be notified immediately, during the observation, that the border has been crossed;

(b)   A request for assistance submitted in accordance with paragraph 1 and outlining the grounds for crossing the border without prior authorisation shall be submitted without delay.

Observation shall cease as soon as the Party in whose territory it is taking place so requests, following the notification referred to in (a) or the request referred to in (b) or where authorisation has not been obtained five hours after the border was crossed.

3. The observation referred to in paragraphs 1 and 2 shall be carried out only under the following general conditions:

(a)   The officers conducting the observation must comply with the provisions of this Article and with the law of the Party in whose territory they are operating; they must obey the instructions of the local responsible authorities.

(b)   Except in the situations provided for in paragraph 2, the officers shall during the observation, carry a document certifying that authorisation has been granted.

(c)   The officers conducting the observation must be able at all times to provide proof that they are acting in an official capacity.

(d)   The officers conducting the observation may carry their service weapons during the observation save where specifically otherwise decided by the requested party: their use shall be prohibited save in cases of legitimate self-defence.

(e)   Entry into private homes and places not accessible to the public shall be prohibited.

(f)   The officers conducting the observation may neither challenge nor arrest the person under observation.

(g)   All operations shall be the subject of a report to the authorities of the Contracting Party in whose territory they took place; the officers conducting the observation may be required to appear in person.

(h)   The authorities of the Contracting Party from which the observing officers have come shall, when requested by the authorities of the Contracting Party in whose territory the observation took place, assist the enquiry subsequent to the operation in which they took part, including legal proceedings.

4. The officers referred to in paragraphs 1 and 2 shall be:

–   As regards the Kingdom of Belgium: members of the "police judiciaire près les Parquets", the "gendarmerie" and the "police communale" as well as customs officers, under the conditions laid down in appropriate bilateral agreements referred to in paragraph 6, with respect to their powers regarding illicit traffic in narcotic

drugs and psychotropic substances, traffic in arms and explosives, and the illicit carriage of toxic and dangerous waste;
–   As regards the Federal Republic of Germany, officers of the "Polizeien des Bundes und der Länder" as well as, with respect only to illegal traffic in narcotic drugs and psychotropic substances and arms traffic, officers of the "Zollfahndungsdienst (customs investigation service) in their capacity as auxiliary officers of the public ministry;
–   As regards the French Republic: officers and criminal police officers of the national police and national "gendarmerie" as well as customs officers, under the conditions laid down in appropriate bilateral agreements referred to in paragraph 6, with respect to their powers regarding illicit traffic in narcotic drugs and psychotropic substances, traffic in arms and explosives, and the illicit carriage of toxic and dangerous waste;
–   As regards the Grand Duchy of Luxembourg: officers of the "gendarmerie" and the police as well as customs officers, under the conditions laid down in appropriate bilateral agreements referred to in paragraph 6, with respect to their powers regarding illicit traffic in narcotic drugs and psychotropic substances, traffic in arms and explosives, and the illicit carriage of toxic and dangerous waste;

5. If, in the process of taking action pursuant to the provisions of this Article, any person, whether natural or legal, suffers loss, damage or injury as a result of negligence or some other fault attributable to the requesting Party or their authorities or agents, or where the action is taken in a manner which is not justified by the terms of this Protocol, that Party shall be liable to pay compensation in respect thereof.

Article 15
Controlled delivery of goods and money

1. Each Party shall undertake to ensure that, at the request of another Party, controlled deliveries may be permitted on its territory in the framework of criminal investigations into extraditable offences.
2. The requested Party may make its assistance subject to specific arrangements with the requesting Party concerning the control of the consignment, the control of the delivery, the future of the goods or money after delivery or in case delivery does not take effect, requirements that the persons assigned to the operation must meet, as well as financial or other arrangements.

Article 16
Undercover agents

1. Where the authorities of a Party are conducting investigative measures within the framework of criminal proceedings in respect of an extraditable offence, and where such measures involve the use of undercover agents, that Party may request assistance from any other Party for the purpose of obtaining authorisation for such agents to continue their activities on the territory of the requested Party.
2. In order to ensure the degree of confidentiality that the security of the undercover agents requires, the requesting Party may request that the assistance sought be granted in general terms, the particulars being agreed upon between an authorised representative of the authorities of the requested Party and an authorised representative of the authorities of the requesting Party.
3. The requested Party may make its assistance subject to specific arrangements concerning the requirements that the undercover agents involved must meet.

Article 17
Use of information

1. The requesting Party may require that the requested Party keep confidential the fact and substance of the request, except to the extent necessary to execute the request. If the requested

Party cannot comply with the requirement of confidentiality, it shall promptly inform the requesting Party.

2. Unless authorised by the requesting Party, the requested Party shall not make use of the substance of the request, nor of the information obtained pursuant to having executed the request, for purposes other than:

(a) those for which it was obtained, or
(b) criminal investigations or proceedings.

3. The requested Party may make the execution of a request dependent on the condition that the evidence obtained will not be used by the authorities of the requesting Party for investigations or proceedings as specified by the requested Party in respect of which that Party could refuse assistance under the Convention.

4. The provisions of this Article shall apply to any information forwarded under Article 6 and to any information laid in accordance with Article 21 of the Convention.

Article 17 bis
Channels of communication

1. Requests for mutual assistance may be forwarded directly by the judicial authorities of the Parties and returned through the same channels.

2. However, any Party may, at any time, by a declaration addressed to the Secretary General of the Council of Europe, reserve the right to make the execution of requests for mutual assistance dependent on one of the following conditions:

(a) that a copy of the request be forwarded to a designated central authority;
(b) that the request be forwarded to a designated central authority.

Article 17 ter
Exchange of information from judicial records

Article 22 of the Convention shall be replaced by the following provisions:

"1. Each Party shall inform any other Party of all criminal convictions and subsequent measures in respect of nationals of the latter Party, entered in the judicial records. Ministries of Justice shall communicate such information to one another at least once a year.

2. Furthermore, any Party which has supplied the above-mentioned information shall communicate to the Party concerned, on the latter's request in individual cases, a copy of the convictions and measures in question as well as any other information relevant thereto in order to enable it to consider whether they necessitate any measures at national level. Requests may be addressed directly to the appropriate authorities of the requested Party, and the replies may be returned directly by those authorities. Communication may also take place between the Ministries of Justice concerned."

Article 17 quinques
Definition of judicial authority

Article 24 of the Convention shall be replaced by the following provisions:

"A Contracting Party may, at any time, by a declaration addressed to the Secretary General of the Council of Europe, define what authorities it will, for the purpose of the Convention, deem judicial authorities."

Article 17 sexies
Friendly settlement

The European Committee on Crime Problems of the Council of Europe shall be kept informed regarding the application of the Convention and this Protocol and shall do whatever is necessary to facilitate a friendly settlement of any difficulty which may arise out of their application.

Article 18
Signature and entry into force

1. This Protocol shall be open for signature by the member States of the Council of Europe, which have signed the Convention. It shall be subject to ratification, acceptance or approval. Instruments of ratification, acceptance or approval shall be deposited with the Secretary General of the Council of Europe.
2. This Protocol shall enter into force on the first day of the month following the expiration of a period of three months after the deposit of the third instrument of ratification, acceptance or approval.
3. In respect of any signatory State which subsequently deposits its instrument of ratification, acceptance or approval, the Protocol shall enter into force on the first day of the month following the expiration of a period of three months after the date of deposit.

Article 19
Accession

1. Any non-member State, which has acceded to the Convention, may accede to this Protocol after it has entered into force.
2. In respect of any acceding State the Protocol shall enter into force on the first day of the month following the expiration of a period of three months after the date of the deposit of the instrument of accession.

Article 20
Territorial application

1. Any State may at the time of signature or when depositing its instrument of ratification, acceptance, approval or accession, specify the territory or territories to which this Protocol shall apply.
2. Any State may, at any later date, by declaration addressed to the Secretary General of the Council of Europe, extend the application of this Protocol to any other territory specified in the declaration. In respect of such territory the Protocol shall enter into force on the first day of the month following the expiration of a period of three months after the date of receipt of such declaration by the Secretary General.
3. Any declaration made under the two preceding paragraphs may, in respect of any territory specified in such declaration, be withdrawn by a notification addressed to the Secretary General. The withdrawal shall become effective on the first day of the month following the expiration of a period of three months after the date or receipt of such notification by the Secretary General.

Article 21
Reservations

1. Any State may, at the time of signature or when depositing its instrument of ratification, acceptance, approval or accession, declare that it avails itself of the right not to accept any one or more of Articles . . .
2. Any State may, at the time of signature or when depositing its instrument of ratification, acceptance, approval or accession, declare that as far as it is concerned any one or more of Articles . . . shall apply only to its relations with those Parties with which bilateral or multilateral agreements to that effect have been concluded.
3. Any State which has made a reservation in accordance with paragraph 2 shall notify the

Secretary General of the Council of Europe of any bilateral or multilateral agreement rendering applicable any of the Articles of this Protocol. The Secretary General shall inform the other Parties of any notification received in accordance with this paragraph.

4. Any State may wholly or partially withdraw a reservation it has made in accordance with the foregoing paragraphs, by means of a declaration addressed to the Secretary General of the Council of Europe, which shall become effective as from the date of its receipt.

5. Any Party which has made a reservation in respect of any Article of this Protocol may not claim the application of that Article by another Party. It may, however, if its reservation is partial or conditional, claim the application of that provision in so far as it has itself accepted it.

Article 22
Denunciation

1. Any Contracting State may, in so far as it is concerned, denounce this Protocol by means of a notification addressed to the Secretary General of the Council of Europe.

2. Such denunciation shall become effective on the first day of the month following the expiration of a period of three months after the date of receipt of the notification by the Secretary General.

3. This Protocol shall, however, continue to apply to the enforcement of sentences of persons who have been transferred in conformity with the provisions of both the Convention and this Protocol before the date on which such denunciation takes effect.

4. Denunciation of the Convention entails automatically denunciation of this Protocol.

Article 23
Notifications

The Secretary General of the Council of Europe shall notify the member States of the Council of Europe and any State which has acceded to this Protocol of:

(a) any signature;
(b) the deposit of any instrument of ratification, acceptance, approval or accession;
(c) any date of entry into force of this Protocol in accordance with Articles . . .;
(d) any other act, declaration, notification or communication relating to this Protocol.

In witness whereof the undersigned, being duly authorised thereto, have signed this Protocol.
Done at . . .

Appendix H

SCHEME RELATING TO MUTUAL ASSISTANCE IN CRIMINAL MATTERS (THE HARARE SCHEME)

as amended in 1999 and

Commentary on the Scheme

Text and Commentary reproduced by kind permission of the Commonwealth Secretariat[1]

Purpose and Scope

(1) The purpose of this Scheme is to increase the level and scope of assistance rendered between Commonwealth Governments in criminal matters. It augments, and in no way derogates from existing forms of cooperation, both formal and informal; nor does it preclude the development of enhanced arrangements in other fora.

(2) This Scheme provides for the giving of assistance by the competent authorities of one country (the requested country) in respect of criminal matters arising in another country (the requesting country).

(3) Assistance in criminal matters under this Scheme includes assistance in
   (a) identifying and locating persons;
   (b) serving documents;
   (c) examining witnesses;
   (d) search and seizure;
   (e) obtaining evidence;
   (f) facilitating the personal appearance of witnesses;
   (g) effecting a temporary transfer of persons in custody to appear as a witness;
   (h) obtaining production of judicial or official records; and
   (i) tracing, seizing and confiscating the proceeds or instrumentalities of crime.

Meaning of Country

2. For the purposes of this Scheme, each of the following is a separate country, that is to say

   (a) each sovereign and independent country within the Commonwealth together with any dependent territories which that country designates; and
   (b) each country within the Commonwealth which, though not sovereign and independent, is not designated for the purposes of the preceding subparagraph.

Commentary

Purpose and scope. The opening words of Paragraph 1 reflect the concern of Law Ministers, expressed in the Communiqué issued after their 1983 Meeting, that there should be more

---

1 The materials reproduced in this appendix are as available in April 1998. Publication of a revised version is anticipated, in 2001.

effective co-operation and mutual assistance within the Commonwealth in criminal matters. The reference to "existing forms of co-operation" is to established channels, such as those of Interpol. The Scheme also recognises, and facilitates, the developing bilateral and regional arrangements between Governments and also between specialist enforcement agencies dealing with matters such as securities regulation or drug-trafficking. Law Ministers were well aware, when adopting the Scheme at their Harare meeting, of the progress made in other contexts but were nonetheless convinced of the great value of a Commonwealth Scheme in this field. The Scheme in no way prevents the full use, and active development, of other forms of co-operation where circumstances make that desirable. It does, however, provide a clear basis for legislative and other action in Commonwealth countries.

The scope of the Scheme is indicated in outline form in paragraph 1(3). The assistance listed is more comprehensive than that available under most existing bilateral and regional arrangements, but the present list was fully supported in the discussions leading up to the adoption of the Scheme. Indeed there was pressure to extend the Scheme to include other forms of assistance, and item (i) (tracing, seizing and confiscating the proceeds of criminal activities) was added in Harare after a special study had been made of the practical issues involved.

Paragraph 1(2) is important in establishing the terminology to be used in the rest of the Scheme. "Competent authorities" is a phrase not further defined; it will include administrative agencies and judicial bodies as appropriate to the particular context. "Country" is defined in paragraph 2, which is based on the corresponding provision in the Scheme for the Rendition of Fugitive Offenders within the Commonwealth (although that Scheme uses the more cumbersome phrase "part of the Commonwealth" throughout, not "country").

CRIMINAL MATTER

3. (1) For the purposes of this Scheme, a criminal matter arises in a country if the Central Authority of that country certifies that criminal or forfeiture proceedings have been instituted in a court exercising jurisdiction in that country or that there is reasonable cause to believe that an offence has been committed in respect of which such criminal proceedings could be so instituted.

(2) "Offence", in the case of a federal country or a country having more than one legal system, includes an offence under the law of the country or any part thereof.

(3) "Forfeiture proceedings" means proceedings, whether civil or criminal, for an order

   (a)   restraining dealings with any property in respect of which there is reasonable cause to believe that it has been

      (i)   derived or obtained, whether directly or indirectly, from; or
      (ii)   used in, or in connection with, the commission of an offence;

   (b)   confiscating any property derived or obtained as provided in paragraph (a)(i) or used as provided in paragraph (a)(ii); or
   (c)   imposing a pecuniary penalty calculated by reference to the value of any property derived or obtained as provided in paragraph (a)(i) or used as provided in paragraph (a)(ii).

Commentary

Criminal matters arising in a country. Paragraph 3, by defining for the purposes of the Scheme when a criminal matter arises in a country, effectively determines the stage of a criminal investigation at which it becomes possible to seek assistance. This issue was fully discussed during the preparation of the Scheme. The prevailing opinion rejected, at one extreme, the view that the Scheme should apply only when criminal proceedings had actually been instituted, and, at the other extreme, the suggestion that assistance could be sought even before the commission of an offence, by way of preventative actin. It was judged appropriate to provide that the Scheme could be invoked when proceedings had been instituted or when there was reasonable cause to believe that an offence in respect of which proceedings could be instituted had been committed. The reference to the possibility of proceedings being instituted refers to matters of evidence rather to any question as to the jurisdiction of the court.

These facts (i.e., the institution of proceedings or the existence of a reasonable belief) would be certified by the requesting country, and the requested country would not normally look behind that certificate and would not examine the basis of jurisdiction asserted by the requesting country. There is, however, a provision in paragraph 5(3) enabling the requested country to seek additional information on any matter relevant to the request for assistance.

No attempt is made in the Scheme to define "criminal proceedings". The definition of "offence" in paragraph 3(2) was inserted to clarify the position in federal or composite countries, and was originally prompted by Canadian difficulties on this point.

The reference to "forfeiture proceedings" in paragraph 3(1) with the whole of paragraph 3(3) were added at Christchurch in 1990 to make it clear that the Scheme provided for full assistance in respect of proceedings for the forfeiture of the proceeds of crime, even if those proceedings were classified as civil proceedings in the requesting country.

CENTRAL AUTHORITIES

4. Each country shall designate a Central Authority to transmit and to receive requests for assistance under this Scheme.

Commentary

Central authorities. The Scheme follows recent international practice in this area in providing for designated persons or offices to act as transmitting and receiving points for requests for assistance, and the term central authority is used in referring to them (paragraph 4). The initiative in seeking assistance will normally lie with some agency in the requesting country which is dealing with the case, and paragraph 5(1) spells this out. The request can be initiated by a law enforcement agency (typically a police force, but it could be, for example, an investigative section of a customs service), a public prosecution authority (but not a private prosecutor; there was a fear of "fishing expeditions" by prospective plaintiffs under the guise of criminal investigation), or a judicial authority. In some circumstances a court could act on the prompting of the defendant or his legal representatives, but it was thought inappropriate to give the defence itself the right to use the Scheme, which is designed essentially for cooperation between official bodies.

The primary duty of the Central Authority of the requesting country is to satisfy itself that the request can properly be made under the Scheme and to ensure that all necessary information is provided to satisfy the detailed provisions of the Scheme and to meet specific queries raised by the Central Authority of the requested country (paragraph 5(2)(3)). Although the request must be transmitted from Central Authority to Central Authority, the Scheme does not prevent responses to the request being made directly to the agency or authority initiating the request. So, for example, if a police force in State A needs assistance in locating a person believed to be in State B, a request under the Scheme would have to be sent via the Central Authorities of the two States (but this would not prevent the use of Interpol or other formal channels: see paragraph 1(1)). Once the person concerned had been located in response to a request under the Scheme, that information could be sent directly to the police force in State A. Administrative requirements could of course be imposed in State B to enable the Central Authority of that State to monitor responses to requests, but that matter is not governed by the Scheme itself.

ACTION IN THE REQUESTING COUNTRY

5. (1) A request for assistance under this Scheme may be initiated by any law enforcement agency or public prosecution or judicial authority competent under the law of the requesting country.

(2) The Central Authority of the requesting country shall, if it is satisfied that the request can properly be made under this Scheme, transmit the request to the central Authority of the requested country and shall ensure that the request contains all the information required by the provisions of this Scheme.

(3) The Central Authority of the requesting country shall provide as far as practicable additional information sought by the Central Authority of the requested country.

ACTION IN THE REQUESTED COUNTRY

6. (1) Subject to the provisions of this Scheme, the requested country shall grant the assistance requested as expeditiously as practicable.

(2) The Central Authority of the requested country shall, subject to the following provisions of this paragraph, take the necessary steps to ensure that the competent authorities of that country comply with the request.

(3) If the Central Authority of the requested country considers

(a) that the request does not comply with the provisions of this Scheme, or

(b) that in accordance with the provisions of this Scheme the request for assistance is to be refused in whole or in part, or

(c) that the request cannot be complied with, in whole or in part, or

(d) that there are circumstances which are likely to cause a significant delay in complying with the request,

it shall promptly inform the Central Authority of the requesting country, giving reasons.

Commentary

Action in the requested country. Paragraph 6(1) indicates the primary duty of the requested country, which is to grant the assistance requested as expeditiously as practicable. This duty is subject to various qualifications in respect of particular types of assistance, and of course arises only if the request is indeed within the scope of the Scheme.

Paragraph 6(2) indicates the responsibility of the Central Authority of the requested country to ensure that the relevant agencies in that country respond to the request. In some cases a request will be thought to be outside the scope of the Scheme; in others the Scheme itself will entitle or require the requested country to refuse to comply with the request; in others again compliance will prove practically impossible or will be subject to great delay. In all these cases paragraph 6(3) requires the Central Authority of the requested country to informal the Central Authority of the requesting country of the circumstances with a full explanation. The quality of communication between the various Central Authorities will be crucial to the Scheme's success.

REFUSAL OF ASSISTANCE

7. (1) The requested country may refuse to comply in whole or in part with a request for assistance under this Scheme if the criminal matter appears to the Central Authority of that country to concern

(a) conduct which would not constitute an offence under the law of that country; or

(b) an offence or proceedings of a political character; or

(c) conduct which in the requesting country is an offence only under military law or a law relating to military obligations; or

(d) conduct in relation to which the person accused or suspected of having committed an offence has been acquitted or convicted by a court in the requested country.

(2) The requested country may refuse to comply in whole or in part with a request for assistance under this Scheme

(a) to the extent that it appears to the Central Authority of that country that compliance would be contrary to the Constitution of that country, or would prejudice the security, international relations or other essential public interests of that country; or

(b) where there are substantial grounds leading the Central Authority of that country to believe that compliance would facilitate the prosecution or punishment of any person on account of his race, religion, nationality or political opinions or would cause prejudice for any of these reasons to any person affected by the request.

(3) The requested country may refuse to comply in whole or in part with a request for assistance to the extent that the steps required to be taken in order to comply with

the request cannot under the law of that country be taken in respect of criminal matters arising in that country.

(4) An offence shall not be an offence of a political character for the purposes of this paragraph if it is an offence within the scope of any international convention to which both the requesting and requested countries are parties and which imposes on the parties thereto an obligation either to extradite or prosecute a person accused of the commission of the offence.

Commentary

Refusal of Assistance. A requested country's duty to provide assistance is not unqualified. The Scheme sets out in paragraph 7 a number of circumstances in which compliance with the request may be refused either in whole or in part. These safeguards are a most important part of the Scheme, and were closely examined by Governments and at the preparatory meetings. There are seven broad grounds on which a requested country may refuse to provide assistance:

(i) "double criminality": (paragraph 7(1)(a))

A "double criminality requirement is a standard feature of extradition treaties; that is, action will not be taken unless the relevant conduct is an offence under the law of both the requesting and requested countries. It is not a standard feature of mutual assistance treaties, especially those in which the types of assistance afforded are relatively limited. In recent practice some treaties expressly exclude the requirement (notably the Canada-U.S.A. Treaty of 1985), but a Draft Model Treaty developed in Australia while not imposing a double criminality requirement does allow a requested country a discretionary power to refuse compliance where the conduct would not constitute an offence under the law of that country. At the January 1986 meeting it was decided to follow the Australian lead. In some parts of the world criminal law reform, influenced by religious or ideological considerations, is defining as offences punishable with heavy penalties conduct which is accepted or much more lightly punished in neighbouring countries. This pointed to a need for some discretionary power to refuse to comply with requests. It was however the tenor of the discussions that the use of this power would be regarded as exceptional and in no way automatic.

(ii) political offences: (paragraph 7(1)(b))

Compliance may be refused where the offence or the proceedings are regarded as having a political character. The double reference to "offence" and proceedings indicates that the formal definition of the offence charged is not necessarily determinative. Paragraph 7(4), which follows closely a provision in the Scheme for the Rendition of Fugitive Offenders, protects the policy behind international conventions designed to secure the prosecution of specific offences.

(iii) military offences: (paragraph 7(1) (c))

It was felt appropriate to enable a requested country to refuse compliance where the offence existed only in a code of military law or concerned the performance of an obligation of military service.

(iv) "double jeopardy": (paragraph 7(1)(d))

Paragraph 7(1)(d) deals with situations in which the person who is accused or suspected of having committed the offence with which the request is concerned has already been proceeded against in the requested country. It would not be desirable to make it obligatory for that country to assist in the bringing of fresh proceedings elsewhere; and this principle is equally relevant whether the original proceedings resulted in a conviction or an acquittal. As before, the requested country is empowered, but not required, to refuse compliance with the request; there may be circumstances, for example, where an acquittal was recorded because a key prosecution witness to the requesting country, where the provision of assistance would be judged appropriate.

(v) State interests – (paragraph 7(2) (a))

Paragraph 7(2) contains two provisions each reflecting aspects of "public policy". One provision is concerned with the interests of the requested country itself. There need be no compliance if a request would prejudice the security, international relations or other essential public interests of that country. This would cover, for example, cases requesting the provision of information which might be relevant to the defence of the State or which might be embarrassing to relations with a neighbouring State, and any requests which were seen as improperly interfering with the business interests of the requested country (perhaps under some claim to extra-territorial anti-trust jurisdiction).

(vi) Discriminatory policies (paragraph 7(2) (b))

The requested country may refuse compliance where there are "substantial grounds" for believing that compliance would facilitate prosecution or punishment or cause prejudice based on racial, religious, nationality or political opinion grounds.

(vii) Unavailability of procedures (paragraph 7(3))

The final ground for refusal is of a quite different nature. Compliance is excused "to the extent that the steps required to be taken in order to comply with the request cannot under the law of that country be taken in respect of criminal matters arising in that country". The general philosophy of the Scheme is that procedures and facilities available in support of criminal investigations and prosecutions initiated in one country should also be made available to assist similar endeavours undertaken in other Commonwealth countries. A requested country is not, however, required to do more than it would do in a purely domestic case. So, for example, if the taking of body samples is not provided for under the relevant law of the requested country it will refuse a request for assistance in obtaining such samples; the availability of procedures under the law of the requesting country is for this purpose quite immaterial.

MEASURES OF COMPULSION

8. (1) The competent authorities of the requested country shall in complying with a request under this Scheme use only such measures of compulsion as are available under the law of that country in respect of criminal matters arising in that country.

    (2) Where under the law of the requested country measures of compulsion cannot be applied to any person to take the steps necessary to secure compliance with a request under this Scheme but the person concerned is willing to act voluntarily in compliance or partial compliance with the terms of the request, the competent authorities of the requested country shall make available the necessary facilities.

Commentary

Measures of Compulsion. The principle just referred to is applied in a slightly more specific context in paragraph 8(1), dealing with "measures of compulsion". It is only if a power of, for example, search and seizure or requiring the provision of samples of blood, would be available in a purely domestic case, that such a power may be used in response to a request under the Scheme. It might happen that an individual named in a request for assistance would be entirely happy to co-operate voluntarily in providing evidence which could not in the circumstances be taken by measures of compulsion. In such a case the duty of the requested country is to make available the necessary facilities (paragraph 8(2)).

SCHEME NOT TO COVER ARREST OR EXTRADITION

9. Nothing in this Scheme is to be construed as authorising the extradition, or the arrest or detention with a view to extradition, of any person.

Commentary

Extradition. Paragraph 9 makes it clear that extradition (and arrest or detention with a view to extradition) is not within this Scheme. Although the present Scheme is complementary to the Scheme for the Rendition of Fugitive Offenders within Commonwealth, it does deal with quite different types of co-operation.

CONFIDENTIALITY

10. The Central Authorities and the competent authorities of the requesting and requested countries shall use their best efforts to keep confidential a request and its contents and the information and materials supplied in compliance with a request except for disclosure in criminal proceedings and where otherwise authorised by the Central Authority of the other country.

LIMITATION OF USE OF INFORMATION OR EVIDENCE

11. The requesting country shall not use any information or evidence obtained in response to a request for assistance under this Scheme in connection with any matter other than the criminal matter specified in the request without the prior consent of the Central Authority of the requested country.

Commentary

Confidentiality and Limitation on Use of Information or Evidence. There is an obvious need for confidentiality in dealing with requests for assistance under the Scheme. Where proceedings have not been commenced, disclosure of the making of a request or of the material supplied in response to it could be embarrassing and prejudicial to either the prosecution agency or the prospective defendant or both. Where proceedings are already in train, similar considerations apply and there is an added danger of interference with the judicial process. To meet this as far as possible, paragraph 10 imposes an obligation of confidentiality on the Central Authorities transmitting and receiving the request and on the agencies dealing with it, in respect both of the existence of the request and of the contents of the request and the response to it. The material may of course be disclosed in criminal proceedings but any other publication requires the consent of the Central Authority of the other country concerned.

A related safeguard is contained in paragraph 11. The information of evidence obtained by the requesting country may only be used in connection with a matter other than the criminal matter specified in the request with the prior consent of the Central Authority of the requested country. The effect is that while disclosure in criminal proceedings is permitted by paragraph 10 that permission is limited to proceedings concerning the criminal matter specified in the request itself; if the evidence provided reveals the existence of further matters in respect of which criminal proceedings are taken, its use in those proceedings requires the consent of the requested country. This provision serves to protect, inter alia, the "political offences" exception in paragraph 7(1)(a); evidence supplied for use in the context of an offence against the person cannot be used instead in proceedings based on a political offence without the approval of the requested country. In general, it is thought that "the criminal matter specified in the request" will be broadly interpreted; if, for example, evidence is sought in order to mount a prosecution against a named individual in respect of a major fraud but the prosecution is ultimately based on a conspiracy between that individual and others to effect the fraud, this would seem to be within the same "criminal matter".

EXPENSES OF COMPLIANCE

12. (1)   Except as provided in the following provisions of this paragraph, compliance with a request under this Scheme shall not give rise to any claim against the requesting country for expenses incurred by the Central Authority or other competent authorities of the requested country.

     (2)   The requesting country shall be responsible for the travel and incidental expenses of witnesses travelling to the requesting country, including those of accompanying officials, for fees of experts, and for the costs of any translation required by the requesting country.

     (3)   If in the opinion of the requested country, the expenses required in order to comply with the request are of an extraordinary nature, the Central Authority of the

requested country shall consult with the Central Authority of the requesting country as to the terms and conditions under which compliance with the request may continue, and in the absence of agreement the requested country may refuse to comply further with the request.

Commentary

Expenses of Compliance. The question of the costs entailed in responding to requests for assistance was fully examined by senior officials at the January 1986 meeting. There was agreement that in most cases the costs would be borne by the requested country. This avoids the necessity for elaborate accounting and payment procedures; and as there will be a two-way traffic in requests for assistance, most countries should find that the expenditure is balanced by the services received from other countries. Paragraph 12 states that the principle that the costs fall on the requested country but indicates three exceptions and a major qualification.

The exceptions concern the travel and subsistence costs of witnesses travelling to the requesting country (and of accompanying officials in the case, for example, of witnesses transferred in custody); fees payable to expert witnesses; and the costs of any translations required by the requesting country. It is thought that these costs, which are readily identifiable, should be met by the requesting country.

The qualification concerns exceptionally heavy costs. It is recognised that in complex cases, prolonged and extensive enquiries may be required. For example, investigations into a commercial fraud may require scrutiny of the records of the financial transactions of a group of companies over an extended period. The costs of such an enquiry would be very great, could be quite prohibitive for a small country, and would not necessarily ever be balanced by any reciprocal service from the requesting country. Paragraph 12(3) enables a requested country to negotiate special terms whenever it regards the potential expenses as "of an extraordinary nature". If terms cannot be agreed – and in some cases the required terms would include the salaries and expenses of officers seconded to a major investigation – the requested country would be entitled to refuse to comply with the request. No attempt is made to define the point at which expenses can properly be regarded as "extraordinary", which must be a matter of experience and judgment.

In 1999 Law Ministers, having considered the concerns of various member countries on the costs associated with the provision of assistance, issued the following guidelines on the issue. These guidelines are to be kept under review.

Law Ministers of the Commonwealth
Recalling that the purpose of the Scheme Relating to Mutual Assistance in Criminal Matters within the Commonwealth (the Harare Scheme) is to increase the level and scope of assistance rendered between Commonwealth governments in criminal matters;

Noting that Clause 12 of the Harare Scheme provides that, subject to sub-clause (2), unless expenses of an extraordinary nature are involved in responding to requests for assistance, the requested country will pay the costs of providing assistance; and

Noting the concern expressed by Law Officers of Small Commonwealth Jurisdictions over the impact on national resources caused by complying with requests for assistance

Adopted the following guidelines to assist member countries to deal with the financial and other costs incurred by jurisdictions in responding to requests for assistance:

Guidelines on the Apportionment of Costs Incurred in Providing Mutual Assistance in Criminal Matters
1. Where the execution of a request for assistance requires that the requesting country be represented before the courts of the requested country and where the human resources available to the Central Authority of the requested country are insufficient to meet that requirement, the Central Authority of the requested country may brief an appropriate member of the private profession to represent the requesting country on its behalf. In such case the [Attorney-General] shall use his or her best endeavours to ensure that the person so briefed has no conflict of interest and that the best interests of the requesting country are protected.
2. Where a request for assistance requires that voluminous or complex documentary or other records be located and retrieved and where the human resources available to the Central Authority of the requested country are insufficient to meet that requirement, the Central Authority of the requested country may secure the services of appropriate specialists to undertake the work necessary to respond to the request.

In such case the Central Authority shall use its best endeavours to ensure that the persons whose services are secured have no conflict of interest and that the best interests of the requesting country are protected.

3. Where the Central Authority of the requested country is of the opinion that the circumstances described in paragraphs 1 and 2 above exist, it shall, before proceeding to secure non-government persons to perform the functions, consult with the requesting country on the proposed action and secure, if necessary, the agreement of the requesting country to pay for the services so contracted for on its behalf, subject to any conditions with respect to the control of costs or of the conduct of the matter agreed by both countries.

4. Where a request for assistance requires the taking of action by police officers in the requested country and the Central Authority of that country is of the opinion that such action would so divert the available police resources as to cause prejudice to the peace of the country the request may be refused.

5. Where a request for assistance seeks the making or enforcement of an order restraining dealings with any property in respect of which there is reasonable cause to believe that it has been derived or obtained, directly or indirectly, from, or used in, or in connection with, the commission of an offence and where the law of the requested country would permit any person with an interest in such property to take action for damages arising from such restraint in the event that the property was not later the subject of an order confiscating it the requested country may, if it considers it appropriate, require from the requesting country an indemnity against any loss incurred by the government of the requested country as a result of such action being successful.

6. In reaching any agreement on the apportionment of costs, the ability to share forfeited or confiscated assets or the existence of any asset sharing agreement between the relevant countries shall be taken into account.

7. Nothing in these guidelines shall be interpreted as detracting from the requirement contained in Clause 12 of the Harare Scheme that countries consult in cases where the requested country is of the opinion that the expenses required in order to comply with a request are of an extraordinary nature.

Contents Request for Assistance

13. (1) A request under the Scheme shall:

(a) specify the nature of the assistance requested;

(b) contain the information appropriate to the assistance sought as specified in the following provisions of this Scheme;

(c) indicate any time-limit within which compliance with the request is desired, stating reasons;

(d) contain the following information:

    (i) the identity of the agency or authority initiating the request;
    (ii) the nature of the criminal matter; and
    (iii) whether or not criminal proceedings have been instituted.

(e) where criminal proceedings have been instituted, contain the following information:

    (i) the court exercising jurisdiction in the proceedings;
    (ii) the identify of the accused person;
    (iii) the offences of which he stands accused, and a summary of the facts;
    (iv) the stage reached in the proceedings; and
    (v) any date fixed for further stages in the proceedings.

(f) where criminal proceedings have not been instituted, state the offence which the Central Authority of the requesting country has reasonable cause to believe to have been committed, with a summary of known facts.

(2) A request shall normally be in writing, and if made orally in the case of urgency, shall be confirmed in writing forthwith.

Commentary

Form and Contents of Requests for Assistance. Requests for assistance will normally be in writing, but it is recognised that the urgency of the case may call for an oral communication. In the latter case the request must be confirmed in writing forthwith (paragraph 13(2)). Paragraph 13 lists the information to be included in all requests; additional items of information are required in connection with requests for particular types of assistance, and these are specified in later paragraphs of the Scheme. It was thought neither necessary nor desirable to settle a Model Form of Request such as is found in some civil procedure conventions. In the present context, the circumstances are too variable and the emphasis is on the inclusion of all useful and helpful information, an emphasis which can be obscured if information is to be presented in a prescribed format of general applicability.

IDENTIFYING AND LOCATING PERSONS

14. (1)   A request under this Scheme may seek assistance in identifying or locating persons believed to be within the requested country.

    (2)   The request shall indicate the purpose for which the information is requested and shall contain such information as is available to the Central Authority of the requesting country as to the whereabouts of the person concerned and such other information as it possesses as may facilitate the identification of that person.

Commentary

Identifying and Locating Persons. The first type of assistance covered by the Scheme is in identifying or locating persons believed to be within the requested country (paragraph 14). In some cases the person concerned will be suspected of crime, and his location could be a prelude to an extradition application; but this is by no means the only type of case. A witness may be sought; or it may be desirable to find someone in order to eliminate him from the field of suspects; or it may be desired to identify some known associates of a person accused of criminal behaviour with a view to obtaining evidence in the requesting country.

SERVICE OF DOCUMENTS

15. (1)   A request under this Scheme may seek assistance in the service of documents relevant to a criminal matter arising in the requesting country.

    (2)   The request shall be accompanied by the documents to be served and, where those documents relate to attendance in the requesting country, such notice as the Central Authority of that country is reasonably able to provide of outstanding warrants or other judicial orders in criminal matters against the person to be served.

    (3)   The Central Authority of the requested country shall endeavour to have the documents served:

        (a)   by any particular method stated in the request, unless such method is incompatible with the law of that country; or

        (b)   by any method prescribed by the law of that country for the service of documents in criminal proceedings.

    (4)   The requested country shall transmit to the Central Authority of the requesting country a certificate as to the service of the documents or, if they have not been served, as to the reasons which have prevented service.

    (5)   A person served in compliance with a request with a summons to appear as a witness in the requesting country and who fails to comply with the summons shall not by reason thereof be liable to any penalty or measure of compulsion in either the requesting or the requested country notwithstanding any contrary statement in the summons.

Commentary

Service of Documents. Assistance can be requested in the service of any document relevant to a criminal matter arising in the requesting country. In early drafts, this provision was limited to judicial documents (originating process, subpoenas, judgements, etc.) but the wider formulation included in the final text will cover any document of which service is required under the procedural rules of the requesting country. For example, notices of appeal by the prosecution and certificates of analysis in drugs cases were cited in Canadian observations.

It is important that the mode of service should satisfy the procedural requirements of the requesting country; hence the obligation in paragraph 15(3) to us a method of service specified in the request unless that method is incompatible with the law of the requested country. Where no special mode of service is desired or available, service will be effected in accordance with the normal procedures used in criminal cases in the requested country; as between Commonwealth countries there should be few difficulties in this provision. A certificate of service (or a statement of the reasons which prevented service) is to be supplied by the requested country: paragraph 15(4).

Paragraph 15(5) was added at Christchurch in 1990 as one of a series of amendments designed to ensure that service of documents, and other types of assistance, would not expose any person to penalties, in either the requesting or requested country, except where the Scheme provides for the use of measures of compulsion.

EXAMINATION OF WITNESSES

16. (1) A request under this Scheme may seek assistance in the examination of witnesses in the requested country.

    (2) The request shall specify, as appropriate and so far as the circumstances of the case permit:

    (a) the names and addresses or the official designations of the witnesses to be examined;

    (b) the questions to be put to the witnesses or the subject matter about which they are to be examined;

    (c) whether it is desired that the witnesses be examined orally or in writing;

    (d) whether it is desired that the oath be administered to the witnesses (or, as the law of the requested country allows, that they be required to make their solemn affirmation);

    (e) any provisions of the law of the requesting country as to privilege or exemption from giving evidence which appear especially relevant to the request; and

    (f) any special requirements of the law of the requesting country as to the manner of taking evidence relevant to its admissibility in that country.

    (3) The request may ask that, so far as the law of the requested country permits, the accused person or his legal representative may attend the examination of the witness and ask questions of the witness.

Commentary

Examination of witnesses. A major objective of the Scheme is the facilitation of the process of obtaining evidence from another country. Paragraph 16 deals with the examination of witnesses, paragraph 17 with search and seizure of property, and paragraph 18 with other types of assistance.

So far as the examination of witnesses is concerned, paragraph 16 indicates the information which a requested country needs to be given if it is to provide the appropriate assistance. It needs to know the name and address of the witness, or at least his official designation (e.g. the Senior Customs Officer at X Airport); the request for assistance could of course be combined with a request for assistance in locating or identifying the witness. It needs to know the questions to be put, or the subject-matter on which the witness is to be examined; the amount of detail will necessarily vary with the nature of the case and the stage which the investigation or actual proceedings have reached. It needs to know of any special procedural requirements as to the taking of evidence. Subject to these requirements (so far as they are permitted by the law of the requested country), that law will establish how the examination is to be conducted, by whom the questions are to be put and before whom the evidence is to be taken. The Scheme avoids going into too much detail on these points, and Central Authorities may need to consult on procedures in particular cases.

There was discussion at the preparatory meeting in January 1986 of the question of the attendance of legal representatives from the requesting country. In some cases this might well be desirable, but there can be difficulties in some jurisdictions over the appearance of counsel from abroad. Paragraph 16(3) contains a modest provision: if the law of the requested country permits, and the request for assistance raises the point, the accused person (where such a person is identified) or his legal representative (which might be limited to a practitioner from the requested country) may attend the examination and ask questions. Nothing in this provision prevents a more generous provision of rights of attendance to interested parties or their representatives, but the obligation of confidentiality in paragraph 10 must be borne in mind.

SEARCH AND SEIZURE

17. (1) A request under this Scheme may seek assistance in the search for, and seizure of property in the requested country.
    (2) The request shall specify the property to be searched for and seized and shall contain, so far as reasonably practicable, all information available to the Central Authority of the requesting country which may be required to be adduced in an application under the law of the requested country for any necessary warrant or authorization to effect the search and seizure.
    (3) The requested country shall provide such certification as may be required by the requesting country concerning the result of any search, the place and circumstances of seizure, and the subsequent custody of the property seized.

Commentary

Search and Seizure. Search and seizure is a sensitive area, and can raise delicate constitutional issues as to rights of privacy etc. It is important to recall in this context the general provisions in paragraph 8, under which the competent authorities of a requested country must use only such measures of compulsion as are available in that country in respect of criminal matters arising in that country, and in paragraph 7(3), which deals with the position where procedures are not available in the requested country.

Bearing these points in mind, paragraph 17(2) refers expressly to the question of warrants or authorizations. The Central Authority of the requesting country must provide all available information which might be required in order to obtain the necessary warrant or authorization to effect the search and seizure. On the other side, the requested country, having complied with a request, must give any certification needed by the requesting country as to the circumstances of search and seizure and the subsequent custody of the property seized as will ensure the admissibility of the resulting evidence: see paragraph 17(3).

OTHER ASSISTANCE IN OBTAINING EVIDENCE

18. (1) A request under this Scheme may seek other assistance in obtaining evidence.
    (2) The request shall specify, as appropriate and so far as the circumstance of the case permit:
        (a) the documents, records or property to be inspected, preserved, photographed, copied or transmitted;
        (b) the samples of any property to be taken, examined or transmitted; and
        (c) the site to be viewed or photographed.

Commentary

Other Assistance in Obtaining Evidence. Paragraph 18 provides for the making of other requests for assistance in obtaining evidence. This covers a wide range of procedures which require neither the examination of witness nor the seizure of property, including copying, measuring, photographing and inspecting property. In some cases, such as that of examining samples referred to in paragraph 18(2)(b) this may be linked to a request for search and seizure; a warrant may be needed to obtain some material which, perhaps because of its chemical properties, need s to be analysed at once; a request under paragraph 18 could seek technical assistance in making that analysis or, in other circumstances, in transmitting the material in conditions which safeguard it for proper analysis.

PRIVILEGE

19. (1) No person shall be compelled in response to a request under this Scheme to give any evidence in the requested country which he could not be compelled to give:

    (a) in criminal proceedings in that country; or
    (b) in criminal proceedings in the requesting country.

   (2) For the purposes of this paragraph any reference to giving evidence includes references to answering any question and to producing any document.

Commentary

Privilege. Following precedents in other international instruments, the Scheme allows claims of privilege by reference to the laws of both the requesting and requested countries: paragraph 19. To assist the authorities of the requested country and to reduce the number of cases in which evidence is obtained there only to be declared privileged in the requesting country, paragraph 16(2) (e) requires that a request for assistance in the examination of a witness should specify any provisions of the law of the requesting country as to privilege or exemption from giving evidence which appear especially relevant to the request. In the end, of course, it will be the courts in the requesting country which will rule on any claim affecting the admissibility of evidence.

PRODUCTION OF JUDICIAL OR OFFICIAL RECORDS

20. (1) A request under this Scheme may seek the production of judicial or official records relevant to a criminal matter arising in the requesting country.

   (2) For the purposes of this paragraph "judicial records" means judgments, orders and decisions of courts and other documents held by judicial authorities and "official records" means documents held by government departments or agencies or prosecution authorities.

   (3) The requested country shall provide copies of judicial or official records which are publicly available.

   (4) The requested country may provide copies of judicial or official records not publicly available, to the same extent and under the same conditions as apply to the provision of such records to its own law enforcement agencies or prosecution or judicial authorities.

Commentary

Production of Judicial or official records. Judicial and official records are of course only a species of documents, and the Scheme could have treated requests for their production in the general context of obtaining documentary evidence. It was, however, felt appropriate to include a separate provision: this form of assistance involves direct co-operation between governments and public agencies in a way which takes the case outside the typical one of obtaining evidence; and it does, for that reason, voice some sensitive issues of confidentiality. After full discussion, it was agreed to distinguish between records which are publicly available in the requested country, which would normally be supplied subject only to the general provisions as to the right to refuse to comply with a request, and records not publicly available. These would be supplied, subject to those general provisions of the Scheme, to the same extent and under the same conditions (as to publication and use, for example) as apply in the requested country to the supply of those types of records to the law enforcement agencies or prosecution or judicial authorities of that country. So, for example, if health service records are treated as confidential and not made available to the police force of the requested country, they will be similarly withheld from the police of a country making a request under the Scheme.

Paragraph 20(2) defines "judicial records" and "official records", the latter including documents held by prosecution authorities as well as by government department or agencies.

TRANSMISSION AND RETURN OF MATERIAL

21. (1) Where compliance with a request under this Scheme would involve the transmission to the requesting country of any document, record or property, the requested country

     (a) may postpone the transmission of the material if it is required in connection with proceedings in that country, and in such a case shall provide certified copies of a document or record pending transmission of the original;

     (b) may require the requesting country to agree to terms and conditions to protect third party interests in the material to be transmitted and may refuse to effect such transmission pending such agreement.

   (2) Where any document, record or property is transmitted to the requesting country in compliance with a request under this Scheme, it shall be returned to the requested country when it is no longer required in connection with the criminal matter specified in the request unless that country has indicated that its return is not desired.

   (3) The requested country shall authenticate material that is to be transmitted by that country.

AUTHENTICATION

22. A document or other material transmitted for the purposes of or in response to a request under this Scheme shall be deemed to be duly authenticated if it:

     (a) purports to be signed or certified by a judge or Magistrate, or to bear in the stamp or seal of a Minister, government department or Central Authority; or

     (b) is verified by the oath of a witness or of a public officer of the Commonwealth country from which the document or material emanates.

Commentary

Transmission and Return of Material Authentication. Paragraphs 21 and 22 of the Scheme contain important practical provisions concerning the supply of material in response to request for assistance; they were revised a Christchurch in 1990. These provisions deal with a number of matters: the fact that some evidence may be required, now or at a later time, for use in the requested country; the fact that third parties may have interests in particular material; and the fact that certain types of material require authentication.

The first matter is dealt with by providing that the supply of material may be postponed where it is needed for proceedings in the requested country (but with an obligation to supply certified copies of documentary material), and that material should be returned to the requested country when it is no longer needed in connection with the criminal matter specified in the request (paragraph 21(1) (a), (2)). The requested country may waive the requirement of return.

The question of third party interests can be a complex one, especially where material has a high intrinsic value and there are several claimants each asserting an interest in it. The Scheme, in paragraph 21 (1)(b), ensures that a requested country need not transmit material unless and until it agrees terms and conditions with the requesting country which are sufficient to protect third party interests; what is appropriate will of course depend on the circumstances of the particular case.

In providing for methods of authentication of material, paragraph 22 goes rather further than other paragraphs of the Scheme. It provides for modes of authentication which will be accepted as sufficient in all countries, whether acting as requesting or requested country in a particular case; implementing legislation will need to address this point accordingly. Authentication may be by signature or certificate of judge or magistrate, the stamp or seal of a Minister, ministry, government department or the Central Authority of the requested country; or reliance may be placed on the sworn evidence of a witness as defined in paragraph 22 (b).

PERSONAL APPEARANCE OF WITNESSES IN THE REQUESTING COUNTRY

23. (1) A request under this Scheme may seek assistance in facilitating the personal appearance of the witnesses before a court exercising jurisdiction in the requesting country.

    (2) The request shall specify

        (a) the subject matter upon which it is desired to examine the witnesses;

        (b) the reasons for which the personal appearance of the witnesses is required; and

        (c) details of the travelling, subsistence and other expenses payable by the requesting country in respect of the personal appearance of the witnesses.

    (3) The competent authorities of the requested country shall invite persons whose appearance as witnesses in the requesting country is desired; and

        (a) ask whether they agree to appear;

        (b) inform the Central Authority of the requesting country of their answer; and

        (c) if they are willing to appear, make appropriate arrangements to facilitate the personal appearance of the witnesses.

    (4) A person whose appearance as a witness is the subject of a request and who does not agree to appear shall not by reason thereof be liable to any penalty or measure of compulsion in either the requesting or requested country.

Commentary

Personal Appearance of Witnesses. Paragraphs 23 to 25 of the Scheme contain a set of related provisions addressing the case in which it is not sufficient to obtain testimony in the requested country; in some circumstances it will be essential that the witness appears at the trial in the requesting country. The Scheme does not propose the use of any measures of compulsion in this area, although some Commonwealth governments are attracted by the idea of providing for the recognition of an international subpoena. The Scheme only provides for assistance designed to facilitate the appearance in the requesting country of a witness who is willing so to appear. Paragraph 23 deals with the usual case, of a potential witness who is resident and at liberty in the requested country; paragraph 24 with the less common, but nonetheless important case, in which the potential witness is in custody in that country; and paragraph 25 guarantees certain immunities to witnesses appearing in response to a request under the Scheme.

In the straightforward case under paragraph 23, the Scheme provides for the passage of an invitation to appear, with reasons and a statement of the travelling, subsistence and other expenses payable by the requesting country, to the potential witness. If he is willing to appear, the requested country helps in making appropriate travel arrangements. As already noted, the costs are borne by the requesting country (paragraph 12(2) of the Scheme).

Paragraph 23(4) was added at Christchurch in 1990 to ensure that refusal to appear attracted no penalties.

PERSONAL APPEARANCE OF PERSONS IN CUSTODY

24. (1) A request under this scheme may seek the temporary transfer of persons in custody in the requested country to appear as witnesses before a court exercising jurisdiction in the requesting country.

    (2) The request shall specify:

        (a) the subject matter upon which it is desired to examine the witnesses;

        (b) the reasons for which the personal appearance of the witnesses is required;

    (3) The requested country shall refuse to comply with a request for the transfer of persons in custody if the persons concerned do not consent to the transfer.

    (4) The requested country may refuse to comply with a request for the transfer of persons in custody and shall be under no obligation to inform the requesting country of the reasons for such refusal.

    (5) A person in custody whose transfer is the subject of a request and who does not

consent to the transfer shall not by reason thereof be liable to any penalty or measure of compulsion in either the requesting or requested country.

(6)   Where persons in custody are transferred, the requested country shall notify the requesting country of:

(a)   the dates upon which the persons are due under the law of the requested country to be released from custody; and

(b)   the dates by which the requested country requires the return of the persons

and shall notify any variations in such dates.

(7)   The requesting country shall keep the persons transferred in custody, and shall return the persons to the requested country when their presence as witnesses in the requesting country is no longer required, and in any case by the earlier of the dates notified under sub paragraph (6).

(8)   The obligation to return the persons transferred shall subsist notwithstanding the fact that they are nationals of the requesting country.

(9)   The period during which the persons transferred are in custody in the requesting country shall be deemed to be service in the requested country of an equivalent period of custody in that country for all purposes.

(10)   Nothing in this paragraph shall preclude the release in the requesting country without return to the requested country of any person transferred where the two countries and the person concerned agreed.

Commentary

Transfer of Witnesses in Custody. Paragraph 24 contains the necessarily more elaborate provisions required to deal with the transfer of persons in custody to appear as witnesses. There can be no transfer if the prisoner refuses his consent (paragraph 24(3)); even if he does consent, the requested country may in its discretion refuse to comply with the request, and need not give any reasons for its refusal (paragraph 24(4)).

Paragraph 24(5) was added at Christchurch in 1990; no penalty attaches to a refusal by the person in custody to agree to a transfer.

A person transferred in custody under paragraph 24 does of course remain in custody in the requesting country. Provisions in paragraph 24(6) and (7) ensure that he will not remain in custody after the expiry of his sentence. Paragraph 24(8) is designed to ensure that a person transferred cannot, by reason of his possessing citizenship of the requesting country, prevent his return in due course to the requested country.

IMMUNITY OF PERSONS APPEARING

25. (1)   Subject to the provisions of paragraph 24, witnesses appearing in the requesting country in response to a request under paragraph 23 or persons transferred to that country in response to a request under paragraph 24 shall be immune in that country from prosecution, detention or any other restriction of personal liberty in respect of criminal acts, omissions or convictions before the time of their departure from the requested country.

(2)   The immunity provided for in that paragraph shall cease:

(a)   in the case of witnesses appearing in response to a request under paragraph 23, when the witnesses having had, for a period of 15 consecutive days from the dates when they were notified by the competent authority of the requesting country that their presence was no longer required by the court exercising jurisdiction in the criminal matter, an opportunity of leaving have nevertheless remained in the requesting country, or having left that country have returned to it;

(b)   in the case of persons transferred in response to a request under paragraph 24 and remaining in custody when they have been returned to the requested country.

Commentary

Immunities. Paragraph 25 of the Scheme confers on witnesses appearing in response to a request under the Scheme immunity from prosecution in respect of acts or omissions before the date on which they left the requested country and from detention in respect of convictions recorded before that date.

TRACING THE PROCEEDS OR INSTRUMENTALITIES OF CRIME

26. (1) A request under this Scheme may seek assistance in identifying, locating and assessing the value of property believed to have been derived or obtained, directly or indirectly, from, or to have been used in, or in connection with, the commission of an offence and believed to be within the requested country.

 (2) The request shall contain such information as is available to the Central Authority of the requesting country as to the nature and location of the property and as to any person in whose possession or control the property is believed to be.

Commentary

Paragraphs 26 to 28 of the Scheme are a revised text approved by Law Ministers in Christchurch in 1990. They replace paragraphs 26 to 29 of the original text. The object of the paragraphs is to provide a framework for co-operation between Commonwealth governments in tracing and seizing the proceeds and instrumentalities of crime.

Tracing the Proceeds of Instrumentalities of Crime. Paragraphs 26 is the counterpart in this context of paragraph 14 which deals with the location of persons. Here assistance may involve not only the location of property but also its identification and the assessment of its value. There may be circumstances in which the relevant property is not to be seized (perhaps because of legitimate third party interests) but penalties are to be imposed by reference to the value of the property; a reliable assessment of that value is clearly important.

Proceeds of Crime. The present text of the Scheme contains no formal definition of "the proceeds of crime", but paragraph 26 indicates the meaning of this term by speaking of property derived or obtained, directly or indirectly, from the commission of an offence. The Scheme does not, of course, prevent a country from adopting a more far-reaching definition for its own purposes in what is still a developing area of law.

SEIZING AND CONFISCATING THE PROCEEDS OF INSTRUMENTALITIES OF CRIME

27. (1) A request under this Scheme may seek assistance in securing:

 (a) the making in the requested country of an order relating to the proceeds of instrumentalities of crime; or
 (b) the recognition or enforcement in that country of such an order made in the requesting country.

 (2) For the purpose of this paragraph, "an order relating to the proceeds of instrumentalities of crime" means:

 (a) an order restraining dealings with any property in respect of which there is reasonable cause to believe that it has been derived or obtained, directly or indirectly, from, or used in, or in connection with, the commission of an offence;
 (b) an order confiscating property derived or obtained, directly or indirectly, from, or used in or in connection with, the commission of an offence; and
 (c) an order imposing a pecuniary penalty calculated by reference to the value of any property so derived, obtained or used.

 (3) Where the requested country cannot enforce an order make in the requesting country, the requesting country may request the making of any similar order available under the law of the requested country.

 (4) The request shall be accompanied by a copy of any order made in the requesting country and shall contain so far as reasonably practicable, all information available to the Central Authority of the requesting country which may be required in connection with the procedures to be followed in the requested country.

 (5) The law of the requested country shall apply to determine the circumstances and

manner in which an order may be made, recognised or enforced in response to the request.

(6) The law of the requested country may provide for the protection of the interests of bona fide third parties in property restrained or confiscated as a result of a request made pursuant to this Scheme, by providing:

    (a) for the giving of notice of the making of orders restraining or confiscating property; and

    (b) that any third party claiming an interest in property so restrained or confiscated may make an application to a court of competent jurisdiction for an order

        (i) declaring that the interest of the applicant in the property or part thereof was acquired bona fide; and

        (ii) restoring such property or the value of the interest therein to the applicant.

Commentary

Seizure and Confiscation and Proceeds and Instrumentalities. Paragraph 27 deals with the seizure and confiscation of proceeds and instrumentalities. The request may *either* seek the making in the requested country of an order of one of the three classes listed in paragraph 27(2) (restraint orders, confiscation orders, or pecuniary penalty orders) *or* the recognition or enforcement in the requested country of such an order already made in the requesting country. Which of these options will be best depends upon the current state of the law in the requested country; some countries will have a full range of possible orders, other will not know, for example, the "pecuniary penalty order" which features in Australian legislation. Again, some countries will have provisions enabling them to enforce foreign confiscation orders on the analogy of foreign money-judgements, but most will not; paragraph 27(3) makes it clear that in such a case the requesting country can adopt the other approach, seeking a fresh order in the requested country.

Paragraph (6) was added in 1999 to meet the concerns of member countries that the Scheme may not adequately reflect the intention that the interests of bona fide third parties in restrained or confiscated property. The provision is intended to operate for the benefit of bona fide third parties **in the requested country**. The law of the requesting country is expected to deal with these interests where the third party's interest is one which ought to be protected under that law. Nothing in this new paragraph is intended to facilitate review by a foreign court of the order itself – it merely recognises that in the requested country, claims of bona fide interests not brought to the attention of the court making the order may exist and may need to be adjudicated.

DISPOSAL OR RELEASE OF PROPERTY

28. (1) The law of the requested country shall apply to determine the disposal of any property

    (a) forfeited; or
    (b) obtained as a result of the enforcement of a pecuniary penalty order
    as a result of a request under this Scheme.

(2) The law of the requested country shall apply to determine the circumstances in which property made the subject of interim seizure as a result of a request under this Scheme may be released from the effects of such seizure.

(3) The law of the requested country may provide that the proceeds of an order of the type referred to in sub-paragraphs 27(2)(b) and (c), or the value thereof, may be

    (a) returned to the requesting country; or
    (b) shared with the requesting country in such proportion as the requested country in its discretion deems appropriate in all the circumstances.

Commentary

Disposal of Property. This paragraph contains provisions formerly in paragraph 27(4) of the Harare text; it makes it clear that the law of the requested country determines what happens to property seized or made the subject of restraint. That law may allow that in appropriate cases, the property of part thereof may be paid over the authorities in the requested country, but arrangements may have to be agreed in particular cases.

Paragraph 3 was added in 1999 to encourage the practice of asset sharing. One motivating factor for the addition of the paragraph was the concern expressed, particularly by small countries and jurisdictions, over the cost implications involved in handling complicated and lengthy requests. The provision is deliberately discretionary and is designed to complement paragraph 1.

CONSULTATION

29. The Central Authorities of the requested and requesting countries shall consult promptly, at the request of either, concerning matters arising under this Scheme.

OTHER ASSISTANCE

30. After consultation between the requesting and the requested countries assistance not within the scope of this Scheme may be given in respect of a criminal matter on such terms and conditions as may be agreed by those countries.

NOTIFICATION OF DESIGNATIONS

31. Designations of dependent territories under paragraph 2 and of Central Authorities under paragraph 4 shall be notified to the Commonwealth Secretary-General.

Commentary

Consultations and Other Assistance. The Scheme will depend for its success on the level of co-operation between Commonwealth Governments in ensuring the enactment of appropriate implementing legislation and between Central Authorities in operating its provisions. Paragraph 30 underlines this by referring to a duty to engage in prompt consultations at the request of another country in relation to matters arising under the Scheme; this should ensure that difficulties are promptly resolved and misunderstandings cleared up. As paragraph 31 makes clear, the Scheme does not seek to limit the scope of co-operation; if particular types of assistance which the Scheme does not cover are desired to meet the circumstances of a particular case, they can be provided by agreement.

LAWS OF COMMONWEALTH COUNTRIES AND JURISDICTIONS WHICH PERMIT THE GRANTING OF ASSISTANCE IN THE INVESTIGATION AND/OR PROSECUTION OF CRIMINAL OFFENCES AND THE RECOVERY OF PROCEEDS OF CRIME.[1]

Reproduced by kind permission of the Commonwealth Secretariat[1]

The following list contains details of laws of Commonwealth countries and jurisdictions which allow the giving of assistance by one country in relation to criminal proceedings or investigations in another country. It also details laws which facilitate the tracing, restraining and confiscation of the proceeds of crime in cases where the criminal conduct occurred in a jurisdiction other than that in which the proceeds of the crime are or have been located.

The laws listed below include laws in force before the introduction of mutual assistance in criminal matters. In most, if not all cases, these laws only apply where criminal proceedings have commenced and are before a court in the requesting country.

Also included are laws giving effect to the Harare Scheme for Mutual Assistance in Criminal Matters and laws enacted to enable countries to fulfill obligations assumed when they became states parties to the 1988 United Nations Convention Against Illicit Traffic in Narcotic Drugs and Psychotropic Substances.

The Commonwealth Secretariat would appreciate advice on the accuracy and completeness of this list which will, like the list of extradition legislation, be updated by the provision of revised or additional pages to be added to the loose-leaf collection of which this forms a part.

The Harare Scheme on Mutual Assistance in Criminal Matters including a commentary on the Scheme follows the table.

Western Samoa has changed its name to Samoa. Individual entries relating to the designation of Western Samoa have not been changed.

May 1998

Anguilla

(1) Evidence (Proceedings in Other Jurisdictions) (Anguilla) Order 1986 (UK S.I. 218 of 1986)

(1) Extends the UK Evidence (Proceedings in Other Jurisdictions) Act 1975 to Anguilla subject to exceptions, adaptations and modifications.

Permits the court to assist in obtaining evidence for criminal proceedings which have been instituted in overseas courts. Assistance available is only examination of witnesses or production of documents.

---

1 The materials reproduced in this appendix are as available in April 1998. Publication of a revised version is anticipated, in 2001.

(2) Criminal Justice (International Co-operation) (Anguilla) Order 1994

(2) Extends, with modifications, the Criminal Justice (International Co-operation) Act 1990 (UK) to Anguilla. Provides for mutual service of proceedings, mutual provision of evidence and transfer of prisoner witnesses to assist in investigating offences involving dangerous drugs.

(3) Mutual Legal Assistance (United States of America) Ordinance 1990

(3) Gives effect to the Treaty between the UK and the USA concerning the Cayman Islands as extended to Anguilla by the 1990 Exchange of Notes.

Antigua and Barbuda

(1) Mutual Assistance in Criminal Matters Act, 1993 (No. 2 of 1993)

(1) Permits Antigua and Barbuda to make and respond to mutual assistance requests. The Act applies to all Commonwealth countries and to foreign states with which treaties have been concluded. The application of the Act in relation to a particular Commonwealth country may be specified as being subject to such conditions, exceptions or qualifications.

The Act provides for the grant of assistance in relation to the proceeds of serious offences.

Australia

(1) Mutual Assistance in Criminal Matters Act 1987 (No. 85 of 1987 as amended by the Crimes Legislation Amendment Act (No. 2) 1988 (No. 66 of 1988), Law and Justice Legislation Amendment Act 1988 (No. 120 of 1988), Crimes Legislation Amendment Act (No. 2 of 1991) (No. 123 of 1991), Cash Transactions Reports Ammendment Act 1991 (No. 188 of 1991) and Crimes and Other Legislation Amendment Act 1994 (No. 182 of 1994) and Mutual Assistance in Criminal Matters Amendment Act 1996 (No. 40 of 1996)

(1) Permits the granting of assistance requiring the use of powers of compulsion to all Commonwealth countries and foreign states **without** prior designation of countries to which assistance may be granted.

The Act provides for the grant of assistance in relation to the proceeds of crimes.

The Act provides that, where a request relates to prosecution or punishment of a person charged with or convicted of an offence which is punishable by the death penalty, the request must be refused unless there are special circumstances. Where the request relates to an investigation in which charges have not been laid but the death penalty could be imposed, the Attorney-General has a broader discretion to refuse the request.

(2) Mutual Assistance in Criminal Matters (United Kingdom) Regulations (No. 2 of 1997)

(2) Provide that the Act applies to the United Kingdom subject to the Australia-United Kingdom Treaty concerning the Investigation of Drug Trafficking and the Confiscation of the Proceeds of Drug Trafficking. In relation to matters not covered by the Treaty, the Act applies to the United Kingdom without qualification.

(3) Various Regulations which apply the Act to certain non-Commonwealth countries with which Australia has general bilateral mutual assistance treaties.

(3) Apply the Act to: Argentina, Austria, Ecuador, Finland, France, Hungary, Israel, Italy, Republic of Korea, Luxembourg, Mexico, Netherlands, Philippines, Portugal, Spain and Switzerland.

(4) Mutual Assistance in Criminal Matters (Canada) Regulations (No. 22 of 1990)

(4) Apply the Act to Canada subject to the treaty between Australia and Canada which deals with mutual assistance in criminal matters

(5) Mutual Assistance in Criminal Matters (Traffic in Narcotic Drugs and Psychotropic Substances) Regulations (No. 401 of 1992 as amended by No. 26 of 1998)

(5) Provides that the Act applies subject to the United Nations Convention against Illicit Traffic in Narcotic Drugs and Psychotropic Substances to parties to the Convention for the purpose of giving effect to the mutual assistance provisions in the Convention.

(6) Mutual Assistance in Criminal Matters (Money Laundering Convention) Regulations (No. 248 of 1997)

(6) Provides that the Act applies subject to the Council of Europe Convention on Laundering, Search, Seizure and Confiscation of the Proceeds of Crime to parties to the Convention for the purposes of giving effect to the international co-operation provisions of the Convention.

(7) Proceeds of Crime Act 1987

(7) Complements the Mutual Assistance in Criminal Matters Act 1987. Permits the registration and enforcement of foreign confiscation and pecuniary penalty orders, search and seizure of tainted property in relation to foreign offences, registration of foreign restraining orders and the use of information gathering powers in relation to foreign offences.

(8) Financial Transaction Reports Act 1988

(8) Gives the Attorney-General access to financial transaction report information for the purpose of dealing with a request made by a foreign country.

(9) Foreign Evidence Act 1994 (No. 59 of 1994)

(9) Establishes rules for the admission in Australian courts of evidence obtained overseas.

(10) Foreign Evidence (Foreign Material – Criminal and Related Civil Proceedings) Regulations (No. 333 of 1994)

(10) Prescribe the types of related civil proceedings, in respect of each State or Territory (of Australia) to which Part 3 of the Foreign Evidence Act 1994 (No. 59 of 1994) (Use of Foreign Material in Criminal and Related Civil Proceedings) applies.

Bahamas

(1) Mutual Legal Assistance (Criminal Matters) Act 1988 (No. 2 of 1988).

(1) Provides for the implementation of treaties for Mutual Legal Assistance in Criminal Matters. A treaty between the Commonwealth of the Bahamas and the United States of America on Mutual Assistance in Criminal Matters executed by the government of the Bahamas on 12 June 1987 is in the schedule.

(2) Mutual Legal Assistance (Criminal Matters) Act, 1988 (Amendment of Schedule) Order 1990 (Subsidiary Legislation No. 54 of 1990)

(2) Adds Canada and the United Kingdom to the Schedule to the Act. The agreement between the Bahamas and the UK relates only to drug trafficking and narcotics offences.

(3) Tracing and Forfeiture of Proceeds of Drug Trafficking Act 1986, s.21 (Act No. 3 of 1986)

(3) Permits the registration and enforcement of specified orders made by courts outside the Bahamas for the purpose of recovering payments or other rewards received in connection with drug trafficking offences or their value. Specified orders are those to which the section applies by order of the Attorney-General.

(4) Tracing and Forfeiture of Proceeds of Drug Trafficking Act (Designated Countries and Territories) Order 1990 (Subsidiary Legislation No. 55 of 1990)

(4) Designates the United Kingdom of Great Britain and Northern Ireland.

(5) Evidence Act 1996 (Act No 4 of 1996)

(5) Section 179 of this Act states that the courts have power to take evidence in relation to criminal proceedings pending before foreign tribunals.

(6) Money Laundering (Proceeds of Crime) Act 1996 (Act No. 8 of 1996)

(6) This legislation facilitates the confiscation of the proceeds of crime in circumstances where the illegal activity was conducted in a jurisdiction other than The Bahamas but the proceeds of that activity have been located in The Bahamas.

Barbados

(1) Mutual Assistance in Criminal Matters Act 1992.

(1) Permits Barbados to make and respond to mutual assistance requests. The Act applies to all Commonwealth countries and to foreign states with which treaties have been concluded. The application of the Act in relation to a particular Commonwealth country may be specified as being subject to such conditions, exceptions or qualifications.

The Act provides for the grant of assistance in relation to the proceeds of serious offences.

No Regulations have been made under the Mutual Assistance in Criminal Matters Act 1993.

(2) Proceeds of Crime Act 1990

(2) S. 67 permits the application of the section to external confiscation and forfeiture orders being orders made by courts for the purpose of recovering proceeds of crime. Where the section has been applied external confiscation and forfeiture orders may be registered and enforced in Barbados. Proceeds of crime are defined as proceeds of scheduled offences being drug trafficking and money laundering offences.

Bermuda

(1) Bermuda (Evidence) Order 1987 (UK S.I. 662 of 1987)

(1) Extends the UK Evidence (Proceedings in Other Jurisdictions) Act 1975 to Bermuda subject to exceptions, adaptations and modifications. Permits the court to assist in obtaining evidence for criminal proceedings which have been instituted in overseas courts. Assistance available is only examination of witnesses or production of documents.

(2) Criminal Justice (International Co-operation) (Bermuda) Act 1994 (1994: 41).

(2) Allows the taking of evidence in connection with criminal proceedings or investigations in foreign countries. In relation to fiscal offences proceedings must have been instituted unless either the request is pursuant to treaty or the dual criminality test is satisfied. Allows the transfer of prisoner witnesses to give evidence or assist investigations overseas. Permits the enforcement in Bermuda of forfeiture orders made by courts in designated countries being orders relating to drug or drug trafficking offences.

(3) Drug Trafficking Suppression Act 1988

(3) Permits the registration and enforcement of external confiscation orders being orders made by courts in designated countries for the purpose of recovering benefits from trafficking in illicit drugs or the value of such benefits.

Botswana

(1) Mutual Assistance in Criminal Matters Act, 1990 (No. 20 of 1990).

(1) Permits the provision of assistance to countries to which the Act applies being countries with which Botswana has an arrangement for mutual assistance in criminal matters. (As at February 1996 the Act had not been applied to any country). The Act provides for the grant of assistance in relation to the proceeds of serious offences.

(2) Proceeds of Serious Crime Act 1990 (No. 19 of 1990)

(2) Applies the provisions of this Act to any order registered under the Mutual Assistance in Criminal Matters Act 1990 by a country to which that Act applies. Also applies the search warrant and production order provisions of this Act to requests transmitted under the Mutual Assistance in Criminal Matters Act.

British Virgin Islands

(1) Criminal Justice (International Co-operation) Act 1993. No. 8 of 1993

(1) Provides for the service of process, taking of evidence and search and seizure at the request of foreign countries. Allows the registration and enforcement of overseas forfeiture orders made in designated countries in respect of offences corresponding to or similar to offences under the Drugs (Pre-

vention of Misuse) Act or drug trafficking offences as defined in the Drug Trafficking Offences Act 1992.

(2)	Mutual Legal Assistance (USA) Act 1990	(2)	Makes provision for giving effect to a treaty made between the Government of the United States of America and the Government of the United Kingdom of Great Britain and Northern Ireland, concerning the Cayman Islands dated 3 July 1986, the terms of which have been extended to the British Virgin Islands.
(3)	Drug Trafficking Offences Act 1992	(3)	Permits the application of the Act to designated countries so as to enable the registration and enforcement of external confiscation orders being orders made by courts in designated countries for the purpose of recovering payments or other rewards received in connection with drug trafficking or their value.

Canada

(1)	Mutual Legal Assistance in Criminal Matters Act 1988. Chapter M-13.6 (R.S. 1985 c.30)	(1)	Provides for the implementation of treaties for mutual legal assistance in criminal matters. Canada has bilateral mutual legal assistance treaties with Hong Kong (drugs only) and the United Kingdom, Australia and the Bahamas. Canada also has mutual legal assistance treaties with the following non-Commonwealth countries: China, France, India, Italy, Korea, Mexico, Netherlands, Spain, Switzerland, Thailand and the United States.
(2)	Evidence Act	(2)	Provides that witnesses can be compelled to appear and testify at the request of a foreign tribunal. Operates only in cases where a criminal matter is pending before a foreign court of justice and when the foreign court has made an order requiring the testimony.
(3)	Forfeited Property Sharing Regulations, 1994	(3)	Permits Canada to share the proceeds of certain crimes with foreign states with which Canada has entered into an agreement under the Seized Property Management Act

Cayman Islands

(1)	The Evidence (Proceedings in Other Jurisdictions) (Cayman Islands) Order 1978 (UK S.I. 1890 of 1978)	(1)	Extends ss. 1 to 3 and 5 to 10 and Schedule 2 to the UK Evidence (Proceedings in Other Jurisdictions) Act 1975 to the Cayman Islands subject to exceptions, adaptations and modifications. Permits the Grand Court to assist in obtaining evidence for criminal proceedings which have been instituted in overseas courts. Assistance available is only examination of witnesses or production of documents.

(2) Mutual Legal Assistance (United States of America) Law 1986 (Law 16 of 1986)

(2) Gives effect to the terms of a treaty between the USA and the UK (including the Cayman Islands) relating to mutual assistance in criminal matters.

(3) Proceeds of Criminal Conduct Law, 1996

(3) Permits the registration and enforcement of confiscation orders made in designated countries in respect of indictable offences other than drug trafficking or tax offences. (Currently UK and USA)

(4) Misuse of Drugs (International Co-operation Law)

(4) Permits the granting of legal assistance to all states parties to the 1988 Convention in drug related investigations and prosecutions

Cyprus

(1) Foreign Tribunal Evidence Law (Cap. 12: 1908)

(1) Permits the Supreme Court to respond to commissions rogatoires and letters of request from foreign courts.

(2) Confiscation of Proceeds of Trafficking of Narcotic Drugs and Psychotropic substances Law of 1992 (Law No. 39(1) of 1992)

(2) Permits the making of regulations applying s.22 to any order of a foreign court being an order of a description specified in the regulations and which is made for the purposes of recovering payments or other rewards received in connection with drug trafficking. Such orders (restraint and confiscation orders) may be registered and enforced in Cyprus.

NOTE: Cyprus has bilateral agreements with the following non-Commonwealth countries: USA, Italy, Greece, Russia, China, Israel, Rumania, Lebanon, Poland, Egypt, Syria, Hungary, Slovakia, Czechia. Negotiations are taking place with the following non-Commonwealth countries: USA, Russia, Jordan, Latvia, China.

Cyprus (Sovereign Base Areas of Akrotiri and Dheklia)

(1) Evidence (Proceedings in Other Jurisdictions) (Sovereign Base Areas of Akrotiri and Dheklia) Order 1987 (UK S.I. 1920 of 1978)

(1) Extends the UK Evidence (Proceedings in Other Jurisdictions) Act 1975 to the Cayman Islands subject to exceptions, adaptations and modifications.

Permits the court to assist in obtaining evidence for criminal proceedings which have been instituted in overseas courts. Assistance available is only examination of witnesses or production of documents.

Dominica

(1) Mutual Assistance in Criminal Matters Act 1990. Act 9 of 1990.

(1) Permits Dominica to make and respond to mutual assistance requests. The Act applies to all Commonwealth countries and to for-

eign states with which treaties have been concluded. The application of the Act in relation to a particular Commonwealth country may be specified as being subject to such conditions, exceptions or qualifications.

The Act provides for the grant of assistance in relation to the proceeds of serious offences.

No orders have been made specifying conditions, exceptions or qualifications to the application of the Act to Commonwealth countries have been made.

The Act has not been applied to any foreign countries under s.30.

(2) Evidence (Proceedings in Other Jurisdictions) Act 1987 (No. 3 of 1987)

(2) S.6 allows the High Court to receive applications for orders for evidence to be obtained in Dominica provided that the application is made by or on behalf of a foreign court or tribunal before which proceedings have been instituted. Order which may be granted relate to examination of witnesses and the production of documents.

Falkland Islands

(1) Evidence (Proceedings in Other Jurisdictions) (Falkland Islands and Dependencies) Order 1978 (UK S.I. 1891 of 1978)

(1) Extends the provisions of the UK Evidence (Proceedings in Other Jurisdictions) Act 1975 to the Falkland Islands and South Georgia and the South Sandwich Islands (since 1985 a separate Territory), subject to modifications.

Permits the court to assist in obtaining evidence for criminal proceedings which have been instituted in overseas courts. Assistance is only available for examination of witnesses or production of documents. Remains in force but is almost entirely superseded by (2) below.

(2) Criminal Justice (Amendment) Ordinance 1991 (sections 3,6,7,9 and 10)

(2) Makes provision corresponding with sections 1,3,5,7 and 9 of the United Kingdom Criminal Justice (International Co-operation) Act 1990.

Section 3 enables overseas criminal process to be served in the Falkland Islands.

Under section 6 evidence (including documents) may be obtained in the Falkland Islands for use in overseas criminal proceedings if the Governor is satisfied:

(a) that an offence has been committed in the requesting country or that there are reasonable grounds for suspecting that such an offence has been committed;

(b) proceedings in respect of that offence have been commenced in the requesting country or that an investigation into that offence is being carried out in the requesting country;

(c) that the requesting country is a Commonwealth country or the request is made pursuant to a treaty to which the UK is a party and which extends to the Falkland Islands; and

(d) that the conduct constituting the offence would constitute an offence of the same or a similar nature if it had been committed in the Falkland Islands.

Section 7 makes provision for the temporary transfer to an overseas country, for the purpose of giving evidence or assisting in an investigation there, of a person serving a custodial sentence in the Falkland Islands.

Section 9 enables powers of entry, search and seizure available in respect of offences in the Falkland Islands to be used in the investigation of an overseas offence. subject to the detailed provisions of the section.

Section 10 empowers the Governor to make Orders enabling forfeiture order made by courts in designated overseas countries to be enforced in the Falkland Islands.

Fiji

(1) Mutual Assistance in Criminal Matters Act, 1997

(1) Permits Fiji to make and respond to mutual assistance requests. The Act applies to any foreign country with which Fiji has an arrangement or a reciprocal agreement. Permits the registration and enforcement of external forfeiture, confiscation and restraining orders. The Act provides for the grant of assistance in relation to the proceeds of serious offences.

(2) Proceeds of Crime Act, 1997

(2) Complements the Mutual Assistance in Criminal Matters Act, 1997. Provides for the registration and enforcement of foreign forfeiture, confiscation and restraining orders and for search for and seizure of property related to foreign serious offences. Action under the Mutual Assistance in Criminal Matters Act is a necessary prerequisite for the operation of this Act.

Gambia

(1) Drug Control Act 1993 (No. 1 of 1993) Part XIII

(1) Permits the Gambia to render assistance to a foreign government or authority which undertakes in writing to render similar assistance to the Government of the Gambia if any request is made to that effect. The assistance available under the Act is available in "drug related matters" which include investigations, inquiries, trials or other proceedings in any foreign country under any law relating directly or indirectly to prohibited or controlled drugs or to property derived from any activity relating to prohibited or controlled drugs. Available assistance includes service of process, transmission of information, examination of witnesses, search, seizure and transfer of prisoner witnesses.

Ghana

(1) Narcotic Drugs (Control, Enforcement and Sanctions) Law 1990

(1) Part VI of the Act permits Ghana to render assistance to a foreign government or authority.

The assistance available under the Act is available in "drug related matters" which include investigations, inquiries, trials or other proceedings in any foreign country under any law relating directly or indirectly to prohibited or controlled drugs or to property derived from any activity relating to prohibited or controlled drugs.

Available assistance includes service of process, transmission of information, examination of witnesses, search, seizure, interception of communications, exercise of investigative powers and transfer of prisoner witnesses.

Gibraltar

(1) Evidence (Proceedings in other Jurisdictions) (Gibraltar) Order 1978 (S.I. 1978 No. 1892: Gibraltar Legal Notice 17 of 1979)

(1) Extends the UK Evidence (Proceedings in Other Jurisdictions) Act 1975 to Gibraltar subject to exceptions, adaptations and modifications.

Permits the court to assist in obtaining evidence for criminal proceedings which have been instituted in overseas courts. Assistance available is only examination of witnesses or production of documents.

Guernsey

(1) Evidence (Proceedings in other Jurisdictions) (Guernsey) Order 1980 (S.I. No. 1956 of 1980)

(1) Extends the UK Evidence (Proceedings in Other Jurisdictions) Act 1975 to Guernsey subject to exceptions, adaptations and modifications.

Permits the court to assist in obtaining evidence for criminal proceedings which have been instituted in overseas courts. Assistance available is only examination of witnesses or production of documents.

(2) Banking Supervision (Bailiwick of Guernsey) Law 1994, s. 44 (No. XIII of 1994)

(3) Financial Supervision Commission (Bailiwick of Guernsey) Law 1987, (Tome XXX)

(4) Drug Trafficking Offences (Bailiwick of Guernsey) Law 1988, SS. 20 & 21 (No. XIX)

(5) Drug Trafficking (Amendment) (Bailiwick of Guernsey) Law 1992 (No. V of 1992)

(5) The Criminal Justice (Fraud Investigation) (Bailiwick of Guernsey) Law 1991 (No. III of 1991)

Guyana

(1) Narcotic Drugs and Psychotropic Substances (Control) Act 1988

(1) Permits Guyana to enter into arrangements with other countries for: (a) the enforcement of Guyanese drug forfeiture orders in drug cases and for the restraint of assets in cases under investigation in Guyana; and (b) recovery and handing over of property located in Guyana which has been confiscated or forfeited by another country in relation to a drug offence.

Isle of Man

(1) Criminal Justice Act 1991 (An Act) of Tynwald)

(1) Permits the Court on application of the Attorney-General to obtain evidence for criminal proceedings which have been instituted in overseas courts or where an investigation is being carried on overseas. Assistance available is normally examination of witnesses or production of documents. There is a power for the Court to grant warrants for the search and seizure of evidence concerning serious offences.

(2) Drug Trafficking Act 1996

(2) Permits the making of regulations applying the Act to external confiscation orders and to proceedings which have been or are to be instituted in the designated country or may

(3) Orders under the Drug Trafficking Act 1996 designate a number of countries for the purposes of the Act.

result in an external confiscation order being made. External confiscation orders are orders made by a court in a designated country for the purpose of recovering payment or other rewards in connection with drug trafficking or their value.

(3) Designate: Afghanistan, Anguilla, Antigua and Barbuda, Argentina, Armenia, Australia, Azerbaijan, Bahamas, Bahrain, Bangladesh, Barbados, Belarus, Bermuda, Bhutan, Bolivia, Boznia-Herzegovina, Brazil, British Virgin Islands, Brunei Darussalam, Bulgaria, Burkino Faso, Burma, Burundi, Cameroon, Canada, Cayman Islands, Chile, China, Colombia, Costa Rica, Croatia, Cyprus, Czech Republic, Denmark, Dominica, Dominican Republic, Ecuador, England and Wales, Egypt, El Salvador, Fiji, Finland, France, Germany, Ghana, Gibraltar, Greece, Grenada, Guatemala, Guernsey, Guinea, Guyana, Honduras, Hong Kong, Hungary, India, Iran, Italy, Ivory Coast, Japan, Jersey, Jordan, Kenya, Latvia, Lesotho, Lithuania, Luxembourg, Macedonia, Madagascar, Malaysia, Mauritania, Monaco, Montserrat, Morocco, Nepal, Netherlands, Nicaragua, Niger, Nigeria, Northern Ireland, Oman, Pakistan, Panama, Paraguay, Peru, Poland, Portugal, Qatar, Romania, Russian Federation, Saudi Arabia, Scotland, Senegal, Seychelles, Slovakia, Slovenia, South Africa, Spain, Sri Lanka, Sudan, Suriname, Sweden, Switzerland, Syria, Togo, Tunisia, Uganda, Ukraine, United Arab Emirates, United Mexican States, United States of America, Uruguay, Venezuela and Yugoslavia, Zambia, Zimbabwe.

(4) Criminal Justice Act 1990 (An Act of Tynwald)

(4) Permits the making of Orders applying the Act to external confiscation orders and to proceedings which have been or are to be instituted in the designated country or may result in an external confiscation order. External Confiscation Orders are orders made by a court in a designated country for the purposes of recovering property obtained as a result of or in connection with a crime other than drug trafficking.

Permits the Attorney-General to give assistance in cases concerning serious or complex fraud wherever committed. The Attorney-General has the power to require the production of documents and may obtain a court warrant to search premises and seize documents for the purposes of the investigation.

Permits the making of an order enabling the enforcement in the Isle of Man of the Orders of courts of designated countries for the

(5) Orders under the Criminal Justice Act 1990 designate a number of countries for the purposes of the confiscation provisions of the Act.

(5) forfeiture, destruction or disposal of instrumentalities of crime.

Designate Bulgaria, Canada, England and Wales, Finland, India, Italy, Lithuania, Netherlands, Nigeria, Northern Ireland, Norway, Romania, Scotland, Sweden, Switzerland, Thailand, United Mexican States, United States of America.

(6) Orders under the Criminal Justice Act 1990 designate a number of countries for the purposes of the forfeiture provisions of the Act relating to drug trafficking offences.

(6) Designate: Afghanistan, Anguilla, Antigua and Barbuda, Argentina, Armenia, Australia, Azerbaijan, Bahamas, Bahrain, Bangladesh, Barbados, Belarus, Bermuda, Bhutan, Bolivia, Boznia-Herzegovina, Brazil, British Virgin Islands, Brunei Darussalam, Bulgaria, Burkino Faso, Burma, Burundi, Cameroon, Canada, Cayman Islands, Chile, China, Colombia, Costa Rica, Croatia, Cyprus, Czech Republic, Denmark, Dominica, Dominican Republic, Ecuador, Egypt, El Salvador, England and Wales, Fiji, Finland, France, Germany, Ghana, Gibraltar, Greece, Grenada, Guatemala, Guernsey, Guinea, Guyana, Honduras, Hong Kong, India, Iran, Italy, Ivory Coast, Japan, Jersey, Jordan, Kenya, Latvia, Luxembourg, Madagascar, Mauritania, Monaco, Montserrat, Morocco, Nepal, Netherlands, Nicaragua, Niger, Nigeria, Northern Ireland, Oman, Pakistan, Panama, Paraguay, Peru, Portugal, Qatar, Romania, Russian Federation, Saudi Arabia, Scotland, Senegal, Seychelles, Slovakia, Slovenia, South Africa, Spain, Sri Lanka, Sudan, Suriname, Sweden, Switzerland, Syria, Togo, Tunisia, Uganda, Ukraine, United Arab Emirates, United Mexican States, United States of America, Uruguay, Venezuela, Yugoslavia, Zambia and Zimbabwe.

(7) Orders under the Criminal Justice Act 1990 designate a number of countries for the purposes of the forfeiture provisions of the Act relating to offences other than drug trafficking offences.

(7) Designate Bulgaria, Canada, England and Wales, India, Italy, Netherlands, Nigeria, Northern Ireland, Scotland, Sweden, Switzerland, United States of America

Jamaica

(1) Mutual Assistance (Criminal Matters) Act, 1995 (Act 5 of 1995 which entered into force on 14 July 1995 pursuant to the Mutual Assistance (Criminal Matters) Act 1995 (Appointed Day) Notice (LN 79 of 1995)

(1) Permits Jamaica to make and respond to mutual assistance requests. The Act applies to designated Commonwealth countries and to foreign states with which relevant treaties have been concluded.

The Act provides for the grant of assistance in relation to the proceeds of prescribed offences being offences related to dangerous drugs.

Jersey

(1) Evidence (Proceedings in Other Jurisdictions) (Jersey) Order 1983

(1) Extends the UK Evidence (Proceedings in Other Jurisdictions) Act 1975 to Jersey subject to exceptions, adaptations and modifications. Permits the Royal Court to assist in obtaining evidence for criminal proceedings which have been instituted in overseas courts. Assistance available is only examination of witnesses or production of documents.

(2) Drug Trafficking Offences (Jersey) Law 1988

(2) Permits the making of regulations applying the Law to external confiscation orders and to proceedings which have been or are to be instituted in a designated country or may result in an external confiscation order being made. External confiscation orders are orders made by a court in a designated country for the purpose of recovering payment or other rewards in connexion with drug trafficking or their value. Also permits production orders and search warrants to be issued in connection with investigations into drug trafficking offences wherever committed.

(3) Investigation of Fraud (Jersey) Law 1991

(3) Enables the investigation of affairs, or any aspect of the affairs, in Jersey of any person where it appears to the Attorney-General that there is a suspected offence of serious or complex fraud committed anywhere.

There are powers enabling the Attorney-General to require the answering of questions and provision of information and to obtain search warrants for documents.

Information obtained which is subject to secrecy obligations imposed by an enactment may only be disclosed for purposes of prosecutions in Jersey or elsewhere. Other information may only be disclosed for the purposes of investigation or prosecution of offences in Jersey or elsewhere or to any company inspector or any body having supervisory, regulatory or disciplinary functions in relation to financial services, any profession or any area of commercial activity. Such disclosures may be further limited to purposes specified under an agreement as to disclosure.

(4) Drug Offences (International Co-operation) Jersey) Law 1996

(4) Permits the Attorney-General to nominate a court or the Viscount of the Royal Court to obtain evidence in connection with drug trafficking offences, wherever committed. Also enables Regulations to be made for the enforcement of overseas forfeiture orders.

(5) Prevention of Terrorism (Jersey) Law 1996

(5) Enables production orders and search warrants to be issued in connection with investigations into terrorist activities or

funds derived from or intended for terrorist activities wherever committed.

Kenya

(1) Fugitive Criminals Surrender Ordinance (Cap. 77, Laws R.E. 1962)

(1) Provides for the taking of evidence by a magistrate or justice of the peace of Kenya for the purposes of any criminal matter pending in any court or tribunal in any foreign state.

The Ordinance also continues in force the UK Foreign Tribunals Evidence Act 1856.

Lesotho

(1) Criminal Procedure and Evidence Act 1981 (No. 7 of 1981)

(1) Section 211 allows courts in Lesotho to issue commissions to authorised persons to take evidence outside Lesotho for the purposes of any trial, preparatory examination or other criminal proceeding.

Malawi

(1) Mutual Assistance in Criminal Matters Act, 1991 (No. 24 of 1991)

(1) Permits Malawi to make and respond to mutual assistance requests. The Act applies to all Commonwealth countries. The application of the Act in relation to a particular Commonwealth country may be specified as being subject to such conditions, exceptions or qualifications.

The Act provides for the grant of assistance in relation to the proceeds of serious offences.

Although the long title of the Act refers to facilitating mutual assistance relations with non-Commonwealth countries there are no substantive provisions in the Act which permit this.

Malaysia

(1) Dangerous Drugs (Forfeiture of Property) Act 1988 (Act No. 340), Part VII

(1) Permits Malaysia to render assistance to a foreign government or authority. The assistance available under the Act is available in "drug related matters" which include investigations, inquiries, trials or other proceedings in any foreign country under any law relating directly or indirectly to prohibited or controlled drugs or to property derived from any activity relating to prohibited or controlled drugs.

Available assistance includes service of

process, provision of information and records and results of investigations in Malaysia, examination of witnesses, search, seizure, interception of communications and transfer of prisoner witnesses.

(2) Extradition Act 1992

(2) Provides for the taking of evidence in Malaysia for the purpose of any *extradition* matter pending in any court or tribunal in any country.

NOTE: The proposed legislation relating to the Harare Scheme is in the process of completion.

Malta

(1) Criminal Code, S.649

(1) Permits the examination of witnesses in connection with offences cognizable by courts outside Malta.

(2) The Dangerous Drugs Ordinance (Cap. 101) as amended by Act XVI of 1996

(2) Allows for the issue of investigation, attachment and freezing orders in connection with drug trafficking offences cognizable by courts outside Malta. It also provides for a procedure to enable the enforcement in Malta of confiscation orders made by a court outside Malta.

(3) The Medical and Kindred Professions Ordinance (Cap. 31) as amended by Act II of 1998

(3) Provides the same forms of assistance as provided in the Dangerous Drugs Ordinance but with respect to drugs specifically falling under the Ordinance

(4) The Prevention of Money Laundering Act 1994 as amended by Act II of 1998

(4) Provides for the same forms of assistance as provided in the Dangerous Drugs Ordinance but with respect to offences of money laundering as defined in the Act and cognizable by courts outside Malta.

NOTE: Assistance to other countries in criminal matters may also be granted in an informal manner where there is no particular legislation which regulates such assistance.

Mauritius

(1) Letters of Request Rules 1985 (GN 95/85)

(1) Permits a judge, upon ex parte application by the Attorney General or other authorised person, to respond to letters of request issued in relation to criminal matters pending before courts or tribunals of another state. The assistance which can be provided is the taking of evidence or the service of process.

Montserrat

(1) The Mutual Legal Assistance Criminal Matters (United States of America) Ordinance, 1991 (No. 1 of 1991)

(1) Extends to Montserrat the Mutual Legal Assistance Treaty between the UK and the US concerning the Cayman Islands. Gives effect to that treaty in Montserrat.

Namibia

(1) Foreign Courts Evidence Act, 1995 (No. 2 of 1995)

(1) Provides for obtaining of evidence of persons in Namibia by courts of law outside Namibia where proceedings are pending. Allows for the endorsement of subpoena issued by proper officers of a competent court in South Africa.

New Zealand

(1) Mutual Assistance in Criminal Matters Act 1992 (1992, No. 86)

(1) Permits New Zealand to make and respond to mutual assistance requests. The Act applies to prescribed countries.

Where the request relates to proceeds of crime, the Act provides for the grant of assistance in relation to the proceeds of serious offences.

Note: Proposed amendments to the Act will permit:
(a) Assistance may be provided in respect of offences covered in the 1973 Convention on the Prevention and Punishment of Crimes against Internationally Protected Persons, Including Diplomatic Agents; the 1979 Convention against the Taking of Hostages; the 1988 Convention against Illicit Traffic in Narcotic Drugs and Psychotropic Substances and the 1994 Convention on the safety of UN and Associated Personnel to any state party to the relevant Convention; and
(b) the granting of assistance to a wider range of countries by permitting the grant of assistance on an *ad hoc* basis to countries which are not prescribed provided certain conditions are met.

(2) Mutual Assistance in Criminal Matters (Prescribed Foreign Country) (United Kingdom) Regulations 1993 (1993/262).

(2) Applies Part III (Requests to New Zealand) of the Mutual Assistance in Criminal Matters Act 1992 to the United Kingdom, subject to clause 2(2) of the Regulations which provides that no request pursuant to Part III of the Act may be made by the UK pursuant to any of the following provisions of that Part of that Act S.38 (assistance in arranging the attendance in a foreign country of prisoners and certain other persons), S.54 (assistance with the enforcement of a

foreign forfeiture order or a foreign pecuniary penalty order): S.59 (a request for the obtaining of the issue of a search warrant in respect of tainted property): S.60 (a request for the obtaining the issue of a restraining order): S.61 (a request for the obtaining of the issue of production order) and S.62 (a request for the obtaining of that issue of a monitoring order).

(3) Mutual Assistance in Criminal Matters (Prescribed Foreign Country) (Australia) Regulations 1993

(3) Applies Part III of the Act to Australia.

(4) Mutual Assistance in Criminal Matters (Prescribed Foreign Country) (Niue) Regulations 1996

(4) Applies Part III of the Act to Niue

(5) Mutual Assistance in Criminal Matters Regulations 1993

(5) Deals with issue of summons, registration or foreign orders and witness expenses: prescribes forms for the purposes of the Act.

(6) Proceeds of Crime Amendment Act 1992 (No. 87 of 1992)

(6) Complements the Mutual Assistance in Criminal Matters Act 1992. Enables the enforcement of registered foreign forfeiture orders, the issue of search warrants in relation to foreign offences and the issue of restraining orders in respect of foreign offences. Permits the use of information gathering powers in relation to foreign serious offences being foreign drug dealing offences.

(7) Evidence Act 1908, ss. 48–48F

(7) Permits a High Court judge to order the examination of witnesses before any person named in the order.

Papua New Guinea

(1) Extradition Act 1975 (Act No. 59 of 1975, as amended by Act No. 17 of 1984)

(1) Section 25 provides for the taking of evidence for the purposes of a criminal matter pending in a designated Commonwealth Country or a foreign state with which Papua New Guinea has an *extradition* treaty.

Designated Commonwealth countries are Australia, Bahamas, Bangladesh, Barbados, Belize, Botswana, Canada, Cyprus, Dominica, Fiji, The Gambia, Ghana, Guyana, India, Jamaica, Kenya, Kiribati, Lesotho, Malawi, Malaysia, Malta, Mauritius, Nauru, New Zealand, Nigeria, Seychelles, Sierra Leone, Singapore, Solomon Islands, Sri Lanka, Swaziland, Tanzania, Tonga, Trinidad and Tobago, Tuvalu, Uganda, United Kingdom, Western Samoa, Zambia and Zimbabwe.

Treaty States are Austria, Belgium, Chile, Czechoslovakia, Ecuador, Greece, Guatemala, Hungary, Iceland, Iraq, Luxembourg,

Monaco, Nicaragua, Paraguay, Poland, Portugal, Switzerland, United States of America, Uruguay and Yugoslavia.

Section 25A provides for the taking of evidence for the purposes of extradition.

St Lucia

(1) Proceeds of Crime Act 1993

(1) Permits the application of the Act to external forfeiture or confiscation orders made in designated countries being countries which are states parties to the United Nations Convention against Illicit Traffic in Narcotic Drugs and Psychotropic Substances.

NOTE: A Mutual Assistance in Criminal Matters Bill has been prepared and placed for the consideration of Cabinet. It is anticipated that this will become law by the end of 1996.

St Vincent and the Grenadines

(1) Mutual Assistance in Criminal Matters Act 1993

(1) Permits St Vincent and the Grenadines to make and respond to mutual assistance requests. The Act applies to all Commonwealth countries and to foreign states with which treaties have been concluded. The application of the Act in relation to a particular Commonwealth country may be specified as being subject to such conditions, exceptions or qualifications.

The Act provides for the grant of assistance in relation to the proceeds of serious offences.

(2) Drug Trafficking Offences Act 1993

(2) Permits the application of the Act to external confiscation orders (in respect of drug trafficking offences, as defined) and to proceedings which have been or are to be instituted in designated countries. External confiscation orders may be registered and enforced

(3) Proceeds of Crime Act 1997

(3) Provides for the registration and enforcement in St Vincent and the Grenadines of external forfeiture orders and external confiscation orders in respect of the proceeds of offences under the Drug Trafficking Offences Act 1993 and scheduled offences (money laundering, organised fraud and the possession of property derived from scheduled offences) where the requesting country is a state party to the UN Convention against Illicit Traffic in Narcotic Drugs and Psychotropic Substances.

Seychelles

(1)   Mutual Assistance in Criminal Matters Act, 1995 (Act No. 7 of 1995).

(1)   The Act applies, subject to such limitation, condition, exemption and qualification as may be specified by regulations, to all Commonwealth countries; to foreign countries with which there is a treaty for bilateral mutual assistance in criminal matters between Seychelles and the foreign country, or for the purpose of giving effect to an international treaty of which Seychelles and the foreign country are parties; and any other foreign country specified by regulations.

(2)   Criminal Procedure Amendment Act 1995 (Act No. 15 of 1995)

(2)   Allows a court, upon application in accordance with a written law which makes provision for mutual assistance in criminal matters between the Seychelles and any other country or jurisdiction, to make an order applying the forfeiture of proceeds of crimes provisions of the Criminal Procedure Act to the foreign order.

Singapore

(1)   Extradition Act 1968 (Cap. 103, 1985 Revision Ed.) as amended by Act No. 35 of 1993.

(1)   Permits the taking of evidence in criminal matters for Commonwealth countries and foreign states.

(2)   Drug Trafficking (Confiscation of Benefits) Act. (Cap. 84A, Laws R.E. 1993)

(2)   Permits the registration and enforcement of foreign confiscation orders being orders made by courts in designated countries for the purpose of recovering payments or other rewards received in connection with drug trafficking or their value. Allows applications to be made for production orders and search warrants in respect of foreign offences.

(3)   Banking Act, Finance Companies Act, Insurance Act, and Futures Trading Act

(3)   Allow the court to make production orders (relating to drug trafficking proceeds) directed at these financial institutions.

South Africa

(1)   International Co-operation in Criminal Matters Act, 1996 (No. 75 of 1996)

(1)   Permits South Africa to make and respond to mutual assistance requests.

Provides for the granting of assistance in obtaining evidence, execution of foreign sentences (recovery of fines and compensatory orders), enforcement of foreign confiscation orders and enforcement of foreign restraint orders.

Provides for the endorsement of subpoena issued by proper officers of a competent court in a country listed in Schedule 1. The countries listed are Lesotho, Swaziland, Botswana, Malawi, Namibia and Zimbabwe. It also provides for compelled attendance of witnesses in court proceedings in these listed countries.

South Georgia and South Sandwich Islands

(1) Evidence (Proceedings in Other Jurisdictions) (Falkland Islands and Dependencies) Order 1978 (UK S.I. 1891 of 1978)

(1) Extends the provisions of the UK Evidence (Proceedings in Other Jurisdictions) Act 1975 to South Georgia and the South Sandwich Islands (since 1985 a separate Territory), subject to modifications.

Permits the court to assist in obtaining evidence for criminal proceedings which have been instituted in overseas courts. Assistance is only available for examination of witnesses or production of documents. Remains in force but is almost entirely superseded by (2) below.

(2) Criminal Justice (Amendment) Ordinance 1991 (sections 3,6,7,9 and 10)

(2) Makes provision corresponding with sections 1,3,5,7 and 9 of the United Kingdom Criminal Justice (International Co-operation) Act 1990.

Section 3 enables overseas criminal process to be served in South Georgia and the South Sandwich Islands.

Under section 6 evidence (including documents) may be obtained in South Georgia and the South Sandwich Islands for use in overseas criminal proceedings if the Governor is satisfied:

(a) that an offence has been committed in the requesting country or that there are reasonable grounds for suspecting that such an offence has been committed;
(b) proceedings in respect of that offence have been commenced in the requesting country or that an investigation into that offence is being carried out in the requesting country;
(c) that the requesting country is a Commonwealth country or the request is made pursuant to a treaty to which the UK is a party and which extends to South Georgia and the South Sandwich Islands; and
(d) that the conduct constituting the offence would constitute an offence of the same or a similar nature if it had been committed in South Georgia and the South Sandwich Islands.

Section 7 makes provision for the temporary transfer to an overseas country, for the purpose of giving evidence or assisting in an investigation there, of a person serving a custodial sentence in South Georgia and the South Sandwich Islands.

Section 9 enables powers of entry, search and seizure available in respect of offences in South Georgia and the South Sandwich Islands to be used in the investigation of an overseas offence, subject to the detailed provisions of the section.

Section 10 empowers the Governor to make Orders enabling forfeiture order made by courts in designated overseas countries to be enforced in South Georgia and the South Sandwich Islands.

Sri Lanka

(1) Foreign Tribunals Evidence Act 1956

(1) Provides for recording evidence in connection with, inter alia, criminal matters pending before a court or tribunal in a foreign country.

Tanzania

(1) Mutual Assistance in Criminal Matters Act 1991 (Act No. 24 of 1991).

(1) Permits Tanzania to make and respond to mutual assistance requests. The Act applies to all Commonwealth countries and to foreign states with which treaties have been concluded. The application of the Act in relation to a particular Commonwealth country may be specified as being subject to such conditions, exceptions or qualifications.

The Act provides for the grant of assistance in relation to the proceeds of serious offences.

(2) Proceeds of Crime Act 1991

(2) Complements the Mutual Assistance in Criminal Matters Act 1991. Provides for the registration and enforcement of foreign restraining, confiscation and pecuniary penalty orders, search and seizure and the exercise of information gathering powers in relation to foreign offences.

(3) Extradition Act 1965

(3) S.25 permits the testimony of any witness to be obtained in relation to any criminal matter pending in any court or tribunal in any other country in like manner as it may be obtained in relation to any civil matter under any rules of court or any enactment for the time being in force. S. 26 permits a magistrate to be required to take evidence for the purpose of any criminal matter pending in any court or tribunal in any other country.

Trinidad and Tobago

(1) Dangerous Drugs (Amendment) Act 1994 (No. 27 of 1994)

(1) Permits the designation of countries for the purposes of the Act. Permits the application

of s.35A of the Dangerous Drugs Act to external confiscation and forfeiture orders. Permits the application of Part VI (restraining orders) of the Dangerous Drugs Act in cases where proceedings in a designated country might result in an external confiscation or forfeiture order being made.

NOTE: A draft Mutual Assistance Bill has been prepared. This Bill has yet to go through other stages in its preparation before there can be a debate on it in Parliament.

Turks and Caicos Islands

(1) Evidence (Proceedings in Other Jurisdictions) (Turks and Caicos Islands) Order 1987 (UK S.I. No. 1266 of 1987)

(1) Extends the UK Evidence (Proceedings in Other Jurisdictions) Act 1975 to the Turks and Caicos Islands subject to exceptions, adaptations and modifications.

Permits the court to assist in obtaining evidence for criminal proceedings which have been instituted in overseas courts. Assistance available is only examination of witnesses or production of documents.

(2) Narcotic Drugs (Evidence) (United States of America) Ordinance 1986 as amended by the Narcotic Drugs (Evidence) United States of America) Amendment Ordinance 1986

(2) Provides for the obtaining of evidence required in investigations and proceedings in the United States of America in pursuant of obligations under the Single Convention on Narcotic Drugs 1961 and its 1972 Protocol.

United Kingdom

(1) Criminal Justice (International Co-operation) Act 1990 (1990 C.5)

(1) Enables the United Kingdom to co-operate with other countries in criminal proceedings and investigations. Permits the provision of assistance to serve process, take evidence and in relation to search and seizure. Allows the registration and enforcement of forfeiture orders made in designated countries and made in respect of drug trafficking offences and other serious offences.

(2) Criminal Justice Act 1988 (c.33)

(2) Allows for the enforcement of restraint and confiscation orders made in designated countries in respect of The serious criminal offences other than drug trafficking.

(3) Drug Trafficking Act 1994 (1994, c.37)

(3) Allows for the enforcement of restraint and confiscation orders made in designated countries in respect of drug trafficking offences.

Vanuatu

(1) Mutual Assistance in Criminal Matters Act No. 52 of 1989.

(1) Permits Vanuatu to make and respond to mutual assistance requests. The Act applies

to all Commonwealth countries and to foreign states with which treaties have been concluded. The application of the Act in relation to a particular Commonwealth country may be specified as being subject to such conditions, exceptions or qualifications.

The Act provides for the grant of assistance in relation to the proceeds of serious offences.

(2) The Serious Offences (Confiscation of Proceeds) Act (No. 50 of 1989)

(2) Complements the Mutual Assistance in Criminal Matters Act 1989. Permits the registration and enforcement of external confiscation and restraining orders made in respect of serious offences being foreign offences the maximum penalty for which is death or imprisonment for not less than three years.

Zambia

(1) The Mutual Legal Assistance in Criminal Matters Act, 1993 (No. 19 of 1993)

(1) Permits the provision of assistance to countries specified in order made under the Act being countries with which Zambia has treaties for mutual legal assistance in criminal matters.

(2) Dangerous Drugs (Forfeiture of Property Act) 1998, Part VII

(2) Permits the provision by Zambia of assistance to a foreign government or authority in a drug related matter. Drug related matter means investigation, inquiry, trial or other proceeding under a law relating directly or indirectly to dangerous drugs or to any property used for or derived from any activity relating to dangerous drugs. Assistance includes provision of information (including documents), service of process, taking of evidence, search, seizure, interception of communications, transfer of prisoner witnesses, provision of results of investigations and exercise of investigative powers.

(3) Narcotic Drugs and Psychotropic Substances Act 1993

(3) S.47 provides that, subject to inconsistencies between the Acts, the Mutual Legal Assistance in Criminal Matters Act 1993 applies to offences under this Act.

Zimbabwe

(1) Criminal Matters (Mutual Assistance) Act (Chapter 9:06)

(1) Permits Zimbabwe to make and respond to mutual assistance requests. The Act may be applied to any country which can provide reciprocity. Evidence can be taken in Zimbabwe for criminal proceedings in any country whether or not the Act applies to that country. This is the only assistance of a compulsory nature which can be provided

in the absence of designation.

(2) Serious Offences (Confiscation of Profits) Act (Chapter 9:17)

(2) Complements the Criminal Matters (Mutual Assistance) Act 1990. Permits the registration and enforcement of foreign restraint, forfeiture and pecuniary penalty orders and the use of information gathering powers in relation to foreign offences.

Appendix J

CONVENTION IMPLEMENTING THE SCHENGEN AGREEMENT OF JUNE 14, 1985

Title III

Chapter 2, Articles 48 to 53

CHAPTER 2
MUTUAL ASSISTANCE IN CRIMINAL MATTERS

Article 48

1. The provisions of this Chapter are intended to supplement the European Convention of 20 April 1959 on Mutual Assistance in Criminal Matters as well as, in relations between the Contracting Parties which are members of the Benelux Economic Union, Chapter 2 of the Benelux Treaty on Extradition and Mutual Assistance in Criminal Matters of 27 June 1962, as amended by the Protocol of 11 May 1974, and to facilitate the implementation of these agreements.
2. Paragraph 1 shall not affect the application of the broader provisions of the bilateral agreements in force between the Contracting Parties.

Article 49

Mutual assistance shall also be granted:

(a)   in proceedings brought by the administrative authorities for offences which are punishable in one of the two Contracting Parties or in both Contracting Parties by virtue of being an infringement of the law and where the decision may give rise to proceedings before a criminal court:
(b)   in damage proceedings for wrongful prosecution or conviction;
(c)   in clemency proceedings;
(d)   in civil proceedings that are combined with criminal proceedings, as long as the criminal court has not yet given a final ruling on the criminal proceedings;
(e)   to communicate legal statements relating to the enforcement of a sentence or a measure, the imposition of a fine or the payment of costs for proceedings;
(f)   in respect of measures relating to the deferral of delivery or suspension of enforcement of a sentence or a detention order, conditional release or a stay of execution or interruption of enforcement of a sentence or a detention order.

Article 50

1. The Contracting Parties undertake to grant each other, in accordance with the Convention and the Treaty referred to in Article 48, mutual assistance as regards infringements of their laws

on excise duties, value added tax and customs duties. Customs provisions shall mean the rules laid down in Article 2 of the Convention of 7 September 1967 between Belgium, the Federal Republic of Germany, France, Italy, Luxembourg and the Netherlands on mutual assistance between customs administrations, as well as Article 2 of Council Regulation (EEC) No 1468/81 of 19 May 1981.

2. Requests regarding evasion of excise duties may not be rejected on the grounds that the requested country does not levy excise duties on the goods referred to in the request.

3. The requesting Contracting Party shall not forward or use information or evidence obtained from the requested Contracting Party for enquiries, proceedings or procedures other than those referred to in its request, without the prior consent of the requested Contracting Party.

4. The mutual assistance provided for in this Article may be refused where the alleged amount of duty underpaid or evaded does not exceed ECU 25 000 or where the presumed value of the goods exported or imported without authorization does not exceed ECU 100 000, unless, given the circumstances or the identity of the accused, the case is deemed to be extremely serious by the requesting Contracting Party.

5. The provisions of this Article shall also apply when the mutual assistance requested concerns infringements punishable only by a fine as infringements of the law in proceedings brought by the administrative authorities, where the request for assistance was made by a judicial authority.

Article 51

The Contracting Parties may not make the admissibility of letters rogatory for search or seizure dependent on any other conditions than the following:

(a)   the offence giving rise to the letters rogatory is punishable under the law of both Contracting Parties by a custodial sentence or a security measure restricting liberty by a maximum of at least six months or is punishable under the law of one of the two Contracting Parties by an equivalent penalty and under the law of the other Contracting Party as an infringement of the regulations, which is prosecuted by the administrative authorities, where the decision may give rise to proceedings before a criminal court.

(b)   enforcement of the letters rogatory is consistent with the law of the requested Contracting Party.

Article 52

1. Each Contracting Party may send procedural documents directly by post to persons who are in the territory of another Contracting Party. The Contracting Parties shall send the Executive Committee a list of the documents which may be forwarded in this way.

2. Where there is reason to believe that the addressee does not understand the language in which the document is written, the document – or at least the important passages thereof – must be translated into (one of) the language(s) of the Contracting Party in the territory of which the addressee is staying. If the authority forwarding the document knows that the addressee speaks only another language, the document – or at least the important passages thereof – must be translated into that other language.

3. Experts or witnesses who have failed to answer a summons to appear, sent to them by post, shall not, even if the summons contains a notice of penalty, be subjected to any punishment or measure of constraint, unless they subsequently voluntarily enter into the territory of the requesting Party and are there again duly summoned. Authorities sending a postal summons to appear shall ensure that this does not involve penalties. This provision shall be without prejudice to Article 34 of the Benelux Treaty on Extradition and Mutual Assistance in Criminal Matters of 27 June 1962, as amended by the Protocol of 11 May 1974.

4. If the offence on which the request for assistance is based is punishable under the law of both Contracting Parties as an infringement of the regulations, which is being prosecuted by the administrative authorities, and where the decision may give rise to proceedings before a criminal court, the procedure outlined in paragraph 1 must in principle be used for the forwarding of procedural documents.

5. Notwithstanding paragraph 1, procedural documents may be forwarded via the judicial authorities of the requested Contracting Party where the addressee's address is unknown or where the requesting Contracting Party requires a formal service.

Article 53

1. Requests for assistance may be made directly between judicial authorities and returned via the same channels.
2. Paragraph 1 shall not prejudice the possibility of requests being sent and returned between Ministries of Justice or through national central offices of the International Criminal Police Organization.
3. Requests for the temporary transfer or transit of persons under temporary arrest or being detained or who are serving a custodial sentence, and the periodic or occasional exchange of information from the judicial records must be effected through the Ministries of Justice.
4. Within the meaning of the European Convention of 20 April 1959 on Mutual Assistance in Criminal Matters, where the Federal Republic of Germany is concerned, Ministry of Justice shall mean the Federal Minister of Justice and the Justice Ministers or Senators in the Federal States.
5. Reports made with a view to proceedings against infringement of the legislation on driving and rest time, in accordance with Article 21 of the European Convention of 20 April 1959 on Mutual Assistance in Criminal Matters or Article 42 of the Benelux Treaty on Extradition and Mutual Assistance in Criminal Matters of 27 June 1962, as amended by the Protocol of 11 May 1974, may be sent by the judicial authorities of the requesting Contracting Party directly to the judicial authorities of the requested Contracting Party.

Appendix K

SEEKING ASSISTANCE IN CRIMINAL MATTERS FROM THE UNITED KINGDOM

Guidelines for Judicial and Prosecuting Authorities

(Second Edition, October 1999)

Contents

Chapter 1: Introduction
Chapter 2: Range of assistance and channels of communication
Chapter 3: Form and content of requests to the UK
Chapter 4: Execution of requests in the UK
Chapter 5: Home Office Code of Practice

Annex A:
Conducting enquiries in, or seeking assistance from, the UK: *The competencies of the Home Office (UK Central Authority) and the National Criminal Intelligence Service (UK National Central Bureau of Interpol)*

Annex B:
The Home Office Code of Practice

Annex C:
Contact details for the Home Office (UK Central Authority) and other relevant UK authorities

Annex D:
Contact details for authorities in the Channel Islands, the Isle of Man and the UK Overseas Territories

Chapter i: Introduction

The United Kingdom Government attaches great importance to assisting judicial and prosecuting authorities in other countries in combating national and international crime.

The UK is able to provide a full range of legal assistance in criminal matters to judicial and prosecuting authorities in other countries under Part I of the Criminal Justice (International Co-operation) Act 1990, the UK's principal mutual legal assistance legislation.

These guidelines:

- give details of the assistance that can be provided under the Act and the procedures to follow when requesting assistance;
- explain the important role of the Judicial Co-operation Unit of the Home Office, in the execution of requests for legal assistance in criminal matters; and
- describe how the Home Office, as the UK Central Authority, works in close co-operation with the UK National Central Bureau of Interpol, which is part of the UK's National Criminal Intelligence Service (NCIS).

The Home Office staff working exclusively on requests for legal assistance and are fully conversant with mutual legal assistance law and practice. The Home Office works to very high professional standards. These are reflected in its published Code of Practice, included in these guidelines.

Extradition matters and international co-operation between, for example, Customs services, tax administrations and regulatory authorities in the financial services industry are not included in these guidelines. Separate guidance on those matters can be obtained from the relevant contact shown in Annex C.

These guidelines are available in English, French, German, Italian and Spanish. Further copies may be obtained from the Judicial Co-operation Unit at the Home Office.

The Home Office is not responsible for judicial co-operation with the Channel Islands, the Isle of Man or the UK Overseas Territories. Contact points for the competent authorities of the Islands and Territories are listed in Annex D.

CHAPTER 2: RANGE OF ASSISTANCE AND CHANNELS OF COMMUNICATION

Range of available assistance: What is possible?

The United Kingdom is able to provide a full range of legal assistance to judicial and prosecuting authorities in other countries and territories for the purposes of criminal investigations and criminal proceedings. The legal assistance that can be provided includes:

- service of summonses, judgements and other procedural documents;
- obtaining witness statements on oath and authenticated documentary evidence, including banking evidence;
- use of the investigation powers of the Serious Fraud Office in London and the Crown Office in Edinburgh in cases of serious or complex fraud;
- exercise of search and seizure powers;
- restraint and confiscation of proceeds of crime, and
- temporary transfer of prisoners, with their consent, to assist with criminal investigations and proceedings.

Which countries can the United Kingdom assist?

The UK can assist any country (or territory) in the world, whether or not that country is able to assist the UK.

Are international agreements required?

The UK can provide most forms of legal assistance without bilateral or international agreements – but assistance in the restraint and confiscation of proceeds of crime is dependent upon a bilateral agreement or other international agreement.

The UK has ratified:

- 1959 European Convention on Mutual Assistance in Criminal Matters and its Additional Protocol;
- the 1990 European Convention on Laundering, Search, Seizure and Confiscation of the Proceeds from Crime, and
- the 1988 United Nations Convention against Illicit Traffic in Narcotic Drugs and Psychotropic Substances (the Vienna Convention).

The UK has also adopted the Commonwealth Scheme Relating to Mutual Assistance in Criminal Matters.

Does the UK require reciprocity?

No, but the UK would expect assistance from countries which are parties to relevant bilateral or international agreements with the UK.

Is dual criminality required?

No usually. The criminal conduct described in any request need not constitute an offence under UK law, had it occurred in the UK, *except* in cases involving the exercise of search and seizure powers or use of the special investigation powers of the Serious Fraud Office (in Scotland, the Crown Office) in cases of serious or complex fraud.

Does the UK assist with requests involving fiscal offences?

In general, yes. But if the request is for evidence on oath, for certified documentary evidence, for search and seizure of evidence or would involved use of the investigation powers of the Serious Fraud Office (in Scotland, the Crown Office), then *one or more* of the following conditions must be satisfied:

- criminal proceedings must have been instituted in the requesting country (meaning that a court has issued a summons or an arrest warrant; the defendant has been charged or indicted; or the facts alleged by the prosecutor have been put to the defendant and will be put before a trial court);
- the request must come from a competent authority in a Commonwealth country or be made under an international agreement, or
- the conduct would constitute an offence of the same or similar nature under UK law had it occurred in the UK.

Which authorities can make requests to the UK? What information should be included in requests?

Details of the authorities which may submit requests for legal assistance to the UK and what information should be included in letters of request (commissions rogatoires) are given in Chapter 3.

Where should requests to the UK be sent?

Requests for legal assistance in criminal matters must be sent to the Home Office.

What does the Home Office do?

The functions of the Home Office as UK Central Authority are described in Chapter 4.

Is it possible to submit requests to the Home Office through diplomatic channels?

Yes. Diplomatic channels, such as Embassies or High Commissions in London, may be used where required by the law and practice of the requesting country. But direct communication with the Home Office is preferred as this can help speed up the execution of requests.

At what stage of investigations or proceedings should requests be sent to the Home Office?

At any stage. In general, requests should be made as soon as the need for legal assistance is known and giving the UK authorities as much time as possible to execute the request. Delay in sending requests to the Home Office can result in an increase in the number of urgent cases, and delay the processing of other requests.

Requests for restraint (freezing) and confiscation of the proceeds of crime may only be considered where proceedings have been instituted or where it is certified when proceedings are to be instituted.

Will the Home Office take account of any requirements or procedures which are specified in requests?

Yes. Testimony may be received or recorded and oaths or cautions administered in any specified form to the extent possible under UK law.

May witnesses in the UK be approached directly without informing the Home Office?

Yes. Contact may be made directly by letter, fax or telephone. If the witness is willing to assist the enquiry voluntarily, an approach may be made through Interpol to record his or her statement or to the Home Office if testimony on oath is required.

How long does it take to execute a request?

This will depend on the circumstances of the request. Requesting authorities are kept informed of progress by the Home Office, in accordance with its Code of Practice, and provided with details of the officer(s) responsible for executing the request. These arrangements help ensure that timely assistance is provided.

Any reasons for urgency such as statutory time limits, pre-trial court appearances or trial dates should be clearly stated in all requests.

May requests be sent to the Home Office via interpol?

Yes, but direct communication with the Home Office is preferred as this helps speed up execution of requests. If requests for legal assistance intended for the Home Office are sent through Interpol channels, they must be marked clearly for the attention of the Home Office.

What assistance does the Home Office, as UK Central Authority, provide which the NCIS, as UK National Central Bureau of Interpol, does not?

The respective competencies of the Home Office and the NCIS are set out in Annex A.

What requests may be sent to the UK National Central Bureau of Interpol at the NCIS?

Examples of requests that may be submitted directly to the UK National Central Bureau of Interpol without involving the Home Office include requests for:

- interviewing witnesses or suspects in criminal investigations where the person to be interviewed is willing to co-operate without appearing or needing to appear before a judicial authority in the UK;
- sharing of information and intelligence concerning investigations into offences which have been committed in the UK (provided that the information or intelligence is *not* being requested for use in proceedings);
- asset tracing enquiries;
- providing details of previous convictions;
- providing, for investigative purposes, details of UK telephone subscribers;
- providing details of keepers of motor vehicles registered in the UK and of driving licences issued in the UK;
- obtaining medical or dental statements or records where the patient has given written consent.

Such requests need not be sent to the Home Office unless it is a requirement of the judicial authority making the request. Requests for *both* legal assistance *and* for investigative assistance may be sent *both* to the Home Office *and* the UK National Central Bureau of Interpol. They will jointly co-ordinate the execution of the request. Any such requests should be clearly marked to show the request had been submitted to both authorities.

May requests for legal assistance be sent direct to courts or prosecuting authorities in the UK?

No. The courts in the UK have no investigative function and the prosecuting authorities do not, in general, have responsibilities for initiating enquiries on behalf of competent authorities abroad. The Home Office handles thousands of requests every year, and is best placed to ensure that requests for legal assistance are dealt with speedily, efficiently and in accordance with the requirements of the requesting authorities.

Requests should always be sent to the Home Office or to the UK National Central Bureau of Interpol at the NCIS.

May evidence be taken away by visiting judicial or investigating officers?

Under law in the UK, all evidence received by a court or seized by a UK investigator must be sent to the Home Office for transmission to the requesting authorities abroad. Once received by the Home Office the evidence may be handed to visiting officials directly or sent to the requesting central or judicial authority.

Are requests kept confidential?

In line with established international practice, the Home Office does not disclose the existence or content of letters of request outside government departments or agencies or the courts or enforcement agencies in the UK. Requests are not disclosed more than is necessary to obtain the co-operation of the witness or other person concerned.

In general, requests are not shown or copied to any witness or other person, nor is any witness informed of the identity of any other witness. In the event that confidentiality requirements make execution of a request difficult or impossible, the Home Office consults the requesting authorities.

Where public statements are made by authorities about the assistance they are requesting from the UK, the Home Office should be notified so that it may respond appropriately to any media or public enquiries.

Where should requests for Scotland and Northern Ireland be sent?

The UK comprises three separate jurisdictions: England and Wales; Scotland; and Northern Ireland. All requests to the UK for assistance in criminal matters should be sent to the Home Office or the UK National Central Bureau of Interpol at NCIS irrespective of from where in the UK the assistance is required. But preliminary, informal enquiries about how to make requests intended for execution in Scotland may be made direct to the Crown Office in Edinburgh.

Where should requests for the Crown Dependencies and the UK Overseas Territories be sent?

The Crown Dependencies, namely the Channel Islands (Guernsey and Jersey) and the Isle of Man, and the UK Overseas Territories[1] are not part of the United Kingdom. The Crown Dependencies and the Overseas Territories are themselves wholly responsible for executing requests within their own jurisdictions (although Interpol London is the Interpol office for the Crown Dependencies and certain of the Overseas Territories[2]). Requests should usually be sent to the Attorney General of the Crown Dependency or Overseas Territory from where the assistance is required.

Are requests ever declined? Is there anything the Home Office cannot do?

Experience so far has shown that requests to the Home Office for legal assistance are rarely declined. However, the UK may decline requests the execution of which may prejudice UK investigations, proceedings, national security or other essential interests. No request will be declined without stating the reason or reasons why the request cannot be executed or without consulting the requesting authority and, where appropriate, inviting it to modify the request so that assistance may be provided.

The UK will decline to execute requests where a trial in the requesting country would involve double-jeopardy (*non bis in idem*). If the subject of a request has been convicted or acquitted in the UK or a third country of an offence arising from the conduct described in the request, the UK will not assist the gathering of evidence for another trial of the same person for the same conduct.

The Home Office cannot facilitate requests for interception of communications for evidential purposes. This is because UK law, section 9 of the Interception of Communications Act 1985, does not permit intercept material lawfully obtained by warrant to be adduced in evidence. Interception is an important intelligence development tool and requests for assistance with intelligence development can be considered by NCIS.

CHAPTER 3: FORM AND CONTENT OF REQUESTS TO THE UK

Which authorities may make requests to the UK?

Requests for legal assistance in criminal matters may made by any competent court or tribunal, judicial or prosecuting authority. Requests may also be made by any other competent authority that the Home Office considers has the function of making requests for the purposes of criminal proceedings or criminal investigations. Such authorities include Attorneys General, investigating judges, examining magistrates, public prosecutors and Ministries or Departments of Justice having responsibilities for criminal matters.

---

1 Anguilla, Bermuda, British Virgin Islands, Cayman Islands, Falklands, Gibraltar, Montserrat, St Helena and the Turks and Caicos Islands
2 Falklands and St Helena: the other Overseas Territories host Interpol Sub-bureaux.

Should requests be made or confirmed in writing?

Yes, requests should always be made in writing, addressed to the Home Office or to the UK National Central Bureau of Interpol, depending on the nature of the assistance requested (see Annex A). They may be sent in advance by fax or e-mail but an undertaking should be given to send the original request by airmail or courier or other method of rapid delivery within a reasonable time, normally 7 days.

What language may requests to the Home Office be made in?

Requests must be made in writing in English or be submitted with an English translation. If no translation is provided the Home Office will ask for one.

What information should be included in requests?

All relevant information must be included. This will vary according to the nature of the assistance required. Omission of any relevant information may delay execution of the request.
    Wherever possible all requests should include:

- Any information which is likely to help the Home Office arrange for execution of the request in accordance with the requirements of the requesting authority.

Letters of request *must* include the following details:

- Details and the address of the judicial or prosecuting authority conducting the investigation or proceedings to which the request relates, and the name, telephone and fax details of the responsible official(s) there.
- Full name(s) of the subject(s) of the investigation or proceedings.
- A summary of the facts of the offence(s) and details of the offence(s) committed or alleged. Where evidence is required, the request should make clear that there are reasonable grounds for suspecting that the offence has been committed and that proceedings have been instituted in relation to the offence or, if proceedings have not been instituted, that the offence is being investigated.
- A description of the evidence or material or other assistance required, clearly stating whether original evidence or certified copies are required.
- The purpose for which the evidence or material or other assistance is required and the relevance of the assistance to the investigation or proceedings.

Requests should also state, to the extent necessary and possible:

- The date of the trial or hearing and any other dates relevant for the purposes of executing the request; and any reasons why the request is urgent, for example because the accused person or suspect is in detention.
- The full name, date of birth and location of any person from whom evidence is required making clear whether there are a witness or an actual or potential accused.
- Available information on the identity and whereabouts of any person to be located.
- Details, including the telephone number, of any British law enforcement officer who is familiar with the investigation.
- The request should also say whether *and why* the presence of officers or officials of the requesting authorities is required during the execution of the request. The names of such persons should be provided (in general, such officers or officials may observe, but may not participate in, the execution of requests).

Requests for service of summonses, judgements and other procedural documents should include:

- The original document(s) with a translation or, if the original documents cannot be provided, a translation *certified* as a true copy of the original.
- The identity, date of birth and location of any person on whom a summons or

judgement is to be served; details of that person's connection with the proceedings; and details of any particular way in which the summons or judgement should be served.

- Details of any allowances and expenses to which a person asked to appear in proceedings abroad is entitled; the address of the court where the proceedings are to take place; and the name and telephone number of an official of the court from whom the person asked to appear can seek further information if necessary.

Requests for witness evidence (testimony), should include

- Where evidence is required to be taken *on oath* before a court in the UK this should be expressly stated in the request. Expressions such as *"to hear"* or *"to examine"* witnesses or suspects should be avoided as they have no precise meaning in UK law. For the avoidance of doubt the requesting authority should set out as clearly as possible the conditions under which any interview or examination should be conducted.
- A list of questions to be asked.
- Details of the procedure to be followed in taking the evidence, including any rules on privilege which a witness or suspect may be entitled to claim.
- Any caution or formal notification of rights which should be given to the witness or suspect under the law of the requesting State.
- If banking evidence is required, the request must provide the name or number of the account and the address or number ("Sort Code") of the branch of the bank where the account is held. This detail is required because there is no central record of bank accounts held in the UK.

Requests for search and seizure of evidence should include

- The full address or a precise description of any place to be searched; full details of the specific material or type of material to be seized and a full description of the criminal conduct concerned. (Requests for search and seizure cannot be executed unless the criminal conduct would be a serious offence under UK law if it had occurred in the UK.)
- An explanation why the material requested is considered both relevant and important evidence to the investigation or proceedings; why the evidence is thought to be on the particular premises or in the possession of the particular person concerned and why the material would not be produced to a UK court if the natural or legal person holding the material were ordered to do so. (This is to help ensure that applications to the UK courts for search warrants are successful and less likely to fail or be subject to subsequent legal challenge.)
- Appropriate undertakings for the safekeeping and return of any seized evidence.

Requests for the restraint (freezing) of property should include:

- The name, address, nationality, date and place of birth and present location of the defendant(s) or person(s) whose criminal conduct has given rise to civil confiscation proceedings.
- Details of the offence with which the defendant has been, or is about to be, charged (or the civil action brought or about to be brought).
- Details of the law applicable to the charges and the evidence against the defendant.
- Particulars of the property which it is intended to restrain in the United Kingdom, the persons holding it and details of the link between the defendant and the property (this is important if the property to be restrained is held in the name of a third party such as a company or another person).
- State clearly whether prior assistance in the case (including asset tracing assistance) has been provided and, if so, give particulars of the UK enforcement or other authority involved and details of the assistance already received.
- Where applicable, details of any court orders already made in the requesting State against the defendant in respect of his or her property. If any court order has been made a *duly authenticated* copy should be included with the request – that is a true copy of that order certified by a person in his or her capacity as a judge, magistrate

or officer of the relevant court of the requesting State, or by an official of the Central Authority in the requesting State.

- Brief details of all known property held by the defendant *outside* the United Kingdom.
- A *certificate* issued by or on behalf of the requesting State's Central Authority stating:

  ☐ that proceedings have been instituted in that country and have not been concluded, or that proceedings are to be instituted in the requesting State and, if so, when;

  ☐ that the confiscation order which it is expected the court of the requesting State will make will have the purpose of recovering property, or the value of property, received in connection with drug trafficking or other serious crime (or, in the case of a forfeiture order, has the purpose of ordering the forfeiture of instrumentalities of crime).

Requests for confiscation of property in the UK should include:

- Information as in requests for restraint.
- An original confiscation order or a *duly authenticated* copy of the confiscation order.
- A *certificate* issued by or on behalf of the requesting State's Central Authority stating:

  ☐ that the confiscation order is in force and that neither the order nor any conviction to which it may relate is subject to appeal;

  ☐ that all or a certain amount of the sum payable under the order remains unpaid in the territory of the requesting State or that other property recoverable under the order remains unrecovered there;

  ☐ that the confiscation order has the purpose of recovering property, or the value of property obtained in connection with drug trafficking or other serious crime (or in the case of a forfeiture order has the purpose of ordering the forfeiture of instrumentalities of crime);

  ☐ and, where the person against whom the confiscation order was made did not appear in the proceedings, that he or she was notified of the proceedings in accordance with the requesting State's law in time to defend them.

Where the request is for the temporary transfer of a UK prisoner to give evidence or otherwise assist in criminal investigations or proceedings outside the UK, it should include:

- Dates on which the presence abroad of the prisoner is required, including the dates on which the court or other proceedings for which the prisoner is required will commence and are likely to be concluded;
- Information for the purpose of obtaining the prisoner's consent to the transfer and satisfying the UK authorities that arrangements will be made to keep the prisoner in secure custody such as:
  - whether the prisoner will have immunity from prosecution for previous offences;
  - details of proposed arrangements for collecting the prisoner from and returning the prisoner to the United Kingdom;
  - details of the type of secure accommodation in which the prisoner will be held in the requesting State;
  - details of the type of escort available abroad to and from the secure accommodation.

The above list is not exhaustive. The Home Office can provide further advice if necessary.

If the assistance requested ceases to be required, the Home Office or the UK National Central Bureau of Interpol should be informed immediately so that enquiries are not made unnecessarily.

Chapter 4: Execution of Requests in the UK

What is the role of the Home Office?

The Home Office's responsibilities include:

- Ensuring that requests for legal assistance conform with the requirements of law in the UK and the UK's international obligations (for example, requests for legal assistance must come from a competent authority and be for the purposes of criminal investigations or proceedings).
- Ensuring that execution of requests is not inappropriate on public policy grounds (for example, requests involving double jeopardy will not be executed).
- Deciding how requests might most appropriately be executed (for example, some requests asking for search and seizure of evidence may be executed effectively by a witness producing the evidence to a court).
- Maintaining confidentiality of requests where necessary.
- Ensuring, so far as possible, that assistance is provided within an appropriate time scale (for example, taking account of trial dates).
- Drawing to the attention of the courts, the police and other UK authorities and agencies requests that evidence be obtained in the presence of foreign police or customs officers or prosecutors or defence lawyers.
- Seeking requesting authorities' agreement to meet extra-ordinary costs of executing requests and for services such as interpreters or stenographers or for duplication of documents. (Ordinarily, costs will be met by the UK authorities, in accordance with established international practice).
- Passing evidence received to the requesting authorities (and checking whether any part of the request remains outstanding).

How are requests executed?

The information below explains the ways requests in which are executed in England and Wales. (Requests seeking assistance from Scotland or Northern Ireland are sent by the Home Office to the Crown Office or the Northern Ireland Office for execution, although the laws and practices in those parts of the UK are similar to those in England and Wales.)

How are requests for service of summonses and judgments executed?

Summonses and judgements received by the Home Office from competent authorities abroad are normally served on the persons to whom they are addressed by recorded delivery post. Where personal service is requested, the Home Office arranges for the document to be served by the police.

Under law in the UK, any person to whom a summons or judgement is addressed must be given a notice explaining, as appropriate, that:

- the document does not impose any obligation under law in the UK to comply with it;
- the person might wish to seek legal advice on the possible consequences under the law of the requesting country of failure to comply, and
- the person may not, as a witness, be accorded the same rights and privileges in the requesting country as they would in criminal proceedings in the UK.

The person on whom a summons or judgement is served is asked to sign a receipt and return it to the Home Office to send to the requesting authority. The Home Office will advise the requesting authority whether the document has been delivered and a receipt has not been received or whether it was not possible to serve the document.

How are requests for evidence on oath executed?

Where a request is made for evidence to be received by a court in the UK or the execution of the request requires judicial authority under UK law, the Home Office may nominate a court to receive such of the evidence *as may appear to the court* to be appropriate. The court has powers to secure the attendance of the witnesses and suspects *named in the request.*

Witnesses and suspects may claim privilege against self-incrimination and refuse to answer questions or produce documents. In particular, a person cannot be compelled to give evidence before the nominated court if he or she could not be compelled to give the evidence in criminal proceedings in the UK or in criminal proceedings in the requesting country.

Where a witness or suspect claims privilege under the law of the requesting country, evidence will not be taken if the requesting authority concedes the claim. Where the claim is not conceded, the evidence may be taken but will not be sent to the requesting authority if a court in the requesting State rules that the claim to privilege is justified.

With the agreement of the UK court, attorneys, law enforcement officers and other interested parties from abroad *named in the request* (or a supplementary request) may observe the proceedings. Such agreement is almost always given.

Under UK law the evidence received by the court *must* be furnished to the Home Office to transmit to the requesting authority. It is possible for the evidence to be received directly from the Home Office by hand or, in urgent cases, for a Home Office official to be present at the court to receive the evidence and pass it directly to the representative of the requesting authority.

If the evidence required does *not* need to be taken on oath, the request may be sent to the UK National Central Bureau of Interpol which may then arrange for the evidence to be obtained directly by the police and the evidence would normally be returned to the requested authorities through Interpol channels or handed to visiting officers.

How are requests for authenticated documentary evidence, including certified banking evidence, executed?

The Home Office may nominate a court to receive such of the documentary evidence *as may appear to the court* to be appropriate. Normally, the custodian of the documents is required by the court to make a statement on oath. This may, for example, indicate whether the documents were created in the ordinary course of business or came into the custodian's possession from a third party and whether the documents are originals or genuine copies of the originals. Such a statement is for "chain of evidence" purposes. If banking evidence is required, the statement is normally provided by an official of the bank concerned.

The bank is under no obligation to inform the account holder that it has been ordered to disclose the information. In most cases, the nominated court will obtain the banking information without itself informing the account holder. This might not be appropriate if the account holder is a third party not complicit in the offence or if the account is administered by, for example, a firm of solicitors (professional legal advisers) or accountants. The decision whether to notify the account holder of the proceedings is entirely a matter for the court.

Before an account holder is notified, the Home Office consults with the requesting authority to ensure that execution of the request would not breach the requesting authority confidentiality requirements.

Under UK law, the evidence received by the court *must* be sent to the Home Office for transmission to the requesting authority.

How can requests for evidence in serious or complex fraud cases be executed?

The Home Office can refer requests for assistance in serious or complex fraud, or any part of such a request, to the Director of the Serious Fraud Office to obtain such of the evidence *as may appear to the Director* to be appropriate. Under law in the UK, the Director must be satisfied on reasonable grounds that the criminal conduct in the requesting country involves "serious or complex fraud". Frauds involving sums less than £1 million would not normally be regarded as "serious".

Before referring a request to the Director, the Home Office will seek a written assurance from the requesting authority that any statement which might be made by a person in response to a requirement imposed by virtue of the Director's investigation powers will not be used in evidence against that person, without the consent of the Home Office. This assurance is required because witnesses do not in general have a right to refuse to answer questions where use is made of the Serious Fraud Office's investigation powers. The assurance is therefore an important safeguard for the witness in the event of self-incrimination. The statement may, of course, be used against the accused person(s) *named in the request* if that is considered appropriate in the requesting country.

Under UK law, the evidence obtained by the Serious Fraud Office *must* be sent by the Director to the Home Office for transmission to the requesting authority.

Further information on what constitutes "serious or complex fraud" and what should be included in a request for legal assistance in cases involving serious or complex fraud may be obtained from the Serious Fraud Office (in Scotland, the Crown Office).

How can requests for search and seizure (search warrants and production orders) be executed?

The Home Office may direct police or Customs to apply to a court for a search warrant or a production order. (A production order is an order of the court requiring the person(s) on whom the order is served to produce the evidence specified in the order).

Where further information is required about the offence or the material to be seized, depending on the particular circumstances, the Home Office will inform the requesting authorities without delay.

Where an application is made for a production order interested parties must by law be notified (by the UK authorities) and be given an opportunity to be represented in the court that is hearing the application. In such cases, the Home Office consults the requesting authorities to ensure that execution of the request would not breach any explicit confidentiality requirement of the requesting authority. Notification of interested parties is not required where an application is made for a search warrant.

There is no authority under UK law to search for and seize, or to compel production of, any items which are subject to "legal privilege". Legal privilege applies to legal advice communicated between lawyers and their clients, but does not apply to communications intended to further a criminal purpose.

Under UK law, the evidence obtained *must* be sent by the police or Customs to the Home Office for transmission to the requesting authorities abroad.

How are requests for restraint (freezing) of assets executed?

In the United Kingdom, a court order to freeze (restrain) assets may be obtained on behalf of a designated foreign jurisdiction when court proceedings which may lead to a confiscation order have been or are about to be instituted there; or if a confiscation order has already been made. It is vital therefore that any request for the restraint of assets in the United Kingdom should make clear whether a confiscation order has been made; and, if not, whether proceedings which may lead to confiscation have been instituted in the requesting state or, if not, when they expect to begin.

UK law enables a restraint or freezing order to be obtained on behalf of another country in our High Court only where that country has been designated by subsidiary legislation. Normally, a country will be designated for assistance in relation to drug assets when it ratifies the 1988 UN (Vienna) Drugs Convention; or for assistance in relation to the proceeds of all crimes when it ratifies the 1990 Council of Europe (Strasbourg) Confiscation or when a bilateral confiscation agreement with the UK is in place.

The Home Office will authorise a relevant prosecuting authority to represent the requesting Government in the High Court proceedings. Applications to the High Court in international restraint and confiscation cases are dealt with in England and Wales by two prosecuting authorities. They are the Central Confiscation Branch of the Crown Prosecution Service and the Asset Forfeiture Unit of HM Customs and Excise. As a general rule, the Central Confiscation Branch of the Crown Prosecution Service will deal with any restraint or confiscation request where a police officer has carried out the preliminary asset tracing enquiries in this country. The Home Office can advise which office might be appropriate in a particular case.

UK law requires that certain UK court orders, including restraint orders, should be served personally on the defendant and/or interested parties. Where the High Court grants a restraint order on behalf of a foreign Government, the order will normally need to be channelled through the Home Office, for service on the appropriate person(s) abroad.

Where a restraint order is granted on behalf of another government, the Home Office will confirm this fact in writing, and request that such service be effected as specified in the order. The requesting country will be asked to complete and return to the Home Office a memorandum of service. It is important that the Home Office receives the completed memorandum quickly since delays could affect the High Court's willingness to continue the order. It is helpful if the completed memorandum is received within two weeks of its despatch and that in the event of unavoidable delay, an advance copy is sent to the Home Office by fax.

How are requests for temporary transfer abroad of UK prisoners executed?

UK law allows for the temporary transfer abroad of UK prisoners, including remand prisoners, *who consent to assist* with criminal investigations and proceedings. Prisoners cannot be transferred from the UK without their consent. Requests for temporary transfer of prisoners must be sent to the Home Office.

The Home Office must be satisfied before agreeing to the transfer that the presence of the prisoner is not already required in the UK for the purposes of investigations or proceedings and that the transfer would not prolong the prisoner's period of detention.

Where the transfer is agreed with the requesting authority, the Home Office arranges for:

- the taking of the prisoner in custody to a departure point in the UK and the delivery of the prisoner into the custody of a person representing the requesting authority;
- the escorting of the prisoner back to the UK by the requesting authority; and
- the subsequent transfer of the prisoner in custody from the arrival point in the UK to his or her place of detention.

The costs of escorting and accommodating prisoners from their point of departure from the UK to their point of return to the UK are borne by the requesting authority.

CHAPTER 5: HOME OFFICE CODE OF PRACTICE

The Home Office aims to ensure that requests for legal assistance are executed promptly, taking account of urgency, and that requesting authorities are kept informed of progress.

All requests received by the Home Office are acknowledged and the requesting authorities are given the name and contact details of the person in the Home Office responsible for co-ordinating its execution. As soon as possible, the Home Office will inform the requesting authority how the request is to be executed. In the relatively few instances where a request cannot be executed in whole or in part, the Home Office will provide an explanation and consult with the requesting authority about whether the assistance can be provided in a different way.

Where possible, the Home Office will give requesting authorities the contact details of the police or Customs officer or court official or other person to whom the request, or part of the request, has been referred for the purposes of executing the request. **That person may then be contacted directly by the requesting authorities.**

Any enquiries about requests that have been sent to the Home Office are also acknowledged and dealt with as quickly as possible. When making enquiries, the Home Office's reference number for the request should be quoted as this speeds up retrieval of information on the status of the request.

The sooner the Home Office is told about any difficulties which the requesting authorities may be having with any requests, the sooner the Home Office is able to reassure the requesting authorities that the matter is being dealt with.

The Home Office has published a Code of Practice. This is a set of standards that the Home Office applies in dealing with requests for legal assistance. The standards are closely monitored. The Code is set out at Annex B.

ANNEX A: CONDUCTING ENQUIRIES IN OR SEEKING ASSISTANCE FROM THE UNITED KINGDOM

THE COMPETENCIES OF THE HOME OFFICE (UK CENTRAL AUTHORITY) AND NCIS (UK NATIONAL CENTRAL BUREAU OF INTERPOL)

The examples below are intended to indicate whether the Home Office, as UK Central Authority for mutual assistance in criminal matters, or the UK National Central Bureau of Interpol (Interpol London) at the UK National Criminal Intelligence Service, is more appropriate for conducting enquiries in or seeking assistance from the UK.

COMPETENCIES OF THE HOME OFFICE INCLUDE:	COMPETENCIES OF THE UK NATIONAL CENTRAL BUREAU OF INTERPOL INCLUDE:
Serving a summons or other judicial document requiring a person to appear before a judicial authority in the requesting country as a witness or defendant in criminal proceedings.	Interviewing witnesses and suspects in criminal investigations where the person to be interviewed is willing to co-operate without appearing before a judicial authority in the UK and where any statement made would be unsworn.
Obtaining sworn evidence or other authenticated or certified evidence, including banking documentation, for use in criminal proceedings or investigations.	Tracing assets in investigations preliminary to prosecution, particularly where the offence involves money laundering.
Authenticating or certifying evidence for use in the requesting country where that evidence has already been obtained by the UK police for their own purposes.	Sharing with the requesting country information concerning investigations into offences which have been committed in the UK.
Exercise of search and seizure powers where evidence is required for use in criminal proceedings or investigations.	Obtaining medical or dental statements or records where the patient has given written consent.
Temporarily transferring prisoners, with their consent, to the requesting country to appear as witnesses in criminal proceedings or to assist in criminal investigations.	Providing details of previous convictions:
	• for the purposes of police investigations, vetting applicants for employment in law enforcement or for work with access to children or suitability for owning firearms and holding gambling licences – when provided with a copy of the person's fingerprints.
	• for police intelligence purposes *only* – without fingerprints.
	Providing telephone subscriber details (UK telephone companies can provide only the family name and the initial of the subscriber and the address where the telephone is located).
	Seizing and securing in the UK property stolen abroad. Police in the UK can seize and retain property where the person in possession of it in the UK is suspected of knowing that the property is stolen.
	Providing passport details (all details held by the UK Passport Agency can be Provided including any photographs held).
	Providing medical samples (body orifice swabs and samples of blood, saliva, semen, hair, urine and other tissue fluids can be obtained with the consent of the person from whom the sample is required).
	Providing details of keepers of motor vehicles registered in the UK and of driving licences issued in the UK.

Requests to the United Kingdom for evidence

The Home Office, being the central authority for the United Kingdom in mutual legal assistance in criminal matters, will:

- acknowledge all requests for evidence upon receipt, giving the name of the Home Office officer handling the request, his or her telephone and fax numbers and a reference number for any queries;
- respond to all enquiries about the execution of requests for assistance within 10 working days of receipt;
- upon receipt of the request where the request is marked "urgent", or no later than 20 working days after receipt in other cases, either: provide the requesting authority with the assistance sought; or inform the requesting authority of the action being taken to obtain the assistance and provide, where possible, the name(s) and other contact details of the person(s) with responsibilities for executing the request, or provide the requesting authority with a full explanation why the request cannot be executed in its entirety or in part and where possible indicate how the assistance might otherwise be obtained;
- if the requesting authority notifies the United Kingdom that it is necessary, provide with 20 working days of receipt of the notification a report on the progress of the request and, where possible, indicate by when the request will be executed and update that report on a similar time scale;
- endeavour to meet all reasonable time scales for the execution of requests, including urgent requests.

Requests to the United Kingdom for service of process (summonses and other procedural documents)

The Home Office will:

- arrange for the execution of all requests for service of summonses within 10 working days of receipt;
- execute all requests for service of process in the manner requested insofar as that is compatible with UK law, and where that is not possible provide the requesting authorities with a full explanation;
- acknowledge simultaneously the receipt and the execution of requests for service of summonses (unless the Home Office has not received signed proof of service at least 10 working days before the hearing date, in which case the acknowledgement will confirm the arrangements made to execute the request);
- acknowledge simultaneously the receipt and the execution of requests for service of judgements and other procedural documents at the same time (unless the Home Office has not received signed proof of service after 30 working days, in which case the acknowledgement will confirm the arrangements made to execute the request);
- when acknowledging requests for service of procedural documents, provide the requesting authorities with the name and other contact details of the officer in the Home Office who has handled the request, including telephone and fax numbers and a reference number for any queries.

ANNEX C: CONTACT DETAILS FOR THE HOME OFFICE AND OTHER RELEVANT UK AUTHORITIES

Requests for legal assistance

Mutual Legal Assistance Section Judicial Co-operation Unit Home Office 50 Queen Anne's Gate London SW1H 9AT

Tel: +44 207 273 2437
Fax: +44 207 273 4400/4584

The Judicial Co-operation Unit at the Home Office has a round-the-clock answer phone facility and may be contacted out-of-hours by dialling: +44 1523 523523 (an operator will take the call who should be given pager number 657782 and a message which will be relayed to the legal assistance duty officer).

Requests for investigative assistance

UK National Central Bureau of Interpol (Interpol London) National Criminal Intelligence Service PO Box 8000 London SE11 5EN

Contact with Interpol London should be made through the National Central Bureau of Interpol in the requesting country.

Tel (24 hours): + 44 207 238 8115
Fax: +44 207 238 8112
Telex: 918734
Encrypted e-Mail: Via X400

Requests in cases of serious or complex fraud

Preliminary, informal enquiries may be sent to: Serious Fraud Office Elm House 10–16 Elm Street London WC1X OBJ

Tel: +44 207 239 7272
Fax: +44 207 833 5430

Requests for execution in Scotland

Preliminary, informal enquiries may be sent to:

Fraud and Specialist Services Unit Crown Office 25 Chambers Street Edinburgh EH1 1LA

Tel: +44 131 226 2626
Fax: +44 131 226 6861

Advice on UK criminal law and procedure

Casework Directorate Crown Prosecution Service 50 Ludgate Hill London EC4M 7EX

Tel: +44 207 273 1382
Fax: +44 207 329 8171

Requests for administrative assistance in Customs matters

HM Customs & Excise International Criminal Division Solicitor's Office New King's Beam House 22 Upper Ground London SE1 9PJ

Tel: +44 207 865 5167
Fax: +44 207 865 5654

Advice on making requests for restraint and confiscation of assets

Central Confiscation Branch Crown Prosecution Service 50 Ludgate Hill London EC4M 7EX

Tel: +44 207 796 8283
Fax: +44 207 796 8270

Asset Forfeiture Unit Solicitor's Office HM Customs and Excise New King's Beam House 22 Upper Ground London SE1 9PJ

Tel: +44 207 865 5187
Fax: +44 207 865 5902

Requests for extradition of fugitives

Extradition Section Judicial Co-operation Unit Home Office 50 Queen Anne's Gate London SW1H 9AT

Tel: +44 207 273 3991
Fax: +44 207 273 2496

Requests for administrative assistance in revenue tax matters

Inland Revenue Solicitor's Office Somerset House London WC2R 1LB

Tel: +44 207 438 7091
Fax: +44 207 438 6246

Requests for regulatory assistance in companies matters

Department of Trade & Industry Investigations & Enforcement Directorate 10 Victoria Street London SW1 ONN

Tel: +44 207 215 3021
Fax: +44 207 215 3115

ANNEX D: CONTACT DETAILS FOR AUTHORITIES IN THE CHANNEL ISLANDS, THE ISLE OF MAN AND THE UK OVERSEAS TERRITORIES

Requests for execution in the Channel Islands and the Isle of Man

Guernsey

HM Attorney General Attorney General's Chambers St James Chambers St Peter Port Guernsey GY1 2PA

Tel: +44 1481 723355
Fax: +44 1481 725439

Isle of Man

Attorney General's Chambers 2nd Floor New Wing Victory House Douglas ISLE OF MAN IM1 3PP

Tel: +44 1624 685452
Fax: +44 1624 629162

Jersey

HM Attorney General Attorney General's Chambers Morier House St Helier Jersey JE1 1DD

Tel: +44 1534 502280
Fax: +44 1534 502299

Requests for execution in the UK Overseas Territories (details of authorities not listed are obtainable from the Home Office)

Anguilla

The Attorney-General The Attorney-General's Chambers The Secretariat The Valley Anguilla

Tel: +1 264 497 3044
Fax: +1 264 497 3126

Bermuda

The Attorney-General's Chambers Global House 43 Church Street Hamilton HM12 Bermuda

Tel: +1 441 292 2463
Fax: +1 441 292 3608

British Virgin Islands

The Attorney-General The Attorney-General's Chambers Government of the British Virgin Islands PO Box 242 Road Town Tortola

Tel: +1 284 494 3701
Fax: +1 284 494 6760

Cayman Islands

The Attorney-General The Attorney-General's Chambers Government Administration Building George Town, Grand Cayman Cayman Islands
Tel: +1 345 949 7900
Fax: +1 345 949 6079

Gibraltar

Attorney-General

Attorney-General's Department 17 Town Range Gibraltar
Tel: + 350 70723
Fax: + 350 79891

Montserrat

The Attorney-General The Attorney-General's Chambers PO Box 129 Olveston Montserrat
Tel: +1 664 491 4686
Fax: +1 664 491 4687

Turks and Caicos Islands

The Governor Government House Grand Turk Turks and Caicos Islands
Tel: +1 649 946 2308
Fax: +1 649 946 2903

JOINT ACTION of 29 June 1998 adopted by the Council on the basis of Article K.3 of the Treaty on European Union, on good practice in mutual legal assistance in criminal matters

(98/427/JHA)

THE COUNCIL OF THE EUROPEAN UNION,

Having regard to the Treaty on European Union, and in particular Article K.3(2)(b) thereof,

Having regard to the Report from the high-level group on organised crime([1]) approved by the European Council held at Amsterdam on 16 and 17 June 1997, and in particular Recommendation No 16 of the Report,

Having regard to the results of the seminar on "Improving judicial cooperation and protecting human rights" held in Luxembourg on 1 and 2 October 1997,

Taking into account the Joint Action 98/428/JHA of 29 June 1998, adopted by the Council on the basis of Article K.3 of the Treaty on European Union, on the creation of a European Judicial Network ([2]), and in particular Articles 4 and 5 thereof,

Having regard to the European Convention on Mutual Assistance in Criminal Matters of 20 April 1959, other conventions in force in this area and the proposed Convention on mutual assistance in criminal matters between the Member States,

Whereas it is necessary to make further practical improvements regarding mutual legal assistance between the Member States, particularly for the purpose of combating serious crime.

Having examined the views of the European Parliament ([3]), following consultation carried out by the Presidency in accordance with Article K.6 of the Treaty,

HAS ADOPTED THE FOLLOWING JOINT ACTION:

Article 1

Statements of good practice

1. Each Member State shall deposit with the General Secretariat of the Council of the European Union within 12 months of the coming into force of this Joint Action a Statement of good practice in executing requests, including transmission of results, from other Member States and sending requests to other Member States for legal assistance in criminal matters.

2. The General Secretariat of the Council shall translate the Statements referred to in paragraph 1 into the official languages of the Community and circulate the translations to Member States.

3. The Statements by each Member State referred to in paragraph 1 shall, without prejudice to the provisions of the proposed Convention on mutual assistance in criminal matters between the Member States, and subject to the Declaration annexed to this Joint Action, include undertakings to promote the following practices in accordance with its national law and legal procedures:

---

1 OJ C 251, 15. 8. 1997, p. 1.
2 See page 4 of this Official Journal.
3 Opinion delivered on 3 April 1998 (OJ C 138, 4. 5. 1998).

(a)   where requested to do so by the requesting Member State, to acknowledge all requests and written enquiries concerning the execution of requests unless a substantive reply is sent quickly; the requesting Member State may not require an acknowledgment unless the request is marked "urgent" by that Member State or, in its view, an acknowledgement is necessary in the light of the circumstances of the case;

(b)   when acknowledging the requests and enquiries referred to in this paragraph, to provide the requesting authority with the name and contact details, including telephone and fax numbers, of the authority, and if possible the person, responsible for executing the request;

(c)   to give priority, as far as it is not contrary to the law of the requested Member State, to requests which have clearly been marked "urgent" by the requesting authority, and to treat requests, whether or not marked "urgent", no less favourably than comparable enquiries made in the requested Member State on behalf of that Member State's own authorities;

(d)   where the assistance requested cannot be executed in whole or in part, to give the requesting authorities a written or oral report explaining the difficulty and where possible offering to consider jointly with the requesting authority how the difficulty might be overcome;

(e)   where it is foreseeable that the assistance cannot, or cannot fully, be provided within any deadline set by the requesting Member State and that this will impair proceedings in the requesting Member State, promptly to give its authority a written or oral report, and any further reports requested by that authority explaining when the assistance requested is likely to be provided;

(f)   to submit requests for assistance as soon as the precise assistance needed is identified and, where a request is marked "urgent" or a deadline is indicated, to explain the reasons for the urgency or deadline; the Statement shall include an undertaking not to mark as "urgent" requests which are of minor importance;

(g)   to ensure that requests are submitted in compliance with the relevant treaty or other international arrangements;

(h)   when submitting requests for assistance, to provide the requested authorities with the name and contact details, including telephone and fax numbers, of the authority and, if possible, the person responsible for issuing the request.

4. Each Member State shall bring its Statement to the attention of its judicial or competent authorities, inviting them to promote measures within their competence as may be necessary with a view to its implementation.

5. Any Statement submitted in accordance with this Article may, without prejudice to paragraph 3, be modified at any time by the Member State which made it by means of a further Statement deposited with the General Secretariat of the Council. Any such further Statement shall be for the purposes of further improving good practice in executing requests for legal assistance in criminal matters.

Article 2

Review of performance

Without prejudice to the mechanism for evaluating the application and implementation at national level of international undertakings in the fight against organised crime, established in Joint Action 97/827/JHA ([1]), each Member State shall periodically review compliance with its Statements made in accordance with Article 1. The mechanism for such review shall be for each Member State to determine having regard to its own arrangements for legal assistance in criminal matters.

Article 3

European Judicial Network

The General Secretariat of the Council shall make the Statements referred to in Article 1(1) available to the European Judicial Network as soon as they are deposited. The Network shall

---

(1) OJ L 344, 15.12.1997, p.7.

take stock of the Statements in the light of its own competencies and experience, and may make any proposals it considers appropriate with a view to improving legal assistance in criminal matters, including finding common methods for evaluation of performance.

Article 4

Review

The Council shall review this Joint Action in the light of the results of the operation of the mechanism for evaluating the application and implementation at national level of international undertakings in the fight against organised crime, established in Joint Action 97/827/JHA.

Article 5

Entry into force

This Joint Action shall enter into force on the day of its publication.

Article 6

Publication

This Joint Action shall be published in the Official Journal.
    Done at Luxembourg, 29 June 1998.
For the Council The President R. COOK

Joint Action on Good Practice in Mutual Legal Assistance in Criminal Matters

Statement of good practice submitted by the United Kingdom in accordance with article 1 of the joint action

Requests to the United Kingdom for evidence

The Home Office, being the central authority for the United Kingdom in mutual legal assistance in criminal matters, will:

- acknowledge all requests for evidence upon receipt, giving the name of the Home Office officer handling the request, his or her telephone and fax numbers and a reference number for any queries;
- respond to all general enquiries about the execution of requests for assistance within 10 working days of receipt;
- upon receipt of the request where the request is marked "urgent", or no later than 20 working days after receipt in other cases, either: provide the requesting authority with the assistance sought; or inform the requesting authority of the action being taken to obtain the assistance and provide where possible the name(s) and other contact details of the person(s) with responsibilities for executing the request; or provide the requesting authority with a full explanation why the request cannot be executed in its entirety or in part and where possible indicate how the assistance might otherwise be obtained;
- if the requesting authority notifies the United Kingdom that it is necessary, provide within 20 working days of receipt of the notification a report on the progress of the request and where possible indicate by when the request will be executed, and update that report on a similar time scale;
- endeavour to meet all reasonable time scales for the execution of requests, including urgent requests.

Requests to the United Kingdom for service of process (summonses and other procedural documents)

The Home Office will:

- arrange for the execution of all requests for service of summonses within 10 working days of receipt;
- execute all requests for service of process in the manner requested insofar as that is compatible with United Kingdom law, and where that is not possible provide the requesting authorities with a full explanation;
- acknowledge simultaneously the receipt and the execution of requests for service of summonses (unless the Home Office has not received signed proof of service at least 10 working days before the hearing date, in which case the acknowledgement will confirm the arrangements made to execute the request);
- acknowledge simultaneously the receipt and the execution of requests for service of judgements and other procedural documents (unless the Home Office has not received signed proof of service after 30 working days, in which case the acknowl- edgement will confirm the arrangements made to execute the request);
- when acknowledging requests for service of procedural documents, provide the requesting authorities with the name and other contact details of the officer in the Home Office who has handled the request, including telephone and fax numbers and a reference number for any queries.

Requests from the United Kingdom to other member states

The Home Office will:

- ensure that requests received from judicial and prosecuting authorities in the United Kingdom for transmission abroad specify the name and contact details of the issuing authority, and include the name of the Home Office officer handling the request, his or her telephone and fax numbers and a reference number for any enquiries;

- ensure that the requests are in conformity with relevant treaty and other international obligations;
- ensure that any request which is of minor importance is not marked "urgent", and that no request is marked "urgent" or sets any deadline for execution of the request unless the reason for the urgency or deadline is stated;
- not ask for a request to be acknowledged where the request is not marked "urgent" or the request does not explain why an acknowledgement is necessary.

Other Matters

The Home Office has brought this Statement to the attention of judicial and other competent authorities in the United Kingdom asking them to:

- take reasonable steps to ensure that requests are submitted as soon as the need for the assistance is identified;
- promote measures within their competence as may be necessary to ensure that the undertakings in this Statement are fulfilled.

The Home Office will review compliance with the undertakings in this Statement before 31 December 2000.

JOINT ACTION of 29 June 1998 adopted by the Council on the basis of Article K.3 of the Treaty on European Union, on the creation of a European Judicial Network

(98/428/JHA)

THE COUNCIL OF THE EUROPEAN UNION,

Having regard to the Treaty on European Union, and in particular K.3(2)(b) thereof,

Having regard to the initiative taken by the Kingdom of Belgium,

Having regard to the Action Plan to combat organised crime approved by the European Council in Amsterdam on 17 June 1997, and in particular Recommendation No 21 thereof,

Bearing in mind the need for coordination between this initiative and the implementation of Recommendation No 19 in that Action Plan,

Taking into account the conclusions of the seminars on "The European judicial network and organised crime", held in Brussels from 8 to 10 May 1996 and on 19 and 20 June 1997, which were organised by the Belgian Ministry of Justice within the framework of a programme partly financed by the European Union, and also of the proceedings of the European Parliament and the European Commission,

Bearing in mind the Joint Action 96/277/JHA of 22 April 1996 concerning a framework for the exchange of liaison magistrates to improve judicial cooperation between the Member States of the European Union (¹),

Whereas it is necessary to make further improvements to judicial cooperation between the Member States of the European Union, particularly in combating forms of serious crime often perpetrated by actual, in most cases transnational, organisations;

Whereas effective improvement of judicial cooperation between the Member States requires the adoption of structural measures at European Union level to enable the appropriate direct contacts to be set up between judicial authorities and other authorities responsible for judicial cooperation and judicial action against forms of serious crime, within Member States;

Whereas this Joint Action is without prejudice to existing conventions and agreements, in particular the European Convention on Mutual Assistance in Criminal Matters of 20 April 1959,

HAS ADOPTED THIS JOINT ACTION:

TITLE I

PRINCIPLES OF THE EUROPEAN JUDICIAL NETWORK

Article 1

Creation

A network of judicial contact points shall be set up between the Member States, hereinafter referred to as "the European Judicial Network".

---

1 OJ L 105, 27, 4. 1996, p. 1.

Article 2

Composition

1. The European Judicial Network shall be made up, taking into account the constitutional rules, legal traditions and internal structure of each Member State, of the central authorities responsible for international judicial cooperation and the judicial or other competent authorities with specific responsibilities within the context of international cooperation, both generally and for certain forms of serious crime, such as organised crime, corruption, drug-trafficking or terrorism.

2. One or more contact points of each Member State shall be established in accordance with its internal rules and internal division of responsibilities, taking care to ensure effective coverage of the whole of its territory and of all forms of serious crime.

3. Each Member State shall ensure that its contact point or points have an adequate knowledge of a language of the European Union other than its own national language, bearing in mind the need to be able to communicate with the contact points in the other Member States.

4. Where the liaison magistrates referred to in Joint Action 96/277/JHA have duties analogous to those assigned by Article 4 to the contact points, they may be linked to the European Judicial Network by the Member State appointing the liaison magistrate in each case, in accordance with the procedures to be laid down by that State.

5. The Commission shall designate a contact point for those areas falling within its sphere of competence.

Article 3

Manner of operation of the network

The European Judicial Network shall operate in particular in the following three ways:

  (a)   it shall facilitate the establishment of appropriate contacts between the contact points in the various Member States in order to carry out the functions laid down in Article 4;

  (b)   it shall organise periodic meetings of the Member States' representatives in accordance with the procedures laid down in Articles 5, 6 and 7;

  (c)   it shall constantly provide a certain amount of up-to-date background information, notably by means of an appropriate telecommunications network, under the procedures laid down in Articles 8, 9 and 10.

TITLE II

CONTACTS WITHIN THE NETWORK

Article 4

Functions of contact points

1. The contact points shall be active intermediaries with the task of facilitating judicial cooperation between Member States, particularly in action to combat forms of serious crime. They shall be available to enable local judicial authorities and other competent authorities in their own country, contact points in the other countries and local judicial and other competent authorities in the other countries to establish the most appropriate direct contacts.

They may if necessary travel to meet other Member State' contact points, on the basis of an agreement between the administrations concerned.

2. The contract points shall provide the legal and practical information necessary to the local judicial authorities in their own country, to the contact points in the other countries and to the local judicial authorities in the other countries to enable them to prepare an effective request for judicial cooperation or to improve judicial cooperation in general.

3. They shall improve coordination of judicial cooperation in cases where a series of requests from the local judicial authorities in a Member State necessitates coordinated action in another Member State.

TITLE III

PERIODIC MEETINGS OF THE EUROPEAN JUDICIAL NETWORK

Article 5

Purpose of the periodic meetings

1. The aims of the periodic meetings of the European Judicial Network shall be as follows:
  (a) to allow the contact points to get to know each other and exchange experience, particularly concerning the operation of the network;
  (b) to provide a forum for discussion of practical and legal problems encountered by the Member States in the context of judicial cooperation, in particular with regard to the implementation of measures adopted by the European Union.

2. The relevant experience acquired within the European Judicial Network shall be passed on to the competent European Union working parties to serve as a basis for discussion of possible legislative changes and practical improvements in the area of international judicial cooperation.

Article 6

Frequency of meetings

1. The European Judicial Network shall first meet within three months following the entry into force of this Joint Action.
  2. The European Judicial Network shall thereafter meet periodically on an *ad hoc* basis, as its members feel the need, at the invitation of the Presidency of the Council, which shall also take account of the Member States' wishes for the Network to meet.

Article 7

Venue of meetings

1. Meetings shall in principle be held on the premises of the Council in Brussels, in accordance with the provisions laid down in the Council's Rules of Procedure.
  2. However, alternative meetings in the Member States should be contemplated, to enable the contact points of all the Member States to meet authorities of the host State other than its contact points and visit specific bodies in that State with responsibilities in the context of international judicial cooperation or of combating certain forms of serious crime.

TITLE IV

INFORMATION AVAILABLE WITHIN THE EUROPEAN JUDICIAL NETWORK

Article 8

Content of the information disseminated within the European Judicial Network

The contact points must have permanent access to the following four types of information:
  1. full details of the contact points in each Member State with, where necessary, an explanation of their responsibilities at national level;

2.   a simplified list of the judicial authorities and a directory of the local authorities in each Member State;
3.   concise legal and practical information concerning the judicial and procedural systems in the 15 Member States;
4.   the texts of the relevant legal instruments and, for conventions currently in force, the texts of declarations and reservations.

Article 9

UPDATING OF INFORMATION

1. The information distributed within the European Judicial Network must without fail be constantly updated.
2. It shall be each Member State's individual responsibility to check the accuracy of the data contained in the system and to inform the Council immediately as soon as data on one of the four points referred to in Article 8 need to be amended.
3. The General Secretariat of the Council shall be responsible for the administration of the Network set up under this Joint Action. In particular, it shall be responsible for making the information referred to in Article 8 available to members of the European Judicial Network and for keeping the information required for the proper functioning of the Network constantly updated.

TITLE V

TELECOMMUNICATIONS NETWORK

Article 10

Report concerning a telecommunications system

1. Within six months of the entry into force of this Joint Action, the Council shall examine, on the basis of a report from the Presidency, drawn up after consultation of the European Judicial Network, whether the Network should be linked by a telecommunications network.
2. The Council shall lay down the details of the configuration of the telecommunications system in a decision taken by a qualified majority, in accordance with Article K.3(2)(b) of the Treaty on European Union.

TITLE VI

FINAL PROVISIONS

Article 11

Territorial application

As regards the United Kingdom, the provisions of this joint Action shall apply to the United Kingdom of Great Britain and Northern Ireland, the Channel Islands and the Isle of Man.

Article 12

Assessment of the operation of the European Judicial Network

The Council shall carry out an initial assessment of the operation of the European Judicial Network at the close of the start-up phase, which shall end one year after the entry into force of this Joint Action.

Thereafter the Council shall, every three years on the Presidency's initiative, carry out an assessment for the operation of the European Judicial Network on the basis of a report drawn up by the Network.

When the first trienial report is examined, the Council shall look at the postion and role that the Network might fulfil *vis-à-vis* Europol, on the basis of experience of the operation of the network and of the development of Europol's powers.

Article 13

Entry into force
This Joint Action shall enter into force one month after the date of its publication in the Official Journal.

Article 14

Publication
The Joint Action shall be published in the Official Journal.

Done at Luxembourg, 29 June 1998.

For the Council
The President
R. COOK

ANNEX

COUNCIL DECLARATION

The Council declares that Article 11 of the Joint Action on the creation of a European Judicial Network is without prejudice to the territorial application of other instruments.

THE MAGISTRATES' COURTS (CRIMINAL JUSTICE (INTERNATIONAL CO-OPERATION)) RULES 1991

S.I. 1991 No. 1074

Made	*25th April 1991*
Laid before Parliament	*8th May 1991*
Coming into force	*10th June 1991*

The Lord Chancellor, in exercise of the powers conferred on him by section 144 of the Magistrates' Courts Act 1980(a) as extended by section 145 of that Act and section 10 of the Criminal Justice (International Co-operation) Act 1990(b), after consultation with the Rule Committee appointed under the said section 144, hereby makes the following Rules:

Citation and commencement

1. These Rules may be cited as the Magistrates' Courts (Criminal Justice (International Co-operation)) Rules 1991 and shall come into force on 10th June 1991.

Interpretation

2. In these Rules "the Act" means the Criminal Justice (International Co-operation) Act 1990.

Service of summons or order outside the United Kingdom

3. Where a summons is issued or order is made by a magistrates' court in accordance with section 2(1) of the Act for service outside the United Kingdom it shall be sent by the justices' clerk to the Secretary of State with a view to its being served there in accordance with arrangements made by the Secretary of State.

Proof of service of summons outside the United Kingdom

4.—(1) The service on any person of a summons issued under section 2(1) of the Act may be proved in any legal proceedings by a certificate given by or on behalf of the Secretary of State.

 (2) A statement in any such certificate as is mentioned in paragraph (1) above:

  (a) that a summons has been served;
  (b) of the manner in which service was effected;
  (c) of the date upon which a summons was served.

shall be admissible as evidence of any facts so stated.

Notice of application for letters of request

5. Notice of an application under section 3(1) (overseas evidence for use in the United Kingdom) of the Act shall be given to the justices' clerk of a magistrates' court and shall—

  (a) be made in writing, save that the court may in exceptional circumstances dispense with the need for notice;

(a) 1980 c. 43.
(b) 1990 c. 5.

(b)   state the particulars of the offence which it is alleged has been committed or the grounds upon which it is suspected that an offence has been committed;

(c)   state whether proceedings in respect of the offence have been instituted or the offence is being investigated; and

(d)   include particulars of the assistance requested in the form of a draft letter of request.

Hearing of application for letters of request

6.—(1) An application under section 3(1) of the Act—

(a)   shall be heard in a petty-sessional court-house;

(b)   may be heard *ex parte*.

(2) When hearing an application under section 3(1) of the Act the court may, if it thinks it necessary in the interests of justice, direct that the public be excluded from the court.

(3) The powers conferred on a magistrates' court by the preceding paragraph shall be in addition and without prejudice to any other powers of the court to hear proceedings in camera.

Letters of request in urgent cases

7. Where in a case of urgency a magistrates' court sends a letter of request direct to any court or tribunal in accordance with section 3(5) of the Act, the justices' clerk shall forthwith notify the Secretary of State of this and send with the notification a copy of the letter of request.

Proceedings before a nominated court

8.—(1) In proceedings before a nominated court pursuant to a notice under section 4(2) of the Act the court may, if it thinks it necessary in the interests of justice, direct that the public be excluded from the court.

(2) The powers conferred on a magistrates' court by the preceding paragraph shall be in addition and without prejudice to any other powers of the court to hear proceedings in camera.

Court register of proceedings before a nominated court

9.—(1) Where a magistrates' court receives evidence in proceedings pursuant to a notice under section 4(2) of the Act, the justices' clerk shall note in the register—

(a)   particulars of the proceedings;

(b)   without prejudice to the generality of (a) above—

    (i)   which persons with an interest in the proceedings were present;

    (ii)   which of the said persons were represented and by whom;

    (iii)   whether any of the said persons were denied the opportunity of cross-examining a witness as to any part of his testimony.

(2) Such part of the register as relates to proceedings mentioned in paragraph (1) above shall be kept in a separate book.

(3) Save as authorised by the Secretary of State, or with the leave of the court, such part of the register as relates to proceedings mentioned in paragraph (1) above shall not be open to inspection by any person.

(4) When so requested by the Secretary of State, the justices' clerk shall send to him a copy of an extract of the register as it relates to any proceedings mentioned in paragraph (1) above.

25th April 1991

Mackay of Clashfern, C.

Explanatory Note

(This note is not part of the Rules)

These Rules govern the procedure to be followed by magistrates' courts in England and Wales in relation to the provisions of Part I of the Criminal Justice (International Co-operation) Act 1990. Rule 3 provides for a summons or order issued under section 2(1) of the Act (for service outside the United Kingdom) to be sent to the Secretary of State for onward transmission and rule 4 provides for the admissibility in evidence of a certificate issued by the Secretary of State stating that a summons so issued has been served, its manner and date of service. Rule 5 provides for a written notice of application to be made where a magistrates' court is to be asked to issue a letter of request, under section 3 of the Act. Rule 6 provides that the public may in the interests of justice be excluded from a hearing of an application for a letter of request. Rule 7 provides that where in urgent cases the court sends a letter of request directly to a court or tribunal outside the United Kingdom, a copy shall be sent to the Secretary of State. Rule 8 makes similar provision to rule 6 for proceedings in a nominated court under section 4(2) of the Act (taking evidence for use overseas). Rule 9 prescribes that the court register of such proceedings shall not be open to public inspection.

THE CROWN COURT (Amendment) RULES 1991

(S.I. 1991 No. 1288)

Made	*27th May 1991*
Laid before Parliament	*10th June 1991*
Coming into force	*1st July 1991*

We, the Crown Court Rule Committee, in exercise of the powers conferred upon us by sections 84(1) and 86 of the Supreme Court Act 1981(a), and section 10 of the Criminal Justice (International Co-operation) Act 1990(b), hereby make the following Rules:

1. These Rules may be cited as the Crown Court (Amendment) Rules 1991 and shall come into force on 1st July 1991.

2. The Crown Court Rules 1982(c) shall be amended by the insertion after rule 29 of the following rules:

"**Service of summons or order outside the United Kingdom**

30. Where a witness summons or order is issued or made by the Crown Court in accordance with section 2(1) of the Criminal Justice (International Co-operation) Act 1990 for service outside the United Kingdom it shall be sent forthwith by the appropriate officer of the Crown Court to the Secretary of State with a view to its being served there in accordance with arrangements made by the Secretary of State.

Application for Letters of Request

31.—(1) Notice of an application under section 3(1) of the Criminal Justice (International Co-operation) Act 1990 (overseas evidence for use in the United Kingdom) shall be given to the appropriate officer of the Crown Court and shall—

    (a)   be made in writing, save that the court may in exceptional circumstances dispense with the need for notice;

    (b)   state the particulars of the offence which it is alleged has been committed or the grounds upon which it is suspected that an offence has been committed;

    (c)   state whether proceedings in respect of the offence have been instituted or the offence is being investigated;

    (d)   include particulars of the assistance requested in the form of a draft letter of request.

(2) The application may be heard ex parte.

(3) When hearing the application the court may, if it thinks it necessary in the interests of justice, direct that the public be excluded from the court.

(4) The powers conferred on the Crown Court by paragraph (3) above shall be in addition and without prejudice to any other powers of the court to hear proceedings in camera.

(5) Where in a case of urgency the Crown Court sends a letter of request direct to any court or tribunal in accordance with section 3(5) of the Criminal Justice (International Co-operation)

(a) 1981 c. 54.
(b) 1990 c. 5.
(c) S.I. 1982/1109, to which there are amendments not relevant to these rules.

Act 1990, the appropriate officer of the Crown Court shall forthwith notify the Secretary of State of this and send with the notification a copy of the letter of request.

Proceedings before a nominated court

32.—(1) Where the Crown Court receives evidence in proceedings before a nominated court in pursuance of a notice under section 4(2) of the Criminal Justice (International Co-operation) Act 1990 the court may, if it thinks it necessary in the interests of justice, direct that the public be excluded from the court.

(2) The powers conferred on the Crown Court by paragraph (1) above shall be in addition and without prejudice to any other powers of the court to hear proceedings in camera.

(3) Where the Crown Court receives evidence in proceedings mentioned in paragraph (10 above the appropriate officer of the Crown Court shall make a record of—

   (a)   which persons with an interest in the proceedings were present;
   (b)   which of the said persons were represented and by whom;
   (c)   whether any of the said persons were denied the opportunity of cross-examining a witness as to any part of his testimony and the reasons for any such denial.

(4) When so requested by the Secretary of State, the appropriate officer of the Crown Court shall send to him a copy of the record as mentioned in paragraph (3) above.

Application for increase in term of imprisonment in default of payment – drug trafficking

33.—(1) The following provisions of this rule shall have effect for the purposes of applications under subsection (2) of section 15 of the Criminal Justice (International Co-operation) Act 1990 (which provides for interest on sums unpaid under confiscation orders in drug trafficking cases).

(2) Notice of application under subsection (2) of the said section 15 to increase the term of imprisonment or detention fixed in default of payment of a confiscation order by a person ("the defendant") shall be made by the prosecutor in writing to the appropriate officer of the Crown Court.

(3) A notice under paragraph (2) above shall—

   (a)   state the name and address of the defendant;
   (b)   specify the grounds for the application;
   (c)   give details of the enforcement measures taken, if any; and
   (d)   include a copy of the confiscation order.

(4) On receiving a notice under paragraph (2) above, the appropriate officer of the Crown Court shall—

   (a)   forthwith send to the defendant and the magistrates' court required to enforce payment of the confiscation order under section 32(1) of the Powers of Criminal Courts Act 1973(a), a copy of the said notice; and
   (b)   notify in writing the applicant and the defendant of the date, time and place appointed for the hearing of the application.

(5) Where the Crown Court makes an order pursuant to an application mentioned in paragraph (1) above, the appropriate officer of the Crown Court shall send forthwith a copy of the order—

   (a)   to the applicant;
   (b)   to the defendant;
   (c)   where the defendant is at the time of the making of the order in custody, to the person having custody of him; and
   (d)   to the magistrates' court mentioned in paragraph (4)(a) above."

Dated 27th May 1991

Mackay of Clashfern, C.,
Lane, C.J.,
Russell, L.J.,
Rougier, J.,
J. A. Henham,
Michael McKenzie,

P. F. Guggenheim,
David Jeffreys,
M. D. L. Kalisher,
S.T. Hammond.

Explanatory Note

(This note is not part of the Rules)

These Rules amend the Crown Court Rules 1982 to govern procedures arising out of the provisions of the Criminal Justice (International Co-operation) Act 1990 and the Drug Trafficking Offences Act 1986 (c.32). Rule 30 provides for a witness summons or order issued under section 2(1) of the 1990 Act (for service outside the United Kingdom) to be sent to the Secretary of State for onward transmission. Rule 31 governs the procedure to be followed where the Crown Court is to be asked to issue a letter of request under section 3 of the 1990 Act. Rule 32 governs the procedure where the Crown Court has been nominated to receive evidence under section 4(2) of the 1990 Act. Rule 33 contains procedural provisions concerning an application under section 15(2) of the 1990 Act for the term of imprisonment or detention fixed in default of payment of a confiscation order under the 1986 Act to be increased to take account of interest on the unsatisfied order.

Appendix P

CRIMINAL JUSTICE ACT 1987
(as amended)

(1987 C. 38)

Arrangement of Sections

Part I
Fraud

Serious Fraud Office

Transfer of cases to Crown Court

Preparatory hearing

Reporting restrictions

Conspiracy to defraud

Part II

General and supplementary

SCHEDULE 2 – Minor and Consequential Amendments.

An Act to make further provision for the investigation of and trials for fraud; and for connected purposes.

[15th May 1987]

BE IT ENACTED by the Queen's most Excellent Majesty, by and with the advice and consent of the Lords Spiritual and Temporal, and Commons, in this present Parliament assembled, and by the authority of the same as follows:—

PART I

FRAUD

The Serious Fraud Office

1. (1) A Serious Fraud Office shall be constituted for England and Wales and Northern Ireland.

(2) The Attorney General shall appoint a person to be the Director of the Serious Fraud Office (referred to in this part of this Act as "the Director"), and he shall discharge his functions under the superintendence of the Attorney General.

(3) The Director may investigate any suspected offence which appears to him on reasonable grounds to involve serious or complex fraud.

(4) The Director may, if he thinks fit, conduct any such investigation in conjunction either with the police or with any other person who is, in the opinion of the Director, a proper person to be concerned in it.

(5) The Director may—

    (a)   institute and have the conduct of any criminal proceedings which appear to him to relate to such fraud; and

    (b)   take over the conduct of any such proceedings at any stage.

(6) The Director shall discharge such other functions in relation to fraud as may from time to time be assigned to him by the Attorney General.

(7) The Director may designate for the purposes of subsection (5) above any member of the Serious Fraud Office who is—

    (a)   a barrister in England and Wales or Northern Ireland:

    (b)   a solicitor of the Supreme Court; or

    (c)   a solicitor of the Supreme Court of Judicature of Northern Ireland.

(8) Any member so designated shall, without prejudice to any functions which may have been assigned to him in his capacity as a member of that Office, have all the powers of the Director as to the institution and conduct of proceedings but shall exercise those powers under the direction of the Director.

(9) Any member so designated who is a barrister in England and Wales or a solicitor of the Supreme Court shall have, in any court, the rights of audience enjoyed by solicitors holding practising certificates and shall have such additional rights of audience in the Crown Court in England and Wales as may be given by virtue of subsection (11) below.

(10) The reference in subsection (9) above to rights of audience enjoyed in any court by solicitors includes a reference to rights enjoyed in the Crown Court by virtue of any direction given by the Lord Chancellor under section 83 of the Supreme Court Act 1981.

(11) For the purposes of giving members so designated who are barristers in England and Wales or solicitors of the Supreme Court additional rights of audience in the Crown Court in England and Wales, the Lord Chancellor may give any such direction as respects such members as he could give under the said section 83.

(12) Any member so designated who is a barrister in Northern Ireland or a solicitor of the Supreme Court of Judicature of Northern Ireland shall have—

    (a)   in any court the rights of audience enjoyed by solicitors of the Supreme Court of Judicature of Northern Ireland and, in the Crown Court in Northern Ireland, such additional rights of audience as may be given by virtue of subsection (14) below; and

    (b)   in the Crown Court in Northern Ireland, the rights of audience enjoyed by barristers employed by the Director of Public Prosecutions for Northern Ireland.

(13) Subject to subsection (14) below, the reference in subsection (12)(a) above to rights of audience enjoyed by solicitors of the Supreme Court of Judicature of Northern Ireland is a reference to such rights enjoyed in the Crown Court in Northern Ireland as restricted by any direction given by the Lord Chief Justice of Northern Ireland under section 50 of the Judicature (Northern Ireland) Act 1978.

(14) For the purpose of giving any member so designated who is a barrister in Northern Ireland or a solicitor of the Supreme Court of Judicature of Northern Ireland additional rights of audience in the Crown Court in Northern Ireland, the Lord Chief Justice of Northern Ireland may direct that any direction given by him under the said section 50 shall not apply to such members.

(15) Schedule 1 to this Act shall have effect.

(16) For the purposes of this section (including that Schedule) references to the conduct of any proceedings include references to the proceedings being discontinued and to the taking of any steps (including the bringing of appeals and making of representations in respect of applications for bail) which may be taken in relation to them.

(17) In the application of this section (including that Schedule) to Northern Ireland references to the Attorney General are to be construed as references to him in his capacity as Attorney General for Northern Ireland.

2. (1) The powers of the Director under this section shall be exercisable, but only for the purposes of an investigation under section 1 above, [or on a request made by] an authority entitled to make such a request]], in any case in which it appears to him that there is a good reason to do so for the purpose of investigating the affairs, or any aspect of the affairs, of any person.

[(1A) The authorities entitled to request the Director to exercise his powers under this section are—

   (a)   the Attorney-General of the Isle of Man, Jersey or Guernsey, acting under legislation corresponding to section 1 of this Act and having effect in the Island whose Attorney-General makes the request, and

   (b)   the Secretary of State acting under section 4(2A) of the Criminal Justice (International Co-operation) Act 1990, in response to a request received by him from an overseas court, tribunal or authority (an "overseas authority").

(1B) The Director shall not exercise his powers on a request from the Secretary of State acting in response to a request received from an overseas authority within subsection (1A)(b) above unless it appears to the Director on reasonable grounds that the offence in respect of which he has been requested to obtain evidence involves serious or complex fraud.]

(2) The Director may by notice in writing require the person whose affairs are to be investigated ("the person under investigation") or any other person whom he has reason to believe has relevant information to [answer questions or otherwise furnish information with respect to any matter relevant to the investigation at a specified place and either at a specified time or forthwith].

(3) The Director may by notice in writing require the person under investigation or any other person to produce at [such place as may be specified in the notice and either forthwith or at such time as may be so specified any specified] documents which appear to the Director to relate to any matter relevant to the investigation or any documents of a specified [description] which appear to him so to relate; and—

   (a)   if any such documents are produced, the Director may—

      (i)   take copies or extracts from them;
      (ii)   require the person producing them to provide an explanation of any of them;

   (b)   if any such documents are not produced, the Director may require the person who was required to produce them to state, to the best of his knowledge and belief, where they are.

(4) Where, on information on oath laid by a member of the Serious Fraud Office, a justice of the peace is satisfied, in relation to any documents, that there are reasonable grounds for believing—

   (a)   that—

      (i)   a person has failed to comply with an obligation under this section to produce them;

(ii) it is not practicable to serve a notice under subsection (3) above in relation to them; or

(iii) the service of such a notice in relation to them might seriously prejudice the investigation; and

(b) that they are on premises specified in the information,

he may issue such a warrant as is mentioned in subsection (5) below.

(5) The warrant referred to above is a warrant authorising any constable—

(a) to enter (using such force as is reasonably necessary for the purpose) and search the premises, and

(b) to take possession of any documents appearing to be documents of the description specified in the information or to take in relation to any documents so appearing any other steps which may appear to be necessary for preserving them and preventing interference with them.

(6) Unless it is not practicable in the circumstances, a constable executing a warrant issued under subsection (4) above shall be accompanied by an appropriate person.

(7) In subsection (6) above "appropriate person" means—

(a) a member of the Serious Fraud Office; or

(b) some person who is not a member of that Office, but whom the Director has authorised to accompany the constable.

(8) A statement by a person in response to a requirement imposed by virtue of this section may only be used in evidence against him—

(a) on a prosecution for an offence under subsection (14) below; or

(b) on a prosecution for some other offence where in giving evidence he makes a statement inconsistent with it.

[(8A) Any evidence obtained by the Director for use by an overseas authority shall be furnished by him to the Secretary of State for transmission to the overseas authority which requested it.

(8B) If in order to comply with the request of the overseas authority it is necessary for any evidence obtained by the Director to be accompanied by any certificate, affidavit or other verifying document, the Director shall also furnish for transmission such document of that nature as may be specified by the Secretary of State when asking the Director to obtain the evidence.

(8C) Where any evidence obtained by the Director for use by an overseas authority consists of a document the original or a copy shall be transmitted, and where it consists of any other article the article itself or a description, photograph or other representation of it shall be transmitted, as may be necessary in order to comply with the request of the overseas authority.]

(9) A person shall not under this section be required to disclose any information or produce any document which he would be entitled to refuse to disclose or produce on grounds of legal professional privilege in proceedings in the High Court, except that a lawyer may be required to furnish the name and address of his client.

(10) A person shall not under this section be required to disclose information or produce a document in respect of which he owes an obligation of confidence by virtue of carrying on any banking business unless—

(a) the person to whom the obligation of confidence is owed consents to the disclosure or production; or

(b) the Director has authorised the making of the requirement or, if it is impracticable for him to act personally, a member of the Serious Fraud Office designated by him for the purposes of this subsection has done so.

(11) Without prejudice to the power of the Director to assign functions to members of the Serious Fraud Office, the Director may authorise any competent investigator (other than a constable) who is not a member of that Office to exercise on his behalf all or any of the powers conferred by this section, but no such authority shall be granted except for the purpose of investigating the affairs, or any aspect of the affairs, of a person specified in the authority.

(12) No person shall be bound to comply with any requirement imposed by a person exercising powers by virtue of any authority granted under subsection (11) above unless he has, if required to do so, produced evidence of this authority.

(13) Any person who without reasonable excuse fails to comply with a requirement imposed on him under this section shall be guilty of an offence and liable on summary conviction to imprisonment for a term not exceeding six months or to a fine not exceeding level 5 on the standard scale or to both.

(14) A person who, in purported compliance with a requirement under this section—

    (a)   makes a statement which he knows to be false or misleading in a material particular; or

    (b)   recklessly makes a statement which is false or misleading in a material particular,

shall be guilty of an offence.

(15) A person guilty of an offence under subsection (14) above shall—

    (a)   on conviction on indictment, be liable to imprisonment for a term not exceeding two years or to a fine or to both; and

    (b)   on summary conviction, be liable to imprisonment for a term not exceeding six months or to a fine not exceeding the statutory maximum, or to both.

(16) Where any person—

    (a)   knows or suspects that an investigation by the police or the Serious Fraud Office into serious or complex fraud is being or is likely to be carried out; and

    (b)   falsifies, conceals, destroys or otherwise disposes of, or causes or permits the falsification, concealment, destruction or disposal of documents which he knows or suspects are or would be relevant to such an investigation,

he shall be guilty of an offence unless he proves that he had no intention of concealing the facts disclosed by the documents from persons carrying out such an investigation.

(17) A person guilty of an offence under subsection (16) above shall—

    (a)   on conviction on indictment, be liable to imprisonment for a term not exceeding 7 years or to a fine or to both; and

    (b)   on summary conviction, be liable to imprisonment for a term not exceeding 6 months or to a fine not exceeding the statutory maximum or to both.

(18) In this section, "documents" includes information recorded in any form and, in relation to information recorded otherwise than in legible form, references to its production include references to producing a copy of the information in legible form; and "evidence" (in relation to subsections (1A)(b), (8A), (8B) and (8C) above) includes documents and other articles.

(19) In the application of this section to Scotland, the reference to a justice of the peace is to be construed as a reference to the sheriff; and in the application of this section to Northern Ireland, subsection (4) above shall have effect as if for the references to information there were substituted references to a complaint.

Notes

In sub-s. (1), the words in the outer pair of square brackets were inserted by the Criminal Justice Act 1988, s. 143 and the words in the inner pair of square brackets were substituted by the Criminal Justice and Public Order Act 1994, s. 164(2). Sub-ss (1A), (1B), (8A), (8B), (8C) and the words in square brackets in sub-s. (18) were inserted by the Criminal Justice and Public Order Act 1994, s. 164(2). The words in square brackets in sub-ss. (2), (3) were substituted by the Criminal Justice Act 1988, s. 170, Sched. 15, para. 113.

3. (1) Where any information subject to an obligation of secrecy under the Taxes Management Act 1970 has been disclosed by the Commissioners of Inland Revenue or an officer of those Commissioners to any member of the Serious Fraud Office for the purposes of any prosecution of an offence relating to inland revenue, that information may be disclosed to any member of the Serious Fraud Office—

    (a)   for the purposes of any prosecution of which that office has the conduct;

    (b)   to any member of the Crown Prosecution Service for the purposes of any prosecution of an offence relating to inland revenue; and

    (c)   to the Director of Public Prosecutions for Northern Ireland for the purposes of any prosecution of an offence relating to inland revenue,

but not otherwise.

(2) Where the Serious Fraud Office has the conduct of any prosecution of an offence which does not relate to inland revenue, the court may not prevent the prosecution from relying on

any evidence under section 78 of the Police and Criminal Evidence Act 1984 (discretion to exclude unfair evidence) by reason only of the fact that the information concerned was disclosed by the Commissioners of Inland Revenue or an officer of those Commissioners for the purposes of any prosecution of an offence relating to inland revenue.

(3) Where any information is subject to an obligation of secrecy imposed by or under any enactment other than an enactment contained in the Taxes Management Act 1970, the obligation shall not have effect to prohibit the disclosure of that information to any person in his capacity as a member of the Serious Fraud Office, but any information disclosed by virtue of this subsection may only be disclosed by a member of the Serious Fraud Office for the purposes of any prosecution in England and Wales, Northern Ireland or elsewhere and may only be disclosed by such a member if he is designated by the Director for the purposes of this subsection.

(4) Without prejudice to his power to enter into agreements apart from this subsection, the Director may enter into a written agreement for the supply of information to or by him subject, in either case, to an obligation not to disclose the information concerned otherwise than for a specified purpose.

(5) Subject to subsection (1) and (3) above and to any provision of an agreement for the supply of information which restricts the disclosure of the information supplied. information obtained by any person in his capacity as a member of the Serious Fraud Office may be disclosed by any member of that office designated by the Director for the purposes of this subsection—

(a)   to any government department or Northern Ireland department or other authority or body discharging its functions on behalf of the Crown (including the Crown in right of Her Majesty's Government in Northern Ireland):

(b)   to any competent authority;

(c)   for the purposes of any prosecution in England and Wales, Northern Ireland or elsewhere; and

(d)   for the purposes of assisting any public or other authority for the time being designated for the purposes of this paragraph by an order made by the Secretary of State to discharge any functions which are specified in the order.

(6) The following are competent authorities for the purposes of subsection (5) above—

(a)   an inspector appointed under Part XIV of the Companies Act 1985 or Part XV of the Companies (Northern Ireland) Order 1986;

(b)   an Official Receiver,

(c)   the Accountant in Bankruptey;

(d)   the official receiver for Northern Ireland;

(e)   a person appointed to carry out an investigation under section 55 of the Building Societies Act 1986;

(f)   a body administering a compensation scheme under section 54 of the Financial Services Act 1986;

(g)   an inspector appointed under section 94 of that Act . . .;

(h)   a person exercising powers by virute of section 106 of that Act;

(i)   an inspector appointed under section 177 of that Act;

[(j)   a person appointed by the Bank of England under section 41 of the Banking Act 1987 to carry out an investigation and make a report;]

(k)   a person exercising powers by virtue of [section 43A or 44(2)] of the Insurance Companies Act 1982;

(l)   any body having supervisory, regulatory or disciplinary functions in relation to any profession or any area of commercial activity, and

(m)   any person or body having, under the law of any country or territory outside the United Kingdom, functions corresponding to any of the functions of any person or body mentioned in any of the foregoing paragraphs.

(7) An order under subsection (5)(d) above may impose conditions subject to which, and otherwise restrict the circumstances in which, information may be disclosed under that paragraph.

Notes

In sub-s. (6), the words omitted from para. (*i*) were repealed by the Criminal Justice Act 1993, s. 79(14), Sched. 6, Pt I, para. (j) was substituted by the Criminal Justice Act 1988, s. 170,

Sched. 15, para. 111. and the words in square brackets in para. (*k*) were substituted by the Insurance Companies (Third Insurance Directives) Regulations 1994, S.I. 1994 No. 1696.

Transfer of Cases to Crown Court

4. (1) If—

(a) a person has been charged with an indictable offence, and
(b) in the opinion of an authority designated by subsection (2) below or of one of such an authority's officers acting on the authority's behalf the evidence of the offence charged—

(i) would be sufficient for the person charged to be committed for trial; and
(ii) reveals a case of fraud of such seriousness or complexity that it is appropriate that the management of the case should without delay be taken over by the Crown Court; and

(c) before the magistrates' court in whose jurisdiction the offence has been charged begins to inquire into the case as examining justices the authority or one of the authority's officers acting on the authority's behalf gives the court a notice (in this Act referred to as a "notice of transfer") certifying that opinion, the functions of the magistrates' court shall cease in relation to the case, except as provided by section 5(3)[, (7A)] and (8) below and by [section 20(4) of the Legal Aid Act 1988].

(2) The authorities mentioned in subsection (1) above (in this Act referred to as "designated authorities") are—

(a) the Director of Public Prosecutions;
(b) the Director of the Serious Fraud Office;
(c) the Commissioners of Inland Revenue;
(d) the Commissioners of Customs and Excise; and
(e) the Secretary of State.

(3) A designated authority's decision to give notice of transfer shall not be subject to appeal or liable to be questioned in any court.

[(4) This section and sections 5 and 6 below shall not apply in any case in which section 51 of the Crime and Disorder Act 1998 (no committal proceedings for indictable offences) applies.]

Notes

In sub-s. (1)(c) the subsection number in square brackets was inserted by the Criminal Justice Act 1988, s. 144(2) and the words in the second pair of square brackets were substituted by the Legal Aid Act 1988, s. 45, Sched. 5, para. 22.

Sub-s. (4) was added by the Crime and Disorder Act 1998, s. 119, Sched. 8, para. 65 partly as from a day to be appointed.

5. (1) A notice of transfer shall specify the proposed place of trial and in selecting that place the designated authority shall have regard to the considerations to which section 7 of the Magistrates' Courts Act 1980 requires a magistrates' court committing a person for trial to have regard when selecting the place at which he is to be tried.

(2) A notice of transfer shall specify the charge or charges to which it relates and include or be accompanied by such additional matter as regulations under subsection (9) below may require.

(3) If a magistrates' court has remanded a person to whom a notice of transfer relates in custody, it shall have power, subject to section 4 of the Bail Act 1976 and regulations under section 22 of the Prosecution of Offences Act 1985—

(a) to order that he shall be safely kept in custody until delivered in due course of law or
(b) to release him on bail in accordance with the Bail Act 1976, that is to say, by directing him to appear before the Crown Court for trial

and where his release on bail is conditional on his providing one or more surety or sureties and in accordance with section 8(3) of the Bail Act 1976, the court fixes the amount in which the surety is to be bound with a view to his entering into his recognizance subsequently in accordance with subsections (4) and (5) or (6) of that section, the court shall in the meantime make an order such as is mentioned in paragraph (a) of this subsection.

(4) If the conditions specified in subsection (5) below are satisfied a court may exercise the powers conferred by subsection (3) above [in relation to a person charged without his] being brought before it in any case in which by virtue of section 128(3A) of the Magistrates' Courts Act 1980 it would have power further to remand him on an adjournment such as is mentioned in that subsection.

(5) The conditions mentioned in subsection (4) above are

(a) that the person [in question] has given his written consent to the powers conferred by subsection (3) above being exercised without his being brought before the court; and

(b) that the court is satisfied that, when he gave his consent, he knew that the notice of transfer had been issued.

(6) Where notice of transfer is given after a person [to whom it relates] has been remanded on bail to appear before [a magistrates' court] on an appointed day, the requirement that he shall so appear shall cease on the giving of the notice, unless the notice states that it is to continue.

(7) Where the requirement that a person [to whom the notice of transfer relates] shall appear before [a magistrates' court] ceases by virtue of subsection (6) above, it shall be his duty to appear before the Crown Court at the place specified by the notice of transfer as the proposed place of trial or at any place substituted for it by a direction under section 76 of the Supreme Court Act 1981.

[(7A) If the notice states that the requirement is to continue, when a person to whom the notice relates appears before the magistrates' court, the court shall have—

(a) the powers and duty conferred on a magistrates' court by subsection (3) above, but subject as there provided; and

(b) power to enlarge, in the surety's absence, a recognizance conditioned in accordance with section 128(4)(a) of the Magistrates' Courts Act 1980 so that the surety is bound to secure that the person charged appears also before the Crown Court.

(8) For the purposes of the Criminal Procedure (Attendance of Witnesses) Act 1965—

(a) any magistrates' court for the petty sessions area for which the court from which a case was transferred sits shall be treated as examining magistrates; and

(b) a person indicated in the notice of transfer as a proposed witness shall be treated as a person who has been examined by the court.

(9) The Attorney General—

(a) shall by regulations make provision requiring the giving of a copy of a notice of transfer, together with a statement of the evidence on which any charge to which it relates is based—

(i)   to any person to whom the notice of transfer relates; and

(ii) to the Crown Court sitting at the place specified by the notice of transfer as the proposed place of trial; and

(b) may be regulations make such further provision in relation to notices of transfer, including provision as to the duties of a designated authority in relation to such notices, as appears to him to be appropriate.

(10) The power to make regulations conferred by subsection (9) above shall be exercisable by statutory instrument subject to annulment in pursuance of a resolution of either House of Parliament.

(11) Any such regulations may make different provision with respect to different cases or classes of case.

6. (1) Where notice of transfer has been given, any person to whom the notice relates, at any time before he is arraigned (and whether or not an indictment has been preferred against him), may apply orally or in writing to the Crown Court sitting at the place specified by the notice of transfer as the proposed place of trial for the charge, or any of the charges, in the case to be dismissed; and the judge shall dismiss a charge (and accordingly quash a count relating to it in any indictment preferred against the applicant) if it appears to him that the evidence against the applicant would not be sufficient for a jury properly to convict him.

(2) No oral application may be made under subsection (1) above unless the applicant has given the Crown Court sitting at the place specified by the notice of transfer as the proposed place of trial written notice of his intention to make the application.

(3) Oral evidence may be given on such an application only with the leave of the judge or by his order, and the judge shall give leave or make an order only if it appears to him, having regard to any matters stated in the application for leave, that the interests of justice require him to do so.

(4) If the judge gives leave permitting, or makes an order requiring, a person to give oral evidence, but he does not do so, the judge may disregard any document indicating the evidence that he might have given.

(5) Dismissal of the charge, or all the charges, against the applicant shall have the same effect as a refusal by examining magistrates to commit for trial, except that no further proceedings may be brought on a dismissed charge except by means of the preferment of a voluntary bill of indictment.

(6) Crown Court Rules may make provision for the purposes of this section and, without prejudice to the generality of this subsection—

 (a) as to the time or stage in the proceedings at which anything required to be done is to be done (unless the court grants leave to do it at some other time or stage):
 (b) as to the contents and form of notices or other documents:
 (c) as to the manner in which evidence is to be submitted: and
 (d) as to persons to be served with notices or other material.

Preparatory Hearings

7. (1) Where it appears to a judge of the Crown Court that the evidence on an indictment reveals a case of fraud of such seriousness or complexity that substantial benefits are likely to accrue from a hearing (in this Act referred to as a "preparatory hearing") before the jury are sworn, for the purpose of—

 (a) identifying issues which are likely to be material to the verdict of the jury;
 (b) assisting their comprehension of any such issues;
 (c) expediting the proceedings before the jury; or
 (d) assisting the judge's management of the trial;

he may order that such a hearing shall be held.

(2) A judge may make an order under subsection (1) above on the application either of the prosecution or of the person indicted or, if the indictment charges a number of persons, any of them, or of his own motion.

(3)–(5) . . .

Notes

The words in square brackets in sub-s. (1) were substituted by the Criminal Justice and Public Order Act 1994, s. 168(1), Sched. 9, para. 30. Sub-ss (3)–(5) were repealed by the Criminal Procedure and Investigations Act 1996, ss. 72, 80, Sched. 3, para. 2, Sched. 5, para. 12.

8. (1) If a judge orders a preparatory hearing, the trial shall begin with that hearing.
(2) Arraignment shall accordingly take place at the start of the preparatory hearing.
9. (1) At the preparatory hearing the judge may exercise any of the powers specified in this section.
(2) The judge may adjourn a preparatory hearing from time to time.
(3) He may determine—

 (a) . . .
 [(a)(a) a question arising under section 6 of the Criminal Justice Act 1993 (relevance of external law to certain charges of conspiracy, attempt and incitement)]
 (b) any question as to the admissibility of evidence; and
 (c) any other question of law relating to the case.

(4) He may order the prosecution—

 (a) to supply the court and the defendant or, if there is more than one, each of them with a statement (a "case statement") of the following—

  (i) the principal facts of the prosecution case;
  (ii) the witnesses who will speak to those facts;

  (iii) any exhibits relevant to those facts,
  (iv) any proposition of law on which the prosecution proposes to rely; and
  (v) the consequences in relation to any of the counts in the indictment that appear
       to the prosecution to flow from the matters stated in pursuance of sub-
       paragraphs (i) to (iv) above;

 (b) to prepare their evidence and other explanatory material in such a form as appears
      to him to be likely to aid comprehension by the jury and to supply it in that form to
      the court and to the defendant or, if there is more than one to each of them;
 (c) to give the court and the defendant or, if there is more than one, each of them notice
      of documents the truth of the contents of which ought in the prosecution's view to
      be admitted and of any other matters which in their view ought to be agreed;
 (d) to make any amendments of any case statement supplied in pursuance of an order
      under paragraph (a) above that appear to the court to be appropriate, having regard
      to objections made by the defendant or, if there is more than one, by any of them.

(5) Where—

 (a) a judge has ordered the prosecution to supply a case statement; and
 (b) the prosecution have complied with the order

he may order the defendant or, if there is more than one, each of them—

  (i) to give the court and the prosecution a statement in writing setting out in general
       terms the nature of his defence and indicating the principal matters on which he
       takes issue with the prosecution;
  (ii) to give the court and the prosecution notice of any objections that he has to the case
       statement;
 (iii) to inform the court and the prosecution of any point of law (including a point as to
       the admissibility of evidence) which he wishes to take, and any authority on which
       he intends to rely for that purpose;
 (iv) to give the court and the prosecution a notice stating the extent to which he agrees
       with the prosecution as to documents and other matters to which a notice under
       subsection (4)(c) above relates and the reason for any disagreement.

(6) Crown Court Rules may provide that except to the extent that disclosure is required—

 (a) by section 5(7) of the Criminal Procedure and Investigations Act 1996 (alibi); or
 (b) by rules under section 81 of the Police and Criminal Evidence Act 1984 (expert
      evidence).

a summary required by virtue of subsection (5) above need not disclose who will give
evidence.

(7) A judge making an order under subsection (5) above shall warn the defendant or, if there
is more than one, all of them of the possible consequence under section 10 below of not
complying with it.

(8) If it appears to a judge that reasons given in pursuance of subsection (5)(iv) above are
inadequate, he shall so inform the person giving them, and may require him to give further or
better reasons.

(9) An order under this section may specify the time within which any specified requirement
contained in it is to be complied with, but Crown Court Rules may make provision as to the
minimum or maximum time that may be specified for compliance.

(10) An order or ruling under this section shall have effect during the trial, unless it appears
to the judge, on application made to him during the trial, that the interests of justice require him
to vary or discharge it.

(11) An appeal shall lie to the Court of Appeal from any order or ruling of a judge under
subsection (3)(b) or (c) above, but only with the leave of the judge or of the Court of
Appeal.

(12) Subject to rules of court made under section 53(1) of the Supreme Court Act 1981
(power by rules to distribute business of Court of Appeal between its civil and criminal
divisions), the jurisdiction of the Court of Appeal under subsection (11) above shall be
exercised by the criminal division of the Court: and the reference in that subsection to the Court
of Appeal shall be construed as a reference to that division.

(13) The judge may continue a preparatory hearing notwithstanding that leave to appeal has
been granted under subsection (11) above, but no jury shall be sworn until after the appeal has
been determined or abandoned.

(14) On the termination of the hearing of an appeal the Court of Appeal may confirm. reverse or vary the decision appealed against.

9A (1) Subsection (2) below applies where

    (a)   a judge orders a preparatory hearing, and

    (b)   he decides that any order which could be made under section 9(4) or (5) above at the hearing should be made before the hearing.

(2) In such case—

    (a)   he may make any such order before the hearing (or at the hearing), and

    (b)   subsections (4) to (10) of section 9 above shall apply accordingly.

10. (1) Any party may depart from the case he disclosed in pursuance of a requirement imposed under section 9 above.

(2) Where—

    (a)   a party departs from the case he disclosed in pursuance of a requirement imposed under section 9 above, or

    (b)   a party fails to comply with such a requirement.

the judge or, with the leave of the judge, any other party may make such comment as appears to the judge or the other party (as the case may be) to be appropriate and the jury may draw such inference as appears proper.

(3) In deciding whether to give leave the judge shall have regard

    (a)   to the extent of any departure or failure, and

    (b)   to whether there is any justification for it.

(4) Except as provided by this section no part—

    (a)   of a statement given under section 9(5) above; or

    (b)   of any other information relating to the case for the accused or, if there is more than one, the case for any of them, which was given in pursuance of a requirement imposed under section 9 above,

may be disclosed at a stage in the trial after the jury have been sworn without the consent of the accused concerned.

Reporting Restrictions

[11. (1) Except as provided by this section—

    (a)   no written report of proceedings falling within subsection (2) below shall be published in Great Britain;

    (b)   no report of proceedings falling within subsection (2) below shall be included in a relevant programme for reception in Great Britain.

(2) The following proceedings fall within this subsection—

    (a)   an application under section 6(1) above;

    (b)   a preparatory hearing.

    (c)   an application for leave to appeal in relation to such a hearing:

    (d)   an appeal in relation to such a hearing.

(3) The judge dealing with an application under section 6(1) above may order that subsection (1) above shall not apply, or shall not apply to a specified extent, to a report of the application.

(4) The judge dealing with a preparatory hearing may order that subsection (1) above shall not apply, or shall not apply to a specified extent, to a report of—

    (a)   the preparatory hearing, or

    (b)   an application to the judge for leave to appeal to the Court of Appeal under section 9(11) above in relation to the preparatory hearing.

(5) The Court of Appeal may order that subsection (1) above shall not apply, or shall not apply to a specified extent, to a report of—

    (a)   an appeal to the Court of Appeal under section 9(11) above in relation to a preparatory hearing.

    (b)   an application to that Court for leave to appeal to it under section 9(11) above in relation to a preparatory hearing, or

    (c)   an application to that Court for leave to appeal to the House of Lords under Part II of the Criminal Appeal Act 1968 in relation to a preparatory hearing.

(6) The House of Lords may order that subsection (1) above shall not apply, or shall not apply to a specified extent, to a report of—

    (a)   an appeal to that House under Part II of the Criminal Appeal Act 1968 in relation to a preparatory hearing, or

    (b)   an application to that House for leave to appeal to it under Part II of the Criminal Appeal Act 1968 in relation to a preparatory hearing.

(7) Where there is only one accused and he objects to the making of an order under subsection (3), (4), (5) or (6) above the judge or the Court of Appeal or the House of Lords shall make the order if (and only if) satisfied after hearing the representations of the accused that it is in the interests of justice to do so; and if the order is made it shall not apply to the extent that a report deals with any such objection or representations.

(8) Where there are two or more accused and one or more of them objects to the making of an order under subsection (3), (4), (5) or (6) above the judge or the Court of Appeal or the House of Lords shall make the order if (and only if) satisfied after hearing the representations of each of the accused that it is in the interests of justice to do so; and if the order is made it shall not apply to the extent that a report deals with any such objection or representations.

(9) Subsection (1) above does not apply to—

    (a)   the publication of a report of an application under section 6(1) above, or

    (b)   the inclusion in a relevant programme of a report of an application under section 6(1) above,

where the application is successful.

(10) Where—

    (a)   two or more persons are jointly charged, and

    (b)   applications under section 6(1) above are made by more than one of them.

subsection (9) above shall have effect as if for the words "the application is" there were substituted "all the applications are"

(11) Subsection (1) above does not apply to—

    (a)   the publication of a report of an unsuccessful application made under section 6(1) above.

    (b)   the publication of a report of a preparatory hearing.

    (c)   the publication of a report of an appeal in relation to a preparatory hearing or of an application for leave to appeal in relation to such a hearing.

    (d)   the inclusion in a relevant programme of a report of an unsuccessful application made under section 6(1) above,

    (e)   the inclusion in a relevant programme of a report of a preparatory hearing, or

    (f)   the inclusion in a relevant programme of a report of an appeal in relation to a preparatory hearing or of an application for leave to appeal in relation to such a hearing.

at the conclusion of the trial of the accused or of the last of the accused to be tried.

(12) Subsection (1) above does not apply to a report which contains only one or more of the following matters—

    (a)   the identity of the court and the name of the judge;

    (b)   the names, ages, home addresses and occupations of the accused and witnesses;

    (c)   any relevant business information;

    (d)   the offence or offences, or a summary of them, with which the accused is or are charged;

    (e)   the names of counsel and solicitors in the proceedings;

    (f)   where the proceedings are adjourned, the date and place to which they are adjourned;

    (g)   any arrangements as to bail;

    (h)   whether legal aid was granted to the accused or any of the accused.

(13) The addresses that may be published or included in a relevant programme under subsection (12) above are addresses—

(a) at any relevant time, and
(b) at the time of their publication or inclusion in a relevant programme;

and "relevant time" here means a time when the events giving rise to the charges to which the proceedings relate occurred.

(14) The following is relevant business information for the purposes of subsection (12) above—

(a) any address used by the accused for carrying on a business on his own account;
(b) the name of any business which he was carrying on on his own account at any relevant time;
(c) the name of any firm in which he was a partner at any relevant time or by which he was engaged at any such time;
(d) the address of any such firm;
(e) the name of any company of which he was a director at any relevant time or by which he was otherwise engaged at any such time;
(f) the address of the registered or principal office of any such company;
(g) any working address of the accused in his capacity as a person engaged by any such company;

and here "engaged" means engaged under a contract of service or a contract for services, and "relevant time" has the same meaning as in subsection (13) above.

(15) Nothing in this section affects any prohibition or restriction imposed by virtue of any other enactment on a publication or on matter included in a programme.

(16) In this section—

(a) "publish", in relation to a report, means publish the report, either by itself or as part of a newspaper or periodical, for distribution to the public;
(b) expressions cognate with "publish" shall be construed accordingly,
(c) "relevant programme" means a programme included in a programme service, within the meaning of the Broadcasting Act 1990.]

Note

ss. 11, 11A were substituted for the original s. 11 by the Criminal Procedure and Investigations Act 1996, s. 72, Sched. 3, para. 6.

[11A—(1) If a report is published or included in a relevant programme in contravention of section 11 above each of the following persons is guilty of an offence—

(a) in the case of a publication of a written report as part of a newspaper or periodical, any proprietor, editor or publisher of the newspaper or periodical;
(b) in the case of a publication of a written report otherwise than as part of a newspaper or periodical, the person who publishes it;
(c) in the case of the inclusion of a report in a relevant programme, any body corporate which is engaged in providing the service in which the programme is included and any person having functions in relation to the programme corresponding to those of an editor of a newspaper.

(2) A person guilty of an offence under this section is liable on summary conviction to a fine of an amount not exceeding level 5 on the standard scale.

(3) Proceedings for an offence under this section shall not be instituted in England and Wales otherwise than by or with the consent of the Attorney General.

(4) Subsection (16) of section 11 above applies for the purposes of this section as it applies for the purposes of that.]

Note

ss. 11, 11A were substituted for the original s. 11 by the Criminal Procedure and Investigations Act 1996, s. 72, Sched. 3, para. 6.

Conspiracy to Defraud

12. (1) If—

(a) a person agrees with any other person or persons that a course of conduct shall be pursued; and

(b)   that course of conduct will necessarily amount to or involve the commission of any offence or offences by one or more of the parties to the agreement if the agreement is carried out in accordance with their intentions,

the fact that it will do so shall not preclude a charge of conspiracy to defraud being brought against any of them in respect of the agreement.

(2) In section 5(2) of the Criminal Law Act 1977, the words from "and" to the end are hereby repealed.

(3) A person guilty of conspiracy to defraud is liable on conviction on indictment to imprisonment for a term not exceeding 10 years or a fine or both.

PART II
GENERAL AND SUPPLEMENTARY

13. (1) An order in Council under paragraph 1(1)(b) of Schedule I to the Northern Ireland Act 1974 (legislation for Northern Ireland in the interim period) which contains a statement that it [is made only for purposes corresponding to] those of any provision of this Act to which this section applies—

(a)   shall not be subject to paragraph 1(4) and (5) of that Schedule (affirmative resolution of both Houses of Parliament); but
(b)   shall be subject to annulment in pursuance of a resolution of either House.

(2) The provision of this Act to which this section applies are sections 4 to 12.

Notes

The words in square brackets in sub-s. (1) were substituted by the Criminal Justice Act 1988, s. 170, Sched. 15, para. 115.

14. There shall be paid out of money provided by Parliament—

(a)   any expenses incurred under this Act by a Minister of the Crown; and
(b)   any increase attributable to the provisions of this Act in the sums payable out of such money under any other Act.

15. The enactments mentioned in Schedule 2 to this Act shall have effect with the amendments there specified (being minor amendments and amendments consequential on the foregoing provisions of this Act).

16. (1) Subject to subsection (3) below, this Act shall come into force on such day as the Secretary of State may by order made by statutory instrument appoint; and different days may be appointed in pursuance of this subsection for different provisions or different purposes of the same provision.

(2) An order under subsection (1) above may make such transitional provision as appears to the Secretary of State to be necessary or expedient in connection with any provision thereby brought into force.

(3) The following provisions shall come into force on the day this Act is passed—

section 13;
this section;
sections 17 and 18.

17. (1) Subject to the following provisions of this section, this Act extends to England and Wales only.

(2) The following provision extend also to Scotland—

section 2;
section 11;
[section 11A;]
section 16;
this section; and
section 18.

(3) The following provisions extend also to Northern Ireland—

section 1 (including Schedule 1); and
section 2 and 3;
section 16;
this section; and
section 18.

(4) section 13 above extends to Northern Ireland only.

(5) The extent of any amendment of an enactment in Schedule 2 to this Act is the same as that of the enactment amended.

(6) Her Majesty may by Order in Council direct that section 2 above shall extend, subject to such modifications as may be specified in the Order, to any of the Channel Islands.

(7) In subsection (6) above "modifications" includes additions omissions and amendments.

Note

The words in square brackets in sub-s. (2) were inserted by the Criminal Procedure and Investigations Act 1996, s. 72, Sched. 3, para. 7

18. This Act may be cited as the Criminal Justice Act 1987.

SCHEDULES

SCHEDULE 1

THE SERIOUS FRAUD OFFICE

General

1. There shall be paid to the Director of the Serious Fraud Office such remuneration as the Attorney General may, with the approval of the Treasury, determine.

2. The Director shall appoint such staff for the Serious Fraud Office as, with the approval of the Treasury as to numbers, remuneration and other terms and conditions of service, he considers necessary for the discharge of his functions.

3. (1) As soon as practicable after 4th April in any year the Director shall make to the Attorney General a report on the discharge of his functions during the year ending with that date.

(2) The Attorney General shall lay before Parliament a copy of every report received by him under sub-paragraph (1) above and shall cause every such report to be published.

Procedure

4. (1) Where any enactment (whenever passed) prohibits the taking of any step—

   (a)   except by the Director of Public Prosecutions or except by him or another, or
   (b)   without the consent of the Director of Public Prosecutions or without his consent or the consent of another

it shall not prohibit the taking of any such step by the Director of the Serious Fraud Office.

(2) In this paragraph references to the Director of Public Prosecutions include references to the Director of Public Prosecutions for Northern Ireland.

5. (1) Where the Director has the conduct of any criminal proceedings in England and Wales, the Director of Public Prosecutions shall not in relation to those proceedings be subject to any duty by virtue of section 3(2) of the Prosecution of Offences Act 1985.

(2) Where the Director has the conduct of any criminal proceedings in Northern Ireland, the Director of Public Prosecutions for Northern Ireland shall not in relation to those proceedings be required to exercise any function under Article 5 of the Prosecution of Offences (Northern Ireland) Order 1972.

6. (1) Where the Director or any member of the Serious Fraud Office designated for the

purposes of section 1[(5)] above ("designated official") gives notice to any justice of the peace that he has instituted, or is conducting, any criminal proceedings in England and Wales, the justice shall—

(a) at the prescribed time and in the prescribed manner; or
(b) in a particular case, at the time and in the manner directed by the Attorney General;

send him every recognizance, information certificate, deposition, document and thing connected with those proceedings which the justice is required by law to deliver to the appropriate officer of the Crown Court.

(2) Where the Director or any designated official gives notice that he has instituted, or is conducting, any criminal proceedings in Northern Ireland—

(a) to a resident magistrate or a justice of the peace in Northern Ireland;
(b) to a clerk of petty sessions in Northern Ireland,

the person to whom the notice is given shall—

(i) at the prescribed time and in the prescribed manner, or
(ii) in a particular case, at the time and in the manner directed by the Attorney General,

send him every recognizance, complaint, certificate, deposition, document and thing connected with those proceedings which that person is required by law to deliver to the appropriate officer of the Crown Court.

(3) The Attorney General may make regulations for the purpose of supplementing this paragraph; and in this paragraph "prescribed" means prescribed by the regulations.

(4) The Director or, as the case may be, designated official shall—

(a) subject to the regulations, cause anything which is sent to him under this paragraph to be delivered to the appropriate officer of the Crown Court; and
(b) be under the same obligation (on the same payment) to deliver to an applicant copies of anything so sent as that officer.

7. (1) The Attorney General may make regulations requiring the chief officer of any police force to which the regulations are expressed to apply to give to the Director information with respect to every offence of a kind prescribed by the regulations which is alleged to have been committed in his area and in respect of which it appears to him that there is a prima facie case for proceedings.

(2) The regulations may also require every such chief officer to give to the Director such information as the Director may require with respect to such cases or classes of case as he may from time to time specify.

8. (1) The Attorney General may, with the approval of the Treasury, by regulations make such provision as he considers appropriate in relation to—

(a) the fees of counsel briefed to appear on behalf of the Serious Fraud Office in any criminal proceedings; and
(b) the costs and expenses of witnesses attending to give evidence at the instance of the Serious Fraud Office and subject to sub-paragraph (2) below, [of] any other person who in the opinion of that Office necessarily attends for the purpose of the case otherwise than to give evidence.

(2) The power conferred on the Attorney General by sub-paragraph (1)(b) above only relates to the costs and expenses of an interpreter if he is required because of the lack of English of a person attending to give evidence at the instance of the Serious Fraud Office.

(3) The regulations may, in particular—

(a) prescribe scales or rates of fees, costs or expenses; and
(b) specify conditions for the payment of fees, costs or expenses.

(4) Regulations made under sub-paragraph (1)(b) above may provide that scales or rates of costs and expenses shall be determined by the Attorney General with the consent of the Treasury.

[(5) In sub-paragraph (1)(b) above "attends" means attends at the court or elsewhere.]

9. (1) Any power to make regulations under this Schedule shall be exercisable by statutory instrument subject to annulment in pursuance of a resolution of either House of Parliament.

(2) Any such regulations may make different provision with respect to different cases or classes of case.

Notes

In para. 6(1) the subsection number in square brackets was substituted by the Criminal Justice Act 1988, s. 170, Sched. 15, para. 116; the word in square brackets in para. 8(1)(*b*) was substituted and para. 8(5) was inserted by s. 166 of the same Act.

SCHEDULE 2

MINOR AND CONSEQUENTIAL AMENDMENTS

Administration of Justice (Miscellaneous Provisions) Act 1933 (c.36).

1. (1) The following paragraph shall be inserted after paragraph (a) of subsection (2) of section

2. (1) of the Administration of Justice (Miscellaneous Provisions) Act 1933 (procedures for indictment of offenders)—

"(aa) the offence is specified in a notice of transfer under section 4 of the Criminal Justice Act 1987 (serious and complex fraud): or".
(2) . . .
2. . . .

Criminal Appeal Act 1968 (c.19)

3. At the end of subsection (1) of section 33 of the Criminal Appeal Act 1968 (right of appeal to House of Lords) there shall be added the words "or section 9 (preparatory hearings) of the Criminal Justice Act 1987".

4. In section 36 of that Act (bail on appeal by defendant) after the word "Lords", there shall be inserted the words "other than a person appealing or applying for leave to appeal from a decision on an appeal under section 9(11) of the Criminal Justice Act 1987 (appeals against orders or rulings at preparatory hearings)".

5. In section 38 of that Act (presence of defendant at hearing) after the word "who" there shall be inserted the words "has been convicted of an offence and".

Prosecution of Offences (Northern Ireland) Order 1972 (S.J., 1972. No. 538 N.I.J.)

6. In Article 5(3) of the Prosecution of Offences (Northern Ireland) Order 1972 (which makes provision, amongst other things, for the functions of the Director of Public Prosecutions in Northern Ireland in relation to the conduct of criminal proceedings) after the word "Director" there shall be inserted the words," subject to any provision contained in the Criminal Justice Act 1987".

7., 8. . . . .

Bail Act 1976 (e.63.)

9. The following sub-section shall be inserted after section 3(8) of the Bail Act 1976—

"(8A) Where a notice of transfer is given under section 4 of the Criminal Justice Act 1987. sub-section (8) above shall have effect in relation to a person in relation to whose case the notice is given as if he had been committed on bail to the Crown Court for trial.

Supreme Court Act 1981 (c.54.)

[10. In section 76 of the Supreme Court Act 1981 (alteration by Crown Court of place of trial)—

(a)   in sub-section (1), after the word "or", in the second place where it occurs, there shall be inserted the words "by substituting some other place for the place specified in a notice under section 4 of the Criminal Justice Act 1987 (notices of transfer from magistrates' court to Crown Court) or by varying".

(b) after sub-section (2), there shall be inserted the following sub-section – "(2A). Where a preparatory hearing has been ordered under section 7 of the Criminal Justice Act 1987, directions altering the place of trial may be given under sub-section (1) at any time before the jury are sworn", and

(c) in sub-section (3), for the word "or", in the second place where it occurs, there shall be substituted the words "as specified in a notice under section 4 of the Criminal Justice Act 1987 or as fixed."

11. In section 77(1) of that Act (by virtue of which Crown Court Rules are required to prescribe the minimum and maximum period which may elapse between a person's committal for trial and the beginning of the trial) after the word "trial", in the first place where it occurs, there shall be inserted the words "or the giving of a notice of transfer under section 4 of the Criminal Justice Act 1987".]

12. In section 81(1)(a) of that Act (power of Crown Court to grant bail to any person committed in custody for appearance before the Crown Court) after the word "Court" there shall be inserted the words "or in relation to whose case a notice of transfer has been given under section 4 of the Criminal Justice Act 1987".

Prosecution of Offences Act 1985 (c.23.)

13. In section 3(2) of the Prosecution of Offence Act 1985 (which makes provision, amongst other things, for the duties of the Director of Public Prosecutions in relation to the conduct of criminal proceedings) after the word "Director" there shall be inserted the words, "subject to any provisions contained in the Criminal Justice Act 1987".

14. The following paragraph shall be inserted after paragraph (a) of section 16(2) of that Act (defendant's costs order)—

"(aa) a notice of transfer is given under section 4 of the Criminal Justice Act 1987, but a person in relation to whose case it is given is not tried on a charge to which it relates; or".

15. The following sub-section shall be inserted after section 16(4) of that Act—

"(4A) The court may also make a defendant's costs order in favour of the accused on an appeal under section 9(11) of the Criminal Justice Act 1987 (appeals against orders or rulings at preparatory hearings)."

16. At the end of subsection (2)(b) of section 18 of that Act (award of costs against accused) there shall be added "or

(c) an appeal or application for leave to appeal under section 9(11) of the Criminal Justice Act 1987;".

Notes

Para. 1(2) was repealed by the Criminal Justice Act 1988, s. 170, Sched. 16. Para. 2 was repealed by the Criminal Procedure and Investigations Act 1996, ss. 74, 80, Sched. 5, para. 9. Paras 7., 8. were repealed by the Legal Aid Act 1988, s. 45, Sched. 6. Paras 10., 11., which were repealed by the Criminal Justice and Public Order Act 1994, s. 168(3), Sched. 11, were reinstated by the Criminal Procedure and Investigations Act 1996, ss. 44, 80, Sched. 5, para. 1.

APPENDIX Q

TREATY BETWEEN THE GOVERNMENT OF THE UNITED KINGDOM OF GREAT BRITAIN AND NORTHERN IRELAND AND THE GOVERNMENT OF THE UNITED STATES OF AMERICA ON MUTUAL LEGAL ASSISTANCE IN CRIMINAL MATTERS WITH EXCHANGE OF NOTES

Washington, 6 January 1994

[The Treaty and Exchange of Notes are not in force]

Presented to Parliament by the Secretary of State for Foreign and Commonwealth Affairs by Command of Her Majesty July 1994

CONTENTS

The Government of the United Kingdom of Great Britain and Northern Ireland and The Government of the United States of America.

Desiring to improve the effectiveness of the law enforcement authorities of both countries in the investigation, prosecution, and combatting of crime through co-operation and mutual legal assistance in criminal matters.

Reaffirming their determination to enhance assistance in the fight against crime as set out in the Agreement Concerning the Investigation of Drug Trafficking Offences and the Seizure and

Forfeiture of Proceeds and Instrumentalities of Drug Trafficking, done at London February 9, 1988.

Have agreed as follows:

Article 1

Scope of Assistance

(1) The Parties shall provide mutual assistance, in accordance with the provisions of this Treaty, for the purpose of proceedings as defined in Article 19 of this Treaty.

(2) Assistance shall include:

(a) taking the testimony or statements of persons:
(b) providing documents, records, and evidence;
(c) serving documents;
(d) locating or identifying persons;
(e) transferring persons in custody for testimony (or other purposes);
(f) executing requests for searches and seizures:
(g) identifying tracing, freezing, seizing, and forfeiting the proceeds and instrumentalities of crime and assistance in related proceedings; and
(h) such other assistance as may be agreed between Central Authorities.

(3) This Treaty is intended solely for mutual legal assistance between the Parties. The provisions of this Treaty shall not give rise to a right on the part of any private person to obtain, suppress, or exclude any evidence, or to impede the execution of a request.

Article 2

Central Authorities

(1) Central Authorities shall be established by both Parties.

(2) For the United States of America, the Central Authority shall be the Attorney General or a person or agency designated by him. For the United Kingdom, the Central Authority shall be the Secretary of State for the Home Department or a person or agency designated by him.

(3) Requests under this Treaty shall be made by the Central Authority of the Requesting Party to the Central Authority of the Requested Party.

(4) The Central Authorities shall communicate directly with one another for the purposes of this Treaty.

Article 3

Limitations on Assistance

(1) The Central Authority of the Requested Party may refuse assistance if:

(a) the Requested Party is of the opinion that the request, if granted, would impair its sovereignty, security, or other essential interests or would be contrary to important public policy;
(b) the request relates to an offender who, if proceeded against in the Requested Party for the offence for which assistance is requested, would be entitled to be discharged on the grounds of a previous acquittal or conviction; or
(c) the request relates to an offence that is regarded by the Requested Party as:

(i)   an offence of a political character; or
(ii) an offence under military law of the Requested Party which is not also an offence under the ordinary criminal law of the Requested Party.

(2) Before denying assistance pursuant to this Article, the Central Authority of the Requested Party shall consult with the Central Authority of the Requesting Party to consider whether assistance can be given subject to such conditions as it deems necessary. If the Requesting Party accepts assistance subject to these conditions, it shall comply with the conditions.

Article 4

Form and Content of Requests

(1) Requests shall be submitted in writing. However, in urgent circumstances, the request may be made orally but shall be confirmed in writing within ten days thereafter.

(2) The request shall include the following:

(a)   the name of the authority conducting the proceedings to which the request relates:

(b)   the subject matter and nature of the proceedings for the purposes of which the request is made;

(c)   a summary of the information giving rise to the request;

(d)   a description of the evidence or information or other assistance sought; and

(e)   the purpose for which the evidence or information or other assistance is sought.

(3) To the extent necessary and possible, a request shall also include:

(a)   the identity, date of birth and location of any person from whom evidence is sought:

(b)   the identity, date of birth and location of a person to be served, that person's relationship to the proceedings, and the manner in which the service is to be made:

(c)   available information on the identity and whereabouts of a person to be located:

(d)   a precise description of the place or person to be searched and of the articles to be seized;

(e)   a description of the manner in which any testimony or statement is to be taken and recorded;

(f)   a list of questions to be asked of a witness;

(g)   a description of any particular procedures to be followed in executing the request;

(h)   information as to the allowances and expenses to which a person asked to appear in the territory of the Requesting Party will be entitled;

(i)   any other information which may be brought to the attention of the Requested Party to facilitate its execution of the request; and

(j)   requirements for confidentiality.

(4) The Requested Party may ask the Requesting Party to provide any further information which appears to the Requested Party to be necessary for the purpose of executing the request.

Article 5

Execution of Requests

(1) As empowered by this Treaty or by national law, or in accordance with its national practice, the Requested Party shall take whatever steps it deems necessary to give effect to requests received from the Requesting Party. The courts of the Requested Party shall have authority to issue subpoenas, search warrants, or other orders necessary to execute the request.

(2) When execution of the request requires judicial or administrative action, the request shall be presented to the appropriate authority by the persons appointed by the Central Authority of the Requested Party.

(3) The method of execution specified in the request shall be followed to the extent that it is not incompatible with the laws and practices of the Requested Party.

(4) If the Central Authority of the Requested Party determines that execution of the request would interfere with ongoing proceedings or prejudice the safety of any person in the territory of the Requested Party, the Central Authority of that Party may postpone execution, or make execution subject to conditions determined necessary after consultation with the Requesting Party. If the Requesting Party accepts the assistance subject to the conditions, it shall comply with the conditions.

(5) The Central Authority of the Requested Party shall facilitate the participation in the execution of the request of such persons as are specified in the request.

(6) The Central Authority of the Requested Party may ask the Central Authority of the

Requesting Party to provide information in such form as may be necessary to enable it to execute the request or to undertake any steps which may be necessary under the laws and practices of the Requested Party in order to give effect to the request received from the Requesting Party.

(7) The Central Authority of the Requesting Party shall inform the Central Authority of the Requested Party promptly of any circumstances which make it inappropriate to proceed with the execution of the request or which require modification of the action requested.

(8) The Central Authority of the Requested Party shall promptly inform the Central Authority of the Requesting Party of the outcome of the execution of the request. If the request is denied, the Central Authority of the Requested Party shall inform the Central Authority of the reasons for the denial.

Article 6

Costs

(1) The Requested Party shall, subject to paragraph (2) of this Article, pay all costs relating to the execution of the request, except for the fees of expert witnesses and the allowances and expenses related to the travel of persons pursuant to Articles 10 and 11 of this Treaty, which fees, allowances, and expenses shall be paid by the Requesting Party.

(2) If the Central Authority of the Requested Party notifies the Central Authority of the Requesting Party that execution of the request might require costs or other resources of an extraordinary nature, or if it otherwise requests, the Central Authorities shall consult with a view to reaching agreement on the conditions under which the request shall be executed and the manner in which costs shall be allocated.

Article 7

Confidentiality and Limitations on Use

(1) The Requested Party shall, upon request, keep confidential any information which might indicate that a request has been made or responded to. If the request cannot be executed without breaching confidentiality, the Requested Party shall so inform the Requesting Party, which shall then determine the extent to which it wishes the request to be executed.

(2) The Requesting Party shall not use or disclose any information or evidence obtained under this Treaty for any purposes other than for the proceedings stated in the request without the prior consent of the Requested Party.

(3) Unless otherwise indicated by the Requested Party when executing the request, information or evidence, the contents of which have been disclosed in a public judicial or administrative hearing related to the request, may thereafter be used for any purpose.

Article 8

Taking Testimony and Producing Evidence in the Territory of the Requested Party

(1) A person in the territory of the Requested Party from whom evidence is requested pursuant to this Treaty may be compelled, if necessary, to appear in order to testify or produce documents, records, or articles of evidence by subpoena or such other method as may be permitted under the law of the Requested Party.

(2) A person requested to testify or to produce documentary information or articles in the territory of the Requested Party may be compelled to do so in accordance with the requirements of the law of the Requested Party. If such a person asserts a claim of immunity, incapacity or privilege under the laws of the Requesting Party, the evidence shall nonetheless be taken and the claim be made known to the Requesting Party for resolution by the authorities of that Party.

(3) Upon request, the Central Authority of the Requested Party shall furnish information in advance about the date and place of the taking of the evidence pursuant to this Article.

(4) The Requested Party shall allow persons specified in the request to ask questions of the person whose testimony or evidence is being taken, through a legal representative qualified to appear before the courts of the Requested Party.

(5) Documentary information produced pursuant to this Article may be authenticated by the attestation of a person competent to do so in the form indicated in Appendix A to this Treaty. No further authentication or certification shall be necessary in order for such documentary information to be admissible in evidence in proceedings in the territory of the Requesting Party. Documentary information produced pursuant to this Article may also be authenticated pursuant to such other form or manner as may be prescribed from time to time by either Central Authority.

Article 9

Records of Government Agencies

(1) The Requested Party shall provide the Requesting Party with copies of publicly available records of government departments and agencies of the Requested Party.

(2) The Requested Party may provide a copy of any record or information in the possession of a government department or agency but not publicly available to the same extent and on the same conditions as to its own law enforcement or judicial authorities. The Requested Party may refuse a request pursuant to this paragraph entirely or in part.

(3) Official records provided pursuant to this Article shall be authenticated by the Central Authority of the Requested Party in the manner indicated in Appendix B to this Treaty. No further authentication or certification shall be necessary in order for such records to be admissible in evidence in proceedings in the territory of the Requesting Party. Records provided pursuant to this Article may also be authenticated pursuant to such other form or manner as may be prescribed from time to time by either Central Authority.

Article 10

Personal Appearance in the Territory of the Requesting Party

(1) A request under this Treaty may seek assistance in facilitating the appearance of any person in the territory of the Requesting Party for the purpose of giving evidence before a court or of being identified in, or otherwise by his presence assisting, any proceedings.

(2) The Central Authority of the Requested Party shall:

    (a)   ask a person whose voluntary appearance in the territory of the Requesting Party is desired whether he agrees to appear: and

    (b)   promptly inform the Central Authority of the Requesting Party of his answer.

(3) If the Central Authority of the Requesting Party so indicates, a person agreeing to appear in the territory of the Requesting Party pursuant to this article shall not be subject to service of process, or be detained or subjected to any restriction of personal liberty, by reason of any acts or convictions which preceded his departure from the territory of the Requested Party.

(4) The safe conduct provided for by this Article shall cease fifteen days after the Central Authority of the Requesting Party has notified the Central Authority of the Requested Party that the person's presence is no longer required, or if the person has left the territory of the Requesting Party and voluntarily returned to it.

Article 11

Transfer of Persons in Custody

(1) A person in the custody of one Party whose presence in the territory of the other Party is sought for the purpose of providing assistance under this Treaty shall be transferred for that purpose if the person and both Parties consent.

(2) For the purposes of this Article:

(a) the Requesting Party shall be responsible for the safety of the person transferred and shall have the authority and the obligation to keep the person transferred in custody unless otherwise authorised by the Requested Party;

(b) the Requesting Party shall return the person transferred to the custody of the Requested Party as soon as circumstances permit and in any event no later than the date upon which he would have been released from custody in the territory of the Requested Party, unless otherwise agreed by both Central Authorities and the person transferred; and

(c) the Requesting Party shall not require the Requested Party to initiate extradition proceedings for the return of the person transferred.

Article 12

Location or Identification of Persons

(1) The Requested Party shall make best efforts to ascertain the location or identity of persons specified in the request.

(2) The Central Authority of the Requested Party shall promptly communicate the results of its inquiries to the Central Authority of the Requesting Party.

Article 13

Service of Documents

(1) The Requested Party shall, as far as possible, effect service of any document relating to or forming part of any request for assistance properly made pursuant to this Treaty by the Requesting Party, including any subpoena or other process requiring the appearance of any person before any authority or tribunal in the territory of the Requesting Party.

(2) Service of any subpoena or other process by virtue of paragraph (1) of this Article shall not impose any obligation under the law of the Requested Party to comply with it.

(3) The Central Authority of the Requesting Party shall transmit any request for the service of a document requiring the appearance of a person before an authority in the Requesting Party a reasonable time before the scheduled appearance.

(4) The Requested Party shall return a proof of service in the manner specified in the request.

Article 14

Search and Seizure

(1) The Requested Party shall execute a request for the search, seizure and delivery of any article to the Requesting Party if the request includes the information justifying such action under the laws of the Requested party and it is carried out in accordance with the laws of that Party.

(2) The Requested Party may refuse a request if it relates to conduct in respect of which powers of search and seizure would not be exercisable in the territory of the Requested Party in similar circumstances.

(3) Every official who has custody of a seized article shall certify the continuity of custody, the identity of the article and the integrity of its condition in the form indicated in Appendix C to this Treaty. No further authentication or certification shall be necessary in order to establish these matters in proceedings in the territory of the Requesting Party. Certification under this Article may also be provided in any other form or manner as may be prescribed from time to time by either Central Authority.

(4) The Central Authority of the Requested Party may require that the Requesting Party agree to terms and conditions which the Requested Party may deem necessary to protect third party interests in the item to be transferred.

Article 15

Return of Documents and Articles

The Central Authority of the Requesting Party shall return any documents or articles furnished to it in the execution of a request under this Treaty as soon as is practicable unless the Central Authority of the Requested Party waives the return of the documents or articles.

Article 16

Assistance in Forfeiture Proceedings

(1) The Parties shall assist each other in proceedings involving the identification, tracing, freezing, seizure or forfeiture of the proceeds and instrumentalities of crime and in relation to proceedings involving the imposition of fines related to a criminal prosecution.

(2) If the Central Authority of one Party becomes aware that proceeds or instrumentalities are located in the territory of the other Party and may be liable to freezing, seizure or forfeiture under the laws of that Party, it may so inform the Central Authority of the other Party. If the Party so notified has jurisdiction, this information may be presented to its authorities for a determination whether any action is appropriate. The said authorities shall issue their decision in accordance with the laws of their country and the Central Authority of that country shall ensure that the other Party is aware of the action taken.

(3) A Requested Party in control of forfeited proceeds or instrumentalities shall dispose of them according to its laws.

Either Party may transfer forfeited assets or the proceeds of their sale to the other Party to the extent permitted by their respective laws, upon such terms as may be agreed.

Article 17

Compatibility with other Arrangements

Assistance and procedures set forth in this Treaty shall not prevent either of the Parties from granting assistance to the other Party through the provisions of other international agreements to which it may be a party, or through the provisions of its national laws. The Parties may also provide assistance pursuant to any arrangement, agreement, or practice which may be applicable between the law enforcement agencies of the Parties.

Article 18

Consultation

(1) The Parties, or Central Authorities, shall consult promptly, at the request of either, concerning the implementation of this Treaty either generally or in relation to a particular case. Such consultation may in particular take place if, in the opinion of either Party or Central Authority, the expenses or other resources required for the implementation of this Treaty are of an extraordinary nature, or if either Party has rights or obligations under another bilateral or multilateral agreement relating to the subject matter of this Treaty.

(2) With respect to any matter for which assistance could be granted under this Treaty, neither Party shall enforce any compulsory measure requiring an action to be performed by any person located in the territory of the other Party, unless the Party proposing such enforcement has first exhausted the procedures established in paragraphs (3) and (4) of this Article.

(3) If a Party is aware that its authorities are intending to take measures referred to in paragraph (2) of this Article, its Central Authority shall inform the other Central Authority, who may request consultations. If the other Party is aware of or considers that the authorities of the first Party have taken or are about to take any such measures, its Central Authority may request consultations. Thereafter, the Central Authorities shall consult with a view to determining whether the assistance sought can be provided under this Treaty, or otherwise resolving the matter.

(4) Where consultations fail to resolve the matter, or unreasonable delay may be jeopardizing the successful completion of a proceeding, either Central Authority may give the other written notice to that effect.

(5) Unless otherwise agreed by the Parties, the obligations under paragraphs (2), (3) and (4) of this Article shall have been fulfilled 21 days after receipt of this written notice, provided that this is not less than 60 days after receipt of the request referred to in paragraph (3) above.

(6) Even in those cases in which the Parties' obligations under this Article have been fulfilled, each Party shall continue to exercise moderation and restraint.

Article 19

Definitions

(1) For the purposes of this Treaty, "proceedings" means proceedings related to criminal matters and includes any measure or step taken in connection with the investigation or prosecution of criminal offences, including the freezing, seizure or forfeiture of the proceeds and instrumentalities of crime, and the imposition of fines related to a criminal prosecution.

(2) In addition, the Central Authorities may at their discretion treat as proceedings for the purpose of this Treaty such hearings before or investigations by any court, administrative agency or administrative tribunal with respect to the imposition of civil or administrative sanctions as may be agreed in writing between the Parties.

Article 20

Territorial Application

This Treaty shall apply:
(1) in relation to the United Kingdom:

(a)   to England and Wales, Scotland, and Northern Ireland; and
(b)   to the Isle of Man, Channel Islands and to any other territory for whose international relations the United Kingdom is responsible and to which this Treaty shall have been extended by agreement between the Parties, subject to any technical modifications agreed by the Parties and to either Party being able to terminate such extension by giving six months written notice to the other through the diplomatic channel; and

(2) to the United States of America.

Article 21

Ratification and Entry into Force

(1) This Treaty shall be ratified, and the instruments of ratification shall be exchanged at London as soon as possible.

(2) This Treaty shall enter into force upon the exchange of instruments of ratification.

Article 22

Termination

Either Party may terminate this Treaty by means of a written notice to the other Party. Termination shall take effect six months following the date of notification.

IN WITNESS WHEREOF, the undersigned, being duly authorized by their respective Governments, have signed this Treaty.

DONE in duplicate at Washington this sixth day of January, 1994.

For the Government of the United Kingdom of Great Britain and Northern Ireland:

For the Government of the United States of America:

MICHAEL HOWARD   JANET RENO

APPENDIX A
CERTIFICATE OF AUTHENTICITY OF BUSINESS RECORDS

I, ————————, attest on penalty of criminal punishment for false statement or false
    (Name)

attestation that I am employed by ————————————————————————
                                      (Name of Business from which documents are produced)

and that my official title is ————————————. I further state that each of the records attached
                       (Official Title)

hereto is the original or a duplicate of the original of records in the custody of

————————————————————————————————. I further state that:
(Name of Business from which documents are produced)

    (A)   such records were made at or near the time of the occurrence of the matters set forth,
           by (or from information transmitted by) a person with knowledge of those mat-
           ters:
    (B)   such records were kept in the course of a regularly conducted business activity:
    (C)   the business activity made the records as a regular practice; and
    (D)   if any of such records is not the original. such record is a duplicate of the original.

—————————————   —————————————
     (Signature)   (Date)

Sworn to or affirmed before me. ————————. a ———————————————————,
                             (Name)   (notary public, judicial officer, etc.)

this _____ day of _____,199__.

APPENDIX B
ATTESTATION OF AUTHENTICITY OF FOREIGN PUBLIC DOCUMENTS

I, ————————, attest on penalty of criminal punishment for false statement or attestation
    (Name)

that my position with the Government of ———————— is ———————— and that in
                                    (Country)   (Official Title)

that position I am authorized by the law of ———————— to attest that the documents
                                (Country)

attached and described below are true and accurate copies of original official records which are

recorded or filed in ———————————— which is a government office or agency of the
              (Name of Office or Agency)

Government of ————————.
              (Country)

Description of Documents:

_____
(Signature)

_____
(Title)

_____
(Date)

APPENDIX C
ATTESTATION WITH RESPECT TO SEIZED ARTICLES

I, ———————, attest on penalty of criminal punishment for false statement or attestation
   (Name)

that my position with the Government of ——————— is ———————. I received
      (Country)   (Title)

custody of the articles listed below from ——————— on ———————, at
      (Name of Person)   (Date)

———————. I relinquished custody of the articles listed below to ——————— on
(Place)   (Name of Person)

———————, at ——————— in the same condition as when I received them (or if
(Date)   (Place)

different, as noted below).

Description of Articles:

Changes in condition while in my custody:

Official Seal

_____
(Signature)

_____
(Title)

_____
(Place)

_____
(Date)

_No. 1_

**Her Majesty's Ambassador at Washington to the Secretary of State of the United States of America**

British Embassy
Washington
6 January 1994

Your Excellency,

    I have the honour to refer to the Treaty between the Government of the United States of America and the Government of the United Kingdom of Great Britain and Northern Ireland on Mutual Legal Assistance in Criminal Matters (the Treaty) signed today. I have the honour to propose that the Treaty be applied in accordance with the provisions set out in this Note.

(a)   The term "important public policy" in Article 3(1)(a) would include a Requested Party's policy of opposing the exercise of jurisdiction which in its view is extraterritorial and objectionable.

(b)   Article 3(1)(b) shall not affect the availability of assistance in respect of other participants in the offence for which assistance is requested who would not be entitled to be discharged on the grounds of previous acquittal or conviction.

(c)   Article 7(2) shall not preclude the use or disclosure of information to the extent that there is an obligation to do so under the Constitution or law of the Requesting Party in a criminal prosecution. Any such proposed disclosure shall be notified by the Requesting Party to the Requested Party in advance.

(d)   The Treaty shall not apply to anti-trust or competition law investigations or proceedings at this time. The Central Authorities may at their discretion treat as proceedings for the purpose of this Treaty such anti-trust or competition law matters, or anti-trust or competition law matters generally, as may be agreed in writing between the Parties at a later date.

(e)   "Compulsory measures" in Article 18, including in the case of the United States a grand jury subpoena, are those measures that require an action to be performed by any person located in the territory of the Party not issuing the measure and that fall within the following categories:

  (i)   any measure for the production of evidence located in the territory of the Party not issuing the measure;

  (ii)   any measure relating to assets in the territory of the Party not issuing the measure; or

  (iii) any measure compelling a natural person who is in the territory of one Party to make a personal appearance in the territory of the other Party unless:

    a)   the Party compelling the appearance has lawfully obtained jurisdiction over that person: or

    b)   the person is a national of the Party compelling the appearance.
    without prejudice to whether a Party objects to these compulsory measures or the jurisdiction claimed by the other Party.

The Central Authorities may add to or amend the categories referred to above as may be agreed in writing between the Parties.

(f)   In the spirit of co-operation, mutual respect, and goodwill, and in the interests of facilitating the co-operative use of the Treaty with respect to proceedings that fall within its scope and of avoiding measures which could result in a conflict of laws, policies, or national interests, the United States Government shall take several practical measures to reduce the number of instances in which conflict may be anticipated. In particular, the United States Department of Justice, on behalf of the United States Government, shall;

  (i)   instruct all federal prosecutors not to seek compulsory measures, as referred to in Article 18(2), with respect to any matter for which assistance could be granted under the Treaty unless the United States Central Authority has concluded that the provisions of Article 18 of the Treaty have been satisfied;

  (ii)   instruct all federal prosecutors not to enforce any compulsory measures, as referred to in Article 18(2), with respect to any matter for which assistance could be granted under the Treaty, unless the United States Central Authority has concluded that the provisions of Article 18 have been satisfied; and

  (iii) undertake to discourage the issue of compulsory measures by other United States Government agencies for evidence located in the United Kingdom in any matter covered by the Treaty by advising all such agencies not to seek such process without consultation and co-ordination with the United States Central Authority.

If the above proposal is acceptable to the Government of the United States of America, I have the honour to propose that this Note and Your Excellency's reply to that effect shall constitute an agreement between our two Governments, which shall enter into force on the date of entry into force of the Treaty.

I have the honour to convey to Your Excellency the assurance of my highest consideration.

ROBIN W RENWICK

No. 2

The Secretary of State of the United States of America to Her Majesty's Ambassador at Washington

Department of State
Washington
6 January 1994

Excellency:

I have the honor to acknowledge receipt of Your Excellency's Note of today's date, which reads as follows:

[As in No. 1]

I have the further honor to inform Your Excellency that the foregoing proposals are acceptable to the Government of the United States of America and that Your Excellency's Note and this Note shall constitute an agreement between our two Governments, which shall enter into force on the date of entry into force of the Treaty.

For the Secretary of State:

THOMAS A WESTON

MODEL BILATERAL CONVENTION ON MUTUAL ADMINISTRATIVE ASSISTANCE FOR THE PREVENTION, INVESTIGATION AND REPRESSION OF CUSTOMS OFFENCES

(June 1967)

Text and Commentary

Contents

1. Historical background

Customs offences have existed ever since frontiers were created and the goods passing across them became subject to duty. The nature and extent of these offences, as well as the means used to commit them, have changed throughout the centuries and vary from country to country. One of the consequences of the considerable expansion of international trade in recent years has been the often alarming increase in Customs offences. They depend on the economic and geographic situation of a country, the rates of duty charged and other local circumstances (quotas and licences, for example).

Present day offenders make full use of all the means that modern technical progress offers to further their own illicit purposes and elude Customs controls or mislead the authorities.

Customs authorities have of course adopted suitable measures for dealing with fraudulent practices which are prejudicial to their national economy. However, experience shows that in many cases action at national level is no longer adequate, in view of the international character of the operations and organisations involved.

Mutual assistance between Customs authorities in the prevention, investigation and repression of Customs offences was considered by the Customs Co-operation Council as far back as 1953. The Member States recognised that such assistance was an efficient means of combating Customs offences and consequently the Council adopted at that time a Recommendation on mutual administrative assistance, which is now applied by 25 Member States.

However, certain States experienced difficulty in granting administrative assistance on the basis of an international instrument merely in the form of a Recommendation. They had therefore concluded bilateral agreements which provide a more effective means of action against Customs offences.

To strengthen mutual administrative assistance at international level, the Council considered the possibility of preparing a multilateral Convention to replace the above Recommendation. However, discussions showed that at present the number of States in a position to ratify such a Convention would be too small to warrant preparation of an instrument of this kind and to guarantee extended and strengthened administrative assistance between States.

As a result, the Council decided that for the time being, it would concentrate its efforts on assisting States which, in these circumstances, may wish to conclude bilateral assistance agreements. Such agreements could be more readily and more speedily concluded if a model bilateral Convention on mutual administrative assistance were available. The Council therefore decided to carry out a detailed survey of the bilateral and, in some cases, multilateral agreements concluded by some States and of the Recommendation on mutual administrative assistance, extracting the principles which might provide a valuable basis for agreements contemplated by other States, leaving aside only those principles which were considered to be too specialised or which seemed suitable only for inclusion in agreements between countries bound by special instruments of association (e.g. Customs Unions).

The principles, suitably adapted, were assembled into the "Model bilateral Convention on mutual administrative assistance for the prevention, investigation and repression of Customs offences", which was approved by the Council at its 29th/30th Sessions in June 1967. The text of this model Convention is shown in the Appendix.

2. PURPOSE OF THE MODEL CONVENTION

The purpose of the Council in adopting this model Convention is to assist States in concluding bilateral mutual administrative assistance agreements for the prevention, investigation and repression of Customs offences. The value of the model is thus similar to that of the Council's International Customs Norms. However, whereas the Norms state only the fundamental principles, the model Convention provides fuller guidance in that it has been given the form and wording of a potentially ready-made Convention. States remain completely free to delete or modify the provisions of the model as they may see fit or insert additional provisions adapted to their needs.

3. STRUCTURE

With one exception, the structure of the model bilateral Convention is the same as that normally adopted in the Council's Conventions. It is divided into 9 Chapters and 21 Articles.

The only departure from the usual lay-out is in Articles 11, 13, 16 and 17 where alternative provisions have been inserted (*). This was done in certain cases where the Council's experts were divided as to the provision best suited to meet particular circumstances. The inclusion of alternatives will enable countries wishing to conclude a bilateral agreement to choose that provision which best meets their requirements.

Since the model was designed to serve as a basis for negotiation between both adjoining countries and countries not having a common frontier, the provisions concerning adjoining countries were grouped together in one Chapter (Chapter III). The model can, therefore, be readily adapted to meet the needs of distant countries by merely leaving out the provisions contained in Chapter III.

4. INCLUSION OF A RESERVATION CLAUSE

No provision is made in the model Convention for entering reservations since it is usual for a bilateral agreement to be negotiated on the basis of what the two States concerned can implement, or could implement after the necessary changes have been made in national legislation.

The Council has taken the view that the implementation of an agreement based on the model Convention would probably entail amending the legislation which the Customs Administration is responsible for enforcing (i.e. Customs law) but that the agreement should not commit the countries concerned to accepting provisions which might call for amendment of other (non-Customs) domestic legislation or encroach upon existing judicial procedures, although the possibility of accepting such provisions, is by no means precluded.

5. PREAMBLE

(a) Designation of signatories to the Convention.

As stated above, the Council's aim is to provide countries with a complete model Convention in order to facilitate and accelerate the conclusion of bilateral agreements. Paragraph I of the

---

(*) In the text of the model Convention, the alternatives for Articles 11, 13, 16 and 17 have been placed between square brackets.

Preamble refers to a "Government signatory", this being a term used in many Conventions concluded between States in which, according to their Constitution, international agreements may only be entered into by the Government. It is recognised, however, that in an actual agreement the wording of this paragraph would in practice need to be adjusted in the light of the respective constitutions of the countries concerned.

(b) Protection of the interests of Contracting States.

The purpose of a bilateral Convention for the prevention, investigation and repression of Customs offences is not only to protect the fiscal interests of the Contracting country but also the legitimate interests of trade as a whole. The Council, aware that the introduction of repressive measures at a national or international level could be misinterpreted in commercial circles, has expressly stated in the Preamble that Customs offences are prejudicial to the economic, fiscal and commercial interests of the countries concerned.

(c) Co-operation in combating Customs offences.

The third paragraph of the Preamble points out that action against Customs offences can be made more effective by co-operation between the Customs Administrations of Contracting States and refers to the corresponding provisions in the Council's Recommendation on mutual administrative assistance.

6. DEFINITIONS AND SCOPE (CHAPTER I)

Chapter I determines the scope of the model Convention by defining the terms "Customs law" and "Customs offence" in Article 1 and, in Article 2, the obligations to which the two Contracting Parties are committed.

(a) Definitions (Article 1).

The term "Customs law" is taken in the widest possible sense, covering all the fields of activity in which Customs Administrations are (or may be) required to implement the provisions of the laws and regulations.

The definition thus covers not only the importation, exportation, transit or circulation of goods but also of capital or means of payment and cites the collection of duties or taxes (or security therefor) and the enforcement of prohibitions, restrictions or controls or of exchange control regulations as functions of the Customs Administration.

Article 1 (b) defines the term "Customs offence" as any breach, or attempted breach, of "Customs law".

(b) Obligations of Contracting States (Article 2).

Article 2 is the fundamental provision of the model Convention. It stipulates the obligations assumed by the two countries in concluding the agreement by which the Customs Administrations undertake to grant each other mutual assistance for the prevention, investigation and repression of Customs offences.

This therefore requires the requested State to assist the requesting State in any action which the latter takes at national level for the purpose of combating Customs offences more effectively. It follows that when requesting assistance from another State, the State whose Customs legislation is violated or under threat of violation must, for its part, take all the measures provided by its own legislation to combat such offences. It is not the purpose of Article 2 to transfer the responsibility for action to the other State.

(c) Reciprocity.

The model Convention does not include a reciprocity clause for the following reasons. There is no reciprocity clause in the bilateral agreements which Member States have brought to the attention of the Council. Moreover, it has been pointed out that the principle of reciprocity is not always desirable in the case of the developing countries. Indeed, developing countries can frequently offer only limited assistance; reciprocity would imply that the assistance from which they might benefit in return would be equally limited. Finally it would be difficult to provide a clause in the model Convention meeting the needs of all the countries concerned, in view of the differences in the Customs legislations and responsibilities of Customs Administrations.

The Council therefore decided not to include a reciprocity clause in the model, leaving the countries concerned to decide, when negotiating an agreement based on the model, to what extent reciprocity should be applicable and select the solution which best meets their requirements.

However, in view of the recent tendency to include a reciprocity clause in bilateral agreements concluded between certain countries, it was felt that some explanation on the subject should be given in this Commentary.

There are several possible solutions.

One would be to limit the scope of the agreement by the inclusion of a clause drafted in general terms, to the effect that mutual assistance shall always be granted on a reciprocal basis, thereby ensuring equivalent, but not necessarily identical, mutual assistance.

Another solution would be a clause drafted in terms designed to ensure reciprocity or a case for case basis. An example of a possible text is given below:

"Assistance shall not be requested where the Customs Administration of the requesting State could not give that assistance if the positions were reversed."

Or, thirdly, each State might be left free to require reciprocity in individual cases if it so desired. This could be done by inserting a clause in the Convention worded along the following lines:

"The Customs Administration of the State which has received a request for assistance may refrain from giving it where the Customs Administration of the requesting State would be unable to furnish that assistance if the positions were reversed."

Since the effect of such clauses would be to limit the scope of the agreement, the relevant text would be appropriately included as a second paragraph to Article 2.

7. PROVISIONS CONCERNING CERTAIN GOODS (CHAPTER II)

If mutual assistance is to be an effective means of combating Customs fraud, each of the two Contracting States must have knowledge of those goods the illicit importation of which is more particularly prejudicial to the other State. Such goods fall into two categories. The first comprises goods the importation of which is forbidden (Article 3) and the second those goods known to be the subject of illicit traffic between the two States (Article 4). Provision has been made for the exchange of lists of such goods between the two States.

(a) Goods the importation of which is forbidden (Article 3).

It is specified that the Customs Administration of one Contracting State shall not permit the exportation to the other Contracting State of goods the importation of which is forbidden in the latter.

The underlying principle of this provision is that if the goods are not permitted to be imported into one of the States, it is pointless to permit their exportation from the other, since the transaction will necessarily be abortive unless the goods are introduced fraudulently. The provision therefore introduces a useful supplement to the controls which are exercised in the country of importation.

This provision has not been included in the part of the Convention relating solely to countries with a common frontier, and is thus applicable to adjoining countries and to others. Whilst its application is certainly more important in relation to the former, there are circumstances in which it can also provide a useful means of assistance between countries which have no common frontier. It is clear, of course, that a country could not prevent the exportation of goods simply on the grounds that it had a mutual administrative assistance agreement with one of the countries at which a vessel which happened to be carrying the goods would call during its voyage. However, the provision could be applied in relation to particular modes of transport where the final destination of the goods is assured (for example, ferry-boats, postal traffic, and certain forms of container and air traffic).

The provision refers to goods the importation of which is "forbidden". This applies to goods which are the subject of an absolute and unconditional prohibition.

Goods the importation of which is limited, restricted or subject to control, in particular for economic reasons, fall under the provisions of Article 4, i.e. assistance can be requested only when the goods in question are known to be the subject of illicit traffic (see page 14, paragraph 7 (b), below).

Implementation of this provision pre-supposes that the Customs Administrations of both countries have the power to prevent the exportation of certain goods on the grounds that the legislation of the importing State precludes their importation. If the legislation of a State does not make such provision, acceptance of this clause entails implicitly the obligation for that State to grant this power to the Customs Administration by amending its legislation accordingly. Moreover, the application of this provision would involve the re-introduction of export controls which have been dismantled in many countries and which may hamper legitimate trade.

(b) Goods known to be the subject of illicit traffic (Article 4).

With regard to goods in the second category, Article 4 merely provides for the exchange of lists of such goods, while measures relating to them are listed in Articles 7, 8(b) and 9(a) and (b).

Although Article 4 does not explicitly state that in order to retain their usefulness these lists should be kept up-to-date, it is implied that the States concerned should also communicate any changes made in the lists.

8. Measures relating to traffic across the common frontier (Chapter III)

If two countries, wishing to grant one another assistance in combating Customs offences, have a common frontier, special arrangements can be made. These are grouped together in Chapter III and cover administrative measures (Article 5), prohibition of exportation in certain circumstances (Article 6) and surveillance of the transport of certain goods (Article 7).

As already stated, the provisions concerning adjoining countries only have been grouped together so as to facilitate use of the model by countries which have no common frontier, by merely leaving these provisions out of their agreement.

(a) Obligation to use competent Customs offices and approved routes (Articles 5 and 6).

Article 5 requires the Customs Administrations of the two States to take such steps as may be appropriate in order to ensure that goods exported and imported over the common frontier pass through the competent Customs offices and along the approved routes. The obligation to channel goods in this way is intended to reduce the opportunity of introducing goods fraudulently into the importing State.

For the application of this provision, each State must have a list of the Customs offices of the other State located on the common frontier and details of the powers and working hours of these offices; paragraph 2 of Article 5 accordingly provides for these particulars to be exchanged.

Since any lack of correlation in the powers and working hours of corresponding Customs offices would render co-operation less effective, paragraph 3 of this Article provides for the necessary correlation.

It should be noted, in this connection, that correlation of competence and working hours of Customs offices in the two States is an administrative measure often provided for in bilateral and multilateral agreements with a view to facilitating rapid movement of goods in legal traffic across frontiers.

(b) Obligation to prevent the exportation of goods which the Customs office of importation is not competent to clear (Article 6).

Article 6 is a related provision which requires the Customs office of exportation to prevent the exportation of goods which the corresponding Customs office in the other State is not competent to clear. This provision is similar to that of Article 3 (2) (see page 13, paragraph 7(a)), since the measures to be taken by the exporting country will depend on the arrangements existing in the importing country.

(c) Surveillance of transport of certain goods towards the common frontier (Article 7).

This Article requires the exporting country to exercise special surveillance of the transport of goods known to be the subject of illicit traffic towards the common frontier.

The extent of this special surveillance by the exporting country depends on national legislation. In countries where legislation provides for a "Customs surveillance zone", the special surveillance may not start until the goods enter this zone. In countries which do not have a formal "Customs surveillance zone" this provision may also be interpreted as entailing the obligation to exercise surveillance in a restricted area of Customs competence along the frontier.

For the purposes of Article 7, the exporting country should make use of the lists of goods known to be the subject of illicit traffic between the two countries communicated to them under the provisions of Article 4 (see page 14, paragraph 7 (b), above).

9. SURVEILLANCE OF PERSONS, GOODS AND MEANS OF TRANSPORT (CHAPTER IV)

Chapter IV consists of one Article (Article 8) and provides for special surveillance in cases where the importing country suspects activities contrary to its Customs legislation. Such surveillance is exercised only on express request and is restricted to the field of competence of the Customs services.

(a) Purpose of surveillance.

Surveillance may be exercised in respect of:

(i) The movements of certain persons suspected of being engaged in activities in breach of the Customs laws of the requesting State;

(ii) Suspicious movements of particular goods stated by the requesting State to be the subject of considerable illicit traffic towards that State;

(iii) Particular places where stocks of goods have been built up, giving reason to assume that they will be used for illicit importation into the requesting State;

(iv) Particular means of transport (e.g., vehicles, ships) suspected of being used for Customs fraud.

(b) Conditions relating to special surveillance.

A request for special surveillance must be based on specific cause for suspicion by the importing country. This supposes knowledge of certain facts likely to result in a breach of its Customs laws. This knowledge may be acquired in different ways. It may have been obtained as a result of the investigation of irregularities in the requesting State itself which give rise to the general suspicion that they resulted from action originating in the territory of the other State, or the requesting State may have been informed of these facts by the other State, e.g. in application of Article 9(a).

The request must specify the particular persons, goods or places to be placed under special surveillance.

(c) Field of application.

The area in which the requested State is bound to exercise such surveillance is limited to the normal zone of activity of the Customs service (see page 15, paragraph 8 (c), above).

10. COMMUNICATION OF INFORMATION (CHAPTER V)

Chapter V consists of Articles 9 and 10 both of which provide for the communication of information of assistance in the prevention or detection of Customs offences. Article 10 also makes provision for the control of goods which are known to be the subject of illicit traffic, by means of a special document.

(a) Decision to communicate information and method of communication.

To avoid imposing an excessive burden on an Administration, Articles 9 and 10 of the model Convention prescribe when (in all cases) and by what method (for certain cases) information should be communicated. It is specified that Customs Administrations should supply information "spontaneously" (Article 9(a)) or "on express request" (Articles 9(b) and 10) or even "on express written request" (Article 9(c)).

Paragraph (b) of Article 9 is a precautionary measure which provides that even though a State may be obliged to communicate certain information spontaneously to the other State, the latter will be entitled to request from the former, where appropriate, any information referred to in paragraph (a). Such a situation might arise for instance when a State considers that an item of information under paragraph (a) is unlikely to be of interest to the other State, whereas in fact the other State attaches considerable importance to it.

Information should be communicated "without delay" in the cases specified in Article 9(a) and "as promptly as possible" in the cases listed in Article 9(c), on the understanding that in all other cases, assistance should nevertheless be granted within a reasonable time-limit.

(b) Limitations on the information to be provided.

The communication of information by one State to another under Article 9, applies only to "available" information. This in effect limits the obligation to information which may have come into the possession of the Customs Administration during the course of its normal activities and routine investigations made for its own purposes; it entails no obligation to carry out any specific or additional investigations for the sole purpose of collecting information of interest only to the requesting State. This principle applies to information communicated either spontaneously (Article 9(a)) or on request (Article 9(b) and (c)).

(c) Information likely to facilitate prevention of Customs offences (Article 9 (a) and (b)).

Contrary to the provisions of Article 8 which states that in a request for surveillance the person or object should be clearly specified, the provisions of Article 9(a) and (b) are drafted in far more general terms, requiring that the other State should be informed of any circumstances likely to entail consequences prejudicial to the Customs interests of that State. If supplied as promptly as possible, this information should enable the State concerned to take necessary measures for preventing the suspected Customs offences. In view of the broad range of possible offences, the information likely to be communicated covers a vast and varied field. In the model Convention it has been classified into four categories:

(i)   *Suspicious operations (Article 9 (a) (i)).*
Information regarding operations which it is suspected will give rise to Customs offences in the other State.
Application of this provision does not pre-suppose full knowledge of the Customs law of the other State. As a rule, the inference that the operation will give rise to an offence may be drawn from the manner in which the operation is prepared or carried out.
(ii)   *Suspected persons and means of transport (Article 9 (a) (ii)).*
This paragraph concerns persons suspected of committing Customs offences in the other State and means of transport likely to be used for that purpose.
(iii)   *Illicit practices (Article 9 (a) (iii)).*
In order to be able to combat fraud effectively, the Customs must be kept informed of any changes in methods used by those engaged in fraudulent activities and their accomplices; States are therefore required to exchange information on any new means or methods used for committing Customs offences.
(iv)   *Goods known to be the subject of illicit traffic (Article 9 (a) (iv)).*
This paragraph supplements Article 4 which provides for exchange of lists of goods known to be the subject of illicit traffic between Contracting States (see page 14, paragraph 7 (b), above). These lists are kept up-to-date by addition of any new information communicated with regard to such goods. If either of the Customs Administrations has noticed that certain goods have recently become the subject of illicit traffic, these are added to the lists while goods which are no longer in this category are deleted. It is pointed out that such notifications should be made even if, for one reason or another, the Contracting States have refrained from exchanging lists.
In addition, paragraph (iv) requires the Customs Administration of one State to report to the Administration of the other on the results of any surveillance carried out in application of Article 7 or 8 (b), when such results can be of interest to that Administration.

(d) Information contained in Customs documents (Article 9 (c) (i)).

This item, which is closely related to paragraphs 9(c) (ii) and (iii) provides for the communication, on express written request, of information contained in Customs documents in the possession of the requested State, relating to exchanges of goods between the two countries, which are suspected to be contrary to the Customs laws of the requesting State. It should be noted that this provision is of rather limited scope since it is specified that the suspected irregularity must relate to the actual exchange of goods; irregularities in connection with declarations and documents are dealt with in paragraphs (ii) and (iii). This provision might prove useful, for instance, in cases of suspected irregularity in connection with trade marks affixed to the goods.

(e) Information enabling false declarations to be detected (Article 9 (c) (ii)).

This item provides for the communication, on express written request, of information enabling false declarations to be detected, in particular with regard to dutiable value. For example, the requested State may have at its disposal a store of information against which subsequent Customs declarations are to be compared with a view to determining their accuracy. There are, of course, a number of respects in which a declaration appended to an official Customs document (e.g. the Goods declaration (inwards)) may be false, but the irregularity most likely to be detected by the method outlined in the example quoted above is in relation to the dutiable value of the goods. Whilst the provision, therefore, refers particularly to irregularity in this respect, it does not preclude requests for information being made in relation to other matters. The most significant limiting factor, as pointed out in connection with paragraph 10 (b) is that the requested Administration is not obliged to make special investigations to obtain the information called for.

(f) Information concerning other documents (Article 9 (c) (iii)).

Subject to the limitation mentioned above regarding availability, this provision enables the requesting State to obtain information from the other State regarding documents other than those referred to in paragraph 10 (d), such as certificates of origin and invoices, which are suspected of being, or known to be, false.

(g) Information directly or indirectly related to formalities conducted by the Customs Administrations (Article 10).

This Article provides for communication, if appropriate in the form of an official document, of information related to the formalities accomplished by the Customs Administration of the requested State in order to test the truth of documents presented or declarations made to the Customs authorities of the requesting State by persons who may be suspected of activities contrary to Customs laws.

Paragraph 1 provides for the communication of information and defines the information to be communicated; under sub-paragraph (a) a Customs Administration may request confirmation of the authenticity of a document issued by another Customs Administration which has been produced in support of a Goods declaration; under sub-paragraph (b), confirmation may be requested that goods which were granted certain benefits, for example tax exemption or duty refund, on exportation from the requesting State because they were declared as intended for home use in the other State, were duly cleared for that purpose by the Customs Administration of that other State.

A Customs Administration may also request confirmation of the lawful exportation of goods from the Customs territory of the other State (sub-paragraph (c)) or the lawful importation, under any Customs procedure, into the Customs territory of the other State (sub-paragraph (d)).

Paragraph 2 of this Article provides for special arrangements which the two States may make for the control of certain goods known to be the subject of illicit traffic, by means of a special document.

This procedure, when applied to the exportation of goods with refund or remission of Customs duties and/or internal taxes, particularly when these are very high, provides protection, for instance against a twofold risk. First, that after exportation such goods may be re-introduced, illicitly, into the country of exportation and, secondly, that they may be introduced illicitly into the country of destination. Such traffic can be detected if the carrier is required to produce to the Customs authorities of the country of importation a document, certified by the Customs authorities of the country of exportation, specifying the quantity and destination of the goods carried. Any discrepancies would be notified to the Customs authorities of the country of exportation in order that they may take appropriate action (e.g. recovery of duties refunded or remitted at exportation, or internal taxes from which exemption was conditional upon the goods being duly imported into another State).

The application of this provision is probably of greatest value in relation to maritime transport, in view of the possible transshipment of goods from one vessel to another whilst on the high seas.

11. INVESTIGATIONS AND NOTIFICATIONS ON BEHALF OF THE OTHER STATE (CHAPTER VI)

Chapter VI (Articles 11 and 12) is designed to meet the difficulties sometimes encountered by a Customs Administration, in respect of a specific offence against its Customs law, in obtaining evidence which is available only in another State, such as statements from persons suspected of the offence, or from witnesses or experts.

Similar difficulties arise when any action or decisions taken by the Customs Administration of one State in connection with an offence committed in its territory are to be notified to the persons concerned in the other State.

(a) Investigations on behalf of the other State (Article 11).

This Article provides for the Customs Administration of one State to carry out investigations, at the express request of the other State, with a view to obtaining evidence concerning a Customs offence committed in the requesting State, and to take statements from the persons concerned, from witnesses or from experts, and to transmit the results of the investigation, as well as any further evidence, such as documents, to the Customs Administration of the requesting State. The Article also provides that duly authorised Customs officials of the requesting State may be present at the enquiries.

In relation to the model Convention as a whole, this provision can be regarded as a means of obtaining specific evidence relating to a Customs offence, as opposed to the more general information normally received under the preceding Articles.

There are, however, certain factors tending to limit the scope of this Article. First, since the Customs offence has not taken place in the country in which the enquiries are made, it may not be possible to carry out an official interrogation of suspected persons or witnesses, and it may be necessary to rely on informal statements. Secondly, whilst the Article makes provision for the attendance of a Customs official of the requesting State, it is clear that his activities would be governed by the legislation of the country where the enquiries were being made.

The obligations implied by this Article for the Customs Administration of the requested State have consequently been qualified by insertion of the optional wording "within the limits of its competence and in accordance with its national legislation". This phrase is intended as a reminder that restrictions may be placed on the action of the officials of the requesting State. Consequently, before a Convention is concluded it may be necessary to ensure that the national legislation permits compliance with requests from the other State.

(b) Notifications on behalf of the other State (Article 12).

Under this Article, the Customs Administration of one State is required, at the request of the other, to notify the persons concerned (or have them notified by the competent authorities) of any action or decisions taken by the administrative authorities of the requesting State in connection with a Customs offence.

This is intended to provide a means, subject to certain limitations, of notifying persons in one State (whether or not residents), of actions taken in connection with a Customs offence in the other State, without going through the normal diplomatic or other channels.

However, in order to avoid encroaching on judicial matters, this provision applies only to decisions or actions taken by administrative authorities. It could be applied, for example, to notify persons of the seizure of goods or the imposition of compromise penalties.

12. ACTION BY CUSTOMS OFFICIALS OF ONE STATE IN THE TERRITORY OF THE OTHER (CHAPTER VII)

This Chapter makes provision for the Customs officials of one State to undertake certain activities in the other State and defines such activities, which are limited to: inspecting documents kept in the Customs Administration offices, extracting information therefrom and, where appropriate, taking copies therefrom (Article 13), and appearing before a court or tribunal in the other State (Article 14).

(a) Circumstances in which enquiry can be made.

The model Convention contains two alternative texts for Article 13, paragraph 1. The difference between the two texts relates to the circumstances in which the enquiry can be made. It will be observed that the first text covers the general case; the only limitation being that the enquiry shall relate to a specific Customs offence. The alternative is a narrower provision, since it provides that an enquiry can be made only when it is necessary to obtain proof of the facts reported against specific persons.

(b) Purpose of the enquiry.

Both texts provide that the visiting Customs officials may inspect, in the offices of the Customs Administration of the other State, the books, registers and other documents kept in these offices which are relevant to the matter under investigation. Paragraph 2 of the Article provides that the visiting officials may be authorised to take copies from the registers, etc., in question.

Such investigations may be necessary, particularly when the information received in application of other provisions in the model Convention is not sufficient to open legal proceedings.

The search should not be indiscriminate but should normally be confined to the books, registers and other documents relevant to the Customs offence under investigation.

Finally, in order to facilitate their investigation, the visiting officials must be afforded all possible assistance and co-operation, as stated in paragraph 3.

(c) Customs officials appearing as witnesses.

Article 14 provides that on the request of the competent authority (i.e. court, tribunal or Customs Administrations as the case may be) of one State, the Customs Administration of the other may authorise its officials to appear as witnesses before a court or tribunal in the requesting State, in the matter of a Customs offence.

Although the wording of the Article does not preclude the officials in question being called as experts, the basic intention is that they should be required to appear to give evidence only in respect of facts ascertained during the course of their official duties.

The term "upon the request of the competent authority" takes account of the fact that, in practice, the Customs official might be able to appear before a court, or tribunal, only if the court or tribunal considered that his presence was desirable or necessary. However, the term does not preclude the possibility of the request being made by the Customs Administration if that Administration wishes to call the official as a witness. For the purposes of this provision, therefore, the Customs Administration is itself regarded as a "competent authority".

13. GENERAL PROVISIONS (CHAPTER VIII)

This Chapter comprises four Articles (Articles 15 to 18), which deal variously with the maintenance of direct personal relations between the responsible officials of the two States; the use to which information received may be put; the circumstances in which the supply of information can be refused; and the establishment of a joint committee for the application of the Convention.

(a) Maintenance of personal relations (Article 15).

The Customs Administrations of the two States should arrange for their investigation staff to maintain direct and personal contact for the purpose of exchanging information.

The purpose of Article 15, paragraph 1, is to establish a link between the two Customs Administrations, to facilitate the exchange of information in the speediest possible way. Moreover, the transmission of the information direct to the persons concerned affords an additional guarantee that its confidential nature is respected (see Article 16). If requests for assistance are to be acted upon as quickly as possible and if information received is to be made use of efficiently and without delay, it is essential that each of the Administrations should have a list of the officials in the other State who have special responsibilities in these respects. Article 15, paragraph 2, provides therefore for the exchange of such lists. The reference to Articles 9 and 10 may be regarded simply as examples: in practice, Administrations could specify the persons to whom any communications under the Convention are to be made.

(b) Use to which information may be put (Article 16).

Information communicated or obtained under a Convention conforming to the model must be treated as confidential, in the sense that it shall be used only for the prevention, investigation and repression of Customs offences. This provision is intended to ensure that the legal requirements for the protection of professional and fiscal secrecy are maintained. The information received from the other State may, however, be used in the interrogation of persons under the provisions of Article 11.

Paragraph 2 of Article 16 specifies the conditions under which the information may be used in the proceedings and prosecutions before administrative or judicial authorities. The model contains alternative texts for this second paragraph.

The first text provides that the information may be so used unless the Administration providing that particular information has made specific reservations to the contrary. If this text were employed in practice it would mean that a specific reservation must be made in relation to each communication that is not available for use in proceedings and prosecutions. This provision is therefore most suitable for inclusion when such reservations are likely to be exceptional.

The alternative text provides that the information may be used in proceedings and prosecutions only with the written consent of the State providing it. Under this text it would be unnecessary to make any reservation at the time the information was provided, since it could not be used without written permission. This, therefore, is a much more restrictive provision.

It should be noted that in both cases where a State withholds consent for the other State to use the information, it is necessary to give the reasons. The intent of this provision is to ensure that the two States set the same standard of refusal, thereby ensuring uniform application of the provision.

(c) Circumstances in which the communication of information may be refused (Article 17).

Article 17 includes an escape clause, by which the Contracting States may in certain cases refuse to abide by the commitments entered into under a bilateral agreement.

The model provides alternative texts for cases in which the requested State may refuse assistance. The first provides that the requested State shall not be required to give the assistance requested if it considers that such assistance is likely to prejudice its sovereignty, security or other essential interests. The wording is sufficiently flexible to allow the requested State some latitude in having recourse to the escape clause. However, it was felt necessary to provide an alternative text extending the right of refusal to requests for assistance which might prejudice the legitimate commercial interest of any enterprise, public or private.

It should be borne in mind that many bilateral agreements include no escape clause of this kind. States contracting such agreements consider that the satisfactory application of an agreement on mutual administrative assistance for the prevention, investigation and repression of Customs offences is dependent on close co-operation based on complete mutual confidence and trust. The inclusion of any provision in disparagement of this trust can detract from the smooth operation of the Convention.

(d) Establishment of a joint Committee (Article 18).

Article 18 provides for the establishment of a joint Committee, consisting of representatives of the Customs Administrations of the two States, to resolve any problems arising out of the application of the Convention. In deciding to include this provision, the Council considered that it was not necessary to lay down in the Article any hard and fast rules regarding the functions of the joint Committee, or the frequency of its meetings.

In practice, it might be desirable to specify that the joint Committee should hold regular meetings to review the working and progress of co-operation between the States. It might also be desirable to define certain rules for making decisions.

14. Final clauses (Chapter IX)

When drawing up a Convention, it is customary for Contracting States to include formal final clauses, depending on the substantive provisions of the Convention and on the wishes of the States concerned. The model Convention suggests possible texts concerning: field of application of the Convention (Article 19); date of entry into force (Article 20) and denunciation procedure (Article 21). These clauses are based on the provisions adopted when drafting other Conventions, and countries remain entirely free to adopt a different formula in an actual Convention. For example, it might be desirable to specify that the denunciation clause should not take effect whilst specific enquiries are under way.

APPENDIX

MODEL
BILATERAL CONVENTION ON MUTUAL ADMINISTRATIVE ASSISTANCE FOR THE PREVENTION, INVESTIGATION AND REPRESSION OF CUSTOMS OFFENCES

Preamble

The Governments signatory to the present Convention,
   Considering that offences against Customs law are prejudicial to the economic, fiscal and commercial interests of their respective countries,
   Convinced that action against these offences can be made more effective by co-operation between their Customs Administrations and having regard, in this respect, to the Recommendation of the Customs Co-operation Council in Brussels on mutual administrative assistance,
   Have agreed as follows:

Chapter i

Definitions and Scope

Article 1

For the purposes of this Convention:

(a)   the term "Customs law" means all the statutory or regulatory provisions applicable by the Customs Administrations on the importation, exportation, transit or circulation of goods, capital or means of payment, whether involving the collection of duties or taxes (or security therefor), or the enforcement of prohibitions, restrictions or controls or of exchange control regulations;

(b)   the term "Customs offence" means any breach, or attempted breach, of Customs law.

Article 2

The Customs Administrations of the two States shall afford each other mutual assistance, on the terms set out in this Convention, for the prevention, investigation and repression of Customs offences.

Chapter II

Provisions concerning certain goods

Article 3

1. The Customs Administrations of the two States shall communicate to each other lists of goods the importation of which is forbidden in their respective territories.

2. The Customs Administration of one State shall not permit the exportation to the other State of goods the importation of which is forbidden in the other State.

Article 4

The Customs Administrations of the two States shall communicate to each other lists of goods known to be the subject of illicit traffic between their territories.

Chapter III

Measures relating to traffic across the common frontier

Article 5

1. The Customs Administrations of the two States shall take such steps as may be appropriate in order to ensure that goods exported and imported over the common frontier pass through the competent Customs offices and along the approved routes.

2. They shall communicate to each other for that purpose a list of the Customs offices located along the common frontier, details of the powers of those offices and their working hours and, when appropriate, any changes in these particulars.

3. The Customs Administrations of the two States shall endeavour to correlate the powers and working hours of corresponding Customs offices.

Article 6

The Customs Administration of one State shall not permit the exportation of goods to the other State where the corresponding Customs office in the other State is not competent to clear them.

Article 7

The Customs Administration of each State shall maintain special surveillance on the transport towards the common frontier of goods known to be the subject of illicit traffic.

Chapter IV

Surveillance of persons, goods and means of transport

Article 8

The Customs Administration of each State shall, at the express request of the other, maintain special surveillance within its field of competence over:

(a) the movements, particularly the entry into and exit from its territory, of particular persons suspected by the requesting State to be habitually or professionally engaged in activities contrary to the Customs law of that State;

(b) suspicious movements of particular goods stated by the requesting State to be the subject of important illicit traffic towards that State;

(c) particular places where stocks of goods have been built up, giving reason to assume that they will be used for illicit importation into the requesting State;

(d) particular vehicles, ships, aircraft, or other means of transport suspected of being used to commit Customs offences in the requesting State.

Chapter V

Communication of information

Article 9

The Customs Administration of one State shall communicate to the Customs Administration of the other State:

(a) spontaneously and without delay, any available information regarding:

    (i) operations which it is suspected will give rise to Customs offences in the other State;

    (ii) persons, and vehicles, ships, aircraft and other means of transport, suspected of being engaged in, or of being used to commit, Customs offences in the other State;

    (iii) new means or methods of committing Customs offences;

    (iv) goods known to be the subject of illicit traffic;

(b) where appropriate and on express request, any information referred to in paragraph (a) above;

(c) on express written request and as promptly as possible, any available information:

    (i) contained in Customs documents relating to exchanges of goods, between the two countries, which are suspected of being contrary to the Customs law of the requesting State;

    (ii) enabling false declarations to be detected, in particular with regard to dutiable value;

    (iii) concerning certificates of origin, invoices, or other documents, known to be, or suspected of being, false.

Article 10

1. On express request, the Customs Administration of one State shall communicate to the Customs Administration of the other State, if appropriate in the form of an official document, information concerning the following matters:

(a) the authenticity of any official document produced in support of a Goods declaration made to the Customs authorities of the requesting State;

(b) whether goods which were granted favourable treatment on departure from the territory of the requesting State, because they were declared as intended for home use in the other State, have been duly cleared for home use in the latter State;

(c) whether goods imported into the territory of the requesting State have been lawfully exported from that of the other State;

(d) whether goods exported from the territory of the requesting State have been lawfully imported into that of the other State.

2. The Customs Administrations of the two States may make special provision for the control of goods which are known to be the subject of illicit traffic. This control may be exercised by means of a special document issued by the Customs authorities of the country of exportation for surrender to the Customs authorities of the country of importation in order that they may certify that the goods were lawfully imported.

CHAPTER VI

INVESTIGATIONS AND NOTIFICATIONS ON BEHALF OF THE OTHER STATE

Article 11

At the express request of the Customs Administration of one State, the Customs Administration of the other State shall [within the limits of its competence and in accordance with its national legislation]:

(a) make enquiries to obtain evidence concerning a Customs offence under investigation in the requesting State and take statements from any persons connected with that offence, or from witnesses or experts;

(b) permit the duly authorised Customs officials of the requesting State to be present at any enquiries made under paragraph (a) above

and transmit the results of the enquiry, as well as any documents or other evidence, to the Customs Administration of the requesting State.

Article 12

At the request of the Customs Administration of one State, that of the other State shall notify the persons concerned or have them notified by the competent authorities, with due respect for the regulations prevailing in that State, of any action or decisions taken by administrative authorities in connection with a Customs offence.

Chapter VII

Action by Customs Officials of one State in the territory of the other

Article 13

[1. In the investigation of a specific Customs offence, officials specifically designated by one State may, on written request by that State and after being duly authorised by the other State, inspect in the offices of the Customs Administration of the other State the relevant books, registers and other documents kept in those offices and extract any information or particulars relating to the offence.]
or
[1. Where it is necessary, in the investigation of a Customs offence, to obtain proof of the facts reported against specific persons, officials specifically designated by one State may, on written request by that State and after being duly authorised by the other State, inspect in the offices of the Customs Administration of the other State the relevant books, registers and other documents kept in those offices and extract any information or particulars relating to the offence.]

2. The officials designated under paragraph 1 above may take copies from the books, registers and documents referred to in that paragraph.

3. In the application of this Article, all possible assistance and co-operation shall be afforded to the officials of the requesting State to facilitate their investigation.

Article 14

Upon the request of the competent authority of one State, the Customs Administration of the other State may authorise its officials to appear before a court or tribunal in the requesting State, as witnesses, in the matter of a Customs offence.

Chapter VIII

General provisions

Article 15

1. The Customs Administrations of the two States shall arrange for the officials responsible for the investigation and repression of Customs offences to maintain personal and direct relations with a view to exchanging information.

2. The communications referred to in Article 9 and paragraph 1 of Article 10 of this Convention shall be made to the officials specially nominated for that purpose by each Customs Administration; a list of these officials shall be furnished to the Customs Administration of the other State.

Article 16

1. Any communication received, or information obtained, under this Convention shall be treated as confidential in the sense that it shall be used only for the purpose of the prevention, investigation and repression of Customs offences.

[2. Any communication received, or information obtained, under this Convention may be made use of during proceedings and prosecutions before administrative or judicial authorities of one State, unless the Customs Administration of the other State has made specific reservations to the contrary. Where such reservations are made the reasons shall be given.]
or

[2. Any communication received, or information obtained, under this Convention may, with the written consent of the Customs Administration of one State, be made use of during proceedings and prosecutions before administrative or judicial authorities of the other State. Where consent is withheld, the reasons shall be given.]

Article 17

The requested State shall not be required to give the assistance provided for by this Convention if it considers that such assistance is likely to prejudice its sovereignty, security or other essential interests [, or the legitimate commercial interests of any enterprise, public or private].

Article 18

A joint Committee shall be established, consisting of representatives of the Customs Administrations of the two States, to consider any problems arising out of the application of this Convention.

CHAPTER IX

FINAL CLAUSES

Article 19

The field of application of this Convention shall extend:

(a)   on the one hand, to the . . . . Customs territory as defined in the . . . . Customs law and to its territorial waters; and

(b)   on the other hand, to the . . . . Customs territory as defined in the . . . . Customs law and to its territorial waters.

Article 20

1. This Convention shall be subject to ratification and the instruments of ratification shall be exchanged at . . . .

2. The Convention shall enter into force . . . . months after the date of exchange of the instruments of ratification.

Article 21

This Convention is of unlimited duration, but either of the two States may denounce it at any time. The denunciation shall take effect . . . . months after the date of the notification thereof to the Ministry of Foreign Affairs of the other State.

In witness whereof . . . . have signed the Convention.

Done at . . . . on the . . . . day of . . . . in the . . . . and . . . . languages, both texts being equally authentic.

APPENDIX R 2

INTERNATIONAL CONVENTION ON MUTUAL ADMINISTRATIVE ASSISTANCE FOR THE PREVENTION, INVESTIGATION AND REPRESSION OF CUSTOMS OFFENCES

(Nairobi, 9 June 1977)

TABLE OF CONTENTS

PREAMBLE

THE CONTRACTING PARTIES to the present Convention, established under the auspices of the Customs Co-operation Council,

Considering that offences against Customs law are prejudicial to the economic, social and fiscal interests of States and to the legitimate interests of trade,

Considering that action against Customs offences can be rendered more effective by co-operation between Customs administrations, and that such co-operation is one of the aims of the Convention establishing a Customs Co-operation Council,

Have agreed as follows:

CHAPTER I

DEFINITIONS

Article 1

For the purposes of this Convention:

(a) the term "Customs law" means all the statutory or regulatory provisions enforced or administrered by the Customs administrations concerning the importation, exportation or transit of goods;

(b) the term "Customs offence" means any breach, or attempted breach, of Customs law;

(c) the term "Customs fraud" means a Customs offence by which a person deceives the Customs and thus evades, wholly or partly, the payment of import or export duties and taxes or the application of prohibitions or restrictions laid down by Customs law or obtains any advantage contrary to Customs law;

(d) the term "smuggling" means Customs fraud consisting in the movement of goods across a Customs frontier in any clandestine manner;

(e) the term "import or export duties and taxes" means Customs duties and all other duties, taxes, fees or other charges which are collected on or in connexion with the importation or exportation of goods but not including fees and charges which are limited in amount to the approximate cost of services rendered;

(f) the term "person" means both natural and legal persons, unless the context otherwise requires;

(g) the term "the Council" means the organization set up by the Convention establishing a Customs Co-operation Council, done at Brussels on 15 December 1950;

(h) the term "Permanent Technical Committee" means the Permanent Technical Committee of the Council;

(ij) the term "ratification" means ratification, acceptance or approval.

CHAPTER II

SCOPE OF THE CONVENTION

Article 2

1. The Contracting Parties bound by one or more Annexes to this Convention agree that their Customs administrations shall afford each other mutual assistance with a view to preventing, investigating and repressing Customs offences, in accordance with the provisions of this Convention.

2. The Customs administration of a Contracting Party may request mutual assistance as provided for in paragraph 1 of this Article in the course of any investigation or in connexion with any judicial or administrative proceedings being undertaken by that Contracting Party. If the Customs administration is not itself conducting the proceedings, it may request mutual assistance only within the limits of its competence in these proceedings. Similarly, if proceedings are undertaken in the country of the requested administration, the latter provides the assistance requested within the limits of its competence in these proceedings.

3. Mutual assistance as provided for in paragraph 1 of this Article shall not extend to requests for the arrest of persons or for the recovery of duties, taxes, charges, fines or any other monies on behalf of another Contracting Party.

Article 3

If a Contracting Party considers that the assistance sought would infringe upon its sovereignty, security or other substantial national interests or prejudice the legitimate commercial interests of any enterprise, public or private, it may decline to provide that assistance or give it subject to certain conditions or requirements.

Article 4

If the Customs administration of a Contracting Party requests assistance which it itself would be unable to give if requested to do so by the other Contracting Party, it shall draw attention to that fact in its request. Compliance with such a request shall be within the discretion of the requested Contracting Party.

CHAPTER III
GENERAL ASSISTANCE PROCEDURES

Article 5

1. Any intelligence, documents or other information communicated or obtained under this Convention:

   (a) shall be used only for the purposes specified in this Convention, including use in judicial or administrative proceedings, and subject to such restrictions as may be laid down by the Customs administration which furnished them; and

   (b) shall be afforded in the receiving country the same protection in respect of confidentiality and official secrecy as applies in that country to the same kind of intelligence, documents and other information obtained in its own territory.

2. Such intelligence, documents or other information may be used for other purposes only with the written consent of the Customs administration which furnished them and subject to any restrictions laid down by that administration and to the provisions of paragraph 1 (b) of this Article.

Article 6

1. The communications between Contracting Parties provided for by this Convention shall pass directly between Customs administrations. The Customs administrations of the Contracting Parties shall designate the services or officials responsible for such communications and shall advise the Secretary General of the Council of the names and addresses of those services or officials. The Secretary General shall communicate this information to the other Contracting Parties.

2. The Customs administration of the requested Contracting Party shall, subject to the laws and regulations in force in its territory, take all necessary measures to comply with a request for assistance.

3. The Customs administration of the requested Contracting Party shall reply to a request for assistance as soon as possible.

Article 7

1. Requests for assistance under this Convention shall normally be made in writing; they shall contain the requisite information and be accompanied by such documents as maybe deemed useful.

2. Requests in writing shall be in a language acceptable to the Contracting Parties concerned. Any documents accompanying such requests shall be translated into a mutually acceptable language, if necessary.

3. Contracting Parties shall in all cases accept requests for assistance and accompanying documents in English or French or accompanied by a translation into English or French.

4. When, for reasons of urgency in particular, requests for assistance have not been made in writing, the requested Contracting Party may require written confirmation.

Article 8

Any expenses incurred under this Convention in respect of experts or witnesses shall be borne by the requesting Contracting Party. The Contracting Parties shall waive all claims for reimbursement of any other costs incurred in the execution of this Convention.

CHAPTER IV
MISCELLANEOUS PROVISIONS

Article 9

The Council and the Customs administrations of the Contracting Parties shall arrange for the services responsible for the prevention, investigation and repression of Customs offences to maintain personal and direct relations with a view to furthering the general aims of this Convention.

Article 10

For the purposes of this Convention any Annex or Annexes to which a Contracting Party is bound shall be construed to be an integral part of the Convention, and in relation to that Contracting Party any reference to the Convention shall be deemed to include a reference to such Annex or Annexes.

Article 11

The provisions of this Convention shall not preclude the application of any more extensive mutual assistance which certain Contracting Parties grant or may grant in future.

CHAPTER V
ROLE OF THE COUNCIL AND OF THE PERMANENT TECHNICAL COMMITTEE

Article 12

1. The Council shall, in accordance with the provisions of this Convention, be responsible for the administration and development of this Convention.

2. To these ends the Permanent Technical Committee shall, under the authority of the Council and in accordance with any directions given by the Council, have the following functions:

    (a)   to submit to the Council proposals for such amendments to this Convention as it may consider necessary;

    (b)   to furnish opinions on the interpretation of provisions of the Convention;

    (c)   to maintain relations with the other international organizations concerned and, in particular, with the competent bodies of the United Nations with UNESCO and with the International Criminal Police Organization/Interpol, as regards action against illicit traffic in narcotic drugs and psychotropic substances, and action against illicit traffic in works of art, antiques and other cultural property;

    (d)   to take any action likely to further the general aims of the Convention and in particular to study new methods and procedures to facilitate the prevention, investigation and repression of Customs offences, to convene meetings, etc.;

    (e)   to perform such tasks as the Council may direct in relation to the provisions of the Convention.

Article 13

For the purposes of voting in the Council and in the Permanent Technical Committee each Annex shall be taken to be a separate Convention.

CHAPTER VI

FINAL PROVISIONS

Article 14

Any dispute between two or more Contracting Parties concerning the interpretation or application of this Convention shall be settled by negotiation between them.

Article 15

1. Any State Member of the Council may become a Contracting party to this Convention:
   (a) by signing it without reservation of ratification;
   (b) by depositing an instrument of ratification after signing it subject to ratification; or
   (c) by acceding to it.

2. This Convention shall be open until 30th June 1978 for signature at the Headquarters of the Council in Brussels by the States referred to in paragraph 1 of this Article. Thereafter, it shall be open for their accession.

3. Each State referred to in paragraph 1 of this Article shall at the time of signing, ratifying or acceding to this Convention specify the Annex or Annexes it accepts, it being necessary to accept at least one Annex. It may subsequently notify the Secretary General of the Council that it accepts one or more further Annexes.

4. The instruments of ratification or accession shall be deposited with the Secretary General of the Council.

5. Customs or economic unions may, together with all their Member States or at any time after all their Member States have become Contracting Parties to this Convention, also become Contracting Parties to this Convention in accordance with the provisions of paragraphs 1, 2 and 3 of this Article. However, such unions shall not have the right to vote.

Article 16

1. This Convention shall enter into force three months after five of the States referred to in paragraph 1 of Article 15 thereof have signed the Convention without reservation of ratification or have deposited their instruments of ratification or accession.

2. For any Contracting Party signing without reservation of ratification, ratifying or acceding to this Convention after five States have signed it without reservation of ratification or have deposited their instruments of ratification or accession, this Convention shall enter into force three months after the said Contracting Party has signed without reservation of ratification or deposited its instrument of ratification or accession.

3. Any Annex to this Convention shall enter into force three months after two States have accepted that Annex. For any Contracting Party which subsequently accepts an Annex after two States have accepted it, that Annex shall enter into force three months after the said Contracting Party has notified its acceptance. No Annex shall however enter into force for a Contracting Party before the Convention has entered into force for that Contracting Party.

Article 17

1. Any State may, at the time of signing this Convention without reservation of ratification or of depositing its instruments of ratification or accession, or any time thereafter, declare by

notification given to the Secretary General of the Council that this Convention shall extend to all or any of the territories for whose international relations it is responsible. Such notification shall take effect three months after the date of the receipt thereof by the Secretary General of the Council. However, the Convention shall not apply to the territories named in the notification before the Convention has entered into force for the State concerned.

2. Any State which has made a notification under paragraph 1 of this Article extending this Convention to any territory for whose international relations it is responsible may notify the Secretary General of the Council, under the procedure of Article 19 of this Convention, that the territory in question will no longer apply the Convention.

Article 18

No reservation to this Convention shall be permitted.

Article 19

1. This Convention is of unlimited duration but any Contracting Party may denounce it at any time after the date of its entry into force under Article 16 thereof.

2. The denunciation shall be notified by an instrument in writing, deposited with the Secretary General of the Council.

3. The denunciation shall take effect six months after the receipt of the instrument of denunciation by the Secretary General of the Council.

4. The provisions of paragraphs 2 and 3 of this Article shall also apply in respect of the Annexes to this Convention, any Contracting Party being entitled, at any time after the date of their entry into force under Article 16 of the Convention, to withdraw its acceptance of one or more Annexes. Any Contracting Party which withdraws its acceptance of all the Annexes shall be deemed to have denounced the Convention.

5. Any Contracting Party which denounces the Convention or withdraws its acceptance of one or more Annexes shall remain bound by the provisions of Article 5 of this Convention for as long as it retains in its possession any intelligence, documents or other information obtained under the Convention.

Article 20

1. The Council may recommend amendments to this Convention.

2. The text of any amendment so recommended shall be communicated by the Secretary General of the Council to all Contracting Parties to this Convention, to the other signatory States and to those States Members of the Council that are not Contracting Parties to this Convention.

3. Any proposed amendment communicated in accordance with the preceding paragraph shall come into force with respect to all Contracting Parties three months after the expiry of a period of two years following the date of communication of the proposed amendment during which period no objection to the proposed amendment has been communicated to the Secretary General of the Council by a State which is a Contracting Party.

4. If an objection to the proposed amendment has been communicated to the Secretary General of the Council by a State which is a Contracting Party before the expiry of the period of two years specified in paragraph 3 of this Article, the amendment shall be deemed not to have been accepted and shall have no effect whatsoever.

Article 21

1. Any Contracting Party ratifying or acceding to this Convention shall be deemed to have accepted any amendments thereto which have entered into force at the date of deposit of its instrument of ratification or accession.

2. Any Contracting Party which accepts an Annex shall be deemed to have accepted any amendments to that Annex which have entered into force at the date on which it notifies its acceptance to the Secretary General of the Council.

Article 22

The Secretary General of the Council shall notify the Contracting Parties to this Convention, the other signatory States, those States Members of the Council that are not Contracting Parties to this Convention, and the Secretary General of the United Nations of:

(a) signatures, ratifications, accessions and notifications under Article 15 of this Convention;

(b) the date of entry into force of this Convention and of each of the Annexes in accordance with Article 16;

(c) notification received in accordance with Article 17;

(d) denunciations under Article 19;

(e) any amendment deemed to have been accepted in accordance with Article 20 and the date of its entry into force.

Article 23

Upon its entry into force this Convention shall be registered with the Secretariat of the United Nations, in accordance with Article 102 of the Charter of the United Nations.

In witness whereof the undersigned, being duly authorized thereto, have signed this Convention.

Done at Nairobi, this ninth day of June nineteen hundred and seventy-seven, in the English and French languages, both texts being equally authentic, in a single original which shall be deposited with the Secretary General of the Council who shall transmit certified copies to all the States referred to in paragraph 1 of Article 15 of this Convention.

Annex I
Assistance by a Customs administration on its own initiative

1. The Customs administration of a Contracting Party shall, on its own initiative, communicate to the Customs administration of the Contracting Party concerned, any information of a substantial nature which has come to light in the course of its normal activities and which gives good reason to believe that a serious Customs offence will be committed in the territory of the other Contracting Party. The information to be communicated shall concern, in particular, the movements of persons, goods and means of transport.

2. The Customs administration of a Contracting Party shall, where deemed appropriate, communicate on its own initiative to the Customs administration of another Contracting Party documents, reports, records of evidence or certified copies thereof in support of the information furnished under paragraph 1.

3. The Customs administration of a Contracting Party shall, on its own initiative, communicate to the Customs administration of another Contracting Party that is directly concerned, any information likely to be of material assistance to it in connexion with Customs offences and, particularly, in connexion with new means or methods of committing such offences.

Annex II
Assistance, on request, in the assessment of import or export duties and taxes

1. At the request of the Customs administration of a Contracting Party which has good reason to believe that a serious Customs offence has been committed in its country, the Customs

administration of the requested Contracting Party shall communicate all available information which may help to ensure the proper assessment of import or export duties and taxes.

2. A Contracting Party shall be taken to have fulfilled its obligations in this respect if, for example, it communicates as appropriate in response to a request the following information or documents available to it:

(a) in respect of the value of goods for Customs purposes: the commercial invoices presented to the Customs of the country of exportation or importation or copies of such invoices, certified or not by the Customs, as the circumstances may require; documentation showing current export or import prices; a copy of the declaration of value made on exportation or importation of the goods; trade catalogues, price lists, etc. published in the country of exportation or in the country of importation;

(b) in respect of the tariff classification of goods: analyses carried out by laboratory services to determine the tariff classification of the goods; the tariff description declared on importation or exportation;

(c) in respect of the origin of goods: the declaration of origin made on exportation, when such declaration is required; the Customs status of the goods in the country of exportation (Customs transit, Customs warehouse, temporary admission, free zone, free circulation, exported under drawback, etc.).

Annex III
Assistance, on request, relating to controls

At the request of the Customs administration of a Contracting Party, the Customs administration of another Contracting Party shall communicate to that Customs administration information concerning the following matters:

(a) the authenticity of official documents produced in support of a Goods declaration made to the Customs authorities of the requesting Contracting Party;

(b) whether goods imported into the territory of the requesting Contracting Party have been lawfully exported from the territory of the other Contracting Party;

(c) whether goods exported from the territory of the requesting Contracting Party have been lawfully imported into the territory of the requested Contracting Party.

Annex IV
Assistance, on request, relating to surveillance

At the request of the Customs administration of a Contracting Party, the Customs administration of another Contracting Party shall, to the extent of its competence and ability, maintain special surveillance for a specified period over:

(a) the movements, particularly the entry into and exit from its territory, of particular persons reasonably believed to be professionally or habitually engaged in Customs offences in the territory of the requesting Contracting Party;

(b) movements of particular goods which are reported by the Customs administration of the requesting Contracting Party as giving rise to important illicit traffic towards or from the territory of that Contracting Party;

(c) particular places where stocks of goods have been built up, giving reason to assume that they are to be used for illicit importation into the territory of the requesting Contracting Party;

(d) particular vehicles, ships, aircraft or other means of transport reasonably believed to be used to commit Customs offences in the territory of the requesting Contracting Party,

and shall communicate a report thereon to the Customs administration of the requesting Contracting Party.

Annex V
Enquiries and Notifications, on Request, on Behalf of Another Contracting Party

1. At the request of the Customs administration of a Contracting Party, the Customs administration of another Contracting Party shall, subject to the laws and regulations in force in its territory, make enquiries to obtain evidence concerning a Customs offence under investigation in the territory of the requesting Contracting Party, and take statements from any persons sought in connexion with that offence or from witnesses or experts, and communicate the results of the enquiry, as well as any documents or other evidence, to the Customs administration of the requesting Contracting Party.

2. At the written request of the Customs administration of a Contracting Party, the Customs administration of another Contracting Party shall, subject to the laws and regulations in force in its territory, notify the persons concerned residing in its territory or have them notified by the competent authorities of any action or decisions taken by the requesting Contracting Party concerning any matter falling within the scope of this Convention.

Annex VI
Appearance by Customs Officials Before a Court or Tribunal Abroad

Where it is not sufficient for evidence to be given solely in the form of a written statement, at the request of the Customs administration of a Contracting Party the Customs administration of another Contracting Party, to the extent of its ability, shall authorize its officials to appear before a court or tribunal in the territory of the requesting Contracting Party as witnesses or experts in the matter of a Customs offence. The request for appearance shall specify, in particular, in what case and in what capacity the official is to be heard. The Customs administration of the Contracting Party accepting the request shall, in authorizing appearance, state any limits with which its officials should comply in giving evidence.

Annex VII
Presence of Customs Officials of One Contracting Party in the Territory of Another Contracting Party

1. At the written request of the Customs administration of a Contracting Party investigating a specific Customs offence, the Customs administration of another Contracting Party shall, where deemed appropriate, authorize officials specially designated by the requesting Contracting Party to consult, in its offices, the relevant books, registers and other documents or data media held in those offices, take copies thereof, or extract any information or particulars relating to the offence.

2. In the application of the provisions of paragraph 1 above, all possible assistance and co-operation shall be afforded to the officials of the requesting Contracting Party to facilitate their investigation.

3. At the written request of the Customs administration of a Contracting Party, the Customs administration of another Contracting Party shall, where deemed appropriate, authorize officials of the requesting administration to be present in the territory of the requested Contracting Party in connexion with enquiries into or the official reporting of a Customs offence of concern to the requesting Contracting Party.

Annex VIII
Participation in Investigations Abroad

Where deemed appropriate by both Contracting Parties, the officials of the Customs administration of a Contracting Party shall, at the request of another Contracting Party, participate in investigations carried out in the territory of that other Contracting Party.

ANNEX IX
POOLING OF INFORMATION

1. The Customs administrations of Contracting Parties shall communicate to the Secretary General of the Council the information specified hereafter insofar as it is of international interest.

2. The Secretary General of the Council shall institute and keep up-to-date a central index of information communicated to him by Contracting Parties and shall use information from it to prepare summaries and studies of new and recurring trends in Customs fraud. He shall periodically review the index to eliminate information which, in his opinion, has outlived its utility or become out-of-date.

3. The Customs administrations of the Contracting Parties shall, upon request by the Secretary General of the Council and subject to the other provisions of the Convention and this Annex, provide the Secretary General with such complementary information as may be necessary to prepare the summaries and studies referred to in paragraph 2 of this Annex.

4. The Secretary General of the Council shall circulate to the services or officials named by the Customs administrations of the Contracting Parties specific information contained in the central index, to the extent that he deems such circulation useful, and any summaries and studies referred to in paragraph 2 of this Annex.

5. The Secretary General of the Council shall, upon request, supply Contracting Parties with any other information available to him under this Annex.

6. The Secretary General of the Council shall honour any restrictions that a Contracting Party having provided information may have placed on its circulation.

7. A Contracting Party having communicated information shall be entitled to require that it be subsequently deleted from the central index and from any registers established by Contracting Parties to which it has been communicated and that no further use be made of it.

PART I: PERSONS
SECTION I: SMUGGLING

8. Notifications under this Section shall provide information concerning:

    (a)   persons finally convicted of smuggling; and
    (b)   where appropriate, persons suspected of smuggling or apprehended in the act of smuggling in the territory of the Contracting Party making the notification, even though legal proceedings have not been completed,

it being understood that when Contracting Parties refrain from notifying the names and descriptions of the persons involved because such notification is prohibited by their national law, they shall nevertheless make a notification containing as many as possible of the items listed in this Section.

In principle, the information notified shall be limited to offences which have resulted in or could lead to imprisonment or a fine exceeding the equivalent of US$2,000.

9. The information to be furnished shall, so far as possible include the following:

(A) Natural persons

    (a)   Surname
    (b)   Forenames
    (c)   Maiden name (if applicable)
    (d)   Nickname or alias
    (e)   Occupation
    (f)   Address (present)
    (g)   Date and place of birth
    (h)   Citizenship/Nationality
    (ij)   Country of residence and countries visited during the past 12 months
    (k)   Type and number of identity papers, including country and date of issue

(l) Physical description
    (1) Sex
    (2) Height
    (3) Weight
    (4) Build
    (5) Hair
    (6) Eyes
    (7) Complexion
    (8) Distinctive marks or peculiarities
(m) Brief particulars of offence (including particulars of type, quantity and origin of goods involved in the offence, manufacturer, shipper and consignor) and circumstances which led to its detection
(n) Nature and amount of penalty and/or sentence imposed
(o) Other observations, including languages spoken and (if available) any previous convictions recorded
(p) Contracting Party furnishing the information (including reference number).

(B) Legal persons (firms)

(a) Name
(b) Address
(c) Names of principal officers or employees of the firm against whom legal action has been taken and, if appropriate, identifying data as indicated under Part (A), Items (a)–(l)
(d) Related multi-national company
(e) Nature of business carried on
(f) Nature of offence
(g) Particulars of offence (including manufacturer, shipper and consignor) and circumstances which led to its detection
(h) Amount of penalty
(ij) Other observations, including (if available) any previous convictions recorded
(k) Contracting Party furnishing the information (including reference number).

10. As a general rule, the Secretary General of the Council shall circulate information relating to natural persons at least to the countries of citizenship/nationality and residence and to the countries visited by the person during the past 12 months.

Section II: Customs fraud other than smuggling

11. Notifications under this Section shall provide information concerning:

(a) persons finally convicted of Customs fraud other than smuggling;
(b) where appropriate, persons suspected of such fraud, even though legal proceedings have not been completed,

it being understood that when Contracting Parties refrain from notifying the names and descriptions of the persons involved because such notification is prohibited by their national law, they shall nevertheless make a notification containing as many as possible of the items listed in this Section.

In principle, the information notified shall be limited to offences which have resulted in or could lead to imprisonment or a fine exceeding the equivalent of US$2,000.

12. The information to be furnished shall, so far as possible, include the following:

(a) Name (or firm name) and address
(b) Names and identifying data of principal officers of the firm against which legal action has been taken
(c) Kind of goods
(d) Country of origin
(e) Related multi-national company

(f)   Name and address of seller
(g)   Name and address of shipper
(h)   Names and addresses of other parties involved (buying or selling agents, other middlemen, etc.)
(ij)   Port(s) or place(s) at which goods were exported
(k)   Brief particulars of offence and circumstances which led to its detection
(l)   Amount of penalty and loss of revenue, if any
(m)   Other observations, including (if available) any previous convictions recorded
(n)   Contracting Party furnishing the information (including reference number).

PART II:
METHODS OF SMUGGLING AND OTHER FRAUD, INCLUDING FRAUD BY FORGERY, FALSIFICATION AND COUNTERFEITING

13. Notifications under this Part shall provide information relating to methods of smuggling and other fraud, including methods of concealment, fraud by forgery, falsification or counterfeiting, in all cases of significant international interest. Contracting Parties shall report each use of a known method of smuggling and other fraud as well as new, unusual or possible methods so that current trends in this field can be detected.

14. The information to be furnished shall, so far as possible, include the following:

(a)   Description of methods of smuggling and other fraud, including fraud by forgery, falsification or counterfeiting. If available, the description (make, model, registration number, etc.) of any means of transport used. Where applicable, data from the approval plate or certificate of containers or vehicles, the designs of which were approved under an international Convention, and information about any violations of seals, bolts, sealing devices or other parts of containers or vehicles
(b)   Description, if applicable, of the place of concealment, including, where possible, a photograph or sketch
(c)   Description of goods concerned
(d)   Nature and description of forgery, falsification or counterfeiting; use to which the forged, falsified or counterfeited documents, Customs seals, registration plates, etc. were put
(e)   Other observations, including the circumstances which led to detection
(f)   Contracting Party furnishing the information (including reference number).

PART III:
VESSELS INVOLVED IN SMUGGLING

15. Notifications under this Part shall provide information relating to vessels, of all types, that have been involved in smuggling, but should be limited, in principle, to cases which are considered to be of international interest.

16. Insofar as it is available and can be communicated under national law, the information to be furnished shall include the following:

(a)   Name and brief identification of vessel (S.S., M.V., tonnage, silhouette, etc.)
(b)   Name and address of owner/charterer
(c)   Flag
(d)   Port of registry and, if different, home port
(e)   Name and citizenship/nationality of master (and, if applicable, principal officers)
(f)   Nature of the offence, including description of goods seized
(g)   Description, if applicable, of the place of concealment (including, where possible, a photograph or sketch) and of the circumstances which led to the discovery
(h)   Country of origin of goods seized
(ij)   First port of lading
(k)   Final port of destination
(l)   Ports of call between (ij) and (k)
(m)   Other observations (number of cases in which the same vessel, shipping company, charterer or other vessel operator has been involved in smuggling, etc.)

(n)   Contracting Party furnishing the information (including reference number).

Annex X
Assistance in action against the smuggling of narcotic drugs and psychotropic substances

1. The provisions of this Annex shall not preclude the application of measures in force at the national level in the matter of co-ordination of the activities of the various authorities competent to take action against the abuse of narcotic drugs and psychotropic substances. They shall also not impede, but complement, the implementation of the provisions of the Single Convention on Narcotic Drugs, 1961, and of the 1971 Convention on Psychotropic Substances by Parties to these Conventions which have also accepted this Annex.

2. The provisions of this Annex concerning the smuggling of narcotic drugs and psychotropic substances shall wherever appropriate and to the extent of the competence of the Customs administrations, apply also to the financial operations undertaken in connexion with such smuggling.

Exchange of information by Customs administrations on their own initiative

3. The Customs administrations of Contracting Parties shall, on their own initiative and without delay, communicate to other Customs administrations which may be directly concerned, any available information concerning:

(a)   operations which are known or suspected to constitute, or which seem likely to give rise to, smuggling of narcotic drugs or psychotropic substances;

(b)   persons known to be engaged in or, insofar as information concerning such persons can be communicated under national law, persons suspected of engaging in operations referred to in paragraph (a) above, and vehicles, ships, aircraft and other means of transport used, or suspected of being used, for such operations;

(c)   new means or methods used for smuggling narcotic drugs or psychotropic substances;

(d)   products which are newly developed or newly used as narcotic drugs or psychotropic substances and which are the subject of smuggling.

Assistance, on request, relating to surveillance

4. At the request of the Customs administration of a Contracting Party, the Customs administration of another Contracting Party shall, to the extent of its competence and ability, maintain special surveillance for a specified period over:

(a)   the movements, particularly the entry into and exit from its territory, of particular persons reasonably believed to be professionally or habitually engaged in the smuggling of narcotic drugs and psychotropic substances in the territory of the requesting Contracting Party;

(b)   movements of narcotic drugs or psychotropic substances which are reported by the Customs administration of the requesting Contracting Party as giving rise to important illicit traffic towards or from the territory of that Contracting Party;

(c)   particular places where stocks of narcotic drugs and psychotropic substances have been built up, giving reason to assume that they are to be used for illicit importation into the territory of the requesting Contracting Party;

(d)   particular vehicles, ships, aircraft or other means of transport reasonably believed to be used for smuggling narcotic drugs or psychotropic substances into the territory of the requesting Contracting Party,

and shall communicate a report thereon to the Customs administration of the requesting Contracting Party.

Enquiries on request on behalf of another Contracting Party

5. At the request of the Customs administration of a Contracting Party, the Customs administration of another Contracting Party shall, subject to the laws and regulations in force in its territory, make enquiries to obtain evidence concerning any smuggling of narcotic drugs or psychotropic substances under investigation in the territory of the requesting Contracting Party, and take statements from any persons sought in connexion with that smuggling or from witnesses or experts, and communicate the results of the enquiry, as well as any documents or other evidence, to the Customs administration of the requesting Contracting Party.

Action by Customs officials of one Contracting Party in the territory of another Contracting Party

6. Where it is not sufficient for evidence to be given solely in the form of a written statement, at the request of the Customs administration of a Contracting Party the Customs administration of another Contracting Party, to the extent of its ability, shall authorize its officials to appear before a court or tribunal in the territory of the requesting Contracting Party as witnesses or experts in the matter of smuggling of narcotic drugs or psychotropic substances. The request for appearance shall specify, in particular, in what case and in what capacity the official is to be heard. The Customs administration of the Contracting Party accepting the request shall, in authorizing appearance, state any limits with which its officials should comply in giving evidence.

7. At the written request of the Customs administration of a Contracting Party, the Customs administration of another Contracting Party shall, where deemed appropriate and to the extent of its competence and ability, authorize officials of the requesting administration to be present in the territory of the requested Contracting Party in connexion with enquiries into or the official reporting of smuggling of narcotic drugs or psychotropic substances of concern to the requesting Contracting Party.

8. Where deemed appropriate by both Contracting Parties and subject to the laws and regulations in force in their territories, the officials of the Customs administration of a Contracting Party shall, at the request of another Contracting Party, participate in investigations carried out in the territory of that other Contracting Party.

Pooling of information

9. The Customs administrations of Contracting Parties shall communicate to the Secretary General of the Council, to the extent that such information is of international interest, information specified hereafter.

10. The Secretary General of the Council shall institute and keep up-to-date a central index of information communicated to him by Contracting Parties and shall use information from it to prepare summaries and studies of new and recurring trends in the smuggling of narcotic drugs or psychotropic substances. He shall periodically review the index to eliminate information which, in his opinion, has outlived its utility or become out-of-date.

11. The Customs administrations of the Contracting Parties shall, upon request by the Secretary General of the Council and subject to the other provisions of the Convention and this Annex, provide the Secretary General with such complementary information as may be necessary to prepare the summaries and studies referred to in paragraph 10 of this Annex.

12. The Secretary General of the Council shall circulate to the services or officials named by the Customs administrations of the Contracting Parties specific information contained in the central index, to the extent that he deems such circulation useful, and any summaries and studies referred to in paragraph 10 of this Annex.

13. The Secretary General of the Council shall, unless advised to the contrary by the Contracting Party furnishing the information, also circulate to the services or officials named by the other Members of the Council, to the competent bodies of the United Nations and to the International Criminal Police Organization/Interpol and to other international organizations with which arrangements have been made in this respect, any information concerning the smuggling of narcotic drugs and psychotropic substances contained in the central index, to the extent that he deems such circulation useful, and any summaries or studies that he may have prepared on this subject under paragraph 10 of this Annex.

14. The Secretary General of the Council shall, upon request, supply a Contracting Party having accepted this Annex with any other information available to him in connexion with the pooling of information provided for by this Annex.

Central index, Part I: Persons

15. Notifications under this Part of the central index shall provide information concerning:

(a)   persons finally convicted of smuggling; and

(b)   where appropriate, persons suspected of smuggling or apprehended in the act of smuggling in the territory of the Contracting Party making the notification, even though legal proceedings have not been completed,

it being understood that when Contracting Parties refrain from notifying the names and descriptions of the persons involved because such notification is prohibited by their national legislation, they shall nevertheless make a notification containing as many as possible of the items listed in this Part of the central index.

16. The information to be furnished shall, so far as possible, include the following:

   (a)   Surname
   (b)   Forenames
   (c)   Maiden name (if applicable)
   (d)   Nickname or alias
   (e)   Occupation
   (f)   Address (present)
   (g)   Date and place of birth
   (h)   Citizenship/Nationality
   (ij)   Country of residence and countries visited during the past 12 months
   (k)   Type and number of identity papers, including country and date of issue
   (l)   Physical description
      (1)   Sex
      (2)   Height
      (3)   Weight
      (4)   Build
      (5)   Hair
      (6)   Eyes
      (7)   Complexion
      (8)   Distinctive marks or peculiarities
   (m)   Brief particulars of offence (including particulars of type, quantity and origin of goods involved in the offence, manufacturer, shipper and consignor) and the circumstances which led to the detection of the offence
   (n)   Nature and amount of penalty and/or sentence imposed
   (o)   Other observations, including languages spoken and (if available) any previous convictions recorded
   (p)   Contracting Party furnishing the information (including reference number).

17. As a general rule, the Secretary General of the Council shall circulate information relating to Part I of the central index at least to the countries of citizenship/nationality and residence and to the countries visited by the person concerned during the past 12 months.

Central index, Part II: Methods

18. Notifications under this Part of the central index shall provide information relating to methods of smuggling narcotic drugs and psychotropic substances, including methods of concealment, in all cases of significant international interest. Contracting Parties shall report each use of a known method of smuggling as well as new, unusual or possible methods so that current trends in this field can be detected.

19. The information to be furnished shall, so far as possible, include the following:

   (a)   Description of methods of smuggling. If available, the description (make, model, registration number, etc.) of any means of transport used. Where applicable, data from the approval plate or certificate of containers or vehicles, the designs of which were approved under an international Convention, and information about any violation of seals, bolts, sealing devices or other parts of containers or vehicles
   (b)   Description, if applicable, of the place of concealment, including, where possible, a photograph or sketch
   (c)   Description of goods concerned
   (d)   Other observations, including the circumstances which led to detection
   (e)   Contracting Party furnishing the information (including reference number).

Central index, Part III: Vessels involved in smuggling

20. Notifications under this Part of the central index shall provide information relating to vessels, of all types, that have been involved in the smuggling of narcotic drugs or psychotropic substances, but should be limited, in principle, to cases which are considered to be of international interest.

21. Insofar as it is available and can be communicated under national law, the information to be furnished shall include the following:

   (a)   Name and brief identification of vessel (S. S., M. V., tonnage, silhouette, etc.)
   (b)   Name and address of owner/charterer
   (c)   Flag
   (d)   Port of registry and, if different, home port
   (e)   Name and citizenship/nationality of master (and, if applicable, principal officers)

(f) Nature of the offence, including description of goods seized
(g) Description, if applicable, of the place of concealment (including, where possible, a photograph or sketch) and a description of the circumstances which led to the discovery
(h) Country of origin of goods seized
(ij) First port of lading
(k) Final port of destination
(l) Ports of call between (ij) and (k)
(m) Other observations (number of cases in which the same vessel, shipping line, charterer or other vessel operator has been involved in smuggling, etc.)
(n) Contracting Party furnishing the information) including reference number).

ANNEX XI

Assistance in action against the smuggling of works of art, antiques and other cultural property
1. The provisions of this Annex apply to works of art, antiques and other "cultural property" which, on religious or secular grounds, is held to be of importance for archaeology, prehistory, history, literature, art or science, within the meaning of paragraphs (a)-(k) of Article 1 of the Unesco Convention on the means of prohibiting and preventing the illicit import, export and transfer of ownership of cultural property (Paris, 14 November 1970), insofar as such works of art, antiques and other cultural property are the subject of smuggling. They do not preclude the application of national measures of co-operation with national services for the protection of the cultural heritage and, in the Customs field, they supplement the implementation of the provisions of the Unesco Convention by Contracting Parties to that Convention which have also accepted this Annex.
2. The provisions of this Annex concerning the smuggling of works of art, antiques and other cultural property shall, wherever appropriate and to the extent of the competence of the Customs administrations, apply also to the financial operations undertaken in connexion with such smuggling.

Exchange of information by Customs administrations on their own initiative
3. The Customs administrations of Contracting Parties shall, on their own initiative and without delay, communicate to other Customs administrations which may be directly concerned, any available information concerning:

(a) operations which are known or suspected to constitute, or which seem likely to give rise to, smuggling of works of art, antiques or other cultural property;
(b) persons known to be engaged in or, insofar as information concerning such persons can be communicated under national law, persons suspected of engaging in operations referred to in paragraph (a) above, and vehicles, ships, aircraft and other means of transport used, or suspected of being used, for such operations;
(c) new means or methods used for smuggling works of art, antiques or other cultural property.

Assistance, on request, relating to surveillance
4. At the request of the Customs administration of a Contracting Party, the Customs administration of another Contracting Party shall, to the extent of its competence and ability, maintain special surveillance for a specified period over:

(a) the movements, particularly the entry into and exit from its territory, of particular persons reasonably believed to be professionally or habitually engaged in the smuggling of works of art, antiques or other cultural property in the territory of the requesting Contracting Party;
(b) movements of works of art, antiques or other cultural property which are reported by the Customs administration of the requesting Contracting Party as giving rise to important illicit traffic from the territory of that Contracting Party;
(c) particular vehicles, ships, aircraft or other means of transport reasonably believed to be used for smuggling works of art, antiques or other cultural property from the territory of the requesting Contracting Party,

and shall communicate a report thereon to the Customs administration of the requesting Contracting Party.

Enquiries on request on behalf of another Contracting Party

5. At the request of the Customs administration of a Contracting Party, the Customs administration of another Contracting Party shall, to the extent of its ability and subject to the laws and regulations in force in its territory, make enquiries to obtain evidence concerning any smuggling of works of art, antiques or other cultural property under investigation in the territory of the requesting Contracting Party, and take statements from any persons sought in connexion with that smuggling or from witnesses or experts, and communicate the results of the enquiry, as well as any documents or other evidence, to the Customs administration of the requesting Contracting Party.

Action by Customs officials of a Contracting Party in the territory of another Contracting Party

6. Where it is not sufficient for evidence to be given solely in the form of a written statement, at the request of the Customs administration of a Contracting Party the Customs administration of another Contracting Party, to the extent of its ability, shall authorize its officials to appear before a court or tribunal in the territory of the requesting Contracting Party as witnesses or experts in the matter of smuggling of works of art, antiques or other cultural property. The request for appearance shall specify, in particular, in what case and in what capacity the official is to be heard. The Customs administration of the Contracting Party accepting the request shall, in authorizing appearance, state any limits with which its officials should comply in giving evidence.

7. At the written request of the Customs administration of a Contracting Party, the Customs administration of another Contracting Party shall, where deemed appropriate and to the extent of its competence and ability, authorize officials of the requesting administration to be present in the territory of the requested Contracting Party in connexion with enquiries into or the official reporting of smuggling of works of art, antiques or other cultural property of concern to the requesting Contracting Party.

8. Where deemed appropriate by both Contracting Parties and subject to the laws and regulations in force in their territories, the officials of the Customs administration of a Contracting Party shall, at the request of another Contracting Party, participate in investigations carried out in the territory of that other Contracting Party.

Pooling of information

9. The Customs administrations of Contracting Parties shall communicate to the Secretary General of the Council, to the extent that such information is of international interest, the information specified hereafter.

10. The Secretary General of the Council shall institute and keep up-to-date a central index of information communicated to him by Contracting Parties and shall use information from it to prepare summaries and studies of new and recurring trends in the smuggling of works of art, antiques or other cultural property. He shall periodically review the index to eliminate information which, in his opinion, has outlived its utility or become out-of-date.

11. The Customs administrations of the Contracting Parties shall, upon request by the Secretary General of the Council and subject to the other provisions of the Convention and this Annex, provide the Secretary General with such complementary information as may be necessary to prepare the summaries and studies referred to in paragraph 10 of this Annex.

12. The Secretary General of the Council shall circulate to the services or officials named by the Customs administrations of the Contracting Parties specific information contained in the central index, to the extent that he deems such circulation useful, and any summaries and studies referred to in paragraph 10 of this Annex.

13. The Secretary General of the Council shall, unless advised to the contrary by the Contracting Party furnishing the information, also circulate to Unesco and to the International Criminal Police Organization/Interpol any information concerning the smuggling of works of art, antiques or other cultural property contained in the central index, to the extent that there has been illicit transfer of ownership and he deems such circulation useful, together with any summaries or studies that he may have prepared on this subject under paragraph 10 of this Annex.

14. The Secretary General of the Council shall, upon request, supply a Contracting Party having accepted this Annex with any other information available to him in connexion with the pooling of information provided for by this Annex.

Central index, Part I: Persons

15. Notifications under this Part of the central index shall provide information concerning:

(a)   persons finally convicted of smuggling; and
(b)   where appropriate, persons suspected of smuggling or apprehended in the act of
       smuggling in the territory of the Contracting Party making the notification, even
       though legal proceedings have not been completed,

it being understood that when Contracting Parties refrain from notifying the names and
descriptions of the persons involved because such notification is prohibited by their national
legislation, they shall nevertheless make a notification containing as many as possible of the
items listed in this Part of the central index.

16. The information to be furnished shall, so far as possible, include the following:

(a)   Surname
(b)   Forenames
(c)   Maiden name (if applicable)
(d)   Nickname or alias
(e)   Occupation
(f)   Address (present)
(g)   Date and place of birth
(h)   Citizenship/Nationality
(ij)   Country of residence and countries visited during the past 12 months.
(k)   Type and number of identity papers, including country and date of issue
(l)   Physical description
       (1)   Sex
       (2)   Height
       (3)   Weight
       (4)   Build
       (5)   Hair
       (6)   Eyes
       (7)   Complexion
       (8)   Distinctive marks or peculiarities
(m)   Brief particulars of offence (including particulars of type and origin of goods
       involved in the offence, and whether there has been an illicit transfer of ownership)
       and the circumstances which led to the detection of the offence
(n)   Nature and amount of penalty and/or sentence imposed
(o)   Other observations, including languages spoken and (if available) any previous
       convictions recorded
(p)   Contracting Party furnishing the information (including reference number).

17. As a general rule, the Secretary General of the Council shall circulate information relating
to Part I of the central index at least to the countries of citizenship/nationality and residence
and to the countries visited by the person concerned during the past 12 months.

Central index, Part II : Methods

18. Notifications under this Part of the central index shall provide information relating to
methods of smuggling works of art, antiques or other cultural property, including methods of
concealment, in all cases of significant international interest. Contracting Parties shall report
each use of a known method of smuggling as well as new, unusual or possible methods so that
current trends in this field can be detected.

19. The information to be furnished shall, so far as possible, include the following:

(a)   Description of methods of smuggling. If available, the description (make, model,
       registration number, in the case of land vehicles, type of vessel, etc.) of any means of
       transport used. Where applicable, data from the approval plate or certificate of
       containers or vehicles, the designs of which were approved under an international
       Convention, and information about any violation of seals, bolts, sealing devices or
       other parts of containers or vehicles
(b)   Description, if applicable, of the place of concealment, including, where possible, a
       photograph or sketch
(c)   Description of goods concerned
(d)   Other observations, including the circumstances which led to detection
(e)   Contracting Party furnishing the information (including reference number).

COMMENTARY

A. GENERAL

1. Historical background

From the very outset, the Council has always sought means of international co-operation which would assist Customs administrations in combating Customs offences. As early as 5 December 1953, it adopted the Recommendation on mutual administrative assistance. This Recommendation enabled the Customs administrations of Members who accepted it to establish very close co-operation, based mainly on direct personal contact between the services concerned.

    The 1953 Recommendation provided for direct mutual assistance between Customs administrations in the field of Customs enforcement, without the need to go through a central agency. The Recommendation of 28 June 1954 for the pooling of information concerning persons convicted of Customs offences established a system whereby information was circulated by the Council General Secretariat. The Recommendation of 8 June 1967 extended this system by providing for the pooling of information concerning not only persons convicted of Customs fraud, but also places of concealment in means of transport, other methods of smuggling, goods particularly liable to be smuggled and known to be the subject of definite smuggling trends and fraud by forgery, falsification or counterfeiting (documents, Customs seals, etc.).

    On 22 May 1975, the Council adopted a new Recommendation on the pooling of information concerning Customs fraud, further broadening the scope of the 1967 Recommendation. In addition to persons finally convicted of Customs fraud, the new Recommendation also covered persons suspected of smuggling or other fraud or apprehended in the act of smuggling provided, however, that the national legislation did not prohibit the communication of such information to other countries. The role of the Council General Secretariat was extended, in that the latter was now required not only to administer the central index and circulate the information contained therein, but also to decide which information should be circulated and to use information from the index to prepare summaries and studies of trends in Customs fraud. Finally, a separate Annex concerning vessels involved in smuggling was included in the new Recommendation.

In 1967, sharing the concern of many countries regarding the alarming increase in the abuse of narcotic drugs and psychotropic substances, the Council adopted a Resolution inviting Members to develop mutual assistance between their Customs administrations, to the greatest possible extent, with a view to preventing and detecting illicit traffic in narcotic drugs and psychotropic substances. This Resolution was followed by the Recommendation of 8 June 1971 on the spontaneous exchange of information concerning illicit traffic in narcotic drugs and psychotropic substances. This Recommendation supplemented the legal means available to Customs services by enabling them to exchange operational intelligence, particularly where the success of an operation depended on speed of action; however, as pointed out in the text of this Recommendation, the sole purpose of this exchange of information was to reinforce the activities of the authorities competent to take action against the abuse of narcotic drugs and psychotropic substances.

From 1973 onwards the Council's attention had been drawn to the problem of preventing and repressing the fraudulent exportation of works of art, antiquities and other cultural property, a matter of concern to the representatives of many countries. In a Resolution adopted on 16 June 1976, the Council drew the attention of its Members to the importance of the UNESCO Convention on the means of prohibiting and preventing the illicit import, export and transfer of ownership of cultural property (1970) and invited them to develop mutual administrative assistance to combat the smuggling of works of art and antiquities, by actively exploiting the possibilities offered by the Recommendations of 1953 and 1967 (as amended in 1975).

The creation of these various legal instruments showed that the Council attached importance to international co-operation to combat Customs fraud, which was assuming an increasingly international character; it had adopted instruments dealing more specifically with the types of smuggling about which its Members were most concerned. However, certain States experienced difficulty in granting administrative assistance merely on the basis of Recommendations and considered that bilateral Conventions on mutual administrative assistance would provide a more effective means of action against Customs offences. In order to facilitate and encourage such agreements, the Council proposed a model bilateral Convention on mutual administrative assistance, for consideration by the countries concerned. In June 1967, the Council in fact adopted the "model bilateral Convention on mutual administrative assistance for the prevention, investigation and repression of Customs offences". This model was given the form and wording of a potentially ready-made Convention. However, States remained completely free to delete or modify the provisions of the model as they saw fit, or insert additional provisions adapted to their mutual needs. Alternatives were even included for certain Articles of the model Convention. This enabled countries wishing to conclude a bilateral agreement to choose the provision which best met their requirements.

However, it became evident that the conclusion of regional bilateral or multilateral agreements, although extremely fruitful and desirable for the countries concerned, could not provide an entirely satisfactory means of international action against Customs fraud, which was becoming increasingly widespread and certain aspects of which concerned all countries. For this reason, in 1974, the Council instructed the Permanent Technical Committee to prepare a draft multilateral Convention on mutual administrative assistance, on the understanding that the resulting instrument should be sufficiently effective and binding, while being acceptable to as many countries as possible. This work culminated in the adoption, on 9 June 1977, at the Council's meeting in Nairobi (Kenya), of an international Convention on mutual administrative assistance for the prevention, investigation and repression of Customs offences. The text of this Convention is reproduced in the Appendix.

2. General scope and structure of the Convention

The Convention consists of a Body and 11 Annexes which may be accepted independently of each other. This system was adopted because it is very flexible. It allows countries which would not, at present, be in a position to implement all the provisions of a mutual administrative assistance Convention to become Contracting Parties to the Convention, accepting only certain Annexes (at least one).

Since States need accept only those Annexes which they are in a position to apply, it was possible to provide that no reservations are permitted (Article 18). The provisions contained in the Annexes therefore have a binding character and this enables a highly developed form of administrative assistance to be organized between States which have accepted the same Annex. Another advantage of this system is that it facilitates the application of the Convention, because the obligations of the various Contracting Parties can be clearly established.

It should also be noted that, as is generally the case in the field of mutual administrative assistance, the Convention is based on the concept of reciprocity, i.e. a Contracting Party has an obligation to render assistance to another Contracting Party only insofar as both have accepted the same Annex.

B. Body of the Convention

1. Preamble

Offences against Customs law are prejudicial not only to the economic and fiscal interests of States but also to the social interests of the international community, particularly as regards the smuggling of narcotic drugs and psychotropic substances, or of cultural property which is part of a country's national heritage.

Although the principal aim of the Customs Co-operation Council is to foster the development of international trade, it must defend the legitimate interests of trade, by repressing abuse which might be facilitated by the simplification of Customs procedures or the reduction of Customs formalities. The Preamble points out that the strengthening of co-operation between Customs administrations is one of the aims of the Convention establishing a Customs Co-operation Council.

2. Definitions (Chapter I)

"*Customs law*" (Article 1, definition (a))

As the competence of Customs administrations varies from country to country, the term "Customs law" will not have the same meaning for all Contracting Parties.

The definition is couched in very general terms. It refers to, for example, the application of control measures (as control is implicit in the Customs activities described in the rest of the definition), the case of financial operations (insofar as the goods themselves are concerned and to the extent of the competence of the Customs administrations), and the case of refunds granted by Members of the European Economic Community in connexion with the exportation of certain agricultural products, insofar as they involve a "provision enforced or administered by the Customs administration" of these countries at exportation.

According to the context in which it is used, the term: "Customs administrations" may designate either the central administration or the outside services. If they consider it necessary, Contracting Parties may introduce appropriate national provisions to define the competence of the various levels. Also, under Article 6, the Contracting Parties have to designate the services or officials responsible for direct communications between Contracting Parties.

"Smuggling" (Article 1, definition (d))

This definition covers not only cases where goods have been concealed to escape Customs control, but also cases where goods, although not concealed, have not been properly declared to the Customs. It covers all modes of transport, including the post.

"Import or export duties and taxes" (Article 1, definition (e))

This definition reproduces the one which appears in other international instruments prepared by the Council, particularly certain Annexes to the international Convention on the simplification and harmonization of Customs procedures (Kyoto Convention).

In this connexion, the Permanent Technical Committee considered that the mutual assistance provided for by the Convention does not apply in cases of dumping (since the GATT anti-dumping Code includes assistance measures on this subject) or of countervailing duties (which are referred to in Article VI of GATT).

"Ratification" (Article 1, definition (ij))

The definition of the term "ratification" facilitates the drafting of the final provisions of the Convention by avoiding the need to repeat the terms "ratification", "acceptance" and "approval" in several Article. The internal legal provisions of individual States concerning the conditions to be met before the competent national authorities may decide on the international instrument declaring the State's willingness to be bound remain applicable. This definition of ratification makes it possible for each State to choose the procedure it prefers for undertaking commitments at international level. It is pointed out that this definition corresponds to the provisions of Article 2 (1) (b) of the Vienna Convention on the Law of Treaties of 23 May 1969.

3. Scope of the Convention (Chapter II)

(a) *Reciprocity* (Article 2, paragraph 1)

As stated above, a Contracting Party has an obligation to render assistance to another Contracting Party only insofar as both have accepted the same Annex (however, see paragraph (e) below).

As specified in the text, although the obligations are assumed by the Contracting Parties, assistance is afforded by their Customs administrations.

(b) *Request for assistance in connexion with judicial proceedings* (Article 2, paragraph 2)

The text of this paragraph is worded in such a way that it does not exclude from the scope of this Convention information which might be of use in connexion with judicial proceedings, since these are precisely the most important cases. However, the text carefully avoids any overlap with possible agreements on mutual assistance in criminal matters. This is why it specifies that this Article applies only in cases where a Customs administration requests assistance from another Customs administration. In all cases, the provisions of the national legislation concerning the competent authorities must be respected. The text of this paragraph could not be interpreted as implying that Customs administrations are empowered to intervene even though under national legislation they are not competent to do so.

(c) *Exclusions* (Article 2, paragraph 3)

This paragraph excludes, on the one hand, requests for the arrest of persons and, on the other hand, requests for assistance with the recovery of duties, taxes, charges, etc., both these measures having been deemed to go beyond what States, at present, normally agree upon in the matter. .

(d) *Escape clause* (Article 3)

The circumstances in which Contracting Parties may refuse assistance are the same as those provided for in the 1967 model bilateral Convention on mutual administrative assistance for the prevention, investigation and repression of Customs offences (Article 17) and in Article IV of the Convention establishing a Customs Co-operation Council, concerning the protection of the legitimate commercial interests of any enterprise, public or private. This clause should be applied only after careful consideration to determine whether the commercial interests in question are legitimate or not. Moreover, Article 3 provides that, while the requested Contracting Party may invoke this text to refuse assistance, it may nevertheless agree to provide such assistance subject to certain conditions or requirements.

(e) *Possible derogation from the principle of reciprocity* (Article 4)

Under the principle of reciprocity, a Customs administration should request from another Customs administration only that assistance which it would itself be able to give if requested to do so. Article 4 provides that, even if this principle cannot be respected, assistance may be requested, provided that the requesting administration draws attention to this fact in its request. However, as specified in connexion with Article 2, paragraph 1, the Convention does not oblige the requested Contracting Party to comply with such a request.

4. General assistance procedures (Chapter III)

(a) *Use which may be made of intelligence, documents and other information* (Article 5)

Article 5 provides that:

— intelligence, documents or other information communicated or obtained under this Convention may be used for the prevention, investigation and repression of Customs offences, including use in judicial or administrative proceedings, without objections on the grounds of their confidentiality, unless the Customs administration which furnished them has expressly laid down restrictions to such use;

— the Contracting Party which receives such intelligence, documents or other information must guarantee protection in respect of confidentiality;

— such intelligence, documents or other information may be used for purposes other than the prevention, investigation or repression of Customs offences with the written consent of the Customs administration which furnished them.

(b) *Procedure for communications between Customs administrations* (Articles 6 and 7)

Articles 6 and 7 lay down the procedures to be followed and the conditions in which communications take place between Customs administrations. Paragraph 2 of Article 6 stresses that all the measures a Customs administration is required to take pursuant to a request are subject to the same restrictions and requirements as are imposed by national law in purely national proceedings of the same kind.

It should also be noted that, for the purposes of Article 7, requests for assistance made by telex, telegram or other means of telecommunication that reproduce the text are regarded as requests made "in writing".

5. Miscellaneous provisions (Chapter IV)

(a) *Personal and direct relations between services responsible for prevention, investigation and repression* (Article 9)

The provisions of Article 9 must be read in conjunction with those of Article 6, paragraph 1, which provides that the Secretary General shall communicate to Contracting Parties the names and addresses of services or officials responsible for direct communications between the Customs administrations of the Contracting Parties. One means of ensuring that personal and direct relations are maintained between the services responsible for the prevention, investigation and repression of Customs offences is, for example, to prepare and keep up-to-date a list of the names and addresses of officials responsible for these various services. Another means of achieving this objective is to convene meetings of officials in charge of these services, as provided for in Article 12, paragraph 2 (d). It is pointed out that, under Article 9, the Council is itself required to make appropriate arrangements in this connexion.

(b) *More extensive mutual administrative assistance* (Article 11)

In general, the more extensive mutual administrative assistance referred to in Article 11 is assistance provided for by bilateral or multilateral (regional) agreements. However, this provision does not prevent Contracting Parties from granting still more extensive assistance than that provided for by such agreements.

Moreover, the Convention is not intended to affect the facilities provided under existing or future bilateral agreements. Bilateral agreements may even be concluded between Contracting Parties to the Convention, to supplement the provisions of the Convention on specific points and to settle certain aspects which are of particular interest to the countries concerned.

6. Role of the Council and of the Permanent Technical Committee (Chapter V)

With regard to Article 12, paragraph 2 (b) it should be noted that the Permanent Technical Committee may furnish opinions on the interpretation of provisions of the Convention, but not on the modes of application of the Convention in particular cases, a task which should be left to the Contracting Parties concerned.

7. Final provisions (Chapter VI)

(a) *Settlement of disputes* (Article 14)

The text of Article 14 differs from the corresponding texts in other Council Conventions in that it does not provide for disputes between Contracting Parties to be referred to the Permanent Technical Committee and to the Council.

(b) *Possibility of Customs or economic unions becoming Contracting Parties* (Article 15, paragraph 5)

The text of this provision is based on the one which appears in the 1975 TIR Convention (Article 52, paragraph 3). The application of this clause may have repercussions on other provisions of the Convention, particularly in respect of the entry into force of the Convention and its Annexes (Article 16), the entry into force of amendments (Article 20) and the acceptance of amendments which have previously entered into force (Article 21). It should be noted that, in these Articles, there is a distinction between the term: "Contracting Parties" which covers both States and, where appropriate, Customs or economic unions and the terms:

"States" and "States which are Contracting Parties", which do not include Customs or economic unions.

(c) *Amendment procedure* (Article 20)

The simplified amendment procedure provided for in Article 20 is based on Article 59 of the 1975 TIR Convention. To take account of the time which might be needed in some countries for consideration by Parliament, paragraph 3 of Article 20 fixes at two years the period during which objections to proposed amendments may be communicated.

C. ANNEXES TO THE CONVENTION

1. General scope of the Annexes

In order to become a Contracting Party to the Convention, it is necessary to accept at least one Annex (Article 15, paragraph 3). An Annex enters into force three months after two States have accepted it, but cannot enter into force for a Contracting Party before the Convention has come into force for that Contracting Party (Article 16, paragraph 3).

Taken together, the Annexes to the Convention cover all categories of goods (including, for example, ship's stores or arms, explosives and ammunition) which might be the subject of a Customs offence. The only restrictions which might possibly exclude certain goods would be derived from the general provisions concerning the scope of the Convention or the scope of the term "Customs law". However, Annex X covers only narcotic drugs and psychotropic substances and Annex XI covers only works of art, antiques and other cultural property. As a result, States which accept any or all of the Annexes from I to IX are obliged to apply them in respect of all goods except narcotic drugs, psychotropic substances, works of art, antiques and other cultural property. On the other hand, States which accept only Annex X or Annex XI are bound only with regard to the goods covered by those Annexes.

2. Assistance by a Customs administration on its own initiative (Annex I)

It is pointed out that the provisions of paragraph 3 of Annex I, which apply to information of direct concern to a Contracting party, do not overlap with the corresponding provisions concerning the pooling of information in Annex IX, X or XI, which apply to information of general interest.

3. Assistance, on request, in the assessment of import or export duties and taxes (Annex II)

The onus is on the requesting Contracting Party to request the assistance provided for by Annex II only when it has good reason to believe that a serious Customs offence has been committed. The requesting Contracting Party judges whether this requirement has been met but, as the requests for assistance must contain the requisite information and be accompanied by such documents as may be deemed useful (Article 7, paragraph 1), the requested administration will be in a position to form its own opinion on the circumstances of the offence.

The obligations of Contracting Parties who accept Annex II are laid down in paragraph 1 of the Annex. The text of paragraph 2 is merely intended to give examples of the ways in which these obligations can be fulfilled.

It should also be noted that wherever the expression: "information or documents available to it" is used in this Annex, it means that the information or documents can be easily and rapidly procured by an administration, without the need for a special investigation.

4. Assistance, on request, relating to controls (Annex III)

It follows from the general intent of the Convention that assistance under the terms of this Annex should be requested only when there is good reason to consider or suspect that an offence has been committed in the territory of the requesting Contracting Party.

5. Assistance, on request, relating to surveillance (Annex IV)

The expression: "to the extent of its competence and ability" used in Annex IV, was inserted to take account of differences which may exist between countries with regard to the territorial competence of Customs administrations (for example, the action of Customs services may be confined to certain parts of the territory) and the means available to Customs administrations for carrying out the surveillance requested.

6. Enquiries and notifications, on request, on behalf of another Contracting Party (Annex V)

The expression: "subject to the laws and regulations in force in its territory" in paragraph 2 of Annex V means that the notifications referred to in this paragraph must be made in the requested country and must comply with the requested country's national laws and regulations applicable to such cases.

The expression: "any matter falling within the scope of this Convention" in paragraph 2 of Annex V obliges Contracting Parties who have accepted this Annex to make such notifications, under the conditions laid down, even in respect of matters covered by Annexes which they have not themselves accepted.

7. Appearance by Customs officials before a court or tribunal abroad (Annex VI)

The reference to the fact that evidence may often be given in the form of a written statement is intended to emphasize that appearances before courts or tribunals in foreign countries should be the exception rather than the rule. Moreover, the requested administration is required to grant the assistance requested only to the extent that the official called upon to give evidence abroad are available and that staffing does not present a problem. However, the provisions of Annex VI apply even where a court or tribunal deals with questions of assessment of import or export duties or taxes in connexion with a Customs offence. If the competent body is not a court or tribunal, recourse may be had to the provisions of other Annexes to the Convention.

This Annex provides that the Customs administration may set limits with which its officials must comply in giving evidence before a foreign court or tribunal. The Convention should not, however, encroach on the rules governing the giving of evidence in the courts.

8. Presence of Customs official of one Contracting Party in the territory of another Contracting Party (Annex VII)

Paragraph 3 of Annex VII provides for the presence of foreign officials in connexion with enquiries of concern to the foreign country; however, in this Annex, only the official's presence is provided for. Cases in which the foreign official participates directly in investigations are dealt with by Annex VIII.

The Convention contains no provisions concerning the legal position of officials of the Customs administration of a Contracting Party in the territory of another Contracting Party, or the protection they should be given. This question should be settled directly between the Contracting Parties concerned.

9. Participation in investigation abroad (Annex VIII)

Under the provisions of this Annex, where two Contracting Parties deem this appropriate, an official may visit a foreign country to assist in an investigation being carried out in that country, without it being specified whether or not this investigation is of concern to the country which sends him. The two Contracting Parties shall agree on the extent of this participation.

10. Pooling of information (Annex IX)

Annex IX incorporates the main provisions of the Council Recommendation of 22 May 1975 on the pooling of information concerning Customs fraud. However, certain amendments have been made to the text of the Recommendation. Essentially, these are as follows:

— under the provisions of paragraph 2, the Secretary General of the Council must periodically review the index to eliminate information which has outlived its utility or become out-of-date; this provision was not included in the 1975 Recommendation;

— under the provisions of paragraph 3, the Secretary General of the Council is entitled, as stated in the Recommendation of 1975, to request complementary information. However, the text specifies that such information must be necessary to prepare summaries and studies.

— paragraph 4 stipulates that the information must be circulated to named services or officials. It is therefore up to the Contracting Parties who accept this Annex to supply a list of names and notify any subsequent amendments thereto;

— race is not mentioned in the list of descriptive elements set out at paragraph 9 (A). It could be included, if necessary, under Item (o) Other observations;

—   the right to refrain from naming suspected persons, when this is prohibited by the national law, has been extended to cover persons finally convicted (paragraphs 8 and 11). The term "national legislation" is to be taken to cover all provisions of general application enacted either by the legislature or by the executive and effective at national level;

—   in addition to the information provided for in the 1975 Recommendation, in paragraphs 9(A) (m), 9 (B) (g), 12 (k) and 14 (e), Contracting Parties who have accepted this Annex are invited to indicate the circumstances which led to the detection of a Customs offence (or a place of concealment). Information of this type can be very useful to other countries participating in the information pooling system;

—   as regards information concerning vessels involved in smuggling, paragraph 16 specifies that such information need be furnished only: "insofar as it is available and can be communicated under national law".

It should also be pointed out that the term: "name" appearing in paragraph 9 (B), must be interpreted in its broadest sense, to include the full trading name of the firm, regardless of its legal status (public company, limited company, etc.).

11. Assistance in action against the smuggling of narcotic drugs and psychotropic substances (Annex X)

(a) *Financial operations undertaken in connexion with the smuggling of narcotic drugs*

Paragraph 2 of Annex X states that, wherever appropriate and to the extent of the competence of the Customs administrations, the provisions of this Annex concerning the smuggling of narcotic drugs and psychotropic substances apply also to financial operations undertaken in connexion with such smuggling. This text was included in the Annex at the request of the United Nations Division of Narcotic Drugs and the International Narcotics Control Board. It takes into account the provisions of the Single Convention on Narcotic Drugs of 1961 (Article 36, paragraph 2, subparagraph (a) (ii) and the 1971 Convention on psychotropic substances (Article 22, paragraph 2, subparagraph (a), (ii) which require that Contracting Parties to these Conventions make any financial operation in connexion with, inter alia, the smuggling of narcotic drugs or psychotropic substances, a punishable offence. With regard to the illicit trafficking in narcotic drugs, on 12 May 1976, the Economic and Social Council of the United Nations adopted a Resolution E/RES/2002(LV) on "Financial transactions related to illicit trafficking in narcotics". In this Resolution, the United Nations Economic and Social Council points out that this traffic requires large sums of money and that leaders of illicit trafficking organizations might be involved in these transactions, without actively participating in the movement of drugs. Close attention by authorities to financial transactions concerning persons suspected of involvement in illicit drug trafficking might therefore lead to the apprehension and conviction of major drug traffickers. It therefore urges governments which have not already done so to enact such legislation as may be necessary to make financial support provided knowingly, by whatever means, in furtherance of drug offences, including smuggling, a punishable offence, and to co-operate with one another in exchanging information to identify drug traffickers committing such an offence.

(b) *Exchange of information by Customs administrations on their own initiative* (paragraph 3)

Paragraph 3 reproduces the substance of the Customs Co- operation Council Recommendation of 8 June 1971 on the spontaneous exchange of information concerning illicit traffic in narcotic drugs and psychotropic substances. However, it should be noted that the expression: "smuggling of narcotic drugs or psychotropic substances" has been used in place of "illicit traffic" and that the obligations concerning the spontaneous communication of information involve only Customs administrations which may be *directly* concerned. Also, with regard to paragraph (b), it is specified that information concerning suspected persons need be communicated only: "insofar as information concerning such persons can be communicated under national law".

(c) *Assistance, on request, relating to surveillance* (paragraph 4)

The text of paragraph 4 reproduces that of Annex IV to the Convention, the one difference being that paragraph 4 concerns only the smuggling of narcotic drugs and psychotropic substances.

(d) *Enquiries on request on behalf of another Contracting Party* (paragraph 5)

Paragraph 5 reproduces the text of paragraph 1 of Annex V to the Convention, but concerns only the smuggling of narcotic drugs or psychotropic substances.

(e) *Action by Customs officials of one Contracting Party in the territory of another Contracting Party.*

Paragraph 6 of this part of the Annex reproduces the provisions of Annex VI, applying them to the smuggling of narcotic drugs and psychotropic substances.

Paragraph 7 reproduces the provisions of paragraph 3 of Annex VII. To make these provisions acceptable to the greatest possible number of countries, it is specified that authorization is granted only to the extent of the competence and ability of the requested administration. During the preparatory work on Annex X it was agreed that when the Customs administration of the requested Contracting Party was not competent in this situation it should forward the request to the competent administration of its country and then transmit the reply to the requesting administration.

Paragraph 8 reproduces the text of Annex VIII, but includes the following expression: "and subject to the laws and regulations in force in their territories".

(f) *Pooling of information*

This part of the Annex is directly based on Annex IX. However, whereas Annex IX is based on the concept of reciprocity, i.e. the information contained in the central index is communicated only to Contracting Parties who have accepted the Annex, paragraph 13 of Annex X provides that, unless the Contracting Party furnishing the information advises to the contrary, information concerning the smuggling of narcotic drugs and psychotropic substances is also circulated to the other Members of the Council, to the competent Bodies of the United Nations, to the International Criminal Police Organization/Interpol and to other international organizations with which arrangements have been made in this respect. Moreover, whereas paragraph 8 of Annex IX provides that, in principle, information notified shall be limited to offences which have resulted in or could lead to imprisonment or a fine exceeding the equivalent of US$2,000, there is no such restriction in Annex X.

12. Assistance in action against the smuggling of works of art, antiques and other cultural property (Annex XI)

Under the provisions of paragraph 2, Annex XI also applies, wherever appropriate and to the extent of the competence of the Customs administration, to the financial operations undertaken in connexion with the smuggling of works of art, antiques and other cultural property. In addition, paragraph 13 of this Annex provides that, unless advised to the contrary by the Contracting Party furnishing the information, the Secretary General of the Council shall also circulate to UNESCO and to the International Criminal Police Organization/Interpol any information concerning the smuggling of works of art, antiques or other cultural property, contained in the central index.

Appendix S

IOSCO
PRINCIPLES FOR MEMORANDA OF UNDERSTANDING

1. Subject Matter

MOUs should provide that investigatory assistance will be granted without regard to whether the type of conduct under investigation would be a violation of the laws of the Requested Authority unless the Requested Authority is not permitted to provide assistance where the type of conduct under Investigation would not be a violation of the laws of the Requested Authority.

In 1989, the Technical Committee endorsed a resolution calling for member organizations to enter into MOUs on information sharing in which they would undertake to provide each other with information on a reciprocal basis, without regard to whether the matter under investigation would be a violation of the laws of the Requested Authority. Most of the existing MOUs cover the broad range of subject matters supported by the Technical Committee. By providing in an MOU for a broad range of matters for which assistance will be provided, each Authority is assured that it will receive as much assistance as possible with respect to all matters falling within its jurisdiction.

If a Requested Authority is not able to provide assistance with respect to matters which would not constitute violations within its own state without breaching its domestic legislation, the Requested Authority should consider recommending that appropriate amendments be made to this legislation to enable the assistance to be given, if it has the power to make such recommendations.

2. Confidentiality

An MOU should provide that an Authority that receives information pursuant to an MOU request will protect the information with the highest possible level of confidentiality which, at a minimum, should provide that the information will be treated with the same level of confidentiality that is given to similar information that it collects in investigations of possible domestic violations. In addition, an MOU should provide the Requested Authority with the opportunity to identify the level of confidentiality that it expects to be attached to information that it transmits pursuant to an MOU request.

The primary purpose of MOUs is to provide information for use in investigations, which are, in most instances, non-public inquiries. In fact, most securities and futures regulators are subject to domestic laws and regulations governing the confidential treatment of information. The confidentiality requirements, however, vary by country and it is possible that the procedures of one authority for maintaining confidentiality will not be consistent with the disclosure or confidentiality provisions of its foreign counterparts. This, in turn, may lead to restrictions on the requested authority's ability to transmit information.

It may be possible to overcome differences between the confidentiality requirements and procedures of the authorities by including confidentiality provisions in the MOU that satisfy the needs of both authorities. In certain instances, however, legislative action may be required to increase the level of confidentiality to encourage the widest possible exchange of information.

3. Implementation Procedures

In a mutually agreeable form, the signatories to an MOU should describe the procedures that they will follow in making and executing requests for information pursuant to the MOU; those procedures should be consistent with both signatories' legal requirements or impediments.

One of the main purposes of an MOU is to create a framework of procedures for exchanging information between regulators. Therefore, it is important that the parties to an MOU clearly set out the manner in which requests will be made and executed.

4. The Rights of Persons Subject to an MOU Request

The fact that an investigation is conducted on behalf of a foreign authority pursuant to an MOU request should not alter the legal rights and privileges granted to persons in the State of the Requested Authority.

Because it is essential that the legal rights and privileges of witnesses be protected, the signatories to an MOU should make sure that the means of executing a request is consistent with the laws, methods and requirements of the Requested Authority. When the laws and policies of the requested authority provide a range of options, requests should be executed in the manner most consistent with the needs of the requesting authority.

Authorities negotiating information-sharing agreements may find it useful to examine the scope and implications of other agreements or treaties between the states of the signatories so that, among other things, they can ensure that the citizens of the signatory countries receive similar guarantees and protections.

5. Consultation

MOUs should contain a provision in which the Authorities agree to consult on relevant issues that arise during the operation of the MOU. Moreover, authorities should consult frequently to discuss developments or proposals likely to affect the other Authority's interests or the available means for cooperation.

Since MOUs are designed to facilitate assistance, and not to create overly formal relations between the signatory authorities, they should contain a provision on consultations. Such a provision could specify circumstances under which it would assist the operation of the MOU to consult, such as where assistance may be or has been denied, and may also provide for consultation when requested by a signatory. By consulting about, for example, a denial of a request for assistance, the Requested Authority may be able to identify certain assistance that it is able to provide, and the Requesting Authority may benefit from learning more about why assistance was denied.

Such consultations also may promote cooperation and avoid misunderstandings and conflicts in situations involving:

— unforeseen circumstances
— overlapping jurisdiction, and
— changes in one authority's laws or procedures.

6. Public Policy Exception

An MOU should provide that the Requested Authority maintains the right to refuse to provide assistance in instances where the provision of assistance would violate the public policy of its state. The concept of public policy would include issues affecting sovereignty, national security, or other essential interests.

Although it is optimal for the scope of an MOU to be as broad as possible, there may be limited instances where, notwithstanding the fact that a request falls within the scope of the MOU, providing assistance would be contrary to the public policy of the state of the Requested Authority. For this reason MOUs should provide a mechanism for dealing with this potential conflict so that the Requested Authority will be able to rely on a public policy exception to the MOU in denying assistance.

7. Types of Assistance

MOUs should provide that the Authorities will take all reasonable steps to ensure that they can utilize their full domestic powers to execute requests for assistance. The available assistance should include, where the Requested Authority has such powers, obtaining documents and the statements or testimony of witnesses, granting access to the Requested Authority's non-public files, and conducting inspections of regulated entities.

Both before and since the Technical Committee's 1989 resolution on information-sharing, several member organizations have obtained the authority to use their full domestic powers to compel the production of documents and statements or testimony on behalf of foreign authorities. In the absence of such authority, a Requested Authority may be limited to providing only information that it can obtain voluntarily or from public files in response to a request for assistance. Since law violators may refuse to produce incriminating information on a voluntary basis, and legal impediments may prevent an innocent intermediary from voluntarily providing information, the Requesting Authority may be unable to obtain critical information at the investigative stage of a matter if production of such information cannot be compelled by the Requested Authority.

Therefore, the ability to compel production of documents and statements or testimony on behalf of a foreign authority greatly enhances the value of MOUs. Authorities that do not have such an ability should take all reasonable steps, including considering recommending amendments to their legislation, where they have such power to recommend, to remove impediments that keep them from utilizing their full domestic powers for providing assistance to foreign authorities.

8. Permitted Uses

MOUs should specify whether and under what circumstances the Requesting Authority may provide information it receives pursuant to an MOU to other domestic authorities for use in related matters, including investigations or proceedings instituted by other authorities and regulators, and SROs.

The civil, criminal and administrative components of a country's securities and futures laws are often enforced by multiple agencies. Since, in the first instance, the Requested Authority is responsible for the use of information located in its files, or which it gathers on behalf of the Requesting Authority, the Requested Authority should have the ability to determine permissible uses of the information. On the other hand, to further the goal of effective law enforcement, MOUs should allow the Requesting Authority to provide information it receives pursuant to an MOU to other regulatory and enforcement groups or agencies that are charged with enforcing securities and futures laws, unless precluded by the laws of the Requested Authority from so doing.

9. Participation by the Requesting Authority

MOUs should provide that, to the extent permitted by the laws and policies of the Requested Authority, the Requesting Authority may be permitted to participate directly in the execution of a request for assistance.

Participation by the Requesting Authority, to the extent permitted by the laws and policies of the State of the Requested Authority, may be desirable to ensure that resources are used effectively in executing requests for assistance.

For example, in executing an MOU request that involves document review and/or the questioning of witnesses, a high degree of familiarity with the investigative record may be necessary in order to elicit the necessary information from witnesses and documents. In many cases, MOU requests are preceded by complex, long-term investigations by the Requesting Authority and the files of the investigation may include far more information than can reasonably be included in a particular MOU request. In such cases, the Requested Authority should consider permitting the persons most familiar with the investigative record to assist in the execution of the request.

10. COST-SHARING

MOUs should provide that, under certain circumstances, the Requested Authority can, if it deems it necessary, Initiate a process for having the Requesting Authority share the costs of providing assistance that are incurred by the Requested Authority.

Requests for assistance may involve extensive use of investigative resources by the Requested Authority. Sharing costs may be appropriate where the cost of a particular request is substantial or where a substantial imbalance has arisen in the cumulative costs incurred by the signatories. Therefore, to minimize the burden that such investigations might place on the Requested Authority, an MOU should provide a mechanism by which the Requesting Authority may be asked to reimburse the Requested Authority for extraordinary costs. An MOU also should provide that the Authorities will consult about the handling of costs in such cases.

Appendix T

MEMORANDUM OF UNDERSTANDING ON MUTUAL ASSISTANCE AND THE EXCHANGE OF INFORMATION BETWEEN THE UNITED ESTATES SECURITIES AND EXCHANGE COMMISSION AND COMMODITY FUTURES TRADING COMMISSION AND THE UNITED KINGDOM DEPARTMENT OF TRADE AND INDUSTRY AND SECURITIES AND INVESTMENTS BOARD

Washington, D.C. September 25, 1991

The United States Securities and Exchange Commission and Commodity Futures Trading Commission on the one hand, and the United Kingdom Department of Trade and Industry and Securities and Investments Board on the other hand, recognising the increasing international activity in the securities, futures and investments markets and the corresponding need for mutual cooperation between the relevant national authorities, have reached the following understanding:

DEFINITIONS

1. For purposes of this Memorandum of Understanding,

  (a) "Authority" means

     (i) for the United States, the Securities and Exchange Commission ("SEC") or the Commodity Futures Trading Commission ("CFTC") acting with respect to their respective areas of jurisdiction;

     (ii) for the United Kingdom, the Department of Trade and Industry ("DTI") or the Securities and Investments Board ("SIB") acting with respect to their respective areas of responsibility.

  (b) "Investment Businesses" means investment businesses, investment companies, other collective investment undertakings and their equivalents, investment banks, merchant banks, brokers, dealers, jobbers, investment advisers and investor advisory services and exchanges.

  (c) "Securities Processing Businesses" means clearing corporations or securities transfer agents.

  (d) "Futures Businesses" means commodity trading advisors, commodity pool operators, futures commission merchants, introducing brokers, associated persons and floor brokers, floor traders, clearing corporations, futures and options brokers and dealers and exchanges.

  (e) "person" means a natural person, unincorporated association, or body corporate, government, or political subdivision, agency, or instrumentality of a government.

  (f) "issuer" means a person who issues or proposes to issue any security.

  (g) (1) "requested Authority" means an Authority to whom a request under this Memorandum is addressed;

     (2) "requesting Authority" means an Authority making a request under this Memorandum.

(h) "legal rule or requirement" means:

(1) for securities, those laws, regulations and requirements of the United States and the United Kingdom relating to:

(A) insider trading in relation to any security;
(B) misrepresentation or the use of fraudulent, deceptive or manipulative practices in connection with the offer, purchase or sale of any security;
(C) the making of a false or misleading statement or any material omission in any application or report made to the Authorities;
(D) the conduct of Investment or Securities Processing Businesses or reporting requirements imposed on such Businesses;
(E) the financial and other qualifications of those engaged in or in control of Investment or Securities Processing Businesses;
(F) the duty to comply with reporting requirements of persons whose securities or sponsored depository receipts in respect of such securities are registered or publicly traded;
(G) the disclosure of interests in the securities of companies; and
(H) the duties of issuers of and offerors for securities to make full and fair disclosure of information relevant to investors.

(2) for futures, those laws, regulations and requirements of the United States and the United Kingdom relating to:

(A) misrepresentation or the use of fraudulent, deceptive or manipulative practices in connection with the offer, purchase or sale of any futures or options contract;
(B) the making of a false or misleading statement or any material omission in any application or report made to the Authorities.
(C) the conduct of futures or options trading on, or subject to the rules of, the markets of the requesting Authority;
(D) the conduct of Futures Businesses or reporting requirements imposed upon such Businesses; and
(E) the financial and other qualifications of those engaged in or in control of Futures Businesses.

2. The parties recognise that while in their laws, regulations and requirements they may define terms differently, requests for assistance will not be denied solely on the grounds of differences in the definitions used by the requesting and requested Authorities.

PART I: CONSULTATIONS ON MATTERS OF MUTUAL INTEREST

3. The Authorities intend to engage in consultations about mutually agreeable approaches designed to enhance the integrity and efficiency of the securities and futures markets of the United States and the United Kingdom, the exercise of market oversight functions and the protection of investors, while avoiding the conflicts that may arise from the application of differing regulatory laws, regulations and practices.

PART II: GENERAL PRINCIPLES

4. This Memorandum sets forth the basis upon which the United States Authorities and the United Kingdom Authorities reciprocally propose to provide assistance for the purpose of facilitating the performance of their respective functions regarding the laws, regulations and requirements of the United States and the United Kingdom. Such assistance will be provided even where the subject matter of the request for assistance does not constitute a violation of the laws, regulations and requirements of the requested Authority. In these circumstances the requesting Authority will determine whether particular conduct could be a violation of its laws, regulations and requirements.

5. This Memorandum sets forth a statement of intent of the Authorities regarding mutual assistance and the exchange of information between the Authorities. Accordingly, the provisions of this Memorandum will not give rise to a right on the part of any private person, directly

or indirectly, to obtain, suppress or exclude any evidence or to challenge the execution of a request for assistance under this Memorandum.

6. In response to requests that satisfy the terms of Part III of this Memorandum, and subject to the conditions set out in Part IV, each Authority will provide the fullest possible measure of mutual assistance to the other subject to its law and national policy. Such assistance may include:

(a) providing access to information in the files of the requested Authority;
(b) questioning or taking the testimony of persons designated by the requesting Authority;
(c) obtaining specified information and documents from persons;
(d) conducting compliance inspections or examinations of Investment or Futures Businesses; and
(e) permitting the representatives of the requesting Authority to participate in the conduct of the enquiries made by the requested Authority pursuant to (b) through (d) of this paragraph.

7. The Authorities recognise the need and desirability of providing mutual assistance and exchanging information to assist each other in securing compliance with their respective legal rules or requirements. However, assistance may be denied on grounds of public interest.

8. The Authorities have defined "legal rule or requirement" to ensure that assistance will be provided in the maximum number of circumstances. However, the Authorities acknowledge that certain requests may relate to a possible breach of laws, regulations and requirements that involve an assertion of jurisdiction not recognised by a requested Authority. Where a requested Authority considers that an assertion of jurisdiction in a matter that is the subject of a request would conflict seriously with an prejudice its sovereign interests the request will be denied.

9. The Authorities recognise that, so long as there are differences in the scope of the laws, regulations and requirements applied in each country, conduct prohibited by the Authorities in one country may not be prohibited by the Authorities in the other. The Authorities intend to engage in consultations about individual cases falling outside the scope of the definition of legal rule or requirement to determine whether assistance will be provided in such cases.

10. Either the DTI or the SIB may refer a request to the other and, if it does so, it will at the same time notify the requesting Authority.

11. This Memorandum does not extend to information held by the DTI solely by virtue of powers and functions that relate to matters other than securities, investments, futures or company law.

PART III: REQUESTS FOR INFORMATION

12. Any request for information made under this Memorandum will satisfy the following requirements:

(a) wherever possible it will be in writing but in cases of urgency it may be oral, and confirmed in writing within 10 days;
(b) it will clearly specify the following:

(i) the information requested;
(ii) the general purpose for which the information is sought, indicating in particular the legal rule or requirement pertaining to the matter that is the subject of the request;
(iii) a description of the conduct and its connection with the jurisdiction of the requesting Authority. However, where the legal rule or requirement in question is that a person be fit or qualified to set up or carry on an Investment, Securities Processing or Futures Business, or otherwise involves the conduct or qualifications of an Investment, Securities Processing or Futures Business, it is sufficient compliance with this subparagraph to specify that information is sought for that purpose;
(iv) the identity of the person, if known, whose conduct causes concern. However, where the relevant rule or requirement falls within paragraph 1 (h) (1) (A) through (C) or 1 (h) (2) (A) and (B) above, it is sufficient compliance with this subparagraph to specify that information is sought concerning the purpose

specified in accordance with (ii) above in order to identify the person(s) against whom proceedings or actions are to be, or may be, taken; and

(v)   where it is apparent to the requesting Authority that another person may obtain the information for a purpose other than securing compliance with or enforcing the legal rule or requirement specified under subparagraph (ii) above in respect of the person(s) (if any) specified under subparagraph (iv) above, to the extent permitted by the laws of the jurisdiction of the requesting Authority, the particulars of that person and that person's interest; and

(vi)   particular procedures contemplated in Part IV of this Memorandum that it requests be utilised for questioning, taking testimony or conducting inspections;

(c)   it will be addressed to one of the requested Authority's contact officers listed in Annex I, or that person's nominee, pursuant to written notice to the requesting Authority; and

(d)   the requested information must be reasonably relevant to securing compliance with the legal rule or requirement specified in the request.

In any case where a requested Authority is not satisfied that a request fully complies with the requirements of this paragraph, it may require the Director of the Office of International Affairs of the SEC or the Director of the Division of Enforcement of the CFTC, or the Under Secretary, Financial Services Division, DTI, or the Group Director, Compliance and Enforcement of the SIB, where applicable, to certify that the request is cognisable under the terms of this Memorandum. A requested Authority may not challenge such a certification except on substantial grounds which will be fully stated in writing.

PART IV: PROCEDURES FOR QUESTIONING OR TAKING TESTIMONY AND CONDUCTING INSPECTIONS

13. In accordance with paragraph 6:

(a)   questioning or taking the testimony of persons, if requested, will be conducted in the same manner and to the same extent as investigations or other proceedings under the laws of the jurisdiction of the requested Authority;

(b)   when requested by the requesting Authority, questioning or taking testimony will be conducted under oath and a transcript will be made;

(c)   a representative of the requesting Authority may be present at the questioning or testimony, may prescribe specific questions to be asked of any witness and, pursuant to paragraph 14 of this Memorandum, may otherwise participate in the examination of any witness.

14. Subject to the following conditions, a requested Authority may grant a request made by the requesting Authority that a person or persons designated by the requesting Authority, including representatives of the requesting Authority, be permitted to conduct the interrogation of any person, or participate in the inspection or examination of the books and records of an Investment or Futures Business or its custodian or agent:

(a)   the requesting Authority must specify the reasons for this request;

(b)   the request may be granted or denied by the requested Authority in its discretion. The requested Authority may impose such conditions on the participation of the requesting Authority as it deems appropriate;

(c)   if the request is granted and the laws of the jurisdiction of the requesting Authority require the opportunity for the witness to consult with legal counsel, or for counsel to the witness to pose questions to the witness, such participation will, subject to (b) above, be permitted; and

(d)   if the request is denied, the Authorities agree to consult pursuant to paragraph 24 of this Memorandum concerning the reasons for the denial and the circumstances under which the request might be granted.

15. Notwithstanding any other provision of this Memorandum, any person providing testimony, information or documents as a result of a request made under this Memorandum will be entitled to all the rights and protections of the laws of the jurisdiction of the requested

Authority. Where assertions are made regarding other rights and privileges arising exclusively pursuant to the laws of the jurisdiction of the requesting Authority, the Authorities will consult to determine the most appropriate way to proceed.

PART V: PERMISSIBLE USES AND CONFIDENTIALITY

16. Information received will be used solely for the purpose of:

    (a)   securing, through enquiries, investigations or litigation, compliance with or enforcement of the legal rule or requirement specified in the request, provided that the information may be used to secure compliance with or enforcement of other applicable legal rules or requirements in proceedings in which a violation of the legal rule or requirement specified in the request is alleged;

    (b)   securing compliance with or enforcement of a legal rule or requirement that was not specified in the request in proceedings in which a violation of the legal rule or requirement specified in the request is not alleged, if prior to such use, the requesting Authority informs the requested Authority of its intention to use the information for such purposes and the requested Authority does not object; or

    (c)   conducting civil or administrative enforcement proceedings, assisting in a criminal prosecution, or conducting any investigation related thereto for any general charge applicable to the violation of the legal rule or requirement identified in the request.

17. The requesting Authority will keep confidential any information provided under this Memorandum subject to the terms of this paragraph, unless it is disclosed in furtherance of the purpose for which it was requested under paragraph 16 above:

    (a)   except as contemplated by paragraph 16 above, the requesting Authority will not offer the information to, and will use its best efforts to ensure that it is not obtained by, any other person. Unless otherwise agreed, in the event that such information is obtained by any public body, the requesting Authority will use its best efforts to ensure that it will not be used by that body in any way that involves its disclosure to any other person;

    (b)   if the requesting Authority becomes aware that the information has been or is likely to be disclosed otherwise than as contemplated by paragraph 16 above, it will inform the requested Authority of the situation; and

    (c)   after the requesting Authority has terminated the matter for which assistance has been requested under this Memorandum, upon request of the requested Authority, it will return to the requested Authority, to the extent permitted by the laws of the jurisdiction of the requesting Authority, all documents and copies thereof not already disclosed in proceedings referred to in paragraph 16 above, and other material disclosing the content of such documents, other than material generated as part of the deliberative, investigative, internal or analytical process of the requesting Authority, which may be retained.

18. Any document or other material provided by an Authority in response to a request under this Memorandum and any copies or other material disclosing its content, other than material generated as part of the deliberative, investigative, internal or analytical process of the requesting Authority, will not become the property of the requesting Authority, and must be redelivered to the requested Authority without delay on demand to the extent permitted by the laws of the jurisdiction of the requesting Authority; provided that such demand may be made only if the requested Authority has reason to believe that the information has been or is likely to be disclosed or used otherwise than as contemplated by paragraph 16 above.

19. Each Authority will keep confidential to the extent permitted by law any request for information made under this Memorandum and any matters arising in the course of its operation, including consultation under this Part or Part I of this Memorandum, unless:

    (a)   such disclosure is absolutely necessary to carry out the request; or

    (b)   the other Authority waives such confidentiality.

A requesting Authority may specify that if the requested Authority considers such disclosure to be absolutely necessary, then the Authority will consult before such disclosure is made.

This paragraph does not apply to general matters of proper public interest relating to the operation of this Memorandum.

Part VI: Other Means of Obtaining Information

20. The Authorities have various powers to obtain information in the exercise of regulatory functions that are within the scope of this Memorandum. If, in the exercise of its powers, any Authority obtains information that it recognises as clearly giving rise to a suspicion of a breach of any legal rule or requirement of any other Authority, then it will, to the extent permitted by law, offer to provide such information to such Authority for any purpose, and subject to compliance by the other with any conditions that would have been applicable had a request pursuant to this Memorandum been made.

21. Where one Authority wishes to make enquiries of, or seek information from, a person within the territory of another Authority on a voluntary basis, the enquiries will be conducted in accordance with arrangements agreed between the Authorities.

22. The execution of this Memorandum will not prejudice the respective positions of the Authorities concerning the use of procedures for obtaining information other than as provided for in this Memorandum.

Part VII: Costs

23. When the costs of providing or obtaining information under this Memorandum are substantial, the requested Authority may require the requesting Authority to undertake to pay those costs. In such an event the relevant Authorities will consult on the issue at the request of either Authority.

Part VIII: Consultations and Waiver

24. The Authorities will keep the operation of this Memorandum under continuous review and consult with a view to improving its operation and resolving any matters. In particular, any Authority will consult another Authority upon request in the event of:

(a)   a request being denied in whole or in part;

(b)   a change in market or business conditions or in the laws, regulations or requirements governing the matters mentioned in paragraph 1(h) above, or any other difficulty arising which makes it necessary to amend or extend this Memorandum in order to achieve its purposes; or

(c)   an assertion by the requested Authority that the provision of assistance would be so burdensome as to disrupt the proper performance of its functions.

25. Where the specific conduct set out in the request for assistance may constitute a breach of a legal rule or requirement in both the territory of the requesting and the requested Authorities, the relevant Authorities will consult in order to determine the most appropriate means for each Authority to provide assistance.

26. In cases where the requested Authority is either the SEC or CFTC, denial of a request under paragraph 7 or 8 will be made by its respective Commission after consultation with relevant officials within the United States Government, and in cases where the requested Authority is a UK Authority, such a denial will be made by the Secretary of State.

27. Any of the conditions of this Memorandum may be relaxed or waived by mutual agreement.

Part IX: Termination

28. This Memorandum will continue to have effect unless terminated by the SEC and CFTC, on the one hand, or the DTI and SIB, on the other hand, by giving 30 days advance written notice

to the other Authorities that the understandings set out herein are no longer to have effect. Such notice may in particular be given in consequence of a change in the laws or regulations applicable to any matter governed by this Memorandum which is regarded by an Authority as material and in the absence of an agreed amendment to take account of the change. The SEC, CFTC, DTI or SIB may withdraw from participation in this MOU only with respect to areas of the Memorandum regarding that Authority's areas of competence and the arrangements relating thereto. Termination by the DTI may take effect with respect to the areas within the competence of the SEC and/or the CFTC and the arrangements relating thereto and will be so specified.

PART X: ENTRY INTO EFFECT

29. This Memorandum will be effective from the date of its signature by the United States Securities and Exchange Commission, the United States Commodity Futures Trading Commission, the United Kingdom Department of Trade and Industry and the United Kingdom Securities and Investments Board.

SIGNED THIS 25TH DAY OF SEPTEMBER 1991

SECURITIES AND   DEPARTMENT OF TRADE
EXCHANGE COMMISSION   AND INDUSTRY

Richard C. Breeden   John Redwood
Chairman   Minister of State for
                                      Corporate Affairs

COMMODITY FUTURES   SECURITIES AND
TRADING COMMISSION   INVESTMENTS BOARD

Wendy Gramm   Sir David Walker
Chairman   Chairman

ANNEX I

CONTACT OFFICERS

DTI: Under Secretary, Financial Services Division
                      Department of Trade and Industry
                      10–18 Victoria Street
                      London SW1H ONN
                      UNITED KINGDOM
                      Telephone: 44 71 215 3160
                      Fax: 44 71 215 3508

SIB: Group Director, Compliance and Enforcement
                      Securities and Investments Board
                      Gavrelle House
                      2–14 Bunhill Row
                      London EC1Y 8RA
                      UNITED KINGDOM
                      Telephone: 44 71 638 1240
                      Fax: 44 71 382 5900

SEC: Director, Office of International Affairs
                              Securities and Exchange Commission
                              450 5th Street, N.W.
                              Washington, D.C. 20549
                              UNITED STATES OF AMERICA
                              Telephone: 1 (202) 272 2306
                              Fax: 1 (202) 504 2282

CFTC: Director, Division of Enforcement
                              Commodity Futures Trading Commission
                              2033 K Street, N.W.
                              Washington, D.C. 20581
                              UNITED STATES OF AMERICA
                              Telephone: 1 (202) 254 9501
                              Fax: 1 (202) 254 3534

Appendix U

COMPANIES ACT 1989, SECTIONS 82 TO 91

Request for assistance by overseas regulatory authority

82—(1) The powers conferred by section 83 are exercisable by the Secretary of State for the purpose of assisting an overseas regulatory authority which has requested his assistance in connection with inquiries being carried out by it or on its own behalf.

(2) An "overseas regulatory authority" means an authority which in a country or territory outside the United Kingdom exercises—

(a) any function corresponding to—

    (i) a function under the Financial Services Act 1986 of a designated agency, transferee body or competent authority (within the meaning of that Act),

    (ii) a function of the Secretary of State under the Insurance Companies Act 1982, the Companies Act 1985 or the Financial Services Act 1986, or

    (iii) a function of the Bank of England under the Banking Act 1987, or

(b) any function in connection with the investigation of, or the enforcement of rules (whether or not having the force of law) relating to, conduct of the kind prohibited by [Part V of the Criminal Justice Act 1993 (insider dealing)], or

(c) any function prescribed for the purposes of this subsection by order of the Secretary of State, being a function which in the opinion of the Secretary of State relates to the companies or financial services.

An order under paragraph (c) shall be made by statutory instrument which shall be subject to annulment in pursuance of a resolution of either House of Parliament.

(3) The Secretary of State shall not exercise the powers conferred by section 83 unless he is satisfied that the assistance requested by the overseas regulatory authority is for the purposes of its regulatory functions.

An authority's "regulatory functions" mans any functions falling within subsection (2) and any other functions relating to companies of financial services.

(4) In deciding whether to exercise those powers the Secretary of State may take into account, in particular—

(a) whether corresponding assistance would be given in that country or territory to an authority exercising regulatory functions in the United Kingdom;

(b) whether the inquiries relate to the possible breach of a law, or other requirement, which has no close parallel in the United Kingdom or involves the assertion of a jurisdiction not recognised by the United Kingdom;

(c) the seriousness of the matter to which the inquiries relate, the importance to the inquiries of the information sought in the United Kingdom and whether the assistance could be obtained by other means[1];

(d) whether it is otherwise appropriate in the public interest to give the assistance sought[2].

(5) Before deciding whether to exercise those powers in a case where the overseas regulatory authority is a banking supervisor, the Secretary of State shall consult the Bank of England.

---

1 For example, the Secretary of State may consider that the procedures available under ss 105/106 of the Financial Services Act 1985 are a more appropriate means of obtaining the information sought, in which event he may make appropriate arrangements.

2 If the matters complained of take place abroad and its effects are limited to overseas, it is unlikely that it would be "in the public interest" to provide the assistance sought.

A "banking supervisor" means an overseas regulatory authority with respect to which the bank of England has notified the Secretary of State, for the purposes of this subsection, that it exercises functions corresponding to those of the Bank under the banking Act 1987.

(6) The Secretary of State may decline to exercise those powers unless the overseas regulatory authority undertakes to make such contribution towards the costs[3] of their exercise as the Secretary of State considers appropriate.

(7) References in this section to financial services include, in particular, investment business, insurance and banking.

Power to require information, documents or other assistance

(1) The following powers may be exercised in accordance with section 82, if the Secretary of State considers there is good reason for their exercise.

(2) The Secretary of State may require any person—

(a)   to attend before him at a specified time and place and answer questions or otherwise furnish information with respect to any matter relevant to the inquiries

(b)   to produce at a specified time and place any specified documents which appear to the Secretary of State to relate to any matter relevant to the inquiries, and

(c)   otherwise to give him such assistance in connection with the inquiries as he is reasonably able to give.[4]

(3) The Secretary of State may examine a person on oath and may administer an oath accordingly.

(4) Where documents are produced the Secretary of State may take copies or extracts from them.

(5) A person shall not under this section be required to disclose information or produce a document which he would be entitled to refuse to disclose or produce on ground of legal professional privilege in proceedings in the High Court or on grounds of confidentiality as between client and professional legal adviser in proceedings in the Court of Session, except that a lawyer may be required to furnish the name and address of his client.

(6) A statement by a person in compliance with a requirement imposed under this section may be used in evidence against him.[5]

(7) Where a person claims a lien on a document, its production under this section is without prejudice to his lien.

(8) In this section "documents" includes information recorded in any form; and, in relation to information recorded otherwise than in legible form, the power to require its production includes power to require the production of a copy of it in legible form.

Exercise of power by office, &c

84.—(1) The Secretary of State may authorise an officer of his or any other competent person to exercise on his behalf all or any of the powers conferred by section 83[6]

(2) No such authority shall be granted except for the purpose of investigating—

(a)   the affairs, or any aspects of the affairs, of a person specified in the authority, or

(b)   a subject-matter so specified, being a person who, or subject-matter which, is the subject of the inquiries being carried out by or on behalf of the overseas regulatory authority,

(3) No person shall be bound to comply with a requirement imposed by a person exercising powers by virtue of an authority granted under this section unless he has, if required, produced evidence of his authority.

---

3 This is a practice that has been adopted in certain MOU's (see the MOU between US SEC and the UK DTI & SIB at App. T above)

4 There is no power to search for or seize material, or to apply for a search warrant under the 1989 Act.

5 Despite this provision, questions of admissibility will be for the requesting jurisdiction to rule upon.

6 Whilst there would appear to be no impediment to the Secretary of State authorising foreign regulators in the UK to exercise such powers, they will be subject to the restrictions on disclosure under s86, which might preclude them from acting in their own jurisdiction upon information collected by them whilst in the UK.

(4) A person shall not by virtue of an authority under this section be required to disclose any information or produce any documents in respect of which he owes an obligation of confidence by virtue of carrying on the business of banking unless—

(a) the imposing on him of a requirement with respect to such information or documents has been specifically authorised by the Secretary of State, or

(b) the person to whom the obligation of confidence is owed consents to the disclosure or production.

In this subsection "documents" has the same meaning as in section 83

(5) Where the Secretary of State authorises a person other than one of his officers to exercise any powers by virtue of this section, that person shall make a report to the Secretary of State in such manner as he may require on the exercise of those powers and the results of exercising them.

Penalty for failure to comply with requirement, &c

85—(1) A person who without reasonable excuse fails to comply with a requirement imposed on him under section 83 commits an offence and is liable on summary conviction to imprisonment for a term not exceeding six months or to a fine not exceeding level 5 of the standard scale, or both,

(2) A person who in purported compliance with any such requirement furnishes information which he knows to be false or misleading in a material particular, or recklessly furnishes information which is false or misleading in a material particular, commits an offence and is liable—

(a) on conviction on indictment, to imprisonment for a term not exceeding two years or to a fine, or both;

(b) on summary conviction, to imprisonment for a term not exceeding six months or to a fine not exceeding the statutory maximum, or both.

Restrictions on disclosure of information[7]

86—(1) This section applies to information relating to the business or other affairs of a person which—

(a) is supplied by an overseas regulatory authority in connection with a request for assistance, or

(b) is obtained by virtue of the powers conferred by section 83, whether or not any requirement to supply it is made under that section.

2. Except as permitted by section 87 below, such information shall not be disclosed for any purpose—

(a) by the primary recipient, or

(b) by any person obtaining the information directly or indirectly from him, without the consent of the person from whom the primary recipient obtained the information and, if different, the person to whom it relates.

3. The "primary recipient" means, as the case may be—

(a) the Secretary of State,

(b) any person authorised under section 84 to exercise powers on his behalf, and

(c) any officer or servant of any such person

---

7 During the Bill's passage through the House of Lords, at the Committee stage, the Secretary of State for Trade & Industry declared that he would not exercise his powers under the Act unless he believed the request to have been made in good faith.

To protect confidentiality, information would only be released:—

(a) under MOU's or similar arrangements providing for limits upon disclosure and its use by the requesting authority; and

(b) in the absence of such arrangements being in place, only subject to similar conditions being imposed on an ad hoc basis.

If for any reason the Secretary of State suspected non-observation of these conditions this would provide grounds for the exercise of his discretion not to initiate such an investigation or pass on all or some of the information obtained during the investigation (504 Parliamentary Debates (Lords) 107)

4. Information shall not be treated as information to which this section applies if it has been made available to the public by virtue of being disclosed in any circumstances in which, or for any purpose for which, disclosure is not precluded by this section.

5. A person who contravenes this section commits an offence and is liable—

(a) on conviction on indictment, to imprisonment for a term not exceeding two years or to a fine, or both;

(b) on summary conviction, to imprisonment for a term not exceeding three months or to a fine not exceeding the statutory maximum, or both.

Exceptions from restrictions on disclosure

1. Information to which section 86 applies may be disclosed—

(a) to any person with a view to the institution of, or otherwise for the purposes of, relevant proceedings,

(b) for the purpose of enabling or assisting a relevant authority to discharge any relevant function, (including functions in relation to proceedings),

(c) to the Treasury, if the disclosure is made in the interests of investors or in the public interest,

(d) if the information is or has been available to the public from other sources

(e) in a summary or collection of information framed in such a way as not to enable the identity of any person to whom the information relates to be ascertained, or

(f) in pursuance of any Community obligation.

2. The relevant proceedings referred to in subsection (1)(a) are—

(a) any criminal proceedings,

(b) civil proceedings arising under or by virtue of the Financial Services Act 1986 and proceedings before the Financial Services Tribunal, and

(c) disciplinary proceedings relating to—

(i) the exercise by a solicitor, auditor, accountant, valuer or actuary of his professional duties, or

(ii) the discharge by a public servant of his duties.

3. In subsection (2)(c)(ii) "public servant" means an officer or servant of the Crown or any public or other authority for the time being designated for the purposes of that provision by order of the Secretary of State.

(4) The relevant authorities referred to in subsection (1)(b), and the relevant functions in relation to each such authority, are as follows—

Authority	Function
The Secretary of State	Functions under the enactments relating to companies, insurance companies or insolvency, or under the Financial Services Act 1986 or Part II, this Part or Part VII of this Act.
[The Treasury	Functions [under the enactments relating to insurance companies] under the Financial Services Act 1986 or under this Part or Part VII of this Act.]
An inspector appointed under Part XIV of 177 of the Financial Services Act 1986	Functions under that Part of that section
A person authorised to exercise powers or appointed under section 43A or 44 of the Insurance Companies Act 1982, section 447 of the Companies Act 1985, section 106 of the Financial Services Act 1986 or section 84 of this Act.	Functions under that section
An overseas regulatory authority	Its regulatory functions (within the meaning of section 82 of this Act).

The Department of Economic Development in Northern Ireland or a person appointed or authorised by that Department	Functions conferred on it or him by the enactments relating to companies or insolvency
A designated agency within the meaning of the Financial Services Act 1986	Functions under that Act or Part VII of this Act
A transferee body or the competent authority within a meaning of the Financial Services Act 1986	Functions under that Act
The body administering a scheme under section 54 of the Financial Services Act 1986	Functions under the scheme
A recognised self-regulating organisation, recognised professional body, recognised investment exchange, recognised clearing house or recognised self regulating organisation for friendly societies (within the meaning of the Financial Services Act 1986)	Functions in its capacity as an organisation, body, exchange or clearing house recognised under that Act
The Chief Registrar of Friendly Societies and the Assistant Registrar of Friendly Societies for Scotland	Functions under the enactments relating to friendly societies or building societies
The Friendly Societies Commission	Functions under the enactments relating to friendly societies or under the Financial Services Act 1986
The Bank of England	[Any of its functions]
[The Financial Services Authority	Functions under the Financial Services Act 1986 (other than as a designated agency within the meaning of that Act), the Banking Act 1987 or section 171 of the Companies Act 1989]
The Deposit Protection Board	Functions under the Bank Act 1987
A body established by order under section 46 of this Act	Functions under Part II of this Act
A recognised supervisory or qualifying body within the meaning of Part II of this Act	Functions as such a body
The Industrial Assurance Commissioner and the Industrial Assurance Commissioner for Northern Ireland	Functions under the enactments relating to industrial assurance
The Insurance Brokers Registration Council	Functions under the Insurance Brokers (Registration) Act 1977
The Official Receiver or, in Northern Ireland, the Official Assignee for company liquidations or for bankruptcy	Functions under the enactments relating to insolvency
A recognised professional body (within the meaning of section 391) of the Insolvency Act 1986)	Functions in its capacity as such a body under the Insolvency Act 1986
The Building Societies Commission	Functions under the Building Societies Act 1986
[The Occupational Pensions Regulatory Authority	Functions under the Pension Schemes Act 1993 or the Pensions Act 1995 or any enactment in force in Northern Ireland corresponding to either of them]
The Director General of Fair Trading	Functions under the Financial Services Act 1986

[A person authorised by the Secretary of State under sections 245C of the Companies Act 1985	Functions relating to the securing of compliance by companies with the accounting requirements of that Act]
[The Director General of the National Lottery	Functions under sections 5 to 10 inclusive and section 15 of the National Lottery etc. Act 1993]

Notes

The table in sub-s. (4) is amended as follows:
the entry relating to the Treasury was inserted by the Transfer of Functions (Financial Services) Order 1992, S.I. 1992 No. 1315, art. 10(1), Sched. 4, para. 12 and amended by the Transfer of Functions (Insurance) Order 1997, S.I. 1997 No. 2781, art. 8, Schedule; the words in square brackets in the entry beginning "A person authorised to exercise powers" were substituted by the Insurance Companies (Third Insurance Directives) Regulations 1994, S.I. 1994 No 1696, reg. 68(1), Sched. 8; the words omitted from the entry beginning "The Chief Registrar of Friendly Societies" were repealed, and the entry relating to the Friendly Societies Commission was inserted by the Friendly Societies Act 1992, s. 120, Sched. 21, para. 11, Sched. 22, Pt I; the words in square brackets in the entry relating to the Bank of England were substituted and the entry relating to the Financial Services Authority was inserted by the Bank of England Act s. 23(1), Sched. 5, para. 66; the entry relating to the Occupational Pensions Authority was inserted by the Pensions Act 1995, s. 122, Sched. 3, para. 19; the entry beginning "A person authorised by the Secretary of State" was added by the Financial Services (Disclosure of Information) (Designated Authorities) (No. 7) Order 1993, S.I. 1993 No. 1826; the entry relating to the Director General of the National Lottery was added by the Financial Services (Disclosure of Information) (Designated Authorities) (No. 8) Order 1994, S.I. 1994 No. 340.

(5) The Secretary of State may be order amend the Table in subsection (4) so as to—

    (a) Add any public or other authority to the Table and specify the relevant functions of that authority,

    (b) remove any authority from the Table, or

    (c) add functions to, or remove functions from, those which are relevant functions in relation to an authority specified in the Table;

and the order may impose conditions subject to which, or otherwise restrict the circumstances in which, disclosure is permitted.

    6. An order under this section shall be made by statutory instrument which shall be subject to annulment in pursuance of a resolution of either House of Parliament.

Exercise of powers in relation to Northern Ireland

88.–(1) The following provision apply where it appears to the Secretary of State that a request for assistance by an overseas regulatory authority may involve the powers conferred by section 83 being exercised in Northern Ireland in relation to matters which are transferred matters within the meaning of the Northern Ireland Constitution Act 1973.

    (2) The Secretary of State shall before deciding whether to accede to the request consult the Department of Economic Development in Northern Ireland, and if he decides to accede to the request and it appears to him—

    (a) that the powers should be exercised in Northern Ireland, and

    (b) that the purposes for which they should be so exercised relate wholly or primarily to transferred matters,

he shall by instrument in writing authorise the Department to exercise in Northern Ireland his powers under section 83.

    (3) The following provisions have effect in relation to the exercise of powers by virtue of such an authority with the substitution for references to the Secretary of State of references to the Department of Economic Development in Northern Ireland—

    (a) section 84 (exercise of powers by officer, &C)

    (b) section 449 of the Companies Act 1985, section 53 or 54 of the Building Societies Act 1986, sections 179 and 180 of the Financial Services Act 1986, section 84 of the Banking Act 1987 and sections 86 and 87 above (restrictions on disclosure of information), and

(c)   section 89 (authority for institution of criminal proceedings);

and references to the Secretary of State in other enactments which proceed by reference to those provisions shall be construed accordingly as being or including references to the Department.

(4) The Secretary of State may after consultation with the Department of Economic Development in Northern Ireland revoke an authority given to the Department under this section.

(5) In that case nothing in the provisions referred to in subsection (3)(b) shall apply so as to prevent the Department from giving the Secretary of State any information obtained by virtue of the authority; and (without prejudice to their application in relation to disclosure of such information by the Secretary of States if it had been obtained by him in the first place.

(6) Nothing in this section affects the exercise by the Secretary of State of any powers in Northern Ireland—

(a)   in a case where at the time of acceding to the request it did not appear to him that the circumstances were such as to require him to authorise the Department of Economic Development in Northern Ireland to exercise those powers, or

(b)   after the revocation by him of any such authority;

and no objection shall be taken to anything done by or in relation to the Secretary of State or the Department on the ground that it should have been done by or in relation to the other.

Prosecutions

89. Proceedings for an offence under section 85 or 86 shall not be instituted—

(a)   in England and Wales, except by or with the consent of the Secretary of State or the Director of Public Prosecutions;

(b)   in Northern Ireland, except by or with the consent of the Secretary of State or the Director of Public Prosecutions for Northern Ireland.

Offences by bodies corporate, partnerships and unincorporated associations

90.—(1) Where an offence under section 85 or 86 committed by a body corporate is proved to have been committed with the consent or connivance of, or to be attributable to any neglect on the part of, a director, manager, secretary or other similar officer of the body, or a person purporting to act in any such capacity, he as well as the body corporate is guilty of the offence and liable to be proceeded against and punished accordingly.

(2) Where the affairs of a body corporate are managed by its members, subsection (1) applies in relation to the acts and defaults of a member in connection with his functions of management as to a director of a body corporate.

(3) Where an offence under section 85 or 86 committed by a partnership is proved to have been committed with the consent or connivance of, or to be attributable to any neglect on the part of, a partner, he as well as the partnership is guilty of the offence and liable to be proceeded against and punished accordingly.

(4) Where an offence under section 85 or 86 committed by an unincorporated association (other than a partnership) is proved to have been committed with the consent or connivance of, or to be attributable to any neglect on the part of, any officer of the association or any member of its governing body, he as well as the association is guilty of the offence and liable to be proceeded against and punished accordingly.

Jurisdiction and procedure in respect of offences

91—(1) Summary proceedings for an offence under Section 85 may, without prejudice to any jurisdiction exercisable apart from this section, be taken against a body corporate or unincorporated association at any place at which it has a place of business and against an individual at any place where he is for the time being.

(2) Proceedings for an offence alleged to have been committed under section 85 or 86 by an unincorporated association shall be brought in the name of the association (and not in that of any of its members), and for the purposes of any such proceedings any rules of Court relating to the service of documents apply as in relation to a body corporate.

(3) Section 33 of the Criminal Justice Act 1925 and Schedule 3 to the Magistrates Courts Act 1980 (procedure on charge of offence against a corporation) apply in a case in which an

unincorporated association is charged in England and Wales with an offence under section 85 or 86 as they apply in the case of a corporation.

(4) (Applies to Scotland only)

(5) Section 18 of the Criminal Justice Act (Northern Ireland) 1945 and Schedule 4 to the Magistrates' Court (Northern Ireland) Order 1981 (procedure on charge of offence against a corporation) apply in a case in which an unincorporated association is charged in Northern Ireland with an offence under section 85 or 86 as they apply in the case of a corporation.

(6) A fine imposed on an unincorporated association on its conviction of such an offence shall be paid out of the funds of the association.

Appendix V

COUNCIL DIRECTIVE OF 19 DECEMBER 1977 CONCERNING MUTUAL ASSISTANCE BY THE COMPETENT AUTHORITIES OF THE MEMBER STATES IN THE FIELDS OF DIRECT TAXATION AND VALUE ADDED TAX

77/799/EEC

The Council of the European Communities,

Having regard to the Treaty establishing the European Economic Community, and in particular Article 100 thereof,

Having regard to the proposal from the Commission,

Having regard to the opinion of the European Parliament,

Having regard to the opinion of the Economic and Social Committee

Whereas practices of tax evasion and tax avoidance extending across the frontiers of Member States lead to budget losses and violations of the principle of fair taxation and are liable to bring about distortions of capital movements and of conditions of competition; whereas they therefore affect the operation of the common market;

Whereas, for these reasons the Council adopted on 10 February 1975 a resolution on the measures to be taken by the Community in order to combat international tax evasion and avoidance.

Whereas the international nature of the problem means that national measures, whose effect does not extend beyond national frontiers, are insufficient; whereas collaboration between administration on the basis of bilateral agreements is also unable to counter new forms of tax evasion and avoidance, which are increasingly assuming a multinational character;

Whereas collaboration between tax administrations within the Community should therefore be strengthened in accordance with common principles and rules;

Whereas the Member States should, on request, exchange information concerning particular cases; whereas the State so requested should make the necessary enquiries to obtain such information;

Whereas the Member States should exchange, even without any request, any information which appears relevant for the correct assessment of taxes on income and on capital, in particular where there appears to be an artificial transfer of profits between enterprises in different Member States or where such transactions are carried out between enterprises in two Member States through a third country in order to obtain tax advantages, or where tax has been or may be evaded or avoided for any reason whatever;

Whereas it is important that officials of the tax administration of one Member State be allowed to be present in the territory of another Member State if both the States concerned consider it desirable;

Whereas care must be taken to ensure that information provided in the course of such collaboration is not disclosed to unauthorised persons, so that the basic rights of citizens and enterprises are safeguarded; whereas it is therefore necessary that the Member States receiving such information should not use it, without the authorisation of the Member State supplying it, other than for the purposes of taxation or to facilitate legal proceedings for failure to observe the tax laws of the receiving State; whereas it is also necessary that the receiving States afford the information the same degree of confidentiality which it enjoyed in the State which provided it, if the latter so requires;

Whereas a Member State which is called upon to carry out enquiries or to provide information shall have the right to refuse to do so where its laws or administrative practices prevent its tax administration from carrying out these enquiries or from collecting or using this information for its own purposes, or where the provision of such information would be contrary to public policy or would lead to the disclosure of a commercial, industrial or professional secret or of a commercial process, or where the Member State for which the information is intended is unable for practical or legal reasons to provide similar information.

Wherease collaboration between the Member States and the Commission is necessary for the permanent study of cooperation procedures and the pooling of experience in the fields considered, and in particular in the field of the artificial transfer of profits within groups of enterprises, with the aim of improving those procedures and of preparing appropriate Community rules,

Has adopted this Directive:

Article 1
General provisions

1 In accordance with the the provisions of this Directive the competent authorities of the Member States shall exchange any information that may enable them to effect a correct assessment of taxes on income and capital.

2 There shall be regarded as taxes on income and on capital, irrespective of the manner in which they are levied, all taxes imposed on total income, on total capital, or on elements of income or of capital, including taxes on gains from the disposal of movable or immovable property, taxes on the amounts of wages or salaries paid by enterprises, as well as taxes on capital appreciation.

3 The taxes referred to in paragraph 2 are at present, in particular: in Belgium:

Impôt des personnes physiques/Personenbelasting
Impôt des sociétés/Vennootschapsbelasting
Impôt des personnes morales/Rechtspersonenbelasting
Impôt des non-résidents/Belasting der niet-vérblijfhouders

in Denmark:

Indkomstskaten til staten
Selskabsskat
Den kommunale indkomstskat
Den amtskommunale indkomstskat
Folkepensionsbidragene
Somandsskat
Den særlige indkomstskat
Kirkeskat
Formueskatten til staten
Bidrag til dagpengefonden

in Greece:

φορο̨ εισοδηματο̨ φνσικων προσωπων
φορο̨ εισοδηματο̨ φνσικων προσωπων
φορο̨ ακινητσν περιονσια̨

in Spain:

Impuesto sobre la Renta de las Personas Fisicas
Impuesto sobre Sociedades
Impuesto Extraordinario sobre el Patrimonio de las Personas Fisicas

in Germany:

Einkommensteuer
Körperschaftsteuer
Vermögensteuer
Gewerbesteuer
Grundsteuer

in France:

Impôt sur le revenu
Impôt sur les sociétés
Taxe professionnelle
Taxe foncière sur les propriétés bâties

Taxe foncière sur les propriétés non bâties
In Ireland:
  Income tax
  Corporation tax
  Capital gains tax
  Wealth tax
in Italy:
  Imposta sul reddito delle persone fisiche
  Imposta sul reddito persone giuridiche
  Imposta locale sui redditi
in Luxembourg:
  Impôt sur le revenu des personnes physiques
  Impôt sur le revenu de collectivités
  Impôt commercial communal
  Impôt sur la fortune
  Impôt foncier
in the Netherlands:
  Inkomstenbelasting
  Vennootschapsbelasting
  Vermogensbelasting
in Austria:
  Einkommensteuer
  Körperschaftsteuer
  Grundsteuer
  Bodenwertabgabe
  Abgabe von land- und fortswirtschaftlichen Betrieben
in Portugal:
  Contribuiáao predial
  Imposto sobre a industria agricola
  Contribuiáao industrial
  Imposto de capitais
  Imposto profissional
  Imposto complementar
  Imposto de mais-valias
  Imposto sobre o rendimento do petroleo
  Os adicionais devidos sobre os impostos precedentes
in Finland:
  Valtion tuloverot/de statliga inkomstskatterna
  Yhteisöjen tulovero/inkomstskatten för samfund
  Kunnallisvero/kommunalskatten
  Kirkollisvero/kyrkoskatten
  Kansaneläkevakuutusmaksu/folkpensionsförsäkringspremien
  Sairausvakuutusmaksu/sjukförsäkringspremien
  Korkotulon lähdevero/källskatten pá ränteinkomst
  Rajoitetusti verovelvollisen lähdevero/källskatten fir begränsat skattskyldig
  Valtion varallisuusvero/den statliga förmögenhetsskatten
  Kiinteistövero/fastighetsskatten
in Sweden:
  Den statliga inkomstskatten
  Sjömansskatten
  Kupongskatten
  Den särskilda inkomstskatten för utomlands bosatta
  Den särskilda inkomstskatten för utomlands bosatta artister m. fl.
  Den statliga fastighetsskatten
  Den kommunala inkomstskatten
  Förmögenhetsskatten
in the United Kingdom:
  Income tax
  Corporation tax

Capital gains tax

Petroleum revenue tax

Development land tax

4 Paragraph I shall also apply to any identical or similar taxes imposed subsequently, whether in addition to or in place of the taxes listed in paragraph 3. The competent authorities of the Member States shall inform one another and the Commission of the date of entry into force of such taxes.

5 The expression "competent authority" means:

in Belgium:

De minister van financiën or an authorised representative

Le ministre des finances or an authorised representative

in Denmark:

Skatteministeren or an authorised representative

in Germany:

Der Bundesminister der Finanzen or an authorised representative

in Greece:

Υπουργειο Οικονομικων or an authorised representative in Spain:

El Ministro de Economia y Hacienda or an authorised representative

in France:

Le ministre de l'économie or an authorised representative

in Ireland:

The Revenue Commissioners or their authorised representative

in Italy:

Il Ministro per le finanze or an authorised representative

in Luxembourg:

Le ministre de finance or an authorised representative

in the Netherlands:

De minister van financiën or an authorised representative

in Austria:

Der Bundesminister für Finanzen or an authorised representative

in Portugal:

O Ministro das Finanças or an authorised representative

in Finland:

Valtiovarainministeriö or an authorised representative

Finansministeriet or an authorised representative

in Sweden:

Ministern med ansuar för skattefrágor or an authorised representative

in the United Kingdom:

–   The Commissioners of Customs and Excise or an authorised representative for information required concerning value added tax and excise duty.

–   The Commissioners of Inland Revenue or an authorised representative for all other information.

[in Portugal:

O Ministro da Finanças e do Plano or an authorised representative]

Article 2
Exchange on request

1 The competent authority of a Member State may request the competent authority of another Member State to forward the information referred to in Article 1(1) in a particular case. The competent authority of the requested State need not comply with the request if it appears that the competent authority of the State making the request has not exhausted its own usual sources of information, which it could have utilised, according to the circumstances, to obtain the information requested without running the risk of endangering the attainment of the sought after result.

2 For the purpose of forwarding the information referred to in paragraph 1, the competent authority of the requested Member State shall arrange for the conduct of any enquiries necessary to obtain such information.

Article 3
Automatic exchange of information

For categories of cases which they shall determine under the consultation procedure laid down in Article 9, the competent authorities of the Member States shall regularly exchange the information referred to in Article 1(1) without prior request.

Article 4
Spontaneous exchange of information

1 The competent authority of a Member State shall without prior request forward the information referred to in Article 1(1), of which it has knowledge, to the competent authority of any other Member State concerned, in the following circumstances:

(a) the competent authority of the one Member State has grounds for supposing that there may be a loss of tax in the other Member State;

(b) a person liable to tax obtains a reduction in or an exemption from tax in the one Member State which would give rise to an increase in tax or to liability to tax in the other Member State;

(c) business dealings between a person liable to tax in a Member State and a person liable to tax in another Member State are conducted through one or more countries in such a way that a saving in tax may result in one or the other Member State or in both;

(d) the competent authority of a Member State has grounds for supposing that a saving of tax may result from artificial transfers of profits within groups of enterprises;

(e) information forwarded to the one Member State by the competent authority of the other Member State has enabled information to be obtained which may be relevant in assessing liability to tax in the latter Member State.

2 The competent authorities of the Member States may, under the consultation procedure laid down in Article 9, extend the exchange of information provided for in paragraph 1 to cases other than those specified therein.

3 The competent authorities of the Member States may forward to each other in any other case, without prior request, the information referred to in Article 1(1) of which they have knowledge.

Article 5
Time limit for forwarding information

The competent authority of a Member State which, under the preceding Articles, is called upon to furnish information, shall forward it as swiftly as possible. If it encounters obstacles in furnishing the information or if it refuses to furnish the information, it shall forthwith inform the requesting authority to this effect, indicating the nature of the obstacles or the reasons for its refusal.

Article 6
Collaboration by officials of the state concerned

For the purpose of applying the preceding provisions, the competent authority of the Member State providing the information and the competent authority of the Member State for which the information is intended may agree, under the consultation procedure laid down in Article 9, to authorise the presence in the first Member State of officials of the tax administration of the other Member State. The details for applying this provision shall be determined under the same procedure.

Article 7
Provisions relating to secrecy

1 All information made known to a Member State under this Directive shall be kept secret in that State in the same manner as information received under its domestic legislation.
    In any case, such information:

— may be made available only to the persons directly involved in the assessment of the tax or in the administrative control of this assessment,
— may in addition be made known only in connection with judicial proceedings or administrative proceedings involving sanctions undertaken with a view to, or relating to, the making or reviewing the tax assessment and only to persons who are directly involved in such proceedings; such information may, however, be disclosed during public hearings or in judgments if the competent authority of the Member State supplying the information raises no objection,
— shall in no circumstances be used other than for taxation purposes or in connection with judicial proceedings or administrative proceedings involving sanctions undertaken with a view to, or in relation to, the making or reviewing the tax assessment.

2 Paragraph I shall not oblige a Member State whose legislation or administrative practice lays down, for domestic purposes, narrower limits than those contained in the provisions of that paragraph, to provide information if the State concerned does not undertake to respect those narrower limits.
    3. Notwithstanding paragraph 1, the competent authorities of the Member State providing the information may permit it to be used for other purposes in the requesting State, if, under the legislation of the informing State, the information could, in similar circumstances, be used in the informing State for similar purposes.
    4 Where a competent authority of a Member State considers that information which it has received from the competent authority of another Member State is likely to be useful to the competent authority of a third Member State, it may transmit it to the latter competent authority with the agreement of the competent authority which supplied the information.

Article 8
Limits to exchange of information

1 This Directive shall impose no obligation to have enquiries carried out or to provide information if the Member State, which should furnish the information, would be prevented by its law or administrative practices from carrying out these enquiries or from collecting or using this information for its own purposes.
    2 The provision of information may be refused where it would lead to the disclosure of a commercial, industrial or professional secret or of a commercial process, or of information whose disclosure would be contrary to public policy.
    3 The competent authority of a Member State may refuse to provide information where the State concerned is unable, for practical or legal reasons, to provide similar information.

Article 9
Consultations

1 For the purposes of the implementation of this Directive, consultations shall be held, if necessary in a Committee, between:

— the competent authorities of the Member States concerned at the request of either, in respect of bilateral questions,
— the competent authorities of all the Member States and the Commission, at the request of one of those authorities or the Commission, in so far as the matters involved are not solely of bilateral interest.

2 The competent authorities of the Member States may communicate directly with each other. The competent authorities of the Member States may by mutual agreement permit

authorities designated by them to communicate directly with each other in specified cases or in certain categories of cases.

3 Where the competent authorities make arrangements on bilateral matters covered by this Directive other than as regards individual cases, they shall as soon as possible inform the Commission thereof. The Commission shall in turn notify the competent authorities of the other Member States.

Article 10
Pooling of experience

The Member States shall, together with the Commission, constantly monitor the cooperation procedure provided for in this Directive and shall pool their experience, especially in the field of transfer pricing within groups of enterprises, with a view to improving such cooperation and, where appropriate, drawing up a body of rules in the fields concerned.

Article 11
Applicability of wider-ranging provisions of assistance

The foregoing provisions shall not impede the fulfilment of any wider obligations to exchange information which might flow from other legal acts.

Article 12
Final provisions

1   Member States shall bring into force, the necessary laws, regulations and administrative provisions in order to comply with this Directive not later than 1 January 1979 and shall forthwith communicate them to the Commission.

2   Member States shall communicate to the Commission the texts of any important provisions of national law which they subsequently adopt in the field covered by this Directive.

Article 13
This Directive is addressed to the Member States.
Done at Brussels, 19 December 1977.

MEMORANDUM OF UNDERSTANDING

Between

The Association of Chief Police Officers, the Crown Prosecution Service of England and Wales, the Serious Fraud Office, Her Majesty's Customs and Excise, the National Crime Squad and the National Criminal Intelligence Service of the United Kingdom of Great Britain and Northern Ireland,

and

The Ministry of the interior of the Russian Federation

on co-operation in the fight against serious crime, organised crime, illicit drug trafficking and in other matters of mutual interest

The Association of Chief Police Officers, representing the police services of England and Wales, the Crown Prosecution Service of England and Wales, the Serious Fraud Office, Her Majesty's Customs and Excise, the National Crime Squad, and the National Criminal Intelligence Service of the United Kingdom of Great Britain and Northern Ireland and The Ministry of the Interior of the Russian Federation (henceforth referred to as the "Participants")

sharing a deep concern over the rise in serious crime, organised crime, illicit drug trafficking and crimes associated therewith, the fight against which comes entirely or partially within the competence of the Participants,

taking into account the provisions of the Agreement between the Government of the Russian Federation and the Government of the United Kingdom of Great Britain and Northern Ireland on co-operation in the fight against crime signed in Moscow on 6th October 1997,

wishing to develop and strengthen practical co-operation in matters of mutual interest, in particular in the fight against the aforesaid crimes,

taking into account the ethical standards referred to in the Annex hereto,

have reached a mutual understanding on the following matters:

Sphere of Application

1. The Participants will, in accordance with the provisions of this Memorandum. co- operate and assist one another as required or on their own initiative while observing the laws, regulations and procedures of their own States.

2. In particular assistance may include:

   1) obtaining evidence, reports and objects where no coercive power is required for this;
   2) providing documents and other materials;
   3) establishing the whereabouts and identity of persons and objects;
   4) the exchange of information, including criminal intelligence, with the aim of preventing, detecting, suppressing and investigating crimes;
   5) within available resources, assistance with the training and development of staff;
   6) Exchange of knowledge and expertise, legislative and regulatory documents and relevant scientific and technical information.
   7) other assistance unless it is prohibited under the legislation of the State of the Participant being asked for assistance.

This Memorandum will not prevent the Participants from using other mutually acceptable forms of co-operation whilst observing the laws regulations and procedures of their own States.

PRINCIPALS

3. With the aim of creating the most favourable conditions for co-operation, the Participants will agree the appointment of Principals to send and receive requests on the basis of this Memorandum.

4. Principals on the British side will be:
on behalf of the Association of Chief Police Officers – the Commissioner of Metropolitan Police;
on behalf of the Crown Prosecution Service – the Director of Public Prosecutions;
on behalf of the Serious Fraud Office – the Director;
on behalf of Her Majesty's Customs and Excise – the Chief Investigation Officer of the National Investigation Service;
on behalf of the National Crime Squad – the Director General;
on behalf of the National Criminal Intelligence Service – the Director General; or a person or persons appointed by them.

Principals on the Russian side will be:
First Deputy Minister of the Interior of the Russian Federation, responsible for the criminal police services;
Deputy Minister of the Interior of the Russian Federation – responsible for combating organised and economic crime;
Deputy Minister of the Interior of the Russian Federation – the Head of the Investigative Committee;
Head of the International Co-operation Department or a person or persons appointed by them.
Participants will immediately inform one another of changes to the list of persons responsible for maintaining working contacts with each other.

5. With the aim of enhancing co-operation, the Participants will communicate directly with one another.
The Ministry of Interior of the Russian Federation will initially contact the Fiscal, Drugs and Crime Liaison Officer for the time being accredited to the British Embassy in Moscow.
Such arrangements do not preclude contacts, where necessary, through diplomatic channels, or through Interpol channels.

RESTRICTIONS WHEN RENDERING ASSISTANCE

6. A Principal of the requested Participant may refuse to execute the request for assistance:
1) if execution of the request may cause damage to the sovereignty, security and/or other essential interests of that Participant's State or contravene the legislative provisions of that Participant's State;
2) if a Principal of the requested Participant believes that the execution of a request will interfere with an ongoing investigation, or proposed investigation, criminal prosecution or court proceedings in his State. However, in this event, consideration will be given to the possibility of postponing the execution of the request or rendering assistance while observing certain conditions; if the requesting Participant accepts assistance under these conditions he will comply with them.

7. Before refusing assistance on the basis of paragraph 6, a Principal of a requested Participant will consult with the Principal of the requesting Participant in order to determine whether assistance can be rendered with conditions being complied with. If the requesting Participant accepts the conditions be will be obliged to comply with them.

8. If the Principal of a requested Participant refuses assistance, the Principal of the requesting Participant will be informed of this in writing within 4 days.

FORM AND CONTENTS OF A REQUEST FOR ASSISTANCE

9. A request for assistance will be submitted in written form, however in case of emergency the Principal of the requested Participant may accept a request in verbal form. A verbal request will

be confirmed in writing within 48 hours unless the Principal of the requested Participant agrees otherwise. The request and annexed documents will be accompanied by a translation into the language of the requested Participant's State unless otherwise agreed.

10. The request will contain:

1) the name of the authority conducting the investigation, court procedure or other measures in connection with which the request has been made;

2) the brief facts of the case and the nature of the investigation, court procedure or criminal prosecution, including a description of the specific criminal act accompanied by the wording of the corresponding articles of the law;

3) the purpose for which evidence, information or other assistance is being requested;

4) a description of the content of evidence, information or other assistance requested;

5) information on the identity, nationality and possible whereabouts of witnesses and/or suspects.

11. Where necessary and to the extent possible the request should also include:

1) a statement by the requesting Participant indicating whether judicial proceedings relating to this matter are pending and if not, a statement as to how soon, if ever, judicial proceedings are likely to occur;

2) a list of questions to be asked of a person;

3) a description of the procedure which it is appropriate to follow when executing the request;

4) information concerning the allowances, expenses and protection to which a person asked to appear is entitled; and

5) any other information which may assist with the execution of the request.

Execution of the Request

12. A request will be executed as fully and as soon as possible in accordance with the procedure provided for by the laws and regulations which govern the activity of the requested Participant.

A requested Participant may ask for additional information if this is necessary in order to execute the request.

13. The requested Participant will aim to act in accordance with the evidential requirements of the requesting Participant provided that this does not conflict with the fundamental principles of law of the requested Participant's State.

14. The requested Participant will use his best efforts to keep confidential a request and/or its contents if such confidentiality is requested by the Principal of the requesting Participant.

If the request cannot be executed without preserving its confidentiality, the Principal of the requesting Participant then determines whether the request should nevertheless be executed.

15. The Principal of the requested Participant will, if asked, advise the Principal of the requesting Participant of progress towards the execution of the request.

16. The Principal of the requested Participant will inform the Principal of the requesting Participant of the outcome of the execution of the request.

17. The requested Participant will pay ordinary costs relating to the execution of a request. Extraordinary costs will be mutually agreed upon by the Participants before the costs are incurred.

18. If the execution of a request does not fall within the competence of the requested Participant he will immediately hand it over to the appropriate competent authority and inform the requesting Participant.

Restrictions on the Use of the Results of an Executed Request

19. The product of a request executed on the basis of this Memorandum may not be used for any purposes other than those for which they were requested and provided, without the permission of the Participant providing them.

20. Information relating to individuals may only be handed over to other competent authorities designated under the Agreement between the Government of the Russian Federation and the Government of the United Kingdom of Great Britain and Northern Ireland on co-operation in the fight against crime, signed in Moscow on 6th October 1997. Such information may only be handed over to other authorities with the prior agreement of the Participant in a position to hand it over.

21. A Principal of a requested Participant may require that the product of a request executed on the basis of this Memorandum be kept secret or used only under the conditions specified. If the requesting Participant accepts the product of the executed request under these conditions, he shall do everything possible to comply with the conditions.

22. Nothing in this Memorandum will preclude the use or disclosure of the product of an executed request where this is necessary under the laws and regulations which regulate the activity of the requesting Participant with regard to an investigation, court procedure or criminal prosecution. The requesting Participant will inform in advance the requested Participant of such possible or proposed use or disclosure.

23. The product of an executed request made public by the requesting Participant in accordance with paragraph 22 may subsequently be used for any purpose.

OBTAINING EVIDENCE AND EXHIBITS IN THE TERRITORY OF THE REQUESTED PARTICIPANT'S STATE

24. A requesting Participant may request that a person be asked to appear before competent authorities of the requested Participant's State to give oral or written evidence and/or to produce exhibits in accordance with the laws and regulations of that State.

25. Upon request, the Principal of the requested Participant will provide information in advance about the date and method of the execution of the request pursuant to this Memorandum and will give full consideration to a request for officers of the requesting Participant to be present during the execution of the request.

PRESENCE OF PERSONS IN THE TERRITORY OF THE REQUESTING PARTICIPANT'S STATE

26. A requesting Participant may apply for the attendance in the territory of his State of a person living in the territory of the requested Participant's State in order to give evidence. The requested Participant will invite such person to appear voluntarily before the competent authorities in the territory of the requesting Participant's State. The Participants will give particular consideration to a request for officers to be present in the territory of the requesting Participant's State for the purpose of giving evidence. In this event the requesting Participant will indicate the extent of the expenses to be reimbursed to such person and the extent of protection to be offered to him.

27. A person who has failed to answer a request to appear, or refuses to appear when requested is not to be subjected to any punishment or measure of restraint in the territory of the requested Participant's State.

PRODUCTION OF RECORDS

28. Upon request, the requested Participant will provide the requesting Participant with copies of publicly available records, including documents or information in the possession of departments and agencies of the requested Participant's State.

29. The requested Participant may provide copies of any records which are in the possession of a department or agency of that Participant's State which are not publicly available, but only to the same extent and under the same conditions as will be available to the competent authorities of that State and if not contrary to the legislation of the requested Participant's State.

ESTABLISHING THE WHEREABOUTS AND IDENTITY OF PERSONS AND PROPERTY

30. If a request is made to establish the whereabouts or identity of any persons or obtain information about property located in the territory of the requested Participant's State the requested Participant will do everything possible in order to execute this request in accordance with the laws and regulations of his own State.

RETURN OF DOCUMENTS, MATERIALS AND PROPERTY

31. If required by a Principal of a requested Participant, a Principal of a requesting Participant will return the documents, materials or property handed over to him as a result of the execution of a request.

32. A requesting Participant may, with the agreement of the requested Participant, delay the return of any documents, materials or property requested, if this is necessary for the purposes of criminal or civil proceedings being conducted.

33. A requested Participant may require the requesting Participant to agree to conditions which are necessary in order to protect the interests of third parties with regard to documents. materials or other property which are to be transferred.

ASSISTANCE WITH THE CONFISCATION OF PROPERTY

34. If the Principal of one Participant becomes aware of proceeds or attributable assets accrued through offences, which are located in the territory of the other Participant's State and which may be forfeitable or subject to confiscation under the laws of that Participant's State, he will so inform the Principal concerned.

CONSULTATION

35. Principals of the Participants will consult one another with the aim of making arrangements for the more effective implementation of this Memorandum.

Any difficulties arising in connection with this Memorandum will be resolved through consultation and negotiation.

OTHER BASES FOR CO-OPERATION

36. This Memorandum will not prevent any of the Participants from co-operating and granting assistance in accordance with the provisions of any applicable international treaties and agreements.

STATUS OF THIS MEMORANDUM

37. This Memorandum is a statement of goodwill and is not intended to impose any legal obligations whatsoever on the Participants.

FINAL PROVISIONS

38. This Memorandum becomes effective upon signature. It continues during the currency of the Agreement between the Government of the Russian Federation and the Government of the United Kingdom of Great Britain and Northern Ireland on co-operation in fighting crime signed at Moscow on 6th October 1997.

39. Any participant to this Memorandum who no longer wishes to participate will give six months' written notice to all other Participants.

40. Amendments or additions may be made to this Memorandum with the written agreement of all Participants. By the consent of the existing Participants other Russian or British law enforcement agencies may be included in this Memorandum.

Signed in London on 18 June 1998, with seven copies in the Russian and English language both texts being equally valid.

For the British side:
For the Association of Chief Police Officers

For the Crown Prosecution Service of
England and Wales

For the Serious Fraud Office

For Her Majesty's Customs and Excise

For the National Crime Squad

For the National Criminal Intelligence Service of the United Kingdom of Great Britain and Northern Ireland

For the Russian side:
For the Ministry of the Interior of the Russian Federation

ANNEX TO THE MEMORANDUM OF UNDERSTANDING

between
the Ministry of the Interior of the Russian Federation
and
the Association of Chief Police Officers,
the Crown Prosecution Service of England and Wales,
the Serious Fraud Office,
Her Majesty's Customs and Excise Service,
the National Crime Squad
and the National Criminal Intelligence Service
of the United Kingdom of Great Britain and Northern Ireland
on co-operation in the fight against serious crimes, organised crime, illicit drug
trafflcking and in other matters of mutual interest

ETHICAL STANDARDS

The operations of the Participants and their working ethos are guided by statements of professional practice which establish the professional standards of behaviour required of staff in the conduct of their affairs and in their dealings with the public. The statements are as follows:

STATEMENT OF THE MINISTRY OF THE INTERIOR OF THE RUSSIAN FEDERATION ON ITS BASIC PURPOSES, TASKS AND VALUES

"The basic purposes and tasks of the Ministry are within its competence to protect the rights and freedom of an individual and citizen, to protect property irrespective of its form of ownership, and ensure public order and public safety; to organise and implement measures to prevent and halt crimes and administrative offences; expose, detect and investigate crimes.

We must respect and protect the individual and the human dignity of a citizen, irrespective of his citizenship, place of residence, social status with regard to means and official status, racial and national origin, sex, age, education, language, religious denomination, political and other convictions, being guided by the Constitution, international legal norms and universal moral principles.

We shall strive to treat the individual as being of the highest importance, humanely, magnanimously and mercifully. Our primary task is to make use disinterestedly and steadfastly of all legal means to protect the innocent from lawlessness and deception, the weak from intimidation, the peace-loving from violence and disorder, not to leave women, the elderly, children, the sick and disabled unprotected in extreme circumstances, and not to permit the tolerance of evil and impunity.

We shall be obliged to display firmness, professional and moral steadiness and intransigence in the fight against crime.

We must be courageous and intelligent in the face of danger in circumstances which require that people's lives are saved, stop crimes which pose a threat to people, and eliminate the consequences of an accident or natural disaster.

When participating in an international partnership we shall strive, first and foremost to increase the effectiveness of the fight against actions such as violent crimes which threaten the life, health and freedom of the individual and his property; gangsters, terrorism and transnational crime; illegal operations involving arms and ammunition, explosives and toxic substances; illegal circulation of narcotic substances and psychotropic substances, historical and cultural objects of value crimes in the economic sphere."

STATEMENT OF THE ASSOCIATION OF CHIEF POLICE OFFICERS ON BEHALF OF THE POLICE SERVICE ON ITS COMMON PURPOSE AND VALUES

"The purpose of the Police Service is to uphold the law fairly and firmly; to prevent crime; to pursue and bring to justice those who break the law, to keep the Queen's Peace; to protect, help and reassure the community and to be seen to do all this with integrity, common sense and sound judgement.

We must be compassionate, courteous and patient, acting without fear or favour or prejudice to the rights of others. We need to be professional, calm and restrained in the face of violence and apply only that force which is necessary to accomplish our lawful duty.

We must strive to reduce the fears of the public and, so far as we can, to reflect their priorities in the action we take. We must respond to well-founded criticism with a willingness to change".

THE CROWN PROSECUTION SERVICE STATEMENT OF PURPOSE AND VALUES

"The Crown Prosecution Service working in the interests of justice, reviews and where appropriate, prosecutes cases, following investigation by others. We also advise the police on matters relating to criminal offences. In each case which we review, we consider whether there is sufficient evidence and, if so, whether the public interest requires a prosecution.

We are committed to providing a high quality prosecution service, working in the interests of justice. As a unified service, we will apply common standards, policy and operational practices throughout England and Wales, ensuring a consistent and timely approach.

Our decisions will be independent of bias or discrimination, but we will always consider the interests of others. We will act with integrity and objectivity, and will exercise sound judgement, with confidence.

In all our dealings with each other and the public, we will be open and honest. We will show sensitivity and understanding to victims and witnesses, and treat all defendants fairly.

We are accountable to Parliament and the public: we will work together with our colleagues to maintain public trust to provide an efficient and effective criminal justice system. In explaining our decisions we will be courteous and helpful.

In order to achieve these high standards, we will report on our performance and respond to criticism positively".

STATEMENT OF THE SERIOUS FRAUD OFFICE ON ITS AIMS AND OBJECTIVES

"The aim of the Serious Fraud Office is to deter fraud and maintain confidence in the United Kingdom business and financial institutions by investigating offences involving serious or complex fraud and by prosecuting persons suspected of committing them.

To achieve this aim the Serious Fraud Office's objectives are:

- To investigate the right cases as quickly and efficiently as their circumstances allow.
- To prosecute cases fairly and in a way that enables a jury to understand complex issues.
- To ensure the Serious Fraud Office's activities and the way they are reported contribute to deterring fraud.

The Serious Fraud Office is accountable to Parliament through the Attorney General. The Serious Fraud Office places great emphasis on international co-operation in achieving its aims and objectives and will exercise it's investigating powers on behalf of a foreign Government in a criminal investigation into matters involving serious or complex fraud".

STATEMENT OF HER MAJESTY'S CUSTOMS AND EXCISE ON ITS COMMON PURPOSE AND VALUES

"The purpose of Her Majesty's Customs and Excise is to collect and manage customs duties and levies and various internal taxes and to undertake functions to protect society by enforcing prohibitions or restrictions upon the importation or exportation of goods.

Her Majesty's Customs and Excise will focus on maintaining high standards of enforcement with regard to the prevention, detection, investigation and prosecution of offences and offenders whilst meeting the needs of those it serves.

Her Majesty's Customs and Excise through international co-operation aims to concentrate a greater proportion of resources to combating criminal activity in international drug smuggling, trans-national organised fiscal fraud and the identification of proceeds of such crime.

Her Majesty's Customs and Excise seeks to maintain these high standards of enforcement with resolve and in line with its traditional values of integrity, impartiality, courtesy and assistance".

THE NATIONAL CRIME SQUAD'S MISSION STATEMENT AND AIMS

"The functions and terms of reference of the National Crime Squad are crystallised in its Mission Statement which identifies the organisational purpose as "To provide leadership and expertise to combat serious and organised crime nationally and internationally".

Based upon the Mission Statement, the National Crime Squad has three strategic aims:

a) to concentrate effort on successfully bringing to justice and/or disrupting those responsible for serious and organised crime;

b) to provide appropriate support to police forces and other law enforcement agencies in relation to serious and organised crime;

c) to create and maintain a recognised, robust, professional and ethical national organisation staffed by people of integrity, ability and commitment".

THE NATIONAL CRIMINAL INTELLIGENCE SERVICE MISSION STATEMENT AND AIM

"The functions and purpose of the National Criminal Intelligence Service are contained within its Mission Statement which identifies the organisational purpose as: "To provide leadership and excellence in criminal intelligence to combat serious and organised crime".

The strategic aims of the organisation are the provision of:

a) strategic assessments on serious and organised crime affecting the UK;

b) criminal intelligence on major criminals and their organisations;

c) criminal intelligence on agreed specialist areas of crime;

d) services to enhance the co-ordination and development of criminal intelligence".

Appendix X

SPECIMEN LETTER OF REQUEST (OUTGOING)

The Competent Legal Authority

The Ministry of Justice

Sir

COMMISSION ROGATOIRE

I [   ], being a designated prosecuting authority, have the honour to request the assistance of the Competent Legal Authority in [   ] in relation to certain enquiries being conducted in the following case [   ]

CONSIDERING the *[prosecution which has been instituted against] [the ongoing investigation involving] the following:—

SUBJECT	DATE OF BIRTH	PLACE OF BIRTH	NATIONALITY	ADDRESS
[ ]	[ ]	[ ]	[ ]	[ ]

[Which may result in charges being brought]/[On charges relating to [*]., namely that [   ]

Extracts from the relevant English Law are annexed hereto.

Brief statement of the case

AND CONSIDERING [narrate international instruments], I do hereby request that with the permission of the Competent Legal Authority and with the co-operation of the Police the evidence detailed below may be obtained. The evidence may be used in any criminal prosecution or other judicial proceedings connected with the above matter, including connected civil proceedings for the confiscation of financial assets held by either the above named suspects or others identified later in the investigation.

RELEVANT RULES OF EVIDENCE — ENGLAND AND WALES

1. **Witness Statements**—In order to be admissible in proceedings, a witness's statement must be signed by the maker and dated. If the witness is under 21, his age should be given. (NB: Although such a witness statement will be admissible at certain preliminary stages of the criminal proceedings, it will usually not be admissible at the trial itself, and so it will very often be necessary to call the witness to give live evidence at the trial. This is due to the operation of the hearsay rule, referred to below.)

2. **Hearsay**—Hearsay evidence includes the testimony of a witness as to the assertions of another person, and documents offered to prove the thrust of what is asserted therein. The basic principle is that a witness must confine his evidence to his own personal observations. In general, hearsay evidence is inadmissible in English Courts. For example, **a summary by a law enforcement officer of the observations made by other officers in his team would be hearsay, and generally inadmissible.**
   An important exception to the hearsay rule is set out in point 3 below.

3. **Business Documents**—The contents of a document shall be admissible as evidence of any fact of which direct oral evidence would be admissible, providing that the document was

1. created or received by a person in the course of a trade, business, profession or other occupation, or as the holder of a paid or unpaid office, and
2. the information contained in the document was supplied by a person (whether or not the person who compiled the document) who had, or may reasonably be supposed to have had, personal knowledge of the matters dealt with.

Where business documents are requested herein, the fact that they were so created or received and that the person supplying the information had such personal knowledge should be included in the statement made to accompany the requested documents.

Further conditions apply to certain special cases, in particular where the document was prepared for the purposes of

1. pending or contemplated criminal proceedings, or
2. a criminal investigation.

The requested authority is therefore asked to contact the above-named officer for further specific details **BEFORE** providing the assistance as set out below.

4. **Computer Records**—In order to be admissible, these must

1. comply with the same criteria as for the admissibility of business documents, and
2. be accompanied by a certificate that the computer was working properly at the relevant time or, if it was not, that any malfunction was not such as to affect the production of the document or the accuracy of its contents. It must also be shown that there are no reasonable grounds to believe that the document produced by the computer is inaccurate because of improper use of the computer.

5. **Chain of Evidence**—When witness statements refer to the physical movement of exhibits, it is necessary to show continuity of transmission. There should be no break in the evidence of such continuity in relation to exhibits.

Witness statements will be required dealing with the matters referred to in 3 to 5 inclusive.

6. **Unused Material**—This has been defined judicially as all material coming into the possession or control or to the knowledge of the prosecuting authority, and which is not served on the defence as part of the prosecution case. The prosecution has a legal duty to serve on the defence any material within its control which may undermine the prosecution case or assist the defence case. Any material held by an assisting state will constitute unused material and will be subject to the principles outlined here.

That material may be considered to be sensitive or non-sensitive. If the prosecuting authority wish to withhold material from the defence on the basis that it is sensitive, even though it may undermine the prosecution case or assist the defence, then the authority must make an application to the trial judge. (This application can be made in respect of material obtained from an assisting State). It is the judge and only the judge who can adjudicate on this matter. If the judge orders disclosure of material which the prosecuting authority are unable or unwilling to disclose, a decision is likely to be made by the prosecuting authority that the prosecution cannot continue.

The requested authority should retain all material in its possession which could be relevant to the on-going prosecution, inform the prosecuting authority of the existence of this material and should be aware that the prosecuting authority may need to view this material at any time.

ASSISTANCE REQUESTED

To have the evidence detailed below taken in a form which complies with the requirements of English Law and Procedure:-

1.}
2.}
3.}
4. Arrangements to permit the officer charged with the investigation of this case [details] on behalf of [   ] to be present when these enquiries are made in your country, to advise in detail on the form in which evidence should be taken in order to comply with the requirements of English Law and Procedure, and to make such physical examination of premises and property as may be necessary for the proper presentation of the case before English courts.

5.   Arrangements to take witness statements from all material witnesses.

6.   Arrangements to allow the attendance at any trial or other judicial hearing of any witnesses who have given testimony.

7.   Arrangements to secure any relevant exhibits and permit their copying and removal to the United Kingdom for use at any trial or other judicial hearing.

8.   Arrangements to permit such other enquiries to be made, persons to be placed under surveillance, persons to be interviewed and exhibits to be secured, the necessity for which becomes apparent in the course of the investigation.

and it is further requested that, in order not to prejudice the investigation, the existence and contents of this Commission Rogatoire and any action taken in response to it, be not notified by the competent authorities in your country to any person outside such authorities (in particular, any of the above subjects), except to the extent that a request to notify such a person in any of the foregoing respects, in contained in, or is necessarily implied by the terms of, any of the above paragraphs 1 –[ ].

1. *[AND it is further requested that action be taken to ensure that [a person from whom evidence is sought e.g. a Bank] does not so notify any other person, including [any of] the above subject[s], consequent on the request[s] for assistance at paragraph[s] [ ] above.]

2. However, there is no objection if your law so requires, for an interested person, including one of the subjects [,] to be informed in advance of an application to a judicial authority for access to property, pursuant to the request[s] for assistance at paragraph[s] [ ] above.

3. The reasons for requesting confidentiality in the above terms are that, [with the exceptions indicated above] [,] [:-] [ ]

[–] if one of the above subjects or an associated party became aware of the existence or contents of this Commission Rogatoire or of action taken in response to it, evidence [, in particular ,] might be interfered with [,] [;]

*[–] assets [, in particular ,] potentially liable to restraint and confiscation might be dissipated [,] [;]

and thus the investigation could be prejudiced.

*[I would especially draw your attention to the fact that]

If it is not possible to preserve confidentiality in the above manner, please notify me prior to executing this Commission Rogatoire.

AND it is further requested that, when forwarding evidence pursuant to this Commission Rogatoire, the appropriate authority indicates to the authorities in the United Kingdom, whether and to what extent the evidence needs to be returned to your country at the conclusion of the proceedings in the United Kingdom.

RECIPROCITY

I confirm that the assistance request in paragraph 1– [ ] above could be obtained under the powers provided for by the current laws of England and Wales, if in a like case a request for such assistance were made to the authorities in England and Wales (noting that a witness cannot be compelled, under those laws, to attend court proceedings abroad).

I extend my thanks for such co-operation and assistance as may be extended to the bearer of this Commission Rogatoire.

I have the honour to be,
Sir your obedient servant

TOWARDS A UNION OF FREEDOM, SECURITY AND JUSTICE: THE TAMPERE MILESTONES

1. From its very beginning European integration has been firmly rooted in a shared commitment to freedom based on human rights, democratic institutions and the rule of law. These common values have proved necessary for securing peace and developing prosperity in the European Union. They will also serve as a cornerstone for the enlarging Union.

2. The European Union has already put in place for its citizens the major ingredients of a shared area of prosperity and peace: a single market, economic and monetary union, and the capacity to take on global political and economic challenges. The challenge of the Amsterdam Treaty is now to ensure that freedom, which includes the right to move freely throughout the Union, can be enjoyed in conditions of security and justice accessible to all. It is a project which responds to the frequently expressed concerns of citizens and has a direct bearing on their daily lives.

3. This freedom should not, however, be regarded as the exclusive preserve of the Union's own citizens. Its very existence acts as a draw to many others world-wide who cannot enjoy the freedom Union citizens take for granted. It would be in contradiction with Europe's traditions to deny such freedom to those whose circumstances lead them justifiably to seek access to our territory. This in turn requires the Union to develop common policies on asylum and immigration, while taking into account the need for a consistent control of external borders to stop illegal immigration and to combat those who organise it and commit related international crimes. These common policies must be based on principles which are both clear to our own citizens and also offer guarantees to those who seek protection in or access to the European Union.

4. The aim is an open and secure European Union, fully committed to the obligations of the Geneva Refugee Convention and other relevant human rights instruments, and able to respond to humanitarian needs on the basis of solidarity. A common approach must also be developed to ensure the integration into our societies of those third country nationals who are lawfully resident in the Union.

5. The enjoyment of freedom requires a genuine area of justice, where people can approach courts and authorities in any Member State as easily as in their own. Criminals must find no ways of exploiting differences in the judicial systems of Member States. Judgements and decisions should be respected and enforced throughout the Union, while safeguarding the basic legal certainty of people and economic operators. Better compatibility and more convergence between the legal systems of Member States must be achieved.

6. People have the right to expect the Union to address the threat to their freedom and legal rights posed by serious crime. To counter these threats a common effort is needed to prevent and fight crime and criminal organisations throughout the Union. The joint mobilisation of police and judicial resources is needed to guarantee that there is no hiding place for criminals or the proceeds of crime within the Union.

7. The area of freedom, security and justice should be based on the principles of transparency and democratic control. We must develop an open dialogue with civil society on the aims and principles of this area in order to strengthen citizens' acceptance and support. In order to maintain confidence in authorities, common standards on the integrity of authorities should be developed.

8. The European Council considers it essential that in these areas the Union should also develop a capacity to act and be regarded as a significant partner on the international scene. This requires close co-operation with partner countries and international organisations, in particular the Council of Europe, OSCE, OECD and the United Nations.

9. The European Council invites the Council and the Commission, in close co-operation with the European Parliament, to promote the full and immediate implementation of the Treaty of

Amsterdam on the basis of the Vienna Action Plan and of the following political guidelines and concrete objectives agreed here in Tampere.

A. A Common EU Asylum and Migration Policy

10. The separate but closely related issues of asylum and migration call for the development of a common EU policy to include the following elements.

I. Partnership with countries of origin

11. The European Union needs a comprehensive approach to migration addressing political, human rights and development issues in countries and regions of origin and transit. This requires combating poverty, improving living conditions and job opportunities, preventing conflicts and consolidating democratic states and ensuring respect for human rights, in particular rights of minorities, women and children. To that end, the Union as well as Member States are invited to contribute, within their respective competence under the Treaties, to a greater coherence of internal and external policies of the Union. Partnership with third countries concerned will also be a key element for the success of such a policy, with a view to promoting co-development.

12. In this context, the European Council welcomes the report of the High Level Working Group on Asylum and Migration set up by the Council, and agrees on the continuation of its mandate and on the drawing up of further Action Plans. It considers as a useful contribution the first action plans drawn up by that Working Group, and approved by the Council, and invites the Council and the Commission to report back on their implementation to the European Council in December 2000.

II. A Common European Asylum System

13. The European Council reaffirms the importance the Union and Member States attach to absolute respect of the right to seek asylum. It has agreed to work towards establishing a Common European Asylum System, based on the full and inclusive application of the Geneva Convention, thus ensuring that nobody is sent back to persecution, i.e. maintaining the principle of non-refoulement.

14. This System should include, in the short term, a clear and workable determination of the State responsible for the examination of an asylum application, common standards for a fair and efficient asylum procedure, common minimum conditions of reception of asylum seekers, and the approximation of rules on the recognition and content of the refugee status. It should also be completed with measures on subsidiary forms of protection offering an appropriate status to any person in need of such protection. To that end, the Council is urged to adopt, on the basis of Commission proposals, the necessary decisions according to the timetable set in the Treaty of Amsterdam and the Vienna Action Plan. The European Council stresses the importance of consulting UNHCR and other international organisations.

15. In the longer term, Community rules should lead to a common asylum procedure and a uniform status for those who are granted asylum valid throughout the Union. The Commission is asked to prepare within one year a communication on this matter.

16. The European Council urges the Council to step up its efforts to reach agreement on the issue of temporary protection for displaced persons on the basis of solidarity between Member States. The European Council believes that consideration should be given to making some form of financial reserve available in situations of mass influx of refugees for temporary protection. The Commission is invited to explore the possibilities for this.

17. The European Council urges the Council to finalise promptly its work on the system for the identification of asylum seekers (Eurodac).

III. Fair treatment of third country nationals

18. The European Union must ensure fair treatment of third country nationals who reside legally on the territory of its Member States. A more vigorous integration policy should aim at granting them rights and obligations comparable to those of EU citizens. It should also enhance non-discrimination in economic, social and cultural life and develop measures against racism and xenophobia.

19. Building on the Commission Communication on an Action Plan against Racism, the European Council calls for the fight against racism and xenophobia to be stepped up. The Member States will draw on best practices and experiences. Co-operation with the European Monitoring Centre on Racism and Xenophobia and the Council of Europe will be further strengthened. Moreover, the Commission is invited to come forward as soon as possible with proposals implementing Article 13 of the EC Treaty on the fight against racism and xenophobia. To fight against discrimination more generally the Member States are encouraged to draw up national programmes.

20. The European Council acknowledges the need for approximation of national legislations on the conditions for admission and residence of third country nationals, based on a shared assessment of the economic and demographic developments within the Union, as well as the situation in the countries of origin. It requests to this end rapid decisions by the Council, on the basis of proposals by the Commission. These decisions should take into account not only the reception capacity of each Member State, but also their historical and cultural links with the countries of origin.

21. The legal status of third country nationals should be approximated to that of Member States' nationals. A person, who has resided legally in a Member State for a period of time to be determined and who holds a long-term residence permit, should be granted in that Member State a set of uniform rights which are as near as possible to those enjoyed by EU citizens; e.g. the right to reside, receive education, and work as an employee or self-employed person, as well as the principle of non-discrimination vis-à-vis the citizens of the State of residence. The European Council endorses the objective that long-term legally resident third country nationals be offered the opportunity to obtain the nationality of the Member State in which they are resident.

IV. Management of migration flows

22. The European Council stresses the need for more efficient management of migration flows at all their stages. It calls for the development, in close co-operation with countries of origin and transit, of information campaigns on the actual possibilities for legal immigration, and for the prevention of all forms of trafficking in human beings. A common active policy on visas and false documents should be further developed, including closer co-operation between EU consulates in third countries and, where necessary, the establishment of common EU visa issuing offices.

23. The European Council is determined to tackle at its source illegal immigration, especially by combating those who engage in trafficking in human beings and economic exploitation of migrants. It urges the adoption of legislation foreseeing severe sanctions against this serious crime. The Council is invited to adopt by the end of 2000, on the basis of a proposal by the Commission, legislation to this end. Member States, together with Europol, should direct their efforts to detecting and dismantling the criminal networks involved. The rights of the victims of such activities shall be secured with special emphasis on the problems of women and children.

24. The European Council calls for closer co-operation and mutual technical assistance between the Member States' border control services, such as exchange programmes and technology transfer, especially on maritime borders, and for the rapid inclusion of the applicant States in this co-operation. In this context, the Council welcomes the memorandum of understanding between Italy and Greece to enhance co-operation between the two countries in the Adriatic and Ionian seas in combating organised crime, smuggling and trafficking of persons.

25. As a consequence of the integration of the Schengen acquis into the Union, the candidate countries must accept in full that acquis and further measures building upon it. The European Council stresses the importance of the effective control of the Union's future external borders by specialised trained professionals.

26. The European Council calls for assistance to countries of origin and transit to be developed in order to promote voluntary return as well as to help the authorities of those countries to strengthen their ability to combat effectively trafficking in human beings and to cope with their readmission obligations towards the Union and the Member States.

27. The Amsterdam Treaty conferred powers on the Community in the field of readmission. The European Council invites the Council to conclude readmission agreements or to include standard clauses in other agreements between the European Community and relevant third

countries or groups of countries. Consideration should also be given to rules on internal readmission.

B. A GENUINE EUROPEAN AREA OF JUSTICE

28. In a genuine European Area of Justice individuals and businesses should not be prevented or discouraged from exercising their rights by the incompatibility or complexity of legal and administrative systems in the Member States.

V. Better access to justice in Europe

29. In order to facilitate access to justice the European Council invites the Commission, in co-operation with other relevant fora, such as the Council of Europe, to launch an information campaign and to publish appropriate "user guides" on judicial co-operation within the Union and on the legal systems of the Member States. It also calls for the establishment of an easily accessible information system to be maintained and up-dated by a network of competent national authorities.

30. The European Council invites the Council, on the basis of proposals by the Commission, to establish minimum standards ensuring an adequate level of legal aid in cross-border cases throughout the Union as well as special common procedural rules for simplified and accelerated cross-border litigation on small consumer and commercial claims, as well as maintenance claims, and on uncontested claims. Alternative, extra-judicial procedures should also be created by Member States.

31. Common minimum standards should be set for multilingual forms or documents to be used in cross-border court cases throughout the Union. Such documents or forms should then be accepted mutually as valid documents in all legal proceedings in the Union.

32. Having regard to the Commission's communication, minimum standards should be drawn up on the protection of the victims of crime, in particular on crime victims' access to justice and on their rights to compensation for damages, including legal costs. In addition, national programmes should be set up to finance measures, public and non-governmental, for assistance to and protection of victims.

VI. Mutual recognition of judicial decisions

33. Enhanced mutual recognition of judicial decisions and judgements and the necessary approximation of legislation would facilitate co-operation between authorities and the judicial protection of individual rights. The European Council therefore endorses the principle of mutual recognition which, in its view, should become the cornerstone of judicial co-operation in both civil and criminal matters within the Union. The principle should apply both to judgements and to other decisions of judicial authorities.

34. In civil matters the European Council calls upon the Commission to make a proposal for further reduction of the intermediate measures which are still required to enable the recognition and enforcement of a decision or judgement in the requested State. As a first step these intermediate procedures should be abolished for titles in respect of small consumer or commercial claims and for certain judgements in the field of family litigation (e.g. on maintenance claims and visiting rights). Such decisions would be automatically recognised throughout the Union without any intermediate proceedings or grounds for refusal of enforcement. This could be accompanied by the setting of minimum standards on specific aspects of civil procedural law.

35. With respect to criminal matters, the European Council urges Member States to speedily ratify the 1995 and 1996 EU Conventions on extradition It considers that the formal extradition procedure should be abolished among the Member States as far as persons are concerned who are fleeing from justice after having been finally sentenced, and replaced by a simple transfer of such persons, in compliance with Article 6 TEU. Consideration should also be given to fast track extradition procedures, without prejudice to the principle of fair trial. The European Council invites the Commission to make proposals on this matter in the light of the Schengen Implementing Agreement.

36. The principle of mutual recognition should also apply to pre-trial orders, in particular to those which would enable competent authorities quickly to secure evidence and to seize assets which are easily movable; evidence lawfully fathered by one Member State's authorities should

be admissible before the courts of other Member States, taking into account the standards that apply there.

37. The European Council asks the Council and the Commission to adopt, by December 2000, a programme of measures to implement the principle of mutual recognition. In this programme, work should also be launched on a European Enforcement Order and on those aspects of procedural law on which common minimum standards are considered necessary in order to facilitate the application of the principle of mutual recognition, respecting the fundamental legal principles of Member States.

VII. Greater convergence in civil law

38. The European Council invites the Council and the Commission to prepare new procedural legislation in cross-order cases, in particular on those elements which are instrumental to smooth judicial co-operation and to enhanced access to law, e.g. provisional measures, taking of evidence, orders for money payment and time limits.

39. As regards substantive law, an overall study is requested on the need to approximate Member States' legislation in civil matters in order to eliminate obstacles to the good functioning of civil proceedings. The Council should report back by 2001.

C. A Unionwide Fight against Crime

40. The European Council is deeply committed to reinforcing the fight against serious organised and transnational crime. The high level of safety in the area of freedom, security and justice presupposes an efficient and comprehensive approach in the fight against all forms of crime. A balanced development of unionwide measures against crime should be achieved while protecting the freedom and legal rights of individuals and economic operators.

VIII. Preventing crime at the level of the Union

41. The European Council calls for the integration of crime prevention aspects into actions against crime as well as for the further development of national crime prevention programmes. Common priorities should be developed and identified in crime prevention in the external and internal policy of the Union and be taken into account when preparing new legislation.

42. The exchange of best practices should be developed, the network of competent national authorities for crime prevention and co-operation between national crime prevention organisations should be strengthened and the possibility of a Community funded programme should be explored for these purposes. The first priorities for this co-operation could be juvenile, urban and drug-related crime.

IX. Stepping up co-operation against crime

43. Maximum benefit should be derived from co-operation between Member States' authorities when investigating cross-border crime in any Member State. The European Council calls for joint investigative teams as foreseen in the Treaty to be set up without delay, as a first step, to combat trafficking in drugs and human beings as well as terrorism. The rules to be set up in this respect should allow representatives of Europol to participate, as appropriate, in such teams in a support capacity.

44. The European Council calls for the establishment of a European Police Chiefs operational Task Force to exchange, in co-operation with Europol, experience, best practices and information on current trends in cross-border crime and contribute to the planning of operative actions.

45. Europol has a key role in supporting unionwide crime prevention, analyses and investigation. The European Council calls on the Council to provide Europol with the necessary support and resources. In the near future its role should be strengthened by means of receiving operational data from Member States and authorising it to ask Member States to initiate, conduct or coordinate investigations or to create joint investigative teams in certain areas of crime, while respecting systems of judicial control in Member States.

46. To reinforce the fight against serious organised crime, the European Council has agreed that a unit (EUROJUST) should be set up composed of national prosecutors, magistrates, or police officers of equivalent competence, detached from each Member State according to its legal system. EUROJUST should have the task of facilitating the proper coordination of

national prosecuting authorities and of supporting criminal investigations in organised crime cases, notably based on Europol's analysis, as well as of co-operating closely with the European Judicial Network, in particular in order to simplify the execution of letters rogatory. The European Council requests the Council to adopt the necessary legal instrument by the end of 2001.

47. A European Police College for the training of senior law enforcement officials should be established. It should start as a network of existing national training institutes. It should also be open to the authorities of candidate countries.

48. Without prejudice to the broader areas envisaged in the Treaty of Amsterdam and in the Vienna Action Plan, the European Council considers that, with regard to national criminal law, efforts to agree on common definitions, incriminations and sanctions should be focused in the first instance on a limited number of sectors of particular relevance, such as financial crime (money laundering, corruption, Euro counterfeiting), drugs trafficking, trafficking in human beings, particularly exploitation of women, sexual exploitation of children, high tech crime and environmental crime.

49. Serious economic crime increasingly has tax and duty aspects. The European Council therefore calls upon Member States to provide full mutual legal assistance in the investigation and prosecution of serious economic crime.

50. The European Council underlines the importance of addressing the drugs problem in a comprehensive manner. It calls on the Council to adopt the 2000–2004 European Strategy against Drugs before the European Council meeting in Helsinki.

X. Special action against money laundering

51. Money laundering is at the very heart of organised crime. It should be rooted out wherever it occurs. The European Council is determined to ensure that concrete steps are taken to trace, freeze, seize and confiscate the proceeds of crime.

52. Member States are urged to implement fully the provisions of the Money Laundering Directive, the 1990 Strasbourg Convention and the Financial Action Task Force recommendations also in all their dependent territories.

53. The European Council calls for the Council and the European Parliament to adopt as soon as possible the draft revised directive on money laundering recently proposed by the Commission.

54. With due regard to data protection, the transparency of financial transactions and ownership of corporate entities should be improved and the exchange of information between the existing financial intelligence units (FIU) regarding suspicious transactions expedited. Regardless of secrecy provisions applicable to banking and other commercial activity, judicial authorities as well as FIUs must be entitled, subject to judicial control, to receive information when such information is necessary to investigate money laundering. The European Council calls on the Council to adopt the necessary provisions to this end.

55. The European Council calls for the approximation of criminal law and procedures on money laundering (e.g. tracing, freezing and confiscating funds). The scope of criminal activities which constitute predicate offences for money laundering should be uniform and sufficiently broad in all Member States.

56. The European Council invites the Council to extend the competence of Europol to money laundering in general, regardless of the type of offence from which the laundered proceeds originate.

57. Common standards should be developed in order to prevent the use of corporations and entities registered outside the jurisdiction of the Union in the hiding of criminal proceeds and in money laundering. The union and Member States should make arrangements with third country offshore-centres to ensure efficient and transparent co-operation in mutual legal assistance following the recommendations made in this area by the Financial Action Task Force.

58. The Commission is invited to draw up a report identifying provisions in national banking, financial and corporate legislation which obstruct international co-operation. The Council is invited to draw necessary conclusions on the basis of this report.

D. Stronger External Action

59. The European Council underlines that all competences and instruments at the disposal of the Union, and in particular, in external relations must be used in an integrated and consistent way to build the area of freedom, security and justice. Justice and Home Affairs concerns must be integrated in the definition and implementation of other Union policies and activities.

60. Full use must be made of the new possibilities offered by the Treaty of Amsterdam for external action and in particular of Common Strategies as well as Community agreements and agreements based on Article 38 TEU.

61. Clear priorities, policy objectives and measures for the Union's external action in Justice and Home Affairs should be defined. Specific recommendations should be drawn up by the Council in close co-operation with the Commission on policy objectives and measures for the Union's external action in Justice and Home Affairs, including questions of working structure, prior to the European Council in June 2000.

62. The European Council expresses its support for regional co-operation against organised crime involving the Member States and third countries bordering on the Union. In this context it notes with satisfaction the concrete and practical results obtained by the surrounding countries in the Baltic Sea region. The European Council attaches particular importance to regional co-operation and development in the Balkan region. The European Union welcomes and intends to participate in a European Conference on Development and Security in the Adriatic and Ionian area, to be organised by the Italian Government in Italy in the first half of the year 2000. This initiative will provide valuable support in the context of the South Eastern Europe Stability Pact.

ANNEX

COMPOSITION METHOD OF WORK AND PRACTICAL ARRANGEMENTS FOR THE BODY TO ELABORATE A DRAFT EU CHARTER OF FUNDAMENTAL RIGHTS, AS SET OUT IN THE COLOGNE CONCLUSIONS

A. COMPOSITION OF THE BODY

(i) Members
  (a)   *Heads of State or Government of Member States*
        Fifteen representatives of the Heads of State or Government of Member States.
  (b)   *Commission*
        One representative of the President of the European Commission.
  (c)   *European Parliament*
        Sixteen members of the European Parliament to be designated by itself.
  (d)   *National Parliaments*
        Thirty members of national Parliaments (two from each national Parliament) to be designated by national Parliaments themselves.

Members of the Body may be replaced by alternates in the event of being unable to attend meetings of the Body.

(ii) Chairperson and Vice-Chairpersons of the Body
The Chairperson of the Body shall be elected by the Body. A member of the European Parliament, a member of a national Parliament, and the representative of the President of the European Council if not elected to the Chair, shall act as Vice-Chairpersons of the Body.

The member of the European Parliament acting as Vice-Chairperson shall be elected by the members of the European Parliament serving on the Body. The member of a national Parliament acting as Vice-Chairperson shall be elected by the members of national Parliaments serving on the body.

(iii) Observers
Two representatives of the Court of Justice of the European Communities to be designated by the Court.

Two representatives of the Council of Europe, including one from the European Court of Human Rights.

(iv) Bodies of the European Union to be invited to give their views
The Economic and Social Committee
The Committee of the Regions
The Ombudsman

(v) Exchange of views with the applicant States
An appropriate exchange of views should be held by the Body or by the Chairperson with the applicant States.

(vi) Other bodies, social groups or experts to be invited to give their views
Other bodies, social groups and experts may be invited by the Body to give their views.

(vii) Secretariat
The General Secretariat of the Council shall provide the Body with secretariat services. To ensure proper coordination, close contacts will be established with the General Secretariat of the European Parliament, with the Commission and, to the extent necessary, with the secretariats of the national Parliaments.

B. WORKING METHODS OF THE BODY

(i) Preparation
The Chairperson of the Body shall, in close concertation with the Vice-Chairpersons, propose a work plan for the Body and perform other appropriate preparatory work.

(ii) Transparency of the proceedings
In principle, hearings held by the Body and documents submitted as such hearings should be public.

(iii) Working groups
The Body may establish *ad hoc* working groups, which shall be open to all members of the Body.

(iv) Drafting
On the basis of the work plan agreed by the Body, a Drafting Committee composed of the Chairperson, the Vice-Chairpersons and the representative of the Commission and assisted by the General Secretariat of the Council, shall elaborate a preliminary Draft Charter, taking account of drafting proposals submitted by any member of the Body.
Each of the three Vice-Chairpersons shall regularly consult with the respective component part of the Body from which he or she emanates.

(v) Elaboration of the Draft Charter by the Body
When the Chairperson, in close concentration with the Vice-Chairpersons, deems that the text of the draft Charter elaborated by the Body can eventually be subscribed to by all the parties, it shall be forwarded to the European Council through the normal preparatory procedure.

C. PRACTICAL ARRANGEMENTS

The Body shall hold its meetings in Brussels, alternately in the Council and the European Parliament buildings.
A complete language regime shall be applicable for sessions of the Body.

Index

The following abbreviations are used in the index:
CJ (IC) A 1990: Criminal Justice (International Co-operation) Act 1990
ECMA 1959: European Convention on Mutual Assistance in Criminal Matters 1959
MLA Section: Mutual Legal Assistance Section of the Home Office
PACE 1984: Police and Criminal Evidence Act 1984